Who's Who

of the

Elite

Members of the:

Bilderbergs
Council on Foreign Relations
&
Trilateral Commission

by

Robert Gaylon Ross, Sr.

Published by

RIE

US & Canadian Sales only: 800-410-5571

Web site: http://www.4rie.com

Copyright 1995

by

Robert Gaylon Ross, Sr.

The purpose of this book is to alert the public of the existence, and activities of the *Elite*, and to encourage active participation by all concerned citizens to stop the takeover of the US, and the rest of the world by the *Elite* in their efforts to form their Global Union (formerly called the New World Order). I encourage every moral, ethical, and legal act, by anyone who cares about their children, grandchildren, and this fine free country, to expose, and stop this takeover attempt.

However, I abhor, and strongly discourage any violent act by anyone for any reason in an effort to stop the *Elite*. It is wrong to break our laws, and to endanger the lives, and property of innocent people.

Our goal is to restore this country to a representative form of constitutional government, which we no longer have. The *Elite*-controlled news media will jump-on any violent act, and blow it out of proportion, in order to stop our efforts. We can return this fine country to one that our children and grandchildren can be safe in, and be proud to live in again, if we just take the time to plan our efforts carefully. Hang in there, and don't give up. It can be done.

This book gives you the "Who" of the *Elite*. My companion book, *They Don't Dare Let Us Tell The People,* will give you the "Where", "Why", "When", and "What" should be done to stop the *Elite* in their efforts to take over the US under their plan for the Global Union. This second book is still in process at the date of this revision, so until notified of the availability of this second book, the reader can find new revelations about the *Elite* by checking our web site on the Internet at: www.4rie.com

US 1st Printing - July, 1995
US 1st Revision - January, 1996
US 2nd Revision – January 2000
US 3rd Revision – February, 2002
US 4th Printing – December 2004

Library of Congress Catalog Card Number: 95-92782
ISBN 0-9649888-0-1

Dedication

**This book is dedicated to Rob, Carrolyn, and Lisa,
whom I love very much.**

In memory of Jack & Bill

Thanks

To Alma, Andrea, Bill R., Jack R., Victor, Ward,
Klaus Kopf, Eric S., Texe Marrs, and Antony C. Sutton
who have made significant contributions to this book.

This book would not be possible without the help of the
competent staff, and excellent references
made available to me by the
Albert B. Alkek Library
Southwest Texas State University
San Marcos, Texas

Special Thanks

To my Assistant - Dee

We suggest that you very carefully read this book, research our materials, check with other sources, and come to your own conclusions. If you do so, you will never read a newsmagazine or newspaper, or watch television the same way again.

Preface

My first exposure to the *Elite*, the people who really run this country, was in 1972, when I first read *None Dare Call It Conspiracy*, by Gary Allen. A friend gave me a copy of this book, asked me to read it, and to give it some thought. I was heavily involved in starting up a new company, and had little interest in political affairs at the time. However, I agreed to read it. After getting started, I became very interested, and could not stop reading until it was finished. This book remained in my subconscious until about 1988, when my concern for the direction that our country was headed began to increase.

I have written hundreds of letters to both my state, and federal representatives regarding things that bothered me. My letters were answered (if they were answered at all) by low-level clerical staffs, who were hired to read, and answer letters from the constituents. This prompted me to write a book titled *What's Wrong in The United States, And How To Fix It*. While conducting the research for this book, I began to run into sources that included brief information about the shadow government that really controls what happens in this country, and around the world, as well. After finishing the writing of the draft of the first book (which will be revised, and published later), I could not rest until I found out more about this hidden oligarchy.

In order to head-off those who would brand me a radical leftist, radical rightist, or other such derogatory terms designed to discredit me (the *Elite's* favorite defense is to "shoot the messenger"), I must declare that I am not an active, or inactive member of any political or religious group of any kind.

I hold a BS degree in Industrial Engineering from Texas A & M University. After graduating, I accepted a commission as a 2nd Lieutenant (later promoted to 1st Lieutenant) in the Army Security Agency (ASA), a branch of the National Security Agency (NSA), which is the BIG BROTHER of the Central Intelligence Agency (CIA). My military training was in the field of cryptoanalysis (the breaking of codes), and I served as a unit commander of an intelligence gathering team on the Demilitarized Zone (DMZ) in the Chorwan valley of South Korea from 1956 to 1957 (after the fighting had ceased).

Upon leaving active duty, I began my professional career in the petroleum industry. I served as an Industrial Engineer for ten years until being promoted into management, and was a manufacturing Plant Manager for over ten years. The remaining seventeen years of my career have been as an International Management Consultant, working in the US, Japan, Mexico, Canada, England, and Iran. The only reason for relating my personal history is to try to set the theme for this book. I pride myself for my ability to back away from a problem, and look at the big picture. Often, this approach will reveal an entirely different image than the one presented by microanalysis. For example, you can be blindfolded, and place your nose against an animal's skin. When the blindfold is removed, you can see hair, and smell an animal. But what kind? You can guess that it is a horse, cow, deer, or other animal, but you cannot be certain. Only after you back far enough away, can you see that it is, in fact, the hide of a moose, hanging on the wall. In this case, microanalysis could not reveal this fact.

The common thread of my formal education, military training, and experience, my engineering training, plus my extensive business management, and consulting background is that I have developed the ability to look for patterns of facts, and events when trying to solve military codes, and/or business problems. I have amassed quite an extensive database (although it is extremely difficult to discover information about secret organizations) on the *Elite*, and have studied it very carefully. My concern is that we are losing control of this great nation, and the world as well, to a group that cares nothing about the present or future quality of life of the majority of citizens of this country, or the rest of the world. The *Elite* are guided by greed, and their insatiable need for control, influence, and power.

This is my first book on the subject of the *Elite*. My second undertaking on this subject is a companion book to be titled *They Don't Dare Let Us Tell The People*. This companion book contains an expanded history of the *Elite,* the Bilderbergs (BB), Council on Foreign Relations (CFR), Trilateral Commission (TC), Skull & Bones Society (S&B), Illuminatti, Round Tables, and Bohemian Club (BC) organizations, their goals, objectives, and their activities in the past, present, and future.

My first inclination was to write just one book with the member lists contained in the index. As the text grew in size, and the lists grew as well, it looked like I was heading for a 600-page book. I decided that it would be more advantageous to split the information into two companion books; one providing the details of the history of the *Elite,* and the other to list the names of *Elite,* along with brief details regarding their connections with these organizations, their positions with these organizations, their "day job" titles, and their employers or affiliations.

The advantage of the approach of splitting the information into two companion books was that the book on details about the *Elite, They Don't Dare Let Us Tell The People*, might be read once, and then placed on the book shelf for future reference. The list of names of the *Elite, Who's Who of the Elite*, should be kept handy by the chair the reader uses while reading the newspaper or news magazines, and/or watching the news on television. As different people appear in newsprint, or on the TV, the reader or observer should reach for *Who's Who Of The Elite* to see if the persons prominent to the news are members, or not. The people in the news never begin their discussions with disclaimers, such as "I am a member of the Bilderberg organization, and would like to give you my opinions of the following subjects from the perspective of a member of this *Elite* organization. My opinion on this subject is..."

The *Elite* controlled news media look for every chance to say, as occasional violent events occur within this nation, and abroad, that many concerned US citizens hate our government, and are interested in overthrowing it when the opportunity presents itself. They fail to mention that their *Elite* leaders are doing just that.

It is extremely important that the reader understands that this book is absolutely not intended to incite violent actions by anyone, for any reason. Wanton attacks on innocent people, violent revolution or armed insurrection is not the answer, for the *Elite*-controlled news media immediately take these violent events as an excuse to first blame foreigners, and then, later, to try to place the blame on the many Militias that have formed around the country. The purpose of the Militias is to defend their arms, property, and families from the confiscation, and abuse by members of various agencies within the federal government. They are not offensive units, but defensive in nature.

Any violent effort to rid the US and the rest of world of the control of the *Elite* is a mistake, for at least the following reasons:

1. It is wrong. It is wrong to break our laws, and to endanger innocent people by violent acts.
2. It is illogical. It is impossible for any armed group to defeat the military capabilities of the *Elite*. It is my opinion that they **own** the US military, NATO, the Secret Service, the CIA, the Supreme Court, and many of the lower courts. They appear to control, either directly or indirectly, most of the state, county, and local law enforcement agencies. To ignore this is pure lunacy.

Even though I am sincerely opposed to violent actions, this should not deter us from using every moral, ethical, political, and legal process at our disposal, in order to stop the *Elite* takeover of the US, and the rest of the world, as well. If you have ever walked into a dirty kitchen at night, and turned on the light, you see the cockroaches scurry out of sight. This book is my efforts to shine a "**Hi-intensity Spotlights**" on the *Elite*, and hope that they will leave this country alone, and leave us alone. Also, if the readers will spread the word about the *Elite*, we have a very good chance of stopping them.

Note: We hope to be able to publish the companion book, ***They Don't Dare Let Us Tell the People***, within 4 – 6 months from the date of the release of this 1999 revision. If you bought this book directly from RIE, your name and address is on a private mailing list, and you will be notified when the next book is available. If you bought this book from any other source, send a postcard or letter to RIE and you will be placed on this private mailing list.

Table of Contents

Table of Contents (Continued)

Table of Contents (Continued)

Introduction

The object of this book is to provide the reader with a list of names of all the current and recent members of the *Elite* secret organizations that dominate in the US, and the rest of the world. They have sister organizations all over the Far East, South and Central America, Africa, the Middle East, Eastern and Western Europe, and the former Soviet States. These groups use different names in different countries. In London, they are called Roundtables, and use the name Royal Institute of International Affairs (RIIA); in the US they go by the name Council on Foreign Relations; in Canada, they are called Canadian Institute of International Affairs, in Chile it is called the Chilean Council on Foreign Relations, and so forth. It is important for the reader to be aware of these sister organizations, but they will be covered in subsequent books. In addition to the CFR, the other secret groups that they belong to are the Bilderbergs, and the Trilateral Commission.

Even though these *Elite* organizations go to a lot of effort, and expense to remain secret, the word seems to get out anyway. There have been many dozens of very good books written since the beginning of this century on this subject, but they remain rather obscure, because the *Elite* conspires to suppress them. My companion book, *They Don't Dare Let Us Tell the People,* covers such efforts to suppress this knowledge in quite lengthy detail.

The names of the members of the CFR, and TC were supplied to me by these two organizations in the form of annual reports from the CFR, and membership lists from the TC. The Bilderberg information was provided by *The Spotlight* weekly newspaper, published by Liberty Lobby in Washington, DC, and from sources that must remain anonymous to protect their lives. Apparently, Spotlight's crack team of investigative reporters have a mole within the Bilderbergs, who provide them with the date, and place of each annual meeting, along with a list of the invited members. However, to my knowledge, no "outsider" has successfully attended one of their meetings, and reported on the subjects covered. The Skull & Bones Society (S&B), and its members were removed from this revision solely to minimize the size of this book, and thereby minimize the cost of publishing. Those who would like to know about the S & B should order a copy of Antony C. Sutton's very informative book, *America's Secret Establishment* (available from RIE). The S & B information is very interesting, but the three major secret groups, the BB, CFR, and TC, are more appropriate to this book. This revision contains much expanded details about the international members, plus the most recent US, and international members of the BB, CFR, and TC.

Should the reader doubt the facts included here, we suggest that he/she contact the CFR, and TC, and ask for the annual reports, and the membership lists, then gather the BB information from *The Spotlight*, check the details in *Who's Who in America*, by Marquis, in their local library, and read most of the recommended references listed at the end of this book. I can assure you that this is a very time consuming, and a grueling task, (for it took me five years part-time, and three years full-time to put this together) but this is the only way to duplicate the contents of this book. I would be very interested to know if, after you're doing so, if you would arrive at the same conclusions that I present in this book.

> *"Although we give lip service to the notion of freedom, we know that government is no longer the servant of the people but, at last, has become the people's master. We have stood by like timid sheep while the wolf killed - first the weak, then the strays, then those on the outer edges of the flock, until at last the entire flock belonged to the wolf."*
> - *From Freedom to Slavery* - by Gerry Spence

> *"Beware of false prophets, which come to you in sheep's clothing, but inwardly they are ravening wolves."*
> - Matthew 7:15

> *"For there is nothing covered that shall not be revealed; neither hid, that shall not be known."*
> - Luke 12:2

> *"As long as the people are well informed, I have confidence in our country's future."*
> - Thomas Jefferson

> *The case for government by the elite is irrefutable ... government by the People is possible but highly improbable"*
> - J. William Fulbright, former Chairman of the Senate Foreign Relations Committee, at a 1963 symposium

"Today Americans would be outraged if U.N. troops entered Los Angeles to restore order; tomorrow they will be grateful! This is especially true if they were told there was an outside threat from beyond, whether real or promulgated, that threatened our very existence. It is then that all people of the world will plead with world leaders to deliver them from this evil. The one thing every man fears is the unknown. When presented with this scenario, individual rights will be willingly relinquished for the guarantee of their well being granted to them by their world government." - Henry Kissinger in an address to the Bilderberg meeting at Evian, France, May 21, 1992. Transcribed from a tape recording made by one of the Swiss delegates.

With these quotes in mind, I will do my very best to reveal the <u>real truth</u> about this cabal that is well along on their schedule of conquering the entire world without firing a single shot. However, I cannot do this alone, so I need your help in spreading the word, for we cannot rely on the *Elite* owned news media, because they are part of the problem.

Brief Descriptions
of the
Bilderberg, Council on Foreign Relations,
and
Trilateral Commission

The brief descriptions of the major *Elite* organizations, the Bilderbergs (BB), Council on Foreign Relations (CFR), and Trilateral Commission (TC), in this book were intended to be brief. For more details, refer to my companion book, *They Don't Dare Let Us Tell the People* (soon to be released). The fundamental differences between these three *Elite* secret organizations are:

1. The BB members are largely from Western Europe, Turkey, Greece, the Scandinavian countries, the US, and Canada.

2. The CFR members were originally from the New York City area, but later expanded to include Washington, DC, and then the rest of the US.

3. The TC members come from all the same above areas, but in this case the Japanese were included because of their dominance of the banking industry. (The largest banks in the world are in Japan.)

4. The BB's are the most secretive of the three. When they meet, they clear out all the guests, and employees in the buildings in which they are to meet, they completely de-bug all the rooms, bring in their own cooks, waiters, housekeepers, heavily armed security guards, etc., and do not allow "outsiders" anywhere near the meeting place just before, during, and immediately after they meet. They claim that there are no written records taken of their discussions, but *The Spotlight* has occasionally acquired very detailed documents that prove otherwise. The attendees are required to maintain complete and absolute secrecy regarding these deliberations. Liberty Lobby's crack investigative reporters on *The Spotlight* have positioned a mole within the BB that somehow acquires a copy of the invitation list, and often a copy of the agenda, but have never penetrated the actual meetings (to date). Each time that they have met on US soil, the meetings were held on Rockefeller owned property.

The object of the formation of these organizations is to enlist key political and economic leaders around the world, in order to gain their assistance in dominating the entire world.

The other differences, and similarities are covered in the following brief descriptions:

Bilderbergs (BB)

John J. McCloy (former Chairman of the CFR, and Chairman of Chase Manhattan Bank) used his position as coordinator of information for the US government to build the framework of what was to become the Office of Strategic Services (OSS), created in 1941-1942 era, headed by Bill Donovan. During 1947, the OSS was rolled into a new group called the Central Intelligence Agency (CIA) by the 1947 National Security Act, which made the activities of the CIA immune from all civil, and criminal laws. In 1950 General Walter Bedel Smith became Director of the CIA. The CIA helped organize, and sponsored the formation, and operation of the Bilderberg Conferences. There is little doubt that the CIA sponsored the formation of the Bilderbergs, and continue to do so, to this day.

Kai Bird's excellent account in *The Chairman, John J. McCoy, The Making of the American Establishment*, states:

> *"In late 1952, Retinger went to America to try the idea out on his American contacts. Among others, he saw such old friends as Averell Harriman, David Rockefeller, and Bedell Smith, then director of the CIA. After Retinger explained his proposal, Smith said, 'Why the hell didn't you come to me in the first place?' He quickly referred Retinger to C. D. Jackson, who was about to become Eisenhower's special assistant for psychological warfare. It took a while for Jackson to organize the American wing of the group, but finally, in May 1954, the first conference was held in the Hotel de Bilderberg, a secluded hotel in Holland, near the German border. Prince Bernhard, and Retinger drew up the list of invitees from the European countries, while Jackson controlled the American list."*

Prince Bernhard, of The Netherlands, became the first Chairman, and served in this post until scandal forced him to resign in 1974. Dr. Retinger became the first Secretary, and remained so until his death.

Liberty Lobby, Inc., 300 Independence Ave., SE, Washington, D.C. 20003, publishes a weekly newspaper titled *The Spotlight*. At my request, they sent me a reprint of a summary of Bilderberg information, titled *Spotlight on the Bilderbergers, Irresponsible Power,* published mid-June, 1975. Page 6 of this document states:

> *"The Congressional Record - U.S. Senate, April 11, 1964, states:*
> *(Speaking) - Mr. (Jacob) Javits - Mr. President, the 13th in a series of Bilderberg meetings on international affairs, in which I participated, was held in Williamsburg, VA, on March 20, 21, and 22.*
> *I ask unanimous consent to have printed in the Record a background paper entitled 'The Bilderberg Meetings.'*

> ### The Bilderberg Meetings

> *The idea of the Bilderberg meetings originated in the early fifties. Changes had taken place on the international politician and economic scene after World War II. The countries of the Western World felt the need for closer collaboration to protect their moral and ethical values, their democratic institutions, and their independence against the growing Communist threat. The Marshall plan and NATO were examples of collective efforts of Western countries to join hands in economic and military matters after World War II.*
> *In the early 1950's, a number of people on both sides of the Atlantic sought a means of bringing together leading citizens, not necessarily connected with government, for informal discussions of problems facing the Atlantic community. Such meetings, they felt, would create a better understanding of the forces, and trends affecting Western nations, in particular. They believed that direct exchanges could help to clear up differences, and misunderstandings that might weaken the West.*
> *One of the men who saw the need for such discussions was the late (Dr.) Joseph H. (Heironymus) Retinger* (as a matter of interest, the name Heironymus is literally translated to be "MEMBER OF THE OCCULT"). *In 1952, he approached His Royal Highness, Prince Bernhard of the Netherlands, with the suggestion of informal and unofficial meetings to discuss the problems facing the Atlantic community. Others in Europe wholeheartedly supported the idea,*

and proposals were submitted to American friends to join in the undertaking. A number of Americans, including C. D. Jackson, the late General Walter Bedell Smith, and the late John Coleman, agreed to cooperate. (Very reliable information from a former CIA member now reveals that the CIA financed Dr. Ritinger's efforts to convince Prince Bernhard to form this group that was later to be called the Bilderbergs. This is confirmed by the fact that General Walter Bedell Smith was the CIA director from 1950 to 1953, so, is it surprising that he would agree to join this group?)

The first meeting that brought Americans and Europeans together took place under the chairmanship of Prince Bernhard at the Bilderberg Hotel in Oosterbeek, Holland, from May 29 to May 31, 1954. Ever since, the meetings have been called Bilderberg meetings.

No Strict Rules of Procedure

From the outset, it was the intentions of the Bilderberg founders, and participants that no strict rules of procedure govern the meetings. Every effort was made to create a relaxed, informal atmosphere conducive to free, and frank discussions.
Bilderberg is in no sense a policy-making body. No conclusions are reached. There is no voting, and no resolutions are passed.
The meetings are off-the-record. Only the participants themselves may attend the meetings.

Participants

It was obvious from the first that the success of the meetings would depend primarily on the level of the participants. Leading figures from many fields - industry, labor, education, government, etc. - are invited, who, through their special knowledge or experience, can help to further Bilderberg objectives. Representatives of governments attend in a personal, and not an official capacity. An attempt is made to include participants representing many political parties, and points of view. American participation has included Members of Congress of both parties.
Over the years, Bilderberg participants have come from the NATO countries, Switzerland, Sweden, Austria, and Finland, and have included prominent individuals such as Dean Rusk, Christian A. Herter, Maurice Faure, Franz-Josef Strauss, Amitore Fanfani, Panayotis Pipinelis, Reginald Maudling, the late Hugh Gaitskell, Omer Becu, Guy Mollet, the late Michael Ross, Herman Abs, C. L. Sulzberger, Joseph Harsch, and T. M. Terkelsen. Individuals with international responsibilities have also participated, among them being Gen. Alfred Gruenther, Lord Ismay, Eugene Black, Gen. Lyman Lemnitzer, Paul-Henry Spaak, and the late Per Jacobsson. `

The Meetings

Bilderberg meetings are held at irregular intervals, but have taken place once or twice a year since 1954. All the early conferences were held in Europe, but a meeting is now held on this side of the Atlantic every few years to provide a convenient opportunity for American, and Canadian participants to attend."

The Spotlight reports that the Bilderberg meetings are highly secret, and are held at random times each year, and rarely at the same location, for security reasons. The responsibility for security for these meetings is in the hands of the government of the country in which the meetings are held. They must supply military security, secret service, national and local police, and private security personnel to protect the privacy and safety of these very powerful international *Elite* members who are not required to conform to regulations that private citizens are subject-to, such as customs searches, visa requirements, or public notice of their meetings. When they meet, no "outsiders" are allowed in or near the building. They bring their own cooks, waiters, telephone operators, housekeepers, and bodyguards.

The Bilderberg membership is made up of Kings, Queens, Princes, Chancellors, Prime Ministers, Presidents, Ambassadors, Secretaries of State, Wall Street investors, international bankers, news media executives, and wealthy industrialist. Their meetings are by "invitation only", and no "outsiders" in the news media are allowed, except by special invitation. However, the news media are **always** present at these meetings such as: Peter

Jennings (BB, and Anchor & Senior Editor of ABC News, World News Tonight), Joseph C. Harsch (BB, CFR, and former Commentator for NBC, Inc.), Bill D. Moyers (BB, and Executive Director of Public Affairs TV, Inc., and former Director of the CFR), William F. Buckley, Jr. (BB, CFR, and Editor-in-Chief of National Review, and host of PBS's Firing Line), Gerald Piel (BB, CFR, and former Chairman of Scientific America, Inc.), Henry Anatole Grunwald (BB, CFR, and former Editor-in-Chief of Time, Inc.), Mortimer B. Zuckerman (BB, CFR, and Chairman & Editor-in-Chief of the US News, and World Report, New York Daily News, and Atlantic Monthly), Robert L. Bartley (BB, CFR, TC, and Vice President of the Wall Street Journal), Peter Robert Kann (BB, CFR, and Chairman & CEO of Dow Jones & Company, and husband of Karen E. House, CFR), William Kristol (BB, and Editor & Publisher of the new The Weekly Standard magazine), Donald (Don) C. Cook (BB, CFR, and former European Diplomatic Correspondent for the Los Angeles Times), Robert Leroy Bartley (BB, CFR, TC, and Vice President of the Wall Street Journal), Albert J. Wohlstetter (BB, CFR, and Writer for the Wall Street Journal), Thomas L. Friedman (BB, CFR, TC, and Columnist for the New York Times), and the "Queen" of the *Elite* - Katharine Graham (BB, CFR, TC, and Owner, and Chairwoman of the Executive Committee of the Washington Post). The 1998 meeting included Leslie Stahl, of CBS' *60 Minutes*. Even though the media moguls attend these secret meetings, they do not file reports about the *Elite* Bilderberg activities during their meetings.

The security measures taken by the Bilderberg Conferences is clearly illustrated in an article appearing in The Spotlight, which stated:

EXCLUSIVE TO THE SPOTLIGHT

By James P. Tucker, JR

Bilderberg is scheduled to meet June 3-6 (1999) at the Caesar Park Penha Longa in Sintra, Portugal. Sintra is a remote resort, about 40 miles from Lisbon. Information about the secret meeting was provided by an agent inside Bilderberg.

Of all the media in the world, only THE SPOTLIGHT, has tracked the Bilderbergers every year and reported on their secret meeting where vital questions and issues are decided which effect every person in the world. American and European financiers, manufacturers, media moguls and politicians meet at remote luxury resorts, allow only "loyal staff" to remain on the job, empty the establishment of all others, employ platoons of police, military and their own private security to seal themselves off. They have tried to keep the meetings secret for 45 years.

But this year following extensive SPOTLIGHT-generated publicity last year in Scotland- and earlier in Germany, Scandinavia, Georgia, and Canada-Bilderberg is taking more extreme steps, its agent confided.

Instead of closing down the Penha Longa to all outsiders one day before the meeting starts on June 2, Bilderberg has ordered the resort shut down a full 48 hours before the internationalist confab.

In addition, Bilderberg will pay hundreds of thousands of dollars to reimburse the Portuguese government for deploying military forces to guard their privacy and for helicopters to seek out intruders.

All Bilderberg participants, their staff members and resort employees will wear photo identification tags that look much like state drivers' licenses. They will have separate colors to identify the wearer as a participant, staff, or employee. A computer chip "fingerprint" will assure the identity of the card's wearer. 'Any intruders are to manhandled-cuffed, jailed, or if resisting or fleeing, shot,' the agent said.

Bilderbergers are greatly disturbed over the growing public knowledge of their control of the world and of resistance to their schemes for a global government as nationalism grows around the world.

Bilderberg was instrumental in tearing down Jean-Marie Le Pen, who founded France's National Front. The French-first party has stunned the Establishment by regularly capturing 15 percent of the vote in that nation.

Expecting recession, Bilderberg feared Le Pen and "nationalists" from other countries would interfere with their "free trade" goals as they fight to protect their domestic industries from exploitation by the global cabal.

Because Bilderberg shares common goals with the Trilateral Commission, the agenda that emerged in Washington (SPOTLIGHT, March 29, 1999) will be major topics in Portugal, too.

This includes a "Globalization summit" called for by Peter D. Sutherland, head of Goldman Sachs International. Sutherland attended the Bilderberg meeting in Scotland last May and is expected in Portugal.

Sutherland is expected to again call for "Supranational institutions to manage the global economy while denouncing nations that "cling tenaciously to their separate identities" while calling for "sharing sovereignty"

In a related topic, there could be renewed calls for the UN to be able to directly tax all people. In the past, Bilderberg has proposed a UN levy on International travel and on the oil at the wellhead, so all who travel or drive will be taxed.

SPOTLIGHT, VOLUME 24, No. 14, Page 3, April, 1999

The Bilderberg's address in Europe is Maja Banck-Polderman, Bilderberg Meetings, Amstel 216, 1017 AJ Amsterdam, The Netherlands. Their US address is Charles W. Muller, American Friends of Bilderberg, Inc., 477 Madison Ave., 6th Floor, New York, NY 10022.

Council on Foreign Relations (CFR)

Let's start with the smoke, and mirrors furnished by the CFR in several of their Annual Reports. Then we will provide the other-side-of-the-coin, as observed by quite a number of independent researchers, and writers.

The *CFR's Annual Report* for July 1, 1993-June 30, 1994, page 4, states:

"The Council on Foreign Relations is a nonprofit, and nonpartisan membership organization dedicated to improving the understanding of U.S. foreign policy, and international affairs through the exchange of ideas.

The Council was founded in 1921 shortly after the end of World War I. Several of the American participants in the Paris Peace Conference decided that it was time for more private American citizens to become familiar with the increasing international responsibilities, and obligations of the United States. This decision led to the creation of an organization dedicated to the continuous study of U.S. foreign policy for the benefit of both its members, and a wider audience of interested Americans."

The New World Order, by Pat Robertson, Copyright 1991, by Word, Inc., Dallas, Texas. All rights reserved, page 66-67, states:

"This august body of 'wise men' has effectively dominated the making of foreign policy by the United States government since before World War II. The CFR has included virtually every key national security, and foreign policy adviser of this nation for the past seventy years."

Page 96: "In government policy, the most visible expression of the Establishment is the Council on Foreign Relations, and its publication, Foreign Affairs. Out of some twenty-nine hundred members, at least five hundred are very powerful, another five hundred are from centers of influence, and the rest are influential in academia, the media, business, and finance, the military, or government. A few are token conservatives."

Page 97: "According to a man who had been a member for fifteen years, Rear Admiral Chester Ward, former judge advocate general of the navy from 1956 to 1960.

'This purpose of promoting disarmament, and submergence of U.S. sovereignty, and national independence into an all-powerful one-world government is the only objective revealed to about 95 percent of 1,551 members [in 1975]. There are two other ulterior purposes the CFR influence is being used to promote; but it is improbable that they are known to more than 75 members, or that these purposes ever have even been identified in writing.'

The goals of the Establishment are somewhat strange, and we will discuss them in detail. At the central core is a belief in the superiority of their own skill to form a world system in which enlightened monopolistic capitalism can bring all of the diverse currencies, banking systems, credit, manufacturing, and raw materials into one government-supervised whole, policed of course by their own world army." (Could this be the army of the United Nations?)

CFR membership is made up of present, and past Presidents, Ambassadors, Secretaries of State, Wall Street investors, international bankers, foundation executives, Think Tank executives, lobbyist lawyers, NATO, and Pentagon military leaders, wealthy industrialist, media owners, and executives, university presidents, and key professors, select Senators, and Congressmen, Supreme Court Justices, Federal Judges, and wealthy entrepreneurs.

They hold regular secret meetings including members, and very select guests. Occasionally they will hold a public meeting, and invite the open press (including C-SPAN), in order to give the impression that they are a harmless group engaged only in social activities.

A number of people, when hearing about the CFR ask, "If you say that the CFR is such a secret organization, why is it that we can get a copy of their annual report, which contains a list of their members? Why should I believe you when you say that they are a secret organization?"

Webster's New Collegiate Dictionary, states that the definition of **attribute** is "To ascribe by way of cause, inherent quality, interpretation, authorship, or classification..." The literal translation is **"You had better not tell the outsiders what we do, or say"**.

The answer then comes from their own document, the *Council on Foreign Relation's 1992 Annual Report*, where they emphatically state, in 20 different places, and in varying terms, that members **better not tell**:

Page 21: *"At all meetings, the Council's rule of <u>non-attribution</u> applies. This assures participants that they may speak openly without others later <u>attributing their statements</u> to them in public media or forums, or <u>knowingly transmitting them to persons who will.</u>"*

Page 122: *"Like the Council, the Committees encourage candid discourse by holding their meetings on a <u>not-for-attribution basis</u>".*

Page 169: *Article II of the by-laws states: "It is <u>an express condition of membership</u> in the Council, to which condition every member accedes by virtue of his or her membership, that members will observe such rules, and regulations as may be prescribed from time to time by the Board of Directors concerning the conduct of Council meetings or the <u>attribution of statements</u> made therein, and that <u>any disclosure,</u> public, or other action by a member in contravention thereof may be regarded by the Board of Directors in its sole discretion as <u>grounds for termination</u> or suspension of membership pursuant to Article I of the by-laws."*

Page 174: *"Full freedom of expression is encouraged at Council meetings. Participants are assured that they may speak openly, as it is the tradition of the Council that others <u>will not attribute or characterize their statements</u> in public media or forums or <u>knowingly transmit them</u> to persons who will. <u>All participants are expected to honor that commitment.</u>"*

Page 175: *"It would not be in compliance with the reformulated Rule, however, for any meeting participant (i) to <u>publish a speaker's statement in attributed form</u> in a newspaper; (ii) to <u>repeat it on television or radio</u>, or on a speaker's platform, or in a classroom; or (iii) to go beyond a memo of limited circulation, by <u>distributing the attributed statement</u> in a company or government agency newspaper. The language of the Rule also goes out of its way to make it clear that a meeting participant is <u>forbidden knowingly to transmit the attributed statement</u> to a newspaper reporter or other such person who is likely to <u>publish it in a public medium</u>. The essence of the Rule as reformulated is simple enough: participants in Council meetings <u>should not pass along an attributed statement in circumstances where there is substantial risk that it will promptly be widely circulated or published.</u>"*

... *"In order to encourage to the fullest a free, frank, and open exchange of ideas in Council meetings, the Board of Directors has prescribed, in addition to the <u>Non-Attribution Rule</u>, the following guidelines. <u>All participants in Council meetings are expected to be familiar with, and adhere to these Guidelines.</u> ..."*

Page 176: *"Members bringing guests should complete a "guest notice card", and acquaint their guests with the Council's <u>Non-Attribution Rule governing what is said at meetings.</u>"*

Later on page 176: *"As a condition of use, the officers of the Council shall require each user of Council records to execute a prior written commitment that he <u>will not directly or indirectly attribute</u> to any living person <u>any assertion of fact or opinion</u> based upon any Council record without first obtaining from such person his written consent thereto."*

In "A letter from the Chairman" in the *1994 Annual Report for the CFR*, Peter G. Peterson states on page 7, that:

"... Members had occasion to meet in intensive <u>off-the-record sessions</u> with Secretary of State [Warren] Christopher, National Security Advisor [Anthony] Lake, Secretary [of State emeritus, George Pratt] Shultz, Ambassador [Mickey] Kantor, Under Secretary of the Treasury [Lawrence H.] Summers, the Joint Chiefs of Staff, and other ranking officials. <u>Next on our agenda are plans for reaching out to congressional leaders as well,</u> an opportunity we will fashion as one component of an enhanced Washington Program."

The CFR's 1999 Annual Report, page 5, states their three goals:
   1. Add value by improving understanding of world affairs and by providing new ideas for U.S. foreign policy.
   2. Transform the Council into a truly national organization to benefit from the expertise and experience of leaders nationwide.
   3. Find and nurture the next generation of foreign policy leaders and thinkers.

These are **"THEIR"** words, not mine. I am simply reporting these facts to you. If this is not a secret organization, then why would they be so emphatic, and state in 20 different ways that **non-attribution** (**or You better not tell**) was so important, in their very own annual report? In addition, if you are proud of what you say, and do, then you don't care whether it becomes public knowledge, or not. The other side of this coin is: if you are doing something illegal, immoral, unethical, unpopular, and/or **unconstitutional**, you will do whatever is necessary to see that it is kept secret. In his book, *"The ANGLO-AMERICAN ESTABLISHMENT"*, Dr. Carroll Quigley writes,

> *"One wintry afternoon in February 1891, three men were engaged in earnest conversation in London. From that conversation were to flow consequences of the greatest importance to the British Empire, and to the world as a whole. For these men were organizing a secret society that was, for more than fifty years, to be one of the most important forces in the formulation, and execution of British imperial and foreign policy.*
>
> *The three men who were thus engaged were already well known in England. The leader was Cecil Rhodes, fabulously wealthy empire builder, and the most important person in South Africa. The second was William T. Stead, the famous, and probably also the most sensational, journalist of the day. The third was Reginald Baliol Brett, later known as Lord Esher, friend, and confidant of Queen Victoria, and later to be the most influential advisor of King Edward VII, and King George V.*
>
> *The details of this important conversation will be examined later. At present we need only point out that the three drew up a plan of organization for their secret society, and a list of original members. The plan for organization provided for an inner circle, to be known as "The Society of the Elect", and an outer circle, to be known as "The Association of Helpers". Within The Society of the Elect, the real power was to be exercised by the leader, and a "Junta of Three". The leader was to be Rhodes, and the Junta was to be Stead, Brett, and Alfred Milner. In accordance with this decision, Milner was added to the society by Stead shortly after the meeting we have described."*
> - Quigley, Carroll (1910-1977), The Anglo-American Establishment, From Rhodes to Cliveden, 1981, Books In Focus, NY, NY pg. 3

> *Of the Secret Societies goals, and methods of operation Quigley writes, "The goals which Rhodes, and Milner sought, and the methods by which they hoped to achieve them were so similar by 1902 that the two are almost indistinguishable. Both sought to unite the world, and above all the English-speaking world, in a federal structure around Britain. Both felt that this goal could best be achieved by a secret band of men united to one another by devotion to the common cause, and by personal loyalty to one another. Both felt that this band should pursue its goal by secret political, and economic influence behind the scenes, and by the control of journalistic, educational, and propaganda agencies... - "* Quigley, Carroll (1910-1977), The Anglo-American Establishment, From Rhodes to Cliveden, 1981, Books In Focus, NY, NY pg. 49

> *Between 1910-1915 the Secret Society evolved into an international group of co-conspirators called Round Table Groups set up in seven nations: Britain, South Africa, Canada, New Zealand, Australia, India, and the United States.* (The British Round Table was actually created in England in Feb. 5, 1891. In the US it is called the Council on foreign Relations, in England it is the Royal Institute for International Affairs, in Canada the Canadian Institute of International Affairs, in Chile it is the Chilean Council on Foreign Relations, and so on.)

> *In 1920 the Secret Society evolved into the Institutes for International Affairs, and the Council on Foreign Relations. Many of the founding fathers belonged to America's first intelligence agency the INQUIRY.*

Note - The above quotes were furnished by " Round Table", who has a web site at: http://www.geocities.com/CapitolHill/2807

The CFR could not accomplish their goals without complicity of the mainstream news media, which they <u>absolutely</u> control with an iron fist. They do this using psychological operations (PSYOPS). The RAND Corp. is one of the chief users of this technique. This is clearly explained by the following Internet message:

"Not many people have heard of the Council on Foreign Relations (CFR) or know how they operate. This is not an accident, the group has purposely maintained a low profile. The CFR is a branch of an international group of co-conspirators called the Round Table Group. This group has been controlling public opinion throughout the world for over 100 years.

The Joint Chiefs of Staff have defined psychological operations (PSYOPS) as those that: "include psychological warfare, and, in addition, encompass those political, military, economic, and ideological actions planned, and conducted to create in neutral or friendly foreign groups the emotions, attitudes, or behavior to support achievement of national objectives." Another proposal "develops the concept of 'strategic psychological operations' as aimed at influencing, and shaping decision-makers' power to govern, or control their followers." The American people, are among the groups being targeted, and controlled.

"Tactics of Deception" are formalized psychological warfare techniques. "Tactics of Deception" build a psychological environment that differs from the material environment. "Tactics of deception" are used to create false reality worlds. In terms of perceptual psychology, "Tactics of Deception" provoke illusory precepts. To influence behavior the deception must follow three basic rules. First, the deception must be "reasonable"; second there must be no simple way of checking the facts in the case; and third the use of deception should not discredit a source which may have valuable future potential.

One way to stop this group is to expose them, and their techniques to the people they are manipulating. One "Tactic of Deception" used to achieve Council on Foreign Relations aims, is to place Council members on both sides of an issue. Another "Tactic of Deception" is to use CFR control of the legal, legislative, and court systems to create the perception that laws are being followed when in fact, Lawyers, Legislators, and Justices are committing blatant illegalities to further CFR aims. A third "Tactic of Deception" is simply to lie."

Source: roundtable's Web Page: http://www.geocities.com/CapitolHill/2807

Another excellent example of deception and cover up is the book, ***The Kennedy Tapes.*** Two CFR members, Ernest R. May and Philip D. Zelikow, supposedly listened to all of President John F. Kennedy audio tapes and wrote this book quoting all of the interesting facts so as to assure the public that there were no other important statements made on these tapes that the public would care to know about. There were to motives involved here: (1) to print only what the *Elite* wanted printed about the JFK assassination, and (2) to throw any other potential researchers off the trail. This was a very grueling task of listening to hundreds of hours of taped conversations. Therefore, other researchers should just " take their word" that they had printed all of the interesting facts from these tapes. I suspect that two non-CFR researchers would have written an entirely different book.

As Peter Grose stated in his Council on Foreign Relations Book, *Continuing the Inquiry* (1996) on page 5:
"They (the British) proposed a permanent Anglo-American Institute of International Affairs, with one branch in London, the other in New York."

The headquarters for the CFR is The Harold Pratt House located at 58 East 68th Street in New York City, New York 10021. Oddly enough, this building is located just across the street from the Russian (former Soviet) Embassy.

Trilateral Commission (TC)

In 1973, David Rockefeller asked Zbigniew Brzezinski to put together an organization of the top political, and business leaders from around the World. He called this group the Trilateral Commission (TC).

According to an information sheet supplied to me by the TC, dated March 23, 1994:

> *"The European Community, North America (U.S. and Canada), and Japan - the three main democratic industrialized areas of the world - are the three sides of the Trilateral Commission. The Commission's members are about 325 distinguished citizens, with a variety of leadership responsibilities, from these three regions. When the first triennium of the Trilateral Commission was launched in 1973, the most immediate purpose was to draw together - at a time of considerable friction among governments - the highest level unofficial group possible to look together at the common problems facing our three areas. At a deeper level, there was a sense that the United States was no longer in such a singular leadership position as it had been in earlier post-World War II years, and that a more shared form of leadership - including Europe, and Japan in particular - would be needed for the international system to navigate successfully the major challenges of the coming years. These purposes continue to inform the Commission's work.*

> *The rise of Japan, and progress of the European Community over the past twenty years - particularly in the world economy - have validated the vision of the Commission's founders. At the same time, the end of the Cold War calls for a fresh vision of what this outward-looking partnership can accomplish in the coming years. The opportunities are remarkable, and yet, with the welcome end of the old Soviet threat, part of the 'glue' holding our regions together has dissolved. Helping meet that leadership challenge is at the heart of the Trilateral Commission effort.*

> *The full Commission gathers once each year - in Lisbon in 1992, in Washington in 1993, in Tokyo in 1994."* (In Copenhagen, Denmark in 1995.)

The above are **their words**. Below are words of those who see this group in a different light.

The New World Order, by Pat Robertson, Copyright 1991, Word, Inc., Dallas, Texas. All rights reserved, Page 102, states:

> *"In 1970 a young Polish intellectual named Zbigniew Brzezinski foresaw the rising economic power of Japan, and postwar Europe. Brzezinski idealized the theories of Karl Marx. In his book, <u>Between Two Ages</u>, as in subsequent writings, he argued that balance-of-power politics was out, and world-order politics was in. The initial world order was to be a trilateral economic linkage between Japan, Europe, and the United States. David Rockefeller funded Brzezinski, and called together an organization, named the Trilateral Commission, with Brzezinski as its first executive secretary, and director.*

> *The stated goals of the Trilateral Commission are: "Close Trilateral cooperation in keeping the peace, in managing the world economy, in fostering economic re-development, and alleviating world poverty will improve the chances of a smooth, and peaceful evolution of the global system."* (Emphasis added.)

The Shadows of Power, by James Perloff, Copyright 1988, pages 154-156, states:
> *"How did the TC begin? 'The Trilateral Commission,' wrote Christopher Lydon in the July 1977 Atlantic, 'was David Rockefeller's brainchild.' George Franklin, North American secretary of the Trilateral Commission, stated that it 'was entirely David Rockefeller's idea originally.' Helping the CFR chairman develop the concept was Zbigniew Brzezinski, who laid the first stone in Foreign Affairs in 1970:*

> *'A new, and bolder approach is needed - creation of a community of the developed nations which can effectively address itself to the larger concerns confronting mankind. In addition to the United States, and Western Europe, Japan ought to be included ... A council representing the United States, Western Europe, and Japan, with regular meetings of the heads of governments as well as some small standing machinery, would be a good start.'*

That same year, Brzezinski elaborated these thoughts in his book <u>Between Two Ages</u>. It shows Brzezinski to be a classic CFR man - a globalist more than lenient toward Communism. He declared that 'National sovereignty is no longer a viable concept', and that 'Marxism represents a further vital, and creative stage in the maturing of man's universal vision. Marxism is simultaneously a victory of the external, active man over the inner, passive man, and a victory of reason over belief...'

The Trilateral Commission was formally established in 1973, and consisted of leaders in business, banking, government, and mass media from North America, Western Europe, and Japan. David Rockefeller was founding chairman, and Brzezinski founding director of the North American branch, most of whose members were also in the CFR.

In the Wall Street Journal, David Rockefeller explained that 'the Trilateral Commission is, in reality, a group of concerned citizens interested in fostering greater understanding, and cooperation among international allies.'

But, it was not all so innocent according to Jeremiah Novak, who wrote in the Atlantic (July 1977):

'The Trilateralists' emphasis on international economics is not entirely disinterested, for the oil crisis forced many developing nations, with doubtful repayment abilities, to borrow excessively. All told, private multinational banks, particularly Rockefeller's Chase Manhattan, have loaned nearly $52 billion to developing countries. An overhauled IMF would provide another source of credit for these nations, and would take the big private banks off the hook. This proposal is the cornerstone of the Trilateral plan.

Senator Barry Goldwater put it less mercifully. In his book <u>With No Apologies,</u> he termed the Commission 'David Rockefeller's newest international cabal', and said, 'It is intended to be the vehicle for multinational consolidation of the commercial, and banking interests by seizing control of the political government of the United States.'

Zbigniew Brzezinski showed how serious TC ambitions were in the July 1973 <u>Foreign Affairs</u>, stating that 'without closer American-European-Japanese cooperation the major problems of today cannot be effectively tackled, and ... the active promotion of such trilateral cooperation must now become the central priority of U.S. policy.' (Emphasis in the ordinal.)

The best way to effect this would be for a Trilateralist to soon become President. One did." (Jimmy Carter.)

... In 1973, Carter dined with the CFR chairman (David Rockefeller) at the latter's Tarrytown, New York estate. Present was Zbigniew Brzezinski, who was helping Rockefeller screen prospects for the Trilateral Commission. Brzezinski later told Peter Pringle of the London Sunday Times that 'we were impressed that Carter had opened up trade offices for the state of Georgia in Brussels, and Tokyo. That seemed to fit perfectly into the concept of the Trilateral.' Carter became a founding member of the (Trilateral) Commission - and his destiny became calculable.

Senator Goldwater wrote:

'David Rockefeller and Zbigniew Brzezinski found Jimmy Carter to be their ideal candidate. They helped him win the nomination, and the presidency. To accomplish this purpose, they mobilized the money power of the Wall Street bankers, the intellectual influence of the academic community - which is subservient to the wealth of the great tax-free foundations - and the media controllers represented in the membership of the CFR, and the Trilateral.'

Seven months before the Democratic nominating convention, the Gallup Poll found less than four percent of Democrats favoring Jimmy Carter for President. But, almost overnight - like Willkie, and Eisenhower before him - he became the candidate."

This is probably one of the very best illustrations of the great power of the *Elite*. They can make or break any president or candidate for president. They <u>made</u> Jimmy Carter in his efforts to become president, and <u>broke</u> Senator Barry Goldwater in his failed attempt.

The TC membership is made up of present, and past Presidents, Ambassadors, Secretaries of State, Wall Street investors, international bankers, foundation executives, Think Tank executives, lobbyist lawyers, NATO, and Pentagon military leaders, wealthy industrialist, media owners, and executives, university presidents, and key professors, select Senators, and Congressmen, and wealthy entrepreneurs.

They hold annual secret meetings including only members, and very select guests.

The TC's US headquarters is located at 345 East 46th Street, Suite 711, New York, NY 10017.

Why Should We Care?

Even though these *Elite* organizations go to a lot of effort and expense to remain secret, the word seems to get out anyway. There have been dozens of very good books written since the beginning of this century on this subject, but they remain rather obscure, because the *Elite* conspire to suppress them.

The BB's are the most secretive of the three. When the BB's meet, they clear out all people in the buildings where they are to meet, they completely de-bug all the rooms, bring in their own cooks, waiters, housekeepers, heavily armed security guards, etc., and they do not allow outsiders anywhere near the meeting place just before, during, and immediately after they meet. These very powerful people do not meet to discuss the latest recipe for blueberry pancakes, or the melting rate of snow at the South Pole. When they meet, they more than likely discuss and decide:

<u>Wars</u> - They decide when wars should start, how long they should last, when they should end, who will and will not participate, the changes in boundaries of countries resulting from the outcome of these wars, who will lend the money to support the war efforts, and who will lend the money to rebuild the countries after they have been destroyed by war.

<u>Money</u> - They own the central banks, such as the Federal Reserve System in the US, and similar organizations in all major countries throughout the world, and therefore are in a position to determine discount rates, prime rates, money supply levels, the prices of gold and other precious metals, and very tightly control who and/or what countries should receive loans (guaranteed by the taxpayers of the respective countries).

<u>Governments</u> - They decide who will be allowed to run for the offices of President, Prime Minister, Chancellor, Governor General, or other names applied to the leaders of all major countries around the world.

<u>Stocks, Bonds, & Commodities</u> - Since the *Elite* own the major banks and the Central banks, they know exactly what interest rates and money supply levels will be, so it is very likely that they regularly run these exchanges up and down to their financial gain.

<u>News and other information</u> - They directly or indirectly own all the major news media, and can therefore tell the public exactly what they want them to hear, and deny the public the information they do not want them to see, hear, or read.

<u>Wages and salaries</u> - They directly or indirectly own all the major banks, businesses, industries, and the like, and therefore can suppress wages and salaries by either shipping the production jobs to the cheapest labor rates around the world, by importing the technical specialists from the cheapest countries around the world, and by employing mostly temporary and/or part time workers in their home countries. The labor unions do not resist such efforts, because the labor leaders are members of the *Elite* as well.

I don't know about you, but these above activities seriously concern me, because my children and grandchildren will suffer many times greater than we do today under the control of these **EVIL MONSTERS** (I have tried to find worse terms for them, but this is the best that I can think of to describe them). My ancestors finally decided to leave Ireland for the New World in 1772 because of economic suppression. The absentee landlords and money merchants of the time had raised the rents on the tenant farmers of Ireland three times in just one year, and the farmers could no longer afford to ply their trade. These brave people risked their lives in this new undeveloped land rather than continue to be persecuted by the *Elite* of that period. The writers of our Constitution took great care in drafting it so as to protect the US from *Elite* domination. We are again being conquered by the *Elite* in ever-increasing ways, and I, for one, have had enough. The best way to stop this cabal's efforts is **"SUNSHINE"**. *Who's Who of the Elite* is my hi-intensity spotlight on this conspiracy.

So, if you want answers to your questions about who is really in charge, this book will open your eyes.

Very Important Note

It is <u>very important</u> that the reader understand the basis of the study that produced the following facts. The names of the *Elite* came directly from very good sources.

The members of the Council on Foreign Relations are listed each year in their annual report. This document is available to the general public from the CFR headquarters, and back issues are available in many public libraries. Most of the back issues are available through inter-library loan services.

The members of the Trilateral Commission came directly from a list of members furnished by the TC headquarters in New York. The TC publishes this list annually, and it is available to the general public.

The members of the Bilderbergs are available only because Liberty Lobby, publishers of *The Spotlight,* has a very good underground network of investigative reporters who stay on the heels of this secret organization. They somehow find out when, and where the secret annual meetings will be held, and somehow get their hands on the lists of attendees. They often also obtain a copy of the agenda. However, to the best of my knowledge, no uninvited outsider has ever been able to slip past the Bilderberg security system, and into the meetings to hear what is actually discussed.

Should the reader care to verify any of this information, I have provided the address of each secret organization at the end of each brief history of the organizations. My sources are also clearly stated.

This study lists each *Elite* members "day job", and affiliation that offers the greatest contribution to the efforts of the *Elite's* plan to snare the US, and the rest of the world, into their Global Union (New World Order).

In order to avoid duplication, and confusion, each *Elite* member had to be linked to only one "day job". In reality, each of these members hold/held a number of important positions in quite a variety of organizations. For example: Robert F. Erburu is/was Chairman & CEO, Times-Mirror Co.; Director & Deputy Chairman, Fed. Reserve Bank of San Francisco; Trustee of, Brookings Institute, Carrie Estelle Doheny Foundation, Fletcher Jones Foundation, Pfaffinger Foundation, J. Paul Getty Trust, Times-Mirror Foundation, Ralph M. Parsons Foundation, & others. However, his greatest contribution to the *Elite* movement is as Chairman & CEO of Times-Mirror Co., so that is how he is listed in the following tables. This information was gathered over a eight year period, and some people have died, moved to new affiliations, been promoted or demoted, and/or hold different jobs within their affiliation. Therefore, these lists are merely a snapshot of where these people were, and their job titles, at the time that they were located. In some cases, I have updated the affiliation of key members of the Elite. However, to do so to all members would become an insurmountable task. The most important message that I provide is not necessarily their names, but the positions of influence that they hold/held.

Also, I have used the term "member" as a generic noun to describe those people who are associated with the *Elite*. This is not exactly correct in the case of the Bilderbergs, because they refer to the people who attend their conferences as "attendees, or invited guests". However, the Bilderbergs do have some, whom they call "members", who belong to their Steering Committee, and/or Advisory Committee.

As you review the following lists of BB, CFR, and TC members, you will notice that there are some members who do not have a "day job" title or affiliation attached to their names. I was successful in identifying the affiliations of 74% of the current members. However, to find the remaining 26% would have resulted in this book being seriously delayed, or never being published. Therefore, I would like to ask the readers to assist in identifying as many of the remaining 26% of unidentified members as possible for future revisions. I would ask that you provide sufficient documentation for your information, as you are willing to share. I cannot use information that is purely speculation, because I have an obligation to protect the innocent, as well. In this same regard, I welcome, and appreciate additions and corrections to my information, because this is a one-man human effort, and to err is human. However, the list of names in this book have been very carefully documented, so the only room for error in their names could be a typographical error in entering their names. Please send your contributions of information to RIE, 24505 Old Ferry Road, Spicewood, TX 78669. I thank you in advance for your help.

Members
of the
Bilderberg, Council on Foreign Relations, and Trilateral Commission's

Sorted by Affiliation

1991-99 Bilderberg Group, Council on Foreign Relations & Trilateral Commission Members

Source: '93 - '99 CFR Annual reports. & TC Master Membership lists ('93-'99); SPOTLIGHT '91 Reprint, + '95, '96, '97 & '99 issues,
Liberty Lobby, Inc., 300 Independence Ave., SE, Washington, DC 20003; attendees at Baden-Baden, Germany meeting of Bilderbergs
Who's Who in America '94, by Marquis, '93 & '94 annual reports., documents from various Think Tanks & other organizations.
Org.: B = US Bilderberg, BA = Austria, BB = Belgium, BC = Canada, BCH = Switzerland, BD = Germany, BK = Denmark, BE = Spain,
BF = France, BFIN = Finland, BGB = Great Britain, BGR = Greece, BH = BB Hungary, BI = Italy, BICE = Iceland, BINT = International
BIRL = Ireland, BL = Luxembourg, BN = Norway, BNL = BB, The Netherlands, BP = BB, Portugal, BPL = Poland, BRUS=Russia, BS = Sweden,
BTR = Turkey, C = Council on Foreign Relations, T = Trilateral Commission, TC = T Canada, TE = T Europe, TJ = T Japan, (fmr.) = former
"Members" applies to Bilderberg Steering Committee and Advisory Committee members, but other participants are Bilderberg "Attendees"

Last Name	First & Mid. Name	Org.	Job Title	Affiliation - Company, Organization	
Federal, State & City Governments					
			Executive Office of the President		
Clinton	William (Bill) J.	B,C,T	President	United States; Governor (fmr.), Arkansas	
Clinton	Hillary Rodham	B	Wife	President Clinton, Senator, New York	
Bush	George Herbert W.	C,T	President (fmr.)	United States; Vice Pres. (fmr.); Director (fmr.), CIA	
Carter	(James Earl) Jimmy	C,T	President (fmr.)	United States	
Ford	Gerald Rudolph, Jr.	B,C	President (fmr.)	United States	
Nixon	Richard Milhaus	C	President (fmr.)	United States	
Eisenhower	Dwight David	C	President (fmr.)	United States	
Hoover	Herbert Clark	C	President (fmr.)	United States	
Murray	Lori Esposito	C	Asst. Director	Arms Cont. & Disarm. Agency, Multilateral Affairs	
Scheinman	Lawrence	C	Asst. Director	Arms Cont. & Disarm. Agency, Nonproliferation	
Nacht	Michael L.	C	Asst. Director	Arms Cont. & Disarm. Agency, Strategic & Eurasian Afrs.	
Earle	Ralph, II	C	Deputy Director	Arms Cont. & Dsrm. Agen.; Dir.,Lawyers Alliance/World Secur.	
Burt	Richard R.	C	Negotiator	Arms Contr. & Disar. Agen., Mbr. (fmr.), Carnegie Endow.	
Lehman	Ronald F., II	C	Director (fmr.)	Arms Control & Disarmament Agency	
Hoinkes	Mary Elizabeth	C	General Counsel	Arms Control & Disarmament Agency	
Hurwitz	Seth L.	C	Counsel (fmr.)	White House, Advisory Committee, Int. Oversight Bd.	
Frankel	Jeffrey A.	C	Member	White House, Council of Economic Advisors	
Hadley	Stephen J.	C	Asst. Secretary (fmr.)	White House, for Int. Security Policy	
Dyke	Nancy Bearg	C	Asst. (fmr.)	White House, for Nat. Security Affairs	
Lampley	Virginia A.	C	Spec. Assits.	White House, Nat. Security Affairs	
Flanagan	Stephen J.	C		White House, Nat. Security Council	
Laipson	Ellen	C	Member	White House, Nat. Security Council	
Witkowsky	Anne A.	C	Director	White House, Nat. Security Council	
Penn	Mark	C	Asian Expert	White House, Nat. Security Council	
DeSouza	Patrick J.	C	Project Dir.	White House, Nat. Security Council	
Feith	Douglas J.	C	Member (fmr.)	White House, Nat. Security Council	
Flournoy	Michael A.	C	Member	White House, Nat. Security Council	
Harris	Elisa D.	C	Director	Nat. Sec. Council, Nonproliferation & Export Control	
Gottemoeller	Rose E.	C	Director	Nat. Sec. Council, Russian, Ukraine & Eurasian Affairs	
Blackwill	Robert D.	B,C	Member (fmr.)	Nat. Sec. Council; Lecturer, JFK School, Harvard Univ.	
Rice	Susan Elizabeth	C	Director	Nat. Security Council, Global Issues & Multinational Afrs.	
Lake	W. Anthony (Tony)	C	Asst. to President	Nat. Security Council; Advisory Bd., Ctr. for Nat. Policy	
Petersen	Howard C.	B,C	Advisor (fmr.)	National Security Council	
Kupchan	Charles A.	C	Member	National Security Council	
Kristoff	Sandra J.	C	Spec. Asst. to Pres.	National Security Council, Asia-Pacific Economic Affairs	
Feaver	Peter D.	C	Director	National Security Council, Defense Policy	
Holl	Jane E.	C	Director	National Security Council, European Affairs	
Schwartz	Eric Paul	C	Director	National Security Council, Global Issues	
Schifter	Richard	C	Special Asst. to Pres.	National Security Council, Washington	
Scowcroft	Brent	B,C,T	Asst. to Pres. (fmr.)	National Security Council; Director (fmr.), CFR	
Kupchan	Clifford A.	C	Member	National Security Council	
Dutton	Frederick G.	C	Special Asst. (fmr.)	White House, to the President	
Nierenberg	Claudia	C		NASA, NOAA, Office of Global Programs	
Kalil	Thomas A.	C	Sr. Director	Nat. Economic Council	
Garment	Leonard	C	White Hse. Council (fmr.)	Nixon Admin.	
Katz	Abraham	C	Chairman	Council for International Business	
Stiglitz	Joseph E.	C	Chairman	Council of Economic Advisers	
Tyson	Laura D'Andrea	B,C,T	Chairwoman (fmr.)	Council of Economic Advisors; Prof., Harvard Univ.	
Gibbons	John Howard	C	Director	Exec. office of the Pres., Office of Sci. & Tech. Policy	
Blacker	Coit Dennis	C	Special Asst.	Exec. Office/Pres., Russian, Ukranian & Eurasian Afrs.	
Brainard	S. Lael	C	Spec. Asst.	Executive Office to President, Int. Economic Affairs	
Keene	Lonnie S.	C	Sr. Policy Analyst	Exec. Office of the President	
Roth	Stanley Owen	C	Spec. Asst.	Executive Office / Pres., Asian Affairs	
Nitze	Paul Hilken	B,C	Director (fmr.)	Fgn. Pol. Plng., Truman, Eisenhower & Nixon Admin.	
Goodman	John B.	C	Special Advisor	for Defense, Conversion & Tech.	
Duffey	Joseph Daniel	C	Director	Information Agency; President (fmr.), American Univ.	
Emerson	Steven A.	C	Specialist	Middle East terrorist	
Richardson	Elliot Lee	C,T	Partner	Milbank, Tweed, Hadley, & McCloy; Dir. (fmr.), CFR	
Esty	Daniel C.	C	Negotiator	NAFTA	
Gates	Robert M.	C	Director	National Intelligence Council; Dir., C.I.A. (fmr.)	
Kolt	George	C	Head	CIA National Intelligence Council, Russia	
Schoettle	Enid C. B.	C		National Intelligence Council	
McFarlane	Robert C.	C	Advisor (fmr.)	National Security , Reagan Admin.	
Berger	Samuel R. (Sandy)	B,C	Asst. to President	National Security Affairs	

Last Name	First & Mid. Name	Org.	Job Title	Affiliation - Company, Organization
Blinken	Anthony (Tony) J.	C	Special Assiostant	to Pres. Clinton, for National Security Affaiors
Soderberg	Nancy E.	B,C	Deputy Asst. to Pres.	Nat. Secur. Afrs.; Fgn. Pol. Adv. to Sen. Ted Kennedy
Odom	William Eldridge	C	Directtor (fmr.)	National Security Agency (NSA)
Garment	Leonard	C	WhiteHse.Coun. (fmr.)	Nixon Admin.
Ponneman	Daniel B.	C	Spec. Asst. to Pres.	Nonproliferation & Export Control
Selin	Ivan	C	Chairman	Nuclear Regulatory Commission (NRC)
Adams	Gordon M.	C	Assoc. Dir.	Office of Management & Budget
Min	Nancy-Ann	C	Associate Director	Office of Management & Budget
Edley	Christopher, Jr.	C	Associate Director	Office of Management & Budget, Economics & Gvt.
Darman	Richard Gordon	C,T	Director (fmr.)	Office of Management & Budget, Bush Admin.
Kramer	Mark Nathan	C	Member	Office of Mgt. & Budget, Coun. on Environ. Quality
Kyle	Robertr D.	C	Spec. Asst. to Pres.	Office of Policy Development
Johns	Lionel Skipwth	C	Assoc. Dir.	Office of Science & Technology
Branscomb	Lewis Mcardy	C	Advisory Council	Off. of Tech. Asmt.; Dir., Mobil Oil Corp.; Dir., Harvard U.
Lederberg	Joshua	C	V. Chair., Adv. Coun.	Off. of Tech. Assessment; Dir., CFR, '89-
Bellamy	Carol	C	Director	Peace Corp., Clinton Admin.; Dir., UNICEF
Barton	Christopher	C	Country Desk Officer	Peace Corps, Costarica, Honduras, Paraguay
Bromley	David Allan	C	Chairman	President's Council for Advancement on Sci. & Tech.
Boskin	Michael Jay	B	Chairman (fmr.)	President's Council of Economic Advisors
Graham	William R., Jr.	C	Science Advisor	to President & Dir. of Office of Sci. & Tech.
Tapia	Raul R.	C	Dep. Spec. Asst.	to President Carter
Carter	William Hodding, III	C	Press Secretary (fmr.)	to President Carter
Cutler	Lloyd Norton	C,T	Counsel	to US Pres. Clinton, '94; Adv. Bd. Mbr., Ctr. for Nat. Pol.
Schlesinger	Arthur Meier, Jr.	C	Special Asst. (fmr.)	to US Pres., '61-64; Adv. Bd. Mbr., Ctr. for Nat. Policy
Sorensen	Theodore Chaikin	C	Special Counsel (fmr.)	to US Pres., '61-64; Bd. Mbr., Ctr. for Int. Pol.; Dir., CFR
Stephanopolos	George R.	B,C	Senior Advisor (fmr.)	to US President Clinton; Rhodes Scholor
Cutter	W. Bowman	C	Deputy Assistant	to US President for Economic Policy
Baker	Howard Henry, Jr.	C	Chief Of Staff (fmr.)	to US President Reagan; Senator (fmr.), Tennessee
Montgomery	Parker Gilbert	C	Member	Trade Representative, Invironmental Pol. Adv. Comm.
Holum	John D.	C	Director	US Defense Dept. Arms Control & Disarmament Agency
Graham	Thomas Wallace, Jr.	C	General Counsel	US Arms Control & Disarmiment Agency
Hills	Carla Anderson	C,T	US Trade Rep. (fmr.)	Exec. Off./Bush Admin.; Trustee, Urban Inst.; Dir., CFR
Spangler	Scott M.	C	Assis. Admin. (fmr.)	USAID
Price	Daniel M.	C	Deputy Gen. Counsel	US Trade Representative
Williamson	Irving A.	C	Deputy Gen. Counsel	US Trade Representative
Bolten	Joshua B.	C	General Counsel	US Trade Representative
Walker	Jenonne R.	C	Spec. Asst. to Pres.	White House, European Affairs
Wales	Jane	C	Associate Director	White House, Interagency Committees
Sonenshine	Tara	C	Deputy Director	White House, National Security Policy; Newsweek Mag.
Wolin	Neal Steven	C	Executive Assistant	White House, Office of National Security Affairs
Duberstein	Kenneth M.	C	Chief-of-Staff (fmr.)	White House, Reagan Administration
Hamburg	Margaret Ann	C	Director (fmr.)	White House Press Conferences; New York City Health Comm.
Administration				
			Agriculture Dept.	
Espy	Mike	B	Secretary	Agriculture Dept.
Freeman	Harry Louis	C	Secretary (fmr.)	Agriculture; Chair., Worldwatch
Hoffman	Michael L.	C	Bureau Chief	Agriculture Dept., Chemistry Div.
			C.I.A.	
Tenet	George J.	C	Director	C.I.A.
Studeman	William Oliver	C	Director (interim)	C.I.A.; Dir. (fmr.), Dept. of Central Intelligence
Deutch	John Mark	B,C,T	Director (fmr.)	C.I.A.; Deputy Secretary (Fmr.) Defense Dept., for Acquis.
Woolsey	R. James	C	Director (fmr.)	C.I.A.; Member, National Security Council
Gates	Robert M.	C	Director (fmr.)	C.I.A.
Webster	William H.	C	Director (fmr.)	C.I.A.
Casey	William J.	C	Director (fmr.)	C.I.A.
Turner	Stansfield	C	Director (fmr.)	C.I.A.
Bush	George H. W.	C	Director (fmr.)	C.I.A.
Colby	William E.	C	Director (fmr.)	C.I.A.
Schlesinger	James	C	Director (fmr.)	C.I.A.
Helms	Richard	C	Director (fmr.)	C.I.A.
McCone	John A.	C	Director (fmr.)	C.I.A.
Dulles	Allen W.	C	Director (fmr.)	C.I.A.
Helms	Richard McGarrah	C	Director (Fmr.)	C.I.A.
Colby	William Egan	C	Director (fmr.)	C.I.A.
Smith	Walter Bedell	C	Director (fmr.)	C.I.A.
Cooper	Charles A.	C,T	Chairman	C.I.A., Nat. Intelligence Council
Rindskopf	Elizabeth R.	C	General Counsel	C.I.A.
Cooper	Chester L.	C	Agent	C.I.A.
Kessler	Martha Neff	C	Assit. NIO	C.I.A., Middle East
Christianson	Geryld B.	C	Agent	C.I.A., Ottawa, 1968-'71
Armstrong	Willis C.	C	Agent	C.I.A., Ottawa, Canada 5862

Last Name	First & Mid. Name	Org.	Job Title	Affiliation - Company, Organization	
			Commerce Dept.		
Brown	Ronald Harmon	C	Secretary	Commerce Dept.	
Kreps	Juanita M.	C,T	Secretary (fmr.)	Commerce Dept.; Director (fmr.), CFR	
Richardson	Elliot Lee	C,T	Secretary (fmr.)	Commerce Dept.	
Peterson	Peter G.	C,T	Secretary (fmr.)	Commerce Dept.	
Connor	John Thomas, Jr.	C	Secretary (fmr.)	Commerce Dept.	
Franklin	Barbara Hackman	C	Secretary (fmr.)	Commerce Dept.; Director, Dow Chemical Co.	
Fitz-Pegado	Lauri J.	C	Asst. Sec.-Designate	Commerce Dept., Foreign Comm. Service	
Haynes	Fred	C	Division Manager	Commerce Dept., Office of Marketing & Product Mgt.	
Meissner	Charles F.	C	Asst. Secretary	Commerce Dept., International Economic Policy	
Rothkopf	David J.	C	Deputy Under Sec.	Commerce Dept., Int. Trade Policy Development	
Carter	Barry Edward	C	Deputy Under Secretary	Commerce Dept., for Export	
Kearney	Jude	C	Dep. Asst. Secretary	Commerce Dept., Service and Finance	
Schuker	Jill	C	Director	Commerce Dept., Office of Public Affairs	
Pollack	Gerald A.	C	Assoc. Director	Commerce Dept., Int. Economics	
Schwab	Susan Carol	C	Asst. Secretary (fmr.)	Commerce Dept.	
Kea	Charlotte G.	C	Spec. Asst. to Assit. Sec	Commerce Dept., Commercial Services	
McEntee	Joan M.	C	Specialist (fmr.)	Commerce Dept., Military Technology	
			Defense Dept.		
Cohen	William Sebastian	C,T	Secretary	Defense; Senator (fmr.), Maine, Armed Svcs., Judiciary	
Perry	William J.	B,T	Secretary (fmr.)	Defense Dept.; Prof., Stanford Univ.	
Aspin	Les	C	Secretary (fmr.)	Defense Dept.; Senator (fmr.)	
Cheney	Richard B.	C,T	Secretary (fmr.)	Defense Dept.	
Carlucci	Frank C., III	C,T	Secretary (fmr.)	Defense Dept.	
Weinberger	Casper Willard	C,T	Secretary (fmr.)	Defense Dept.; Chairman, Forbes magazine	
Brown	Harold	C,T	Secretary (fmr.)	Defense Dept.; Councelor, Ctr. for Strategic & Int. Stud.	
Rumsfeld	Donald H.	B,C	Secretary (fmr.)	Defense Dept.	
Schlesinger	James R.	C	Secretary (fmr.)	Defense Dept.	
Richardson	Elliot Lee	C,T	Secretary (fmr.)	Defense Dept.	
Laird	Melvin R.	T	Secretary (fmr.)	Defense Dept.	
McNamara	Robert Strange	B,C,T	Secretary (fmr.)	Defense Dept.	
McElroy	Neil H.	C	Secretary (fmr.)	Defense Dept.	
Wilson	Charles E.	C	Secretary (fmr.)	Defense Dept.	
Marshall	George C.	C	Secretary (fmr.)	Defense Dept.	
Forrestal	James V.	C	Secretary (fmr.)	Defense Dept.	
White	John P.	C	Deputy Secretary	Defense Dept.; Chair., Concord Coalition	
Stone	Michael P. W.	C	Secretary (fmr.)	Defense Dept., Dept. of the Army	
West	Togo D.	C	Secretary (fmr.)	Defense Dept.,, of the Army	
Patterson	Robert P.	C	Secretary (fmr.)	War Department	
Stimson	Henry L.	C	Secretary (fmr.)	War Department	
Davis	Dwight F.	C	Secretary (fmr.)	War Department	
Weeks	John W.	C	Secretary (fmr.)	War Department	
Baker	Newton D.	C	Secretary (fmr.)	War Department	
Horton	Frank B., III	C	Prin. Deputy	Defense Dept., to Assist. Secretary	
Mark	Gregory A.	C	Secretary (fmr.)	Air Force, Carter Admin.; Chancellor, Univ. of Texas, Austin	
Owens	William Arthur	C	Vice Chairman	Defense Dept., Joint Chiefs of Staff	
Shalicashvilli	John M.	C	Chairman (fmr.)	Defense Dept., Joint Chiefs of Staff	
Powell	Colin Luther	B,C	Chairman (fmr.)	Defense Dept., Joint Chiefs of Staff	
Crowe	William J., Jr.	C,T	Chairman (fmr.)	Defense Dept., Joint Chiefs of Staff	
Vessey	John W.	C	Chairman (fmr.)	Defense Dept., Joint Chiefs of Staff	
Jones	David Charles	C	Chairman (fmr.)	Defense Dept., Jt. Chiefs of Staff; Dir., Gen. Electric Co.	
Taylor	Gen. Maxwell D.	C	Chairman (fmr.)	Defense Dept., Joint Chiefs of Staff	
Lemnitzer	Gen. Lyman	C	Chairman (fmr.)	Defense Dept., Joint Chiefs of Staff	
McCloy	John J., II	B,C	Commander-in-Chief	Defense Dept., Air Force, Headquarters, Euro. Command	
Smith	Leighton Warren, Jr.	C	Commander-in-Chief	Defense Dept., Naval Operations	
Thurman	Maxwell R.	C	Cmdr.-in-Chief (fmr.)	Defense Dept., Southern Command, Panama	
Rogers	Bernard William	C	Cmdr.-in-Chief (fmr.)	Defense Dept., European Command	
Turner	Stansfield	C	Cmdr.-in-Chief (fmr.)	Def. Dept., N. A. T. O., Allied Forces Southern Europe	
Butler	George Lee	C	Cmdr.-in-Chief (fmr.)	Defense Dept., USAF, Strategic	
Train	Harry Depue, II	C	Cmdr.-in-Chief (fmr.)	Def. Dept., Atlantic Flt. & Supreme Allied Commander	
Goodpaster	Andrew Jackson	B,C	Cmdr.-in-Chief (fmr.)	Def. Dept.; Superintendent (fmr.), US Military Academy	
Boyd	Charles Graham	C	ep. Cmdr.-in-Chief (fmr	Defense Dept., US European Command	
Galvin	John Rogers	B,C	Supr. Ald. Cdr. (fmr.)	Defense Dept., SHAPE, Europe	
Fogleman	Ronald R.	C	Chief-of-Staff	Defense Dept., Air Force, Air Mobility Command	
McPeak	Merrill Anthony	C	Chief-of-Staff	Defense Dept., Air Force	
Chain	John T., Jr.	C	Chief-of-Staff	Defense Dept., Air Force; CO of Strategic Air Command	
Reimer	Dennis J.	C	Chief-of-Staff	Defense Dept., Army	
Allen	Lew, Jr.	C	Chief-of-Staff (fmr.)	Defense Dept., Air Force	
Dugan	Michael J.	C	Chief-of-Staff (fmr.)	Defense Dept., Air Force	
Gabriel	Charles Alvin	C	Chief-of-Staff (fmr.)	Defense Dept., Air Force	
Welch	Larry D.	C	Chief-of-Staff (fmr.)	Defense Dept., Air Force	

Last Name	First & Mid. Name	Org.	Job Title	Affiliation - Company, Organization
Sullivan	Gordon Russell	C	Chief-of-Staff (fmr.)	Defense Dept., Army
Wickham	John Adams, Jr.	C	Chief-of-Staff (fmr.)	Defense Dept., Army
Meyer	Edward Charles	C	Chief-of-Staff (fmr.)	Defense Dept., Army, Carter Admin.
Ralston	Joseph W.	C	Dep. Chief-of-Staff	Defense Dept., Air Force
Boorda	Jeremy Michael	C	Chief (fmr.)	Defense Dept., Naval Operations
Johnson	Jerome L.	C	Vice Chief	Defense Dept., Naval Operations
Dur	Philip A.	C	Rear Admiral	Defense Dept., Navy
Johnson	Jay L.	C	Chairman	Defense Dept., of Naval Operations
Kross	Walter	C	Commander in Chief	Defense Dept., Transportation Command
Marshall	Andrew W.	C	Director	Defense Dept., Net Assessment
Marshall	Anthony D.	C	Director	Defense Dept., Net Assessment
Caulfield	Matthew Patrick	C	Director	Defense Dept., Marine Corps, WFG
Harshberger	Edward R.	C	Director	Defense Dept., Navy, Acquisition Policy
Horn	Sally K.	C	Director	Defense Dept., Threat Reduction Policy
Merritt	Jack Neil	C	Director (fmr.)	Defense Dept., Joint Chiefs of Staff
Hanson	Thor	C	Director (fmr.)	Defense Dept., Joint Chiefs of Staff, Joint Staff
Slocombe	Walker Becker	C	Under Secretary	Defense Dept.; Advisory Board, Center for Nat. Policy
Warner	Edward L., III	C	Assistant Secretary	Defense Dept.
Carter	Ashton B.	C	Assistant Secretary	Defense Dept., Nuclear Section
Freeman	Charles W., Jr.	B	Asst. Sec. (fmr.)	Defense Dept., for Int. Security
Wallerstein	Mitchel B.	C	Deputy Asst. Sec.	Defense Dept., Counterproliferation Policy
Sewall	Sarah	C	Deputy Asst. Sec.	Def. Dept., Peacekeeping & Peace Enforcement Policy
Irvin	Patricia L.	C	Deputy Asst. Sec.	Defense Dept., Humanities & Refugee Affairs
Kruzel	Joseph J.	C	Deputy Asst. Sec.	Defense Dept., European & N. A. T. O. Policy
Sherwood	Elizabeth D.	C	Deputy Asst. Sec.	Defense Dept., Nuclear Security
Duffy	Gloria Charmian	C	Dep. Asst. Sec. (fmr.)	Defense Dept., Special Coordinatyor for Threat Reduction
Goodman	Sherri Wasserman	C	Deputy Under Sec.	Defense Dept., Environmental Security
Lodal	Jan M.	C	Prin. Dep. Under Sec.	Defense Dept., for Policy
Eberhart	Ralph E.	C	Vice Chief-of-Staff	Defense Dept. HQ U. S. Airforce, Wash.
Stein	Paul E.	C	Superintendent	Defense Dept., Air Force Academy
Stofft	William A.	C	President	Defense Dept., Army War College
Summers	Harry G., Jr.	C	Fellow	Defense Dept., Army War College
Stevenson	Charles A.	C	Professor	Defense Dept., National War College
Deibel	Terry L.	C	Prof. & Chairman	Defense Dept., National War College, Nat. Security Pol.
Rokke	Ervin Jerome	C	President	Defense Dept., National Defense University
Cerjan	Paul G.	C	President (fmr.)	Defense Dept., National Defense University
Kramer	Steven Philip	C	Professor	Defense Dept., Nat. Defense Univ., Ind. College
Bennett	Donald Vivian	C	Superintendent (fmr.)	Def. Dept.; Superintendent (fmr.), US Military Academy
Rostow	Eugene Victor	B,C	Dist. Vis. Resch. Prof.	Defense Dept., National Defense University
Clark	Wesley Kanne	C	Comdr.-in-Chief	Defense Dept., Southern Command
Hunter	Robert E.	B,C	US Representative	Defense Dept., N. A. T. O.
Taft	William H., IV	C	US Ambassador (fmr.)	Defense Dept., N. A. T. O.
Keel	Alton Gold, Jr.	C	US Ambassador (fmr.)	Defense Dept., N. A. T. O.
Knowlton	William Allen	C	Representative (fmr.)	Defense Dept., N. A. T. O., US Army
Hayward	Thomas B.	C	Admiral (fmr.)	Defense Dept., Chief of Naval Oper.
Pustay	John S.	C	Major General	Defense Dept.
Smith	DeWitt C., Jr.	C	Major General	Defense Dept.
Pustay	John S.	C	Major General	Defense Dept.
Gregson	Wallace C.	C	Brig. General	Defense Dept., U.S. Marine Corp, Asst. Deputy Chief of Staff
Mize	David M.	C	Brig. General	Defense Dept., Deputy Dir., European Command
Smith	Perry M.	C	Brigadear General	Defense Dept.
Sewall	John O. B.	C	Maj. General (fmr.)	Defense Dept. Army
McCarthy	James P.	C	General	Defense Dept., Air Force
Ross	James D.	C	General	Defense Dept., Army
Woerner	Fred F.	C	General	Defense Dept., Southern Command
Richardson	William R.	C	Lt. General	Defense Dept., Army
Rowny	Edward L.	C	Lt. General	Defense Dept.
Kern	Paul J.	C	Lt. General	Defense Dept., Army Acquisions Corp.
Vuono	Carl E.	C	General (fmr.)	Defense Dept., Army
Cisneros	Marc A.	C	Commander (fmr.)	Defense Dept., Fifth U.S. Army
Horton	Alan W.	C	Colonel	Defense Dept., Air Force
Golden	James R.	C	Lt. Col. (fmr.)	US Army
Snyder	David M.	C	Captain	Defense Dept., Air Force
Flynn	Stephen E.	C	Member	Defense Dept., Cost Guard
Krulak	Charles C.	C	Commandant	Defense Dept., Marine Corps
Mundy	Carl Epting, Jr.	C	Commandant (fmr.)	Defense Dept., Marine Corps
Kelley	Paul Xavier	C	Commandant (fmr.)	Defense Dept., Marine Corps
Wilkerson	Thomas L.	C	Maj. General	Defense Dept., Marine Corps Plans
Pilling	Donald L.	C	Division Director	Defense Dept., Navy, General Planning
Cebrowski	Arthur K.	C	Director for Command	Defense Dept., Control, Communications & Computer Syst.
Smith	William Young	C	President (fmr.)	Defense Dept., Defense Analyses
Ikle	Fred Charles	C	Member (fmr.)	Defense Dept., Defense Policy Advisory Commission
Miller	Franklin C.	C	Sr. Counselor	Defense Dept., Forces Policy
Hilton	Robert Parker, Sr.	C	Vice Director (fmr.)	Defense Dept., Office Joint Chiefs-of-Staff
Smith	Larry K.	C	Counselor	Defense Dept., Office of the Secretary
Spalter	Jonathan	C	Special Assistant	Defense Dept., Principal Deputy Under Secretary
Longstreth	Thomas K.	C	Prin. Dep. Asst. Sec.	Defense Dept., Strategy, Requirements & Resources

Last Name	First & Mid. Name	Org.	Job Title	Affiliation - Company, Organization	
Cisler	Walker Lee	B,C	Chf., Pub. Util. (fmr.)	Defense Dept., Supreme Allied Com., Euro. Command	
McNeill	John Henderson	C	Deputy Gen. Counsel	Defense Dept.	
Sullivan	Margaret C.	C	Special Asst. to Sec.	Defense Dept.	
Marr	Phebe A.	C		National Defense Univ.; Mid-East Specialist	
Campbell	Kurt M.	C		Defense Dept.	
			Education Dept.		
Kearns	David T.	C,T	Dep. Sec. of Educ.	Education Dept.; Chairman (fmr.) XEROX Corp.	
			Energy Dept.		
Richardson	William (Bill) Blaine	B,C	Secretary	Energy Dept.; US Ambassador (fmr.) to the UN	
Schlesinger	James Rodney	C	Secretary (fmr.)	Energy Dept.	
Duncan	Charles William, Jr.	C	Secretary (fmr.)	Energy Dept.	
Whitaker	Mark	C	Director	Energy Dept., Defense Nuclear Facility Safety Board	
Young	Alison (Alice) I.	C	Division Director	Energy Dept., Planning & Restoration	
			Federal Bureau of Iinvestigation (FBI)		
Webster	William H.	C	Director (fmr.)	F.B.I.	
Ruckelshaus	William D.	C,T	Director (fmr.)	F.B.I.	
			H.H.S. Dept.		
Shalala	Donna E.	C,T	Secretary	H. H. S. Dept.; Member (fmr.), TC ; Director, CFR	
Califano	Joseph Anthony, Jr.	C	Secretary (fmr.)	H.H.S. Dept.	
Weinberger	Casper Willard	C,T	Secretary (fmr.)	H.H.S. Dept.	
Richardson	Elliot Lee	C,T	Secretary (fmr.)	H.H.S. Dept.	
Ribicoff	Abraham A.	C	Secretary (fmr.)	H.H.S. Dept.	
Chow	Jack C.	C	Int. Coord. & Liason	H. H. S. Dept., Fogerty International Center	
Smith	Wayne S.	C	Division Director	H. H. S. Dept., Office of Survey & Certification	
			H.U.D. Dept.		
Cisneros	Henry G.	C,T	Secretary (Frm.)	H. U. D. Dept.; Mayor (fmr.), San Antonio; Bd., Ctr./Nat. Pol.	
Hills	Carla Anderson	C,T	Secretary (Frm.)	H. U. D. Dept.	
Lynn	James Thomas	C,T	Secretary (Frm.)	H. U. D. Dept.	
Young	Joan P.	C	Administrative Officer	H. U. D. Dept., Office of Ethics	
			Interior Dept.		
Babbitt	Bruce Edward	C,T	Secretary	Interior Dept.	
			Justice Dept.		
Thornburgh	Richard	C	Attorney Gen. (fmr.)	Justice Dept.	
Rogers	William P.	C	Attorney Gen. (fmr.)	Justice Dept., '58-'61; Hon. Dir., Foreign Policy Assoc.	
Thornburgh	(Richard L.) Dick	C	Attorney Gen. (fmr.)	Justice Dept.; Under Secretary General (fmr.), UN	
Richardson	Elliot Lee	C,T	Attorney Gen. (fmr.)	Justice Dept.	
Katzenbach	Nicholas deB.	C	Attorney Gen. (fmr.)	Justice Dept.	
Rogers	William P.	C	Attorney Gen. (fmr.)	Justice Dept.	
Meissner	Doris M.	C	Commissioner	Justice Dept., Immigration & Naturalization Service	
Ewing	William Hickman, Jr.	C	US Attorney (fmr.)	Justice Dept.	
Guthman	Edwin O.	C	Press Secretary (fmr.)	Justice Dept., to Rob. F. Kennedy	
Seigenthaler	John L.	C	Admin. Asst. (fmr.)	Justice Dept., to Robert F. Kennedy	
			Labor Dept.		
Martin	Lynn	C	Secretary (fmr.)	Labor Dept.	
Williamson	Thomas Samuel, Jr.	C	Solicitor	Labor Dept.; Ptnr., Covington & Burling, Washington	
			State Dept.		
Albright	Madeleine K.	C	Secretary	State, State Dept.; Amb. (fmr.), United Nations	
Richardson	William (Bill) Blaine	C	Secretary (fmr.)	State Dept.	
Christopher	Warren M.	C,T	Secretary (fmr.)	State Dept.; Chairman, Carnegie Corp. of New York	
Eagleburger	Lawrence S.	C,T	Secretary (fmr.)	State Dept.; Director, Phillips Petroleum	
Baker	James A., III	C	Secretary (fmr.)	State Dept.	
Schultz	George P.	C	Secretary (fmr.)	State Dept.	
Haig	Alexander Meigs, Jr.	C,T	Secretary (fmr.)	State Dept.; Chairman & President, Worldwide Assoc., Inc.	
Muskie	Edmund Sixtus	C	Secretary (fmr.)	State Dept.	
Vance	Cyrus Robert	C,T	Secretary (fmr.)	State Dept.	
Kissinger	Henry Alfred	B,C,T	Secretary (fmr.)	State Dept., Nixon, Carter Admin.; Chair., Kissinger Assoc.	
Rogers	William P.	C	Secretary (fmr.)	State Dept.	
Rusk	Dean	B,C	Secretary (fmr.)	State Dept.	
Herter	Christian A., Jr.	B,C	Secretary (fmr.)	State Dept.	
Dulles	John Foster	C	Secretary (fmr.)	State Dept.	
Acheson	Dean G.	C	Secretary (fmr.)	State Dept.	
Marshall	George C.	C	Secretary (fmr.)	State Dept.	
Stettinius	E. R., Jr.	C	Secretary (fmr.)	State Dept.	
Hull	Cordell	C	Secretary (fmr.)	State Dept.	
Stimson	Henry L.	C	Secretary (fmr.)	State Dept.	
Kellogg	Frank B.	C	Secretary (fmr.)	State Dept.	
Lansing	Robert	C	Secretary (fmr.)	State Dept.	
Rusk	Dean	B,C	Secretary (fmr.)	State Dept.; Adv. Bd. mbr., Ctr. for Int. Pol. & Nat. Policy	

Last Name	First & Mid. Name	Org.	Job Title	Affiliation - Company, Organization	
Herter	Christian A., Jr.	B,C	Secretary (fmr.)	State Dept.	
Talbott	Strobe	C,T	Deputy Secretary	State Dept.; US Ambassador (fmr.), to Russia; Dir., CFR	
Wharton	Clifton R., Jr.	C,T	Deputy Secr. (fmr.)	State Dept.; Member (fmr.), TC; Director, CFR	
Cohen	Herman Jay	C	Assistant Secretary	State Dept., African Affairs	
Gati	Toby Trister	C	Assistant Secretary	State Dept., Intelligence & Research Bureau	
Kelly	John H.	C	Assistant Secretary	State Dept., Near Eastern & South Asian Affairs	
Lord	Winston	B,C,T	Assistant Sec. (fmr.)	State Dept., East Asian & Pacific Affairs; Mbr. (fmr.) TC	
Oxman	Stephen A.	C	Assistant Secretary	State Dept., European & Canadian Affairs	
Watson	Alexander Fletcher	C	Assistant Secretary	State Dept., Inter-American Affairs	
Shattuck	John	C	Assistant Secretary	State Dept., Democracy, Human Rights & Labor	
Raphel	Robin L.	C	Asst. Secretary	State Dept., South Asian Affairs	
Dallara	Charles H.	B	Asst. Secretary (fmr.)	State Dept., International Affairs	
Derian	Patricia Murphy	C	Asst. Secretary (fmr.)	State Dept., Human Rights	
Korb	Lawrence J.	C	Asst. Secretary (fmr.)	State Dept., Bush Admin.; Brookings Inst.	
Atwood	John Brian	C	Under Secretary	State Dept., Mgt..; Admin., US Int. Devel. Coop. Agency	
Eizenstat	Stuart E.	C	Under Secretary	St. Dept, Int. Trade; V. Ch., Powell, Goldstein, Frazer & Murphy	
Davis	Lynn E.	B,C,T	Under Secretary	State Dept., International Security Affairs	
Moose	Richard M.	C	Under Secretary	State Dept., For Management	
Spero	Joan Edelman	C,T	Under Secretary	State Dept., Econ. & Agric. Affairs; Member (fmr.), TC	
Tarnoff	Peter	C,T	Under Secretary	State Dept.; President (fmr.) Council on Fgn. Relations	
Samuels	Nathaniel	C	Dep. Under Sec. (fmr.)	State Dept.	
Fort	Randall Martin	C	Deputy Asst. Sec.	State Dept.	
Freeman	Bennett	C	Deputy Asst. Sec.	State Dept., Public Affairs	
Harris	Martha Caldwell	C	Deputy Asst. Sec.	State Dept., Center for Defense Trade	
Kurtzer	Daniel C.	C	Deputy Asst. Sec.	State Dept.	
Niehuss	John M.	C	Deputy Asst. Sec.	State Dept., International Monitary Affairs	
Valenzuela	Arturo A.	C	Deputy Asst. Sec.	State Dept., Mexican Affairs	
Verville	Elizabeth Giavani	C	Deputy Asst. Sec.	State Dept., Bureau of Political-Military Affairs	
Rickard	Stephen A.	C	Dep. Assis. Sec.	State Dept., South Asian Affairs	
Kartman	Charles	C	Princ. Dep. Assis. Sec.	State Dept., East Asian and Pacific Affairs	
Gibney	Frank Bray	C	Director	State Dept., Commission for Pacific Econ. Cooperation	
Perkins	Edward J.	C	Director	State Dept., Personnel; Amb. (fmr.), United Nations	
Steinberg	James B.	B,C	Director	State Dept., Policy Planning; Dep., Nat. Security Council	
Hanscom	Patricia L.	C	Deputy Director	State Dept., Conventional Arms Control	
Lancaster	Carol J.	C	Deputy Director	State Dept., Int. Development Cooperation Agency	
Inderfurth	Karl F. (Rick)	C	Alt. Representative	State Dept., Special Policy Affairs	
Dine	Thomas A.	C	Asst. Administrator	State Dept., A. I. D., Bureau of Euro. & New Ind. States	
Hicks	John F.	C	Asst. Administrator	State Dept., A. I. D., Africa	
Lancaster	Carol J.	C	Deputy Administrator	State Dept., A. I. D.	
Gallagher	Dennis J.	C	Asst. Legal Adviser	State Dept., Office of Legal Advisor	
Donilon	Thomas E.	B,C	Chief of Staff (fmr.)	State Dept.; Asst. Sec., for Public Affairs	
Reed	Joseph Verner, Jr.	C	Chief of Protocol	State Dept.; Director, Foreign Policy Association	
Williams	Maurice Jacoutot	C	Chief US Delegate	State Dept., US-North Vietnam Jt. Econ. Commission	
Rubin	James P.	C	Communications Dir.	State Dept., Office of the UN Ambassador	
Holland	Mary Sue	C	Division Director	State Dept., Office of Information Security Technology	
Barnett	Robert Warren	C	Econ. Counsel (fmr.)	State Dept., US Embassy, The Hague	
Courtney	William Harrison	C	Fgn. Service Officer	State Dept.	
Goldgeier	James M.	C	Member	State Dept., National Security Council	
Sofaer	Abraham David	C	Legal Advisor	State Dept.; Partner, Hughes, Hubbard & Reed, Wash.	
Moose	George E.	C	Alt. Representative	State Dept., African Affairs, UN Security Council	
Romberg	Alan D.	C	Member (fmr.)	State Dept.	
Feierstein	Mark	C	Policy Advisor	State Dept., O. A. S., to US Representative	
Ely-Raphel	Nancy Halliday	C	Prin. Dep. Asst. Sec.	State Dept.	
Binnendijk	Hans	C	Principal Deputy Dir.	State Dept., E. E. O. C., Policy Planning	
Brimmer	Esther Diane	C	Spec. Asst./Und. Sec.	State Dept., Policy Affairs	
Nix	Crystal	C	Special Assistant	State Dept., Office of Legal Adviser	
Clapp	Priscilla A.	C	Special Rep.	State Dept., Food Security	
Mirsky	Yehudah	C	Spec. Advisor	State Dept., Bureau of Democracy, Human Rights & Labor	
Ross	Dennis B.	C	Peace Negotiator	State Dept., Middle-East Peace Talks, Clinton Admin.	
Richard	Anne C.	C	Member	State Dept., Research, Plans & Policy	
Einaudi	Luigi R.	C	Sr. Advisor	State Dept., Policy Planning Staff	
Moran	Theodore H.	C	Sr. Advisor	State Dept., Policy Planning Staff	
Scheffer	David J.	C	Sr. Advisor & Counsel	State Dept., Office of the Secretary	
Murphy	Sean David	C	Staff Assistant	State Dept., Bureau of Political-Military Affairs	
Hollick	Ann L.	C	Staff Director	State Dept., Economic Policy Staff	
Mattox	Gale A.	C	Staff Member	State Dept., Policy Planning Staff	
Pezullo	Lawrence A.	C	US Special Envoy	State Dept., on Haiti	
Camps	Miriam	B,C	Vice President (fmr.)	State Dept., Planning Council	

Last Name	First & Mid. Name	Org.	Job Title	Affiliation - Company, Organization	
Sestanovich	Stephen R.	C	US Ambassador	State Dept., at Large	
Todman	Terence A.	C	US Ambassador	State Dept., Argentina; Amb. (fmr.), Spain, Denmark	
Bodie	William C.	C	US Ambassador	State Dept., Asia Pacific Economic Cooperation Forum	
Phillips	Christopher H.	C	US Ambassador	State Dept., Brunei	
Bohlen	Avis T.	C	US Ambassador	State Dept., Bulgaria	
Cook	Frances D.	C	US Ambassador	State Dept., Cameroon, Yaounde	
Ney	Edward N.	C	US Ambassador	State Dept., Canada; Director, Foreign Policy Assoc.	
Guerra-Mondragon	Gabriel	C	US Ambassador	State Dept., Chile	
Basora	Adrian A.	C	US Ambassador	State Dept., Czech Republic	
Black	Shirley Temple	C	US Ambassador	State Dept., Czechoslovakia; Actress (fmr.)	
Aponte	Mari Carmen	C	US Ambassador	State Dept., Dominican Republic	
Pelletreau	Robert Halsey, Jr.	C	US Ambassador	State Dept., Egypt, Tunesia	
Kelly	John Hubert	C	US Ambassador	State Dept., Finland	
Harriman	Pamela D. Churchill	C	US Ambassador	State Dept., France, Hon. Mbr. Exec. Com., Brookings Inst.	
Redman	Charles E.	B	US Ambassador	State Dept., Bonn, Germany, Chief of Mission	
Burns	R. Nicholas	C	US Ambassador	State Dept., Greece	
Arcos	Cresencio S.	C	US Ambassador	State Dept., Honduras	
Bartholomew	Reginald	C	U.S. Ambassador	State Dept., Italy	
Mondale	Walter Fritz	B,C,T	US Ambassador	State Dept., Japan	
Courtney	William Harrison	C	U.S. Ambassador	State Dept., Kazakhstan	
Bosworth	Stephen W.	C,T	US Ambassador	State Dept., S. Korea	
Jeter	Howard F.	B	US Ambassador	State Dept., Liberia	
Spain	James William	C	US Ambassador	State Dept., Maldives & Sri Lanka; US Amb. (fmr.), Turkey	
Jones	James R.	C,T	US Ambassador	State Dept., Mexico; Chair./CEO (fmr.), Amer. Stock Exch.	
Vogelgesang	Sandra (Sandy) L.	C	US Ambassador	State Dept., Nepal	
Carrington	Walter C.	C	US Ambassador	State Dept., Nigeria	
Cowal	Sally Grooms	C	US Ambassador	State Dept., Port of Spain, Trinidad & Tobago	
Negroponte	John Dimitri	C	US Ambassador	State Dept., Philippines	
Rey	Nicholas A.	C	US Ambassador	State Dept., Poland	
Simons	Thomas W., Jr.	C	US Ambassador	State Dept., Poland	
Hicks	Irvin	C	US Ambassador	State Dept., Republic of Seychelles	
Wendt	E. Allan	C	US Ambassador	State Dept., Republic of Slovenia	
Moses	Alfred Henry	C	US Ambassador	St.Dept.,Romania;Ptnr.,Covington&Burling;Pres.,Amer.Jew.Cong.	
Pickering	Thomas R.	B,C	US Ambassador	State Dept., Russia, Moscow,'94; Ambassador (fmr.), UN	
Shriver	Robert Sargent, Jr.	C	US Ambassador	State Dept., S.A.L.T.; Adv. Bd., Ctr. for Int. Pol., Nat. Pol.	
Oakley	Robert B.	C	US Ambassador	State Dept., Somalia	
Lyman	Princeton Nathan	C	US Ambassador	State Dept., South Africa	
Gardner	Richard Newton	C,T	US Ambassador	State Dept., Spain; Ambassador (fmr.) to Italy	
Ross	Christopher W.S.	C	US Ambassador	State Dept., Syrian Arab Republic	
Crowe	William J., Jr.	C,T	US Ambassador	State Dept., U. K.; Chair. (fmr.), Joint Chiefs-of-Staff	
Miller	William Green	C	US Ambassador	State Dept., Ukraine	
Litt	David G.	C	US Ambassador	State Dept., United Arab Emerites	
Leddy	John M.	C	US Ambassador	State Dept., USIA	
Hummel	Arthur W., Jr.	C	US Ambassador	State Dept., USIA	
Zimmermann	Warren	C	US Ambassador	State Dept., Yugoslavia; Mbr. (fmr.), Carnegie Endow.	
Leonard	James F.	C	US Ambassador	State Dept.	
Macomber	William B.	C	US Ambassador	State Dept.	
Petree	Richard W.	C	US Ambassador	State Dept.	
Schaufele	William E., Jr.	C	US Ambassador	State Dept.	
Whitehouse	Charles S.	C	US Ambassador	State Dept.	
Garthoff	Raymond L.	C	US Ambassador	State Dept., to USIA	
Gallucci	Robert L.	C	US Amb.-at-Large	State Dept., Political-Military Affairs	
Holmes	Henry Allen	C	US Amb. at Large	State Dept., Burdensharing	
Wolf	Milton Albert	C	US Ambassador (fmr.)	State Dept., Austria	
Coon	Jane Abell	C	US Ambassador (fmr.)	State Dept., Bangladesh	
Mark	David E.	C	US Ambassador (fmr.)	State Dept., Barundi, Romania	
Dawson	Horace Greeley, Jr.	C	US Ambassador (fmr.)	State Dept., Botswana	
Swank	Emory Coblentz	C	US Ambassador (fmr.)	State Dept., Cambodia, '70-73	
Spiro	Herbert John	C	US Ambassador (fmr.)	State Dept., Cameroon, Equitorial Guinea	
Schmidt	Adolph William	B	US Ambassador (fmr.)	State Dept., Canada	
Strausz-Hupe	Robert	C	US Ambassador (fmr.)	State Dept., Ceylon, Belgium, Sweden, N.A.T.O., Turkey	
Davis	Nathaniel	C	US Ambassador (fmr.)	State Dept., Chile	
Lilley	James R.	C	US Ambassador (fmr.)	State Dept., China	
Tuthill	John Wills	B,C	US Ambassador (fmr.)	State Dept., EEC, Brazil	
Vest	George Southall	C	US Ambassador (fmr.)	State Dept., EEC, Brussels	
Wisner	Frank G., II	B,C	US Ambassador (fmr.)	State Dept., Egypt	
Duke	Angier Biddle	C	US Ambassador (fmr.)	State Dept., El Salvador, Spain, Denmark	
Bloomfield	Richard J.	C	US Ambassador (fmr.)	State Dept., Equador, Portugal	
Korry	Edward M.	C	US Ambassador (fmr.)	State Dept., Ethopia	
Greenwald	Joseph A.	C	US Ambassador (fmr.)	State Dept., European Communities	
Rush	Kenneth	C	US Ambassador (fmr.)	State Dept., France	
Samuels	Michael A.	C	US Ambassador (fmr.)	State Dept. GATT	
Talbot	Phillips	C	US Ambassador (fmr.)	State Dept., Greece	
Stroock	Thomas Frank	C	US Ambassador (fmr.)	State Dept., Guatemala	
Bergold	Harry Earl, Jr.	C	US Ambassador (fmr.)	State Dept., Hungary, Nicaragua	
Kaiser	Philip Mayer	C	US Ambassador (fmr.)	State Dept., Hungary; Sr. Cons.,SRI Int.; Adv. Bd., Nat. Pol.	
Cobb	Charles E., Jr.	C	US Ambassador (fmr.)	State Dept., Iceland, Reykjavik	

Last Name	First & Mid. Name	Org.	Job Title	Affiliation - Company, Organization	
Lewis	Samuel Winfield	C	US Ambassador (fmr.)	State Dept., Israel; Dir., St. Dept., pol. plng. staff	
Rabb	Maxwell M.	C	US Ambassador (fmr.)	State Dept., Italy; Chairman, Ecomarine	
Hewitt	William Alexander	B,C,T	US Ambassador (fmr.)	State Dept., Jamaica	
Day	Arthur R.	C	US Ambassador (fmr.)	State Dept., Jaruselem	
Ferguson	Glenn Walker	C	US Ambassador (fmr.)	State Dept., Kenya; President, Radio Free Europe	
Hinton	Deane Roesch	C	US Ambassador (fmr.)	State Dept., Kinshasa, Zaire	
Laney	James Thomas	C	US Ambassador (fmr.)	State Dept., S. Korea; Pres. (fmr.), Emory Univ.	
Lowenstein	James Gordon	C	US Ambassador (fmr.)	State Dept., Luxemburg; Sr. Consultant, APCO Assoc.	
Palmer	Ronald Dewayne F.	C	US Ambassador (fmr.)	State Dept., Malaysia Kuala Lumpur	
Blake	Robert O.	C	US Ambassador (fmr.)	State Dept., Mali	
Bloch	Julia Chang	C	US Ambassador (fmr.)	State Dept., Nepal; Gp. Exec. V. Pres(fmr.), Bankamerica	
Joseph	Geri Mack	C	US Ambassador (fmr.)	State Dept., Netherlands, The Hague	
Shad	John S. R.	B	US Ambassador (fmr.)	State Dept., Netherlands; Director, various companies	
Easum	Donald B.	C	US Ambassador (fmr.)	State Dept., Nigeria	
Platt	Nicholas	C	US Ambassador (fmr.)	State Dept., Pakistan	
Solomon	Richard Harvey	C	US Ambassador (fmr.)	State Dept., Phillipines	
Simmons	Thomas W.	B	US Ambassador (fmr.)	State Dept., Poland	
Strauss	Robert Schwarz	C,T	US Ambassador (fmr.)	State Dept., Russia; Pt., Akin, Gump, Strauss, Hauer & Feld	
Akins	James E.	C	US Ambassador (fmr.)	State Dept., Saudi Arabia	
Djerejian	Edward Peter	C	US Ambassador (fmr.)	State Dept., Syria; Asst. Sec. (fmr.),Near E. & S. Asian Afrs.	
Smith	David Shiverick	C	US Ambassador (fmr.)	State Dept., Sweden	
Cutler	Walter Leon	C	US Ambassador (fmr.)	State Dept., Tunesia, Saudi Arabia	
Hartman	Arthur A.	B,C	US Ambassador (fmr.)	State Dept., U.S.S.R.; Bd. Mbr., Center for Fgn. Pol. Devel.	
Matlock	Jack Foust, Jr.	B,C	US Ambassador (fmr.)	State Dept., U.S.S.R.; Columbia Univ.	
Okun	Herbert S.	C	US Ambassador (fmr.)	State Dept., Yugoslavia	
Grove	Brandon H., Jr.	C	US Ambassador (fmr.)	State Dept., Zaire; Dir., Off. of Foreign Scvs. Inst.	
Smith	Gerard C.	T	Amb.-at-Lge., (fmr.)	State Dept.; Chief Negotiator, S. A. L. T.	
Guest	Michael E.	C	Foreign Officer	State Dept., Czech Republic	
Snyder	Jed C.	C	Team Leader	State Dept., INSS, Middle East & South Asia	
Cowhey	Peter F.	C	Bureau Chief	State Dept., Int. Bureau Fed. Communications Commission	
Precht	Henry	C	Head	State Dept., Iran Desk	
Sapiro	Miriam	C	Member	State Dept., Legal Affairs	
Hunsberger	Warren S.	C	Chief of Research (fmr.)	State Dept., Japan and Korea	
Wilkinson	Sharon	C	Member	State Dept.	
Bernstein	David S.	C	Member	State Dept.	
			Transportation Dept.		
Coleman	William Thaddeus, Jr.	C,T	Secretary (fmr.)	Transportation Dept.	
Goldschmidt	Neil	C,T	Secretary (fmr.)	Transportation Dept.; Governor (fmr.), Oregon	
Davis	Jerome	C	Division Chief	Transportation Dept., Supply & Space Management	
			Treasury Dept.		
Summers	Lawrence H.	B,C	Secretary	Treasury Dept.	
Rubin	Robert E.	B	Secretary (fmr.)	Treasury Dept.; Ch., Thrift Deposit Prot. & Oversight Bd.	
Bentsen	Lloyd	B	Secretary (fmr.)	Treas. Dept.;Ptrn.,Verner Liipferi Bernhard McPherson & Hand	
Brady	Nicholas Frederick	B,C	Secretary (fmr.)	Treasury Dept.; Director, NCR Corp.	
Baker	James A., III	C	Secretary (fmr.)	Treasury Dept.	
Reagan	Donald T.	C	Secretary (fmr.)	Treasury Dept.	
Blumenthal	Werner Michael	C,T	Secretary (fmr.)	Treasury Dept.	
Simon	William E.	C	Secretary (fmr.)	Treasury Dept.	
Schultz	George P.	C	Secretary (fmr.)	Treasury Dept.	
Kennedy	David Michael	B	Secretary (fmr.)	Treasury Dept.	
Fowler	Henry Hamill	C	Secretary (fmr.)	Treasury Dept.	
Dillon	C. Douglas	B,C	Secretary (fmr.)	Treasury Dept.	
Anderson	Robert B.	C	Secretary (fmr.)	Treasury Dept.	
Morgenthau	Henry	C	Secretary (fmr.)	Treasury Dept.	
Woodin	William H.	C	Secretary (fmr.)	Treasury Dept.	
Mills	Ogden L.	C	Secretary (fmr.)	Treasury Dept.	
Houston	David F.	C	Secretary (fmr.)	Treasury Dept.	
Altman	Roger C.	C	Deputy Sec. (fmr.)	Treas. Dept.; Actg. CEO of RTC; V. Chair., Blackstone Gp.	
Knight	Edward S.	C	Gen. Counsel	Treasury Dept.	
Apgar	David Puschel	C	Sr. Policy Advisor	Treasury Dept., Controller of the Currency	
Bergsten	Rand V	T	Asst. Secretary (fmr.)	Treasury Dept., Int. Affairs; Dir., Inst. of Int. Economics	
Bestani	Robert M.	C	Deputy Asst. Sec.	Treasury Dept., Int. Monetary Affairs	
Glauber	Robert R.	C	Under Secretary	Treasury Dept., Clinton Admin.	
Hill	J. French	C	Deputy Asst. Sec.	Treasury Dept., Corp. Finance	
Levine	Susan B.	C	Deputy Asst. Sec.	Treasury Dept., Int. Devel., Dept. of Environmental Pol.	
Smith	John T., II	C	Bureau Chief	Treasury Dept., Procurement, Tax Systems Admin.	
Nye	J. Benjamin H.	B,C,T	Exec. Secretary	Treasury Dept.	
Powell	Jerome H.	C	Assit. Sec. (fmr.)	Treasury Dept., Domestic Finance	

Last Name	First & Mid. Name	Org.	Job Title	Affiliation - Company, Organization
			United Nations	
Richardson	William Blaine	C	US Ambassador (fmr.)	U.N.; Congressman (fmr.), New Mexico
Albright	Madeleine K.	C	US Ambassador (fmr.)	U.N.
Perkins	Edward J.	C	US Ambassador (fmr.)	U.N.
Pickering	Thomas R.	C	US Ambassador (fmr.)	U.N.
Kirkpatrick	Jeane Duane Jordan	C,T	US Ambassador (fmr.)	U.N.
McHenry	Donald F.	B,C	US Ambassador (fmr.)	U.N.
Young	Andrew	C,T	US Ambassador (fmr.)	U.N.
Scranton	William W.	C,T	US Ambassador (fmr.)	U.N.
Moynihan	Daniel Patrick	C	US Ambassador (fmr.)	U.N.
Scali	John Alfred	C	US Ambassador (fmr.)	U.N.
Bush	George H. W.	C,T	US Ambassador (fmr.)	U.N.
Yost	Charles W.	C	US Ambassador (fmr.)	U.N.
Ball	George W.	B,C	US Ambassador (fmr.)	U.N.
Goldberg	Arthur J.	C	US Ambassador (fmr.)	U.N.
Stevenson	Adlaii Ewing, III	B,C	US Ambassador (fmr.)	U.N.
Wadsworth	James J.	C	US Ambassador (fmr.)	U.N.
Lodge	Henry Cabot	C	US Ambassador (fmr.)	U.N.
Acheson	Dean G.	C	US Ambassador (fmr.)	U.N.
Johnson	Herschel V.	C	US Ambassador (fmr.)	U.N.
Abram	Morris B.	C	US Ambassador (fmr.)	United Nations European office, Geneva
Catto	Henry Edward, Jr.	C	US Ambassador (fmr.)	United Nations, Geneva, U. K.
Scranton	William W.	C,T	US Ambassador (fmr.)	United Nations, Geneva
Young	Andrew	C,T	US Ambassador (fmr.)	United Nations; Congressman (fmr.), Georgia
McHenry	Donald F.	B,C	US Ambassador (fmr.)	UN; Mbr., Carnegie Endow.; Dir., Coca-Cola Co.
Prendergast	Kieran	B	Under Sec. Gen.	U.N., for Political Affairs,
Vanden Heuvel	William J.	C	Chairman	U.N. Assoc. of the U.S.A.
Walker	William N.	C	Head	U.N. Observers, Bosnia
Mills	Susan R.	C	Director	U.N., Dept. of Admin. & Management, Finance Mgmt. Office
Rosenstock	Robert	C	Chairman	U.N., Int. Law Commission
Feissel	Gustave	C	Resident Rep. (fmr.)	U.N., to Cyprus
Aaron	David L.	C	Representative	UN; (fmr.) Nat. Security Advisor, Jimmy Carter
Baker	James Estes	C	Director	UN, Dept. of Humanitarian Affairs
Battle	Lucius Durham	C	Chairman (fmr.)	UNESCO General Conference
Brown	Carroll	C	Member (fmr.)	UN General Assembly
Calabia	Dawn T.	C		UN Office of High Commissioner for Refugees
Draper	William Henry, III	C	CEO	UN Development Programme
Fromuth	Peter	C	Special Assistant	UN, Mission to the
Hinerfeld	Ruth J.	C	Vice Chairman	UN Association of the US
Moore	Jonathan	C	Representative	UN Mission; Sr. Assoc., Carnegie Endow. for Int. Peace
Morse	F. Bradford	B,C	Under Secretary	United Nations
Pyle	Cassandra A.	C	Chairwoman	United Nations, Academy for Educ. Devel.
Sorensen	Gillian Martin	C	Under Secretary	UN, Special Advisor for Information & Public Policy
Speth	James Gustav	C	Und. Sec.-Gen., Adm.	UN Development Prog.; Bd. Member, Ctr. for Int. Policy
Spiers	Ronald Ian	C	Under Secretary	UN, for Political Affairs
Stassen	Harold E.	C	Signer	United Nations Charter; Gov. (fmr.), Minnesota
Rubin	Nancy H.	C	Hd. Of Deligation	U.N. Human Rights Commission
White	P. Maureen	C	US Representative	UNICEF
			Other Government Agencies	
Langdon	George Dorland, Jr.	C	President (fmr.)	American Museum of Natural History, NYC
Norman	William Stanley	C	Exec. Vice President	AMTRAK, Washington
Johnston	Philip	C	President & CEO	C. A. R. E.
Hurwitz	Sol	C	President	Commission for Economic Development, NYC
Strock	James Martin	C	Asst. Administrator	E. P. A.; Secretary, St. of California, Environ. Protection
Nitze	William Albert	C	Asst. Administrator	E. P. A.; Pres., Alliance to Save Energy, Wash.
Lawrence	Richard D.	C	Director	Environmental Protection Agency, Eng. Oper. Division
Tigert	Ricki Rhodarmer	C	Chairman	F. D. I. C., Board of Directors
Powell	Michael K.	C	Member	Federal Communications Commission
Miller	Paul David	C	Inspector General	Federal Labor Relations Authority
Billington	James Hadley	C	Librarian	Library of Congress
Hardt	John P.	C	Sr. Specialist	Library of Congress, Post-Soviet Economy
Stewart	Ruth Ann	C	Asst. Librarian	Library of Congress, National Programs
Kupperman	Robert Harris	C	Sr. Fellow	Los Alamos Laboratory: mbr., Strat. & Int. Studies
Deffenbaugh	Ralston H., Jr.	C	Executive Director	Lutherin Immigration & Refugee Service
Press	Frank	C	President	National Academy of Science
Hodgson	James D.	C	Head (fmr.)	O.S.H.A., Nixon Admn.
Hills	Laura Hume	C	Sr. Comm. Counsel	Overseas Private Development Corp.
Unger	Leonard L.	C	Office Manager	S. E. C., Office of Inspection & Financial Responsibility
Mann	Michael D.	C	Director	Security Exchange Commission, Office of Int. Affairs
Lader	Philip	C	Administrator	Small Business Administration
Loomis	Henry	C	Trustee	Smithsonian Institute
Nooter	Robert H.	C	Board Member	Smithsonian Inst.
Katzenstein	Peter J.	C	Staff Member	Smithsonian Inst.
Newman	Constance Berry	C	Under Secretary	Smithsonian Inst.
Baroody	William J., Jr.	C	Chairman	Smithsonian Inst., Center for Scholars
Manilow	Lewis	C	Chairman	U. S. I. A., Advisory Commission on Public Diplomacy

Last Name	First & Mid. Name	Org.	Job Title	Affiliation - Company, Organization	
Miller	Marcia E.	C	Chairwoman	U.S. Int. Trade Commission	
Wells	Samuel F., Jr.	C	Deputy Director	Woodrow Wilson International Center for Scholors	
West	Togo D.	C	Secretary	Veterans Affairs; Defense Dept., (fmr.) Sec. of the Army	
Greenberg	Arthur N.	C	Office Director	Veterans Administration, Quality Management	
White	Robert M.	C	Associate Director	Veterans Admin., Compensation & Pension Service	
Congress					
			House of Representatives		
Bereuter	Douglas K.	C	Congressman	Nebraska, Banking & Finance, Int. Relations	
Berman	Howard Lawrence	C	Congressman	California, Judiciary, Int. Relations, Judiciary	
Bishop	Sanford D., Jr.	C	Congressman	Geoegia	
Burton	Daniel Farrell, Jr.	C	Congressman	Indiana, Foreign Affairs Committee	
Conable	Barbara B.	T	Congresswoman	New York; Commissioner, UN Comm. On Global Governance	
Dicks	Norman D.	C	Congressman	Washington, Appropriations, Select Intelligence/Ranking	
Frank	Barney	C	Congressman	Massachusetts, Banking & Finance, Judiciary	
Gejdenson	Sam	C	Congressman	Connecticut, House Oversight, Int. Relations	
Gephardt	Richard Andrew	C	Congressman	Missouri, Minority Leader	
Gingrich	Newton L.	C	Congressman	Georgia; Speaker of the House	
Goss	Porter J.	C	Congressman	Florida	
Hamilton	Lee Herbert	B,C,T	Congressman	Indiana, Int. Relations/Ranking, Joint Economic	
Harman	Jane L.	C	Congresswoman	California, National Security, Select Intelligence	
Houghton	Amory, Jr. (Amo)	C	Congressman	New York, Int. Relations, Ways & Means	
Hyde	Henry B.	C	Congressman	Illinois, Int. Relations, Chairman, Judiciary,	
Johnson	Nancy Lee	C	Congresswoman	Connecticut, Ways & Means	
Kolbe	Jim	C	Congressman	Arizona	
LaFarce	John J.	C	Congressman	New York	
Leach	James Albert Smith	C,T	Congressman	Iowa, Int. Relations, Chair., Banking & Fin. Services	
Lewis	John P.	C	Congressman	Georgia, Ways & Means	
Matsui	Robert Takeo	C	Congressman	California, Ways & Means	
McDermott	James (Jim) A.	C	Congressman	Washington, Ways & Means	
Molinari	Susan K.	C	Congresswoman	New York, Budget, Transportation & Infrastructure	
Pastor	Ed	C	Congressman	Arizona	
Payne	Donald M.	C	Congressman	New Jersey, Int. Relations, Education & the Workforce	
Petri	Thomas Everet	C	Congressman	Wisconsin, Educ. & Workforce, Transport. & Infrastructure	
Porter	John Edward	C	Congressman	Illinois, Appropriations	
Rangel	Charles B.	C,T	Congressman	New York, Ways & Means/Ranking; Joint Taxation	
Schumer	Charles E.	C	Congressman	New York, Banking & Finance, Judiciary	
Spratt	John McKee, Jr.	C	Congressman	South Carolina, Budget/Ranking, National Security	
Stokes	Louis	C	Congressman	Ohio, Appropriations	
Anderson	John Bayard	C,T	Congressman (fmr.)	Illinois; '80 candidate for President	
Barnes	Michael Darr	C	Congressman (fmr.)	Maryland	
Beilenson	Anthony C.	C	Congressman (fmr.)	California, Rules	
Bolling	Landrum Rymer	C	Congressman (fmr.)	Montana	
Brademas	John	B,C,T	Congressman (fmr.)	New York; Dir., Texaco Inc.; Pres. (fmr.), NYU.	
Clinger	William F., Jr.	C	Congressman (fmr.)	Pennsylvania, Chairman, Govt. Reform & Oversight	
Dymally	Mervyn Malcolm	C	Congressman (fmr.)	California	
Fascell	Dante B.	C	Congressman (fmr.)	Florida	
Ferraro	Geraldine Anne	C	Congresswoman (fmr.)	New York; US Amb. to the UN Human Rights Comm.	
Foley	Thomas Stephen	B,C,T	Spkr. of House (fmr.)	House of Represenbtatives; Amb. to Japan	
Fraser	Donald M.	T	Congressman (fmr.)	Minnesotta	
Gray	William H., III	T	Congressman (fmr.)	Pennsylvania; Pres. & CEO, United Negro College Fund	
Green	Bill	C	Congressman (fmr.)	New York	
Levine	Mel	C	Congressman (fmr.)	California; Assoc., Builders for Peace	
McCurdy	Dave Keith	C	Congressman (fmr.)	Oklahoma	
Moody	Jim	C	Congressman (fmr.)	Wisconsin	
Reid	Ogden R.	C	Congressman (fmr.)	(Council of American Ambassadors)	
Schroeder	Patricia Scott	C	Congresswoman (fmr.)	Colorado, Armed Svcs., Judic., Post Office & Civ. Svcs.	
Solarz	Stephen Joshua	C	Congressman (fmr.)	New York ; Sr. Counselor, APCO Assoc. Consultants	
Weber	Vin	C	Congressman (fmr.)	Minnesota; Empower America mbr.	
Whalen	Charles William, Jr.	C	Congressman (fmr.)	Ohio	
Wolpe	Howard	C	Congressman (fmr.)	Michigan	
Browne	Robert Span	C	Staff Director (fmr.)	Hse. Bkg. Subcom.,Int. Dev. Trade & M. P., Ctr./Nat. Pol.	
Falk	Pamela S.	C	Staff Dir.	House of Representatives	
Goldman	Andrew	C	Sr. Policy Analyst	House Republican Research Committee	
Hovey	Justus Allan, Jr.	C	Staff Member (fmr.)	House of Representatives, Commission of Fgn. Affairs	
Norton	Eleanor Holmes	C	Delegate (fmr.)	Dist. of Columbia, Pub. Bldg. & Gnds., Pub. Wks. & Tran.	
Rademaker	Stephen Geoffrey	C	Repres. Chief Counsel	House of Representatives, Commission of Fgn. Affairs	
Shelton	Joanna Reed	C	Prof. Staff Member	US House of Representatives, Ways & Means	
van Dusen	Michael H.	C	Min. Chief-of-Staff	House Committee on Int. Relations	
Wessel	Michael R.	C	Member	House Democratic Leaders Office	

Last Name	First & Mid. Name	Org.	Job Title	Affiliation - Company, Organization	
			Senate		
Bayh	Evan	B	Senator	Indiana	
Chafee	John Hubbard	B,C,T	Senator	Rhode Island, Environ. & P.W./Chair., Fin., Sel. Intellig.	
Clinton	Hillary Rodham (Rosenberg)	B	Senator	New York	
Dodd	Christopher J.	B,C	Senator	Connecticut, Bkg., Hsg. & Urban Afrs., Fgn. Rel., Rules	
Feinstein	Dianne	B,T	Senator	California; Foreign Operations, Judiciary, Rules & Admin.	
Frist	William H.	C	Senator	Tennessee, Senate Majority Leader	
Glenn	John H.	T	Senator	Ohio, Armed Svcs., Gvt. Afrs./Ranking, Sel. Intel.	
Graham	Bob	C	Senator	Florida, Intelligence, Vet. Afrs., Fin., Env. & Pub. Wks.	
Hagel	Chuck	B	Senator	Nebraska	
Johnston	J. Bennett	B	Senator	Louisiana, Democrat	
Kerry	John Forbes	C	Senator	Massachusetts, Banking, Commerce, Fgn. Rel., Intell.	
Lieberman	Joseph I.	C	Senator	Connecticut, Armed Svcs.,Govt.Afrs.,Envir./ Pub. Wks.	
McCain	John	C	Senator	Arizona, Armed Svcs., Commerce, Chair., Science & Tran.	
Moynihan	Daniel Patrick	C	Senator	New York, Fin./Ranking, Joint Taxation, Rules & Admin.	
Reed	Jack		Senator	Rhode Island	
Robb	Charles Spittal	C,T	Senator	Virginia; Armed Services, Foreign Relations, Intelligence	
Rockefeller	John D. (Jay), IV	C,T	Senator	West Virginia, Commerce, Fin., Veterans Affairs/Ranking	
Roth	William V., Jr.	C,T	Senator	Delaware, Finance/Chair., Joint Taxation/V. Chair.	
Sarbanes	Paul S.	C	Senator	Maryland, Banking, Housing/Ranking, Budget, Fgn. Rel.	
Schumer	Charles E.	C	Senator	New York	
Snowe	Olympia J.	C	Senator	Maine; Cong. (fmr.), Budget, Armed Svcs., Commerce	
Torricelli	Robert G.	C	Senator	New Jersey; Congressman (fmr.)	
Warner	John	C	Senator	Virginia	
Agnew	Harold M.	C	Senator (fmr.)	New Mexico	
Boren	David Lyle	C	Senator (fmr.)	Oklahoma, Fin., Agriculture, Select Com. on Intel.	
Boschwitz	Rudy	C	Senator (fmr.)	Minnesota	
Bradley	William L.	B,C	Senator (fmr.)	New Jersey; Fin., Energy & Nat. Res.; Rhodes Scholar	
Brooke	Edward	B	Senator (fmr.)	Massachusetts	
Clark	Dick	C	Senator (fmr.)	Iowa; Ambassador-at-Large, US State Dept.	
Cranston	Alan	T	Senator (fmr.)	California	
Culver	John C.	C,T	Senator (fmr.)	Iowa	
Danforth	John C.	T	Senator (fmr.)	Missouri	
Harris	Fred R.	B	Senator (fmr.)	Oklahoma	
Hart	Gary	C	Senator (fmr.)	Colorado; Presidential Candidate	
Johnston	J. Bennett	B	Senator (fmr.)	Louisiana, Appropriations, Budget, Energy, Aging	
Mathias	Charles McC., Jr.	B,C	Senator (fmr.)	Maryland	
McGovern	George Stanley	C	Senator (fmr.)	South Dakota; Principal, Mid-East Political Council	
Mitchell	George John	C	Senator (fmr.)	Maine; Majority Leader, Finance, Veterans Affairs	
Nunn	Sam	B	Senator (fmr.)	Georgia, Armed Svcs. Rnkg. Mbr., Gvt. Affrs., Small Bus.	
Pell	Claiborne	C	Senator (fmr.)	Rhode Island, Foreign Relations, Labor, Rules	
Pressler	Larry	C	Senator (fmr.)	S. Dakota, Chair., Commerce; Fgn. Relations, Judiciary	
Ribicoff	Abraham A.	C	Senator (fmr.)	Connecticut	
Riegle	Donald W.	B	Senator (fmr.)	Michigan, Budget, Finance, Banking, Hsg. & Urban Afrs.	
Sanford	Terry	C	Senator (fmr.)	North Carolina; Bd. Mbr., World Fed of NC	
Scott	Hugh	B	Senator (fmr.)	Pennsylvania	
Stevenson	Adlaii Ewing, III	B,C	Senator (fmr.)	Illinois	
Wirth	Timothy Endicott	C	Senator (fmr.)	Colorado; State Dept., Under Secretary for Global Affairs	
Wofford	Harris Llewellyn	C	Senator (fmr.)	Pennsylvania, Foreign Relations, Labor, Small Business	
Edelstein	Julius C. C.	C	Admin. Asst. (fmr.)	to Senator Herbert H. Lehman	
Hoehn	William Edwin, Jr.	C	Sr. Advisor	to Senator Sam Nunn	
Stone	Roger D.	C	Campaign Manager	Arlen Spector	
Blum	John (Jack) A.	C	Staff Member	Senate Foreign Relations Committee	
Holt	Pat M.	C	Chief of Staff (fmr.)	Senate Foreign Relations Committee	
Battaglia	Charles	C	Staff Director	Senate Veteran's Affair Committee	
Thiessen	Marc A.	B,C	Aide	Senate, to Jesse Helms	
Hess	John B.	C	Sr. Advisor	Senator Barbara Boxer	
Judiciary			**Supreme Court**		
Breyer	Stephen G.	C	Associate Justice	Supreme Court; Chief Judge (fmr.), Court of Appeals	
Ginsburg	Ruth Bader	C	Associate Justice	Supreme Court	
O'Connor	Sandra Day	C	Associate Justice	Supreme Court	
Frankfurter	Felix	C	Associate Justice (fmr.)	Supreme Court	
Hughes	Charles E.	C	Associate Justice (fmr.)	Supreme Court	
Aldrich	George H.	C	Legal Assistant	Supreme Court, Justice Byron A. White	
			Other Federal Courts		
Allison	Richard Clark	C	Judge	Iran-US Claims Tribunal, The Hague	
Bonsal	Dudley Baldwin	C	US District Judge	New York	
Brower	Charles Nelson	C	Counsel & Advocate	US International Court of Justice, The Hague	
Cabranes	Jose Alberto	C	US District Judge	Connecticut	
Carey	John	C	Judge	Westchester County Court, White Plains	
Harper	Conrad Keith	C	Chairman	US Court of Appeals, Admin. & Grievance commission	
Schwarzer	William W.	C	US District Judge	California, San Francisco	
Schwebel	Stephen Myron	C	Judge	International Court of Justice, The Hague	
Silberman	Laurence Hirsch	C	Judge	Circuit Court of Appeals, Washington	
Stevenson	John Reese	C	Judge (fmr.)	Permanent Court of Arbitration, The Hague	
Tannenwald	Theodore, Jr.	C	Sr. Judge	US Tax Court	
Paine	George C., II	C	Judge	Bankruptcy Court, Nashville	
Parker	Barrington D., Jr.	C	Dist. Judge	New York	

Who's Who of the Elite

Last Name	First & Mid. Name	Org.	Job Title	Affiliation - Company, Organization
City & State Governments				
			City	
Bradley	Tom	C,T	Mayor (fmr.)	Los Angeles
Cortines	Ramon C.	B	Chancellor	New York City, Board of Education
Dinkins	David	C	Mayor (fmr.)	New York
Goldin	Harrison J.	C	Mayor (fmr.)	New York City
O'Cleireacain	Carol	C	Member (fmr.)	New York City Office of the Budget; Brookings Inst.
Lythcott	George I.	C		New York City Health Dept.
Hawkins	Ashton	C	Exec. V. Pres./Counsel	Metropolitan Museum of Art, Board of Trustees, NYC
Romero-Barcelo	Carlos Antonio	C	Resident Commission	Puerto Rico; Education & Labor, Natural Resources
Schmoke	Kurt L.	C,T	Mayor	Baltimore
			States	
Torres	Art	C	Senator (State)	California
Chiles	Lawton	T	Governor	Florida
Asencio	Diego C.	C	Executive Director	Florida International Affairs Commission
Dukakis	Michael Stanley	C	Governor (fmr.)	Massachusetts; Candidate for US President (fmr.)
Florio	James J.	B	Governor (fmr.)	New Jersey
Whitman	Christine Todd	B,C	Governor	New Jersey
Apodaca	Jerry	C	Governor (Fmr)	New Mexico, '75-'79
Cuomo	Mario Matthew	C	Governor (fmr.)	New York
Goodman	Roy Matz	C	State Senator	New York
Shaffer	Gail S.	C	Secretary of State	New York
Schwarzman	Stephen Allen	C	Observer	New York, State Finance Control Board
Kaminer	Peter H.	C	Special Master	New York, Supreme Court
Hernandez-Colon	Rafael	C	Governor	Puerto Rico
McCall	H. Carl	C	Comptroller	State of New York
Wilder	Lawrence Douglas	B	Governor (fmr.)	Virginia
			Universities	
Picker	Harvey	C	Board Member	Academy of Politcal Science
Herzstein	Jessica	C	Professor	ACOEM Post Graduate Seminars
Hamilton	Michael P.	C	Professor	Adirondack Community College
Alderman	Michael Harris	C	Department Chairman	Albert Einstein College of Medicine
Parker	Jason H.	C	Exec. Associate	American Council of Learned Societies
Herter	Frederic P.	C	President (fmr.)	American Univ.
Rubin	Seymour Jeffrey	C	Professor (fmr.)	American Univ.
Broad	Robin	C	Professor	American Univ., School of Int. Service
Perlmutter	Louis	C	Professor	American Univ., Wash.
Olson	William Clinton	C	Professor (fmr.)	American Univ., Washington
Huebner	Lee W.	C	President	American Univ., Paris
Zogby	James J.	C	President	Arab American Institute
Berkowitz	Bruce D.	C	Assoc. Director	Aspen Strategy Group
Rosenzweig	Robert Myron	C	President	Association of American Universities, Washington
Link	Troland S.	C	Board Member	AUC
Regan	Edward V.	C	Professor	Bard College, Economic Inst.
Lichtenstein	Cynthia C.	C	Professor	Boston College
Cromwell	Adelaide M.	C	Professor	Boston Univ.
Fanning	Katherine Woodruff	C	Adjunct Professor	Boston Univ.
Norton	Augustus Richard	C	Professor	Boston Univ.
Fromkin	David	C	Professor	Boston Univ., Int. Relations
Cheever	Daniel Sargent	C	Professor (fmr.)	Boston Univ., Political Science & International Relations
Eilts	Hermann Frederick	C	Department Chairman	Boston Univ.; US Ambassador (fmr.), Saudi Arabia
Coles	James Stacy	C	Pres. (fmr.)	Bowdin College
Edwards	Robert Hazard	C	President	Bowdoin College
Roche	John P.	C	Professor	Brandeis Univ., Fletcher Sch./Law & D., Civil & Fgn. Afrs.
Brown	Seyom	C	Professor	Brandeis Univ.; Member, Carnegie Endowment
Fry	Earl H.	C	Chairman	Brigham Young Univ., Canadian Studies
Hughes	John	C	Professor	Brigham Young Univ., Journalism
Lynch	William, Jr.	C	Professor	Brooklyn College
Gregorian	Vartan	C	President	Brown Univ.
Skidmore	Thomas E.	C	Professor	Brown Univ.
Weiss	Thomas G.	C	Professor	Brown Univ.
Gaer	Felice D.	C	Director	Brown Univ., Advancement of Human Rights
Garrison	Mark J.	C	Board Member	Brown Univ., Center for Foreign Policy Development
Kalicki	Jan H.	C	Sr. Advisor	Brown Univ., Center for Foreign Policy Development
Baird	Charles Fitz	C	Trustee	Bucknell Univ.
Mitchell	Jacquelyn A.	C	Dean	Buffalo Univ., Graduate School
Munger	Edwin Stanton	C	Professor	California Institute of Technology, Political Geography
Pedersen	Richard Foote	C	Director	California Poly Pomona Univ., International Programs
Arciniega	Tomas Abel	C	President	California State Univ., Bakersfield
Hazard	John Newbold	C	Professor (fmr.)	Cambridge Univ.
Bean	Atherton	C	Professor (fmr.)	Carleton College
Lewis	Stephen Richard, Jr.	C	President	Carleton College; Trustee, Carnegie Endowment
Goodby	James Eugene	C	Dist. Service Prof.	Carnegie Mellon Univ.
Bundy	McGeorge	B,C	Chairman	Carnegie Univ., Committee for Reducing Nuclear Danger

Last Name	First & Mid. Name	Org.	Job Title	Affiliation - Company, Organization
Ragone	David Vincent	C	President (fmr.)	Case Western Research Univ., Cleveland
Perez	Antonio F.	C	Professor	Catholic Univ. of America, Law
Spencer	William Courtney	C	Managing Director	Centre for International Education
Clark	Kenneth Bancroft	C	Professor (fmr.)	City College of New York
Murphy	Joseph S.	C	President	City Univ. of New York, Graduate School, NYC
Finger	Seymour Maxwell	C	Adjunct Professor	City Univ. of New York, NYC
Harleston	Bernard Warren	C	President	City Univ. of New York, NYC
LeMelle	Tilden John	C	Interim President	City Univ. of New York, NYC
Gotbaum	Victor	C	Director	City Univ. of New York, NYC, Ctr. For Social Research
Rustow	Dankwart A.	C	Professor	City Univ. of New York, NYC, Political Science and Sociology
Cotter	William Reckling	C	President	Colby College
Nathan	Andrew J.	C		Colombia Univ.
Anderson	Lisa	C	Professor	Colombia Univ., Political Science
Hendrickson	David C.	C	Assoc. Professor	Colorado College
Newton	Quigg	C	President (fmr.)	Colorado Univ.
Goldman	Emily O.	C	Assoc. Professor	Colorado Univ.., Political Science
Bialer	Seweryn	C	Professor	Columbia Univ.
Dennis	Everette Eugene, Jr.	C	Executive Director	Columbia Univ.
Elliott	Osborn	C	Professor	Columbia Univ.
Graff	Henry Franklin	C	Professor (fmr.)	Columbia Univ.
Henkin	Louis	C	Professor (fmr.)	Columbia Univ.
Hohenberg	John	C	Professor (fmr.)	Columbia Univ.
Jervis	Robert L.	C	Professor	Columbia Univ.
Milner	Helen V.	C	Professor	Columbia Univ.
Richards	Paul Granston	C	Professor	Columbia Univ.
Sassen	Saskia	C		Columbia Univ.
Skinner	Elliott P.	C	Professor	Columbia Univ.
Sovern	Michael Ira	C	President (fmr.)	Columbia Univ.
Stepan	Alfred C.	C	Dean (fmr.)	Columbia Univ.
Zuckerman	Harriet	C	Sr. Research Scholar	Columbia Univ.
Clurman	Richard Michael	C	Chairman	Columbia Univ., Board of Governors
Beim	David Odell	C,T	Professor	Columbia Univ., Business School
Bresnan	John J.	C	Sr. Research Scholar	Columbia Univ., East Asian Institute
Hamilton	Charles V.	C	Professor	Columbia Univ., Government
Simon	Francoise L.	B	Professor	Columbia Univ., Graduate School of Business
Sick	Gary G.	C	Executive Director	Columbia Univ., Gulf/2000 Project; Author
Stern	Fritz Richard	C	Professor	Columbia Univ., History
Neuman	Stephanie G.	C	Adj. Professor	Columbia Univ., Int. Affairs
Patrick	Hugh T.	C	Professor	Columbia Univ., Int. Business
Yu	Frederick T. C.	C	Professor (fmr.)	Columbia Univ., Int. Journalism
Wriggins	W. Howard	C	Professor(fmr.)	Columbia Univ., Int. Politics
Schilling	Warner R.	C	Professor	Columbia Univ., Int. Relations
Janow	Merit E.	C	Professor	Columbia Univ., Int. Trade
Ginsburg	Jane C.	C	Professor	Columbia Univ., Law
Young	Michael K.	C	Professor	Columbia Univ., Law
Schachter	Oscar	C	Professor	Columbia Univ., Law School
Baldwin	David A.	C	Professor	Columbia Univ., Polit. Sci.
Betts	Richard K.	C	Professor	Columbia Univ., Political Science
Marx	Anthony William	C	Professor	Columbia Univ., Political Science
Curtis	Gerald L.	C,T	Professor	Columbia Univ., Political Science, East Asian Institute
Speyer	Jerry I.	C	Chairman	Columbia Univ., Trustees
Baldwin	Richard Edward	C	Professor	Columbia Univ., World Order Studies
Kirk	Grayson Louis	C	Pres. & Trustee (fmr.)	Columbia Univ.; Vice Chairman (fmr.) & Director, CFR
Hilsman	Roger	C	Professor (fmr.)	Columia Univ.
Miller	David Charles, Jr.	C	Professor	Computer Science
Gaudiani	Claire Lynn	C	President	Connecticut College
Greene	Joseph Nathaniel, Jr.	C	Member	Connecticut College, Ctr. for Int. Studies & Lib. Arts
Iselin	John Jay	C	President	Cooper Union for Advancement of Science & Art
Gottfried	Kurt	C	Department Chairman	Cornell Univ.
Marks	Paul Alan	C	Professor	Cornell Univ.
Sagan	Carl Edward	C	Prof., Astronimer	Cornell Univ.
Thomas	Lewis	C	Professor	Cornell Univ. Medical School, Medicine
Reppy	Judith V.	C	Professor	Cornell Univ. Peace Studies
Einaudi	Mario	C	Professor	Cornell Univ., Center for Int. Studies
Telhami	Shibley	C	Assoc. Professor	Cornell Univ., Near Eastern Studies
Lewis	John Wilson	C	Professor	Cornell Univ., Political Science
Rhodes	Frank Harold Trevor	C	President	Cornell Univ.; Director, General Electric Co.
Lyons	Gene Martin	C	Professor	Dartmouth College
Kean	Thomas H.	C	President	Drew Univ.; Board Member, Carnegie Corp. of New York
Embree	Ainslie Thomas	C	Professor (fmr.)	Duke Univ.
Gann	Pamela B.	C	Professor	Duke Univ., Law
Keohane	Nannerl Overholster	C,T	President	Duke Univ.; Director, IBM Corp.
Morley	James William	C	Professor (fmr.)	East Asian Inst., Political Science
Passin	Herbert	C	Professor (fmr.)	East Asian Inst., Sociology
Pitts	Joe W., III	C	Professor	Eastern College, St. Davids PA
Laney	James Thomas	C	President	Emory Univ.; Director, Coca-Cola Company
Stone	Jeremy Judah	C	President	Federation of American Scientists, Washington

Last Name	First & Mid. Name	Org.	Job Title	Affiliation - Company, Organization
Stiehm	Judith Hicks	C	Provost (fmr.)	Florida International Univ., Miami
Harris	Joseph E.	C	Professor	Florida State Univ.
O'Hare	Joseph Aloysius	C	President	Fordham Univ.
van den Haag	Ernest	C	Professor	Fordham Univ., Jurisprudence & Public Policy
O'Connor	Walter F.	C	Director	Fordham Univ., Taxation and Accounting Program
Lipset	Seymour Martin	C		George Mason Univ.
Wilkins	Roger W.	C	Professor	George Mason Univ., History
Ratchford	J. Thomas	C	Director	George Mason Univ., Science, Trade & Technology
Harding	Harry	C	Dean	George Wash. Univ.; Brookings Inst.; Trustee, Asia Found.
Buergenthal	Thomas	C	Professor	George Washington Univ.
Sohn	Louis Bruno	C	Dist. Research Prof.	George Washington Univ.
Trachtenberg	Stephen Joel	C	President	George Washington Univ.
Vaky	Viron Peter	C	Adjunct Professor	George Washington Univ., Dipolmacy
Nau	Henry R.	C	Professor	George Washington Univ., Political Science & Int. Affairs
Roberts	Walter Ronald	C	Diplomat-in-Residence	George Washington Univ., Washington
Bello	Judith Hipper	C	Adjunct Professor	Georgetown Univ.
Feshbach	Murry	C	Professor	Georgetown Univ.
Hudson	Michael Craig	C	Professor	Georgetown Univ.
Lieber	Robert J.	C	Professor	Georgetown Univ.
Mikell	Gwendolyn	C	President	Georgetown Univ.
Muravchik	Joshua	C	Res. Scholar	Georgetown Univ.
Quigley	Kevin F. F.	C	Guest Scholar	Georgetown Univ.
Shelton-Colby	Sally A.	C	Member	Georgetown Univ.
van Cott	Donna Lee	C	Doctoral Cand.	Georgetown Univ.
Luttwak	Edward Nicolae	C	Chairman in Strategy	Georgetown Univ., Center for Strategic & Int. Studies
Mujal-Leon	Eusebio M.	C	Chairman	Georgetown Univ., Government Dept.
Stent	Angela E.	C	Professor	Georgetown Univ., Governmlent
Haddad	Yvonne Yazbeck	C	Professor	Georgetown Univ., History
Tucker	Nancy Bernkopf	C	Professor	Georgetown Univ., History, Sch. of Fgn. Service
Newsom	David Dunlop	C	Professor	Georgetown Univ., International Relations
Stromseth	Jane E.	C	Professor	Georgetown Univ., Law
Green	Carl J.	C	Director	Georgetown Univ., Law Ctr.
Weiss	Edith Brown	C	Vice Chairwoman	Georgetown Univ., Law Ctr.
Krogh	Peter F.	B	Dean	Georgetown Univ., School of Foreign Service
Hyland	William George	C,T	Distinguished Prof.	Georgetown Univ.; Editor (fmr.), CFR, Foreign Affairs
Smalley	Patricia Tolles	C	Charter Trustee	Hamilton College
Rizk	Nayla M.	C	Director	Harvard Business School Assoc. of North Carolina
Barker	Robert R.	C	President (Fmr)	Harvard Magazine, Board of Overseers
Cooper	Richard Newell	B,C,T	Professor	Harvard U.;Dir.,CFR;Und.Sec.(fmr.),St. Dept.,Econ.Afrs.
Brown	Michael E.	C		Harvard Univ.
Falkenrath	Richard A.	C		Harvard Univ.
Glazer	Nathan	C	Professor	Harvard Univ.
Hirschman	Albert Otto	C	Professor (fmr.)	Harvard Univ.
Houthakker	Hendrik	T	Prof. of Economics	Harvard Univ.
Maier	Charles Steven	C	Professor	Harvard Univ.
Mickiewicz	Ellen Propper	C	Subcom. Member	Harvard Univ.
Oettinger	Anthony Gervin	C	Member of Faculty	Harvard Univ.
Peretz	Don	C	Professor	Harvard Univ.
Pharr	Susan J.	C	Member	Harvard Univ.
Price	Donald K.	B	Professor (fmr.)	Harvard Univ.
Rudenstine	Neil Leon	C	President	Harvard Univ.
Said	Edward W.	C	Professor	Harvard Univ.
Spar	Debra L.	C		Harvard Univ.
Vogel	Ezra F.	B,C	Professor	Harvard Univ.
Wells	Louis T., Jr.	C	Member	Harvard Univ.
Yergin	Daniel Howard	C	Research Associate	Harvard Univ.
Meselson	Matthew Stanley	C	Associate Professor	Harvard Univ., Biology
Kanter	Rosabeth Moss	C	Professor	Harvard Univ., Business School
Stobaugh	Robert Blair	C	Professor	Harvard Univ., Business School
Yoffie	David B.	C	Professor	Harvard Univ., Business School, Int. Business
Meyer	John Robert	C	Professor	Harvard Univ., Capital Formation & Economic Growth
Doty	Paul M., Jr.	C	Director (fmr.)	Harvard Univ., Center for Science
Zinberg	Dorothy Shore	C	Sr. Research Assoc.	Harvard Univ., Center for Science & International Affairs
Harpel	James W.	C	Professor	Harvard Univ., Ctr. for Business and Government
Grose	Peter	C	Research Fellow	Harvard Univ., Ctr. for Scince & Int. Affairs
Dominguez	Jorge Ignacio	C	Department Chairman	Harvard Univ., Cuban Studies
Friedman	Benjamin Morton	C	Department Chairman	Harvard Univ., Dept. of Economics
Blendon	Robert Jay	C	Department Chairman	Harvard Univ., Dept. of Health Policy & Management
Rosovsky	Henry	C,T	Professor	Harvard Univ., Economics
Froot	Kenneth A.	C	Professor	Harvard Univ., Finance
Keohane	Robert Owen	C	Professor	Harvard Univ., Government
Pipes	Richard Edgar	C	Professor	Harvard Univ., History
Gates	Henry Louis, Jr.	C	Professor	Harvard Univ., humanities
Kelman	Herbert C.	C	Fellow	Harvard Univ., Int. Conflict Analysis
Krasner	Stephen D.	C	Professor	Harvard Univ., Int. Relations
Mottahedeh	Roy	C	Professor	Harvard Univ., Islamic History
Neustadt	Richard Elliott	C	Professor (fmr.)	Harvard Univ., J. F. K. School of Government

Last Name	First & Mid. Name	Org.	Job Title	Affiliation - Company, Organization
Bower	Joseph Lyon	C	Member of Faculty	Harvard Univ., JFK School of Government
Vagts	Detlev Frederick	C	Professor	Harvard Univ., Law
Echols	Marsha A.	C	Professor	Harvard Univ., Law School
Glendon	Mary Ann	C	Professor	Harvard Univ., Law School
Thornell	Richard P.	C	Professor	Harvard Univ., Law School
Trainor	Bernard Edmund	C	Director	Harvard Univ., National Security Program
Wiener	Jonathan Baert	C	Assoc. Professor	Harvard Univ., Risk Analysis
Goldman	Marshall I.	C	Assoc. Director	Harvard Univ., Russian Research Ctr.
Yalman	Nur	C	Professor	Harvard Univ., Social Anthropology
Jackson	Eric K.	C	Fellow	Harvard Univ., Social Politics
Szporluk	Roman	C	Professor	Harvard Univ., Ukranian History
Blackmer	Donald Laur. Morton	C	Research Associate	Harvard Univ., West European Studies
Safran	Nadav	C	Professor (fmr.)	Harvard Univ.; author of "The Embattled Ally"
Putnam	Robert D.	C,T	Director	Harvard Univ.; Chairman & CEO (fmr.), Levi Strauss & Co.
Hehir	J. Bryan	C	Member	Harvard Univ.; Georgetown Univ. TheoligaN
Dodge	William S.	C	Professor	Hastings of the Law
Reisman	W. Michael	C	Professor	Hebrew Univ., Jurisprudence
Haynes	Ulric St. Clair, Jr.	C	Dean	Hofstra Univ., School of Business
Smythe	Mabel M.	C	Member	Howard Univ., Advisory Commission
Chayes	Abram J.	C	Professor	Howard Univ., Law School; Adv. Bd. Mbr., Ctr./Nat. Pol.
Turner	J. Michael	C	Assoc. Professor	Hunter College
Crahan	Margaret E.	C	Chairwoman	Hunter College, Env. Justice: Response
Wells	Herman B.	C	Chancellor	Indiana Univ.
Ehrlich	Thomas	C	Professor	Indiana Univ. System, Law
O'Connell	Mary Ellen	C	Professor	Indiana Univ., Int. Law
Calkins	Hugh	C,T	President & Director	Initiatives in Urban Education
Weston	Burns H.	C	Professor	Iowa Univ., Law
Wing	Adrien K.	C	Professor	Iowa Univ., Law
Gati	Charles	C	Professor	John's Hopkins Univ.
Brzezinski	Zbigniew	B,C,T	Counselor	Johns Hop.,Ctr./Strat. & Int. Stud.; Nat. Sec. Advis. (fmr.)
Wohlforth	William C.	C	Assoc. Editor	Johns Hopkins Press
Adams	Robert McCormick	C	Professor	Johns Hopkins Univ.
Cohen	Eliot A.	C	Professor	Johns Hopkins Univ.
Frank	Isaiah	C	Professor	Johns Hopkins Univ.
Weiss	Charles, Jr.	C	Professor	Johns Hopkins Univ.
Zartman	I. William	C	Professor	Johns Hopkins Univ., Advanced Int. Studies
Hinshaw	Randall Weston	C	Professor (fmr.)	Johns Hopkins Univ., Claremont Graduate School
Jordan	Amos Azariah, Jr.	C	Vice Chairman	Johns Hopkins Univ., Crt. for Strat. & Int. Studies
Abshire	David M.	C,T	President	Johns Hopkins Univ., Ctr. for Strat. & Int. Studies
Armstrong	Anne Legendre	C,T	Chairman	Johns Hopkins Univ., Ctr. for Strat. & Int. Studies
Cordesman	Anthony H.	C	Co-Director	Johns Hopkins Univ., Ctr. for Strat. & Int. Studies
Fairbanks	Richard Monroe, III	C	Sr. Counsel	Johns Hopkins Univ., Ctr. for Strat. & Int. Studies
Taylor	William Jesse, Jr.	C	Member	Johns Hopkins Univ., Ctr. for Strat. & Int. Studies
Zoellick	Robert Bruce	B,C,T	Pres. & CEO	Johns Hopkins Univ., Crt. for Strat. & Int. Studies
Zimmerman	Peter D.	C	Member	Johns Hopkins Univ., Crt. for Strat. & Int. Studies
Fore	Henrietta Holsman	B,C	Sr. Associate	Johns Hopkins Univ., Crt. for Strat. & Int. Studies
Baer	M. Delal	C	Sr. Fellow & Dir.	Johns Hopkins Univ., Crt. for Strat. & Int. Studies
Miller	Debra L.	C	Director	Johns Hopkins Univ., Crt. for Strat. & Int. Studies
Muller	Steven	C	President	Johns Hopkins Univ., Fed. Reserve Bank
Litwak	Robert S.	C	Director	Johns Hopkins Univ., Int. Studies
Grant	James Pineo	C	Director (fmr.)	Johns Hopkins Univ., International Vol. Services
Barnett	Arthur Doak	C	Professor (fmr.)	Johns Hopkins Univ., Sch of Advanced Int. Studies
Levy	Walter James	B,C	Oil Consultant	Johns Hopkins Univ., Sch of Advanced Int. Studies
Mandelbaum	Michael E.	C	Fgn. Policy Specialist	Johns Hopkins Univ., Sch of Advanced Int. Studies
Packard	George Randolph	C	Dean	Johns Hopkins Univ., Sch of Advanced Int. Studies
Wolfowitz	Paul Dean	B,C,T	Dean	Johns Hopkins Univ., Sch of Advanced Int. Studies
Doran	Charles F.	C	Professor	Johns Hopkins Univ., School of Medicine
Brown	Frederic Joseph	C	Director	Johns Hopkins Univ., Southeast Asian Studies
Rotberg	Robert Irvin	C	President	Lafayette College, Pennsylvania
Gardner	James Albert	C	President (fmr.)	Lewis & Clark College, Portland
Sudarkasa	Niara	C	President	Lincoln Univ., Pennsylvania
Steinberg	David Joel	C	President	Long Island Univ., Brooklyn
Howard	John R.	C	Trustee	Louis & Clark College
Schneider	Jan	C	Professor	Medical College of Pennsylvania
McPherson	Melville Peter	C	President	Mich. St. Univ.;Grp.Exec.V. P. (fmr.) Bankamerica Corp.
Hamilton	Ruth Simms	C	Project Director	Michigan State University, African Research Project
Garber	Larry	C		Michigan Univ.
Eisendrath	Charles R.	C	Director	Michigan Univ., Journalism Flow. Prog.
Widner	Jennifer	C	Assoc. Proffesor	Michigan Univ., Political Science

Last Name	First & Mid. Name	Org.	Job Title	Affiliation - Company, Organization
Bloomfield	Lincoln Palmer	C	Professor (fmr.)	MIT
Gell-Mann	Murray	C	Professor	MIT
Intriligator	Michael David	C	Professor	MIT
Stratton	Julius Adams	C	President (fmr.)	MIT
Tsipis	Kosta Michael	C	Sr. Research Scientist	MIT
Wheelon	Albert Dewell	C	Visiting Prof. (fmr.)	MIT
Wiesner	Jerome Bert	C	President (fmr.)	MIT
Weiner	Myron	C	Sr. Staff Member	MIT & Harvard Univ.
Seamans	Robert Channing, Jr.	C	Sr. Lecturer	MIT, Aeronautics & Astronomics
Berger	Suzanne	C	Department Chairman	MIT, Dept. of Political Science
Rathjens	George William	C	Professor	MIT, Dept. of Political Science
Thurow	Lester C.	T	Professor	MIT, Economics, Alfred P. Sloan School of Management
Rattray	Gregory J.	C		MIT, PHd. Candidate, Law School
Kaysen	Carl	B,C	Professor (fmr.)	MIT, Political Economy
Griffith	William E.	C	Professor	MIT, Political Science
Johnson	Willard Raymond	C	Professor	MIT, political science
Posen	Barry R.	C	Professor	MIT, Political Science
Samuels	Richard J.	C	Professor	MIT, Political Science
Skolnikoff	Eugene B.	C	Professor	MIT, Political Science
Pye	Lucian Wilmot	C	Professor	MIT, Political Science; Director (fmr.), CFR
Keniston	Kenneth	C	Professor	MIT, Science Technology and Society
Potter	William C.	C	Professor	Monterey Inst. for Int. Studies
Gard	Robert G., Jr.	C	President	Monterey Inst. of Int. Studies
Kennan	Elizabeth Topham	C	President	Mt. Holyoke College
Jastrow	Robert	C	Chairman	Mt. Wilson Institute
Taylor	Arthur Robert	C,T	President	Muhlenberg College, Allentown, Pennsylvania
Mills	Karen Gordon	C	Director	N.Y. Univ.
Edelman	Gerald Maurice	C	Director	Neuroscience Institute
Utton	Albert E.	C	Professor	New Mexico Univ.
Jacoby	Tamar	C	Instructor	New School for Social Research, NYC
Zolberg	Aristide Rodolphe	C	Professor	New School for Social Research, NYC
Denoon	David Baugh Holden	C	Professor	New York Univ., NYC
Nadiri	M. Ishaq	C	Professor	New York Univ., NYC
Oliva	Lawrence Jay	C	President	New York Univ., NYC
Samuelson	Paul Anthony	B	Professor	New York Univ., NYC
Fox	Eleanor Mae Cohen	C	Professor	New York Univ., NYC, Law
Franck	Thomas Martin	C	Professor	New York Univ., NYC, Law
Lowenfeld	Andreas Frank	C	Professor	New York Univ., NYC, Law
Finkelstein	Lawrence S.	C	Professor	Northern Illinois Univ.
Bienen	Henry S.	C	President	Northwestern Univ.
Revesz	Richard L.	C	Professor	NYU Law School
Sherry	George Leon	C	Professor	Occidental College, Diplomacy & World Affairs
Millett	Allan R.	C	Professor	Ohio State Univ.
Mansfield	Edward D.	C	Assoc. Professor	Ohio State Univ., Political Science
Gaddis	John Lewis	C	Distinguished Prof.	Ohio Univ.
Bartlett	Thomas Alva	C	Member	Oregon State System of Higher Education
Meron	Theodor	C	Professor	Oxford Univ., England
Cox	Robert Gene	C	Governor	Oxford Univ., Manchester College
Davis	Vincent	C	Director	Patterson School of Diplomacy & Int. Communications
Ferguson	John Henry	B	Professor (fmr.)	Pennsylvania State Univ.
Larson	Charles Robert	C	President	Pioneers Science & Technology History Association
Sonnenfeldt	Richard Wolfgang	C	Professor	Poly Institute of New York, Brooklyn
Bugliarello	George	C	President	Polytechnical Univ., Brooklyn
Stanley	Peter William	C	President	Pomona College, California
Wheat	Francis Millspaugh	C	Vice Chairman	Pomona College, California
Calder	Kent Eyring	C	Professor	Princeton Univ.
Falk	Richard A.	C	Professor	Princeton Univ.
Friedberg	Aaron L.	C		Princeton Univ.
Gilpin	Robert G., Jr.	C	Professor	Princeton Univ.
Grossman	Gene M.	C	Professor	Princeton Univ.
Kennan	George Frost	C	Professor (fmr.)	Princeton Univ.
Lewis	Bernard	C	Professor (fmr.)	Princeton Univ.
Sinding	Steven W.	C	Professor	Princeton Univ.
Stokes	Donald Elkinton	C	Professor	Princeton Univ.
Suleiman	Ezra N.	C	Professor	Princeton Univ.
Waterbury	John	C	Professor	Princeton Univ.
Turkevich	John	C	Professor	Princeton Univ., Chemistry
Kenen	Peter Bain	C	Professor	Princeton Univ., Economics & Finance
Patterson	Gardner	C	Professor	Princeton Univ., Economics Dept.
Geertz	Clifford James	C	Professor	Princeton Univ., Institute for Advanced Studies
Woolf	Harry	C	Director	Princeton Univ., Institute for Advanced Studies
Udovitch	Abraham L.	C	Professor	Princeton Univ., Near Eastern Studies
Herbst	Jeffrey	C	Professor	Princeton Univ., Political and Int. Affairs
Sigmund	Paul Eugene	C	Professor	Princeton Univ., Politics
Brown	Leon Carl	C	Director	Princeton Univ., Program of Near Eastern Studies
Hippel, von	Frank N.	C	Professor	Princeton Univ., Public & Int. Affairs
Levy	Marion J. Jr.	C	Professor	Princeton Univ., Sociolgy and Int. Affairs

Last Name	First & Mid. Name	Org.	Job Title	Affiliation - Company, Organization
Goheen	Robert Francis	C	Sr. Fellow	Princeton Univ.,Woodrow Wilson Sch.;Amb. (fmr.),India
Shapiro	Harold Tafler	C	President	Princeton Univ.; Director, Dow Chemical Co.
Godwin	I. Lamond	C	Professor	Princton Univ.
Gullion	Edmund A.	C	Professor	Princton Univ.
Grossman	Gene M.	B	Professor	Princton Univ., Int. Economics
Snyder	Jack L.	C	Professor	Princton Univ., Int. History
Jansen	Marius B.	C	Professor	Princton Univ., Japanese Studies
Doyle	Michael William	C	Professor	Prinseton Univ.
Mulholland	William D.	B	Trustee	Queen's University
Horner	Matina Souretis	C	President (fmr.)	Radcliffe College
Khuri	Nicola Najib	C	Professor	Rockefeller Univ.
Pais	Abraham	C	Professor	Rockefeller Univ.
Piore	Emanuel Rubin	B	Adjunct Professor	Rockefeller Univ.
Seitz	Frederick	C	President (fmr.)	Rockefeller Univ.
Wiesel	Torsten Nils	C	President	Rockefeller Univ.
Ausubel	Jesse Huntley	C	Director	Rockefeller Univ., Prog. for the Human Environment
Sawoski	Mark	C	Professor	Roger Williams Univ.
Alexander	Robert Jackson	C	Professor (fmr.)	Rutgers Univ.
Horowitz	Irving Louis	C	Professor	Rutgers Univ.
Shafer	D. Michael	C	Director	Rutgers Univ., CASE
Mendlovitz	Saul H.	C	Professor	Rutgers Univ., Peace & World Studies, Law School
Salk	Jonus Edward	C	Founding Director	Salk Institute of Biological Studies
Berger	Marilyn	C	Professor	Seattle Univ., Law
Conway	Jill Kathryn Ker	C	President (fmr.)	Smith College
Pye	August Kenneth	C	President	Southern Methodist Univ., Dallas
Wildenthal	Claud Kern	C	President	Southwest Medical School
Carmichael	William Daniel	C	Executive Director	Soviet Union & East Euro. Programs Inst. for Int. Educ.
Stewart	Donald M.	C	President (fmr.)	Spelman College, Director, Ctr. for International Policy
Cole	Johnnetta Betsch	C	President	Spelman College; Director, Coca-Cola Co.
Shultz	George Pratt	C,T	Honorary Fellow	Stanford U., Hoover Inst., Calif.; Sec. (fmr.), State Dept.
Abel	Elie	C	Professor	Stanford Univ.
Casper	Gerhard	C	President	Stanford Univ.
Fuerbringer	Otto	C	Professor	Stanford Univ.
Kennedy	David Michael	B	Professor	Stanford Univ.
Krueger	Anne O.	C	Professor	Stanford Univ.
Smith	Clint E.	C	Professor	Stanford Univ.
Oksenberg	Michael	C,T	Sr. Fellow	Stanford Univ., Asia Pacific Research Ctr.
Runge	Carlisle Ford	C	Professor	Stanford Univ., Economics
Mickelson	Sig	C	Research Fellow	Stanford Univ., Hoover Institute
Skinner	Kiron Kanian	C		Stanford Univ., Hoover Institute
Wolf	Charles, Jr.	C	Sr. Fellow	Stanford Univ., Hoover Institute
Raisian	John	C	Sr. Fellow	Stanford Univ., Hoover Institute, California
Campbell	Wesley Glenn	C	Counselor	Stanford Univ., Hoover Institute, California
Lapidus	Gail W.	C	Sr. Fellow	Stanford Univ., Inst. for Int. Studies
Naylor	Rosamond Lee	C	Professor	Stanford Univ., Inst. for Int. Studies
Dallin	Alexander	C	Dept. Chairman	Stanford Univ., International Relations
Ely	John Hart	C	Professor	Stanford Univ., Law School
Drell	Sidney David	C	Executive Director	Stanford Univ., Linear Accelerator Center
Panofsky	Wolfgang Kurt H.	C	Director (fmr.)	Stanford Univ., Linear Accellerator
Sagan	Scott D.	C	Assoc. Professor	Stanford Univ., Political Science
Rohlen	Thomas P.	C	Professor	Stanford Univ., School of Humanities
Rosen	Arthur H.	C	Chairman	Stanford Univ., Sino-judaic Inst.
Lyman	Richard Wall	C	President (fmr.)	Stanford Univ.; Director, IBM Corp.
Perry	William J.	B,T	Professor	Stanford Univ.; Sec. (fmr.) Defense Dept.
Enthoven	Alain C.	C	Professor	Stanfore Univ., Public and Private Management
Cox	Edward F.	C	Member	State Univ. of New York, Plng. Committee Steering Committee
Herskovits	Jean	C	Professor	State Univ. of New York, African History
Plimpton	Calvin Hastings	C	Professor (fmr.)	State Univ. of New York, Downstate Medical Center
Travis	Martin Bice, Jr.	C	Professor	State Univ. of New York, Stony Brook, Politicl Science
Reed	Charles Bass	C	Chancellor	State Univ. System of Florida
Speidel	Kirsten E.	C	Professor	Swarthmore College
Kurth	James R.	C	Professor	Swarthmore Univ.
Cooke	Goodwin	C	Professor	Syracuse Univ.
Hermann	Charles F.	C	Director	Texas A&M Bush School of Government and Public Service
Madrid	Arturo	C	Professor	Trinity Univ. San Antonio
Stoessinger	John G.	C	Professor	Trinity Univ., Int. Affairs
Burlingame	John F.	C	Teaching Assit.	Tufts Univ.
Fawaz	Leila	C	President (fmr.)	Tufts Univ.
Robinson	Pearl T.	C	Member	Tufts Univ.
Salacuse	Jeswald William	C	Dean	Tufts Univ.
Terry	Sarah M.	C	Assoc. Professor	Tufts Univ.
Meagher	Robert F.	C	Professor	Tufts Univ., Law School
Farer	Tom Joel	C	Visiting Professor	Tulane Law School
Bauman	Robert Poe	C	Professor (fmr.)	Univ. of Alabama
Green	Jerrold D.	C	Director	Univ. of Arizona, Ctr. for Mideast Studies

Last Name	First & Mid. Name	Org.	Job Title	Affiliation - Company, Organization
Wakeman	Frederick Evans, Jr.	C	Professor	Univ. of California
Cornelius	Wayne	C	Specialist	Univ. of Cal., Ctr. of U.S.-Mexico Studies
van Evera	Stephen W.	C	Assoc. Professor	UC Berkeley, Political Science
Wildavsky	Aaron	C	Professor (fmr.)	UC, Berkelely, Political Science & Public Policy
Zysman	John	C	Professor	UC, Berkeley, Political Science
Rosberg	Carl Gustaf	C	Professor (fmr.)	Univ. of Cal. Berkeley
Lyons	Richard K.	C	Professor	Univ. of Cal. Berkeley, Business School
Eichengreen	Barry	C	Economist	Univ. of Cal., Berkeley
Teece	David John	C	Professor	Univ. of California, Berkeley
Chaudhry	Kiren Aziz	C	Professor	U.C. Berkeley, Political Science
Waltz	Kenneth Neal	C	Professor	Univ. of California, Berkeley, Political Science
Seaborg	Glenn Theadore	C	Department Chairman	Univ. of California, Berkley, Science
Katz	Milton	B,C	Advisory Board Mbr.	Univ. of California, Consortium/Competition and Coop.
Boecker	Paul Harold	C	President	Univ. of California, Inst. of the Americas
MacDougal	Gary E.	C	Professor	UCLA
Rosecrance	Richard N.	C	Professor	UCLA
Higgins	Robert F.	C	Assoc. Professor	UCLA, Civil Engineering
Korbonski	Andrzej	C	Professor	UCLA, Russia and East European Studies
Shirk	Susan L.	C	Professor	UCLA, San Diego
Goldberger	Marvin Leonard	C	Professor	Univ. of California, L. A., Physics
Gourevitch	Peter Alexis	C	Professor	Univ. of California, San Diego
Erb	Guy F.	C		Univ. of Cal., San Diego
Schake	Kori Naomi	C	Professor	Univ. of Cal. San Diego
Kahler	Miles	C	Professor	Univ. of Cal. San Diego, Int. Relations
Hoston	Germaine A.	C	Professor	Univ. of Cal. San Diego, Political Science
Haggard	Stephen	C	Adj. Professor	Univ. of Cal., San Diego, Political Science
Klein	David	C	Visiting Professor	Univ. of California, San Diego
MacDonald	Gordon James F.	C	Professor	Univ. of California, San Diego
Sheldon	Eleanor Harriet B.	C	Visiting Professor	Univ. of California, Santa Barbara
Hanrieder	Wolfram F.	C	Professor (fmr.)	U.C. Santa Barbara, German Foreign Policy
Lary	Hal B.	C		Univ. of Chicago
Lynn	Laurence Edwin, Jr.	C	Director	Univ. of Chicago, Ctr./Urban Resources & Pol. Science
Gottlieb	Gidon Alain Guy	C	Professor	Univ. of Chicago, Law School
Rudolph	Susanne Hoeber	C	Professor	Univ. of Chicago, Political & Social Science
Rudolph	Lloyd Irving	C	Professor	Univ. of Chicago, Political Science
Gray	Hanna Holborn	C	President	Univ. of Chicago; Dir., Atl. Richfield Co.,Concord Coal.
Smith	Michael Bryant	C	Professor	Univ. of Connecticut
Benbow	Terence H.	C	Dean	Univ. of Connecticut, Law School
Karns	Margaret P.	C		Univ. of Dayton
Himes	James Albert	C	Professor (fmr.)	Univ. of Florida
Lee	William L.	C	Professor	Univ. of Georgia
Cleveland	James Harlan	B,C	President (fmr.)	Univ. of Hawaii
Kanet	Roger Edward	C	Professor	Univ. of Illinois
Linowes	David Francis	C	Professor (fmr.)	Univ. of Illinois
Kolodziej	Edward Albert	C	Research Professor	Univ. of Illinois, Political Science
Stempel	John D.	C	Professor	Univ. of Kentucky
Kahin	George McTurnan	C	Honorary Fellow	Univ. of London, Sch. of Org. and African Studies
Quester	George Herman	C	Professor	Univ. of Maryland, Political Science
Foote	Edward Thaddeus, II	C	President	Univ. of Miami
Moss	Amber Holmes, Jr.	C	Dean	Univ. of Miami, Graduate School
Jackson	John Howard	C	Professor	Univ. of Michigan
Light	Timothy	C	Professor	Univ. of Michigan
McCracken	Paul Winston	B,C,T	Professor (fmr.)	Univ. of Michigan
Power	Philip H.	C	Regent	Univ. of Michigan
Tanter	Raymond	C	Professor	Univ. of Michigan
Hovey	Graham	C	Professor	Univ. of Michigan, Communications Studies
Stein	Eric	C	Professor (fmr.)	Univ. of Michigan, Law School
Jacobson	Harold Karan	C	Professor	Univ. of Michigan, Political Science
Clark	Noreen Morrison	C	Department Chairman	Univ. of Michigan; Director, Aaron Diamond Foundation
Ruttan	Vernon Wesley	C	Professor	Univ. of Minnesota
Schuh	George Edward	C	Dean	Univ. of Minnesota, Humphrey Institute
Brinkley	Douglas G.	B	Director	Univ. of New Orleans, Eisenhower Ctr. for American Studies
Behrman	Jack Newton	C	Professor (fmr.)	Univ. of North Carolina
Black	Stanley Warren. III	C	Professor	Univ. of North Carolina
Nugent	Walter Terry King	C	Professor	Univ. of Notre Dame
Hesburgh	Theodore Martin	B,C,T	President (fmr.)	Univ. of Notre Dame; Director (fmr.), CFR
Frankel	Francine Ruth	C	Professor	Univ. of Pennsylvania
Meyerson	Martin	C	President (fmr.)	Univ. of Pennsylvania
Oliver	Covey T.	C	Professor (fmr.)	Univ. of Pennsylvania, Law School
Lustick	Ian S.	C	Professor	Univ. of Pennsylvania, Political Science
Coffey	Joseph Irving	C	Professor (fmr.)	Univ. of Pittsburgh
Mesa-Lago	Carmelo	C	Distinguished Prof.	Univ. of Pittsburgh
Huizenga	John W.	C	Professor (fmr.)	Univ. of Rochester
O'Brien	Dennis J.	C	Professor	Univ. Of Rochester

Last Name	First & Mid. Name	Org.	Job Title	Affiliation - Company, Organization
Lowenthal	Abraham Frederic	C	Director, Leader	Univ. of S. Cal., Int. Studies; Advis. Bd., Ctr. for Nat. Pol.
Brand	Laurie A.	C	Director	Univ. of Southern Cal., Center for Int. Studies
Bender	Gerald J.	C	Assoc. Prof.	Univ. of Southern Cal., International Relations
Aronson	Jonathan D.	C	Professor	Univ. of Southern Cal.
Puchala	Donald J.	C	V.P. of Programs	Univ. of Southern Cal.
Rhodes	Edward	C	Professor	Univ. of Southern Cal.
Odell	John	C	Professor	Univ. of Southern California
Sample	Steven Browning	C	President	Univ. of Southern California, Los Angeles
Bobbitt	Philip Chase	C	Professor	Univ. of Texas, Austin
Jordan	Barbara	T	LBJ Cent. Chr. (fmr.)	Univ. of Texas, Austin
Louis	William Roger	C	Department Chairman	Univ. of Texas, Austin
Mark	Hans Michael	C	Chancellor	Univ. of Texas, Austin
Weinberg	Steven	C	Professor	Univ. of Texas, Austin
Weintraub	Sidney	C	Professor	Univ. of Texas, Austin
Rostow	Walt Whitman	C	Professor	Univ. of Texas, Austin, Political Economics
Donaldson	Robert Herschel	C	President	Univ. of Tulsa
Reinhardt	John Edward	C	Professor (fmr.)	Univ. of Vermont
Turner	Robert Foster	C	Associate Professor	Univ. of Virginia
Cronin	Audrey Kurth	C	Professor (fmr.)	Univ. of Virginia, Politics of NATO
Miles	Edward L.	C	Professor	Univ. of Wash., Seattle
Denny	Brewster Castberg	C	Dean (fmr.)	Univ. of Washington, Seattle
Pyle	Kenneth Birger	C	Professor	Univ. of Washington, Seattle
Reiss	Mitchell B.	C	Adjunct Professor	Univ. of Washington, Seattle
Baldwin	Robert Edward	C	Research Professor	Univ. of Wisconsin
Lyall	Katherine Culbert	C	President	Univ. of Wisconsin
Young	Mervin Crawford	C	Professor	Univ. of Wisconsin
Krause	Lawrence B.	C	Professor	Univer. Of Cal. San Diego
Hosmer	Bradley Clark	C	Superintendent	USAF Academy
Smith	Edwin M.	C	Professor	USC, Law School
Whitaker	C. S.	C	Professor	USC, Los Angeles
Firmage	Edwin B.	C	Professor	Utah Univ., Law
Mehta	Ved Parkash	C	Professor	Vassar College
Schwartz	Thomas Alan	C	Assoc. Professor	Vermont Univ.
Gause	F. Gregory, III	C	Asst. Professor	Vermont Univ., Political Science
Trani	Eugene Paul	C	President	Virginia Commonwealth Univ.
Weidenbaum	Murray Lew	C	Department Chairman	Washington Univ., Economics
Danforth	William Henry	C	President	Washington Univ.; Director, McDonnell Douglas Corp.
Danforth	William Henry	C	Chancellor	Washington Univ.; Director, McDonnell Douglas Corp.
Marshall	Dale Rogers	C	President	Weaton College, Mass.
Miller	Linda B.	C	Professor	Wellesley College
Barrett	Nancy Smith	C	Provost & Vice Pres.	Western Michigan Univ.
Christman	Daniel William	C	Superintendent	West Point
Barnett	Michael N.	C	Assoc. Professor	Wisconsin Unvi., Madison, Political Science
Altman	Sidney	C	Professor	Yale Univ.
Apter	David Ernest	C	Professor	Yale Univ.
Sutterlin	James S.	C	Professor	Yale Univ.
McDougal	Myres S.	C	Professor (fmr.)	Yale Univ. Law School
Stith-Cabranes	Kate	C	Secretary	Yale Univ., Board of Directors
Smith	Gaddis	C	Professor	Yale Univ., History
Ranis	Gustav	C	Professor	Yale Univ., International Economics
Lipson	Leon	C	Professor (fmr.)	Yale Univ., Jurisprudence
LaPalombara	Joseph	C	Professor	Yale Univ., Political Science
Marmor	Theodore R.	C	Professor	Yale Univ., Public Policy & Mgt.
Garten	Jeffrey E.	C	Dean	Yale Univ.; Under Sec. (fmr.) Commerce Dept., Int. Trade
			Financial Organizations	
International Banking				
Newburg	Andre W. G.	C	General Counsel	Euro. Bank of Reconstruction & Development, London
Lawson	Eugene K.	C	1st V. Pres.,V. Chair.	Export-Import Bank of US
Cline	William Richard	C	Adv. Bd. Mbr. (fmr.)	Export-Import Bank of US
Rodriguez	Rita Maria	C	Director	Export-Import Bank of US
Fessenden	Hart	C	General Council	Export-Import Bank of US
Brody	Kenneth D.	C	President & Chairman	Export-Import Bank of US
Macomber	John D.	C	President & Chairman	Export-Import Bank of US; Prin., JDM Inv. Gp.; Dir., Xerox
Rudman	Warren Bruce	C	Deputy Chairman	Fed, Boston; Sen. (fmr.), N. H.; Co-Fnd.r, Concord Coal.
Reynolds	A. William	C	Chairman	Fed, Cleveland; Pres. & CEO, GenCorp, Akron
Greenberg	Maurice R.	B,C,T	Deputy Chair. (fmr.)	Fed, New York; Ch. & CEO, Amer. Int. Gp., Inc.; Dir., CFR
Futter	Ellen Victoria	C	Chairman	Fed, New York; President, Barnard College, NYC
Greenspan	Alan	C,T	Chairman	Fed. Res. Syst.,Bd./Gov.;TC mbr.(fmr.);Dir.(fmr.),CFR
Patrikis	Ernest T.	C	Deputy Gen. Counsel	Fed. Reserve Bank of NY
McDonough	William J.	B,C	President	Fed. Reserve Bank of NY
Sobol	Dorothy Meadow	C		Fed. Reserve Bank of NY
Black	Eugene R.	C	Chairman (fmr.)	Fed. Reserve Sustem
Burns	Arthur F.	C	Chairman (fmr.)	Fed. Reserve Sustem
Martin	William McC.	C	Chairman (fmr.)	Fed. Reserve Sustem
McCabe	Thomas B.	C	Chairman (fmr.)	Fed. Reserve Sustem
Meyer	Eugene	C	Chairman (fmr.)	Fed. Reserve Sustem

Who's Who of the Elite

Last Name	First & Mid. Name	Org.	Job Title	Affiliation - Company, Organization
Miller	G. William	C	Chairman (fmr.)	Fed. Reserve Sustem
Anderson	Harold W.	C	President (fmr.)	Fed. Reserve Sustem, Kansas City
Greene	Margaret L.	C	Deputy Manager	Fed. Reserve System, Foreign Opperations
Johnson	Willene A.	B	Sr. Officer	Fed. Reserve, New York
Volcker	Paul Adolph	B,C,T	Chairman (fmr.)	Fed.Res.Sys.;Mbr.,Brkgs. Inst.,Dir.,Concord Coal, CFR
Solomon	Anthony M.	C		Federal Reserve Bank
Cross	Sam Y.	C	Manager	Federal Reserve Board, F.O.M. Account
Forrestal	Robert Patrick	C	President	Federal Reserve Syst., Federal Reserve Bank of Atlanta
Exter	John	C	Monetary Econ. (fmr.)	Federal Reserve System
Truman	Edwin M.	C	Staff Dir., Economist	Federal Reserve System
Blinder	Alan Stuart	C	Vice-Chairman	Federal Reserve System
Kamarck	Andrew M.	C		Int. Bank for Reconstruction and Development, Wash.
Preston	Lewis Thompson	C	President	Int. Bank of Reconstruction & Devel.; Treas. (fmr.), CFR
Dale	William Brown	C	Dep. Mng Dir. (fmr.)	International Monitary Fund, Geneva
Junz	Helen B.	C	Spec. Trade Repr., Dir.	International Monitary Fund, Geneva
Erb	Richard David	C	Deputy Managing Dir.	International Monitary Fund, Washington
Rivlin	Alice Mitchell	C,T	Vice Chairman	Rederal Reserve Board, Federal Reserve System
Einhorn	Jessica P.	C,T	Managing Director	The World Bank, for Finance & Resource Mobilization
Wolfensohn	James David	B,C	President	The World Bank; Council Member, Brookings Inst.
Vernon	Raymond	B,C	Visiting Prof. (fmr.)	The World Bank; Professor (fmr.), Harvard Univ.
McNamara	Robert Strange	B,C,T	President (fmr.)	The World Bank; Sec. of Def. (fmr.); Member Brookings Inst.
Broadman	Harry G.	C	Writer	The World Bank
Page	John M., Jr.	C	Chief Econ.	The World Bank
Wirth	David A.	C	Economic Assistant	The World Bank
Martin-Brown	Joan	C		The World Bank
Herz	Barbara	C	Division Chief	The World Bank, Population and Human Resources
Hamilton	Ann O.	C	Director	The World Bank, Population and Humanities
			Commercial Banks	
Lozano	Ignacio E., Jr.	C	Director	Bank of America, San Francisco
Coombe	George William, Jr.	C	Exec. Vice Pres. (fmr.)	Bank of America, San Francisco
Buchman	Mark Edward	C	President & CEO	Bank of Los Angeles, Liberty Bank, Honolulu
Bacot	John Carter	C	Chairman & CEO	Bank of New York Co., Inc.
Clausen	A. W.	T	Chair. & CEO (fmr.)	Bankamerica Corp., San Diego
Peterson	Rudolph A.	B,C	Chair., Exec. Comm.	Bankamerica Corp., San Diego
Binkley	Nicholas Burhs	C	Chairman & CEO	Bankamerica Corp., San Diego
Staheli	Donald L.	C	Director	Banker's Trust
Vojta	George J.	C	Vice Chairman	Bankers Trust Co., NYC
Sanford	Charles Stedman, Jr.	C	Chairman & CEO	Bankers Trust Co., NYC
Ireland	Robert Livingston, III	C	General Partner	Brown Brothers Harriman & Co.
Erckclentz	Alexander Tonio	C	Partner	Brown Brothers Harriman & Co.
Brown	Walter H.	C	Limited Partner	Brown Brothers Harriman & Co.
Hoch	Frank W.	C	Limited Partner	Brown Brothers Harriman & Co.
Goldstein	Jeffrey A.	C	Vice-Chairman	BT Wolfensohn & Co.
Aburdene	Odeh Felix	C	Managing Partner	Capital Trust
Lipsky	John P.	C	Chief Economist	Chase Manhattan Bank
Wilson	John Donald	C	Sr. Vice Pres. (fmr.)	Chase Manhattan Bank
Douglass	Robert Royal	C	Vice Chairman (fmr.)	Chase Manhattan Bank; Director, Rockefeller Ctr.
Rockefeller	David	B,C,T	Ch., Int. Advis. Com.	Chase Manhattan Bank; Hon. Chair., CFR; Chair., TC
Labrecque	Thomas G.	C,T	President & COO	Chase Manhattan Bank; Mbr., Brookings Inst.
Roett	Riordan	C	Director (fmr.)	Chase National Bk., Nat. Rel. of Emerging Markets
Whitman	Marina v. N.	C,T	Director	Chase,Proctor & Gambel;Dist.Vis.Prof.,U./Mich.;Dir. (fmr.),CFR
Shipley	Walter Vincent	C,T	Chairman & CEO	Chase; Chr. & CEO (fmr.), Chemical Banking Corp.
Price	John Roy, Jr.	C	Managing Dir. (fmr.)	Chemical Bank Corp., NYC, Govt. & Community Afrs.
McGillicuddy	John Francis	C	Chair. & CEO (fmr.)	Chemical Bank Corp., NYC; Dir., Texaco, Inc.
Callander	Robert John	C	President (fmr.)	Chemical Banking Corp.
McCouch	Donald G.	C	Sr. Mng. Dir. (fmr.)	Chemical Banking Corp.; Bd. Mbr., Council of the Amer.
Bains	Leslie Elizabeth	C	Managing Director	Citibank, N.A., NYC
Rhodes	William Reginald	C	Vice Chairman	Citibank, N.A., NYC
Freytag	Richard A.	C	President & CEO	Citicorp Banking Corp.
Wriston	Walter Bigelow	B	Chairman (fmr.)	Citicorp; Director (fmr.), CFR
Theobald	Thomas Charles	C	Chairman & CEO	Continental Bank Corp., Chicago; Dir., Xerox Corp.
Huber	Richard Leslie	C	Vice Chairman	Continental Bank Corp./Continental Bank, N.A.
Hennessy	John M.	C	President & CEO	Credit Suisse First Boston Corp
Mulford	David C.	C	Vice Chairman	Credit Suisse First Boston Corp
Huyck	Philip M.	C	Sr. Advisor	Credit Suisse First Boston Corp
Shoemaker	Alvin V.	C	Chairman (fmr.)	Credit Suisse First Boston Corp
Parsons	Richard Dean	C	Chairman & CEO	Dime Savings Bank of N. York, NYC; Pres., Time-Warner
Wilmers	Robert George	C	President & CEO	ENY Savings Bank, NYC
Gilbert	Jackson B.	C	2nd Chairman	Espirito Santo Bank of Florida, Miami
Raines	Franklin Delano	C,T	Chairman & CEO	Fed. Nat. Mortgage Assoc. (FNMA)
Shapiro	Eli	C	Chairman (fmr.)	Federal Home Loan Bank, Boston
Petty	John Robert	C	Chairman	Federal National Payables Inc., Washington
Toll	Maynard Joy, Jr.	C	Managing Director	First Boston Corp., NYC
Abboud	Alfred Robert	C	Chairman & CEO	First City BankCorp, Houston
Terracciano	Anthony Patrick	C	Chair., Pres. & CEO	First Fidelity Bancorp, New Jersey
Thayer	Artemas Branson	C	Chairman	First Florida Banks Inc., Tampa

Last Name	First & Mid. Name	Org.	Job Title	Affiliation - Company, Organization
Carson	Edward Mansfield	C	Chairman & CEO	First Interstate Bancorp, L. A.
Porzecanski	Arturo C.	C	Chief Economist	ING-Berings
Rice	Joseph Albert	C	Chair. & CEO (fmr.)	Irving Bank Corp.
Weatherstone	Dennis	C	Chairman & CEO	J. P. Morgan & Co.; Director, General Motors Corp.
Bashawaty	Albert C.	C	Sr. Officer	J.P. Morgan
Stern	Ernest	C		J.P. Morgan & Co., Inc.
Mathis	Brian Pierre	C		J.P. Morgan, N.Y.
Dalton	James Edward	C	President	Logicon RDA, Corp.
Pilliod	Charles J., Jr.	C	Director	Manufacturers Hanover Corp.
Johnson	Thomas Stephen	C	President (fmr.)	Manufacturers Hanover Corp.
Mason	Elvis L.	C	Managing Partner	Mason Best Co.
Cahouet	Frank Vondell	C	Chairman & CEO	Mellon Bank, N. A.
Baldwin	Henry Furlong	C	Chairman	Mercantile Bankshares Corp.
Moragoda	Milinda	C		Merchantile Merchant Bank
Vagliano	Alexander Marino	C	Chairman	Michelin Financial Corp.
de Vries	Rimmer	C	Sr. Vice President	Morgan Guaranty Trust Co., NYC
Smith	Peter Bennett	C	Chairman, Credit Com.	Morgan Guaranty Trust Co.; Congr. (fmr.), Vermont
Considine	Jill M.	C	President	N.Y. Clearinghouse Assn.
Deming	Frederick Lewis	B	Director	National City Bancorp
Beeman	Richard E.	C	Exec. Vice President	National City Bank, Cleveland
Knight	Robert Huntington	C	Director	National Leadership Bank
McColl	Hugh Leon, Jr.	T	Chair., Pres. & CEO	NationsBank Corp.
Offit	Morris Wolf	C	President	Offitbank, NYC; Council Member, Brookings Institute
Solomon	Peter J.	C	Founder	Peter J. Solomon Co.
Allbritton	Joe Lewis	C	Chairman	Riggs AP Bank Ltd., London
Istel	Yves-Andre	C	Vice Chairman	Rothschild, Inc., N.Y.
Zwick	Charles J.	C	Chairman (fmr.)	Southeast Banking Corp.; Trustee, Carnegie Endow.
Holbrooke	Richard C.	B,C,T	US Ambassador	U.N. Designate; V. Chr., Credit Suissse First Boston Corp.
Holcomb	M. Staser	C	Exec. Vice President	USAA , San Antonio
Jacobs	Nehama	C	Director	Wells Fargo Bank
Sonenshine	H. Marshall	C	Partner	Wolfensohn & Co.
			Investment Organizations	
Mai	Vincent A.	C	President & CEO	AEA Investors Inc.; Bd. Mbr., Carnegie Corp. of NY
Baird	Zoe E.	C	V.P. & Gen. Counsel	Aetna Life & Casualty, Hartford, CT.
Keough	Donald Raymond	T	Chairman	Allean & Co., Inc.; President (fmr.), Coca-Cola Co.
Savage	Frank	C	Chairman	Alliance Capital Management Int.
Yanney	Michael B.	C	Chair & CEO	America First Cos.
Linen	Jonathan S.	C	Vice Chairman	American Express
Abboud	Labeeb M.	C	Group Counsel	American Express Bank, LTD.
Clark	Howard Longstreth	C	Chair. & CEO (fmr.)	American Express Co.
Chenault	Kennethy Irving	C	President	American Express Co., Consumer Card & Fin. Svcs.
Youngman	William Sterling	C	Chairman (fmr.)	American Home Assurance Co.
Roberts	John Joseph	C	Chairman	American International Underwriters Corp.
Duval, Raoul	Michael	C	Limited Partner	Anthem Partners
Soros	Paul	C	Co-Owner	APEX Silvermines, LTD. Caman Islands
Lazarus	Steven M.	C	Managing Dir.	Arch Ventures Partner
Arnhold	Henry H.	C	Chairman	Arnhold & Bleichroeder
Parsky	Gerald Lawrence	C,T	Chairman	Aurora Capital Partners, L. A.
McDonald	Alonzo Lowry, Jr.	C	Chairman & CEO	Avenir Group, Inc.
Vermilye	Peter Hoagland	C	Sr. Advisor	Baring Asset Management
Hoguet	George R.	C		Baring Asset Management, Brookline, MA
Hurford	John Boyce	C	Vice Chairman	BEA Associates, NYC
Hallingby	Paul, Jr.	C	Sr. Managing Director	Bear Sterns & Co.
Bovin	Dennis Alan	C	Vice Chairman	Bear Sterns & Co.
Woods	Ward W., Jr.	C	President & CEO	Bessimer Securities
Brock	William E., III	C	Chairman	Blackstone Gp., NYC; Sec. (fmr.), Labor Dept., '85-'87
Stockman	David Allen	C,T	General Partner	Blackstone Gp., NYC; Dir. (fmr.), Office of Mgt. & Budget
Fenster	Steven R.	C	Limited Ptnr. (fmr.)	The Blackstone Group
Hutchins	Glenn H.	C	Member	The Blackstone Group
Brock	Bill	T	Chairman	Brock Group, Wash.
Bullock	Hugh	C	Investment Banker	Bullock Co., NYC
Culver	David	T	Chairman	CAI Capital Corp.
Nachmanoff	Arnold	C	Man. Director	Capital Advisors Limited
Kotecha	Mahesh K.	C	Sr. Vice President	Capital Markets Assurance Corp.
Lovelace	Jon B., Jr.	C	Chairman	Capital Research & Management Co., L. A.
Carter	Marshall Nichols	C	Sr. Vice President	Chase Manhattan Corp.
Chubb	Hendon	C	CEO	Chubb Insurance Co. of Canada
Taylor	Wilson H.	T	Chair., Pres. & CEO	CIGNA Corp.
Trebat	Thomas J.	C	Man. Director	Citicorp Securities Inc., Emerging Markets Research
Stein	Elliot, Jr.	C	Man. Director	Commonwealth Capital Partners, L.P.
Davis	Shelby Cullom	C	Managing Partner	Cullom Davis & Co.
Wells	Damon, Jr.	C	Owner & CEO	Damon Wells Interests, Houston
Flanigan	Peter Magnus	C	Director	Dillon, Read & Co., Inc.
Haskell	John Henry F., Jr.	C	Managing Director	Dillon, Read & Co., Inc.
Birkelund	John Peter	C	Chairman & CEO	Dillon, Read & Co., Inc.; Honorary Officer, CFR
Albright	Archie Earl	C	Chairman	Ecogen, Inc.

Last Name	First & Mid. Name	Org.	Job Title	Affiliation - Company, Organization
Small	Lawrence M.	C	Chief Oper. Officer	Federal National Mortgage Association
Perkins	George William, II	B	President & Chairman	Financial Marketing System, Inc.
Ganoe	Charles Stratford	C	Exec. Vice President	FMS Group Inc.
Greenberg	Evan G.	C	Dir. & Exec. V.P.	Foreign General Insurance
Russell	George F.	T	Chairman & CEO	Frank Russell Company
Oppenheimer	Michael Frank	C	Exec. Vice President	Futures Group, Inc.
Frank	Charles Raphael, Jr.	C	Exec. Vice President	GE Capital Corp.
Altschul	Arthur Goodhart	C	Chairman	General American Investors Co.
Gfoeller	Joachim, Jr.	C	Principal	Gfoeller Investments, N.Y.
Corzine	Jon S.	B	Chr. & Sr. Partner (fmr.)	Goldman Sachs & Co.
Hurst	Robert Jay	C	General Partner	Goldman Sachs & Co.
Friedman	Stephen James	B,C,T	Sr. Ch. & Ltd. Partner	Goldman Sachs & Co.
Weinberg	John Livingston	C	Sr. Chairman	Goldman Sachs & Co.; Director, Du Pont Co.
Fowler	Henry Hamill	C	General Partner	Goldman Sachs & Co.; Director, Foreign Policy Assoc.
Thornton	John L.	B	Pres. & co-COO	Goldman Sachs Group, Inc.
Corrigan	E. Gerald	B,C,T	Partner & Mng. Dir.	Goldman Sachs; Pres. (fmr.), Fed. Res. Bk., NY;Dir.,CFR
Hormats	Robert D.	C,T	Vice Chairman	GoldmanSachs;Ast.Sec./St.(fmr.);Carnegie End.;Dir.,CFR
McCann	Edward	C	Prin., Invest. Banking	Hamilton & Quist, Inc., NYC
Eberle	William Denman	C	Chairman	Holders Capital Corp.
Tomlinson	Alexander Cooper	C	President	Hungarian-American Enterprise Fund, Washington
Stewart	Gordon Curran	C	President	Insurance Information Institute, NYC
Sinkin	Richard N.	C		InterAmerican Holding C.
Araskog	Rand Vincent	C,T	Chair., Pres. & CEO	ITT Corp.
Goldman	Charles Norton	C	Vice President	ITT Corp., NYC
Cappello	Juan C.	C	Sr. V. President	ITT Corp.; Bd. Mbr., Council of the Americas
Lynch	Edward Stephen	C	Treasurer	ITT Europe, Inc., Brussels
Epstein	Jeffrey E.	T	President	J. Epstein & Co.; Wexner Investment Co.
Lehman	John F., Jr.	C	Chairman	J. F. Lehman & Co., NYC
Miller	Robert Stevens, Jr.	C	Sr. Partner	James D. Wolfensohn, Inc.
Elliott	Byron Kauffman	C	Chairman (fmr.)	John Hancock Mutual Insurance Co.
Kaufman	Henry	C	President	Henry Kaufman & Co.
Kubarych	Roger M.	C	Gen. Manager	Henry Kaufman & Co.
Johnson	Howard Wesley	C	Chairman	Kenan Systems Corp.; Director, Du Pont Co.
Gordon	Albert Hamilton	C	Chairman	Kidder, Peabody & Co.
Knowlton	Winthrop	C	Chairman	Knowlton Brother, Inc. (Investing)
Kravis	Henry R.	B,C	Founding Partner	Kohlberg Kravis Roberts; Member, Brookings Institute
Sudarkasa	Michael E. M.	C	Director	Labat-Anderson, Inc., Int. Trade Inv. Promotion Service
Newman	Richard T.	C		Lake Forest Capital Management
Baeza	Mario Leon	C	Chairman & CEO	Latin American Equity Partners
Rohatyn	Felix George	C,T	Senior Partner	Lazard Freres & Co.
Lynn	James Thomas	C	Sr. Advisor	Lazard Freres & Co.
Rattner	Steve Lawrence	B,C	Head Committee Gp.	Lazard Freres & Co., LLC
Blumenthal	Werner Michael	C,T	Limited Partner	Lazard Freres & Co.; Director (fmr.), CFR
Schlesinger	James Rodney	C	Sr. Advisor	Lehman Bros.; Sec. (fmr.), Engy. Dept.;Dir. (fmr.), CIA
Seitz	Raymond G. H.	T	Vice-Chair.	Lehman Brothers, Europe; Amb. (fmr.) to UK
Roosevelt	Theodore, IV	C	Managing Dir. (fmr.)	Lehman Brothers, Inc., NYC
Caldwell	Philip	C,T	Sr. Managing Director	Lehman Brothers, Inc.; Director, Digital Equip. Corp.
Green	Ernest G.	C	Managing Director	Lehman Brothers; Chair., African Development Foundation
Ball	George Wildman	B,C	Sr. Mng. Director	Lehman Brothers; fmr. Undersec., State
Kimmitt	Robert Michael	B,C	Managing Director	Lehman Brothers; US Amb. (fmr.), St. Dept., Germany
Olsen	Leif H.	C	President	Leif H. Olso Investments, Inc.
Lipper	Kenneth	C	Chairman	Lipper Analytical Service; Trustee, Rockefeller Bros. Fund
Loeb	John Langeloth	C	Vice Chairman	Loeb Partners Corp., NYC
Lovejoy	Thomas Eugene	C	Chairman	Manhattan Life Insurance Co., NYC
Tasco	Frank J.	C	Chair. Exec. Comm.	Marsh & McLennan Cos.
Schreyer	William Allen	C	Chairman	Merrill Lynch & Co.
Smith	Winthrop Hiram, Jr.	C	Exec. V. Pres. & Chair.	Merrill Lynch International
Heimann	John Gaines	C	Chairman	Merrill Lynch, Glob.Fin. Inst. Gp.;Mbr. Brookings Inst.
Luce	Charles Franklin	C	Specia Counsel	Metropolitan Life Insurance Co.
Samuels	Barbara C., II	C	Member	Moody's Investors Service, Inc.
Bohn	John Augustus, Jr.	C	President	Moody's Investors Service, Inc.
Fisher	Richard B.	T	Chairman	Morgan Stanley Dean Witter
Galbraith	Evan Griffith	C	Int. Dir., Sr. Advisor	Morgan Stanley Group, Inc.
Gilbert	S. Parker	C	Chairman	Morgan Stanley
Evans	John C.	C	Advisory Dir.	Morgan Stanley & Co.
Whittemore	Frederick B.	C	Partner	Morgan, Stanley & Co.
Wadsworth-Darby	Mary	C	Member	Morgan, Stanley & Co., N.Y.
Palmieri	Victor Henry	C	CEO	Mutual Life Insurance Co.
Sullivan	Barry F.	T	President & CEO	New York City Partnership
Phelan	John J., Jr.	C	Chair. & CEO (fmr.)	New York Sock Exchange, NYC
Donaldson	William Henry	C	Chairman & CEO	New York Stock Exchange; Trustee, Carnegie Endow.
Shelp	Ronald Kent	C	President & CEO	NYC Partnership
Balick	Kenneth D.	C	Director	Nomoura Securities, Int. Business Development
Sekulow	Eugene A.	C		NYNEX Corp.
Gantcher	Nathan	C	President & Co-CEO	Oppenheimer
Mills	Bradford	C	Chairman & CEO	Overseas Private Investors, Ltd.
Marron	Donald Baird	C	CEO	PaineWebber Inc., NYC

Last Name	First & Mid. Name	Org.	Job Title	Affiliation - Company, Organization
McAfee	W. Gage	C		PC Asset Management, Hong Kong
Lilienthal	Sally	C	Founder & Pres.	Ploughshares Fund
Shulman	Colette	C	Advisor	Ploughshares Fund
Tang	David K. Y.	C	Man. Partner	Preston, Gayes & Ellis; Investment Banker, Hong Kong
Dawkins	Peter Miller	C	Chairman & CEO	Primerica Financial Services
Zinder	Norton Donald	C	Invest. Consultant	Private
Freund	Gerald	C	President	Private Funding Association
Winters	Robert Cushing	T	Chair. & CEO (fmr.)	Prudential Insurance Co. of America
Stevens	James William	C	Exec. Vice President	Prudential Insurance Co., Newark
McQuade	Lawrence Carroll	C	Vice Chairman	Prudential Mutual Fund Mgt., NYC
Teeters	Nancy Hays	C	Director & Trustee	Prudential Mutual Fund Mgt., NYC
Greenberg	Sanford David	C	Chairman	Realty Capital Inc.
Barry	Thomas Corcoran	C	President & CEO	Rockefeller & Co., Inc.; Partner, CZ Ltd.
Rockefeller	David, Jr.	C	Chairman	Rockefeller Fin. Services, Inc.; Mbr., Brookings Inst.
Victor	Alice	B	Executive Assistant	Rockefeller Fin. Services; Rapporteur, Bilderberger Gp.
Ackerman	Peter	C	Managing Dir.	Rockport Finabcial Ltd., Dir., Cato Institute
Rockefeller	Nicholas	C		Rockvest Int. Development Group
Salomon	William R.	C	Hon. Chairman	Salomon Brothers Inc.
Gutfreund	John H.	C,T	Chair. & CEO (fmr.)	Salomon Bros. Inc.; Council Member, Brookings Inst.
Owen	Henry David	C,T	Sr. Advisor	Salomon Bros.; Brookings Inst.; Bd. Mbr., Ctr./Int. Pol.
Barber	Charles Finch	C	Director (fmr.)	Salomon Brothers Inc.
Enders	Thomas O.	C	Managing Dir.	Salomon Brothers Inc.
Maughan	Deryck C.	T	Co-Chair. & Co-CEO	Salomon Smith Barney Inc.
Hill	James Tomilson	C	Co-Head	Shearson Lehman Brothers, Investment Banking Div.
Zarb	Frank Gustave	C	Pres., Chair. & CEO	Smith, Barney, Harris, Upham & Co.; Dir., CFR
Soros	George	B,C,T	President	Soros Fund Mgt.; Fdr.& Chair., Open Society Institute
Burns	Patrick Owen	C	Sr. Consultant	Stage Interprises, ENJ
Martinuzzi	Leo Sergio, Jr.	C	Chairman	Strategic Dimensions, Inc.
Tanner	Harold	C	President	Tanner & Co., Inc., NYC
Malek	Frederic Vincent	C	Chairman	Thayer Capital Partners; Pres. Bush's Campaign Mgr., '92
Seidman	Herta Lande	C	Co-Founder	Tradenet Corp., NYC
Tierney	Paul E., Jr.	C	Chairman	TW Holdings, Inc., S. C.
Leone	Richard C.	C	President	Twentieth Century Fund
Wasserstein	Bruce	C	President	Wasserstein, Perella & Co., NYC; Ch. (fmr.) Maybelline
Wiener	Malcolm Hewitt	C	Chairman	Willburn Corp., NYC; Member, Brookings Institute
Stamas	Stephen	C	Private Invest. Exec.	Windcrest Partners, NYC; Director (fmr.), CFR
Pardee	Scott E.	C		Yamaichi Int. (America Inc.)
Foundations				
Robinson	Leonard Harrison, Jr.	C	President	African Devel. Found.; COO, Wash. Strat. Consulting Gp.
Dawson	Marion M.	C	Member-Designate	African Development Foundation
Waters	Cherri D.	C	Director	African Development Foundation, Office of Learning
Winston	Michael Russell	C	President	Alfred Harcourt Foundation
Gomory	Ralph Edward	C	President	Alfred P. Sloan Foundation
Greenwood	Ted	C	Program Officer	Alfred P. Sloan Foundation
van Fleet	James Alward	C	Chairman (fmr.)	American-Korean Foundation
Emerson	Alice Frey	C	Sr. Fellow	Andrew W. Mellon Found.; Dir., Eastman Kodak Co.
Bell-Rose	Stephanie	C	Found. Counsel	Andrew W. Mellon Foundation
Bowen	William Gordon	C	President	Andrew W. Mellon Foundation
Sawyer	John Edward	C	President (fmr.)	Andrew W. Mellon Foundation
Fuller	William P.	C	President	Asia Foundation
Slawson	Paul S.	C	Trustee	Asia Foundation
Williams	Haydn	C	President (fmr.)	Asia Foundation
Howell	Ernest M.	C	Trustee	Asia Foundation; Vice President, Smith Barney
Celeste	Richard F.	C	Board Member	Carnegie Corp. of New York
Finberg	Barbara Denning	C	Exec. Vice President	Carnegie Corp. of New York
Heinz	Teresa	C	Trustee	Carnegie Corp. of New York
Richardson	Yolonda	C	Program Officer	Carnegie Corp. of New York
Robinson	David Z.	C	Sr. Counselor to Pres.	Carnegie Corp. of New York
Rosenfield	Patricia L.	C	Program Chairman	Carnegie Corp. of New York
Stremlau	John J.	C	Executive Director	Carnegie Corp. of New York
Minow	Newton N.	C	Chairman	Carnegie Corp. of New York; Dir., Sara Lee Corp.
Kaplan	Helene L.	C	Board Member	Carnegie Corp. of NY, Mobil Oil Corp.; Dir., CFR
Hamburg	David A.	C	President	Carnegie Corp. of NY; Adv. Bd., Ctr. for Nat. Policy
Beattie	Richard Irwin	C	Board Member	Carnegie Corp. of NY; Bd. Mbr., Ctr. for Int. Policy
Haskins	Caryl Parker	C	Honorary Trustee	Carnegie Corp. of NY; Trustee, Asia Foundation
Boyer	Ernest Leroy	C	President	Carnegie Foundation
Pifer	Alan Jay Parrish	C	Vice President	Carnegie Foundation for Advancement in Teaching
Saunders	Harold H.	C	Member	Charles F. Kettering Foundation
Yankelovich	Daniel	C	Director	Charles F. Kettering Foundation
Edelman	Marian Wright	C	President	Children's Defense Fund, Mbr. of Bd., Ctr. for Int. Policy
Mahoney	Margaret Ellerbe	C	President	Commonwealth Foundation, NYC
Tepper-Marlin	Alice	C	Founder	Council on Economic Priorities (Foundation)
Aguirre	Horacio	C	Advisor/Bd.	Cuban American Nat. Foundation
Joseph	James Alfred	C	President	Cummins Foundation
Straus	Oscar S., II	C	President	Daniel & Florence Guggenheim Foundation
Robinson	Marshall Alan	C	Vice President	Daniele Agostino Foundation

Last Name	First & Mid. Name	Org.	Job Title	Affiliation - Company, Organization
Bell	Peter D.	C	Member	Edna McConnell Clark Foundation, Inc.
Stewart	Patricia Carry	C	Vice President	Edna McConnell Clark Foundation, Inc.
Friend	Theodore Wood, III	C	President	Eisenhower Exchange Fellowship Inc.
Bader	William Banks	C	President	Eurasia Foundation, Washington
Bell	David Elliott	B,C	Exec. Vice President	Ford Foundation
Berresford	Susan Vail	C	President	Ford Foundation
Ispahani	Mahnaz Z.	C	Director	Ford Foundation
Thomas	Franklin Augustine	C	President	Ford Foundation
Kazemi	Farhad	C	Member (fmr.)	Ford Foundation, Rockefeller Foundation
Heard	George Alexander	C	Trustee	Ford Foundation; Chancellor (fmr.), Vanderbilt U.
Hedstrom	Mitchell Warren	C	Trustee	Ford Foundation; Vice President, Citibank, N. A.
Dubow	Arthur Myron	C	President	Fourth Estate, Inc.
Loy	Frank Ernest	C	President	Ger. Marshall Fund of US; Adv. Bd. Mbr., Ctr. for Nat. Pol.
Debs	Barbara Knowles	C	Trustee	Geraldine R. Dodge Foundation
Leland	Marc Ernest	C	Sr. Advisor	Gordon P. Getty Trust, Washington
Dedrick	Fred T.	C	Director	Greater Philadelphia First Foundation, Econ. Development
Ruebhausen	Oscar Melick	C	Board Member	Greenwall Foundation
Atherton	Alfred Leroy, Jr.	C	Board Member	Hariri Foundation
Percy	Charles Harting	C	Chairman & President	Hariri Foundation
Hester	James Mcnaughton	C	President	Harry Frank Guggenheim Foundation
Hauser	Rita Eleanore A.	C	Member	Hauser Foundation; Director, CFR
Ellis	James Reed	C	Trustee	Henry M. Jackson Foundation
Fisher	Richard W.	C	Member	Heritage Foundation
Heinz	Teresa	C	Chairwoman	Howard Heinz Foundation
Beinecke	William S.	C	Chairman	Hudson River Foundation
Sloane	Ann Brownell	C	Private Board Member	Inter-American Foundation
Stevens	Norton	C	Private Board Member	Inter-American Foundation
Williams	Harold Marvin	C	President & CEO	J. Paul Getty Trust
Heyns	Roger William	C	Board Member	James Irving Foundation
Adams	Ruth Salzman	C	Dir. & Senior Advisor	John D. & Catherine T. MacArthur Foundation
Benedict	Kenneth M.	C	Program Director	John D. & Catherine T. MacArthur Foundation
McCormack	Elizabeth J.	C	Trustee	John D. & Catherine T. MacArthur Foundation
Rabinowitch	Victor	C	Sr. Vice President	John D. & Catherine T. MacArthur Foundation
Simmons	Adele Smith	C	President	John D. & Catherine T. MacArthur Foundation
Pond	Elizabeth	C	Fellow	John D., & Katherine T. Mac Arthur Foundation
Smith	Malcolm Bernard	C	Chairman	John Simon Guggenheim Memorial Found., Fin. Comm.
Holmes	Kim R.	C	Vice President & Dir.	Kathran & Shelton Cullom Davis Int. Studies Ctr.
Cook	Howard A.	C	President (fmr.)	Mac Jannet Foundation
Morrisett	Lloyd N.	C	President	Markle Foundation
Gershman	Carl Samuel	C	President	National Endowment for Democracy
Duderstadt	James J.	C	Chairman	National Science Foundation, National Science Board
Bullock	Mary Brown	C	Head, Spec. Proj. Sect.	National Science Foundation, Public Affairs
Weil	Frank A.	C	President	Norman Foundation
Ingersoll	Robert Stephen	C,T	Chairman	Panasonic Foundation
LeMelle	Wilbert J.	C	President	Phelps-Stokes Fund; Trustee, Carnegie Endowment
Schubert	Richard Francis	C	President & CEO	Points of Light Foundation
Fanton	Jonathan Foster	C	Trustee	Rockefeller Bro. Fund.; Pres., New School for Social Resch.
Moody	William S.	C	Prog. Officer	Rockerfeller Brothers Fund
Starr	Stephen Frederick	C,T	Director	Rockefeller Bros. Found.; Adj. Fellow, Hudson Inst.
Train	Russell Errol	C,T	Trustee	Rockefeller Bros. Found.; Chair., World Wildlife Fund, Wash.
Luers	William Henry	C	Trustee	Rockefeller Bros. Fund.; Pres., Metro. Museum of Art, NYC
Segal	Sheldon Jerome	C	Director	Rockefeller Brothers Found., Population Science
Campbell	Colin Goetze	C	President	Rockefeller Brothers Foundation
Phillips	Russell A., Jr.	C	Exec. Vice President	Rockefeller Brothers Foundation
Chasin	Dana	C	Trustee	Rockefeller Family Fund
Arthurs	Alberta Bean	C	Director	Rockefeller Foundation
Davidson	Ralph Kirby	C	Assoc. Director (fmr.)	Rockefeller Foundation
Goldmark	Peter Carl, Jr.	C	President	Rockefeller Foundation
Prewitt	Kenneth	C	Sr. Vice President	Rockefeller Foundation
Sutton	Francis Xavier	C	Consultant	Rockefeller Foundation, USAID, World Bank
Price	Hugh B.	C	Vice President	Rockefeller Foundation; Member, N.Y. Times
Ilchman	Alice Stone	C	Chairman	Rockefeller Foundation; Pres., Sarah Lawrence College
Biemann	Betsy	C		Rockerfeller Foundation
Cohen	Joel Ephraim	C	Trustee	Russell Sage Foundation
Davis	Kathryn Wasserman	C	President	Shelby Cullom Davis Foundation
Cooper	Kerry	C	Member	Stanford A. Winter & Brian L. Weiner Endowment Found.
Truitt	Nancy Sherwood	C	Sr. Advisor	The Foundation Ctr.
Muse	Martha Twitchell	C	Chairman	Tinker Foundation, NYC; Bd. Mbr., Council of the Amer.
Williams	Earl Carter	C	Director	Wolf Trap Foundation
Heckscher	August	C	President (fmr.)	Woodrow Wilson Foundation
Fuller	Kathryn Scott	C	President & CEO	World Wildlife Fund, Washington
Neal	Stephen L.	C	President	Z. Smith Reynolds Foundation

Last Name	First & Mid. Name	Org.	Job Title	Affiliation - Company, Organization
Industry				
			Aerospace	
Bossidy	Lawrence A.	T	Chairman & CEO	Alliedsignal
Clarkson	Lawrence William	C	Corp. Vice President	Boeing Co., Seattle, Planning & Int. Development
Wilson	T. A.	T	Chairman (fmr.)	Boeing Company
Pigott	Charles M.	C	Director	Boeing Company, Chevron Corp.
Deagle	Edwin Augustus, Jr.	C	Director	Hughes Aircraft Co., Int. Business Planning
Currie	Malcolm Roderick	C	Chairman & CEO	Hughes Aircraft Co., missile systems group
Puckett	Allen E.	C		Hughs Aircraft Corp.
Blackwell	James Augusta, Jr.	C	Vice Pres. & Gen. Mgr.	Lockheed Aerospace Systems Co., Burbank
Jones	Thomas V.	C,T	Chairman (fmr.)	Northrop Corp.
O'Donnell	Kevin	C	Chr. Ex. Com. (fmr.)	SIFCO Industries
Seigle	John William	C	Vice President	United Technologies Corp., Sikorsky Aircraft Div.
Carlson	Robert John	C	President & Director	United Technologies, Hartford
			Apparel	
Haas	Robert D.	C,T	Chairman & CEO	Levi Strauss & Co.; Council Mbr., Brookings Inst.
Haas	Walter A.	T	Hon. Chairman	Levi Strauss & Co.
Haas	Peter E.	C	Director	Levi Strauss & Co.
Krueger	Harvey	C	Director	Bernard Chaus, Inc. (mfg. Of women's clothes)
Wachner	Linda Joy	C	Chairwoman & CEO	WARNACO, Inc.
			Beverages	
Goizueta	Roberto C.	C,T	Chairman & CEO	Coca-Cola; Dir., Eastman Kodak Co., Ford Motor Co.
Llewellyn	J. Bruce	C	Chairman	Coca-Cola Bot. Co., Phil.; Cousin of Colin Powell
Clendenin	John L.	C	Director	Coca-Cola Co.
Duncan	Charles William, Jr.	C	Director	Coca-Cola Co., Council Member, Brookings Institute
Bronfman	Edgar M., Jr.	C	President & CEO	Joseph E. Seagram's & Sons (liquor); Dir., Du Pont Co.
Enrico	Roger A.	T	Chair. & CEO	PepsiCo, Inc.
Calloway	D. Wayne	T	Chair. & CEO (fmr.)	PepsiCo, Inc.
Kendall	Donald M.	C,T	Chairman (fmr.)	PepsiCo Inc.
Akers	John F.	C	Director	PepsiCo, Inc.
			Building Materials	
Houghton	James R.	C,T	Chairman & CEO (fmr.)	Corning Inc.
Cholmondeley	Paula H. J.	C	V.P.	Owens Corning
			Chemicals	
Johnson	Samuel Curtis	T	Chairman & CEO	Johnson, S. C. & Son, Inc
Cabot	Thomas Dudley	C	Honorary Chairman	Cabot Corp.
Liffers	William Albert	C,T	Vice Chairman	Cyanamid International
Popoff	Frank P.	C	Chairman & CEO	Dow Chemical Co.
Johnson	Nancie S.	C	Vice President	E.I. du Pont de Nemours & Co.
Brimmer	Andrew F.	C,T	Director	E.I. du Pont de Nemours & Co.
Bronfman	Edgar M.	C	Director	E.I. du Pont de Nemours & Co.
Carey	Hugh L.	C	Exec. Vice President	Grace, W. R. & Co.; Governor (fmr.), NY St.
Huntsman	Jon Meade, Jr.	C	President	Huntsman Chem.Co.;Mbr.(fmr.),St.Dept.,US Pacif. Isl.Jt.Com.Cor
Shapiro	Robert B.	B	Chairman & CEO	Monsanto Company
Stookey	John Hoyt	C	Chairman & CEO	Quantum Chemical Corp.
Jamieson	John Kenneth	C	Director	Raychem Corp.
Duncan	John C.	C	Vice President (fmr.)	St. Joe Minerals Corp
			Computers, Office Equipment	
MacGregor	Ian K.	C	Chair. & CEO (fmr.)	AMAX, Inc.
Gerstner	Louis V., Jr.	B,C,T	Chairman & CEO	IBM Corp.
Trowbridge	Louis V., Jr.	B,T	Chair. & CEO (fmr.)	IBM Corp.;Chair./CEO (fmr.),RJR Nabisco Holding Corp.
Pfeiffer	Ralph A., Jr.	C	Chairman (fmr.)	IBM, World Trade Corp.
Hancock	Ellen M.	C	Sr. V. Pres./Gen. Mgr.	IBM Corp.
Opel	John R.	C	Director	IBM Corp.
Wertheim	Mitzi Mallina	C	Member	IBM Corp., Federal Sector Div.
Jackson	Lois M.	C	Member	IBM Corp., Latin America
Armstrong	John Alexander	C	Vice President	IBM Corp.; Professor (fmr.), Univ. of Wisconsin
Hope	Judith Richards	C	Director	IBM Corp.; Sr. Ptnr., Paul Hastings, Janofsky & Walker
Garwin	Richard Lawrence	C		IBM; Consultant, Los Alamos Scientific Laboratory
Cummiskey	Frank J.	C		IBM
Packard	David	T	Chairman	Hewlett-Packard Company
			Construction	
Bechtel	Riley P.	T	Chairman & CEO	Bechtel Group, Inc.
			Electric & Gas Utilities	
McGrath	Eugene R.	C	President & CEO	Consolidated Edison Co., of New York, NYC
Willrich	Mason	C	CEO (fmr.)	Pacific Gas & Electric, San Francisco
Bryson	John E.	C	Chairman & CEO	Southern California Edison Co.; Dir., CFR

Last Name	First & Mid. Name	Org.	Job Title	Affiliation - Company, Organization
			Electronic, Electrical Equipment	
Welch	John F.	C	Chairman & CEO	General Electric Company; Owner, Kidder-Peabody
Ellsworth	Paolo	T	Vice Chairman & CEO	General Electric Company, USA
Heineman	Benjamin W., Jr.	C	Sr. Vice President	General Electric Company; Bd. Member, Ctr. for Nat. Pol.
Dammerman	Dennis D.	T	V. Chr. & Exec. Officer	General Electric Xompany
Armstrong	C. Michael	C	Chairman & CEO	GM Hughes Electronics Corp.
Binger	James H.	C	President (fmr.)	Honeywell
Schulhof	Michael Peter	C	Vice Ch., Pres. & CEO	Sony USA, Inc.
Rice	Donald Blessing	C,T	President & COO	Teledyne, Inc.; Sec. (fmr.), Defense Dept., Air Force
Shepherd	Mark	T	General Director	Texas Instruments, Inc.
Pino	John Anthony	C	CEO	ACT Management
			Food	
McCarthy	John G.	C	President	American Crop Protection Assoc.
Andreas	Dwayne Orville	B,C,T	Chairman & CEO	Archer Daniels Midland Co. (ADM)
MacMillan	Whitney	T	Chair. & CEO (fmr.)	Cargill, Inc.
Pearce	William R.	C,T	Vice President	Cargill; Pres. & CEO, I.D.S. Mutual Fund Group
Johnson	Robbin S.	C	Corp. V.P.	Cargill Inc., Minn.
Fletcher	Phillip Douglas	C	President	Con Agra
Fribourg	Michel	C	Chairman (fmr.)	Continental Grain Co.
Ferguson	James L.	C	Chair. & CEO (fmr.)	General Foods Corp.
McCain	H. Harrison	T	Chairman	McCain Foods Limited, Toronto
Urban	Thomas Nelson	C	President	Pioneer Hi-Bred Int., Inc.
Hart	Augusta Snow, Jr.	C	Vice Chairman (fmr.)	Quaker Oats Co.
Hafner	Joseph A., Jr.	C	President & CEO	Riviana Foods Inc.
Sticht	J. Paul	C	Chair. & CEO (fmr.)	RJR Nabisco, Inc., Winston-Salem
Bryan	John H.	B,T	Chairman & CEO	Sara Lee Corp.
Gilbert	Jarobin, Jr.	C	Director	Whitman Corp.
Wilbur	Brayton, Jr.	B,C	President	Wilbur-Ellis Co., San Franciscop; Dir., Safeway Stores
Swanson	David Heath	C	President & CEO	World Grain Div., Continental Grain Co.
			Forest & Paper Products	
Miller	Charles Daly	C	Chairman & CEO	Avery Dennison Corp.
Fox	Joseph Carter	C	President & CEO	Chesapeake Corp.
Georges	John A.	T	Chairman & CEO (fmr.)	International Paper Co.
Luke	John Anderson, Jr.	C	President & CEO	Westvaco Corp., NYC
Weyerhaeuser	George H.	T	Chairman & CEO	Weyerhaeuser Company
			General Merchandisers	
Hawley	Philip M.	T	Consultant	Broadway Stores, Inc.
Goldsmith	Jack Landman, III	C	Chair. & CEO (fmr.)	Federated Department Stores, Inc.
			Healthcare	
Wehrle	Leroy Snyder	C	President	Healthcare Cost Analysid, Inc.
			Hotels & Motels	
Sheeline	Paul Cushing	C	CFO (fmr.)	Intercontinental Hotels Corp.
			Industrial & Farm Equipment	
Morgan	Lee L.	T	Chairman (fmr.)	Caterpillar Inc.
Frey	Donald Nelson	C	Director	Clark Equipment Co.
Condon	Joseph F.	C	Sr. Vice President	Combustion Engineering Int. Sales, Inc.
Miller	Joseph Irwin	C	Chair., Exec. Comm.	Cummins Engine Co., Inc.
Becherer	Hans Walter	C	Chairman & CEO	Deere & Co.
Hanson	Robert A.	T	Chairman (fmr.)	Deere & Co.
Alvarado	Donna M.	C	Director	Harnischfeger Ind, Inc.
Schacht	Henry Brewer	C,T	Chair. & CEO (fmr.)	Lucent Technologies Inc.; Chair., Carnegie Corp. of NY
Weller	Ralph Albert	C	Chairman (fmr.)	Otis Elevator Co.
			Internet	
Glusker	Peter H.	B	Vice President	Prodigy
Olvey	Lee D.	C	Vice President	OCLC
			Metals	
O'Neill	Paul H.	T	Chairman & CEO	ALCOA
Levin	Michael S.	C	Chairman	e-Steel LLC (USA)
Paul	Ronald Arthur	C	General Counsel	Howmet Corp.
Armstrong	Roland Arthur	C	V. Pres./Gen. Counsel	Howmet Corp.
Ellsworth	Robert Fred	C	Chairman	Howmet Corp.; Dep. Secretary, Defense Dept, Ford Admin.
Hand	Scott M.	C	President	INCO Limited
Munroe	George Barber	C	Chairman & CEO	Phelps Dodge Corp.

Last Name	First & Mid. Name	Org.	Job Title	Affiliation - Company, Organization
			Motor Vehicles & Parts	
Russell	Thomas W., Jr.	C	Chair. & CEO (fmr.)	American Brake Shoe Co. (ABEX)
Magowan	Peter A.	C	Director	Chrysler Corp.
Califano	Joseph Anthony, Jr.	C	Director	Chrysler;Sec.(fmr.),HEW Dept.;Adv. Bd.,Ctr./Nat.Pol.
Margolis	David Israel	C	Chairman & CEO	Coltec Industries, Inc.
Powers	William Francis, Jr.	C	Exec. Dir. of Research	Ford Motor Co.
Trotman	Alexander J.	B	Chairman	Ford Motor Company
Ford	Henry, II	B	President	Ford Motor Company
Golightly	Niel L.	C	Spokesman	Ford Motor Company
Miller	Arjay	T	President (fmr.)	Ford Motor Company
Gorman	Joseph T.	C,T	Chairman, Pres. & CEO	TRW Inc.; Director, Proctor & Gambel Co.
Mettler	Ruben F.	C,T	Chairman (fmr.)	TRW, Inc.; Dir., Council on Foreign Relations, '86-'92
			Petroleum Refining & Service	
Sunderland	Jack B.	C	President	America Ind. Oil Co.
Goodman	Herbert Irwin	C	Chairman	Applied Trading Systems, Houston
Bowlin	Mike R.	C	President & COO	Atlantic Richfield Co.
Edwards	Howard Lee	C	Corp. Secretary	Atlantic Richfield Co.
Anderson	Robert Orville	B,C	Chairman (fmr.)	Atlantic Richfield Co. (ARCO)
Bonney	J. Dennis	C	Vice Chairman	Chevron Corp.
Keller	Geoirge M.	T	Chairman (fmr.)	Chevron Corp.
Smart	Stephen Bruce, Jr.	C	Director	Chevron Corp.; Sr. Fellow, World Resources Inst.
Renfrew	Charles B.	C	Director	Chevron; Adv. Bd. Mbr., Ctr./Int. Pol.; Ctr./Nat. Pol.
Rice	Condoleezza	C	Director	Chevron; Prov.,Stanford U.;Bd. Mbr.,Carnegie Corp.
Chen	Kimball C.	C	Co-Chairman	Energy Transportation Group, Inc.
Raymond	Lee R.	C,T	Chairman & CEO	EXXON Corp.
Clarke	J. G.	C	Director	EXXON Corp.
Rawl	Lawrence G.	C	Chair. & CEO (fmr.)	EXXON Corp., NYC
Cattarulla	Elliot R.	C	Vice President	EXXON Corp., Public Affairs
Bromery	Randolph Wilson	C	Director	EXXON Corp.; (fmr.) Chase Manh. Bk.; Prof., Univ./Mass.
Gerson	Emelio Gabriel	B	Exec. Vice President	EXXON Corp.; Dir. & Cons., Grace Geothermal Corp.
Wilhelm	Robert E.	C	Sr. Vice Pres. & Dir.	EXXON Corp.;V.,Chair.,Coun.of the Americas;Fgn. Pol. Assoc.
Cheney	Richard (Dick) B.	C,T	Chair., Pres. & CEO	Halliburton Co.;Wyoming,Cong.(fmr.);Dir.CFR;Sec.(fmr.),Def.D
Huffington	Roy Michael	C	Founder & CEO (fmr.)	Huffco Oil
McGhee	George Crews	B,C	Oil Producer	McGhee Production Co.
Noto	Lucio A.	T	Chair. & CEO	Mobil Corp.
Murray	Allen E.	C,T	Chr., Pres./CEO (fmr.)	Mobil Corp.; Council Member, Brookings Institute
Peters	Aulana L.	C	Director	Mobil Oil Corp.; Partner, Gibson, Dunn & Crutcher
Mosbacher	Robert A.	C	Chairman	Mosbacher Energy Co.; Campaign Mrg., George Bush.'92
Morrell	Gene Paul	C	Vice Chairman	Petro United Terminals, Inc., Houston
Lichtblau	John H.	C	Chairman	Petroleum Independent Research Associates, Inc., NYC
Roff	John Hugh, Jr.	C	Chairman	PetroUnited Terminals, Inc., Houston
Tobias	Randall L.	C	Director	Phillips Petroleum Co.
Silas	Cecil Jesse	C,T	Chairman & CEO (fmr.)	Phillips Petroleum Company
Baird	Euan	T	Chairman	Schlumberger, Ltd.
Richardson	Frank H.	C	President & CEO	Shell Oil Co.
Bookout	John Frank, Jr.	C	Dir./Mbr. Exec. Com.	Shell Petroleum, Inc.
Mead	Dana George	C	Chief Oper. Officer	Tenneco, Inc., Houston
Pham	Kien D.	C		Tennaco Inc.
Granville	Maurice Fryer	C	Chairman (fmr.)	Texaco Inc.
DeCrane	Alfred C., Jr.	C	Chair. & CEO (fmr.)	Texaco Inc.
Malin	Clement B.	C	V. President	Texaco Inc., Int. Rel.; Bd. Mbr., Council of the Americas
Stegemeier	Richard Joseph	C	Chairman & CEO	Unocal Corp.
			Pharmaceuticals	
Gelb	Richard Lee	C	Pres., Chair. & CEO	Bristol-Myers Squibb Co.
Furlaud	Richard Mortimer	C	Director	Bristol-Myers Squibb Co.
Burke	James E.	C,T	Chair. & CEO (fmr.)	Johnson & Johnson; Dir.,IBM Corp.; Dir., CFR
Wilson	Robert N.	T	Vice Chairman	Johnson & Johnson
Knoppers	Antoine T.	B,C	Sr. Vice Pres. (fmr.)	Merck & Co., Inc.
Kogan	Richard J.	C	President & CEO	Schering-Plough Corp.
Leschly	Jan	C	CEO	Smith Kline Beecham p.l.c.
Wendt	Henry	T	Chairman (fmr.)	Smith Kline Beecham p.l.c.
Vink	Lodewijk J.R. de	C	President & CEO	Warner-Lambert Company
			Pipelines	
Lay	Kenneth L.	T	Chair. & CEO	Enron Corp.
Mark	Rebecca P.	C	Chair. & CEO (fmr.)	Enron Development Corp.
West	J. Robinson	C	Chairman	Gas Ventures Advisers
Williams	Joseph Hill	C	Chairman & CEO	Williams Companies, Tulsa

Last Name	First & Mid. Name	Org.	Job Title	Affiliation - Company, Organization
			Sciectific, Photographic, & Control Equipment	
Fisher	George Myles C.	T	Chairman & CEO	Eastman Kodak Co.
Collins	Paula J.	C	Director	Eastman Kodak Co., Trade Relations
Currie	Donald Henry	B	Chairman & CEO	General Instruments Corp., Chicago
Nicholas	N. J., Jr.	C	Director	Xerox Corp
Allaire	Paul Arthur	B,C,T	Ch./CEO/Ch.,Ex.Com.	Xerox Corp.; Dir., Sara Lee Corp.; Dir., CFR
Thoman	G. Richard	B,C	President & COO	Xerox Corp.
			Soap, Cosmetics	
Lewis	W. Walker	B,C	Exec. V. Pres. & Pres.	Avon Products
Godchaux	Frank Area, III	C	Vice President	Colgate-Palmolive Co., NYC
Lauder	Leonard Alan	C	President & CEO	Estee Lauder, Inc.
Artzt	Edwin L.	C	Chairman & CEO	Proctor & Gamble Co.
			Telecommunications	
Allen	Robert E.	C	Chairman & CEO	AT&T; Dir., Pepsico, Inc.; Dir., CFR
Tobias	Randall L.	T	Vice Chairman	AT&T; Dir., Phillips Petroleum Co.
Collado	Robert E.	C	Chairman (fmr.)	AT&T
Berndt	John Edward	C	President	AT&T Int. Communications Services
Levy	Reynold	B	Managing Dir.	AT&T, NYC, Int. Pub. Afrs.; Bd. Mbr., Coun. of the Amer.
McGinn	Richard A.	B	Chairman & CEO	Lucent Technologies
Penzias	Arno A.	C	V. P. Research	AT&T Bell Labs.
Tipson	Frederick S.	C		AT&T
Schmults	Edward Charles	C,T	Sr. Vice President	GTE Corp., external relations
Schacht	Henry Brewer	C	Chairman & CEO	Lucent Technologies Inc.; Chair., Carnegie Corp. of NY
Jacobs	Eli S.	C	Chairman	Memorex-Telex
Forester	Lynn	B,C	CEO	Netwave Inc. (Communications)
Swid	Stephen Claar	T	Chairman & CEO	SCS Communications, NYC
Esrey	William T.	C	Chair. & CEO	Sprint Corp.
Straus	R. Peter		Chairman	Straus Communications, Inc.
			Truck Leasing	
Burns	M. Anthony	T	Chair., Pres. & CEO	Ryder System, Inc.
			Trains & Trucking	
Davison	Daniel Pomeroy	C	Chairman	Burlington N. Santa Fe Corp.
Reed	John Shed	C	Chairman & CEO	Santa Fe Southern Pacific Corp.
Martin	William F.	C	Vice President	Yellow Freight System, Inc.
			Waste Management	
Ruckelshaus	William D.	C,T	Chairman & CEO	Bwng. Ferris;Adm (fmr.)EPA;Dep.Gen.(fmr.),Just. Dpt.
			Other	
Ball	David George	C	President	AMAX Cen. Services
Townley	Preston	C	President & CEO	Conference Board
Raymond	David Alan	C	President	Ebasco Services Int., NYC
Gerson	Ralph Joseph	C	Exec. Vice President	Guardian Industries Corp.
Hines	Gerald D.		Developer	Industrial & Residential, Houston
Pigott	Maceo Nathaniel	T	Owner	International Resources Exchange Corp.
Ryan	John Thomas, III	C	Pres., Chair. & CEO	Mine Safety Appliances Co., Pitt.
Trowbridge	Alexander Buel, Jr.	C	Director	NAM, Washington
Hoopes	Townsend Walter	C	Vice Chairman	Reseal International Corp., NYC
Voell	Richard Allen	C	President & CEO	Rockefeller Group, NYC (real estate service co.)
Ecton	Donna R.	C	President & CEO	Van Houten N. America
Winokur	Herbert S., Jr.	C	Executive	various companies; NY Historical Society
Kelly	James P.	C	Chair & CEO	UPS of America
Public Relations & Advertising				
Dilenschneider	Robert Louis	C	Principal	Dilenschneider Group, Inc. NYC (public relations)
Ross	Thomas Bernard	C	Sr. Vice President	Hill & Knowlton, NYC (P. R. firm)
Schmertz	Herbert	C	President	Schmertz Co., Inc. (P. R. firm)
Wexler	Anne	C	Chairman	Wexler, Reynolds, Harrison & Schule, Inc. (P. R. firm)
Georgescu	Peter Andrew	C	President	Young & Rubicam, Inc. (advertising agency)
Consultants				
Laudicina	Paul A.	C	Vice President	A.T. Kearney, Global Business
Roskens	Ronald William	C	President	Action International, Inc., Omaha
Zumwalt	Elmo Russell, Jr.	C	President	Admiral Zumwalt & Consultants, Inc.
Zorthian	Barry	C	Partner	Alcalde, Rousselot & Fay, Arlington
Gross	Patrick Walter	C	Vice Chairman	American Management Systems, Inc.
Rossotti	Charles Ossola	C	President	American Management Systems, Inc., Arlington
Ravenal	Earl Cederic	C	President	Ames Associates, Wash.
Hoeber	Amoretta M.	C	President	AMH Consulting
Turner	William Cochrane	C	Chairman & CEO	Argyle Atlantic Corp., Phoenix
Dunn	Kempton	C	Environ. Analyst	Arthur D. Little (Consultant)
Matthews	Eugene A.	C	President	Ashta International (Consulting)
Gadiesh	Orit	C	Chairman	Bain & Company (consulting)
Odeen	Philip A.	C	President & CEO	BDM

Last Name	First & Mid. Name	Org.	Job Title	Affiliation - Company, Organization
Freidheim	Cyrus F., Jr.	C	Vice Chairman	Booz, Allen & Hamilton Inc., NYC
Rhodes	John Bower, Sr.	C	Of Counsel	Booz, Allen & Hamilton Inc., NYC
Treat	John Elting	C	Vice Pres. & Partner	Booz, Allen & Hamilton Inc., NYC
Motley	Joel W.	C	Co-Owner	Carmona, Motley & Co.
Cook	Gary M.	C	President	Cook Co.
Sato	Kumi	C	President	Cosmo Relations Corp., (Consultants)
Evans	Daniel J.	T	Chairman	Daniel J. Evans Associates
Diebold	John	B,C	President & Chairman	Diebold Group; Chairman, Griffenhagen-Kroeger, Inc.
Ramo	Simon	C	Consultant	Engineering
Vanblen	Tom Clayton	C	Managing Director	Enterprise Consultants, Inc., Washington
Groves	Ray John	C	Chairman & CEO	Ernst & Young, NYC
Abegglen	James C.	C	Chairman	Gemini Consulting, (Asia)
Gilmore	Richard	C	Founder	GIC Group
Huberman	Benjamin	C	Principal	Huberman Consulting Group
Tucker	Robert W.	C	President	INTERED
Sharp	Daniel Asher	C	Sr. Int. Advisor	InterMatrix Group
Goekjian	Samuel V.	C	Chair. & CEO	Intracon Assoc. (Consultants)
Sterner	Michael Edmund	C	Managing Director	IRC Group, Inc.
Meister	Irene W.	C	Principal	Irene Meister and Assoc.
Raymond	Jack	C	President	JR Consulting Servives, Inc.
Bremer	L. Paul, III	C	Mng. Director	Kissinger & Assoc.; Dir., Foreign Policy Assoc.
Haley	John Charles	C	Deputy Chair. (fmr.)	Kissinger & Associates
Oh	Kongdan	C	Analyst	Korean Policy
Malmgren	Harold Bernard	C	Managing Director	Malmgren, Golt, Kingston, Ltd., London
Zonis	Marvin	C	President	Marvin Zonis & Associates
Mihaly	Eugene Bramer	C	Chairman	Mihaly International of Canada, Ltd.
Solomon	Anne G. K.	C	Consultant	N.Y. City
Hatfield	Robert Sherman	C	Chairman & CEO	National Executive Services Corp., NYC
Lake	William Thomas	C	Financial Consultant	New York City
Peters	Arthur King	C	President & Owner	Peters, A. K. Co., NYC
Marshall	Charles Burton	C	Consultant	Political Science
Tang	David K. Y.	C		Preston, Gayes & Ellis; Investment Banker, Hong Kong
Connor	Joseph E.	C	Partner	Price Waterhouse & Co.
Galpin	Timothy J.	C	Principal	Pritchett & Assoc., Dallas (Consultants)
Bissell	Richard Mervin, Jr.	C	Business Consultant	private practice, Connecticut
Bowman	Richard Carl	C	Vice President	RBI, Inc.
Rhinesmith	Stephen Headley	C	Principal	Rhinesmith & Associates, Inc., NYC
Sisco	Joseph John	C,T	Principal	Sisco Associates, Washington
Spencer	John H.	C	President	Spencer & Spencer, Inc.
Zakheim	Dov Solomon	C	CEO	System Planning Corp., Int., Inc.
Szanton	Peter L.	C	President	Szanton & Assoc.
Ho	Christine M.Y.	C	President	Think Inc. N.Y. (Consultants)
van Dyk	(Frederick T.) Ted	C	President	van Dyk, Associates
Strauss	Simon David	C	Consultant	various industrial firms in US
Walker	Charles E.	C	Chairman	Walker/Free Assoc.
Ward	Haskell G.	T	President	Ward Associates, Inc.
Nolte	Richard Henry	C	General Partner	Washburn Island Res. L. P.
Marks	Russell Edward, Jr.	C	Director	Webb, Johnson & Klemmer
Whalen	Richard James	C	Chairman	Whalen Co., Inc.
Law Firms				
Andrews	David R.	C	Lawyer	ABA, Natural Resources Section
Jordan	Vernon Eulion, Jr.	B,C,T	Sr. Partner	Aikin, Gump, Strauss, Hauer & Feld; Dir., RJR Nabisco
Hargrove	John Lawrence	C	Attorney	Amer. Society of Law and Medicine
Stevens	Paul Schott	C	Chairman	American Bar Assoc. Standing Committee
Karamanian	Susan L.	C	Vice President	American Society of Int. Law
Ku	Charlotte	C	Exec. Dir. & Exec. V.P.	American Society of Int. Law
Juster	Kenneth I.	C	Partner	Arnold & Porter
Clarizio	Lynda	C	Partner	Arnold & Porter Law Firm, Wash.
Gerber	Louis Emil	C	Sr. Partner	Arter & Hadden, Columbus
Rovine	Arthur William	C	Partner	Baker & McKenzie, NYC
Lougheed	E. Peter	T	Sr. Partner	Bennet Jones Verchere, Barristers & Soilicitors
Benson	Lucy Peters Wilson	C,T	President	Benson & Associates, Amherst & Washington
Blumrosen	Alexander B.	C	Attorney	Bernard-Hertz Bojot
Raul	Alan Charles	C	Principal	Beverage & Diamond P. C., Washington
Butler	William Joseph	C	Partner	Butler, Jablow & Geller, NYC
Cohen	Benjamin Jack	C	Partner	Cahill, Gordon & Reindel, NYC
Friedman	Bart	C	Sr. Partner	Cahill, Gordon, & Reindale
Kass	Stephen L.	C	Partner	Carter, Ledyard & Milburn
Tillinghast	David Rollhaus	C	Partner	Chadbourne & Parke, NYC
Fremont-Smith	Marion R.	C	Partner	Choate, Hall & Stewart, Boston
Da Silva	Russell J.	C	Partner	Christy & Viener

Last Name	First & Mid. Name	Org.	Job Title	Affiliation - Company, Organization	
Unger	David G.	C		New York Times	
Rosenthal	Jack	C	Asst. Managing Editor	New York Times	
Rosenthal	A. M.	C	Columnist	New York Times	
Semple	Robert B., Jr.	C	Columnist	New York Times	
Sulzberger	Cyrus Leo	B	Columnist (fmr.)	New York Times	
Wicker	Thomas Grey	B	Columnist (fmr.)	New York Times	
Weisman	Steven	C	Editorial Bd. Mem.	New York Times	
Meyer	Karl Ernest	C	Editorial Bd. Member	New York Times	
Weinstein	Michael M.	C	Editorial Columnist	New York Times	
Friedman	Thomas L.	B,C,T	Fgn. Affrs. Columnist	New York Times	
Greenfield	James L.	C	Mbr. Editorail Bd.	New York Times	
Crittenden	Ann	C	Reporter (fmr.)	New York Times	
Levitas	Mitchel Ramsey	C	Sr. Editor	New York Times	
Oakes	John Bertram	C	Sr. Editor (fmr.)	New York Times	
Krauss	Clifford	C	Writer	New York Times	
Sciolino	Elaine F.	C	Writer	New York Times	
Brooke	James B.	C	Writer	New York Times	
Uhlig	Mark	C	Writer	New York Times	
Whitney	Craig R.	C	Writer	New York Times	
Greenfield	James L.	C		New York Times	
Munyan	Winthrop R.	C		New York Times, Dir., Manufacturers Hanover	
Lewis	Flora	C,T	Sr. Columnist	New York Times, Paris	
Gordon	Michael R.	C	Correspondent	New York Times, Pentagon	
Miller	Judith	C	Correspondent	New York Times; Dep. Asst Sec. (fmr.), Def. Dept., Manpower	
Hoge	Warren M.	C	Asst. Mng. Editor	New York Times	
Bernstein	Richard	B	Book Critic	New York Times	
Murdock	Rupert	C	Founder & CEO	News Corp.	
Thomas	Barbara Singer	C	Director	News International, London, Business & Legal Affairs	
Dreyfuss	Joel	C	Editor-in-Chief	Our World News	
Lee-Kung	Dinah	C		Oversees Press Club, N.Y.	
Rubin	Trudy	C	Columnist	Philidelphia Inquirer	
Posner	Michael H.	C		Reuters News Service	
Warren	Gerald Lee	C	Editor	San Diego Union-Tribune	
Chickering	Allen Lawrence	C	Columnist	San Francisco Chronicle	
Assousa	George E.	C	Writer	Scientific America	
Riesel	Victor	C	Columnist (fmr.)	Syndicated Labor	
Kahn	Harry	C	Founding Sponsor	The American Prospect	
Parkinson	Roger P.	C	Publisher & CEO	The Globe and Mail	
Kohut	Andrew	C		Times Mirror Co.	
Hessler	Curtis Alan	C	Executive	Times Mirror Co.	
Erburu	Robert F.	C,T	Chair. & CEO (fmr.)	Times Mirror Co.;Coun. Mbr., Brookings Inst.;Dir., CFR	
Adelman	Kenneth Lee	C	Syndicated Columnist	Tribune Media Services; Asst. Sec. (fmr.), Defense Dept.	
Dergham	Raghida	C	President	U.N. Correspondent's Association	
Bennett	Susan J.	C	Editor, Writer	USA Today	
Reston	James Barrett	B	Co-Chairman	Vineyard Gazette	
Brauchli	Marcus W.	C	Writer	Wall Street Journal	
Bartley	Robert Leroy	B,C,T	Editor	Wall Street Journal	
Shlaes	Amity	C	Editorial Board Mbr.	Wall Street Journal	
Lipsky	Seth	C	Mem. Ed. Board	Wall Street Journal	
Robbins	Carla Anne	C	Staff Reporter	Wall Street Journal	
Gigot	Paul A.	B,C	Wash. Columnist	Wall Street Journal	
Wohlstetter	Albert J.	B,C	Writer	Wall Street Journal	
Melloan	George R.	C	Writer	Wall Street Journal	
Fifield	Russell Hunt	C	Contributer	Wall Street Journal, Asia	
Henninger	Daniel Paul	C	Deputy Editor	Wall Street Journal, Editorial Page	
Kempe	Frederick Schumann	C	Managing Editor	Wall Street Journal, Europe, Brussels	
Steiger	Paul Ernest	C	Managing Editor	Wall Street Journal, NYC	
Train	John	C	Writer	Wall Street Journal, Worth magazine, Forbes magazine	
Lescaze	Lee	C	Foreign Editor	Wall Street Journal; Accociate, Foreign Policy Assoc.	
Seib	Gerald	C	Nat. Policy Corespond.	Wall Street Journal; Accociate, Foreign Policy Assoc.	
Hume	Ellen	C	Columnist	Wall Street Journal; PBS	

Last Name	First & Mid. Name	Org.	Job Title	Affiliation - Company, Organization
Lindsay	John Vliet	C	Of Counsel	Mudge, Rose, Guthrie, Alex. & Ferdon; Mayor (fmr.) NYC
Martinez	Vilma Socorro	C	Partner	Munger, Tolles & Olson, L. A.
Williams	Avon Nyanza, III	C	Attorney (fmr.)	Nashville, TNN
Dalley	George Albert	C	Partner	Neill, Dalley, Carroll, Nealer & Assev.
Mitchell	George H., Jr.	C	Attorney-at-Law	O'Connor, Cavanagh, Phoenix
Tung	Ko-Yung	C,T	Chairman	O'Melveny & Myers, Global Practice Group,
Hight	B. Boyd	C	Partner	O'Melveny & Myers, L. A.
Roney	John Harvey	C	Partner	O'Melveny & Myers, L. A.
Masin	Michael Terry	C	Managing Partner	O'Melveny & Myers, NYC
Horlick	Gary Norman	C	Partner	O'Melveny & Myers, Washington
Coleman	William Thaddeus, Jr.	C,T	Sr. Partner	O'Melveny & Myers; Sec. (fmr.) Transportation
Jessup	Philip Caryl, Jr.	C	Secretary-Treasurer	Obor, Inc.
Horton	Scott	C	Partner	Patterson, Belknap, Webb & Tyler
Irwin	John Nichol, II	C	Partner	Patterson, Belknap, Webb & Tyler
Wender	Ira Tensard	C	Partner	Patterson, Belknap, Webb & Tyler
Merkling	Christian	C	Attorney	Paul Weiss Rifkind Wharton & Garrison
Cohen	Jerome Alan	C	Partner	Paul, Weiss, Riffind, Wharton, & Garrison
Nimetz	Matthew	C	Partner	Paul, Weiss, Rifkind, Wharton & Garrett
Quigley	Leonard Vincent	C	Partner	Paul, Weiss, Rifkind, Wharton & Garrett
Wiley	Richard Arthur	C	Director	Powers & Hall, P.C.
Barrett	Barbara McConnell	C	Lawyer	private practice, Paradise Valley, Arizona
Connolly	Gerald Edward	C	Partner	Quarles & Brady
Ogden	Alfred	C	Of Counsel	Reboul, MacMurphy, Hewett, Maynard & Kristoff
Young	Nancy	C	Partner	Richards & O'Neil, NYC
Katzenbach	Nicholas deB.	C	Of Council	Riker, Danzig, Scherer, Hyl. & Perr.; Dir. (fmr.), CFR
Rogovin	Mitchell	C	Partner	Rogovin, Huge & Schiller, Washington
Rose	Elihu	C	Partner	Rose Associates, NYC
Sanders	Edward G.	C	Attorney	Sanders, Barnet, Goldman, Simons & Mosk
Dubin	Seth H.	C	Partner	Satterle, Stephens, Burke & Burke
Rivkin	Donald Herschel	C	Member	Schnader, Harrison, Segal & Lewis
Gerson	Allan	C	Attorney	Shapiro & Olander, Baltimore
Rhinelander	John Bassett	C	Partner	Shaw, Pittman, Potts & Trowbridge
Tuck	Edward Hallam	C	Of Counsel	Shearman & Sterling, NYC
Volk	Stephen Richard	C	Sr. Partner	Shearman & Sterling, NYC
Burand	Deborah K.	C	Member	Shearman & Sterling
Connor	John Thomas, Jr.	C	Partner	Sills, Cummis, Radin, Newark
Kraemer	Lillian Elizabeth	C	Partner	Simpson, Thacher & Bartlett, NYC
Walker	John Lockwood	C	Partner	Simpson, Thacher & Bartlett, NYC
Bialkin	Kenneth Jules	C	Partner	Skadden, Arps, Slate Meagher & Flom
Kaplan	Mark Norman	C	Member of Firm	Skadden, Arps, Slate Meagher & Flom
Shapiro	Isaac	C	Partner	Skadden, Arps, Slate Meagher & Flom
Mallery	Richard K.	C	Exec. Comm. Member	Snell & Wilmer, Phoenix
Davidson	Daniel I.	C	Attorney	Spiegel McDiarmid, Wash.
Squadron	Howard Maurice	C	Partner	Squadron, Ellenoff, Plesent Sheinfeld & Sork.
White	Walter H., Jr.	C	Attorney	Steptoe & Johnson, Wash.
Carey	Sarah Collins	C	Partner	Steptoe & Johnson, East-West Trade
Leigh	Monroe	C	Partner	Steptoe & Johnson, Washington
Olmstead	Cecil Jay	C	Member	Steptoe & Johnson, Washington
Brock	Mitchell	C	Partner	Sullivan & Cormwell, NYC
Grant	Stephen Allen	C	Partner	Sullivan & Cromwell, NYC
Rodriguez	Vincent Angel	C	Partner	Sullivan & Cromwell, NYC
Horn	Garfield H.	C	Sr. Counsel	Sullivan & Cromwell, N.Y.
Taft	Robert	T	Attorner-Partner	Taft, Stettinius & Hollister
Lubman	Stanley B.	C	Partner	Thelen, Marrin, Johnson & Bridges
Hurlock	James Bickford	C	Partner	White & Case, NYC
Kempner	Maximilian Walter	C	Of Council	Will & Emery McDermott, NYC
Kester	John Gordon	C	Partner	Williams & Connolly, Washington
Bruemmer	Russell J.	C	Attorney	Wilmer, Cutler & Pickering
Thompson	James	T		Winston & Strawn
Wesley	Edwin Joseph	C	Lawyer	Winthrop Stimson, et al, NYC
Silkenat	James Robert	C	Partner	Winthrop, Stimson, Putnam & Roberts
Anthoine	Robert	C	Senior Counsel	Winthrop, Stimson, Putnam & Roberts, London
Shestack	Jerome Joseph	C	Partner	Wolf, Block, Schorr & Solis-Cohen, Philadelphia
Steiner	Daniel	C	Lobbyist	to the U.S. Senate
Gardner	Nina Luzzatto	C	Int. Lawyer	

Last Name	First & Mid. Name	Org.	Job Title	Affiliation - Company, Organization
Mainstream News Media				
			Authors	
Andreas	Terry	C	Author	"The Flock Report in Perspective"
Asmus	Ronald D.	C	Author	"A United Germany"
Avedon	John F.	C	Author	"In Exile from the Land of Snows"
Baldwin	Sherman	C	Author	"Ironclaw"
Barger	Teresa C.	C	Author	"Private Capital Flow and the Poor"
Barnds	William J.	C	Author	"Intelligence & Fgn. Policy: Dilemmas of a Democracy"
Beitler	Ruth Margolies	C	Author	"The Intifada"
Bell	J. Bowyer	C	Author	"The Irish Troubles"
Bodea	Sorin A.	C	Author	"Information Technology & Economic Performance"
Bonsal	Philip W.	C	Author	"Cuba, Castro, and the United States"
Bouis	Antonina W.	C	Author/Translator	"Mothers and Daughters"
Coles	Isobel	C	Author	"Built-in Impediments"
Crawford	John F.	C	Author	"Notes on the Uses of Edgar Poe"
de Menil	Lois Pattison	C	Author	"Chirac's France in the New Europe"
Denton	E. Hazel	C	Author	"Srilanka", Harvard Business School
Duffy	James Henry	C	Author	"Fiction & Non-fiction books"
Dunn	Lewis A.	C	Author	"Kuwait, the Outbreak of Hostilities and the Aftermath"
Edington	Mark D. W.	T	Author	"Fog of the Familiar Paradigm:On the Dangers of Appl. Theory"
Ellsburg	Daniel	C	Author	"The Pentagon Papers"
Feltman	Jeffrey	C	Author	"Culturism, Autonomy, Women's Rights & Subjugation"
Gates	Philomene A.	C	Author	"Suddenly Alone: A Woman's Guide to Womanhood"
Gerhart	Gail M.	C	Author	"Black Power in South Africa"
Goldstein	Gordon	C	Author	"Consequences of the Information Revolution"
Goodman	George Jerome W.	C	Author	(Adam Smith)
Helprin	Mark	C	Author	"Ellis Island", '81; Bob Dole's speech writer, '96 campaign
Holgate	Laura S. Hayes	C	Co-Author	"Collective Security in a Changing World"
Ikenberry	G. John	C	Author	"Salvaging the G-7"
Jackson	Bruce P.	C	Co-Author	"Space, Power, and Strategy"
Janis	Mark W.	C	Co-Author	"European Rights Law"
Kandell	Jonathan	C	Author	"Passage through El Dorado"
Katz	Daniel Roger	C	Co-Author	"Reviving the Rainforest in Southeast Asia"
Lewis	Loida Nicholas	C	Author/Attorney	"How to Get a Green Card"
MacFarquar	Emily	C	Co-Author	"Non-Govt Org., Early Warning and Preventive Diplomacy"
Maxwell	Kenneth	C	Author	"LA Capital : The Biography of Mexico City"
May	Ernest R.	C	Co-Author	"The Kennedy Tapes"
Meers	Sharon I.	C	Co-Author	"Foreign Exchange Regimes"
Meyer	Cord	C	Author	"Facing Reality: From World Federalism to the CIA"
Oye	Kenneth A.	B	Author	"Cooperation under Anarchy"
Roosa	Ruth AmEnde	C	Author	"Entrepreneurship in Imperial Russia and the Soviet Union"
Rosenthal	Joel H.	C	Author	"Today's Offic Corps, A Repsit. of Vrtu in/Archiac Wld"
Schell	Orville H., Jr.	C	Author	"The China Reader : The Reform Era "
Sick	Gary G.	C	Author	"October Surprise; State Dept., Carter Admin."
Todaro	Michael P.	C	Author	"Urbanization, Unemployment & Migration In Africa"
Walinsky	Adam	C	Author	"The Crisis of Public Order"
Wiarda	Howard J.	C	Author	"Ethnocentricity & Foreign Policy"
Wilson	Gretchen	C	Author	"With All Her Might"
Winters	Francis X.	C	Author	"The Year of the Hare: America in Viet Nam"
Wirth	John D.	C	Author	"The CEC"
Wohl	Richard H.	C	Author	"Practice by Foreign Lawyers in Japan"
Wohlstetter	Roberta	C	Author	"Pearl Harbor: Warning and Decision"
Zelikow	Philip D.	C	Co-Author	"The Kennedy Tapes"
			Book Publishing	
Thomas	Brooks	C	President	Butterfield House
Bessie	Simon Michael	C	Publisher	Cornelia & Michael Bessie Books
Burlingame	Edward Livermore	C	Publisher	Edward Burlingame Books
Sifton	Elizabeth	C	Publisher	Hill & Wang
Bernstein	Robert Louis	C	Publisher-at-large	John Wiley & Sons
Lauinger	Philip C., Jr.	C	Principal	Lauinger Publishing Co., Tulso
Lyons	James Edward	C	President	Littlefield Publish., Inc.
Barlow	William Edward	C	Owner & Pres. (fmr.)	MIN Publishing, N.Y.C.
Silvers	Robert Benjamin	C	Co-Editor	New York Rev. Books
Snyder	Richard Elliot	C	Chairman & CEO	Paramount Publications, NYC
Osnos	Peter Lionel Winston	C	V. Pres. & Assoc. Pub.	Random House Trade Books
Epstein	Jason	C	V. Pres. & Editor, Dir.	Random House, Inc.
Vitale	Alberto Aldo	C	Chair., Pres. & CEO	Random House, NYC
Morse	Kenneth Pratt	C	Chairman (fmr.)	Standard Register Co., Dayton
Lamm	Donald Stephen	C	Chairman	W. W. Norton & Co.
Swenson	Eric Pierson	C	Sr. Edit./V. Ch. (fmr.)	W. W. Norton & Co.
Kaminsky	Howard	C	President & Publisher	Warner Books, Inc.

Last Name	First & Mid. Name	Org.	Job Title	Affiliation - Company, Organization
			Magazine Publishing	
Tyrrell	Robert Emmett, Jr.	C	Editor-in-Chief	American Spectator
Powers	Thomas Moore	C	Author & Contr. Edit.	Atlantic
Wilson	Donald Malcolm, III	C	Publisher	Business for Central N.J., Princeton
Smith	Stephen Grant	C	Editor	Civilization
Podhoretz	Norman	B,C	Editor-in-Chief	Commentary
Rauch	Rudolph Stewart, III	C	Managing Editor	Constitution
Bassow	Whitman	C	Contributing Edit.	Environmental Protection
Hillgren	Sonja Dorothy	C	Washington Editor	Farm Journal
Lansner	Kermit Irvin	C	Editor, Director	Financial World
Novak	Michael John	C	Columnist	Forbes; Scholar, American Enterprise Inst.
Doebele	Justin	C	Writer	Forbes
Kraar	Louis	C	Reporter	Fortune
Hoge	James Fulton, Jr.	B,C,T	Editor	Foreign Affairs, Director (fmr.), CFR
Maynes	Charles William	B,C	Editor	Foreign Policy; Carnegie Endow./Int. Peace
Lind	Michael E.	C	Sr. Editor	Harper's, New Republic
Lapham	Lewis Henry	C	Editor	Harper's
Lyons	Gene Martin	C		Harper's; Prof., Dartmouth College
de Borchgrave	Arnaud	C	Editor-in-Chief (fmr.)	Insight & Washington Times
Crile	George, III	C	Editor/Publisher (fmr.)	Medical Tribune; Physician
Pipes	Daniel	C	Editor	Middle East Quarterly
Sims	Robert B.	C	V.P.	National Geographic
Stokes	Bruce	C	Int. Econ. Corr.	National Journal; Fellow, CFR
Buckley	William Frank, Jr.	B,C	Editor-at-Large	National Review; PBS-Firing Line
Rodman	Peter Warren	C	Sr. Editor	National Review
Wieseltier	Leon	C	Literary Editor	New Republic
Lane	Charles M.	C	Sr. Editor	New Republic
Ellingwood	Susan K.	C	Asst. Editor	New Republic
Hertzberg	Hendrik	C	Executive Editor	New Yorker; Speach Writer for Jimmy Carter
Blumenthal	Sidney	C	Spec. Political Corresp.	New Yorker; Prof. (fmr.), Univ. of Miami
Kramer	Jane	C	Author	New Yorker
Viorst	Milton	C	Staff Writer	New Yorker
Danner	Mark	C	Staff Writer	New Yorker
Isenberg	Steven Lawrence	C	Deputy Publisher	Newsday, Inc.
Klurfeld	James Michael	C	Associate Editor	Newsday, Inc.
Sexton	William Cottrell	C	Columnist, Edt. (fmr.)	Newsday, Inc.
Smith	Richard Mills	C	Editor-in-Chief, Pres.	Newsweek
Parker	Maynard Michael	C	Editor	Newsweek
Nagorski	Andrew	C	Writer	Newsweek
Levinson	Marc	C	Writer	Newsweek
Klein	Joe	C	Columnist	Newsweek; Consultant, CBS News
Thomas	Evan W., III	C	Member	Newsweek, Author, "The Very Best Men"
Palmer	Norman Dunbar	C	Member	Orbis, Global Futures Digest, Editorial Board
Morse	Edward L.	C	Publisher	Petroleum Intelligence Weekly
Art	Robert J.	C	Member	Political Science Quarterly, Ed. Adv. Board
Kristol	Irving	C	Co-Editor	Public Interest.; Dist. Fellow, Amer. Enter. Inst.
Grune	George Vincent	C	Chairman & CEO (fmr.)	Reader's Digest Assn.
Greene	Kenneth Otto	C	Director	Reader's Digest Assn.
Laird	Melvin R.	T	Sr. Counsellor	Reader's Digest Assn.
Kondracke	Morton	C	Executive Editor	Roll Call
Cohen	Patricia	C	Political Editor	Rolling Stone
Allen	Jodi T.	C	Editor	Slate
Piel	Gerald	B,C	Chairman (fmr.)	Scientific America, Inc.
Levin	Gerald	T	Chairman & CEO	Time Warner Inc., NYC
McManus	Jason Donald	C	Editor-in-Chief (fmr.)	Time Warner Inc., NYC
Pearlstine	Norman	C	Editor-in-Chief	Time Warner Inc., NYC; Editor, Time, Inc.
Davidson	Ralph Parsons	C	Chairman	Time, Inc., JFK Center for the Performing Arts
Loeb	Marshall Robert	C	Managing Editor	Time, Inc., magazine development
Grunwald	Henry Anatole	B,C	Editor-in-Chief (fmr.)	Time, Inc.; US Ambassador (fmr.), to Austria
Gart	Murray Joseph	C	Counseler (fmr.)	Time, Inc.
Cloud	Stanley Wills	C	Wash. Contrib. Edit.	Time
Duncan	Richard L.	C	Executive Editor	Time
Gaines	James R.	C	Managing Editor	Time
Isaacson	Walter Seff	C	Editor	Time, of New Media
Rudolph	Barbara	C	Writer	Time
Donnelly	Sally B.	C	Correspondent	Time, Moscow
Kramer	Michael	C	Chief Polit. Corr.	Time
McAllister	Jef Alivarius	C		Time
Muller	Henry	C	Editorial Director	Time; Board Member, Carnegie Corp. of NY
Stacks	John F.	C	Deputy Mng. Editor	Time
van Voorst	L. Bruce	C	Sr. Correspondent	Time
Zuckerman	Mortimer Benjamin	B,C,T	Chr. & Edit.-in-Chief	US News/World Reports,NY Daily News,Atlantic Monthly
Gergen	David R.	B,C,T	Editor-at-Large	US News & World Report; Spec. Asst. to Pres. Clinton
Fallows	James MacKenzie	C	Editor	US News & Wrld. Rept.; Wash. Edit. (fmr.), Atlantic Mthly.
Fromm	Joseph	C	Asst. Editor (fmr.)	US News & World Report
Lief	Louis	C	Diplom. Correspond.	US News & World Report
Ajami	Fouad	C	Contributing Editor	US News & World Report

Last Name	First & Mid. Name	Org.	Job Title	Affiliation - Company, Organization
Horn	Miriam	C	Sr. Editor	US News & World Report
Klein	Edward Joel	C	Contributing Editor	Vanity Fair, NYC
O'Shaughnessy	Elise	C	Writer	Vanity Fair
Karalekas	Anne	C	Publisher	Washington Post Magazine
Merrill	Philip	C	Owner/Pres./Publisher	Washintonian
Kristol	William (Bill)	B	Editor & Publisher	Weekly Standard; Chair., Project/Republican Future
Chace	James	B,C		World Policy Journal
LeoGrande	William Mark	C	Director	World Policy Journal
			Newspaper Publishing	
Decherd	Robert William	T	Chairman	A. H. Belo Corp.
Hultman	Tamela	C	Exec. Editor	African News Service
Kramer	J. Reed	C	Pre. & Man. Editor	African News Service
Topping	Seymour	C	President (fmr.)	American Newspaper Editors
Doyle	James S.	C	V. P., Exec. Editor	Army Times, The Independent Weekly
Rosenblum	Mort	C	Spec. Corresp.	Associated Press
King	John A., Jr.	C	Writer	Associated Press
Erbsen	Claude Ernest	C	V. Pres. & Director	Associated Press, World Services
Hutzler	Charles	C	Correspondent	Associated Press, Bejing
Veliotes	Nicholas Alexander	C	President	Association of American Publishers
Trewhitt	Henry L.	C	Cont. Editor	Baltimore Sun
Winship	Thomas	C	Editor (fmr.)	Boston Globe
Greenway	Hugh Davids Scott	C	Editorial Page Editor	Boston Globe
Shepard	Stephen B.	C	Editor-in-Chief	Business Week
Young	Stephen B.	C	Writer	Center of the American Experiment
Nenneman	Richard Arthur	C	Editor-in-Chief (fmr.)	Christian Science Monitor
Goodsell	James Nelson	C	Member	Christian Science Monitor
Handelman	Stephen	C	Journalist	Comrade Criminal
Cowles	John	T	CEO (fmr.)	Cowles Media Co.
Kruidenier	David	C	Chairman	Cowles Media Co.
Chambers	Anne Cox	C	Board Member	Cox Enterprises, Inc.
Townsend	Alair	C	Publisher	Crain's New York Business
Graubard	Stephen Richard	C	Managing Editor	Daedalus
Cullum	Lee	C	Columnist	Dallas Morning News
Chavira	Ricardo	C	Foreign Edit.	Dallas Morning News
Landers	James Michael	C	International Editor	Dallas Morning News
Pederson	Rena	C	V.P./Editorial Page	Dallas Morning News
Overholster	Geneva	C		Des Moines Register
Stroud	Joe Hinton	C	Sr. Vice President	Detroit Free Press
Snow	Robert Anthony(Tony)	C	Journalist	Detroit News, USA Today
House	Karen Elliott	C	Int. Vice President	Dow Jones & Co.; wife/Peter Kann, Pub., Wall St. Journ.
Kann	Peter Robert	B,C	Chairman & CEO	Dow Jones & Co.; Pub.,Wall St. Jour.;wife/Karen E. House
Ferre	Antonio Luis	C	President & Publisher	El Nuevo Dia
Decter	Midge	C	Distinguished Fellow	Institute on Religion & Public Life
Krisher	Bernard	C	Editor-at-large	Japan Avenue; Asia Wired
Herling	John	C	Edit., Publisher (fmr.)	John Herling's Labor Letter
Shoemaker	Don Cleavenger	C	Columnist	Knight-Ridder Newspapers
Estabrook	Robert Harley	C	Publisher (fmr.)	Lakeville Journal, Connecticut
Healy	Melissa	C	Journalist	Los Angeles Times
Healy	Melissa	C		Los Angeles Times
Nelson	Jack	C	Wash. Bureau Chief	L. A. Times; PBS TV, Washington Week in Review
del Olmo	Frank	C	Deputy Editor	Los Angeles Times
Coffey	C. Shelby, III	C	Editor, Exec. V. Pres.	Los Angeles Times
Cook	Donald (Don) C.	B,C	Euro. Dip. Cor. (fmr.)	Los Angeles Times
Toth	Robert Charles	C	Nat. Security Corresp.	Los Angeles Times
Laventhol	David Abram	C	Publisher & CEO	Los Angeles Times
Day	Anthony	C	Sr. Correspondent	Los Angeles Times
Wright	Robin	C	Wash. Correspondent	Los Angeles Times
Geyer	Georgie Anne	C	Syndicated Columnist	Los Angeles Times Syndicate
White	Robert James	C	Columnist	Minneapolis Star Tribune
McKinney	Robert Moody	C	Chairman	New Mexican, Inc.
Sheinbaum	Stanley K.	C		New Perspectives Quarterly
O'Neill	Michael James	C	Vice President (fmr.)	New York Daily News
Breindel	Eric Marc	C	Editor & Columnist	New York Post

Last Name	First & Mid. Name	Org.	Job Title	Affiliation - Company, Organization
Unger	David G.	C		New York Times
Rosenthal	Jack	C	Asst. Managing Editor	New York Times
Rosenthal	A. M.	C	Columnist	New York Times
Semple	Robert B., Jr.	C	Columnist	New York Times
Sulzberger	Cyrus Leo	B	Columnist (fmr.)	New York Times
Wicker	Thomas Grey	B	Columnist (fmr.)	New York Times
Weisman	Steven	C	Editorial Bd. Mem.	New York Times
Meyer	Karl Ernest	C	Editorial Bd. Member	New York Times
Weinstein	Michael M.	C	Editorial Columnist	New York Times
Friedman	Thomas L.	B,C,T	Fgn. Affrs. Columnist	New York Times
Greenfield	James L.	C	Mbr. Editorail Bd.	New York Times
Crittenden	Ann	C	Reporter (fmr.)	New York Times
Levitas	Mitchel Ramsey	C	Sr. Editor	New York Times
Oakes	John Bertram	C	Sr. Editor (fmr.)	New York Times
Krauss	Clifford	C	Writer	New York Times
Sciolino	Elaine F.	C	Writer	New York Times
Brooke	James B.	C	Writer	New York Times
Uhlig	Mark	C	Writer	New York Times
Whitney	Craig R.	C	Writer	New York Times
Greenfield	James L.	C		New York Times
Munyan	Winthrop R.	C		New York Times, Dir., Manufacturers Hanover
Lewis	Flora	C,T	Sr. Columnist	New York Times, Paris
Gordon	Michael R.	C	Correspondent	New York Times, Pentagon
Miller	Judith	C	Correspondent	New York Times; Dep. Asst Sec. (fmr.), Def. Dept., Manpower
Hoge	Warren M.	C	Asst. Mng. Editor	New York Times
Bernstein	Richard	B	Book Critic	New York Times
Thomas	Barbara Singer	C	Director	News International, London, Business & Legal Affairs
Dreyfuss	Joel	C	Editor-in-Chief	Our World News
Lee-Kung	Dinah	C		Oversees Press Club, N.Y.
Rubin	Trudy	C	Columnist	Philidelphia Inquirer
Posner	Michael H.	C		Reuters News Service
Warren	Gerald Lee	C	Editor	San Diego Union-Tribune
Chickering	Allen Lawrence	C	Columnist	San Francisco Chronicle
Assousa	George E.	C	Writer	Scientific America
Riesel	Victor	C	Columnist (fmr.)	Syndicated Labor
Kahn	Harry	C	Founding Sponsor	The American Prospect
Parkinson	Roger P.	C	Publisher & CEO	The Globe and Mail
Kohut	Andrew	C		Times Mirror Co.
Hessler	Curtis Alan	C	Executive	Times Mirror Co.
Erburu	Robert F.	C,T	Chair. & CEO (fmr.)	Times Mirror Co.;Coun. Mbr., Brookings Inst.;Dir., CFR
Adelman	Kenneth Lee	C	Syndicated Columnist	Tribune Media Services; Asst. Sec. (fmr.), Defense Dept.
Dergham	Raghida	C	President	U.N. Correspondent's Association
Bennett	Susan J.	C	Editor, Writer	USA Today
Reston	James Barrett	B	Co-Chairman	Vineyard Gazette
Brauchli	Marcus W.	C	Writer	Wall Street Journal
Bartley	Robert Leroy	B,C,T	Editor	Wall Street Journal
Shlaes	Amity	C	Editorial Board Mbr.	Wall Street Journal
Lipsky	Seth	C	Mem. Ed. Board	Wall Street Journal
Robbins	Carla Anne	C	Staff Reporter	Wall Street Journal
Gigot	Paul A.	B,C	Wash. Columnist	Wall Street Journal
Wohlstetter	Albert J.	B,C	Writer	Wall Street Journal
Melloan	George R.	C	Writer	Wall Street Journal
Fifield	Russell Hunt	C	Contributer	Wall Street Journal, Asia
Henninger	Daniel Paul	C	Deputy Editor	Wall Street Journal, Editorial Page
Kempe	Frederick Schumann	C	Managing Editor	Wall Street Journal, Europe, Brussels
Steiger	Paul Ernest	C	Managing Editor	Wall Street Journal, NYC
Train	John	C	Writer	Wall Street Journal, Worth magazine, Forbes magazine
Lescaze	Lee	C	Foreign Editor	Wall Street Journal; Accociate, Foreign Policy Assoc.
Seib	Gerald	C	Nat. Policy Corespond.	Wall Street Journal; Accociate, Foreign Policy Assoc.
Hume	Ellen	C	Columnist	Wall Street Journal; PBS

Last Name	First & Mid. Name	Org.	Job Title	Affiliation - Company, Organization
Graham	Katharine	B,C,T	Chair., Exec. Comm.	Washington Post, Newsweek, Brookings Inst.
Graham	Donald E.	B	Publisher	Washington Post
Hoagland	Jimmie Lee	B,C	Associate Editor	Washington Post
Diehl	Jackson	C	Asst. Managing Editor	Washington Post
Getler	Michael	C	Asst. Managing Editor	Washington Post
Ignatius	David	C	Asst. Mng. Editor	Washington Post
Rowen	Hobart	C	Columnist	Washington Post
Weymouth	Lally	C	Columnist	Washington Post
Roberts	Chalmers McGeagh	C	Contrib. Columnist	Washington Post
Greenfield	Meg	C	Editorial Page Editor	Washington Post
Downie	Leonard, Jr.	C	Executive Editor	Washington Post
DeYoung	Karen	C	Member	Washington Post
Kaiser	Robert Greeley	C	News Editor	Washington Post
Constable	Pamela	C	Staff Writer	Washington Post
Krauthammer	Charles	C	Syndicated Columnist	Washington Post
Smith	R. Jeffrey	C	Writer	Washington Post
Pincus	Walter Haskell	C	National Reporter	Washington Post
Rosenfeld	Stephen Samuel	C	Deputy Editor	Washington Post, Editorial Page
Murphy	Caryle Marie	C	Fgn. Correspondent	Washington Post, Middle East, Cairo
Geyelin	Philip L.	C		Washington Post, Newsweek
Oberdorfer	Don	C	Journalist	Washington Post; Mbr., Johns Hopkins Univ.
Mazarr	Michael J.	C	Editor	Washington Quarterly
Shiner	Josette	C	Managing Editor	Washington Times
Grenier	Richard	C	Columnsist	Washington Times
			Radio Broadcasting	
Schorr	Daniel Louis	C	Sr. Analyst	National Public Radio, CNN
Tiido	Harri	TE	Editor-in-Chief	Radio KUKU Tallinn
			Television Broadcasting	
Murphy	Thomas S.	C	Chairman & CEO	Cap. Cities ABC Inc.; Dir., IBM, Johnson & John., Texaco
Arledge	Roone	C	President	ABC News; Creator of Wide World of Sports
Amos	Deborah	C	Correspondent	ABC News
Brinkley	David	C	Anchorman	ABC, This Week
Isham	Christopher	C	Sr. News Producer	ABC, World News Tonight
Jennings	Peter	B	Anchor & Sr. Editor	ABC News, World News Tonight
Sawyer	L. Diane	C	Co-Anchor	ABC, Prime Time Live
Scali	John Alfred	C	Sr. Correspondent	ABC News, Washington
Sherwood	Ben	C	News Producer	ABC-TV
Utley	Garrick	C	Correspondent	ABC News; Director, CFR
Walters	Barbara	C	Co-Host	ABC, 20/20
Will	George	T	Panelist	ABC, This Week; Columnist, GFW Inc.
Zelnick	Carl Robert	C	Pentagon Corresp.	ABC News, Washington
Tisch	Laurence Alan	C	Chair., Pres. & CEO	CBS Inc.
Wyman	Thomas H.	C	Chairman	CBS; Director, General Motors Corp.
Cochran	Barbara Cohen	C	Exec. Producer	CBS News
Stahl	Lesley R.	C	Correspondent	CBS, National Affairs,
Bradley	Edward R.	C	Principal Corresp.	CBS, 60 Minutes
Cohen	Stephen Frand	C	Commentator	CBS News; Prof., Princeton Univ.
Hottelet	Richard C.	C	Journalist	CBS News, UPI
Kalb	Marvin	C	Chief Dip. Corr. (fmr.)	CBS, NBC, Moder., Meet the Press; Prof., Harvard U.
Rather	Dan	C	Anchor, Mng. Editor	CBS, Evening News
Richman	Joan F.	C	V. President (fmr.)	CBS News
Cooney	Joan Ganz	C	Chair., Exec. Comm.	Children's TV Wkshop; Dir., Johnson & Johnson, Xerox
Johnson	Wyatt Thomas, Jr.	C,T	President	CNN
Oliver	April	C	Producer	CNN, Special Assignment
Evans	Rowland, Jr.	C	Sy. Col. & C0-Anchor	CNN, Evans & Novak
Jackson	Jesse Louis, Sr.	C	Host	CNN, Both Sides; founder, PUSH; Rainbow Coalition
Kalb	Bernard	C	Moderator	CNN, Reliable Sources
Schneider	William	C	Correspondent	CNN; Member, American Enterprise Institute
Sesno	Frank	C	Anchor	CNN
Rowan	Carl T.	T	President	CTR Productions Inc.
Cross	June Victoria	C	Producer	Frontline Station, WGBH-TV
Brokaw	Thomas (Tom) John	C	Anchor	NBC Nightly News
Chancellor	John	C	Commentator (fmr.)	NBC News
Agronsky	Martin	C	Comentator	NBC News
Drew	Elizabeth	C	Commentator	NBC, Meet The Press; Columnist; Director (fmr.), CFR
Harsch	Joseph C.	B,C	Commentator (fmr.)	NBC, Inc.; Christian Science Monitor
Levine	Irving Raskin	C	Chief Econ. Cor.(fmr.)	NBC, Wash.; now Dean, Lynn Univ., Sch. of Int. Stud.
Pfeiffer	Jane Cahill	C	Chairwoman (fmr.)	NBC, Inc., NYC
Schlosser	Herbert S.	C	President (fmr.)	NBC, Inc.
Crystal	Lester Martin	C	Executive Producer	PBS TV, MacNeil Lehrer News Hour
Hunter-Gault	Charlayne	C	Commentator	PBS, McNeil/Lehrer; McNeil Lehrer News
Beschloss	Michael R.	C	Commentator	PBS, Jim Lehrer Newshour
Karnow	Stanley	C	Narrator (fmr.)	PBS TV
Lehrer	Jim Charles	C	Assoc. Ed., Co-Anchor	PBS TV, MacNeil Lehrer News Hour
Mosettig	Michael David	C	Sr. Producer	PBS TV, MacNeil Lehrer News Hour

Last Name	First & Mid. Name	Org.	Job Title	Affiliation - Company, Organization
Smith	Hedrick Lawrence	C	Commentator	PBS TV, Washington Week in Review
Moyers	Bill D.	B	Executive Director	Public Affairs TV, Inc.; Director (fmr.), CFR
Frederick	Robert R.	C	Chair. & CEO (fmr.)	RCA
Collins	Joseph J.	C	Chairman	Time Warner Cable
Bell	S. (Steve) Scott	C	News Anchor	USA Network Updates
Eisner	Michael	C	Chairman	Walt Disney Company
Rockefeller	Sharon Percy	C	President & CEO	WETA-TV and FM radio
			Movie Industry	
Ovitz	Michael	C	President (fmr.)	Walt Disney
Fairbanks	Douglas, Jr.	C	Actor	Hollywood
Walton	Anthony J. (Tony)	C	Designer/Illustrator	Theater & Films, Book Illustrator

Charities, Race & Religion

Last Name	First & Mid. Name	Org.	Job Title	Affiliation - Company, Organization
Bernadin	Joseph Louis C.	C	Archbishop (Late)	Chicago
Bond	Jean Carey	C	Member	Black Radical Congress
Chao	Elaine L.	C	President	United Way America (wife of Senator Mitch McConnell)
Hertzberg	Arthur	C	Rabbi (fmr.)	Temple Emanu El
Hoenlein	Malcolm, Rabbi	C	Exec. Vice Chairman	Conf. Pres. of Major Jewish Organizations
Hooks	Benjamine Lawson	C	Executive Director	NAACP, NYC
Jacobs	John Edward	C	President & CEO	National Urban League, NYC; Director, Coca-Cola Co.
Lelyveld	Arthur Joseph	C	Sr. Rabbi (fmr.)	Fairmont Temple, Cleveland
Maguire	John David	C	Chairman	MLK Center for Social Change, Atlanta
Moore	Paul, Jr.	C	Diocese Bishop	New York
Rockwell	Hays H.	C	Bishop	Missouri
Schneier	Arthur	C	Rabbi & Hon. Chair.	World Jewish Congress, American Sect.
Shriver	Donald Woods, Jr.	C	Professor	Christianity Union Theology Seminary, NYC
Siegman	Henry	C	Exec. Committee Mbr.	Interreligious Commission on Peace
Stein	Jonathan B.	C	President (fmr.)	B'nai Israel Usy
Sullivan	Leon Howard	C	Chairman	Zion Home for Retired
Yzaguirre	Raul H.	C	President	Nat. Council of La Raza

Think Tanks

Last Name	First & Mid. Name	Org.	Job Title	Affiliation - Company, Organization
Derryck	Vivian Lowery	C	President	African-American Institute
Garment	Suzanne	C	Resident Scholar	American Enterprise Institute; Author
Hellmann	Donald Charles	C	Trustee	American Enterprise Institute
Huntington	Samuel Phillips	C	Trustee	American Enterprise Institute
Kirkpatrick	Jeane Duane Jordan	C,T	Sr. Fellow	American Enterprise Inst.; US Ambassador (fmr.), UN
Ornstein	Norman Jay	C	Resident Scholar	American Enterprise Institute, Washington
Perle	Richard Norman	C	Resident Fellow	American Enterprise Institute, Public Policy Resolution
Wattenberg	Ben J.	C	Sr. Fellow	American Enterprise Institute; Syndicated Columnist
Lamont	Lansing	C	Sr. Fellow	Americas Society, Canadian Affairs
Keeny	Spurgeon Milton, Jr.	C	Pres. & Exec. Dir.	Arms Control Association, Wash.
Spielvogel	Carl	C	Director	Asia Society
Bouton	Marshall M.	C	V.P.	Asia Society, Texas
Anderson	David	C	Director	Aspen Inst., Berlin; US Ambassador (fmr.) to Yugoslavia
McLaughlin	David Thomas	B,C	President & CEO	Aspen Institute
Low	Stephen	C	President	Association for Diplomatic Studies
Ridgway	Rozanne Lejeanne	B,C,T	Co-Chairman	AtlanticCoun.;Amb. (fmr.),Germ.;Dir.,RJR Nab.,Sara Lee
Sloss	Leon	C	Assoc. Councilor	Atlantic Council
Witunski	Michael	C	Councelor	Atlantic Council Councelor's (Law)
Yost	Casimir A.	B,C	Hon. Chairman	Bilderberg; Dir., Gorbachev State of the World Adv. Bd.
Eliot	Theodore Lyman, Jr.	B,C	US Hon. Sec. Gen.	Bilderberg Group; US Ambassador (fmr.), Afghanistan
Winthrop	Grant F.	B	Rapporteur	Bilderberg Gp.; Partner, Milbank, Wilson, Winthrop, Inc.
Armacost	Michael Hayden	C,T	President	Brookings Inst.; Mbr.,Asia Found.; Amb. (fmr.), Japan
Bergsten	C. Fred	B,C,T	Sr. Fellow	Brookings Institution
Cabot	Louis Wellington	B,C	Chairman (fmr.)	Brookings Institute; Chairman (fmr.), Cabot Corp.
Dam	Kenneth W.	B,C	Council Member	Brookings Inst.; Deputy Sec. (fmr.), St. Dept.; Dir., CFR
Daniel	David Ronald	C	Council Member	Brookings Institute; Managing Director, McKinsey & Co.
Fried	Edward R.	C	Sr. Fellow	Brookings Institute
Giffen	James H.	C	Council Member	Brookings Inst.; Chair. & President, Mercator Corp.
Gordon	Lincoln	B,C	Guest Scholar	Brookings Institute
Hellman	Frederick Warren	C	Council Member	Brookings Institute; Partner, Matrix Partners
Joffe	Robert David	C	Member	Brookings Inst.; Partner, Cravath, Swaine & Moore, NYC
Lardy	Nicholas R.	C		Brookings Institute
Lincoln	Edward J.	C	Sr. Fellow	Brookings Institute
MacLaury	Bruce King	C,T	President	Brookings Institute
Mann	Thomas Edward	C	Sr. Fellow	Brookings Institute
Martin	William McC., Jr.	C	Council Member	Brookings Institute
Newhouse	John	B,C	Dir. of Scholars	Brookings Institute
Nolan	Janne E.	C	Sr. Fellow	Brookings Institute
Pincus	Lionel Irwin	C	Council Member	Brookings Inst.; Chair./CEO, E.M. Warburg, Pincus & Co.
Quandt	William Bauer	B,C	Sr. Fellow	Brookings Institute; Univ. of Virginia
Robinson	James Dixon, III	C	Council Member	Brookings Inst.; Pr., Robinson, J.D., Inc.; Dir.,Coca-Cola
Rose	Daniel	C	Council Member	Brookings Inst.; Dir., Foreign Policy Association
Saul	Ralph Southey	C	Chair., Exec. Comm.	Brookings Institute; CIGNA Corp.
Silk	Leonard Solomon	C	Sr. Fellow	Brookings Institute

Last Name	First & Mid. Name	Org.	Job Title	Affiliation - Company, Organization
Solomon	Robert	C	Guest Scholar	Brookings Institute
Sonnenfeldt	Helmut	B,C,T	Guest Scholar	Brookings Inst.; Edit. Bd. Mbr., Carnegie Endow. mag.
Trezise	Philip Harold	C,T	Sr. Fellow	Brookings Institute
Whitehead	John Cunningham	B,C,T	Chairman	Brookings Institute; Chairman, AEA Investors Inc., NYC
Zilkha	Ezra K.	C	Council Member	Brookings Institute
Bryant	Ralph C.	C	Sr. Fellow	Brookings Inst.
Epstein	Joshua M.	C	Sr. Fellow	Brookings Inst.
Kaplan	Stephen S.	C	Member	Brookings Inst.
Morris	Bailey-Eck	C	Vice President	Brookings Inst., Communications
Cohen	Roberta	C	Guest Scholar	Brookings Inst., Fgn. Pol. Studies
Weiss	Stanley A.	B	Chairman	Business Executives for National Security, Inc.
Beckler	David Zander	C	Associate Director	Carnegie Commission for Science Tech. & Government
Drayton	William, Jr.	C	Mbr. Advisory Council	Carnegie Commission for Science Tech. & Government
Mathews	Jessica Tuchman	B,C,T	President	Carnagie End. for Int. Peace
Abramowitz	Morton I.	C	Pres. & Mbr. Edit. Bd.	Carnegie Endow.; US Ambassadore (fmr.), to Turkey
Arnold	Millard W.	C	Member (fmr.)	Carnegie Endowment for International Peace
Bailey	Charles Waldo, II	C	Trustee	Carnegie Endowment; Editor (fmr.), Nat. Public Radio
Baker	Pauline H.	C	Director	Carnegie Endowment; Member, Aspen Institute
Carothers	Thomas	C	Co-Director	Carnegie Endowment for International Peace
Carswell	Robert	C	Chairman	Carnegie Endowment for International Peace
Dean	Jonathan	C	Member (fmr.)	Carnegie Endowment for International Peace
Debs	Richard A.	C	Trustee	Carnegie Endowment; Chairman, Debs, R. A. & Co.
Destler	I. M.	C	Member (fmr.)	Carnegie Endowment for International Peace
Ellis	Patricia	C	Co-Chairman	Carnegie Endowment, Foreign Policy Group
Falco	Mathea	C	Sr. Associate	Carnegie Endowment for International Peace
Goldring	Natalie J.	C	Member (fmr.)	Carnegie Endowment for International Peace
Gwin	Catherine B.	C	Member (fmr.)	Carnegie Endowment for International Peace
Haass	Richard	C,T	Member	Carnegie Endowment for Internsational Peace
Halsted	Thomas A.	C	Member (fmr.)	Carnegie Endowment for International Peace
Hamilton	Daniel S.	C	Sr. Associate	Carnegie Endowment for International Peace
Harrison	Selig Seidenman	C	Sr. Associate	Carnegie Endowment for International Peace
Hoffman	Adonis Edward	C		Carnegie Endowment for International Peace
Balaran	Paul	C	V.P.	Carnegie Endow. for International Peace
Colbert	Evelyn	C	Sr. Res. Analyst	Carnegie Endowment for Int. Peace
Hoffman	Adonis Edward	C	Sr. Assoc	Carnegie Endowment for Int. Peace
Horelick	Arnold L.	C	V.P. & Dir.	Carnegie Endowment for Int. Peace
Hufstedler	Shirley Mount	C	Trustee	Carnegie Endow.; Part., Hufstedler, Kaus & Ettinger
Hughes	Thomas Lowe	C,T	President (fmr.)	Carnegie Endowment for Int. Peace, Ch., Mid-Atl. Club
Kemp	Geoffrey	C	Director	Carnegie Endowment, Arms Control Project
Kennedy	Donald	C	Trustee	Carnegie Endowment; President (fmr.), Stanford U.
Kreisberg	Paul H.	C	Member (fmr.)	Carnegie Endowment; Director (fmr.), CFR
Li	Victor H.	C	Member (fmr.)	Carnegie Endowment for International Peace
Lodge	George Cabot	C	Trustee	Carnegie Endowment; Professor , Harvard Univ.
Marder	Murrey	C	Member (fmr.)	Carnegie Endowment for International Peace
Newell	Barbara Warne	C	Trustee	Carnegie Endowment; Counselor, Florida Dept. of Labor
O'Flaherty	J. Daniel	C	Member (fmr.)	Carnegie Endowment for International Peace
Omestad	Thomas E.	C	Associate Editor	Carnegie Endowment, Foreign Policy
Pierre	Andrew J.	C	Sr. Associate	Carnegie Endowment for Int. Peace; Johns Hopkins Univ.
Posvar	Wesley W.	C	Trustee	Carnegie Endowment; Pres. (fmr.), Univ. of Pittsburgh
Rogers	William D.	C	Editorial Bd. Mbr.	Carnegie Endowment, Foreign Policy magazine
Simes	Dimitri Konstantin	C	Sr. Assoc. & Director	Carnegie Endow., Study Gp./Russian/Commonw'lth Afrs.
Spector	Leonard S.	C	Sr. Associate	Carnegie Endowment for International Peace
Spencer	Edson W.	C,T	Trustee	Carnegie Endowment for International Peace
Spiro	Peter J.	C	Resident Associate	Carnegie Endowment for International Peace
Steel	Ronald	C	Member (fmr.)	Carnegie Endowment for International Peace
Straus	Donald Blun	C	Trustee (fmr.)	Carnegie Endowment for International Peace
Teitelbaum	Michael S.	C	Member (fmr.)	Carnegie Endowment for International Peace
Ullman	Richard Henry	C	Editorial Bd. Mbr.	Carnegie Endow. magazine; Professor, Princeton U.
Ungar	Sanford J.	C	Member (fmr.)	Carnegie Endowment for International Peace
Layne	Christopher	C	Sr. Fellow	Cato Institute
Hillenbrand	Martin Joseph	C	Co-Director	Center for East-West Trade Policy
Freeman	Harry Louis	C	Principal	Center for Excellence in Government

Last Name	First & Mid. Name	Org.	Job Title	Affiliation - Company, Organization
Bator	Francis Michael	C	Advisory Bd. Member	Center for International Policy
Blechman	Barry M.	C	Advisory Bd. Member	Center for Int. Policy; Chair., Henry Stimson Ctr.
Branson	William H.	C	Advisory Bd. Member	Center for International Policy
Cahn	Anne H.	C	Advisory Bd. Member	Center for International Policy
Cooper	John Milton, Jr.	C,T	Advisory Bd. Member	Center for International Policy
Ferre	Maurice A.	C	Advisory Bd. Member	Center for Int. Policy; Advisory Bd., Ctr. for Nat. Policy
Fetter	Steve	C	Advisory Bd. Member	Center for International Policy
Forman	Shepard	C	Advisory Bd. Member	Center for International Policy
Garcia-Passalacqua	Juan Manuel	C	Advisory Bd. Member	Center for International Policy
Ginsburg	David	C	Advisory Bd. Member	Center for International Policy
Halperin	Morton H.	C	Advisory Bd. Member	Center for International Policy; Dir., ACLU, Wash. office
Kelleher	Catherine M.	C	Advisory Bd. Member	Center for International Policy, Center for Nat. Policy
Legvold	Robert H.	C	Advisory Bd. Member	Center for Int. Policy; Trustee, Carnegie Endowment
Lehman	Orin	C	Advisory Bd. Member	Center for International Policy
Livingston	Robert Gerald	C	Advisory Bd. Member	Center for International Policy, Center for Nat. Policy
Marshall	Ray	C	Advisory Bd. Member	Center for International Policy
Polsby	Neilson Woolf	C	Advisory Bd. Member	Center for International Policy, Center for Nat. Policy
Radway	Laurence I.	C	Advisory Bd. Member	Center for International Policy, Center for Nat. Policy
Rivers	Richard Robinson	C	Advisory Bd. Member	Center for International Policy, Center for Nat. Policy
Robison	Olin C.	C	Advisory Bd. Member	Center for International Policy, Center for Nat. Policy
Roth	William Matson	C,T	Trustee	Center for Int. Policy; Center for Nat. Policy
Steinbrener	John D.	C	Advisory Bd. Member	Center for International Policy, Center for Nat. Policy
Warnke	Paul Culliton	C,T	Trustee	Center for Int. Policy; Council Mbr., Brookings Inst.
Wolff	Alan William	C	Advisory Bd. Member	Center for International Policy
Yarmolinsky	Adam	C	Trustee	Center for Int. Policy; Provost, Univ. of Maryland
Cowan	L. Gray	C	Consultant	Center for Int. Studies, African Studies
Baldwin	Robert H. B.	C	Founding Chair.	Center for Int. Studies, Inc.
Aidinoff	Merton Bernard	C	Board Member	Center for National Policy
Allison	Graham Tilletty, Jr.	B,C,T	Advisory Bd. Member	Center for National Policy; Director (fmr.), CFR
Cooke	John F.	C	Board Member	Center for National Policy
Harman	Sidney	C	Board Member	Center for National Policy; Sidney Harman Ind.
Ladner	Joyce A.	C	Vice Chairwoman	Center for National Policy
Tempelsman	Maurice	C	Board Member	Center for National Policy
Wiener	Carolyn Seely	C	Board Member	Center for National Policy
McFate	Patricia Ann	C	Program Director	Center for National Security Negotiations
Zimmerman	William	C	Program Director	Center for Political Studies
Booker	Salih	C	Consultant	CFR Conference
Bradford	Zeb	C	Military Fellow (fmr.)	Council on Foreign Relations
Bundy	William P.	C	Editor & Dir. (fmr.)	Council on Foreign Relations, Foreign Affairs magazine
Campbell	John Coert	C	Director (fmr.)	Council on Foreign Relations
Clough	Michael	C	Director	CFR, Domestic Policy & Fgn. Policy
Cohen	Stephen S.	C	Director	Council on Foreign Relations
Cyr	Arthur	C	Vice President	Council on Foreign Relations, Chicago
Dillon	C. Douglas	B,C	Vice Chairman (fmr.)	CFR, '76-'78; Mbr., Brookings Inst.
Dobriansky	Paula	T	V.P & Wash. Dir.	Council on Foreign Relations
Fabian	Larry Louis	C	Sr. V. P. & CEO	CFR; Carnegie Endow., Rockefeller Found.
Figueras	Ana	C	Asst. Treasurer	Council on Foreign Relations
Fishlow	Albert	C	Member	Council on Foreign Relations, Economic Studies
Franklin	George S.	C,T	Director (fmr.)	CFR; (David Rockefeller's roommate at Harvard Univ.)
Frye	Alton	C	Sr. V. P. & Nat. Dir.	Council on Foreign Relations, '94
Gelb	Leslie Howard	C,T	President	CFR; Columnist, New York Times
Geyelin	Philip L.	C	Director	Council on Foreign Relations, '77-'87
Gleysteen	William H., Jr.	C	Vice President (fmr.)	Council on Foreign Relations; The Japan Society
Gustafson	Judith	C	Secretary	Council on Foreign Relations
Halaby	Najeeb E.	C	Director	CFR, '70-'72; Mbr., Brookings Inst.
Kapstein	Ethan B.	C	Vice President	CFR, for Studies
Hauser	William L.	C	Director	Council on Foreign Relations
Hoffmann	Stanley H.	B,C	Director, '83-92	CFR; Editorial Bd., Carnegie Endow.; Harvard Univ.
Horn	Karen N.	C	Director	Council on Foreign Relations
Inman	Bobby Ray	C,T	Vice Chairman	Council on Foreign Relations; Dir., Xerox Corp.
Keller	Edmoud J.	C	Acting Sr. V. Pres.	Council on Foreign Relations
Keller	Kenneth Harrison	C	Sr. V. P.	Council on Foreign Relations
Lewis	Elise Carlson	C	Asst. Secretary	Council on Foreign Relations
Loranger	Donald E., Jr.	C	Military Fellow (fmr.)	Council on Foreign Relations
Manning	Bayless	C	President (fmr.)	Council on Foreign Relations, '71-'77
McColough	C. Peter	C	Dir. & Treasurer (fmr.)	Council on Foreign Relations; Dir., Xerox Corp.
Millington	John A.	C	Vice President	Council on Foreign Relations, Planning & Development
Murphy	Richard W.	C	Sr. Fellow	Council on Foreign Relations, Middle East Countries
Osmer-McQuade	Margaret	C	Vice President (fmr.)	Council on Foreign Relations, Meetings
Peterson	Peter G.	C,T	Chairman	CFR, Blackstone Group; Prin., Concord Coal.
Rielly	John Edward	C	Executive Director	Council on Foreign Relations, Chicago; Cargagie Endow.
Rizopoulos	Nicholas X.	C	Vice President	Council on Foreign Relations, Studies
Roosa	Robert V.	B,C	Director	Council on Foreign Relations, '66-'81
Rubin	Barnett R.	C	Director	Council on Foreign Relations, Ctr. for Preventive Action
Scalapino	Robert A.	B,C	Director, '82-89	Council on Fgn. Rel.; Adv. Bd. Mbr., Ctr. for Nat. Pol.
Shulman	Marshall D.	B,C	Director	Council on Foreign Relations, '72-'77
Sughrue	Karen M.	C	Vice President	Council on Foreign Relations, Meetings

Last Name	First & Mid. Name	Org.	Job Title	Affiliation - Company, Organization
Swing	John Temple	C	Exec. V. President	CFR, 1993; President, Fgn. Pol. Assoc.
Usher	William R.	C	Military Fellow (fmr.)	Council on Foreign Relations
Woodbridge	David	C	Treasurer	Council on Foreign Relations
Shinn	James J.	C	Sr. Fellow	Council on Foreign Relations
Whitaker	Jennifer Seymour	C	Dep.Nat. Director	Council on Foreign Relations
Wilkie	Edith B.	C	Legislative Spec.	Council on Foreign Relations
Motulsky	Dan T.	C	Member	CFR, N.Y. Committee
Wilson	Serena Lynn	C	Member	CFR, Wash. Committee
Landau	George Walter	C	President (fmr.)	Coun./Amer.;US Amb.(fmr.),St.Dept.,Paraguay,Chile,Venezuela
Osborne	Richard de J.	C	Treasurer	Council of the Americas
Kennan	Christopher J.	C	US Representative	Advisory Council of the Americas
Galvis	Sergio J.	C	General Counsel	Council of the Americas; Partner, Sullivan & Cromwell
Purcell	Susan Kaufman	C	Managing Dir.	Council of the Americas
Herzstein	Robert Erwin	C	Board Member	Coun. of the Amer.; Ptnr. In Chg., Shearman & Sterling, Wash.
Rockefeller	Rodman C.	C	Board Member	Council on the Americas; Mbr., Pocantico Assoc.
Stoga	Alan	C	Board Member	Council of the Americas; Mng. Dir., Kissinger & Assoc.
Batkin	Alan R.	C	Mbr. Advisory Bd.	Council of the Americas; V. Chair., Kissinger & Assoc.
Carbonell	Nestor T.	C	Mbr. Advisory Bd.	Council of the Americas; Sr. V. Pres., PepsiCo F.&B. Int.
Helander	Robert Charles	C	Mbr. Advisory Bd.	Council of the Amer.; Ptnr., Jones, Day, Reavis & Pogue, NYC
Segal	Susan L.	C	Mbr. Advisory Bd.	Council of the Americas; Sr. Mng. Dir., Chemical Bank
Viscusi	Enzo	C	Mbr. Advisory Bd.	Council of the Americas; Rep./ the Amer., ENI Americas
Barnes	Harry G., Jr.	C	Consultant	Ctr. for Fgn. Policy Devel.; US Amb.(fmr.) to India,Chili
Vance	Cyrus Robert	C,T	Board Member	Ctr./Fgn. Pol. Devel.; Sec. (fmr.) St. Dept., Carter Adm.
Watson	Thomas J., Jr.	C	Chairman	Ctr. for Fgn. Policy Development; US Amb. (fmr.), USSR
Muskie	Edmund Sixtus	C	Chairman	Ctr. for Nat. Policy; Hon. Director, Foreign Policy Assoc.
Fesharaki	Fereidun	C	Member	East-West Center
Lefever	Ernest W.	C	Sr. Fellow	Ethics and Public Policy Center
Yochelson	John N.	C	Member	European Institute, Washington
Baumann	Carol Edler	C	Director	Foreign Policy Association
Bennett	W. Tapley, Jr.	C	Director	Foreign Policy Association
Curran	R. T.	C	President	Foreign Policy Association
Fredericks	J. Wayne	C	Director	Foreign Policy Association
Goldberg	Samuel	C	Director	Foreign Policy Association
Hayes	Samuel P.	C	Honorary Director	Foreign Policy Association
Hoepli	Nancy L.	C	Editor-in-Chief	Foreign Policy Association
Hoyt	Mont Powell	C	Director	Foreign Policy Association
Lindsay	Robert V.	C	Honorary Director	Foreign Policy Association
Marks	Leonard Harold	C	Chair., Exec. Comm.	Foreign Policy Association
Merow	John E.	C	Director	Foreign Policy Association
Niehuss	Rosemary Neaher	C	Director	Foreign Policy Association; member, Kissinger Assoc.
Pierce	Ponchitta A.	C	Director	Foreign Policy Association
Ross	Arthur	C	Director	Foreign Policy Association
Ruggie	John G.	C	Director	Foreign Policy Association
Krepon	Michael	C	President	Henry L. Stimson Ctr.
Fisher	Cathleen S.	C	Sr. Associate	Henry L. Stimson Ctr. Wash.
Eberstadt	Mary	C	Professor	Hudson Institute
Kravis	Marie-Josee	C	Sr. Fellow	Hudson Institute
Abrams	Elliott	C	Sr. Fellow	Hudson Institute; Secretary (fmr.), State Dept.
Carlucci	Frank C., III	C,T	Adjunct Fellow	Hudson Inst.; Sec. (fmr.), Def. Dept.; V. Ch., Carlyle Gp.
Coleman	James S.	T	Trustee	Hudson Institute
Fisher	Roger Dummer	C	Trustee	Hudson Inst.; Dir., Harvard Univ., Negotiation Project
Golden	William Theodore	C	Public Member	Hudson Institute
Herzfeld	Charles Maria	C	Fellow (fmr.)	Hudson Institute
Zraket	Charles A.	C	Trustee	Hudson Institute; Trustee, MITRE Corp.
Henkin	Alice H.	C	Vice Chairwoman	Human Rights Watch Advisory Commity
Jones	Sidney R.	C	Executive Director	Human Rights Watch/Asia
Lesch	Ann Mosely	C	Board Member	Human Rights Watch
Goldman	Merle	C	Member	Human Rights Watch
Marcum	John Arthur	C	Member	Human Rights Watch
Burkhalter	Holly J.	C	Director	Human Rights Watch/Africa Watch
Utgoff	Victor A.	C		Institute for Defense Analysis
Frost	Ellen Louise	C	Sr. Fellow	Inst. for Int. Econ.; Adv. Bd. Member, Ctr. for Nat. Pol.
Mroz	John Edwin	C	President	Institute for East-West Studies
Solomon	Anthony S.	T	Chairman	Inst. for East-West Security Studies,Econ. Progr., N.Y.
Hurewitz	Jacob Coleman	C	Consultant	Institute for Foreign Policy Analisis
Pfaltzgraff	Robert Louis, Jr.	C	President	Institute for Foreign Policy Analisis
Hufbauer	Gary Clyde	C	Sr. Fellow	Institute for International Economics
Barnet	Richard Jackson	C	Trustee	Institute for Policy Studies
DeWind	Adrian W.	C	Trustee	Institute for Policy Studies
Weiss	Cora	C	Member	Institute for Policy Studies; 30th Anniversary Comm.
Ink	Dwight A.	C	President (fmr.)	Institute of Public Administration, NYC
Taubman	William Chase	C	Member	Int. Academy Advisory Gp., Russian Fgn. Min. Archives
Stanley	Timothy Wadsworth	C	President	International Economics Studies Institute
DeVecchi	Robert P.	C	President	International Rescue Committee
Myerson	Toby Salter	C	Secretary (fmr.)	Japan Society, Inc., NYC
Slater	Joseph Elliott	C	Department Chairman	John J. McCloy International Center
Williams	Eddie Nathan	C	President	Joint Center for Political & Economic Studies, Wash.

Last Name	First & Mid. Name	Org.	Job Title	Affiliation - Company, Organization
Burns	Haywood	C	President	Nation Institute
Styron	Rose	C	Trustee	Nation Institute
Feldstein	Martin S.	B,C,T	Pres. & CEO	National Bureau of Economic Research; Prof., Harvard U.
Lindsay	Franklin Anthony	B,C	Mbr. Exec. Committee	National Bureau of Economic Research
Lampton	David M.	C	President	National Committee on U.S.-China Relations
Richardson	John	C	Chairman (fmr.)	National Endowment for Democracy
Johnson	Robert Henry	C	Member	National Planning Association
Davis	Jacquelyn Kay	C	President	National Security Planning Association
Neier	Aryeh	C	President	Open Society Inst..(Funded by George Soros);Adj.Prof.,N.Y.Univ
Asher	Robert E.	C	Member	Overseas Development Council
Assevero	Vicki-Ann E.	C	Member	Overseas Development Council
Beyer	John C.	C	Member	Overseas Development Council
Bissell	Richard Etter	C	Sr. Fellow	Overseas Development Council, Wash.
Bowie	Robert R.	B,C,T	Member	Overseas Development Council
Brainard	Lawrence J.	C	Member	Overseas Development Council
Bruce	Judith	C	Member	Overseas Development Council
Challenor	Herschelle S.	C	Member	Overseas Development Council
Chayes	Antonia Handler	C	Member	Overseas Development Council; Ctr. for Int. Policy
Dulany	Peggy	C	Director	Overseas Development Council
Dunlop	Joan Banks	C	Member	Overseas Development Council
Farmer	Thomas Laurence	C	Director	Overseas Development Council
FitzGerald	Frances	C	Member	Overseas Devel. Council; Edit. Bd. Carnegie Endow.
Freeman	Orville L.	C	Member	Overseas Devel. Council; Sec. (fmr.), Agriculture
Hamilton	Edward K.	C	Director	Overseas Devel. Council; Director (fmr.), CFR
Heldring	Frederick	C	Director	Overseas Development Council
Helmboldt	Niles E.	C	Member	Overseas Development Council
Jacobson	Jerome	C	Director	Overseas Development Council
Jaquette	Jane	C	Member	Overseas Development Council
Kipper	Judith	C	Director	Overseas Development Council
Lucas	C. Payne	C	Director	Overseas Devel. Council; Adv. Bd., Ctr. for Nat. Pol.
Martin	Edwin McCammon, Jr.	B,C	Member	Overseas Development Council
McLean	Sheila Avrin	C	Member	Overseas Development Council
Murray	Douglas P.	C	Member	Overseas Development Council
Nelson	Marlin E.	C	Member	Overseas Development Council
Perkins	James A.	B,C	Member	Overseas Development Council; Dir., CFR
Richardson	Henry J., III	C	Member	Overseas Development Council
Robinson	Charles W.	B,C,T	Member	Overseas Development Council, Brookings Institute
Sacks	Paul M.	C	Member	Overseas Devel. Council; Muntinational Strategies, Inc.
Schaetzel	J. Robert	C,T	Member	Overseas Development Council
Sewell	John Williamson	C	President	Overseas Development Council
Sheffield	Jill W.	C	Member	Overseas Development Council
Timpson	Sarah L.	C	Member	Overseas Development Council
Van Vlierden	Constant M.	C	Member	Overseas Development Council
Wilson	Ernest James, III	C	Director	Overseas Development Council
Zeidenstein	George	C	Counsel	Overseas Development Council
Stern	Paula	C,T	Senior Fellow	Progressive Policy Inst., Pres., The Stern Group
Thomson	James Alan	C	President & CEO	RAND Corp., Santa Monica
Rowen	Henry Stanislaus	C	President	RAND Corp.; Prof., Stanford Univ., Public Policy
Stanton	Frank	C	Chairman (fmr.)	RAND Corp.
Gompert	David C.	C	V.P. & Dir.	RAND Corp., Defense Research Inst.
Fukuyama	Francis	C	Sr. Researcher	RAND Corp.
Kanter	Arnold Lee	C	Sr. Fellow	RAND Corp., Wash.; The Scowcroft Group
Lambeth	Benjamin S.	C	Specialist	RAND Corp, Russian Military Affrairs
Larrabee	F. Stephen	C	Sr. Staff Member	RAND Corp., Int. Policy Dept.
Rich	Michael David	C	Sr. Vice President	RAND Corp.
Shubert	Gustave Harry	C	Sr. Fellow	RAND Corp., Santa Monica
Tanham	George Kilpatrick	C	Dep. to V. Pres. (fmr.)	RAND Corp.
Buchheim	Robert W.	C	Member	RAND Corp.
Lesser	Ian O.	C	Researcher	RAND Corp.
Gordon	Philip H.	C	Consultant	RAND Corp.
Treverton	Gregory F.	C	Director	RAND Corp., Int. Security & Defense Policy Ctr.
Khalilzad	Zalmay	C	Director	RAND Corp., Middle East Studies
Tedstrom	John E.	C	Investigator	RAND Corp., Russian, Ukranian & Eurasian Affairs
Ames	Oakes	C	Chairman	Rhodes Scholarship Selection Commission
Ayers	Harry Brandt	C	Board Member	Southern Center for International Studies, Atlanta
Brittenham	Raymond Lee	C	Vice Chairman	Spanish Institute
Robinson	Randall	C	Member	Trans-Africa
Heck	Charles B.	C,T	Director	Trilateral Commission
Revay	Paul	T	Director	Trilateral Commission
Luck	Edward Carmichael	C	President	UN Association of the US
Cline	Ray Steiner	C	Chairman	US Global Strategy Council
Crocker	Chester Arthur	C	Chairman	US Institute of Peace
Kampelman	Max M.	C	Vice Chairman	US Institute of Peace

Last Name	First & Mid. Name	Org.	Job Title	Affiliation - Company, Organization
Moore	John Norton	C	Chairman (fmr.)	US Inst. for Peace; Adj. Prof., Georgetown Law School
Rostow	Elspeth Davies	C	Vice Chairman	US Inst. for Peace; Prof. (fmr.), Univ. of Texas, Austin
Hentges	Harriet	C	Exec. Vice President	US Institute of Peace
Kintner	William Roscoe	C	Director	US Institute for Peace
Little	David	C	Sr. Scholor	US Institute for Peace
Thompson	W. Scott	C	Director	US Inst. for Peace; Mbr. (fmr.), Carnegie Endowment
Kapp	Robert A.	C	President	US-China Business Council
Sullivan	Roger Winthrop	C	President (fmr.)	US-China Business Council
Jorden	William John	C	Chairman	US-Panama Consultive Commission
Sullivan	William H.	C	Chairman	US-Vietnam Trade Council; Mbr., Dean Whitter
Fischer	David J.	C	President	World Affairs Council
Jarvis	Nancy A.	C	Chairman (fmr.)	World Affairs Council
Knight	Jessie J., Jr.	C	Chairman	World Affairs Council, Nom. & Elect. Comm.
Rieff	David	C		World Policy Institute
Rosenberg	Tina	C		World Policy Institute
Brown	Lester Russell	C	President	Worldwatch Institute, Washington
			Unions	
Sweeney	John J.	C	President	AFL-CIO Union 1995 -
Meany	George	(--)	President (fmr.)	AFL-CIO Union 1955 - '79; CIA Agent
Kirkland	Joseph Lane	C,T	President (fmr.)	AFL-CIO Union ('79-'95); Dir. (fmr.), CFR; TC since '73
Chavez-Thompson	Linda	C	Executive V.P.	AFL-CIO; Sec. (fmr.) Labor Dept.; Newspaper Columnist
Lucy	William	C	Int. Sec./Treasurer	AFL-CIO, AFSCME
Donahue	Thomas Reilly	C,T	Sec./Treasurer (fmr.)	AFL-CIO Union; Dir., CFR
Williams	Lynn Russell	B	Int. President	United Steel Workers of America
Woodcock	Leonard	T	President	United Auto Workers Union
Shanker	Albert	T	President	American Federation of Teachers Union
Kemble	Eugenia	C	Director	American Fed. of Teachers (Union), Educational Issues
Joyce	John T.	C	President	Bricklayers & Allied Craft., Int.; V. Chair., Ctr./Nat. Pol.
Watts	Glenn Ellis	C,T	President (fmr.)	Communications Workers of Amererica; Director, CFR
Mazur	Jay	C,T	President	Union of Needletrades, Industrial and Textile Employees
Sheinkman	Jack	B,C	President	Amalgamated Clothing and Textile Workers Union
Starobin	Herman	C	Research Dir. (fmr.)	Int. Ladies Garment Workers Union
Miscellaneous				
Dean	Robert W.	C	Director	AGC, Membership & Marketing
McGowan	Alan	C	Director	American Assoc. for the Advancement of Science
Andreae	Charles N., III	C	President	Andreae & Associates
Ravitch	Richard	C	Chairman	Aquarius Management Corp.
Moss	Richard H.	C		Battelle Pacific N.W. Nat. Laboratory
Steinberg	Richard H.	C	Member	Berkeley Roundtable on the Int. Economy
Lall	Betty Goetz	C	Editor (fmr.)	Bulletin of Atomic Scientists
Denison	Robert J.	C	Vice Chairman	CalArts; Chair. First Security Mgt., N.Y.
Landy	Joanne	C		Campaign for Peace and Democracy
Nagorski	Zygmunt, Jr.	C		Canadian Diplomatic Corps
Basek	John T.	C	President	Clintondale Aviation
Auspitz	Josiah Lee	C	Advisor	Comm. For the Study of the Amer. Electorate
Burns	William F.	C	Member	Committee on Int. Security & Arms Control
Marton	Kati	C	Chairwoman	Committee to Protect Journalists
Eggers	Thomas E.	C	Majority Partner	Computer Sciences Corp.
Hunter	Shireen T.	C	Sr. Assoc.	Ctr. For European Studies, Brussels
Karl	Terry Lynn	C	Director	Ctr. for Latin American Studies
Kahan	Jerome H.	C	Director	Ctr. for Navel Analysis for Regional Issues
Morey	David E.	C	President & CEO	DMG, Inc.
de Menil	George	C	Son	Dominique de Menil, art collector & philanthropist
Martin	Daniel R.	C	President & CEO	E-Z-EM Inc.
Prestowitz	Clyde V.	C	President	Economic Strategy Institute
Singer	Christine-Eibs	C		Energy House
Weigel	George	C	Sr. Fellow	Ethics & Public Policy Ctr.
Nilsson	A. Kenneth	C		Eureka Group, Inc.
Serfaty	Simon	C	Director	European Studies
Johnson	James A.	C,T	Chairman & CEO	Fannie Mae
Di Martino	Rita	C	Director	Fed. Gov. Affairs
Edwards	Claude A.	TC	President	Fed. Superannuates Nat. Assoc.
Kenney	F. Donald	C	Honorary Dir.	Finland Trade
Goldman	Guido	C	Chairman	First Spring Corp.
Lateef	Noel V.	C	President & CEO	Foreign Policy Assoc., N.Y.
Karatnycky	Adrian	C	President	Freedom House
Lord	Bette Bao	C	Chairman	Freedom House; wife of Winston Lord
Bernstein	Tom A.	C	Member	Fund for Free Expression
Sanchez	Nestor D.	C	Exec. V.P.	George C. Marshall Int. Ctr.
Votaw	Carmen Delgado	C		Girl Scouts of the USA
Kim	Hanya Marie	C		Global Advanced Technology Corp. N.Y.
Nichols	Carole	C		Global Kids, Inc.
Gardels	Nathan P.	C	Editor	Global Viewpoint
Jabber	Paul	C	President	Globicaom, Inc.
Villar	Arturo	C	Director	Gorbachev State of the World Advisory Board

Last Name	First & Mid. Name	Org.	Job Title	Affiliation - Company, Organization
Fung	Victor K. K.	B,C	Chairman	Hong Kong Trade Development Council.
Pearson	John E.	C	Manager	Hoover's Online, Human Resources
Cherne	Leo	C	Chairman (fmr.)	I.R.C.
de Janosi	Peter E.	C	Director	IIASA, Luxemburg, Austria
Skarzynski	Michael P.	C	President	Inferno Network Software
Lipscomb	Thomas H.	C		Infosafe Systems
Krasno	Richard M.	C	President & CEO	Inst. of International Education
Ritch	John B., III	C	US Ambassador	Int. Atomic Energy Agency
Smith	Gordon	T	Chairman	Int. Development Research Centre, Canada
Comstock	Phil	C	Representitive	Int. Guard, Joint Warrighter Ctr.
Evans	Gordon W.	C	Life Trustee	Int. House
DuBrul	Stephen M., Jr.	C	Trustee	Int. House
Goins	Charlynn	C	Member	Int. Planned Parenthood Federation, Pres. Council
Matuszewski	Daniel C.	C	President	Int. Research and Exchange Board
van der Vink	Gregory E.	C		Int. Research Inst. for Seismology
Davis	Maceo N.	C	Chairman & CEO	Int. Resource Exchange Corp.
Germain	Adrienne	C	V.P. & Prog. Dir.	Int. Women's Health Coalition
Hakim	Peter	C	Member	Inter American Dialogue
Morris	Max K.	C	Chairman	Jacksonville Electric Authority
Clemons	Steven C.	C	Director	Japan Policy Research Inst.
Levin	John A.	C	Principal	John A. Levin and Co., N.Y.
Deutch	Michael J.	C	Father of	John Deutch, DCI (fmr.)
Doherty	William C., Jr.	C	Son	Joseph Doherty, formerly with Merrill Lynch
Kamsky	Virginia Ann	C	Principal	Kamsky Assoc.
Pursley	Robert E.	C	Chairman	Logistics Management Inst.
Cooper	James H.S.	C	Member	Medical Quality Commission
Perlman	Janice E.	C	Fdr. & Exec. Dir.	Megacities Project
Hernandez	Antonia	C	President	Mexican American Legal Defense & Education Fund
Melville	Richard A.	C	Member	MOFTE/CICETE, Bristole, ME
Muller	Charles W.	C	President	Murden & Co.
Smith	Carleton Sprague	C	President (fmr.)	Music Library Assoc.
Kiley	Robert R.	C	President	N.Y.C. Partnership
Anthony	John Duke	C	President & CEO	Nat. Counsil on U.S.-Arab Relations, Wash.
Farrington	Thomas A.	C	Chairman	Nat. Ctr. For Afro/American Artists, Boston
Roche	James G.	C	Director (fmr.)	Nat. Ctr. for Volunteer Action
Jacobs	Norman	C	Chairman (fmr.)	Nat. Heritage, Football Licensing Authority
Hewlett	Sylvia Ann	C	Director	Nat. Parenting Assoc.
Geiger	Theodore	C	Chief	Nat. Planning Assoc., Wash., Int. Studies
Nye	Joseph S., Jr.	C	Chairman	Nat. Intelligence Council; Dean, Harvard Univ., School of Govt.
Clark	Ralph L.	C	Member	National Science Foundation
Sawhill	John Crittenden	C,T	President & CEO	Nature Conservancy; Pres. (fmr.), New York Univ., NYC
Mayer	Gerald M., Jr.	C	Officer	New Hampshire Council on World Affairs
Thorup	Cathryn L.	C	Dep. Co-odinator	New Partnership Initiative
Heginbotham	Stanley J.	C	Member	New York Academy of Sciences
Combs	Richard E., Jr.	C	Director	Newly Independent States Non Proliferation Project
Bullard	Edward P.	C	Executive	Non-Profit organization
Voljc	Marko	TE	CEO	Nova Ljublijanska Banka, Ljubljana
Albright	Alice Patterson	C	Daughter	of Madeline Albright, UN Ambassador
Cuomo	Kerry Kennedy	C	Daughter	of Robert Kennedy, wife of Andrew Cuomo
Debevoise	Eli Whitney, II	C	Son	of Thomas McElrath Debevoise, Veremont Law School
Greenberg	Karen J.	C	V.P.	OSI, Programs
Owen	Robert B.	B	President	Owen Research Inc.
Mochizuki	Kiichi	C		Pacific Inst., N.Y.
Cloherty	Patricia M.	C	Pres. & General Ptn.	Patricof Co. (Venture Cap.)
Hansen	Carol Rae	C	Member	Peace Task Force
Harris	Irving B.	C	Chairman	Pittway Corp., Exec. Committee
Ferrari	Frank E.	C	V.P.	Pro Space Ventures Inc.
Corrigan	Kevin	C	Member	Prodemca, National Council
Karis	Thomas G.	C	Sr. Resident Fellow	Ralph Bunche Inst.
Portes	Richard D.	C	Sec. General	RES Conference
Rose	Frederick Phineas	C	Chairman	Rose & Associates
Seibold	Frederick C., Jr.	C	V.P. & Treas. (fmr.)	Sears World Trade, Wash.
Mayer	Lawrence A.	C	Economist	St. Louis
Auer	James E.	C	Physician	St. Lukes Medical Center, Milwaukee
Shulman	Stanley S.	C		Stanton Reality Trust
Melby	Eric D.K.	C	Sr. Associate	The Forum for Int. Policy
Wimpfheimer	Jacques D.	C	Member	The Jockey Club of South Africa
Herberger	Roy A., Jr.	C	President	The Maricopa Partnership (Finance)
Douglas	Paul W.	C	Chair& CEO (Fnr.)	The Pittston Co.
Bales	Carter F.	C	Founder	The Wicks Group of Companies
Clifford	Donald K., Jr.	C	Founder and Pres.	Threshold Management Inc.
Conners	Leila	C	Founder	TRA Mulitmedia Content Provider
Sisk	Timothy D.	C	Prog. Officer	U.S. Inst. of Peace
Mahoney	Thomas H., IV	C	Co-Leader	United World Federalist
Youngblood	Kneeland C.	C	Board Memb.	US Enrichment Corp.
Haltzel	Michael	C	Staff Director	US Inst. Of Peace
Aron	Adam M.	C	Chairman & CEO	Vail Resorts (Real Estate)

Last Name	First & Mid. Name	Org.	Job Title	Affiliation - Company, Organization
Satloff	Robert Barry	C	Member	Wash. Inst. for Near East Affairs
Woon	Eden	C	Exec. Director	Washington State China Realtions Council
Ravenholt	Albert	C	Member	World Affairs Council
Churchill	Buntzie Ellis	C	President (fmr.)	World Affairs Council of Philadelphia
Dougan	Diana, Lady	C	Chairwoman	World Communications Advisory Council
Mello	Judy Hendren	C	President	World Learning
Martinez	Armando Bravo	C	Sr. Fellow	World Policy Inst.
Thomas	Lee B., Jr.	C	Benifactor of Assoc.	World Resources Inst.
Foreign Countries				
			Austria	
Androsch	Hannes	B	Minister	Austria, Finance
Dalma	Alfons	B	Editor-in-Chief (fmr.)	ORF, Austrian radio & television
Igler	Hans	B	President (fmr.)	Federation of Austrian Industriaslists
Jankowitsch	Peter	B	Minister of State	European Integration & Development Cooperation
Janssen	Baron Paul-Emmanuel	TE	Hon. Chairman	Generale de Banque, Brussels
Karner	Dietrich	B	Chair., Mng. Board	Erste Allgemeine-Generali Aktiengesellschaft
Kothbauer	Max	B	Deputy Chairman	Creditanstalt-Bankverein
Maculan	Alexander R.	B	Chairman	Maculan Holding AG
Mitterbauer	Peter	B,T	President	The Federation of Austrian Industry, Vienna
Necci	Antonio Lorenzo	T	CEO	PS-Ferrovie dello Stato
Neisser	Heinrich	T	Member	Austrian Parliament; 2nd President, National Assembly
Puhringer	Othmar	B	Chairman	VA-Technologie AG
Randa	Gerhard	B	Chairman/Mng. Bd.	Bank of Austria
Schenz	Richard	B	Chairman & CEO	OMV AG. Austria
Schmidt-Chiari	Guido	B,T	Chairman of Mng. Bd.	Creditanstalt Bankverein
Scholten	Rudolf	B	Exec. Bd. Member	Oesterreichische Kontrollbank AG, Austria
Verzetnitsch	Fredrich	T	Member	Austrian Parl. (SPOe); Pres., Austrian Fed. of Trade Unions
Vranitzky	Franz	B	Federal Chancellor (fmr.)	Austria
Zimmermann	Norbert	B	Chairman	Berndorf AG, Austria
			Belgium	
Cadieux	Jean-Louis	BB	Dir.-General, Deputy	EEC, for Foreign Affairs, from Belgium
Callebaut	Pierre	T	Chairman	Amylum, Brussels
Camu	Louis	BB	Chairman (fmr.)	Banque de Brouxelles
Claes	Willy	BB	Secretary-General	NATO; Minister of Fgn. Affairs, Belgium
Davignon	Viscounte Etienne	BB,TE	Honorary Chairman	Bilderbergs Soc.Generale de Belgique;V.Ch.(fmr.)Com./Euro.
Donnea	Francois X.	B	Minister (fmr.)	Defense
Goossens	John J.	B	Pres. & CEO	Belgacom
Groothaert	Baron Jacques	T	Honorary Chairman	Generale Bank, Brussels; Ambassador to Belgium
Hinnekens	Jan	T	Chairman	Belgian Boerenbond(Farmers Union);Bd.Mbr.,Bank/Belgium
Houthuys	Jozef	BB	President	C. S. C. Belgique; Vice President, C. M. T.
Huyghebaert	'Jan	BB	President	Almanij N.V., Belgium
Janssen	Baron Daniel E.	BB,TE	Chair., Exec. Comm.	Solvay & Co., Brussels
Keersmaeker	Paul de	T	Chairman	Interbrew, Leuven; (fmr.) Mbr. of thge Belgian Govt.
Lambert	Baron	BB	Chairman	Compagnie Bruxelles Lambert pour la Fin. et l'Indust.
Leysen	Andre	T	Chairman & CEO	Gevaert, Antwerp
Martens	Wilfried	BB	Prime Minister	Belgium
Maystadt	Philippe	BB	Vice-Prime Minister	Belgium; Minsiter, Finance & Foreign Trade
Philippe	H.R.H. Prince	B	Prince	Belgium
Simonet	Henri	BB,TE	Member	
Snoy	et d'Oppuers, Baron	BB	Minister (fmr.)	Belgium, Finance
Spitaels	Guy	BB	Minister	Belgium, of State; Chairman, Socialist Party
Thierry	Jacques	T	Hon. Chairman	Banque Bruxelles Lambert; Ch.,Artois Piedboeuf Interbrew
Vits	Mia de	B	Gen. Secretary	ABVV-FGTB
			Bulgaria	
Kamov	Nikolai	B	Member	Bulgarian Parliament
			Canada	
Aird	John B.	BC	Sr. Partner (fmr.)	Aird, Zimmerman & Berlis
Alford	William Parker	CC	Professor (fmr.)	Univ. of Western Ontario
Axworthy	Lloyd	BC	Minister	Canadian Foreign Affairs
Bassett	Isabel	B	Parl. Asst.	to Min. of Finance, Gvt./Ontario
Belanger	Michel	TC	Chairman & CEO	National Bank of Canada
Black	Conrad M.	BC,TC	Chairman & CEO	Hollinger Inc., Toronto
Bosley	John	TC	Member	Canadian House of Commons; Spkr., House of Commons
Bouey	Gerald K.	TC	Governor (fmr.)	Bank of Canada
Bougie	Jacques	TC	President & CEO	Alcan Aluminium, Ltd., Montiral
Bourassa	Robert	BC	Prime Minister (fmr.)	Quebec
Chastelain	John A. D. de	B	Chairman	Independent Int. Comm. On Decommissioning
Chretien	Jean	BC	Prime Minister	Canada
Chretien	Raymond A.J.	B	Ambassador	to the US
Cohen	Marshall A.	TC	Counsel	Cassels, Brock & Blackwell, Barristers & Solicitors, Toronto
Cook	Gail C. A.	TC	Exec. Vice President	Bennecon Ltd.
Courtis	Kenneth	B	1st Vice-President	Deutsche Bank Group
Cross	Devon G.	B	Head	Donner Canadian Foundation

Last Name	First & Mid. Name	Org.	Job Title	Affiliation - Company, Organization
Cyr	Raymond	TC	President	Bell Canada Enterprises
Deans	Ian	TC	Chairperson	Public Service Staff Relations Board of Canada, Ottawa
Delorme	Jean-Claude	BC	Chairman	Caisse de depot et placement du Quibec
Desmarais	Andre'	TC	Chairman & CEO	Power Corp. of Canada, Montrial
Deutsch	John H.	BC	Professor (fmr.)	Queen's Univ., Canada
Dion	Stephane	B	Minister	Intergovt. Affairs
Dobell	Peter C.	TC	Founding Director	Parliament Centre for Fgn. Affairs & Fgn. Trade, Ottowa
Dobson	Wendy K.	T	Prof. & Director	Ctr. For Int. Business, Toronto Univ.; Deputy (fmr.), G-7
Drouin	Marie-Josee	BC,TC	Executive Dir.	Hudson Inst. of Canada, Montreal
Dupuy	Michel	BC	Asst. Und. sec. (fmr.)	Canada, State Dept.
Eaton	Frederik S.	BC	Chair., Exec. Comm.	Eaton's of Canada
Eyton	John Trevor	TC	Member	Canadian Senate; Pres. & CEO, Brascan Ltd., Toronto
Flood	A. L.	BC	Chairman	Canadian Imperial Bank of Commerce
Fortier	L. Yves	TC	Sr. Partner	Ogilvy Renault, Barr. & Solic.; Canadian Amb. (fmr.) UN;
Frum	David	B	Polit. Commentator	
Garneau	Raymond	TC	Member	Canadian Parliament
Godsoe	Peter C.	B,T	Chairman & CEO	Bank of Nova Scotia
Gordon	Duncan L.	BC	Partner	Clarkson, Gordon & Co.
Gotlieb	Allen E.	BC,TC	Chairman	Trilateral Commission, Canada; Ambassador (fmr.) to US
Graham	William (Bill) C.	TC	Chairman	Canadian Hse. of Com., Standing Comm. on Fgn. Affairs, Ottawa
Gratton	Robert	TC	Chairman & CEO	Power Financial Corp. of Canada, Montrial
Griffin	Anthony G.S.	BC	Hon. Chair. & Dir.	Guardian Group
Harris	Michael	BC	Premier	Ontario
Hennigar	David J.	TC	Chairman	Crownx Inc., Nova Scotia
Herrndorf	Peter A.	B	Chairman & CEO (fmr.)	TV Ontario; Sr. Visiting Fellow, Toronto Univ.
Jackson	Sarah Jeanette	CC	Sculptor, Graphic Art.	Canada
Kirby	Michael J. L.	TC	Member	Canadian Senate
Klein	Ralph P.	B	Premier	Alberta
MacDonald	William A.	BC	Partner	McMillan, Binch
MacLaren	Roy	BC,TC	High Commissioner	for Canada in Britain
MacMillan	Margaret O.	B	Editor	International Journal, CIIA
Manning	Preston	B	Leader	Reform Party
Martin	Paul	BC	Minister	Finance, Canada
McDougall	Barbara	B	Minister	External Affairs
McGrath	James A.	TC	Lt. Governor	Newfoundland
McKenna	Frank	BC	Premier	New Brunswick, Canada
McKeough	W. Darcy	TC	Director	McKeough Sons Company Ltd.
Morris	Joseph	BC	President (fmr.)	Canadian Labour Congress
Munroe-Blum	Heather	B	Vice President	Univ. of Toronto, Res. & Int. Rel.
Mureray	Lowell	TC	Minister of State	Canadian Senate
Mustard	J. Fraser	B	President	Canadian Institute for Advanced Research
O'Donnell	Anthony G. S.	BC	Director	of Companies, Canada; Chairman (fmr.), Home Oil Co.
Ostry	Sylvia	BC	Chairman	Univ. of Toronto, Int. Studies
Pattison	James A.	TC	Chair., Pres. & CEO	Jim Pattison Group, Inc., Vancouver
Phelps	Michael E.J.	TC	Chair. & CEO	Westcoast Energy Inc., Vancouver
Polanyi	John	BC	Professor	Univ. of Toronto, Canada
Prichard	J. Robert	B	President	University of Toronto
Roblin	Duff	T	Member	Canadian Senate
Rogers	Edward S.	BC	President & CEO	Rogers Communications, Inc.
Sabia	Maureen	B	President & Dir.	Maureen Sabia Int.
Sauve	Jeanne (Mrs.)	BC	Minister (fmr.)	Canada, State of Science & Technology
Sharp	Mitchell	TC		Ontario
Southern	Ronald D.	TC	Chair., Pres. & CEO	ATCO Ltd., Calgary; Ch., Canadian Util., Ltd. Edmonton
Thorsell	William	BC	Editor	Globe and Mail
Trudeau	Pierre	BC	Prime Minister (fmr.)	Canada
Turner	William I. M., Jr.	TC	Chairman & CEO	EXSULTATE Inc., Montrial
Wielingen	G. A., van	TC	President & CEO	NuGas Limited, Alberta
Warren	J. H.	T	Ptin. Trade Pol. Adv.	Bureau de Quebec
Wexler	Conrad Moffat	TC	Chairman & CEO	Hollinger Inc., Toronto
White	Peter G.	BC	Chairman	Unimedia; Head (fmr.), of Prime Minister's office
Wilson	L. R.	BC,T	Chair., Pres. & CEO	BCE Inc., Montrial
Wilson	Michael	BC	Minister	of Industry, Science & Technology & Int. Trade, Canada
Winegard	William C.	TC	Chairman	Canadian House of Commons
			China	
Burmester	Sven	TE	Representative	UN Population Fund, Beijing
			Czech Republic	
Dlouhy	Vladimir	TE	Min. of Econ. (fmr.)	Czechoslovakia; Sr. Advisor, ABB
Kovanda	Karel	B	Hd. of Mission	Czech Rep. to NATO & WEU
Kunert	Jiri	T	Chair. & CEO	Zivnostenska Banka, Prague
Schwarzenberg, of	Prince Karel	TE	Foun. & Dir.	Nadace Bohemiae, Prague; Chancellor (fmr.) to Pres Havel
Zantovsky	Michael	B	Chairman	Comm. On Fgn. Affairs, Defense & Security, Czech Senate

Last Name	First & Mid. Name	Org.	Job Title	Affiliation - Company, Organization
			Denmark	
Andersen	Bodil Nyboe	B	Governor	Central Bank of Denmark
Andersen	K. B.	BDK	Minister (fmr.)	Denmark, Foreign Affairs
Bjerregaard	Ritt	BDK,TE	Member	European Commission; Mbr., Parl., Danmark ; Chr., SDP Gp.
Deleuran	Aage	BDK	Editor-in-Chief	Berlingske Tidende, Denmark
Ellemann-Jensen	Uffe	BDK	Member	Danish Parliament; Minister (fmr.), Foreign Affairs
Lykketoft	Mogens	B	Minister	of Finance
Schleimann	Jorgen	BDK,TE	Sr. Columnist	"Berlingske " Gp. of Newspapers, Chr., Euro. Mvmt, Denmark
Seidenfaden	Toger	BDK	Editor-in-Chief	Politiken A/S
Sorensen	Svend O.	BDK	Mng. Director (fmr.)	Den Danske Landmandsbank
Terkelsen	Terkel M.	BDK	Editor-in-Chief (fmr.)	Berlingske Tidende, Denmark
Thygensen	J. V.	BDK	President (fmr.)	Export Credit Council of Denmark
Wilhjelm	Nils	BDK	President	Industrial Mortgage Fund, Denmark; Min. of Ind. (fmr.)
			Finland	
Ahlstrom	Krister Harry	BFIN,TE	Chairman	Ahlstrom Group, Helsinki
Aho	Esko	BFIN	Prime Minister	Finland
Ahtisarri	Martti	BFIN	President	Republic of Finland
Ehrnrooth	Georg	BFIN	President & CEO	Metra Corp., Finland
Erkko	Aatos	BFIN,TE	Chairman	Sanoma Corp., Helsinki, Finland
Hamalainen	Sirkka	BFIN,TE	Member	Euro. Cent. Bank, Chair., (fmr.) Bank of Finland, Helsinki
Harmaia	Jukka	B,T	President & CEO	Enso-Gutzeit Oy
Ihamuotila	Jaako	BFIN	Chairman & CEO	Neste Corp.
Iloniemi	Jaakko	BFIN	Managing Director	Center for Finnish Business & Policy Studies
Jakobson	Max	BFIN,TE	Ambassador (fmr.)	to US; Consultant & Sr. Columnist, Helsinki
Jarimo-Lehtinen	Marja	BFIN	Organizer	Bilderberg Group, meeting in Helsinki
Kohler	Jarl	BFIN	President	Finnish Forest Industries Federation
Lipponen	Paavo	B	Prime Minister	Finland
Lloniemi	Jaakko	BFIN	Ambassador (fmr.)	to US; Managing Dir., Council of Econ. Organizations
Mattsson	Bjorn	B	President & CEO	Cultor Ltd.
Niinisto	Sauli V.	B	Minister	of Finance
Nykopp	Johan	B	fmr. Ambassador	President, Tampella
Ollila	Jorma	BFIN	Chairman & CEO	Nokia Corp.
Rossi	Reino	BFIN	Mng. Director (fmr.)	Finska Socker
Vanhala	Matti	B	Chairman	Bank of Finland
Vartia	Pentti	B	Mng. Director	Research Inst. Of the Finnish Economy (ETLA)
Virkkunen	Janne	B	Sr. Editor-in-Chief	Helsingin Sanomat
Voutilainen	Pertti	B	President	Merita Bank Ltd.
Wendt	Gerhard M. H.	BFIN	President	Kone Corp.
			France	
Albert	Michel	B,T	Member	l'Inst.de France;Mbr.,Coun./Mon.Pol.,Banque de France
Alphand	Herve	BF	Sec. General (fmr.)	French Foreign Office
Alphandery	Edmond	T	Chairman	Caisse Nationale de Prevoyance, Paris
Attali	Jacques	BF	Professor (fmr.)	Ecole Polytechnique
Barre	Raymond	T	Prime Minister (fmr.)	France, de ; Member, National Assembly
Baumgartner	Wilfred S.	BF	Hon. Governor (fmr.)	Banque de France
Bebear	Claud	B	Chairman & CEO	AXA Group
Bergougnoux	Jean	T	Chairman	S.N.C.F. (French Railways), Paris
Biedenkopf	Kurt	B,T	Ministry President	Free State of Saxony; Mbr.)Fmr.) German Bundestag
Boiteux	Marcel	T	Honorary Chairman	French Electric Board, Paris
Bon	Michel	T	Chairman	France Telecom, Paris
Boucher	Eric Le	B	Chief Editor, Int.	Le Monde, France
Casanova	Jean-Claude	T	Professor	Economic Inst. for Policy Studies, Paris; Editor, Commentaire
Catroux	Diomede	BF	Minister (fmr.)	France, de
Cavasse	Felicia	B	Organizer	1992 Bilderbern Conference
Chalandon	Albin	BF	Member (fmr.)	French National Assembly
Collom	Bertrand	BF,TE	Chairman & CEO	Lafarge-Coppee, Paris
Cotta	Alain	T	Professor	Univ. of Paris, Economics & Management
Coutinho	Vasco Pereira	B	Chairman	IPC Holding
David-Weill	Michel	T	Sr. Partner	Lazard Freres & Co., Paris & New York
Devedjian	Patrick	T	Member	French National Assembly, Paris
Dromer	Jean	T	Chairman	Financiere Agache, Paris
Fabius	Laurent	BF,TE	Member	Parliament; fmr. Prime Min., fmr. Ch. Parl.
Faure	Edgar	BF	President (fmr.)	French National Assembly
Faure	Lucie, Madam	BF	Author	French
Fontaine	Andre	BF	Editor-in-Chief (fmr.)	Le Monde, France
Gergorin	Jean-Louis	B	Bd. Member	Matra Hachette
Giscard d'Estaing	Valery	BF	President (fmr.)	French Republic, '74-'81; Pres., Euro. Movement Inst.
Guetta	Bernard	B	Editor-in-Chief	Le Nouvel Observateur
Guindey	Guillaume	BF	President (fmr.)	Compagnie Int. des Wagons-Lits et du Tourisme
Hague	William	B	Leader	Conservative Party
Herzog	Maurice	BF	Member (fmr.)	French National Assembly
Imbert	Claude	BF,TE	Editor-in-Chief	"Le Point", Paris
Jaffre	Philippe	BF	Chairman & CEO	Elf Aquitaine
Joly	Alain	T	Chairman & CEO	L'Air Liquide, Paris
Jospin	Lionel	BF	First Secretary	Socialist Party; Minister (fmr.) d'Etat

Last Name	First & Mid. Name	Org.	Job Title	Affiliation - Company, Organization
Julliard	Jacques	T	Associate Director	Le Nouvel Observateur, Paris
Kessler	Denis	TE	Chairman	French Insurance Assoc., (Ffsa), Paris
Lacharriere	Marc Ladreit, de	B	Chairman	Fimalac
Lamassoure	Alain	T	Budget Minister	& Govt. Spokesman, France
Larre	Rene	BF	Director (fmr.)	Bank of International Settlement
Lellouche	Pierre	BF,TE	Member	National Assembly, Paris
Leprince-Ringuet	Louis	BF	Member (fmr.)	Academie Francaise
Levy	Maurice	T	Chairman	Publicis, Paris
Levy-Lang	Andre	BF,TE	Chairman	Banque Paribas, Compagnie Financiere de Paribas, Paris
Martinet	Gilles	T	Ambassador	France, de; Pres. Assoc. for Euro. Cultural Comm., Paris
Mestrallet	Gerard A.	B	Chairman & CEO	Suez Lyonnaise des Eaux
Moisi	Dominique	B	Deputy Director	IFRI, France
Montbrial, de	Thierry	BF,TE	Member	de l'Institut de France
Morali	Veronique	BF	Organizer, '92 Conf.	Bilderberg Group, 1991 Baden-Baden Meeting
Noir	Michel	BF	Mayor	Lyon, France; Sec. of State for Foreign Trade (fmr.)
Pompidou	Georges Jean R.	BF	President (fmr.)	French Republic
Raimond	Jean-Bernard	BF	Member	French National Assembly; Minister (fmr.), Fgn. Affairs
Richard	Alain	T	Minister	Defense, France
Rose, de	Francois	T	Ambassador	France, de; Permanent Representative to NATO
Rothschild, de	Baron Edmond	BF	Chairman	Banque Rothschild of Paris
Rothschild, de	Baron Guy Edmound, de	BF	President & Exec. Dir.	Compagnie du Nord, Paris
Roy	Olivier	B	Professor	Laboratoire Monde Iranien, CNRS
Sampermans	Francoise	B	Chairman	Groupe Express
Schacht	Serge	T	Chairman	Compagnie de Distrib. de Mat. Elect.
Schweitzer	Louis	T	Chair. & Mng. Dir.	Regie Renault, Paris
Sonnenfeldt	Jean	T	Director General	French Electric Board, Paris
Southern	Marcel	T	Honorary Chairman	French Electric Board, Paris
Stoleru	Lionel	BF	Econ. Counsel. (fmr.)	to President of French Republic
Trichet	Jean-Claud	B	Governor	Banque de France
Uri	Pierre	BF	Professor	Paris IX
Vedrine	Hubert	T	Minister	Foreign Affairs, France
Veil	Simone	T	Minister (fmr.)	France, de, State for Social, Health & Urban Affairs
			Germany	
Abs	Herman	BD	Chairman (fmr.)	Deutsche Bank AG, Frankfurt am Main
Angermeyer	Joachim-Hans	BD	Member (fmr.)	German Bundestag, FDP; Chair., Siko-Consult GmbH & Co.
Bahr	Egon Karlheinz	BD	Director	IFS Hamburg; Fed. Min. (fmr.) for spec. tasks; SPD mbr.
Bangemann	Martin	BD	Minister (fmr.)	Economics; Mbr., Commission of the European Union
Barzel	Rainer	BD	Member (fmr.)	German Bundestag; Pres. (fmr.) Bundestag; CDU mbr.
Becker	Kurt	BD	Editor (fmr.)	Stadtanzeiger
Beitz	Berthold	BD	Chairman (fmr.)	Gen. Authorized Rep. of Friedrich GmbH
Berg	Fritz	BD	President (fmr.)	BDI (Bundesverband der dt. Industrie)
Bertram	Christoph	BD	Dipl. Correspondent	"Die Zeit", Hamburg, Ger.; Mbr. BB Steering Committee
Biedenkopf	Kurt	BD,TE	Ministry President	Free State of Saxony; Mbr. Comm. on Global Governance
Birrenbach	Kurt	BD,TE	Chairman (fmr.)	August-Thyssen-Huette AG; Mbr. (fmr.) CDC, EP
Blomeyer-Bartensteun	H. H.	BD	Personal Assistant	to Alois Mertes, Minister of State (fmr.)
Boden	Hans C.	BD	Hon. President (fmr.)	Int. Trade Chamber, Paris
Brandt	Willy	BD	Chancellor (fmr.)	Germany; Fdr., Comm. on Global Governance 1992
Brautigam	Hans-Otto	B	Minister	of Justice, Brandenburg
Brauer	Max	BD	Mayor (fmr.)	Freie u. Hansestadt Hamburg; Mbr. (fmr.) Bundestag
Breuel	Birgit	BD	Board Member	Treuhandanstalt, Germany
Buelow	Andres, von	BD	Member (fmr.)	German Bundestag, SPD; Sec. of State (fmr.), Min. (fmr.) Def.
Burda	Hubert	B	Chairman	Burda Media
Cartellieri	Ulrich	BD	Bd. Member	Deutsche Bank, A.G.
Dethleffsen	Erich	BD	Attendee	Bilderberg Group, 1966, Wiesbaden, Germany
Dicke	Gunther F. W.	B	First VP	Deutsche Bank AG, Organizer '91 BB Conf.
Dieter	Werner H.	BD	Chairman	Mannesmann A.G., Duesseldorf, Germany
Dohnanyi	Klaus, von	BD	Member (fmr.)	Ger. Bundestag; Mayor (fmr.), Freie u. Hansestadt; SPD
Eckardt	Felix, von	BD	Ambassador (fmr.)	United Nations; Mbr. (fmr.) Budnestag; CDU
Ehmke	Horst	T	Member (fmr.)	German Bundestag, SPD
Emminger	Otmar	BD	President (fmr.)	Deutsche Bundesbank;Mbr. (fmr.) BIZ, Basel, Switzerland
Engelen-Kefar	Ursula	B	Deputy Chair.	Deutscher Gewerkschaftsbund
Engholm	Bjoern	BD	Chairman	Ger. Bundestag; Min. (Fmr.(, Trade & Commerce; CDU
Falkenheim	Ernst G.P.	BD	Attendee	Bilderberg Group, 1966, Wiesbaden, Germany
Fuchs	Michael	T	President	Nat. Federation of German Wholesale & Export Trade
Genscher	Hans-Dietrich	BD	Foreign Min. (fmr.)	Germany;Mbr.(fmr.)Bundestag;Min.(fmr.)Fgn.Afrs.;FDP
Geyer	Gerhard	BD	Chairman (fmr.)	ESSO AG, Hamburg; Bd. Mbr. (fmr.) Dresdner Bank AG
Giersch	Herbert	BD	Director (fmr.)	Institut fuer Weltwirtschaft, Kiel
Gross	Herbert	BD	Attendee	Bilderberg Group, 1955, Garmisch-Partenkirchen, Germany
Gutowski	Armin	T	Director (fmr.)	Hamburger Weltwirtschasftsarchiv (HWWA)
Hahn	Carl	T	Supervisory Bd. Mbr.	Volkswagen AG, Wolfsburg
Hallstein	Walter	BD	Member (fmr.)	Ger. Bundestag; Pres. (fmr.), European Movement; CDU
Hartwig	Hans	T	Chairman (fmr.)	Bundesverband des dt. Gross-und Aussenhandels
Hassen	Uwe	T	Chairman	Allianz Versicherungs-Aktiengesellschaft, Munich
Haussmann	Helmut	BD	Member	German Bundestag, Free Democratic Party
Herrhausen	Alfred	BD	President (fmr.)	Deutsche Bank AG, Frankfurt am Main
Herwarth von Bittenfeld	Hans-Heinrich	BD	Chairman (fmr.)	Deutsche Unilever GmbH; Under Secretary (fmr.)

Last Name	First & Mid. Name	Org.	Job Title	Affiliation - Company, Organization
Heyn	Rolf	BD	Attendee	Bilderberg Group, 1955, Garmisch-Partenkirchen, Germany
Hoffmann	Dieter H.	T	Lawyer	Gurland/Lambsdorff;Hd.(fmr.)UnternehmensgruppeNeueHeima
Kohlhaussen	Martin	T	Chair., Mng. Bd.	Commerzbank, Frankfurt-am-Main; Pres., Assoc./German Banks
Hornhues	Karl-Heinz	T	Member	German Bundestag (CDU), Chair. Fgn. Affairs Comm.
Hundt	Dieter	T	President	Confederation of German Employers' Assoc. (BDA), Cologne
Ischinger	Wolfgang	B	State Secretary	Ministry of Fgn. Affairs, Germany
Issing	H. C. Otmar	B	Exec. Bd. Member	European Central Bank
Jannott	Horst K.	T	Chairman	Muenchner Rueckversicherung AG, Munich
Joffe	Josef	T	Foreign Editor	"Sueddeutsche Zeitung", Munich
Kaiser	Karl	BD,TE	Director	Research Inst. of German Society for Fgn. Affairs (DGAP)
Kaske	Karlheinz	BD	Chairman (fmr.)	ZVEI - Central Association of Electro-Technical Ind.
Kastrup	Dieter	BD	Director	Political Dept., Minister of Foreign Affairs, Germany
Keitel	Hans-Peter	B	Chairman	Hochtief AG
Kiep	Walter Leisler	BD,TE	Treasurer	Christian Democratic Party; Member (fmr.), German Parl.
Kiesinger	Kurt-George	BD	Chancellor (fmr.)	Germany; Fed. Chairman (fmr.) CDU Partyt
Kloten	Norbert	T	President (fmr.)	Landeszentralbank, Baden-Wuerttemberg
Kohl	Helmut	BD	Chancellor (fmr.)	Germany; Chairman, CDU Party
Kohler	Horst	T	President	Deutscher Sparkassen-u. Giroverband, Bonn, Germany
Kopper	Hilmar	B	Chairman, Sup. Bd.	Deutsche Bank AG, Frtankfurt am Main
Krapf	Franz	B	Ambassador (fmr.)	Tokyo, Japan
Kristoffersen	Erwin	T	Head	Int. Abteilung des Deutschen Gewerkschaftsbundes
Kuehlmann-Stumm	Knut Freiherr, von	BD	Member (fmr.)	Ger. Bundestag; Vice-Party Whip (fmr.) FDP
Lafontaine	Oskar	BD	Party Leader SPD	Ministry Pres., Saarland; Mbr. German Bundestag
Lambsdorff	Count Otto	BD,TE	Partner	Wessing Beerenberg-Gossler
Lamers	Karl F.	B	Member	Parliament (Spokesman, Fgn. Affrs. CDU/CSY)
Lauk	Kurt	BD,TE	Board Member	DaimlerChrysler, Stuttgart
Leisler-Kiep	Walter	BD, TE	Treasurer	CDU Party; Mbr. (fmr.) German Bundestag
Leister	Klaus-Dieter	T	Board Member	Westdeutsche Landesbank Girozentrale, Dusseldorf
Leonhard	Wolfgang	BD	Professor (fmr.)	Yale Univ., Soviet History
Leverkuehn	Paul M. Adolf	BD	Commissioner (fmr.)	German Property, German Embassy, Washington, DC
Liesen	Klaus	BD	Chairman	VW AG, Wolfsburg; Chair. (fmr.) Exec. Bd., Ruhrgas AG
Loewenthal	Richard	BD	Political Scientist	Freie Universitaet Berlin
Majonica	Ernst	BD	Member (fmr.)	Ger. Bundestag CDU; Mbr. (fmr.) European Parliament
Markmann	Heinz	T	Director	Wirtschafts-und Sozialwissenschaftliches Institut (WWI)
Martini	Eberhard	T	Spokesman	Bayerische Hypotheken-und Wechsel Bank, Munich
Matuschka	Count Albrecht	T	Chairman	Matuschka-Gruppe, Munich
Maull	Hanna W.	T	Co-Director	German Institut for Foreign Affairs, Bonn
Mehnert	Klaus	BD	Political Scientist	Editor-In-Chief (fmr.), "Osteuropaq" magazine
Meister	Edgar	T	Bd. Member	Deutsche Bandesbank, Frankfort-am-Main
Menne	Alexander W.	BD	Member (fmr.)	Ger. Bundestag. FDP; Bd. Mbr., Hoechst AG, Frankfurt
Merkel	Hans	BD	Attendee	Bilderberg Mtg., 1967
Mertes	Alois	BD	Member (fmr.)	Ger. Bundestag; Spokesman (fmr.), Fgn. Afrs., CDU/CSU
Mommer	Karl	BD	Member (fmr.)	Ger. Bundestag, SPD; Mbr. (fmr.) Council of Europe
Mueller	Rudolf	BD	Member	German Bundestag, SPD
Mueller-Armack	Alfred	BD	Economics Scientist	Mbr. (fmr.) "Freiburg Schule";Undersec. (fmr.) Euro. Afrs.
Muenchmeyer	Alwin	T	President (fmr.)	Deutscher Industrie und Handelstag-"DIHT"
Murmann	Klaus	T	Hon. Chairman	Federation of German Employees Association, (BDA)
Narjes	Karl-Heinz	T	Vice President (fmr.)	Com. of European Union; Mbr. (fmr.) Ger. Bundestag, CDU
Nass	Matthias	B	Deputy Editor	Die Zeit
Neumann	Friedrich	T	Chairman	Arbeitgeberverband Nordrhein-Westfalen
Oetker	Rudolf August	BD	Head	Oetker-Gruppe, Bielefeld
Offergeld	Rainer	BD	Minister (fmr.)	Economic C0-Operation
Pereger	Werner A.	B	Polit. Correspondent	Die Zeit
Pierer, von	Heinrich	TE	Chair. & CEO	Siemens AG, Munich
Ploetz	Hans-Friedrich, von	B	State Secretary	Ministry for Fgn. Affairs
Pohl	Karl Otto	B	President	Deutsche Bundesbank
Ponto	Juergen	BD	Chairman (fmr.)	Dresdner Bank AG, Frankfurt am Main
Porzner	Konrad	T	Member (fmr.)	German Bundestag; Sec. (fmr.) State, SPD
Reitzle	Wolfgang	BD		BMW AG, Munich
Renger	Adalbert, von	BD	Director	Fed. Industrial Board, Policy Planning
Richter	Klaus	T	Director	Optische Werke G. Rodenstock
Riesenhuber	Heinz	T	Member	German Bundestag; (fmr.) Fed. Min. of Research & Tech., Bonn
Ringel	Johannes	T	Bd. Member	Westdeutsche Landesbank Girozentrale, Dusseldorf
Rosenberg	Ludwig	BD	Trade Union Ldr. (fmr.)	Chairman (fmr.) Deutscher Gewerkschaftsbund (DGB)
Ruhe	Volker	BD,TE	Minister of Defense	Gernamy; General Sec. (fmr.), Bundestag, CDU
Ruge	Friedrich	BD	Vice-Admiral (fmr.)	(fmr.) Heeresgruppe B; (fmr.) Uni-Prof. Tuebingen
Ruhnau	Heinz	BD	Chairman	Deutsche Lufthansa AG, Koeln
Scharping	Rudolf	B	Minister	Defense, Germany
Scheel	Walter	BD	Fed. President (fmr.)	Germany; Chairman (fmr.) Bilderberg Mtg.; FDP
Schiller	Karl	BD	Member (fmr.)	German Bundestag; Prof., Economics; SPD
Schmidt	Helmut	BD,TE	Chancellor (fmr.)	Germany; Co-Editor, "Die Zeit", Hamburg
Schmitz	Ronald	T	Board Member	Deutsche Bank, Germany
Schneider	Ernst-Georg	BD	President	Industrie- u. Handelskammer (IHK), Duesseldorf
Schneider-Lenne	Ellen	T	Board Member	Deutsche Bank, Frankfurt
Schrempp	Jurgen F.	B	Chair./Bd. of Mgt.	Daimler Chrysler AG
Schroeder	Gerhard	BD,TE	Member (fmr.)	German Bundestag; Minister (fmr.) of Defence; CDU
Simon	Gunar	BD	Personal Assistant	to Manfred Woerner, Germany

Last Name	First & Mid. Name	Org.	Job Title	Affiliation - Company, Organization
Sohl	Hans-Gunther	BD,TE	Hon. President (fmr.)	Fed. Assoc./German Ind.; Dir. (fmr.), A.-Thyssen-Huette AG
Sommer	Theo	BD,TE	Editor-in-Chief	"Die Zeit", Freie und Hansestadt HamburgGermany
Speidel	Hans	BD	General	Cmdr.-In-Chief (fmr.), NATO land forces, Mid, Europe
Springer, Sr.	Axel Caesar	BD	Publisher (fmr.)	Springer-Publishing house; Frei u. Hansestadt Hamburg
Sternberger	Dolf	BD	Political Scientist	Prof. (fmr.), Heidelberg; Pres. (fmr.), P.E.N.-Ctr. of Ger.
Stoltenberg	Gerhard	BD,TE	Member	German Bundestag; Minister (fmr.), Defence; CDU
Strauss	Franz-Joseph	BD	Min. President (fmr.)	Free State of Baveria; Fed. Min. (fmr.) Finance; CSU
Strube	Jurgen	B	CEO	BASF Aktiengesellschaft
Teltschik	Horst	BD,TE	Moard Member	BMW AG, Munich; Chancellor-Advicer (fmr.)
Teufel	Erwin	B	Prime Minister	Daden-Wurtemberg
Tidemann	Heinrich	T	Chairman	Siemens AG, Munich/Berlin, Munich
Toepfer	Klaus	BD	Minister	House Building, Ger.; Mbr. (fmr.), Ger. Bundestag; CDU
Troeger	Heinrich	BD	Vice President (fmr.)	Dewutsche Bundesbank; Mbr. (fmr.), Bundestag; SPD
Verheugen	Gunter	B	Secretary General	Social Democratic Party
Voigt	Karsten D.	TE	Co-ordinator	for German-American Relations, Berlin
Voscherau	Henning	BD	Mayor	Hamburg
Wechmar	Ruediger von	BD	Diplomat	Pres. (fmr.) UN-Generalk Assby.; Mbr., Euro. Parliament
Weiss	Heinrich	T	Chairman	SMS Company, Duesseldorf
Weizsaecker	Richard von	BD	Fed. President (fmr.)	Ger.; Mayor (fmr.), Berlin; Mbr. (fmr.), Ger. Bundestag
Westrick	Ludger	BD	Fed. Minister (fmr.)	Germany, Special Tasks, CDU; Chief, Bundeskanzleramt
Wieczorek	Norbert	T	Member	German Bundestag,SPD; Cghair., Comm./ Eoro. Union Affrs.
Wischnewski	Hans-Juergen	BD	Member (fmr.)	German Bundestag
Wissmann	Matthias	B	Fed. Minister	for Transportation
Wolff von Amerongen	Otto	BD,TE	Chairman	East Comm./the German Ind.; Ch. & CEO, Otto Wolff Ind.
Zahn	Joachim	T	Chairman (fmr.)	Daimler-Benz AG, Sindelfingen/Stuttgart
			Great Britain	
Armstrong	Lord of Ilminster	T	Director	R.T.Z. Corp.,London;Chief Cabinet Off.(fmr.)/Prime Min.
Asher	Bernard	T	Chairman	HSBC Investment Bank, London
Baring	Sir John	BGB		Baring Brothers & Co.
Bennett	Frederic, Sir	BGB	Member (fmr.)	British Parliament
Blair	Tony	B	Prime Minister	England
Bonfield	Peter, Sir	T	CEO	British Telecom
Brown	Gordon	BGB	Member	British Parliament, Labour Party
Browne	E. John P.	B	Group CEO	British Petroleum Co., plc
Buchanan	Robin W.T.	B	Sr. Partner	Bain & Company Inc.UK
Carrington	Peter Rupert, Lord	BGB	Chairman	Bilderberg Gp., Christie's Int. plc; Sec. Gen. (fmr.), NATO
Clarke	Kenneth	B	Member	Parliament; Chancellor. (fmr.) of the Exchequer
Cooper	Yvette	TE	Member	British Parliament
Cradock	Percy	BGB	Ambassador (fmr.)	to China, Great Britain
Cranborne	Robert M.J.C.	B	Leader	Opposition Party, House/Lords
Emmott	Bill	T	Editor	"The Economist", London
Evans	Robert	T	CEO & Board Member	British Gas Corp., London
Freedman	Lawrence	BGB	Head of Department	of War Studies, King's College, U. K.
Garel-Jones	Tristan, Lord	T	Member (fmr.)	British Parl.; Advisor to Union Bank of Switzerland, London
Garton Ash	Timothy	BGB	Fellow	St. Antony's College, Oxford
Gilbert of Dudley	John, Lord	T	Minister	Def.Procurement;(fmr.)Mbr.,British Parl.;Training/Trans.Min.(fm
Giles	Frank T. R.	BGB	Deputy Editor (fmr.)	Sunday Times
Green	Stephen	TE	Chairman	HSBC Investment Bank, London
Greenhill	Lord	BGB	Banker (fmr.)	Great Britain
Grieson	Ronald	B	Vice Chair. (fmr.)	GEC
Hall	Arnold, Sir	BGB	Chr./Mng. Dir. (fmr.)	Hawker Siddeley Group, Ltd.
Hannay	David	B	Perm. Representative	U.K. Mission to the U.N.
Harding	Sir William	T	Director	LLoyds Bank, London; British Ambassador (fmr.)
Harrowby	Earl of	T	Chairman	Private Bank, The, London
Healey	Denis	BGB	Chan. to Exchequer	Great Britain
Heath	Edmund	BGB	Prime Minister (fmr.)	Great Britain
Henderson	Nicholas	BGB	Ambassador (fmr.)	to Poland, from Great Britain
Hogg	Christopher	B	Chairman	Reuters Group plc
Home	Lord of the Hirsel	BGB	Chairman (fmr.)	Bilderberg Group
Horam	John	BGB	Member (fmr.)	British Parliament
Howell of Guildford	David, Lord	T	Member (fmr.)	British Parliament; Chairman, Foreign Affairs Comm.
Hutton	Will	B	Editor	The Observer
Ilminister, of	Armstrong, Lord	T	Director	R. T. Z. Corp., London
Jacobi	Mary Jo	B	Hd./Gp. Pub. Affrs.	HSBC Holdings plc
Jenkins	Sir Michael	BGB,TE	Vice Chairman	Dresdner Kleinwort Benson Group; (fmr.) British Ambassador
Job	Peter	BGB	CEO	Reuters Holding PLC
Jones	Aubrey	BGB	Chairman (fmr.)	Cornhill Insurance Co., Ltd.
Kaletsky	Anatole	B	Asst. Editor	The Times
Karamanlis	Koetas A.	B	Leader	Opposition Party
Knight	Andrew	B	Editor	"The Economist Newspaper Ltd."; Exec. Chair., News Int., plc
Kogg	Christopher	B	Chairman	Courtauids plc, U. K.
Laing	Martin, Sir	T	Chairman	John Laing, London
Lee Williams	Alan	T	Director	British Atlantic Council; Member (fmr.), Parliament
Mabro	Robert E.	B	Director	Oxford Inst. for Energy Studies
MacFarquar	Roderick	TE	Member (fmr.)	British Parliament; Professor , Harvard Univ.
Mandelson	Peter A.	B	Member	British Parliament

Who's Who of the Elite

Last Name	First & Mid. Name	Org.	Job Title	Affiliation - Company, Organization
Maude	Francis	TE	Member	British Parliament; Shadow Chancellor of the Exchequer
Micklethwait	R. John	BGB	Business Editor	The Economist
Monks	John	BGB	General Secretary	Trades Union Congress (TUC)
Moody-Stuart	Mark	T	Chairman	Shell Trans.& Tdg.Co.;Gp.Mng.Dir.,Ryl. Dutch/Shell Gp.,London
Nixon	Sir Edwin	T	Deputy Chairman	National Westminster Bank, London
Norrington	Humphrey	T	Vice Chairman	Barclays Bank, London
Owen	Lord	B,T	Chairman	Middlesex Holdings
Patten	Chris	T	Governor (fmr.)	Hong Kong; (fmr.) Mbr., British Cabinet
Perry	Sir Michael	T	Chairman	Centrica & Dunlop Slazenger Gp.; (fmr.) Chr., Unilever, London
Porrit	Jonathon	B	Programsme Dir.	Forum for the Future
Prideaux	John Francis, Sir	BGB	Chairman (fmr.)	National Westminster Bank, London
Purves	William	B	Gp. Chairman	HSBC Holdings plc
Radice	Giles H.	B	Member	Parliament; Chair., European Movement
Rell	Eric	B	Sr. Advisor	SBC Warburg
Richardson	Gordon	BGB	Governor (fmr.)	Bank of England
Rifkind	Malcolm	BGB	Foreign Secretary	Great Britain
Rippon of Hexham	Lord	BGB,TE	Chairman	Unichem & Dun & Bradstreet, London
Robertson	George	B	Secretary	of State for Defence
Robertson	Simon	BGB	Chairman	Kleinwort Benson Group plc
Robins	David	TE	CEO	ING Barings, London
Rodgers	William	BGB	Minister (fmr.)	British State, for Defence
Roll of Ipsden	Eric, Lord	BGB,TE	Sr. Advisor	SBC Warburg, London
Rothschild, de	Emma	B	Director	Centre, Hist. & Econ.; Fellow, Cambridge U.
Rothschild, de	Evelyn	B	Chairman	N.M. Rothschild & Sons
Shore	Peter, Lord	T	Member	British House of Lords, London
Simon of Highbury	David, Lord	T	Chairman	British Pet., London; Min., (fmr.), Trade/Competitiveness in Euro.
Smith	John	BGB	Member	British Parl., Lab. Party; Shadow Chancellor, Exchequer
Stevenson	H. Dennis	B	Chairman	SRU Groupe; Tate Gallery
Tapsell	Peter, Sir	T	Member	British Parliament
Taylor	J. Martin	BGB	CEO (fmr.)	Barclays Bank, London
Taylor	Geoffrey	T	Chairman	Daiwa European Bank, London
Thatcher	Margaret, Lady	BGB	Prime Minister (fmr.)	Great Britain
Thompson	Gerald F.M.P.	BGB	Chairman (fmr.)	Kleinwort Benson Ltd. (investment bank)
Tuke	Anthony	BGB	President (fmr.)	Barclays Bank, London
Villeneuve	Andre-Francois H.	B	Exec. Dir.	Reuters Group Holding plc
Waldegrave	William A.	B	Secretary of State	Minister of Agriculture, Fisheries & Food
Warburg	Sir Siegmund George	BGB	Chairman (fmr.)	S. G. Warburg & Co., Lond.; Ptnr., Kuhn, Loeb & Co.
Williams	Alan	TE	Member	British Parliament, London
Windsor	HRH Prince Philip	B	Prince & , Duke of	of England
Wolf	Martin	B	Assoc. Editor	The Finantial Times, Economic Commentastor
Wooldridge	Adrian D.	B	Fgn. Correspondent	The Economist
Wright	Patrick	BGB	Perm. Under Sec.	of State; Head, Diplomatic Service, U. K.
Yahuda	Michael B.	B	Professor	Int. Rel., London School of Economics
			Greece	
Argyros	Sterios	B,T	Member	European Parliament
Arsenis	Gerasimos	BGR	Minister of Defense	Greece
Carras	Costa	BGR	Director	of various companies, Greece
Christodoulou	Efthymios	BGR	Minister	of Economic Affairs, Greece
Costopoulos	Yannis	B		
Couloumbis	Theodore A.	B	President	Greek Foreign Policy Institute
David	George A.	B	Chairman	Hellenic Bottling Company S.A.
Karras	K.	B		
Kiranidiotis	Yannos	B	Deputy Minister	for Foreign Affairs, Greece
Liras	G.	B		
Livanos	G.	B		
Manos	Stephanos	TE	Member	Greek Parliament
Mitsotakis	Konstantinos	B	Prime Minister	Greece
Niarchos	Stavros Spyros	BGR	Head	Niarchos Group; Shipowner
Pangalos	Theodoros G.	BGR	Minister	Greece, Foreign Affairs
Papademos	Lucas	T	Governor	Bank of Greece, Athens
Papandreou	George A.	B	Alt. Minister	for Foreign Affairs
Papkonstandinov	Michael	B	Foreign Minister	Greece
Peratikos	Michael	B		
Pesmazoglu	John S.	BGR	Dep. Governor (fmr.)	Bank of Greece
Veremis	Thomas M.	B	Professor	Athens Univ., Political History
Vourloumis	Panagis	TE	Chair.& Man. Dir.	Alpha Finance, Athens
Zombanakis	Minos	BGR	Chairman	Group for International Study & Evaluation, Greece
			Hungary	
Orban	Viktor	TE	Prime Minister	Hungary
Suranyi	Gyorgy	B	President	National Bank of Hungary

Last Name	First & Mid. Name	Org.	Job Title	Affiliation - Company, Organization
			Iceland	
Bjarnason	Bjorn	BICE	Member	Parliament, Iceland, Independence Party
Hallgrimsson	Geir	BICE	Prime Minister (fmr.)	Iceland
Oddsson	David	B	Prime Minister	Iceland; Mayor (fmr.), Reykjavik; Ch., Independence Party
Schmidheimy	Stephan E.	B	Chairman	ANOVA Holdings Ltd.
			Ireland	
Bruton	John	BIRL	Leader	of Fine Gael.
Burrows	Richard	T	Chairman & CEO	Irish Distillers, Dublin
Conroy	Richard	TE	Chairman & CEO	Conroy Diamonds/Gold; Sen. Mbr., Irish Repub.; Chair., ARCON
FitzGerald	Garret	BIRL,TE	Prime Minister (fmr.)	Ireland; Member, Irish Dail
Gleeson	Dermot	B	Attorney General	
Keating	Justin	T	Minister (fmr.)	Irish Industry & Comm.; Leader (fmr.), Labor Party
Lawlor	Liam	TE	Member	Irish Dail, Dublin
Quinn	Lochlann	B	Chairman	Allied Irish Bank Gp.
Schmertz	Richard	T	Chairman	Conroy Petroleum; Member/Senate, Irish Republic
Staunton	Myles	TE	Member	Senate, Irish Republic
Sutherland	Peter D.	B,T	Chair. & Mng. Dir.	Goldman Sachs Int.,London;Dir.Gen.(fmr.),GATT & WTO
			Italy	
Adler	Lionello	T	Chairman	Banca Commerciale Italiana, Milan
Agnelli	Giovanni	BI	Hon. Chairman	Fiat S.P.A., Italy; Strg. Comm. Mbr., Bilderberger Gp.
Agnelli	Umberto	BI,TE	CEO & V.-Chair.	IFI; Chair., IFIL - Fianziaria di Partecipazioni S.p.A.
Ambrosetti	Alfredo	BI	Chairman	Ambrosetti Group, Italy
Armenise	Giovanni Auletta	T	Chairman	Banca Nazionale dell' Agricoltura, Rome
Bassetti	Piero	T	President	Assocamerestro, Rome; Ch. (fmr.)Chmbr. of Com. & Ind., Milan
Bernabe'	Franco	B,T	CEO	Telecom Italia, Rome
Bettiza	Enzo	BI	Journalist (fmr.)	Corriere della Sera, Italy
Biancheri Chiappori	Boris	T	Chairman	Agenzia ANSA; Chair., I.S.P.I., Milan; Chair., ANSA, Milan
Boniver	Margherita	T	Minister	Tourism, Italy
Callieri	Carlo	T	Mng. Director	Iniziativa Piemonte;Ex.V.P.,(fmr.)Fiat, Turin;V.Chr.,Confindustri
Cantoni	Giampiero	BI	Chairman	Banca Nazionale del Lavoro, Italy
Cappuzzo	Umberto	T	Member	Italian Senate, Def. Comm.;Chief/Staff (fmr.)Army,Rome
Carli	Guido	BI	Governor (fmr.)	Bank of Italy
Carruba	Salvatore	T	Culture Alderman	Municipality of Milan; Man. Editor, (fmr.), Il Sole 24 Ore, Milan
Cavalchini	Luigi G.	B	Perm. Representative	European Union
Cereti	Fausto	T	Chairman & CEO	Alitalia, Rome
Cerretelli	Adriana	B	Correspondent	"Il Sole/24 Ore."
Cipolletta	Innocenzo	BI	Director General	Confindustria, Italy
Cittadini	Cesi Il Marchese	BI	President (fmr.)	Association pour l'Etude des Problemes de l'Europe
Colombo	Umberto	T	Chairman	Foundation LEAD Euirope, Rome
Colonna di Paliano	Don Guido, Prince	BI	Chairmen (fmr.)	La Rinascente
Del Turco	Ottaviano	T	General Secretary	Italian Socialist Party (PSI), Rome
Draghi	Mario	BI	Director General	Italian Ministry of the Treasury
Ducci	Roberto	BI	Director General (fmr.)	Political Affairs, Minister for Foreign Affairs
Ferragamo	Ferruccio	T	Mng. Director	Salvatore Ferragamo Italia, Florence
Forte	Francesco	BI	Professor (fmr.)	Univ. of Torino
Fresco	Paolo	B,T	Chairman	Fiat S.p.A.
Gazzoni Frascara	Giuseppe	T	Chair. & Mng. Dir.	Gazzoni; Pres., Fed. of Italian Food Ind., Bologna
Giavazzi	Francesco	B	Professor	Bocconi Univ., Milan, Economics
Guidi	Marcello	T	Chairman	ISPI, Milan; Ambassador (fmr.) of Italy
Kohnstamm	Max	BI,TE	President (fmr.)	European Univ.,Florence,fmr.Sec.Gen.,Action/Euro.
La Malfa	Giorgio	BI	Professor (fmr.)	Milan State Univ.
Levi	Arrigo	BI,TE	Political Columnist	"Corriere dela Sera", Rome
Malfatti	Franco Maria	BI	Minister (fmr.)	Italian Dept. of Education
Masera	Rainer S.	B	Dir. General	I.M.I.S. p.A.
Merlini	Cesare	T	Chair., Exec. Comm.	Council for the United States and Italy
Michelis, De	Gianni	BI	Minister	Foreign Affairs, Italy
Monti	Mario	BINT,TE	Member	European Commission, Brussels
Moratti	Gian Marco	T	President	Saras-Raffinerie Sade; Chair., Petrolifera Italiana, Rome
Olivetti	Roberto	BI	President (fmr.)	Soc. Gen. Semiconduttori S.P.A.
Padoa-Schioppa	Tommaso	B	Exec. Bd. Member	European Central Bank
Pirelli	Alberto	BI	Mng. Partner (fmr.)	Pirelli & Co., Milan
Pirelli	Leopoldo	BI	Partner	Pirelli & Co.
Profumo	Alessandro	B	CEO	Credito Italiano
Ratti	Giuseppe	T	Board Member	CoeClerici, Genoa
Rocca	Gianfelice	T	Chairman	Techint Europe, Milano
Rognoni	Virginia	BI	Minister	Defense, Italy
Romano	Sergio	TE	Editorialist	Corriere della Sera, Milan; Italian Amb. (fmr.), to USSR
Ronchey	Alberto	BI	Dir. & Corresp. (fmr.)	"La Stampa", Italy
Rossella	Carlo	B	Editor	Editrice La Stampa S.P.A.
Ruggiero	Pierre	T	Executive V. Chairman	Fiat, Turin
Santo	Espirito	BI	President & CEO	Banco Espirito
Saracoglu	Rusdu	B	"Mediator"	EU Community
Savona	Paolo	T	Minister	Industry ,Italy, of
Schmidt-Chiari	Guido	BI,TE	Chairman	Constantia Gp.; (fmr.) Chair., Creditanstalt Bankverein, Vienna
Sheeline	Umberto	T	Vice Chairman	Fiat, Turin

Who's Who of the Elite

Last Name	First & Mid. Name	Org.	Job Title	Affiliation - Company, Organization
Siglienti	Sergio	T	Chairman	Banco Commerciale Italiana, Milan
Silvestri	Renato	T	CEO	Tecnitel, Rome
Silvestri	Stefano	B	Vice President	Istituto Affari Int.
Silvestri	Umberto	TE	Chairman	STET Int., Netherlands; Chairman (fmr.) Telecom Italia
Siniscalco	Domenico	B	Professor	Economics; Dir., Fendazione ENI
Townley	Umberto	T	Mng. Dir. & CEO	STET, Rome (telecommunications)
Tronchetti Provera	Marco	T	Chair. & CEO	Pirelli, Milan
Veltroni	Walter (Valter)	BI	Vice Prime Min.	Italy
Vittorelli	Paolo B.	T	Chairman	Institute Studi Ricerche Defesa, Rome
Zandano	Gianni	T	Chairman	Instuto Bancario San Paolo di Torino
Zannoni	Paolo	BI	Sr. Vice President	Defense & Space, Fiat S.P.A., Italy
			Japan	
Akiyama	Tomiichi	TJ	Sr. Corp. Advisor	Sumitomo Corp.
Amaya	Naohiro	TJ	Executive Director	Dentsu Institute for Human Studies
Aoi	Joichi	TJ	Chairman	Toshiba Corp.
Chino	Yoshitoki	TJ	Vice Chairman	Daiwa Anglo-Japanese Found.;Advisor,Daiwa Securities Co.,Ltd
Ejiri	Koichiro	TJ	Sr. Bd. Advisor	Mitsui & Co., Ltd.
Ejiri	Takashi	TJ	Attorney	Ashai Law Office
Fujii	Hirokai	TJ	President	The Japan Foundation
Fukukawa	Shinji	TJ	Chairman & CEO	Dentsu Inst./Human Stud.;Ex.V.Pres.(fmr.),Kobe Steel Co.
Funabashi	Yoichi	TJ	Columnist	"The Asahi Shimbun"
Gyohten	Toyoo	TJ	President	The Inst. for Int. Monetary Affairs
Hasegawa	Norishige	TJ	Counsellor	Sumitomo Chemical Co., Ltd.
Hashida	Taizo	TJ	Counsellor	Fuji Bank, Ltd.
Hashimoto	Toru	TJ	Chairman	Fuji Bank, Ltd.
Hata	Tsutomu	TJ	Prime Minister (fmr.)	Diet, Japanese ; Min. for Fgn. Afrs.; Minister (fmr.), Fin.
Higuchi	Hirotaro	TJ	Hon. Chairman	Asahi Breweries, Ltd.
Hirose	Gen	TJ	Honorary Chairman	Nippon Life Insurance, Ltd.
Hori	Tetsuya	TJ	President	Long-Term Credit Bank of Japan, Ltd.
Horie	Tetsuya	TJ	Dir. & Sr. Counsellor	The Long-Term Credit Bank of Japan, Ltd.
Hosomi	Takashi	TJ	Chairman	NLI Resch. Inst.; Ch. (fmr.), Overseas Econ. Coop. Fund
Ichimura	Shin'ichi	TJ	Director	Int. Centre for the Study of East Asian Devel., Kitakyushu
Inouye	Kaoru	TJ	Honorary Chairman	Dai-Ichi Kangyo Bank, Ltd.
Ishihara	Hideo	TJ	Chairman	Goldman Sachs (Japan) Ltd.
Ishikawa	Rokuro	TJ	Chairman	Kajima Corp.
Ishikawa	Takeru	TJ	Chairman	Mitsui Marine & Fire Insurance Co., Ltd.
Ito	Tadashi	TJ	Chairman	Sumitomo Corp.
Kadono	Kin'ichi	TJ	Senior Advisor	Toshiba Corp.
Kaji	Motoo	TJ	Chairman	The Int. House of Japan
Kakizawa	Koji	TJ	Member	Diet, Japanese ; Parliament V. Minister of Fgn. Affairs
Kamiya	Fuji	TJ	Dean	Toyo-Eiwa Women's Univ.; Visiting Professor, Keio U.
Kamiya	Ken'ichi	TJ	Director & Counsellor	Sakura Bank, Ltd.
Kaneko	Hisashi	TJ	President	NEC Corp.
Kato	Koichi	TJ	Member	Diet, Japanese ; Chief Cabinet Secretary (fmr.)
Kawaguchi	Yoriko	TJ	Mng. Director	Suntory Ltd.
Kawakatsu	Kenji	TJ	Chairman	Sanwa Bank, Ltd.
Kitamura	Toshi	TJ	Sr. Advisor	Hitachi, Ltd.
Kobayashi	Koji	TJ	Chairman (fmr.)	NEC Corp.
Kobayashi	Shoichiro	TJ	Chairman	Kansai Electric Power Co., Ltd.
Kobayashi	Yotaro	TJ	Chairman & CEO	Fuji Xerox Co., Ltd.
Kojima	Akira	TJ	Director	"The Nikon Keizai Shimbun", and Editorial Page Editor
Kondo	Takeshi	TJ	Man. Director	ITOCHU Corp.
Kono	Shunji	TJ	Chairman	The Tokio Marine and Fire Insurance Co., Ltd.
Kosai	Yutaka	TJ	Chairman	Japan Center for Economic Research
Kosaka	Kenji	TJ	Member	Japanese House of Representatives
Kume	Yutaka	TJ	Chairman	Nissan Motor Co., Ltd.
Kusukawa	Toru	TJ	Chairman	Fuji Research Institute Corp.
Kuwata	Yoshio	TJ	Sr. Exec. Mgr.	Hitachi. Ltd.
Maeda	Shonosuke	TJ	President	Toray Industries, Inc.
Makihara	Minoru	TJ	President	Mitsubishi Corp.
Matsukawa	Michiya	TJ	Sr. Advisor (fmr.)	Nikko Research Ctr., Ltd.
Matsuoka	Seiji	TJ	Special Advisor	Nippon Credit Bank, Ltd.; Chairman (fmr.)
Miyauchi	Yoshihiko	TJ	Pres. & CEO	ORIX Corp.
Miyazaki	Isamu	TJ	Sr. Advisor	Daiwa Institute of Research, Ltd.
Miyazawa	Kiichi	TJ	Prime Minister (fmr.)	Diet, Japanese, now Member of Diet
Miyoshi	Masaya	TJ	Counsellor	Keidanren
Mogi	Yuzaburo	TJ	President & CEO	Kikkoman Corp.
Morikawa	Toshio	TJ	President	Sumitomo Bank, Ltd.
Morishita	Yoichi	TJ	President	Matsushita Electric Industrial Co., Ltd.
Morita	Akio	TJ	Chairman & CEO	Sony Corp.
Morita	Kazuo	TJ	Vice President	Hitachi, Ltd.
Motono	Moriyuki	TJ	Advisor to Board	Nomura Securities Co., Ltd.
Mukaibo	Takashi	TJ	Chairman	Japanese Atomic Ind. Forum; Pres. (fmr.), U. of Tokyo
Murase	Jiro	TJ	Managing Partner	Bingham Dana Murase
Murofushi	Minoru	TJ	President & CEO	ITOCHU Corp.
Nagai	Yonosuke	TJ	Professor	Aoyama Gakuin Univ.

Who's Who of the Elite

Last Name	First & Mid. Name	Org.	Job Title	Affiliation - Company, Organization
Nagasue	Eiichi	TJ	Member (fmr.)	Diet, Japanese
Nakahara	Nobuyuki	TJ	Honorary Chairman	Tonen Corp.
Nakamura	Kaneo	TJ	Counsellor	The Industrial Bank of Japan, Ltd.
Nakamura	Toshio	TJ	Counsellor	The Bank of Tokyo-Mitsubishi, Ltd.
Nishihara	Masashi	TJ	Professor	Nat. Defense Academy, Int. Relations
Noguchi	Teruo	TJ	Chairman & CEO	Koa Oil Co., Ltd.
Ogasawara	Toshiaki	TJ	Publisher-Chairman	"The Japan Times, Ltd."; President, Nifco Inc.
Ogata	Sadako	TJ	High Commissioner	UN High Commission for Refugees
Ogata	Shijuro	TJ	Deputy Gov. (fmr.)	Japan Development Bank
Ohga	Norio	TJ	Chair. & CEO	Sony Corp.
Ohnishi	Masafumi	TJ	Chairman	Osaka Gas Co., Ltd.
Okano	Mitsuyoshi	TJ	President	The Suruga Bank, Ltd.
Okawara	Yoshio	TJ	President	Inst. for Int. Pol. Studies; (fmr.) Amb. to the US
Okita	Yoichi	TJ	Professor	Nat. Inst. for Policy Research
Okuda	Hiroshi	TJ	President	Toyota Motor Corp.
Okumura	Ariyoshi	TJ	Sr. Advisor	IBJ NW Asset Management Co., Ltd.
Owada	Hisashi	TJ	Ambassador (fmr.)	to the U.N.; Vice Minister (fmr.) of Foreign Affairs
Saba	Shoichi	TJ	Advisor to the Board	Toshiba Corp. Ltd.
Saeki	Kiichi	TJ	Sr. Advisor	Institute for International Policy Studies
Saito	Yutaka	TJ	Chairman & CEO	Nippon Steel Corp.
Sato	Seizaburo	TJ	Director	Inst. for Int. Policy Studies
Shibusawa	Masahide	TJ	Director	East-West Seminars
Shiina	Motoo	TJ	Member	House/Councillors; Japanese Chair., UK-Japan 2000 Gp.
Shiina	Takeo	TJ	Chairman & CEO	IBM Japan, Ltd.
Shimokobe	Atsushi	TJ	Chairman	The Tokio Marine Research Institute
Shiozaki	Yasuhisa	TJ	Member	Japanese House of Councillors
Suzuki	Tetsuo	TJ	President	HOYA Corp.
Taida	Hideya	Tj	Man. Director	Marubeni Corp.
Takagi	Tsuyoshi	TJ	President	ZENSEN (Text.,Gmnt,Chem.,Merch.& Allied Ind.Wkrs.Un.)
Takemi	Keizo	TJ	Member	Japanese House of Councillors
Tanaka	Akihiko	TJ	Associate Professor	Univ. of Tokyo, Institute of Oriental Culture
Tanaka	Naoki	TJ	Presodent	The 21st Century Public Policy Institute
Tateishi	Nobuo	TJ	Chair. & Rep. Dir.	OMRON Corp
Tatsumi	Sotoo	TJ	President (fmr.)	Sumitomo Bank, Ltd.
Tomabechi	Toshihiro	TJ	Director	Toppan Moore Co., Ltd.; CEO, Tomabechi Consultants
Toyoda	Eiji	TJ	Honorary Chairman	Toyota Motor Corp.
Toyoda	Tatsuro	TJ	Vice. Chairman	Toyota Motor Corp.
Toyonaga	Keiya	TJ	Vice President	Matsushita Electric Industrial Co., Ltd.
Tsutsumi	Seiji	TJ	Chairman	Saison Corp.
Uetani	Hisamitsu	TJ	Chairman (fmr.)	Yamaichi Securities Co., Ltd, Tokyo
Umemura	Shoji	TJ	Chairman	Nikko Securities Co., Ltd.
Washio	Etsuya	TJ	President	Japan Trade Union Confederation (RENGO)
Watanabe	Fumio	TJ	Counsellor	Tokyo Marine & Fire Insurance Co., Ltd.
Watanabe	Takeshi	TJ	Chairman	Japan Silver Volunteers
Yakushiji	Taizo	TJ	Vice President	Keio Univ.
Yamamoto	Tadashi	TJ	President	Japan Center for International Exchange
Yamashita	Isamu	TJ	Chairman (fmr.)	Trilateral Commission, Japan
Yashiro	Masamoto	TJ	Exec. V. President	Citicorp/Citibank, NA; Country Corp. Officer
Yoneura	Noriyuke	TJ	Man. Director	Fuji Xerox Co. LTD.
Yoshino	Bunroku	TJ	Chairman	Inst. for Int. Economic Studies; Amb. (fmr.) to Germany
			Luxembourg	
Jaans	Pierre	BL	General Manager	Institut Monetaire Luxembourgeois
Santer	Jacques	BL	Prime Minister	Luxemburg
Thorn	Gaston	T	Chairman	Bank Int. a'Luxembourg; President (fmr.), EEC
			The Netherlands	
Banck	Maja	B	Executive Secretary	Bilderberg meetings
Bergh	Maarten A. van den	B	Gp. Mng. Dir.	Royal Dutch/Shell
Beugel	Ernst H., van der	B	Vice President	Royal Dutch Airlines,fmr.Min./State,Fgn.Affrs.
Bolkestein	Fritz	BNL	Parliamentary Leader	VVD (Liberal Party)
Brinkhorst	Laurens-Jan	BNL	Minister (fmr.)	The Netherlands, Foreign Affairs Dept.
Goudswaard	Johan M.	B	Vice Chairman (fmr.)	Unilever N. V.
Grave	Frank H. G. de	BNL	Minister	Defense, The Netherlands
Halberstadt	Victor	BNL	Hon. Sec. General	Bilderberg Gp., Europe & Canada; Professor, Leiden Univ.
Herkstroter	Cor A. J.	B	Chairman	Royal Dutch Shell, The Neatherlands
Hoeven	Cess H. van der	BNL	President	Royal Ahold
Justman Jacob	Poul Louis	BNL	Chairman (fmr.)	Kon. Ned. Hoogovens & Staalfabrieken N.V.
Karsten	C. Frits	BNL	Managing Dir. (fmr.)	AMRO Bk. N.V.; Hon. Treas. (fmr.), Bilderberger Gp.
Knapen	Ben	BNL	Editor-in-Chief (fmr.)	"NRC Handelsblad", The Netherlands
Korteweg	Pieter	BNL	President & CEO	Robeco Gp., The Netherlands; Hon. Treas., Bilderberger Gp.
Lede, van	Cees	TE	Chairman & CEO	Akzo Nobel, Arnheim; Pres. (fmr.), Fed./Netherlands Ind.
Lubbers	Ruud F.M.	B	Prime Minister	The Netherlands
Maas	Cees	T	Exec. Bd. Mbr.	Int. Nederlanden Group (insurance), Amsterdam
Melkert	Ad P. W.	B	Minister	of Social Affairs and Employment
Oort	Conrad J.	BNL	Advisor - Bd. of Mgt.	Algemene Bank Nederland NV
Ruding	H. Onno	T	Vice Chairman	Citicorp/Citibank, New York; Dutch Minister (fmr.) of Finance

Last Name	First & Mid. Name	Org.	Job Title	Affiliation - Company, Organization
Rykens	Paul	B	Hon. Treasurer (fmr.)	Bilderberg Group
Schaik	Gerard, van	T	Chairman	Heineken Breweries, Amsterdam
Scheepbouwer	Ad J.	BNL	Chairman & CEO	TNT Post Group
Scherpenhuijsen Rom	Willem	TE	Chairman (fmr.)	Internationale Nederlanden Group (insurance), Amsterdam
Tabaksblat	Morris	BNL	Chairman	Unilever N.V.
Traa	Maarten, van	T	Member	Dutch Parliament
van Oranje Nassau	Beatrix Wilhelmina	BNL	Queen	The Netherlands
van Oranje Nassau	Johan Friso Bernhard	BNL	Prince	The Netherlands
Voorhoeve	Joris	TE	Member	Dutch Parliament
Vuursteen	Karel	B,T	Chairman/Exec Bd.	Heineken N.V., Amsterdam
Waal	Lodewjk J. de	B	Chairman	Dutch Confed. of Trade Unions (FNV)
Wallage	Jacques	B	Parliamentary Leader	PvdA (Labor Party)
Wijffels	Herman H. F.	B	Chairman	Robobank Nederland
Zijlstra	Jelle	B	President (fmr.)	The Netherlands Bank
Zwan, van der	Arie	TE	Dean	Nijenrode Univ., Breukelen
			Norway	
Brundtland	Arne Olav	B,T	Sr. Research Fellow	Norwegian Institute of International Affairs, Oslo
Clement	Kristin	B	Deputy Dir. Gen.	Norwegian Confed. Of Business & Industry
Ditlev-Simonsen	Per	B	Managing Director	Sverre Ditlev-Simonsen & Co.
Faremo	Grete	T	Vice President	Storebrand; (fmr.) Norwegian Min. of Devel. Cooperation
Hegge	Per Egil	B	Editor	Aftenposten, Norway
Heiberg	Gerhard	T	Partner	Norscan Consulting, Oslo; Chair., Aker. Oslo
Hoegh	Leif	BN	Owner (fmr.)	Norwegian ships
Hoegh	Westye	BN	Chairman	Leif Hoegh & Co.; Pres., Norwegian Shipowners Assoc.
Hojdahl	Odd	B	Vice Chairman (fmr.)	Norwegian Trade Union
Holst	Johan Jorgen	T	Minister	Norway, of Defense
Jagland	Thorbjorn	T	Member	Norwegian Parliamjent; Chairman, Norwegian Labor Party
Lorck	Karl	B	Managing Dir. (fmr.)	Elkem-Spigerverket
Munthe	Preben	T	Professor	Univ. of Oslo; Counselor, Norwegian Nobel Institute
Myklebust	Egil	BN	CEO	Norsk Hydro
Myrvoll	Ole	B	Member (fmr.)	Norwegian Parliament
Petersen	Jan	B	Parliamentary Leader	Censewrvative Party
Stoltenberg	Thorvald	B,T	Co-Chairman (UN) (fmr.)	Steering Comm. of the Int. Conf. on former Yugoslavia
Storvik	Kjell	B	Governor	Bank of Norway
Svanholm	Poul Johan	T	Chairman	Den Danske Bank, Copenhagen
Tidemand	Otto Grieg	B	Shipowner	Oslo, Norway; Min. (fmr.) Norwegian Defense & Econ. Afrs.
Udgaard	Nils M.	BN	Fgn. Editor	Aftemposten
Vaarvik	Dagfinn	BN	Editor-in-Chief (fmr.)	Nationen
Warring	Niels	B	Chairman	Wilhelm Wilhelmsen Limited A/S, Norway
			Poland	
Baczynski	Jerzy	T	Editor-in-Chief	Polityka, Warsaw
Belka	Marek	T	Adv. To President	of Poland; Prof., Inst. Of Economics, Warsaw
Olechowski	Andrzej	B,T	Chairman	Bank Handlowy W Warszawie
Sito	Jerzy	T	Vice President	Polish PEN Club, Warsa; Amb. (fmr.) to Denmark
Suchocka	Hanna	B	Minister	of Justice
Zieba	Father Maciej	TE	Principal	Polish Province of the Dominican Order, Warsaw
			Portugal	
Amaral	Joaquim Freitas do Amaral	BP	Member	Portugese Parliament
Balsemao	Francisco Pinto	BP	Prime Min. (fmr.)	Portugal
Barrosso	Jose Manuel Durao	B	Minister, Fgn. Affairs	Portugal
Borges	Antonio	B,T	Dean	INSEAD
Braga de Macedo	Jorge	T	Professor	Nova Univ., Econ., Lisbon; Min., Portugal, of Finance
Carrilho	Maria	B	Professor	Sociology
Cravinho	Joao Cardona G.	B	Minister	for Infrastructure, Planning & Territorial Admin.
Durao Barrosso	Jose Manuel	B	Minister	Foreign Affairs
Grilo	Eduardo C. Marcal	B	Minister	Portugese Education
Guedes	Salvador	B	Bd. Member	Sogrape, Porto, Portugal
Horta e Costa	Miguel	B	Vice President	Portugal Telecom
Lamego	Jose	T	Secretary	State for Fgn. Affairs & Cooperation, Portugal
Marante	Margarida	BP	Journalist	Television, Portugese
Mateus	Rui	T	Chairman	Emaudio International, Lisbon
Mello, de	Antonio Vasco	B,TE	Chairman	Sociedad de Reparacao e Montagem de Equip. Ind., Lisbon
Menezes Ferreira	Joao de	T	Director	Euroamer, Lisbon; (fmr.) Mbr. of Portugese Parliament
Mexia	Antonio	TE	Chairman	Gas de Portugal & Trangas, Lisbon
Monjardino	Carlos A.P.V.	B	President	Fundacao Oriente, Portugal
Nabo	Francisco Murteira	B	President & CEO	Portugal Telecom
Pimenta	Carlos	B	Member	Eoro. Parliament; fmr. Sec., St.,Environment
Pinho	Ilidio, de	T	Chairman	Colep, Lisbon
Pinto Balsemao	Francisco	T	Chairman	SIC; Prime Minister (fmr.), Portugal
Salgado	Ricardo E. S.	B	President & CEO	Grupo Espirito Santo
Sampaio	Jorge	B	President	of Portugal
Santos	Nicolau	B	Editor-in-Chief	Expresso
Silva	Artur Santos	B	President & CEO	BPI Group
Sousa	Marcelo Robelo de	B	Leader	PSD Party

Last Name	First & Mid. Name	Org.	Job Title	Affiliation - Company, Organization
Tavares	Carlos	T	Chairman	Banca Nacional Ultramarino, Lisbon
Teles	Jose M. Galvao	B	Member	Council of State
Veiga	Miguel	BP	Lawyer	Portugese
Vitorino	Antonio	B	Dep. Prime Minister	and Minister of Defence
			Russia	
Chubais	Anatoli B.	B	1st V. Prim., Chair. (fmr.)	
Shevtsova	Lilia	B	Member	Carnegie Moscow Center
Trenin	Dmitri V.	B	Deputy Director	Carnegie Moscow Center
			Spain	
Aguirre y Gil de Biedma	Esperanza	B	President	Spanish Senate
Almunia Amann	Joaquin	B	Sec. General	Socialist Party
Ballve'	Pedro	T	Chairman	Campofrio Alimentacion, Madrid
Boada Vilallonga	Claudio	T	Honorary Chairman	Banco Hispano-Americano, Madrid
Borbon	H.R.M. Sofia	B	Queen	of Spain
Camps	Victoria	T	Member	Spanish Senate; Prof., Philosophy, Barcelona Univ.
Carvajal Urquijo	Jaime	B,T	Chairman	Dresdner Klainwort Benson S.A.(Spain);Ch.,Ford Espana,Madrid
Ceron Ayuso	Jose' Luis	T	Minister (fmr.)	Trade, Spain; Chairman, ASETA, Madrid
Esperanza	Aguirre y Gil de Biedma	B	President	Spanish Parliament
Etxenike	Pedro Miguel	T	Professor	Basque County U.;(fmr.)Basque Min./Educ,San Sebastian,Spain
Fanjul	Oscar	T	Hon. Chairman	Repsol, Madrid (energy)
Feo	Julio	T	Chairman	Conssultores de Comunicacion y Direccion, Madrid
Ferrer	Carlos	T	Chairman	Ferrer Int. Group; Chair., Int. Vienna Council
Garrigues Walker	Antonio	T	Chairman	Garrigues & Anderson, Madrid
H.R.M.	Sofia	B	Queen	Spain
Herrero de Minon	Miguel	T	Lawyer/Int. Consult.	Private; Member (fmr.), Spanish Parliament
Iglesias	Carmen	T	Member	Royal Spanish Academy of History
Luzon Lopez	Francisco	BE	Chairman & CEO	Argentaria
Maragall	Pascual	T	Mayor (fmr.)	Barcelona
March Delgado	Carlos	T	Chairman	Banca March, Madrid
Pujol	Jordi	BE	President	Generalitat de Catalunya, Spain
Rato Figaredo	Rodrigo, de	B	Parliamentary Leader	Spanish Parliament, Minority Group
Rodriguez Inciarte	Matias	B	Exec. Vice Chairman	BSCH, Spain
Sarasqueta	Antxon	T	Exec. President	Muntimedia Capital; Editor, "Echos", Madrid
Schwartz	Pedro	T	Exec. President	Fundesco, Madrid; Prof., Econ., Autonomous U. of Madrid
Segurado	Jose'	T	Chairman	Jasinas,Madrid;Hon.Chair.,CEIM;Mbr.(fmr.)Span.Parl.
Serra	Narcis	B	Dep. Prime Minister	Spain
Solbes Mira	Pedro	B,T	Member	Spanish Parliament; (fmr.) Min. of Fin. & Agriculture, Madrid
Trillo Figueroa	Federico	B	VP & Member	Parliament (Partido Popular)
Urquijo	Jaime Carvajan	B	Chair. & Gen. Mgr.	Iberfomento
Vargas Llosa	Mario	TE	Writer	Member of the Royal Spanish Academy
Vila Marsans	Jose	T	Chairman	Rhone Poulenc Fibras,Barcelona;Dir.,Banco Central,Madrid
Villalonga	Juan	T	Chairman	The National Telephone Co. (Telefonica), Madrid
Yanez-Barnuovo	Juan A.	B	Permanent Rep.	United Nations, from Spain
Ybarra	Emelio	T	Exec. Chairman	Banco Bilbao-Vizcaya, Madrid
			Sweden	
Aberg	Carl Johan	TE	Board Member	Skandinaviska Enskilda Banken, Stockholm
Aslund	Anders	B	Sr. Associate	Carnegie Endowment for Int. Peace, Swedish
Barnevik	Percy	B	Chairman	Investor AB
Belfrage	Erik	T	Sr. Vice President	Skandinaviska Enskilda Banken, Stockholm
Bergstrom	Hans	B	Political Editor	"Dagens Nyheter"
Bildt	Carl	B,T	Prime Minister (fmr.)	Sweden; Mbr., Swedish Parliament; Chair, Moderate Party
Dennis	Bengt	T	Senior Advisor	Skandinaviska Enskilda Banken, Stockholm
Gustafsson	Stan	B	Chairman	AB Astra, Sweden
Hedelius	Tom C.	BS	Chairman	Svenska Hendelsbanken
Jonung	Lars	BS	Professor	Stockholm School of Economics
Larsson	Stig	BS	President & Dir. Gen.	Swedish Railways
Lundvall	D. Bjorn H.	BS	President (fmr.)	Telefon AB L.M. Ericsson
Palme	S. Olaf	BS	Prime Minister (fmr.)	Sweden
Ramfors	Bo C.E.	B	Mng. Dir. & CEO	Skandinaviska Enskilda Banken, Stockholm
Rojas	Mauricio	B	Assoc. Professor	Lund Univ., Economic History
Rosengren	Bjorn	BS	Minister	Swedish Industry, Employment & Communication
Sahlin	Mona	B	Member	Swedish Parliament
Svanholm	Poul Johan	T	Chairman	Den Danske Bank; (fmr.) Chair., Carlsberg, Copenhagen
Svedberg	Bjorn	B,T	Chairman	Ericsson;(fmr.)Gp.CEO,Skandinaviska Enskilda Banken,Stockhol
Thygesen	Niels	T	Professor	Copenhagen Univ., Economics, Enonomic Institute
Uusmann	Ines J.	B	Minister	Transportation & Communications
Wallenberg	Jacob	B	Chairman	Skandinaviska Enskilda Banken
Wallenberg	Marcus, Dr.	B	Chairman	Skanvinaska Enskilda Banken
Wallenberg	Peter	T	1st Vice Chairman	Skandinaviska Enskilda Banken, Stockholm
Wickman	Krister	B	Governor (fmr.)	Bank of Sweden

Last Name	First & Mid. Name	Org.	Job Title	Affiliation - Company, Organization
			Switzerland	
Ackermann	Josef	B,T	Board Mbr.	Deutsche Bank, Frankfurt-am-Main
Butler	Hugo	BCH	Editor-in-Chief	Neue Zurcher Zeitung
Cotti	Flavio	B	Minister	Switzerland, Foreign Affairs
Delamuraz	Jean-Pascal	B	Vice President	Federal Council; Minister of the Economy
Frehner	Walter	BCH	Chairman	Swiss Bank Corp.
Gasteyger	Curt	BCH	Professor (fmr.)	Graduate Institute of International Studies
Gerber	Fritz	BCH	Chairman	F. Hoffmann-La Roche AG, Switzerland
Gysling	Erich	B	Head (fmr.)	Foreign Dept. of
Heckmann	Hans	BCH	Vice Chairman	Union Bank of Switzerland
Krauer	Alex	BCH	Chair. & Mng. Dir.	Ciba-Geigy, Ltd., Switzerland
Liotard-Vogt	Pierre	B	Chairman (fmr.)	Nestle Alimentana S.A.
Markstaller	Margrit	B		
Maucher	Helmut O.	BCH	Chairman & CEO	Nestle Ltd.
Monnier	Claude	B	Editor-in-Chief (fmr.)	Journal de Geneve
Pury	David, de	BCH	Chairman	de Pury Pictet Turrettini & Co.
Ringier	Michael	BCH	Publisher & Chairman	Ringier Inc., Switzerland
Schmidheiny	Stephan	BCH	Chairman	ANOVA Holdings Ltd.
Schurer	Wolfgang	BCH	Chairman	MS Management Service AG
Sommaruga	Cornelio	BCH	President	Int. Committee of the Red Cross
Umbricht	Victor H.	B	Director (fmr.)	Ciba-Geigy, Ltd., Switzerland
Vasella	Daniel L.	BCH	Chairman & CEO	Novartis AG
Widmer	Siegmund	B	Mayor (fmr.)	Zurich, Member (fmr.), Swedish Parliament
			Turkey	
Akbil	Semih	B	Head (fmr.)	Ministry of Foreign Affairs, Information Dept.
Alp	Ali Hikmet	B	Ambassador	Perminent Representative to the C.S.C.E.
Bayar	Ugur	B	Chairman	Privatazation Admin.
Beyazit	Selahattin	BTR	Director	various companies in Turkey
Bilgin	Dinc	BTR	Chairman	Sabah A.S.
Birgi	M. Nuri	BTR	Turkish Amb. (fmr.)	N.A.T.O.
Boyazit	Selattin	B	Director	Compa, Turkey
Boyner	Cem	BTR	Chairman	New Democracy Movement
Caglayangil	Ihsan S.	B	Minister (fmr.)	Turkish Foreign Affairs
Cem	Ismail	B	Minister	for Foreign Affairs
Cetin	Hikmet	BTR	Deputy Prime Minister	fmr. Minister for Foreign Affairs
Demirel	Suleyman	BTR	Prime Minister (fmr.)	Turkey
Dogramaci	Ihsan	BTR	Professor (fmr.)	Hacettepe Univ., Turkey
Ecevit	Bulent	BTR	Member (fmr.)	Turkish Parliament
Ercel	Gazi	B	Governor	Central Bank of Turkey
Erguder	Ustun	BTR	Rector	Bosporus Univ.
Feyzioglu	Turan	B	Dep. Prm. Min. (fmr.)	Turkey
Gezgin Eris	Meral	BTR	President	IKV (Econ. Devel. Foundation)
Gokmen	Oguz	BTR	Head (fmr.)	Minister of Foreign Affairs, Econonics Dept.
Gonensay	Emre	BTR	Minister	Turkish Foreign Affairs
Halefoglu	Vahit	BTR	Minister(fmr.)	Foreign Affairs, Turkey
Inan	Kamuran	BTR	Member (fmr.)	Turkish Senate
Isik	Hasan F.	BTR	Member (fmr.)	Turkish Parliament
Kazgan	Gulten (Mrs.)	B	Professor (fmr.)	Univ. of Istanbul
Kirac	Suna	BTR	Vice Chairman	Koc Holding A.S.
Koc	Rahmi M.	B	Chairman	Koc Holding, A.S.
Mardin	Serif	BTR	Chairman	American U., Wash. D.C., Dep., Islamic Stud.
Ozceri	Tugay	B	Under Secretary	Ministry of Foreign Affairs, Turkey
Tara	Sinan	BTR	Vice President	Enka Construction & Ind. Inc.
Tunc	Halil	BTR	Chairman (fmr.)	Federation of Turkish Workers Unions
Yasa	Memduh	BTR	Professor (fmr.)	Univ. of Istanbul
Yasar	Selcuk	B	Director (fmr.)	several companies, Izmir
Yucaoglu	Erkut	B	Chairman	Tusiad, Turkey
			Ukraine	
Mityukov	Ihor	B	Minister	Finance, Ukraine
			International	
Bartelds	Hans	TE	Chairman of Exec. Com.	Fortis NL, Utrecht
Berthoin	Georges	T	Int. Hon. Chairman	European Movement: Honorary European Chairman, TC
Bildt	Carl	B,T		The High Representative
Bokros	Lojos	B	Sr. Advisor	The World Bank
Bonino	Emma	BINT	Member	European Parliament
Bottelier	Pieter P.	B	Chief of Mission	The World Bank, Resident Mission in China
Brittan	Leon	B	Vice President	European Commission
Brock	Hans, van den	B	Commissioner	European Communities
Carmoy	Herve' de	TE	Hon. Chairman	Banque Industrialle et Mobiliere Privee (B.I.M.P.), Paris
Clercq	Willy, de	T	Member	Euro. Parliament; Chair., Commission for Fgn. Econ. Rel.
Crockett	Andrew	B	Gen. Mgr.	Bank for Int. Settlement
Cutileiro	Jose	BINT	Secretary General	Western European Union
Dahrendorf	Ralf	B	Director (fmr.)	London School of Economic & Political Science
Declercq	Baron Guido	TE	Hon. Chairman	ORDA-B; Hon. Gen. Admin., Catholic Univ., Leuven

Who's Who of the Elite

Last Name	First & Mid. Name	Org.	Job Title	Affiliation - Company, Organization
Deflassieux	Jean	T	Chairman	Banque des Eschanges Int.;Hon. Chair.,Credit Lyonnais
Dunkel	Arthur	B	Director General	GATT (General Agreement on Tariffs & Trade)
Fischer	Stanley	B,T	1st Dep. Mng. Dir.	IMF
Holm	Niels W.	T	Chairman	Nat. Inst. of Animal Science & Danish Stds. Assoc.
Jochimsen	Reimut	T	President	Central Bank of Northrhine-Westphalia, Dusselodorf
Johnstone	Donald J.	B	Sec. General	OECD
Lahnstein	Manfred	T	Sup. Board Member	Bertelsmann AG, Gutersloh; Fed. Min. (fmr.), Finance
Lennep	Jonkheer Emile, van	BINT	Sec. General (fmr.)	O. E. C. D.
Liikanen	Erkki	B	Member (fmr.)	European Commission (EC)
Lissakers	Karin M.	C	US Executive Director	International Monetary Fund (IMF)
Luns	Joseph M.A.H.	BINT	Sec. General (fmr.)	N. A. T. O.
Owen	Lord	B,T	Co-Chairman (fmr.)	EEC Steering Comm., Int. Confederation of Yugoslavia
Palliser	Sir Michael	T	Vice Chairman	Samuel Montagu & Co.
Roper	John	T	Associate Fellow	Royal Institute of Internastional Affairs (RIIA), London
Ruckelshaus	Hans	T	Chairman of Exec. Bd.	Fortis;Ch./Mng. Dir., Amev, Utrecht; Dir. (fmr.), CFR
Ruggiero	Renato	BINT,TE	Dir. General	WTO/OMC, Geneva; Ex. V.P. (fmr.),FIAT S.p.A., Int. Adv. Bd.
Saracoglu	Rusdu	B	Mediator	EU Community
Schmults	Otto	T	Chairman	East-West Trade Commission; Chair. & CEO O. Wolff I.
Solana Madarings	Javiar	B	Secretary Gen.	N.A.T.O.
Steeg	Helga	BINT	Executive Director	International Energy Agency
Tamaron	El Marques, de	T	Director	Instituto de Cuestiones Internationales y Politica Exterior
Thayer	Lord	T	Director	RTZ Corp.; Chief Cabinet Secretary (fmr.) & Prime Min.
Tidbury	Antonio	T	Chairman	S. e Reparacio e Montagem de Eq. Ind.
Vasco de Mello	Antonio	T	Chairman	Sociedade de Reparacao e Montagem de Equip. Ind., Lisbon
Vries	Gijs M. de	B	Leader	Liberal Group, European Parl.
Wegener	Henning	BINT	Asst. Sec. General	N. A. T. O., for Political Affairs
Weinberg	Serge	T	Chair. & Dir. Gen.	Pinault-Printemps-Redoute Group, Paris;Ch. (fmr.), Rexel
Woerner	Manfred	B	Secretary General	N. A. T. O.

Unidentified at publication date

(The following people are members of the "ELITE", but their affiliations has not been determined at the time
of publication. If you can identiify the job and affiliation of any of the below, and can provide proof,
please send the facts to RIE. We sincerely do appreciate your help.)

Last Name	First & Mid. Name	Org.	Job Title	Affiliation - Company, Organization
Abbot	Charles S.	C		
Abbott	Wilder K.	C		
Abdel-Meguid	Terek	C		
Abercrombie-Winstanley	Gina	C		
Abernethy	Robert John	C		
Adler	Allen R.	C		
Ahern	William Edward	C		
Ahmad	Kamal	C		
Ahn	Woodrow	C		
Aho	C. Michael	C		
Aizenman	Nurith	C		
Akins	James E.	C		
Albright	Alice Patterson	C		
Alexander	Sarah Elizabeth	C		
Allan	F. Aley	C		
Allen	Richard V.	C		
Almond	Michael	C		
Alpern	Alan N.	C		
Alterman	Jon B.	C		
Altman	Emily	C		
Altshuler	David	C		
Andelman	David	C		
Anderson	Charles N., III	C		
Anderson	Joseph A.	C		
Anderson	Laurence Desaix	C		
Anderson	Paul F.	C		
Anderson	Robert	C		
Andrews	David R.	C		
Ansour	M. Michael	C		
Archambeau	Shelly L.	C		
Areizaga-Soto	Jaime A.	C		
Armstrong	DeWitt C., III	C		
Arnavat	Gustavo	C		
Arredondo	Fabiola R.	C		
Ashton	Sarah Scott	C		
Axelrod	Robert M.	C		
Babbitt	Eileen F.	C		
Babbitt	Hasrriet C	C		
Bacon	Kenneth H.	C		
Bagley	Elizabeth Frawley	C		
Baird	Peter W.	C		
Baker	John R.	C		
Baker	Nancy Kassebaum	C		
Bakhash	Shaul	C		

Last Name	First & Mid. Name	Org.	Job Title	Affiliation - Company, Organization
Baldwin	David A.	C		
Band	Laurence Merrill	C		
Barashefsky	Charlene	C		
Barber	James A., Jr.	C		
Barkan	Joel D.	C		
Barr	Michael S.	C		
Barry	Lisa B.	C		
Barshay	Jill	C		
Bartlett	Richard Allen	C		
Bass	Peter Evan	C		
Bauer	Joanne R.	C		
Baumann	Roger R.	C		
Bechky	Perry	C		
Bedrosian	Gregory R.	C		
Beim	Nicholas F.	C		
Bell	Burwell B.	C		
Bell	Gordon P.	C		
Bell	Holley Mack	C		
Bell	Rober G.	C		
Bellamy	Carol	C		
Bellinger	John B. III	C		
Bennett	Andrew	C		
Beplat	Tristan E.	C		
Bergen	Peter	C		
Berkowitz	Bruce D.	C		
Berkowsky	Pamela	C		
Bernard	Kenneth W.	C		
Berrie	Scott D.	C		
Berring	Helle	C		
Berris	Jan	C		
Bersin	Alan D.	C		
Beshar	Peter Justus	C		
Bessie	Simon Michael	C		
Best	William A., III	C		
Beutner	Austin M.	C		
Bewkes	Jeffrey	C		
Bicksler	Barbara	C		
Biddle	George	C		
Biegun	Stephen E.	C		
Biel	Eric R.	C		
Bindenagel	James D.	C		
Birdsall	Nancy	C		
Birenbaum	David E.	C		
Birnbaum	Eugene A.	C		
Bishop	Sanford D., Jr.	C		
Bjorklund	Eric C.	C		
Black	Joseph E.	C		
Blahous	Charles P., III	C		
Blair	Sally Onesti	C		
Blake	Robert O.	C		
Blake	Vaughn R.	C		
Blank	Stephen	C		
Bleier	Edward	C		
Blinken	Donald	C		
Bliss	Richard M.	C		
Bloom	Evan Todd	C		
Bloomberg	Michael R.	C		
Blum	Richard C.	C		
Boardman	Harry	C		
Bob	Daniel E.	C		
Boecker	Paul H.	C		
Bogert	Carrol R.	C		
Boggs	Michael D.	C		
Bohen	Frederick M.	C		
Bollinger	Martin J.	C		
Bond	Robert D.	C		
Booker	Salih	C		
Boone	Theodore S.	C		
Bose	Meena	C		
Bossert	Philip A., Jr.	C		
Botts	John C.	C		
Bowen	Vincent E., III	B		
Bowles	Erskin B.	C		
Bowman	Frank Lee	C		
Braathen	Erik	C		
Bracken	Paul	C		
Bradford	Zeb	C		

Last Name	First & Mid. Name	Org.	Job Title	Affiliation - Company, Organization
Brady	Connor	C		
Brady	Linda Parrish	C		
Brady	Rose	C		
Braitwaite	Rodric	C		
Bramlett	David A.	C		
Brandler	Donald K.	C		
Braunschvig	David	C		
Breck	Henry Reynolds	B		
Brederode	Santos Nuno	C		
Breed	Henry Eltinge	C		
Breindel	Eric M.	C		
Brinkman	L. C.	C		
Britt	David V. B.	C		
Broda	Frederick C.	C		
Brody	Christopher W.	C		
Broitman	Elana	C		
Bronson	Rachel	C		
Brookins	Carol	C		
Brooks	Harvey	C		
Brown	Brian A.	C		
Brown	Cynthia	C		
Brown	Gwendolyn	C		
Brown	L. Dean	C		
Brown	Michael A.	C		
Brown	Tobias Josef	C		
Brown	Kathleen	C		
Browning	David S.	C		
Bruemmer	Melissa L. S.	C		
Brunley	James H. IV	C		
Bryan	Greyson L.	C		
Brzezinski	Ian J.	C		
Brzezinski	Mark F.	C		
Bueno	De mesquita Bruce	C		
Bullard	Edward P.	C		
Bunzel	Jeffrey H.	C		
Burck	William A.	C		
Burgess	Geoffery P.	C		
Busbee	R. Christopher	C		
Bush	Robert C. Jr.	C		
Bushner	Rolland H.	C		
Bussey	Donald S.	C		
Busuttil	James	C		
Buttenheim	Lisa M.	C		
Buultjens	Ralph	C		
Buxbaum	Richard M.	C		
Buyske	Gail	C		
Byrne	Patrick M.	C		
Byrnes	Robert F.	C		
Cabot	Elizabeth	C		
Caesar	Camille M.	C		
Cahill	Kevin M.	C		
Cain	Kenneth L.	C		
Caldwell	Dan	C		
Calhoun	Michael J.	C		
Calingart	Daniel	C		
Callaghy	Thomas M.	C		
Callahan	David L.	C		
Callander	Robert John	C		
Callen	Michael A.	C		
Calleo	David P.	C		
Callwood	Kevin R.	C		
Campbell	Carolyn	C		
Campbell	Thomas J.	C		
Canal	Carlos M., Jr.	C		
Canavan	Christopher	C		
Canfield	Franklin O.	C		
Cannon	James M.	C		
Caputo	Lisa M.	C		
Carey	William D.	C		
Carlos	Manuel Luis	C		
Carlson	Scott A.	C		
Carlson	Steven E.	C		
Carnesale	Albert	C		
Carpendale	Andrew Michael	C		
Carpenter	Ted Galen	C		
Carr	John W.	C		
Carruth	Reba Anne	C		

Last Name	First & Mid. Name	Org.	Job Title	Affiliation - Company, Organization
Carson	C. W., Jr.	C		
Carter	George E.	C		
Carter	James H.	C		
Carter	Mark Andrew	C		
Carter	Theodore N.	C		
Case	Robert A.	C		
Cassidy	Eileen E.	C		
Cates	John M., Jr.	C		
Caufield	Frank J.	C		
Cavanagh	Richard Edward	C		
Cave	Ray	B		
Cebrian	Juan Luis	C		
Cebrowski	Arthur K.	C		
Cha	Victor /d.	C		
Chain	John T., Jr.	C		
Chan	Gerald L.	C		
Chang	David C.	C		
Chang	Gareth C. C.	C		
Chang	Joyce	C		
Chanin	Clifford	C		
Chanis	Jonathan A.	C		
Chao	Victor Tzu-Ping	C		
Chapman	Margaret Holt	C		
Charles	Robert B.	C		
Charpie	Robert A.	C		
Chartener	Robert	C		
Chase	Anthony R.	C		
Chatterjee	Purnendu	C		
Chaves	Robert J.	C		
Checki	Terrence J.	C		
Cheney	Elizabeth L.	C		
Cheney	Stephen A.	C		
Cheremeteff	Kyra	C		
Chickering	A. Lawrence	C		
Choi	Andrey	C		
Chollet	Derek H.	C		
Chorlins	Marjorie	C		
Choucri	Nazli	C		
Christensen	Thomas J.	C		
Christianson	John F.	C		
Christman	Walter L.	C		
Cimbalo	Jeffery L.	C		
Cirincione	Joseph	C		
Clark	J. H. Collum	C		
Clark	Mark E.	C		
Clark	Stephen C.	C		
Clark	Susan Lesley	C		
Clark	William, Jr.	C		
Clarke	Donald C.	C		
Cleveland	Peters Mathews	C		
Cloonan	Edward T.	C		
Clough	Michael	C		
Coan	Louisa	C		
Cobb	Paul Whitlock, Jr.	C		
Cohen	Ariel	C		
Cohen	Betsy H.	C		
Colby	Jonathan E.	C		
Cole	Samual A.	C		
Cole	Thomas Winston Jr.	C		
Coleman	Lewis W.	C		
Coles	Julius E.	C		
Collier	David	C		
Connaughton	James L.	C		
Cook	Gretchen R.	C		
Coolidge	Nicholas J.	C		
Coombs	Philip H.	C		
Cooper	Kathleen B.	C		
Cooper	Rebecca J.	C		
Cott	Suzanne	C		
Cousens	Elizabeth M.	C		
Covey	James "Jock" P.	C		
Cowen	Jeffery	C		
Craner	Lorne W.	C		
Cressey	Roger W., III	C		
Crichton	Kyle C.	C		
Crocker	Bathsheba N.	C		
Cross	Devon G.	C		

Last Name	First & Mid. Name	Org.	Job Title	Affiliation - Company, Organization
Crown	Lester	C		
Cruise	Daniel L.	C		
Cummings	Robert L., Jr.	C		
Cumpiano	Flavio	C		
Curtis	Charles B.	C		
Cusimano	Maryanne K.	C		
Cutshaw	Kenneth A.	C		
Daalder	Iao H.	C		
Dahlman	Michael Keith	C		
Dalton	Gregory	C		
Dam	Marcia W.	C		
Damrosch	Lori Fisler	C		
Daniel	Ana R.	C		
Dash	Michele Samantha	C		
David	Jack	C		
Davis	Allison S.	C		
Davis	Nathaniel	C		
Davis	Stephen M.	C		
Davis	Kim Gordon	C		
Davison	Kristina Perkin	C		
Davison	W. Phillips	C		
Dawisha	Karen Lea	C		
Days	Drew Saunders, III	C		
de Cuba	Jose	C		
de Menil	George	C		
de Menil	Joy	C		
Decyk	Roxanne J.	C		
Del Toro	Carlos	C		
Denham	Robert E.	C		
Denton	James S.	C		
DePalma	Samuel	C		
DePoy	Philip E.	C		
Derr	Kenneth T.	C		
Dertouzos	Michael	C		
DeShazer	Mac Arthur	C		
Deutch	Philip J.	C		
Devine	Caroline M.	C		
Devine	M. Colette	C		
Devine	Thomas J.	C		
Dickey	Christopher S.	C		
Dickson	R. Russell, Jr.	C		
Diebold	William, Jr.	C		
Dinh	Viet D.	C		
DiPaola	Joseph, Jr.	C		
Dixon	Carmen R.	C		
Doerge	David J.	C		
Doherty	William C., Jr.	C		
Donnell	Ellsworth	C		
Donnelly	Harold C.	C		
Dorsen	Norman	C		
Dory	Amanda Jean	C		
Doty	Grant R.	C		
Dowling	John N.	C		
Drittel	Peter Marc	C		
Drucker	Joy E.	C		
Drucker	Richard A.	C		
Druckerman	Pamela	C		
Drumwright	J. R.	C		
Duberstein	Kenneth M.	C		
Due	Johnita P.	C		
Duersten	Althea L.	C		
Duffy	Gloria Charmian	C		
Duke	Robin Chandler	C		
Dunbar	Charles F.	C		
Dunigan	Andrew	C		
Dunigan	P. Andrew	C		
Dunkerley	Craig G.	C		
Dunn	Michael M.	C		
Dunston	Stronica	C		
Dyson	Esther	C		
Earner	William A.	C		
Eberstadt	Nicholas N.	C		
Eckartsberg, von	K. Gayle	C		
Economy	Elizabeth C.	C		
Edelman	Albert I.	C		
Edwards	Mickey	C		
Efros	Laura L.	C		

Last Name	First & Mid. Name	Org.	Job Title	Affiliation - Company, Organization
Einhorn	Robert J.	C		
Eldeman	Richard Winston	C		
Elliott	Inger McCabe	C		
Ellison	Keith P.	C		
Elson	Edward E.	C		
Emerson	Steven A.	C		
English	Robert D.	C		
Ensor	David B.	C		
Entwistle	L. Brooks	C		
Epstein	Barbara	C		
Espy	Charisse	C		
Estrada	Alfredo	C		
Esty	Daniel C.	C		
Evans	Carol V.	C		
Evans	Gail H.	C		
Evans	Tatjana H.	C		
Ewing	Anthony P.	C		
Fairbanks	Charles H., Jr.	C		
Fairman	David M.	C		
Feigenbaum	Evan A.	C		
Feinberg	Richard B.	C		
Feiner	Ava S.	C		
Feinstein	Lee Andrew	C		
Feist	Samuel H.	C		
Ferguson	Charles Henry	C		
Ferguson	Ronald E.	C		
Ferlic	Suzanne	C		
Fernandez	Jose W.	C		
Ferrell	Lisa C.	C		
Fields	Bertram M.	C		
Fields	Craig I.	C		
Fierce	Mildred C.	C		
Fife	Eugene V.	C		
Findakly	Hani K.	C		
Finlayson	Grant Ellison	C		
Finn	James	C		
Finney	Paul B.	C		
Firestone	Charles M.	C		
Fisher	Daniel S.	C		
Fitts	Sarah Watkins	C		
Fitzgibbons	Harold E.	C		
Flaherty	Peter	C		
Flanagan	Peter	C		
Fleischmann	Alan H.	C		
Fleishman	Rachel	C		
Flournoy	Michael A.	C		
Flynn	George J.	C		
Foege	William H.	C		
Foley	S. R., Jr.	C		
Folsom	George A.	C		
Forrester	Anne	C		
Foster	Brenda Lei	C		
Foulon	Mark	C		
Fraga	Arminio	C		
Frank	Andrew D.	C		
Frank	Richard A.	C		
Frankel	Andrew V.	C		
Franklin	William E.	C		
Frazer	Jendayi E.	C		
Fredman	Jonathan M.	C		
Freedman	Eugene M.	C		
Freeman	Bennett	C		
Freeman	Constance J.	C		
Freeman	Roger C.	C		
Freidheim	Stephen C.	C		
Frelinghuysen	Peter H. B.	C		
Freytag	Richard A.	C		
Fribourg	Paul	C		
Friedman	David S.	C		
Friedman	Jennifer	C		
Friedman	Jordana D.	C		
Froman	Michael B. G.	C		
Frye	William R.	C		
Fudge	Ann M.	C		
Fuld	Richard S., Jr.	C		
Fullerton	William Bewick	C		
Galvis	Carlos	C		

Last Name	First & Mid. Name	Org.	Job Title	Affiliation - Company, Organization
Gannon	John C.	C		
Gardner	Antony Laurence	C		
Garnett	Sherman	C		
Gaston	Patricia E.	C		
Gay	Catherine	C		
Gayle	Helen D.	C		
Gebhard	Paul R.S.	C		
Gedo	Inge	C		
Geithner	Timothy F.	C		
Gelb	Amos	C		
Gelb	Bruce S.	C		
George	John M.	C		
Gerson	Eliot F.	C		
Geyelin	Henry R.	C		
Gfoeller	Michael	C		
Gfoeller	Tatiana C.	C		
Ghiglione	Loren	C		
Gibbs	Nancy Reid	C		
Gibney	James Suydam	C		
Gil	Andres V.	C		
Gil	Peter P.	C		
Ginn	Sam	C		
Ginsberg	Marc Charles	C		
Glauber	Robert R.	C		
Globerman	Norma	C		
Gluck	Carol	C		
Glueck	Jeffrey Scott	C		
Goldberg	Andrew C.	C		
Goldberg	Ronnie Lee	C		
Goldin	Harrison J.	C		
Golob	Paul D.	C		
Goodman	John B.	C		
Gordon	John A.	C		
Gorelick	Jamie S.	C		
Gornick	Alan L.	C		
Goss	Porter J.	C		
Gottsegen	Peter M.	C		
Gould	Peter G.	C		
Graff	Robert D.	C		
Graham	Carol Lee	C		
Graham	Lawrence Otis	C		
Graham	Thomas Wallace	C		
Grand	Stephen R.	C		
Grayson	Judy S.	C		
Greathead	R. Scott	C		
Green	Michael Jonathan	C		
Greenberg	David	C		
Greene	James C.	C		
Greene	Wade	C		
Griego	Linda	C		
Griffin	Anne-Marea	C		
Griffith	Alessandra J.	C		
Grimes	Joseoh A., Jr.	C		
Grimes	Julie M.	C		
Guisinger	Stephen E.	C		
Gundlach	Andrew S.	C		
Guptepranay	Haasmimil	C		
Guth	John H.J.	C		
Gutmann	Henning P.	C		
Gwertzman	Bernard M.	C		
Hagel	Chuck	C		
Hagen	Katherine A.	C		
Hale	David D.	C		
Hall	C. Barrows	C		
Hall	John P.	C		
Hallerberg	Mark S.	C		
Halperin	David R.	C		
Halstad	Edward	C		
Hamburg	Jill	C		
Hamilton	Doug N.	C		
Hamilton	Jonathan Carroll	C		
Hammonds	D. Holly	C		
Hansen	Keith Eric	C		
Harari	Maurice	C		
Harmon	James A.	C		
Harris	John M.	C		
Hart	Bill, Jr.	C		

Last Name	First & Mid. Name	Org.	Job Title	Affiliation - Company, Organization
Hart	Brett J.	C		
Hart	Parker T.	C		
Hart	Todd C.	C		
Hartman	J. Lise	C		
Haschigian	Ninial	C		
Hauge	John R.	C		
Hauser	William L.	C		
Havel	Theresa Ann	C		
Hayes	Margaret Daly	C		
Hayward	Thomas B.	C		
Hearn	Ruby P.	C		
Hecker	Siegfried S.	C		
Heep-Richter	Barbara D.	C		
Heifetz	Elaine F.	C		
Heimbold	Charles A., Jr.	C		
Heimowitz	James B.	C		
Heineman	Melvin L.	C		
Heintz	Stephen B.	C		
Heintzen	Harry L.	C		
Hejlik	Dennis J.	C		
Helm	Robert W.	C		
Helton	Arthur C.	C		
Henry	Nancy L.	C		
Hersman	Rebecca K. C.	C		
Heslin	Sheila N.	C		
Hiatt	Fred	C		
Hicks	Irvin, Jr.	C		
Hicks	Kathleen H.	C		
Higginbotham	F. Michael	C		
Higgins	Tracy Eliane	C		
Hill	Joseph C.	C		
Hillen	John	C		
Hobbs	Tammany D.	C		
Hoffenberg	Mark R.	C		
Hoffman	Bruce	C		
Holdren	John P.	C		
Holloway	Dwight F., Jr.	C		
Holmas	Stephen T.	C		
Holtquist	Timothy A.	C		
Hood	Robert E.	C		
Hope	Richard O.	C		
Hornik	Richard H.	C		
Horton	Frank B., III	C		
Horton	Sharon Freeman	C		
Hottelet	Richard C.	C		
Howard	Lyndsay	C		
Howard	M. William, Jr.	C		
Howell	Peter	C		
Howson	Nicholas C.	C		
Hrynkow	Sharon Hemond	C		
Huber	Robert T.	C		
Hughes	Jeffrey L.	C		
Hughes	John	C		
Hughs	Duane L.	C		
Hume	Cameron R.	C		
Huntington	Patricia S.	C		
Hurlock	Matthew	C		
Hutchings	Robert L.	C		
Ignatius	David	C		
Immergut	Mel M.	C		
Irwin	Steven M.	C		
Isaacs	Maxine	C		
Itoh	William M.	C		
Ivester	M. Douglas	C		
Izlar	William H., Jr.	C		
Jaffe	Amy Myers	C		
James	Francis J.	C		
Jebb	Cindy R.	C		
Jessup	Alpheus W.	C		
Johnson	L. Oakley	C		
Johnson	Larry D.	C		
Johnson	Lionel Skipwith	C		
Johnson	Suzanne Nora	C		
Johnstone	V.	C		
Jones	Alan	C		
Jones	Anita K.	C		
Jones	Benjamin Felt	C		

Last Name	First & Mid. Name	Org.	Job Title	Affiliation - Company, Organization
Jones	Kerri-Ann	C		
Jones	Thomas W.	C		
Joost	Peter Masrtin	C		
Jordan	Eason	C		
Joseph	Ira B.	C		
Joseph	Richard A.	C		
Jumper	John P.	C		
Kadlec	Robert	C		
Kagan	Robert W.	C		
Kanak	Donald Perry	C		
Kandell	Jonathan	C		
Kang	C. S. Eliot	C		
Kansteiner	Walter H., III	C		
Kantor	Mickey	C		
Kaplan	Gilbert E.	C		
Kaplan	Harold J.	C		
Karatz	Bruce	C		
Kasdin	Robert	C		
Kassalow	Jordan S.	C		
Kassof	Allen H.	C		
Kathwari	M. Farooq	C		
Kaufman	Daniel J.	C		
Kaufman	Robert R.	C		
Kaufmann	William W.	C		
Kaye	Charles R.	C		
Kaye	Dalia Dassa	C		
Kean	Christopher	C		
Kearns	David T.	C		
Kellen	Stephen M.	C		
Kellerman	Barbara	C		
Kellner	Peter B.	C		
Kellogg	David	C		
Kelly	Arthur L.	C		
Kennedy	Craig	C		
Kerr	Ann	C		
Keydel	John F.	C		
Kezirian	A. Peter, Jr.	C		
Khalidi	Rashid Islam	C		
Kiermaier	John	C		
Kiernan	Robert Edward, III	C		
Kimsey	James V.	C		
Kinde	Lawrence John	C		
King	Charles	C		
King	John A., Jr.	C		
Kirkland	Richard I., Jr.	C		
Kissee-Sandoval	Catherine J.	C		
Kitchen	Helen	C		
Kitchen	Jeffrey C.	C		
Kittrie	Orde F.	C		
Klasky	Helaine S.	C		
Kleiman	Robert	C		
Klein	George	C		
Klemperer, von	Alfred H.	C		
Klissas	Nicholas S.	C		
Klotz	Frank G.	C		
Knox	John H.	C		
Kobak	Deborah J.	C		
Koch	Wendy M.	C		
Kolbe	James T.	C		
Koltai	Steven R.	C		
Korn	Jessica	C		
Kosiw	Michael V., Sr.	C		
Kraeutler	Kirk	C		
Kramek	Robert E.	C		
Kramer	David J.	C		
Kramer	Helen M.	C		
Kranenburg	Hendrik J.	C		
Kranwinkle	C. Douglas	C		
Kriegel	J. L.	C		
Kubisch	Jack B.	C		
Kull	Steven Gordon	C		
Kuniholm	Bruce R.	C		
Kuntstadter	Geraldine	C		
Kuntz	Carol R.	C		
Kutchins	Alison B.	C		
Kwoh	Stewart	C		
Laber	Jeri	C		

Last Name	First & Mid. Name	Org.	Job Title	Affiliation - Company, Organization
Ladd	Edward H.	C		
LaFleur'	Vinca S.	C		
Laird	Venessa	C		
Lamar	Stephen E.	C		
Lamb	Denis	C		
Lambert	Brett B.	C		
Lambeth	Benjamin S.	C		
Landau	Christopher	C		
Landis-Guzman	Lauren R.	C		
Langlois	John D.	C		
Lasser	Lawrence J.	C		
Lauder	Ronald S.	C		
Laurenti	Jeffrey	C		
Lavin	Franklin L.	C		
Leavy	David C.	C		
LeClerc	Paul	C		
Lederer	Ivo John	C		
Lee	Chong-Moon	C		
Lee	Ernest S.	C		
Lee	Janet	C		
Lee	John J.	C		
Lee	John M.	C		
Leebron	David W.	C		
Leeds	Roger S.	C		
Leet	Mildred Robbins	C		
Leghorn	Richard S.	C		
Lehr	Deborah H.	C		
Leich	John Foster	C		
Lempert	Robert J.	C		
Leness	Amanda V.	C		
Leonard	James G.	C		
Lerner-Lam	Eva	C		
Levin	Neal D.	C		
Levine	Marne L.	C		
Levy	Philip I.	C		
Levy	Samuel J.	C		
Lewis	Clifford M.	C		
Lewis	David A.	C		
Li	Lehman	C		
Libby	I. Lewis	C		
Lieber	James Edmund	C		
Lieberman	Henry R.	C		
Lieberman	Jodi B.	C		
Lieberman	Nancy A.	C		
Lieberthal	Kenneth	C		
Lighthizer	Robert E.	C		
Lincoln	Edward J.	C		
Lindquist	Warren T.	C		
Litan	Robert E.	C		
Liu	Maragret	C		
Lockwood	John E.	C		
Loeb	Frances Lehman	C		
Long	Jeffrey W.	C		
Long	Susan M.	C		
Long	T. Dixon	C		
Long	William J.	C		
Loranger	Donald E., Jr.	C		
Lorena	Inmaculada de H.	C		
Lorentzen	Oivind, III	C		
Lovdahl	Randall John	C		
Lowenkron	Barry F.	C		
Lowrey	Dennis Allen	C		
Loy	James Milton	C		
Lozano	Monica C.	C		
Lubin	Nancy	C		
Luu	Thien-Ky	C		
Luzzatto	Ann R.	C		
Lynch	Thomas F., III	C		
Lynn	James T.	C		
Lynn-Jones	Sean M.	C		
Lyons	Richard Kent	C		
Ma	Christopher Yi-Wen	C		
Mabus	Raymond Edwin, Jr.	C		
MacArthur	Douglas, II	C		
MacCormick	Charles F.	C		
MacDonald	Shawn A.	C		
MacGillivray	Adrien	C		

Last Name	First & Mid. Name	Org.	Job Title	Affiliation - Company, Organization
Mackay	Leo Sydney, Jr.	C		
Macy	Robert M., Jr.	C		
Mahoney	Catherine F.	C		
Makins	Christopher J.	C		
Mako	William P.	C		
Malley	Robert	C		
Malmgren	Karen Philippa	C		
Malone	Alice Kimball	C		
Mamdani	Mahmoud	C		
Manca	Marie Antoinette	C		
Mann	Hillary	C		
Manzi	Jim	C		
Marchick	David	C		
Marcucci	Anna Patricia	C		
Marinzoli	A. Roger	C		
Markusen	Ann R.	C		
Marshall	Anthony D.	C		
Marshall	Katherine	C		
Marshall	Z. Blake	C		
Martin	Lisa L.	C		
Martin	Malcolm W.	C		
Martinez	Leo S., Jr.	C		
Massey	L. Camille	C		
Massey	Walter E.	C		
Massie	Suzanne	C		
Mastanduno	Michael	C		
Mastanduno	Michael	C		
Mathews	Eugene A.	C		
Mathews	Michael S.	C		
Mathews	Sylvia M.	C		
Matsukata	Naotaka	C		
Matsuoka	Tama	C		
Maxwell	Kenneth	C		
May	Michael M.	C		
Mayhew	Alice E.	C		
Mc Carter	John W.	C		
Mc Donald	Tom	C		
Mc Keon	Elizabeth	C		
Mc Laughin	Charles J.	C		
Mc Lean	Mora L.	C		
Mc Namara	Thomas E.	C		
McCartan	Patrick F.	C		
McCarthy	James P.	C		
McCarthy	Paul B.	C		
McClary	Topnya D.	C		
McCormick	David H.	C		
McDermott	James A.	C		
McDevitt	Sean Daniel	C		
McFarlane	Jennifer A.	C		
McFarlane	Robert C.	C		
McGuire	Raymond J.	C		
McGurn	William	C		
McHale	Thomas R.	C		
McLin	Jon B.	C		
McManus	Doyle	C		
McNamara	Kathleen R.	C		
McNaugher	Thomas L.	C		
McNeill	Robert L.	C		
McNerney	Michael J.	C		
Meacham	Jon	C		
Mead	Walter R.	C		
Medina	Kathryn B.	C		
Mendelson	Sarah E.	C		
Mendez	Jose F.	C		
Mendlovitz	Saul H.	C		
Mendoza	Roberto G.	C		
Menges	Carl B.	C		
Menke	John R.	C		
Menon	Rajan	C		
Mentzl	Jamie F.	C		
Merkel	Claire Sechler	C		
Merkel	David A.	C		
Merszei	Zoltan	C		
Mertus	Julie A.	C		
Messite	Zach	C		
Mestres	Ricardo A., Jr.	C		
Metcalf	George R.	C		

Last Name	First & Mid. Name	Org.	Job Title	Affiliation - Company, Organization
Meyer	Cord	C		
Meyer	Michael Ryder	C		
Meyerman	Harold J.	C		
Midgley	Elizabeth	C		
Midgley	John J., Jr.	C		
Milestone	Judith B.	T		
Miller	Judith	C		
Miller	Ken	C		
Miller	Matthew L.	C		
Miller	Michelle Beth	C		
Mims	Valerie A.	C		
Mishkin	Alexander	C		
Mitchell	Arthur M., III	C		
Moe	Sherwood G.	C		
Moffett	George	C		
Moffett	Julia	C		
Molano	Walter Thomas	C		
Monroe	Hunter	C		
Montgomery	Mark C.	C		
Montgomery	Philip O'Bryan, III	C		
Moock	Joyce Lewinger	C		
Moore	John J., Jr.	C		
Moore	John M.	C		
Morgan	Thomas E.	C		
Morgenthau	Lucinda L. Franks	C		
Morris	Milton D.	C		
Moskow	Kenneth A.	C		
Moskow	Michael H.	C		
Moss	David	C		
Mudd	Margaret F.	C		
Muller	Edward R,	C		
Muller	Steven	C		
Mullins	Janet	C		
Munyan	Winthrop R.	C		
Murase	Emily Moto	C		
Murdock	Deroy	C		
Murdy	William F.	C		
Murray	Ian P.	C		
Murray	Janice L.	C		
Murray	Leonard, III	C		
Nagl	John A.	C		
Najera	Peter F.	C		
Najjar	Mitri J.	C		
Namkung	K. A.	C		
Nasher	Raymond D.	C		
Nathan	James A.	C		
Nathoo	Raffiq A.	C		
Natt	Ted M.	C		
Navab	Alexander	C		
Nelson	Daniel N.	C		
Nelson	Marie E.	C		
Nelson	Mark A.	C		
Newberg	Esther R.	C		
Newcomb	Nancy	C		
Newman	Frank Neil	C		
Newman	Pricilla A.	C		
Nichols	Nancy Stephenson	C		
Nichols	Rodney W.	C		
Nicholson	Jamie E.	C		
Nielsen	Nancy	C		
Nielsen	Suzanne C.	C		
Nielsen	Waldemar A.	C		
Nizich	Ivan Astrid	C		
Noam	Eli M.	C		
Nolan	Kimberly	C		
Noland	Marcus	C		
Nonacs	Eric S.	C		
Norquist	Grover Glenn	C		
Northrop	Michael F.	C		
Nossel	Suzanne F.	C		
Novicki	Margaret A.	C		
Nuechterlein	Jeffrey D.	C		
O'Malley	Cormac K. H.	C		
O'Prey	Kevin P.	C		
Oakes	John G. H.	C		
Ogden	William S.	C		
Olmer	Lionel H.	C		

Last Name	First & Mid. Name	Org.	Job Title	Affiliation - Company, Organization
Olson	Ronald L.	C		
Ondaatji	Elizabeth Heneghan	C		
Orlins	Stephen A.	C		
Orr	Robert C.	C		
Orszag	Peter R.	C		
Osborn	George K., III	C		
Osisek	Elizabeth M.	C		
Osnos	Susan Sherer	C		
Osterander	F. Taylor, Jr.	C		
Ostermann	Christian	C		
Ostlund	William Brian	C		
Otero	Joaquin F.	C		
Overholster	Geneva	C		
Owen	Vance	C		
Oxman	Bernard H.	C		
Oxnan	Robert B.	C		
Pakula	Hannah C.	C		
Palmer	Mark	C		
Paperin	Stuart J.	C		
Pardew	James W., Jr.	C		
Parent	Alexander	C		
Park	H. K.	C		
Parker	Jay	C		
Parker	Karen E.	C		
Parks	Michael Christopher	C		
Passer-Muslin	Juliette M.	C		
Pastor	Ed	C		
Pastor	Robert A.	C		
Patricof	Alan J.	C		
Patterson	Hugh B., Jr.	C		
Pauker	Guy J.	C		
Paul	Michael G.	C		
Pavel	Barry	C		
Peckham	Gardner G.	C		
Penfield	James K.	C		
Perea-Henze	Raul	C		
Perez	David	C		
Permutter	Amos	C		
Perritt	Henry H., Jr.	C		
Perry	William J.	C		
Peruzzi	Hillary Kircher	C		
Peters	Michael P.	C		
Petersen	Erik R.	C		
Petersen	Holly	C		
Petree	Richard W., Jr.	C		
Petschek	Stephen R.	C		
Phillips	Cecil M.	C		
Piedra	Alberto M., Jr.	C		
Pieezenik	Steve R.	C		
Piercy	George T.	C		
Piercy	Jan	C		
Pierson	Jeffrey D.	C		
Pike	John E.	C		
Pillar	Russell I.	C		
Pilliod	Charles J., Jr.	C		
Pillsbury	Michael	C		
Pilon	Juliana Geran	C		
Pinder	Jeanne	C		
Pinkerton	W. Stewart	C		
Pitts	Joseph W., III	C		
Plank	John N.	C		
Platt	Alan A.	C		
Platt	Alexander Hartley	C		
Plattner	Mark F.	C		
Platz	Stephanie S.	C		
Plaut	Peter G.	C		
Plepler	Richard	C		
Plumeri	Joseph J., II	C		
Pocalyko	Michael N.	C		
Polk	George W.	C		
Polk	William R.	C		
Pollack	Kenneth M.	C		
Pool	Marquita J.	C		
Popkin	Anne Brandeis	C		
Portes	Jonathan D.	C		
Posner	Michael H.	C		
Prager	Robert J.	C		

Last Name	First & Mid. Name	Org.	Job Title	Affiliation - Company, Organization
Prasso	Sheri	C		
Prieto	Daniel B., III	C		
Pruitt	Lisa R.	C		
Pryce	Jeffrey F.	C		
Pryce	William T.	C		
Pulling	Thomas L.	C		
Pusey	Nathan M.	C		
Pyle	Cassandra A.	C		
Quilter	Peter A.	C		
Rabinowitch	Alexander	C		
Radtke	Robert W.	C		
Ralph	Regan Elizabeth	C		
Ramirez	Lilia L.	C		
Ramo	Joshua Cooper	C		
Rankin	Clyde E., III	C		
Rappaport	Alan H.	C		
Rashish	Myer	C		
Rasmussen	Nicholas J.	C		
Ravitch	Samantha F.	C		
Reback	Sanford C.	C		
Reese	William S.	C		
Reeves	Jay B. L.	C		
Reichart	William M.	C		
Reichert	Douglas D.	C		
Reid	Whitelaw	C		
Reinhart	Carmen M.	C		
Reinharz	Jehuda	C		
Reinke	Fred W.	C		
Reynolds	Carolyn A.	C		
Rhodes	Thomas L.	C		
Rice	Susan E.	C		
Rich	Bryan A.	C		
Rich	John H., Jr.	C		
Richards	Stephen H.	C		
Richardson	David B.	C		
Richardson	Richard W.	C		
Richardson	William R.	C		
Richardson	Yolanda C.	C		
Richter	Anthony H.	C		
Richter	Anthony H.	C		
Ries	Hans A.	C		
Rifkind	Robert S.	C		
Rivas-Vasquez	A. Victoria	C		
Robert	Joseph E., Jr.	C		
Roberts	Brad	C		
Roberts	Richard T.	C		
Robinson	Barbara Paul	C		
Robinson	Elizabeth L.	C		
Robinson	Eugene Harold	C		
Roche	James G.	C		
Rocke	Mark D.	B		
Rohan	Karen	C		
Roman	Nancy E.	C		
Romberg	Alan D.	C		
Romero	Anthony D.	C		
Rondeau	Ann E.	C		
Rose	Charlie Peete, Jr.	C		
Rosen	Daniel H.	C		
Rosen	Jane K.	C		
Rosen	Robert L.	C		
Rosen	Stephen P.	C		
Rosenblatt	David S.	C		
Rosenthal	Mitchell	C		
Rosenwald	E. John, Jr.	C		
Rosin	Axel G.	C		
Ross	Anne	C		
Ross	James D.	C		
Ross	Robert S.	C		
Ross	Roger	C		
Roth	Katheryn G.	C		
Rottenberg	Linda D.	C		
Route	Ronald A.	C		
Rowny	Edward L.	C		
Ruenitz	Robert M.	C		
Ruga	Raimundo L.	C		
Rugh	William A.	C		
Rupp	George	C		

Last Name	First & Mid. Name	Org.	Job Title	Affiliation - Company, Organization
Russin	Elizabeth	C		
Rustow	Dankwart A.	C		
Ryan	John Thomas, Jr.	C		
Saenz	Thomas A.	C		
Sakoian	Carl	C		
Salazar	Ana Maria	C		
Salem	George R.	C		
Samore	Gary	C		
Samuels	Nathaniel	C		
Sanchez	Miguel A.	C		
Sanchez	Orlando	C		
Sandberg	Sheryl K.	C		
Sandel	Michael J.	C		
Sander	Alison B.	C		
Sanders	Robin Renee	C		
Sargeant	Stephen T.	C		
Saunders	Paul J.	C		
Saunders	Phillip C.	C		
Saylor	Lynne S.	C		
Schadlow	Nadia C.	C		
Schaffer	Howard B.	C		
Schaffer	Teresita C.	C		
Schecter	Jerrold	C		
Schenk	James R.	C		
Scher	Robert M.	C		
Schiff	Frank W.	C		
Schlefer	Mark P.	C		
Schlesinger	Jacob M.	C		
Schmenann	Anya	C		
Schoen	Douglas E.	C		
Schrage	Elliot J.	C		
Schroeder	Christopher M.	C		
Schultz	William F.	C		
Schumacher	Edward	C		
Schuyler	C. V. R.	C		
Schwab	William B.	C		
Schwartz	Adam	C		
Schwartz	Ethan	C		
Schwarz	Benjamin C.	C		
Scott	David Wilson	C		
Seagrave	Norman P.	C		
Seaton	James B., III	C		
Seidenberg	Ivan	C		
Selin	Douglas	C		
Shailor	Barbara	C		
Shair	Beth L.	C		
Shambaugh	David	C		
Shapiro	Andrew J.	C		
Shaplen	Jason T.	C		
Shayne	Herbert M.	C		
Sheehan	Kevin P.	C		
Sheffield	James R.	C		
Shelley	Sally Swing	C		
Shenk	Maury David	C		
Sherman	Michael	C		
Sherman	Wendy R.	C		
Shields	Lisa Katherine	C.		
Shiffman	Gary M.	C		
Shire	Jacqueline	C		
Shoemaker	Christopher Cole	C		
Shore	Jennifer	C		
Shorr	David	C		
Showalter	Vinca	C		
Sigal	Leon V.	C		
Silver	Allison	C		
Simmons	P. J.	C		
Simmons	Ruth J.	C		
Simons	Julie A.	C		
Sims	Albert G.	C		
Sinclair	Paula J.	C		
Slade	David R.	C		
Smith	Clint N.	C		
Smith	DeWitt C., Jr.	C		
Smith	Gare A.	C		
Smith	John McCall	C		
Smith	Perry M.	C		
Smith	Peter Hopkinson	C		

Last Name	First & Mid. Name	Org.	Job Title	Affiliation - Company, Organization
Smith	Theodore M.	C		
Smith	Tony	C		
Snider	Don M.	C		
Snyder	Craig	C		
Snyder	David M.	C		
Snyder	L. Britt	C		
Snyder	Scott A.	C		
Solbert	Peter O. A.	C		
Solomon	Andrew W.	C		
Solomon	Anthony M.	C		
Solomon	Joshua N.	C		
Solomon	Lisa J.	C		
Sonne	Christian R.	C		
Southwick	James D.	C		
Speedie	David C.	C		
Spiegal	John W.	C		
Spindler	J. Andrew	C		
Springer	Jenny	C		
Stackpole	D. Andrew	C		
Stalson	Helena	C		
Stankard	Francis X.	C		
Stanton	R. John, Jr.	C		
Staples	Eugene S.	C		
Starr	Jeffrey M.	C		
Steadman	Richard C.	C		
Stebbins	James H.	C		
Stedman	Louellen	C		
Stein	Mark B.	C		
Steinberg	Mark R.	C		
Steiner	Steven E.	C		
Steinfeld	Edward S.	C		
Stern	David Joel	C		
Stern	H. Peter	C		
Stern	Jeffrey	C		
Stern	Jessica E.	C		
Stern	Todd D.	C		
Sternlight	David	C		
Stetson	Anne	C		
Stevens	Charles R.	C		
Stid	Daniel D.	C		
Stifel	Laurence D.	C		
Stiles	Deborah F.	C		
Stiles	Ned B.	C		
Stockton	Paul Noble	C		
Stone	Randall	C		
Strmecki	Marin J.	C		
Stromseth	Jane E.	C		
Suits	Christopher D.	C		
Sulkin	Seth R.	C		
Sullivan	Louis W.	C		
Sullivan	Margaret C.	C		
Suslow	Leo A.	C		
Sutphen	Mona K.	C		
Sweig	Julia E.	C		
Sweitzer	Brandon W.	C		
Swiers	Peter Bird	C		
Swigert	James W.	C		
Tahir-Kheli	Shirin R.	C		
Taliaferro	Jeffery	C		
Talwar	Puneet	C		
Tang	Angelica	C		
Tarter	C. Bruce	C		
Tashkovich	Geligor A.	C		
Taylor	Kathryn Pelgrift	C		
Teeter	Robert M.	C		
Tellis	Ashley J.	C		
Temple-Raston	Dina Simone	C		
Tennyson	Leonard B.	C		
Thery	Jane L. Barber	C		
Thomas	Evan W., III	C		
Thomas	James P.	C		
Thomas-Lake	Hillary	C		
Thompson	Robert L.	C		
Thomson	James C., Jr.	C		
Thornton	Thomas P.	C		
Thoron	Louisa	C		
Tien	Chang-Lin	C		

Last Name	First & Mid. Name	Org.	Job Title	Affiliation - Company, Organization
Tien	John K., Jr.	C		
Tiersky	Ronald	C		
Tillman	Seth P.	C		
Timothy-Lankester	Kristen	C		
Tindell	Cynthia A.	C		
Tirana	Amina	C		
Todd	Maurice Linwood	C		
Ton	Tuong-Vy	C		
Topping	Audrey Ronning	C		
Torano	Maria Elena	C		
Tornz	Michael R.	C		
Torres	Art	C		
Torres	Esteban Edward	C		
Trenkle	Timothy Paul	C		
Trice	Robert H., Jr.	C		
Trimble	Charles R.	C		
Trojan	Vera M.	C		
Tsehai	Elizabeth	C		
Tu	Lawrence P.	C		
Tucher	H. Anton	C		
Tucker	Katherine K.	C		
Tucker	Richard F.	C		
Tuminez	Astrid S.	C		
Turck	Nancy B.	C		
Ulman	Cornelius M.	C		
Ungeheuer	Frederick	C		
Urfer	Richard P.	C		
Usher	William R.	C		
Utgoff	Victor A.	C		
Vagliano	Sara	C		
Valenta	Jiri	C		
Van Ouderan	John	C		
Vanden Heuvel	Jon	C		
Vanderlugt	Robert D.	C		
Varanini	Jeffery Paul	C		
Varela	Marta B.	C		
Vecchi	Sesto	C		
Vecchio	Mark S.	C		
Veit	Carol M.	C		
Veit	Lawrence A.	C		
Venable	Nicole Y.	C		
Verleger	Philip K., Jr.	C		
Verstandig	Toni Grant	C		
Vessey	John W.	C		
Vidal	David J.	C		
Viebranz	Curtis G.	C		
Viederman	Stephen	C		
Viets	Richard Noyes	C		
Vincent	Eric	B		
Vine	Richard D.	C		
Volgelson	Jay M.	C		
von Lipsey	Rod	C		
Wacsh	Michael H.	C		
Waddell	Rick	C		
Wahl	Nicholas	C		
Wahlestedt	April	C		
Waldron	Arthur Nelson	C		
Walker	G. R.	C		
Walker	Jaceques P.	C		
Walking	Sarah K.	C		
Wallace	Roger Windham	C		
Wallander	Celeste A.	C		
Wallich	Christine	C		
Walton	Anthony J.	C		
Walton	Reginald K.	C		
Ward	Jennifer C.	C		
Ward	John W.	C		
Ward	Katherine T.	C		
Ward	Patrick J.	C		
Ware	Carl	C		
Warner	John William	C		
Warren	Lewis, Jr.	C		
Washburn	Abbott M.	C		
Washburn	John L.	C		
Watson	Peter S.	C		
Watts	John H.	C		
Watts	William	C		

Last Name	First & Mid. Name	Org.	Job Title	Affiliation - Company, Organization
Way	Alva O.	C		
Weaver	David R.	C		
Weaver	George L. P.	C		
Webb	Hoyt K.	C		
Webble	Steven	C		
Weber	Doron	C		
Weber	Steven	C		
Webster	William H.	C		
Wechsler	William F.	C		
Wedgwood	Ruth N. Glushien	C		
Weeks	Jennifer R.	C		
Weiksner	George B., Jr.	C		
Weinert	Richard S.	C		
Weinrod	W. Bruce	C		
Weisberg	Jacob	C		
Weiss	Andrew S.	C		
Weissman	Ivan S.	C		
Welch	Jasper A., Jr.	C		
Welch	Larry D.	C		
Wells	Walter N.	C		
Wesbrook	Stephen D.	C		
Weschler	Joanna	C		
Wesley	Edwin J.	C		
West	Owen O' Driscoll	C		
Wheeler	John K.	C		
Whitaker	Jennifer Seymour	C		
White	Julia A.	C		
White	Peter C.	C		
White	Timothy J.	C		
Wilds	Walter W.	C		
Wiley	W. Bradford	C		
Wilhelm	Harry E.	C		
Willey	Fay	C		
Williams	Christine	C		
Williams	Melvin F., Jr.	C		
Williams	Paul R.	C		
Williamson	Edwin A.	C		
Williamson	Richard S.	C		
Wilson	Heather A.	C		
Wilson	Karen	C		
Wilson	Margaret Scarbrough	C		
Wilson	Percy C.	C		
Winokur	Herbert S., Jr.	C		
Winslow	Richard S.	C		
Wolf	Ira	C		
Wolosky	Lee S.	C		
Wood	Joseph R.	C		
Wood	Suzanne	T		
Woolsey	Suzanne H.	C		
Worden	Mary Stuart "Minky"	C		
Wormuth	Christine E.	C		
Wright	Abi E.	C		
Wright	L. Patrick	C		
Wright-Carozza	Paolo G.	C		
Wyatt-Walter	Holly	C		
Yacoubian	Mona	C		
Yang	James Ting-Yeh	C		
Yang	Linda Tsao	C		
Yang	Phoebe L.	C		
Yee	Melinda C.	C		
Yordan	Jaime E.	C		
Young	Edgar B.	C		
Young	M. Crawford	C		
Young	Peter Joel C.	C		
Yu	Peter M.	C		
Yudkin	Richard A.	C		
Zaccaro	Donna A.	C		
Zagoria	Donald S.	C		
Zaleski	Michael	C		
Zegart	Amy B.	C		
Zeikel	Arthur	C		
Zelikow	Philip D.	C		
Zemmol	Jonathan I.	C		
Zinni	Anthony Charles	C		
Zinser	Alan	C		
Zipp	Brian R.	C		
Zisk	Kimberly Marten	C		

Bilderberg, Council on Foreign Relations
& Trilateral Commission Members

Sorted by Name

1991-99 Bilderberg Group, Council on Foreign Relations & Trilateral Commission Members

Source: '93 - '99 CFR Annual reports. & TC Master Membership lists ('93-'99); SPOTLIGHT '91 Reprint, + '95, '96, '97 & '99 issues,
Liberty Lobby, Inc., 300 Independence Ave., SE, Washington, DC 20003; attendees at Baden-Baden, Germany meeting of Bilderbergs
Who's Who in America '94, by Marquis, '93 & '94 annual reports., documents from various Think Tanks & other organizations.
Org.: B = US Bilderberg, BA = Austria, BB = Belgium, BC = Canada, BCH = Switzerland, BD = Germany, BK = Denmark, BE = Spain
BF = France, BFIN = Finland, BGB = Great Britain, BGR = Greece, BH = BB Hungary, BI = Italy, BICE = Iceland, BINT = International
BIRL = Ireland, BL = Luxembourg, BN = Norway, BNL = BB, The Netherlands, BP = BB, Portugal, BPL = Poland, BRUS=Russia, BS
BTR = Turkey, C = Council on Foreign Relations, T = Trilateral Commission, TC = T Canada, TE = T Europe, TJ = T Japan, (fmr.) = f
"Members" applies to Bilderberg Steering Committee and Advisory Committee members, but other participants are Bilderberg "Attende

Last Name	First & Mid. Name	Org.	Job Title	Affiliation - Company, Organization
Aaron	David L.	C	Representative	UN; (fmr.) Nat. Security Advisor, Jimmy Carter
Abbot	Charles S.	C		
Abbott	Wilder K.	C		
Abboud	Alfred Robert	C	Chairman & CEO	First City BankCorp, Houston
Abboud	Labeeb M.	C	Group Counsel	American Express Bank, LTD.
Abdel-Meguid	Terek	C		
Abegglen	James C.	C	Chairman	Gemini Consulting, (Asia)
Abel	Elie	C	Professor	Stanford Univ.
Abercrombie-Winstanley	Gina	C		
Aberg	Carl Johan	TE	Board Member	Skandinaviska Enskilda Banken, Stockholm
Abernethy	Robert John	C		
Abram	Morris B.	C	US Ambassador	United Nations European office, Geneva
Abramowitz	Morton I.	C	Pres. & Mbr. Edit. Bd.	Carnegie Endow.; US Ambassadore (fmr.), to Turkey
Abrams	Elliott	C	Sr. Fellow	Hudson Institute; Secretary (fmr.), State Dept.
Abs	Herman	BD	Chairman (fmr.)	Deutsche Bank AG, Frankfurt am Main
Abshire	David M.	C,T	President	Ctr. for Strat. & Int. Stud.; Amb. (fmr.), N. Atlan. Coun.
Aburdene	Odeh Felix	C	Managing Partner	Capital Trust
Ackerman	Peter	C	Managing Dir.	Rockport Finabcial Ltd., Dir., Cato Institute
Ackermann	Josef	B,T	Board Mbr.	Deutsche Bank, Frankfurt-am-Main
Ackley	Gardner	T	Disting. Prof. (fmr.)	Univ. of Michigan
Adams	Gordon M.	C	Assoc. Dir.	O. M. B.
Adams	Robert McCormick	C	Professor	John Hopkins Univ.
Adams	Ruth Salzman	C	Dir. & Senior Advisor	John D. & Catherine T. MacArthur Foundation
Adelman	Kenneth Lee	C	Syndicated Columnist	Tribune Media Services; Asst. Sec. (fmr.), Defense Dept.
Adler	Allen R.	C		
Adler	Lionello	TE	Chairman	Banca Commerciale Italiana, Milan
Agnelli	Giovanni	BI	Hon. Chairman	Fiat S.P.A., Italy; Strg. Comm. Mbr., Bilderberger Gp.
Agnelli	Umberto	BI,TE	CEO & V.-Chair.	IFI; Chair., IFIL - Fianziaria di Partecipazioni S.p.A.
Agnew	Harold M.	C	Senator (fmr.)	New Mexico
Agronsky	Martin	C	Comentator	NBC News
Aguirre	Horacio	C	Advisor/Bd.	Cuban American Nat. Foundation
Aguirre y Gil de Biedma	Esperanza	BE	President	Spanish Senate
Ahern	William Edward	C		
Ahlstrom	Krister Harry	BFIN,TE	Chairman	Ahlstrom Group, Helsinki
Ahmad	Kamal	C		
Ahn	Woodrow	C		
Aho	C. Michael	C		
Aho	Esko	BFIN	Prime Minister	Finland
Ahtisarri	Martti	BFIN	President	Republic of Finland
Aidinoff	Merton Bernard	C	Board Member	Center for National Policy
Aird	John B.	BC	Sr. Partner (fmr.)	Aird, Zimmerman & Berlis
Aizenman	Nurith	C		
Ajami	Fouad	C	Contributing Editor	U.S. News & World Report
Akbil	Semih	BTR	Head (fmr.)	Ministry of Foreign Affairs, Information Dept.
Akers	John F.	C	Director	Pepsico, Inc.
Akins	James E.	C	Ambassador (fmr.)	Saudi Arabia
Akiyama	Tomiichi	TJ	Sr. Corp. Advisor	Sumitomo Corp.
Albert	Michel	B,T	Member	l'Inst.de France;Mbr.,Coun./Mon.Pol.,Banque de France
Albright	Alice Patterson	C	Daughter	of Madeline Albright, UN Ambassador
Albright	Archie Earl	C	Chairman	Ecogen, Inc.
Albright	Madeleine K.	C	Secretary	State, State Dept.; Amb. (fmr.), United Nations
Alderman	Michael Harris	C	Department Chairman	Albert Einstein College of Medicine
Aldrich	George H.	C	Legal Assistant	Supreme Court, Justice Byron A. White
Alexander	Robert Jackson	C	Professor (fmr.)	Rutgers Univ.
Alexander	Sarah Elizabeth	C		
Alford	William Parker	CC	Professor (fmr.)	Univ. of Western Ontario
Allaire	Paul Arthur	B,C,T	Ch.,CEO/Ch.,Ex.Com.	Xerox Corp.; Dir., Sara Lee Corp.; Dir., CFR
Allan	F. Aley	C		
Allbritton	Joe Lewis	C	Chairman	Riggs AP Bank Ltd., London
Allen	Jodi T.	C	Editor	Slate
Allen	Lew, Jr.	C	Chief-of-Staff (fmr.)	Air Force
Allen	Robert E.	C	Chairman & CEO	AT&T; Dir., Pepsico, Inc.; Dir., CFR
Allen	Richard V.	C		
Allison	Graham Tillety, Jr.	B,C,T	Advisory Bd. Member	Center for National Policy; Director (fmr.), CFR
Allison	Richard Clark	C	Judge	Iran-US Claims Tribunal, The Hague
Almond	Michael	C		

Last Name	First & Mid. Name	Org.	Job Title	Affiliation - Company, Organization
Almunia Amann	Joaquin	BE	Sec. General	Socialist Party
Alp	Ali Hikmet	B	Ambassador	Perminent Representative to the C.S.C.E.
Alpern	Alan N.	C		
Alphand	Herve	BF	Sec. General (fmr.)	French Foreign Office
Alphandery	Edmond	T	Chairman	Caisse Nationale de Prevoyance, Paris
Alterman	Jon B.	C		
Altman	Emily	C		
Altman	Roger C.	C	Deputy Sec. (fmr.)	Treas. Dept.;Actg. CEO/RTC; V. Chair., Blackstone Gp.
Altman	Sidney	C	Professor	Yale Univ.
Altschul	Arthur Goodhart	C	Chairman	General American Investors Co.
Altshuler	David	C		
Alvarado	Donna M.	C	Director	Harnischfeger Ind, Inc.
Amaral	Joaquim Freitas do Amaral	BP	Member	Portugese Parliament
Amaya	Naohiro	TJ	Executive Director	Dentsu Institute for Human Studies
Ambrosetti	Alfredo	BI	Chairman	Ambrosetti Group, Italy
Ames	Oakes	C	Chairman	Rhodes Scholarship Selection Commission
Amos	Deborah	C	Correspondent	ABC News
Andelman	David	C		
Andersen	Bodil Nyboe	BDK	Governor	Central Bank of Denmark
Andersen	K. B.	BDK	Minister (fmr.)	Denmark, Foreign Affairs
Anderson	Charles N., III	C		
Anderson	David	C	Director	Aspen Inst., Berlin; US Ambassador (fmr.) to Yugoslavia
Anderson	Harold W.	C	President (fmr.)	Kansas City Fed. Reserve Sustem
Anderson	John Bayard	C,T	Congressman (fmr.)	Illinois; '80 candidate for President
Anderson	Joseph A.	C		
Anderson	Laurence Desaix	C		
Anderson	Lisa	C	Professor	Colombia Univ., Political Science
Anderson	Marcus A.	C	Air Force I.G.	Defense Dept., Air Force, Lt. General
Anderson	Paul F.	C		
Anderson	Robert	C		
Anderson	Robert Orville	B,C	Chairman (fmr.)	Atlantic Richfield Co. (ARCO)
Andreae	Charles N., III	C	President	Andreae & Associates
Andreas	Dwayne Orville	B,C,T	Chairman & CEO	Archer Daniels Midland Co. (ADM)
Andreas	Terry	C	Author	"The Flock Report in Perspective"
Andrews	David R.	C	Lawyer	ABA, Natural Resources Section
Androsch	Hannes	BA	Minister	Austria, Finance
Angermeyer	Joachim-Hans	BD	Member (fmr.)	German Bundestag, FDP; Chair., Siko-Consult GmbH & Co.
Angulo	Manuel Rafael	C	Partner	Curtis, Mallet-Prevost, Colt & Mosle, NYC
Ansour	M. Michael	C		
Anthoine	Robert	C	Senior Counsel	Winthrop, Stimson, Putnam & Roberts, London
Anthony	John Duke	C	President & CEO	Nat. Counsil on U.S.-Arab Relations, Wash.
Aoi	Joichi	TJ	Chairman	Toshiba Corp.
Apgar	David Puschel	C	Sr. Policy Advisor	Treasury Dept., Controller of the Currency
Apodaca	Jerry	C	Governor (Fmr)	New Mexico, '75-'79
Aponte	Mari Carmen	C	U.S. Amb.	to Dominican Republic
Apter	David Ernest	C	Professor	Yale Univ.
Araskog	Rand Vincent	C,T	Chair., Pres. & CEO	ITT Corp.
Archambeau	Shelly L.	C		
Arciniega	Tomas Abel	C	President	California State Univ., Bakersfield
Arcos	Cresencio S.	C	US Ambassador	State Dept., Honduras
Areizaga-Soto	Jaime A.	C		
Argyros	Sterios	BGR,TE	Member	European Parliament
Arledge	Roone	C	President	ABC News; Creator of Wide World of Sports
Armacost	Michael Hayden	C,T	President	Brookings Inst.; Mbr.,Asia Found.; Amb. (fmr.), Japan
Armenise	Giovanni Auletta	TE	Chairman	Banca Nazionale dell' Agricoltura, Rome
Armstrong	Anne Legendre	C,T	Chairman	Ctr. for Strat. & Int. Stud.; US Amb. (fmr.), U. K.
Armstrong	C. Michael	C	Chairman & CEO	GM Hughes Electronics Corp.
Armstrong	DeWitt C., III	C		
Armstrong	John Alexander	C	Vice President	IBM Corp.; Professor (fmr.), Univ. of Wisconsin
Armstrong	Lord of Ilminster	TE	Director	R.T.Z. Corp.,London;Chief Cabinet Off.(fmr.)/Prime Min.
Armstrong	Roland Arthur	C	V. Pres./Gen. Counsel	Howmet Corp.
Armstrong	Willis C.	C	Agent	CIA, Ottawa, Canada 5862
Arnavat	Gustavo	C		
Arnhold	Henry H.	C	Chairman	Arnhold & Bleichroeder
Arnold	Millard W.	C	Member (fmr.)	Carnegie Endowment for International Peace
Aron	Adam M.	C	Chairman & CEO	Vail Resorts (Real Estate)
Aronson	Jonathan D.	C	Professor	Univ. of Southern Cal.
Arredondo	Fabiola R.	C		
Arsenis	Gerasimos	BGR	Minister of Defense	Greece
Art	Robert J.	C	Member	Political Science Quarterly, Ed. Adv. Board
Arthurs	Alberta Bean	C	Director	Rockefeller Foundation
Artzt	Edwin L.	C	Chairman & CEO	Proctor & Gamble Co.
Asencio	Diego C.	C	Executive Director	Florida International Affairs Commission
Asher	Bernard	T	Chairman	HSBC Investment Bank, London
Asher	Robert E.	C	Member	Overseas Development Council
Ashton	Sarah Scott	C		
Aslund	Anders	BS	Sr. Associate	Carnegie Endowment for Int. Peace, Swedish

Last Name	First & Mid. Name	Org.	Job Title	Affiliation - Company, Organization
Asmus	Ronald D.	C	Author	"A United Germany"
Aspin	Les	C	Secretary (fmr.)	Defense Dept.; Senator (fmr.)
Assevero	Vicki-Ann E.	C	Member	Overseas Development Council
Assousa	George E.	C	Writer	*Scientific America*
Atherton	Alfred Leroy, Jr.	C	Board Member	Hariri Foundation
Attali	Jacques	BF	Professor (fmr.)	Ecole Polytechnique
Atwood	John Brian	C	Under Secretary	St. Dept., Mgt.; Admin., US Int. Devel. Coop. Agency
Auer	James E.	C	Physician	St. Lukes Medical Center, Milwaukee
Auspitz	Josiah Lee	C	Advisor	Comm. For the Study of the Amer. Electorate
Ausubel	Jesse Huntley	C	Director	Rockefeller Univ., Prog. for the Human Environment
Avedon	John F.	C	Author	"In Exile from the Land of Snows"
Axelrod	Robert M.	C		
Axworthy	Lloyd	BC	Minister	Canadian Foreign Affairs
Ayers	Harry Brandt	C	Board Member	Southern Center for International Studies, Atlanta
Babbitt	Bruce Edward	C,T	Secretary	Interior Dept.
Babbitt	Eileen F.	C		
Babbitt	Hasrriet C	C		
Bacon	Kenneth H.	C		
Bacot	John Carter	C	Chairman & CEO	Bank of New York Co., Inc.
Baczynski	Jerzy	TE	Editor-in-Chief	Polityka, Warsaw
Bader	William Banks	C	President	Eurasia Foundation, Washington
Baer	M. Delal	C	Sr. Fellow & Dir.	CSIS, Mexico Project
Baeza	Mario Leon	C	Chairman & CEO	Latin American Equity Partners
Bagley	Elizabeth Frawley	C		
Bahr	Egon Karlheinz	BD	Director	IFS Hamburg; Fed. Min. (fmr.) for spec. tasks; SPD mbr.
Bailey	Charles Waldo, II	C	Trustee	Carnegie Endowment; Editor (fmr.), Nat. Public Radio
Bains	Leslie Elizabeth	C	Managing Director	Citibank, NYC
Baird	Charles Fitz	C	Trustee	Bucknell Univ.
Baird	Euan	T	Chairman	Schlumberger, Ltd.
Baird	Peter W.	C		
Baird	Zoe E.	C	V.P. & Gen. Counsel	Aetna Life & Casualty, Hartford, CT.
Baker	Howard Henry, Jr.	C	Chief Of Staff (fmr.)	to US President Reagan; Senator (fmr.), Tennessee
Baker	James A., III	C	Secretary (fmr.)	State Dept.
Baker	James Estes	C	Director	State Dept., UN, Dept. of Humanitarian Affairs
Baker	John R.	C		
Baker	Nancy Kassebaum	C		
Baker	Pauline H.	C	Director	Carnegie Endowment; Member, Aspen Institute
Bakhash	Shaul	C		
Balaran	Paul	C	V.P.	Carnegie Endow. for International Peace
Baldwin	David A.	C	Professor	Columbia Univ., Polit. Sci.
Baldwin	Henry Furlong	C	Chairman	Mercantile Bankshares Corp.
Baldwin	Richard Edward	C	Professor	Columbia Univ., World Order Studies
Baldwin	Robert Edward	C	Research Professor	Univ. of Wisconsin
Baldwin	Robert H. B.	C	Founding Chair.	Center for Int. Studies, Inc.
Baldwin	Sherman	C	Author	"Ironclaw"
Bales	Carter F.	C	Founder	The Wicks Group of Companies
Balick	Kenneth D.	C	Director	Nomoura Securities, Int. Business Development
Baliles	Gerald L.	C	Member	Legal Draft. Sub-Comm.,St.Water Study Comm., Virginia
Ball	David George	C	President	AMAX Cen. Services
Ball	George Wildman	B,C	Sr. Mng. Director	Lehman Brothers; fmr. Undersec., State
Ballve'	Pedro	TE	Chairman	Campofrio Alimentacion, Madrid
Balsemao	Francisco Pinto	BP	Prime Min. (fmr.)	of Portugal
Banck	Maja	BNL	Executive Secretary	Bilderberg meetings
Band	Laurence Merrill	C		
Bangemann	Martin	BD	Minister (fmr,)	Economics; Mbr., Commission of the European Union
Barashefsky	Charlene	C		
Barber	Charles Finch	C	Director (fmr.)	Salomon Brothers Corp.
Barber	James A., Jr.	C		
Barger	Teresa C.	C	Author	"Private Capital Flow and the Poor"
Baring	Sir John	BGB		Baring Brothers & Co.
Barkan	Joel D.	C		
Barker	Robert R.	C	President (Fmr)	Harvard Magazine, Board of Overseers
Barlow	William Edward	C	Owner & Pres. (fmr.)	MIN Publishing, N.Y.C.
Barnds	William J.	C	Author	"Intelligence & Fgn. Policy: Dilemmas of a Democracy"
Barnes	Harry G., Jr.	C	Consultant	Ctr./Fgn. Policy Devel.; US Amb. (fmr.) to India, Chili
Barnes	Michael Darr	C	Congressman (fmr.)	Maryland
Barnet	Richard Jackson	C	Trustee	Institute for Policy Studies
Barnett	Arthur Doak	C	Professor (fmr.)	John Hopkins Univ., Sch of Advanced Int. Studies
Barnett	Michael N.	C	Assoc. Professor	Wisconsin Unvi., Madison, Political Science
Barnett	Robert Warren	C	Econ. Counsel (fmr.)	State Dept., US Embassy, The Hague
Barnevik	Percy	B	Chairman	Investor AB
Baroody	William J., Jr.	C	Chairman	Smithsonian Inst., Center for Scholars
Barr	Michael S.	C		
Barr	Thomas Delbert	C	Partner	Cravath, Swaine & Moore, N.Y.C.
Barre	Raymond	TE	Prime Minister (fmr.)	France, de ; Member, National Assembly
Barrett	Barbara McConnell	C	Lawyer	private practice, Paradise Valley, Arizona
Barrett	John Adams	C	Partner	Fulbright & Jaworski, Houston

Last Name	First & Mid. Name	Org.	Job Title	Affiliation - Company, Organization
Barrett	Nancy Smith	C	Provost & Vice Pres.	Western Michigan Univ.
Barrosso	Jose Manuel Durao	BP	Minister, Fgn. Affairs	Portugal
Barry	Lisa B.	C		
Barry	Thomas Corcoran	C	President & CEO	Rockefeller & Co., Inc.; Partner, CZ Ltd.
Barshay	Jill	C		
Bartelds	Hans	TE	Chairman of Exec. Com.	Fortis NL, Utrecht
Bartholomew	Reginald	C	U.S. Ambassador	State Dept., Italy
Bartlett	Joseph Warren	C	Partner	Mayer, Brown & Platt
Bartlett	Richard Allen	C		
Bartlett	Thomas Alva	C	Member	Oregon State System of Higher Education
Bartley	Robert Leroy	B,C,T	Editor	Wall Street Journal
Barton	Christopher	C	Country Desk Officer	Peace Corps, Costa Rica, Honduras, Paraguay
Barzel	Rainer	BD	Member (fmr.)	German Bundestag; Pres. (fmr.) Bundestag; CDU mbr.
Basek	John T.	C	President	Clintondale Aviation
Bashawaty	Albert C.	C	Sr. Officer	J.P. Morgan
Basora	Adrian A.	C	US Ambassador	State Dept., Czech Republic
Bass	James E.	C	Lawyer	Gibson, Dunn & Crutcher
Bass	Peter Evan	C		
Bassett	Isabel	B	Parl. Asst.	to Min. of Finance, Gvt./Ontario
Bassetti	Piero	TE	President	Assocamerestro, Rome; Ch. (fmr.)Chmbr. of Com. & Ind., Milan
Bassow	Whitman	C	Contributing Edit.	*Environmental Protection Magazine*
Batkin	Alan R.	C	Mbr. Advisory Bd.	Council of the Americas; V. Chair., Kissinger & Assoc.
Bator	Francis Michael	C	Advisory Bd. Member	Center for International Policy
Battaglia	Charles	C	Staff Director	Senate Veteran's Affair Committee
Battle	Lucius Durham	C	Chairman (fmr.)	UNESCO General Conference
Bauer	Joanne R.	C		
Bauman	Robert Poe	C	Professor (fmr.)	Univ. of Alabama
Baumann	Carol Edler	C	Director	Foreign Policy Association
Baumann	Roger R.	C		
Baumgartner	Wilfred S.	BF	Hon. Governor (fmr.)	Banque de France
Bayar	Ugur	BTR	Chairman	Privatazation Admin.
Bayh	Evan	B	Senator	Indiana
Bean	Atherton	C	Professor (fmr.)	Carleton College
Beard	Ronald Stratton	C	Chair. & Mng. Partner	Gibson, Dunn & Crutcher
Beattie	Richard Irwin	C	Board Member	Carnegie Corp. of NY; Bd. Mbr., Ctr. for Int. Policy
Bebear	Claud	B	Chairman & CEO	AXA Group
Bebear	Claud	BF	Chairman & CEO	AXA Group
Becherer	Hans Walter	C	Chairman & CEO	Deere & Co.
Bechky	Perry	C		
Bechtel	Riley P.	T	Chairman & CEO	Bechtel Group, Inc.
Becker	Kurt	BD	Editor (fmr.)	Stadtanzeiger
Beckler	David Zander	C	Associate Director	Carnegie Commission for Science Tech. & Government
Bedrosian	Gregory R.	C		
Beeman	Richard E.	C	Exec. Vice President	National City Bank, Cleveland
Begley	Louis	C	Partner	Debevoise & Plimpton, NYC
Behrman	Jack Newton	C	Professor (fmr.)	Univ. of North Carolina
Beilenson	Anthony C.	C	Congressman (fmr.)	California, Rules
Beim	David Odell	C	Professor	Columbia Univ., Business School
Beim	Nicholas F.	C		
Beinecke	William S.	C	Chairman	Hudson River Foundation
Beitler	Ruth Margolies	C	Author	"The Intifada"
Beitz	Berthold	BD	Chairman (fmr.)	Gen. Authorized Rep. of Friedrich GmbH
Belanger	Michel	TC	Chairman & CEO	National Bank of Canada
Belfrage	Erik	TE	Sr. Vice President	Skandinaviska Enskilda Banken, Stockholm
Belka	Marek	TE	Adv. To President	of Poland; Prof., Inst. Of Economics, Warsaw
Bell	Burwell B.	C		
Bell	David Elliott	B,C	Exec. Vice President	Ford Foundation
Bell	Gordon P.	C		
Bell	Holley Mack	C		
Bell	J. Bowyer	C	Author	"The Irish Troubles"
Bell	Peter D.	C	Member	Edna McConnell Clark Foundation, Inc.
Bell	Rober G.	C		
Bell	S. (Steve) Scott	C	News Anchor	USA Network Updates
Bell-Rose	Stephanie	C	Found. Counsel	Andrew W. Mellon Foundation
Bellamy	Carol	C	Director	Peace Corp., Clinton Admin.; Dir., UNICEF
Bellinger	John B. III	C		
Bello	Judith Hipper	C	Adjunct Professor	Georgetown Univ.
Benbow	Terence H.	C	Dean	Univ. of Connecticut, Law School
Bender	Gerald J.	C	Assoc. Prof.	U.S.C., International Relations
Benedict	Kenneth M.	C	Program Director	John D. & Catherine T. MacArthur Foundation
Bennet	Douglas Joseph, Jr.	B,C	Assistant Secretary	State Dept., International Organization Affairs
Bennett	Andrew	C		
Bennett	Donald Vivian	C	Superintendent (fmr.)	Def. Dept.; Superintendent (fmr.), US Military Academy
Bennett	Frederic, Sir	BGB	Member (fmr.)	British Parliament
Bennett	Susan J.	C	Editor, Writer	USA Today
Bennett	W. Tapley, Jr.	C	Director	Foreign Policy Association
Benson	Lucy Peters Wilson	C,T	President	Benson & Associates, Amherst & Washington

Last Name	First & Mid. Name	Org.	Job Title	Affiliation - Company, Organization
Bentsen	Lloyd	B	Secretary (fmr.)	Treas. Dept.;Ptrn.,Verner Liipferi Bernhard McPherson & Hand
Beplat	Tristan E.	C		
Bereuter	Douglas K.	C	Congressman	Nebraska, Banking & Finance, Int. Relations
Berg	Fritz	BD	President (fmr.)	BDI (Bundesverband der dt. Industrie)
Bergen	Peter	C		
Berger	Marilyn	C	Professor	Seattle Univ., Law
Berger	Samuel R. (Sandy)	B,C	Asst. to President	National Security Affairs
Berger	Suzanne	C	Department Chairman	MIT, Dept. of Political Science
Bergh	Maarten A. van den	BNL	Gp. Mng. Dir.	Royal Dutch/Shell
Bergold	Harry Earl, Jr.	C	US Ambassador (fmr.)	State Dept., Hungary, Nicaragua
Bergougnoux	Jean	TE	Chairman	S.N.C.F. (French Railways), Paris
Bergsten	C. Fred	B,C,T	Sr. Fellow	Brookings Institution
Bergsten	Rand V	T	Asst. Secretary (fmr.)	Treasury Dept., Int. Affairs; Dir., Inst. of Int. Economics
Bergstrom	Hans	B	Political Editor	"Dagens Nyheter"
Berkowitz	Bruce D.	C	Assoc. Director	Aspen Strategy Group
Berkowsky	Pamela	C		
Berman	Howard Lawrence	C	Congressman	California, Judiciary, Int. Relations, Judiciary
Bernabe'	Franco	BI,TE	CEO	Telecom Italia, Rome
Bernadin	Joseph Louis C.	C	Archbishop (Late)	Chicago
Bernard	Kenneth W.	C		
Berndt	John Edward	C	President	AT&T Int. Communications Services
Bernstein	David S.	C		State Dept.
Bernstein	Richard	B	Book Critic	New York Times
Bernstein	Robert Louis	C	Publisher-at-large	John Wiley & Sons
Bernstein	Tom A.	C	Member	Fund for Free Expression
Berresford	Susan Vail	C	President	Ford Foundation
Berrie	Scott D.	C		
Berring	Helle	C		
Berris	Jan	C		
Bersin	Alan D.	C		
Berthoin	Georges	TE	Int. Hon. Chairman	European Movement: Honorary European Chairman, TC
Bertram	Christoph	BD	Dipl. Correspondent	"Die Zeit", Hamburg, Ger.; Mbr. BB Steering Committee
Beschloss	Michael R.	C	Partipitant	PBS, Jim Lehrer Newshour
Beshar	Peter Justus	C		
Besley	John	TC	Member	Canadian House of Commons
Bessie	Simon Michael	C	Publisher	Cornelia & Michael Bessie Books
Best	William A., III	C		
Bestani	Robert M.	C	Deputy Asst. Sec.	Treasury Dept., Int. Monetary Affairs
Bettiza	Enzo	BI	Journalist (fmr.)	Corriere della Sera, Italy
Betts	Richard K.	C	Professor	Columbia Univ., Political Science
Beugel	Ernst H., van der	BNL	Vice President	Royal Dutch Airlines,fmr.Min./State,Fgn.Affrs.
Beutner	Austin M.	C		
Bewkes	Jeffrey	C		
Beyazit	Selahattin	BTR	Director	various companies in Turkey
Beyer	John C.	C	Member	Overseas Development Council
Bialer	Seweryn	C	Professor	Columbia Univ.
Bialkin	Kenneth Jules	C	Partner	Skadden, Arps, Slate Meagher & Flom
Biancheri Chiappori	Boris	TE	Chairman	Agenzia ANSA; Chair., I.S.P.I., Milan; Chair., ANSA, Milan
Bicksler	Barbara	C		
Biddle	George	C		
Biedenkopf	Kurt	BD,TE	Ministry President	Free State of Saxony; Mbr. Comm. on Global Governance
Biegun	Stephen E.	C		
Biel	Eric R.	C		
Biemann	Betsy	C		Rockerfeller Foundation
Bienen	Henry S.	C	President	Northwestern Univ.
Bierley	John Charles	C	Partner	Macfarlane Ferguson, Tampa
Bildt	Carl	BE,TE	Prime Minister (fmr.)	Sweden; Mbr., Swedish Parliament; Chair, Moderate Party
Bilgin	Dinc	BTR	Chairman	Sabah A.S.
Billington	James Hadley	C	Librarian	Library of Congress
Bindenagel	James D.	C		
Binger	James H.	C	President (fmr.)	Honeywell
Binkley	Nicholas Burhs	C	Chairman & CEO	Bankamerica Corp., San Diego
Binnendijk	Hans	C	Principal Deputy Dir.	State Dept., E. E. O. C., Policy Planning
Birdsall	Nancy	C		
Birenbaum	David E.	C		
Birgi	M. Nuri	BTR	Turkish Amb. (fmr.)	N.A.T.O.
Birkelund	John Peter	C	Chairman & CEO	Dillon, Read & Co., Inc.; Honorary Officer, CFR
Birnbaum	Eugene A.	C		
Birrenbach	Kurt	BD,TE	Chairman (fmr.)	August-Thyssen-Huette AG; Mbr. (fmr.) CDC, EP
Bishop	Sanford D., Jr.	C	Congressman	Geoegia
Bissell	Richard Etter	C	Sr. Fellow	Overseas Development Council, Wash.
Bissell	Richard Mervin, Jr.	C	Business Consultant	private practice, Connecticut
Bjarnason	Bjorn	BICE	Member	Parliament, Iceland, Independence Party
Bjerregaard	Ritt	BDK,TE	Member	European Commission; Mbr., Parl., Danmark ; Chr., SDP Gp.
Bjorklund	Eric C.	C		
Bjorklund	Conrad M.	BC,TC	Chairman & CEO	Hollinger Inc., Toronto
Black	Joseph E.	C		

Who's Who of the Elite

Last Name	First & Mid. Name	Org.	Job Title	Affiliation - Company, Organization
Black	Shirley Temple	C	US Ambassador	State Dept., Czechoslovakia; Actress (fmr.)
Black	Stanley Warren. III	C	Professor	Univ. of North Carolina
Blacker	Coit Dennis	C	Special Asst.	Exec. Office/Pres., Russian, Ukranian & Eurasian Afrs.
Blackmer	Donald Laur. Morton	C	Research Associate	Harvard Univ., West European Studies
Blackwell	James Augusta, Jr.	C	Vice Pres. & Gen. Mgr.	Lockheed Aerospace Systems Co., Burbank
Blackwill	Robert D.	B,C	Member (fmr.)	Nat. Sec. Council; Lecturer, JFK School, Harvard Univ.
Blahous	Charles P., III	C		
Blair	Sally Onesti	C		
Blair	Tony	B	Prime Minister	England
Blake	Robert O.	C	Ambassador (fmr.)	Mali
Blake	Vaughn R.	C		
Blank	Stephen	C		
Blechman	Barry M.	C	Advisory Bd. Member	Center for Int. Policy; Chair., Henry Stimson Ctr.
Bleier	Edward	C		
Blendon	Robert Jay	C	Department Chairman	Harvard Univ., Dept. of Health Policy & Management
Blinder	Alan Stuart	C	Vice-Chairman	Federal Reserve System
Blinken	Anthony (Tony) J.	C	Special Assiostant	to Pres. Clinton, for National Security Affairs
Blinken	Donald	C		
Bliss	Richard M.	C		
Bloch	Julia Chang	C	US Ambassador	St. Dept., Nepal; Gp. Exec. V. Pres. (fmr.), Bankamerica
Blomeyer-Bartensteun	H. H.	BD	Personal Assistant	to Alois Mertes, Minister of State (fmr.)
Bloom	Evan Todd	C		
Bloomberg	Michael R.	C		
Bloomfield	Lincoln Palmer	C	Professor (fmr.)	MIT
Bloomfield	Richard J.	C	US Ambassador (fmr.)	State Dept., Equador, Portugal
Blum	John (Jack) A.	C	Staff Member	Senate Foreign Relations Committee
Blum	Richard C.	C		
Blumenthal	Sidney	C	Spec. Political Corresp.	New Yorker Magazine; Prof. (fmr.), Univ. of Miami
Blumenthal	Werner Michael	C,T	Limited Partner	Lazard Freres & Co.; Director (fmr.), CFR
Blumrosen	Alexander B.	C	Attorney	Bernard-Hertz Bojot
Boada Vilallonga	Claudio	TE	Honorary Chairman	Banco Hispano-Americano, Madrid
Boardman	Harry	C		
Bob	Daniel E.	C		
Bobbitt	Philip Chase	C	Professor	Univ. of Texas, Austin
Bodea	Sorin A.	C	Author	"Information Technology & Economic Performance"
Boden	Hans C.	BD	Hon. President (fmr.)	Int. Trade Chamber, Paris
Bodie	William C.	C	Ambassador	Asia Pacific Economic Cooperation Forum
Boecker	Paul Harold	C	President	Univ. of Calif., Inst. of the Americas
Bogert	Carrol R.	C		
Boggs	Michael D.	C		
Bohen	Frederick M.	C		
Bohlen	Avis T.	C	U.S. Amb.	State Department to Bulgaria
Bohn	John Augustus, Jr.	C	President	Moody's Investors Service
Boiteux	Marcel	TE	Honorary Chairman	French Electric Board (EDF), Paris
Bokros	Lojos	BINT	Sr. Advisor	The World Bank
Bolkestein	Fritz	BNL	Parliamentary Leader	VVD (Liberal Party)
Bolling	Landrum Rymer	C	Congressman (fmr.)	Montana
Bollinger	Martin J.	C		
Bolten	Joshua B.	C	General Counsel	US Trade Representative
Bon	Michel	TE	Chairman	France Telecom, Paris
Bond	Jean Carey	C	Member	Black Radical Congress
Bond	Robert D.	C		
Bonfield	Peter, Sir	TE	CEO	British Telecom
Bonino	Emma	BINT	Member	European Parliament
Boniver	Margherita	TE	Minister	Tourism, Italy
Bonney	J. Dennis	C	Vice Chairman	Chevron Corp.
Bonsal	Dudley Baldwin	C	US District Judge	New York
Bonsal	Philip W.	C	Author	"Cuba, Castro, and the United States"
Booker	Salih	C	Consultant	CFR Conf. on
Bookout	John Frank, Jr.	C	Dir., Mbr. Exec. Com.	Shell Petroleum, Inc.
Boone	Theodore S.	C		
Boorda	Jeremy Michael	C	Chief/Nav. Oper.(fmr.)	Defense Dept., US Navy
Borbon	H.R.M. Sofia	BE	Queen	of Spain
Borchgrave	Arnaud, de	C	Editor-in-Chief (fmr.)	Insight Magazines & Washington Times
Boren	David Lyle	C	Senator (fmr.)	Oklahoma, Fin., Agriculture, Select Com. on Intel.
Borges	Antonio	BP,TE	Dean	INSEAD
Boschwitz	Rudy	C	Senator (fmr.)	Minnesota
Bose	Meena	C		
Boskin	Michael Jay	B	Chairman (fmr.)	President's Council of Economic Advisors
Bosley	John	TC	Member	Canadian House of Commons; Spkr., House of Commons
Bossert	Philip A., Jr.	C		
Bossidy	Lawrence A.	T	Chairman & CEO	Alliedsignal
Bosworth	Stephen W.	C,T	US Ambassador	S. Korea
Bottelier	Pieter P.	BINT	Chief of Mission	The World Bank, Resident Mission in China
Botts	John C.	C		
Boucher	Eric Le	BF	Chief Editor, Int.	*Le Monde*, France
Bouey	Gerald K.	TC	Governor (fmr.)	Bank of Canada

Last Name	First & Mid. Name	Org.	Job Title	Affiliation - Company, Organization
Bougie	Jacques	TC	President & CEO	Alcan Aluminium, Ltd., Montrial
Bouis	Antonina W.	C	Author/Translator	"Mothers and Daughters"
Bourassa	Robert	BC	Prime Minister (fmr.)	Quebec
Bouton	Marshall M.	C	V.P.	Asia Society, Texas
Bovin	Dennis Alan	C	Vice Chairman	Bear Sterns & Co.
Bowen	Vincent E., III	C		
Bowen	William Gordon	C	President	Andrew W. Mellon Foundation
Bower	Joseph Lyon	C	Member of Faculty	Harvard Univ., JFK School of Government
Bowie	Robert R.	B,C,T	Member	Overseas Development Council
Bowles	Erskin B.	C		
Bowlin	Mike R.	C	President & COO	Atlantic Richfield Co.
Bowman	Frank Lee	C		
Bowman	Richard Carl	C	Vice President	RBI, Inc.
Boyazit	Selattin	BTR	Director	Compa, Turkey
Boyd	Charles Graham	B,C	Dep. Cmd.-in-Chief (fmr.)	Defense Dept., US European Command
Boyer	Ernest Leroy	C	President	Carnegie Foundation
Boyner	Cem	BTR	Chairman	New Democracy Movement
Braathen	Erik	B		
Bracken	Paul	C		
Brademas	John	B,C,T	Congressman (fmr.)	New York; Dir., Texaco Inc.; Pres. (fmr.), NYU.
Bradford	Zeb	C	Military Fellow (fmr.)	CFR
Bradley	Bill	C		
Bradley	Edward R.	C	Principal Corresp.	CBS, 60 Minutes
Bradley	Tom	C,T	Mayor (fmr.)	Los Angeles
Bradley	William (Bill) L.	B,C	Senator (fmr.)	New Jersey; Fin., Energy & Nat. Res.; Rhodes Scholar
Brady	Connor	B		
Brady	Linda Parrish	C		
Brady	Nicholas Frederick	B,C	Secretary (fmr.)	Treasury Dept.; Director, NCR Corp.
Brady	Rose	C		
Braeutigam	Hans-Otto	BD	Minister	Justice, Brandenberg, Germany
Braga de Macedo	Jorge	TE	Professor	Nova Univ., Econ., Lisbon; Min., Portugal, of Finance
Brainard	Lawrence J.	C	Member	Overseas Development Council
Brainard	S. Lael	C	Spec. Asst.	Executive Office to President, Int. Economic Affairs
Braitwaite	Rodric	B		
Bramlett	David A.	C		
Brand	Laurie A.	C	Director	U.S.C., Center for Int. Studies
Brandler	Donald K.	C		
Brandt	Willy	BD	Chancellor (fmr.)	Germany; Fdr., Comm. on Global Governance 1992
Branscomb	Lewis Mcardy	C	Advriory Council	Off./Tech. Asmt.; Dir., Mobil Oil Corp.; Dir., Harvard U.
Branson	William H.	C	Advisory Bd. Member	Center for International Policy
Brauchli	Marcus W.	C	Writer	*Wall St. Journal*
Brauer	Max	BD	Mayor (fmr.)	Freie u. Hansestadt Hamburg; Mbr. (fmr.) Bundestag
Braunschvig	David	C		
Brautigam	Hans-Otto	B	Minister	of Justice, Brandenburg
Breck	Henry Reynolds	C		
Brederode	Santos Nuno	B		
Breed	Henry Eltinge	C		
Breindel	Eric Marc	C	Editor & Columnist	New York Post
Bremer	L. Paul, III	C	Mng. Director	Kissinger & Assoc.; Dir., Foreign Policy Assoc.
Bresnan	John J.	C	Sr. Research Scholar	Columbia Univ., East Asian Institute
Breuel	Birgit	BD	Board Member	Treuhandanstalt, Germany
Breyer	Stephen G.	C	Associate Justice	Supreme Court; Chief Judge (fmr.), Court of Appeals
Brimmer	Andrew F.	C,T	Director	Du Pont (E. I, Du Pont De Nemours & Co.)
Brimmer	Esther Diane	C	Spec. Asst./Und. Sec.	State Dept., Policy Affairs
Brinkhorst	Laurens-Jan	BNL	Minister (fmr.)	The Netherlands, Foreign Affairs Dept.
Brinkley	David	C	Anchorman	ABC, This Week
Brinkley	Douglas G.	B	Director	Univ. of New Orleans, Eisenhower Center for American Studies
Brinkman	L. C.	B		
Britt	David V. B.	C		
Brittan	Leon	BINT	Vice President	European Commission
Brittenham	Raymond Lee	C	Vice Chairman	Spanish Institute
Broad	Robin	C	Professor	American Univ., School of Int. Service
Broadman	Harry G.	C	Writer	World Bank
Brock	Hans, van den	BINT	Commissioner	European Communities
Brock	Mitchell	C	Partner	Sullivan & Cornwell, NYC
Brock	William E., III	C,T	Chairman	Blackstone Gp., NYC; Sec. (fmr.), Labor Dept., '85-'87
Broda	Frederick C.	C		
Brody	Christopher W.	C		
Broitman	Elana	C		
Brokaw	Thomas (Tom) John	C	Anchor	NBC Nightly News
Bromery	Randolph Wilson	C	Director	EXXON Corp.; (fmr.) Chase Manh. Bk.; Prof., Univ./Mass.
Bromley	David Allan	C	Chairman	President's Council for Advancement on Sci. & Tech.
Bronfman	Edgar M., Jr.	C	President & CEO	Joseph E. Seagram's & Sons (liquor); Dir., Du Pont Co.
Bronson	Rachel	C		
Brooke	Edward	B	O	Massachusetts
Brooke	James B.	C	Writer	*New York Times*
Brookins	Carol	C		

Last Name	First & Mid. Name	Org.	Job Title	Affiliation - Company, Organization
Brooks	Harvey	C		
Brower	Charles Nelson	C	Counsel & Advocate	US International Court of Justice, The Hague
Brown	Brian A.	C		
Brown	Carroll	C	Member (fmr.)	State Dept., UN General Assembly
Brown	Cynthia	C		
Brown	Frederic Joseph	C	Director	Johns Hopkins Univ., Southeast Asian Studies
Brown	Gordon	BGB	Member	British Parliament, Labour Party
Brown	Gwendolyn	C		
Brown	Harold	C,T	Secretary (fmr.)	Defense Dept.; Councelor, Ctr. for Strategic & Int. Stud.
Brown	L. Dean	C		
Brown	Leon Carl	C	Director	Princeton Univ., Program of Near Eastern Studies
Brown	Lester Russell	C	President	Worldwatch Institute, Washington
Brown	Michael A.	C		
Brown	Michael E.	C		Harvard Univ.
Brown	Richard P., Jr.	C	Associate	Morgan, Lewis & Bockius, Philadelphia
Brown	Ronald Harmon	C	Secretary	Commerce Dept.
Brown	Seyom	C	Professor	Brandeis Univ.; Member, Carnegie Endowment
Brown	Tobias Josef	C		
Brown	Walter H.	C	Limited Partner	Brown Brothers Harriman
Brown	Kathleen	C		
Browne	E. John P.	BGB	Group CEO	British Petroleum Co., plc
Browne	Robert Span	C	Staff Director (fmr.)	Hse. Bkg. Subcom.,Int. Dev. Trade & M. P., Ctr./Nat. Pol.
Browning	David S.	C		
Bruce	Judith	C	Member	Overseas Development Council
Bruemmer	Melissa L. S.	C		
Bruemmer	Russell J.	C	Attorney	Wilmer, Cutler & Pickering
Brundtland	Arne Olav	BN,TE	Sr. Research Fellow	Norwegian Institute of International Affairs, Oslo
Brunley	James H. IV	C		
Bruton	John	BIRL	Leader	of Fine Gael.
Bryan	Greyson L.	C		
Bryan	John H.	B,T	Chairman & CEO	Sara Lee Corp.
Bryant	Ralph C.	C	Sr. Fellow	Brookings Inst.
Bryson	John E.	C	Chairman & CEO	Southern California Edison Co.; Dir., CFR
Brzezinski	Ian J.	C		
Brzezinski	Mark F.	C		
Brzezinski	Zbigniew	B,C,T	Counselor	Johns Hop.,Ctr./Strat. & Int. Stud.; Nat. Sec. Advis. (fmr.)
Buchanan	Robin W.T.	BGB	Sr. Partner	Bain & Company Inc.UK
Buchheim	Robert W.	C	Member	Rand Corp.
Buchman	Mark Edward	C	President & CEO	Bank of Los Angeles, Liberty Bank, Honolulu
Buckley	William Frank, Jr.	B,C	Editor-at-Large	National Review; PBS-Firing Line
Buelow	Andres von	BD	Member (fmr.)	German Bundestag, SPD; Sec. of State (fmr.), Min. (fmr.) Def.
Bueno	De mesquita Bruce	C		
Buergenthal	Thomas	C	Professor	George Washington Univ.
Bugliarello	George	C	President	Polytechnical Univ., Brooklyn
Bullard	Edward P.	C	Executive	Non-Profit organization
Bullock	Hugh	C	Investment Banker	Bullock Co., NYC
Bullock	Mary Brown	C	Head, Spec. Proj. Sect.	National Science Foundation, Public Affairs
Bundy	McGeorge	B,C	Chairman	Carnegie Univ., Committee for Reducing Nuclear Danger
Bundy	William P.	C	Editor & Dir. (fmr.)	Council on Foreign Relations, Foreign Affairs magazine
Bunzel	Jeffrey H.	C		
Burand	Deborah K.	C	Member	Shearman & Sterling
Burck	William A.	C		
Burda	Hubert	BD	Chairman	Burda Media
Burgess	Geoffery P.	C		
Burgess	John Allen	C	Lawyer	Hale & Dorr, Boston
Burke	James E.	C,T	Director	IBM Corp.; Director, CFR
Burkhalter	Holly J.	C	Director	Human Rights Watch/Africa Watch
Burlingame	Edward Livermore	C	Publisher	Edward Burlingame Books
Burlingame	John F.	C	Teaching Assit.	Tufts Univ.
Burmester	Sven	TE	Representative	UN Population Fund, Beijing
Burns	Haywood	C	President	Nation Institute
Burns	M. Anthony	T	Chair., Pres. & CEO	Ryder System, Inc.
Burns	Patrick Owen	C	Sr. Consultant	Stage Interprises, ENJ (Venture Cap.)
Burns	R. Nicholas	C	U. S. Amb.	State Dept., to Greece
Burns	Patrick Owen	C	Sr. Consultant	Stage Interprises, ENJ (Venture Cap.)
Burns	William F.	C	Member	Committee on Int. Security & Arms Control
Burrows	Richard	TE	Chairman & CEO	Irish Distillers, Dublin
Burt	Richard R.	C	Negotiator	Arms Contr. & Disar. Agen.,Mbr. (fmr.),Carnegie Endow.
Burton	Daniel Farrell, Jr.	C	Congressman	Indiana, Foreign Affairs Committee
Busbee	George	T	Partner	King & Spalding
Busbee	R. Christopher	C		
Bush	George Herbert W.	C,T	President (fmr.)	United States; Director (fmr.), CIA, CFR
Bush	Robert C. Jr.	C		
Bushner	Rolland H.	C		
Bussey	Donald S.	C		
Busuttil	James	C		
Butler	George Lee	C	Comdr.-in-Chief (fmr.)	Defense Dept., USAF, Strategic

Last Name	First & Mid. Name	Org.	Job Title	Affiliation - Company, Organization
Butler	Hugo	B	Editor-in-Chief	*Neue Zurcher Zeitung*
Butler	Samuel Coles	C	Partner	Cravath, Swaine & Moore, N.Y.C.
Butler	William Joseph	C	Partner	Butler, Jablow & Geller, NYC
Buttenheim	Lisa M.	C		
Buultjens	Ralph	C		
Buxbaum	Richard M.	C		
Buyske	Gail	C		
Byrne	Patrick M.	C		
Byrnes	Robert F.	C		
Cabot	Elizabeth	C		
Cabot	Louis Wellington	B,C	Chairman (fmr.)	Brookings Institute; Chairman (fmr.), Cabot Corp.
Cabot	Thomas Dudley	C	Honorary Chairman	Cabot Corp.
Cabranes	Jose Alberto	C	US District Judge	Connecticut
Cadieux	Jean-Louis	BB	Dir.-General, Deputy	EEC, for Foreign Affairs, from Belgium
Caesar	Camille M.	C		
Caglayangil	Ihsan S.	BTR	Minister (fmr.)	Turkish Foreign Affairs
Cahill	Kevin M.	C		
Cahn	Anne H.	C	Advisory Bd. Member	Center for International Policy
Cahouet	Frank Vondell	C	Chairman & CEO	Mellon Bank, N. A.
Cain	Kenneth L.	C		
Calabia	Dawn T.	C		U.N. Office of High Commissioner for Refugees
Calder	Kent Eyring	C	Professor	Princeton Univ.
Caldwell	Dan	C		
Caldwell	Philip	C,T	Sr. Managing Director	Lehman Brothers, Inc.; Director, Digital Equip. Corp.
Calhoun	Michael J.	C		
Califano	Joseph Anthony, Jr.	C	Director	Chrysler; Sec.(fmr.), HEW Dept.; Adv. Bd., Ctr./Nat.Pol.
Calingart	Daniel	C		
Calkins	Hugh	C,T	President & Director	Initiatives in Urban Education
Callaghy	Thomas M.	C		
Callahan	David L.	C		
Callander	Robert John	C	President (fmr.)	Chemical Banking Corp.
Callebaut	Pierre	TE	Chairman	Amylum, Brussels
Callen	Michael A.	C		
Calleo	David P.	C		
Callieri	Carlo	TE	Mng. Director	Iniziativa Piemonte,Turin;Exec.V.P.,(fmr.)Fiat, Turin
Calloway	D. Wayne	T	Chairman & CEO	PepsiCo, Inc.
Callwood	Kevin R.	C		
Campbell	Carolyn	C		
Campbell	Colin Goetze	C	President	Rockefeller Brothers Foundation
Campbell	John Coert	C	Director (fmr.)	Council on Foreign Relations
Campbell	Kurt M.	C		Defense Dept.
Campbell	Thomas J.	C		
Campbell	Wesley Glenn	C	Counselor	Stanford Univ., Hoover Institute, California
Camps	Miriam	B,C	Vice President (fmr.)	State Dept., Planning Council
Camps	Victoria	TE	Member	Spanish Senate; Prof., Philosophy, Barcelona Univ.
Camu	Louis	BB	Chairman (fmr.)	Banque de Brouxelles
Canal	Carlos M., Jr.	C		
Canavan	Christopher	C		
Canfield	Franklin O.	C		
Cannon	James M.	C		
Cantoni	Giampiero	BI	Chairman	Banca Nationale del Lavoro, Italy
Cappello	Juan C.	C	Sr. V. President	ITT Corp.; Bd. Mbr., Council of the Americas
Cappuzzo	Umberto	TE	Vice. President	Alcide De Gasperi Found.;Mbr.(fmr.),Italian Senate,Def.Comm.
Caputo	Lisa M.	C		
Carbonell	Nestor T.	C	Mbr. Advisory Bd.	Council of the Americas; Sr. V. Pres., PepsiCo F.&B. Int.
Carey	Hugh L.	C	Exec. Vice President	W. R. Grace & Co.; Governor (fmr.), NY St.
Carey	John	C	Judge	Westchester County Court, White Plains
Carey	Sarah Collins	C	Partner	Steptoe & Johnson, East-West Trade
Carey	William D.	C		
Carli	Guido	BI	Governor (fmr.)	Bank of Italy
Carlos	Manuel Luis	C		
Carlson	Robert John	C	President & Director	United Technologies, Hartford
Carlson	Scott A.	C		
Carlson	Steven E.	C		
Carlucci	Frank C., III	C,T	Adjunct Fellow	Hudson Inst.; Sec. (fmr.)f, Def. Dept.; V. Ch., Carlyle Gp.
Carmichael	William Daniel	C	Executive Director	Soviet Union & East Euro. Programs Inst. for Int. Educ.
Carmoy	Herve' de	TE	Hon. Chairman	Banque Industrialle et Mobiliere Privee (B.I.M.P.), Paris
Carnesale	Albert	C		
Carothers	Thomas	C	Co-Director	Carnegie Endowment for International Peace
Carpendale	Andrew Michael	C		
Carpenter	Ted Galen	C		
Carr	John W.	C		
Carras	Costa	BGR	Director	of various companies, Greece
Carrilho	Maria	BP	Professor	Sociology
Carrington	Peter Rupert, Lord	BGB	Chairman	Bilderberg Gp., Christie's Int. plc;Sec. Gen. (fmr.), NATO
Carrington	Walter C.	C	US Ambassador	State Dept., Nigeria
Carroll	J. Speed	C	Partner	Cleary, Gottlieb, Steen & Hamilton

Last Name	First & Mid. Name	Org.	Job Title	Affiliation - Company, Organization
Carruba	Salvatore	TE	Culture Alderman	Municipality of Milan; Man. Editor, (fmr.), Il Sole 24 Ore, Milan
Carruth	Reba Anne	C		
Carson	C. W., Jr.	C		
Carson	Edward Mansfield	C	Chairman & CEO	First Interstate Bancorp, L. A.
Carswell	Robert	C	Chairman	Carnegie Endowment for International Peace
Cartellieri	Ulrich	BD	Bd. Member	Deutsche Bank, A.G.
Carter	(James Earl) Jimmy	C,T	President (fmr.)	United States
Carter	Ashton B.	C	Assistant Secretary	Defense Dept., Nuclear Section
Carter	Barry Edward	C	Deputy Under Secretary	Commerce Dept., for Export
Carter	George E.	C		
Carter	James H.	C		
Carter	Mark Andrew	C		
Carter	Marshall Nichols	C	Sr. Vice President	Chase Manhattan Corp.
Carter	Theodore N.	C		
Carter	William Hodding, III	C	Press Secretary (fmr.)	to President Carter
Carvajal Urquijo	Jaime	B,T	Chairman	Dresdner Klainwort Benson S.A.; Chairman, Ford Espana, Madri
Casanova	Jean-Claude	TE	Professor	Economic Institute for Policy Studies, Paris; Editor, Commentaire
Case	Robert A.	C		
Casper	Gerhard	C	President	Stanford Univ.
Cassidy	Eileen E.	C	0	
Cates	John M., Jr.	C		
Catroux	Diomede	BF	Minister (fmr.)	France, de
Cattarulla	Elliot R.	C	Vice President	EXXON Corp., Public Affairs
Catto	Henry Edward, Jr.	C	US Ambassador (fmr.)	United Nations, Geneva, U. K.
Caufield	Frank J.	C		
Caulfield	Matthew Patrick	C	Director	Defense Dept., Marine Corps, WFG
Cavalchini	Luigi G.	BI	Perm. Representative	European Union
Cavanagh	Richard Edward	C		
Cavasse	Felicia	B	Organizer	1992 Bilderbern Conference
Cave	Ray	C		
Cebrian	Juan Luis	B		
Cebrowski	Arthur K.	C	Director for Command	Defense Dept., Control, Communications & Computer Syst.
Celeste	Richard F.	C	Board Member	Carnegie Corp. of New York
Cem	Ismail	BTR	Minister	for Foreign Affairs
Cereti	Fausto	TE	Chairman & CEO	Alitalia, Rome
Cerjan	Paul G.	C	President (fmr.)	Defense Dept., National Defense University
Ceron Ayuso	Jose' Luis	TE	Minister (fmr.)	Trade, Spain; Chairman, ASETA, Madrid
Cerretelli	Adriana	BI	Correspondent	"Il Sole/24 Ore."
Cetin	Hikmet	BTR	Deputy Prime Minister	fmr. Minister for Foreign Affairs
Cha	Victor /d.	C		
Chace	James	B,C		World Policy Journal
Chafee	John Hubbard	B,C,T	Senator	Rhode Island, Environ. & P.W./Chair., Fin., Sel. Intellig.
Chain	John T., Jr.	C	Chief-of-Staff	Defense Dept., Air Force; CO of Strategic Air Command
Chalandon	Albin	BF	Member (fmr.)	French National Assembly
Challenor	Herschelle S.	C	Member	Overseas Development Council
Chambers	Anne Cox	C	Board Member	Cox Enterprises, Inc.
Chan	Gerald L.	C		
Chancellor	John	C	Commentator (fmr.)	NBC News
Chang	David C.	C		
Chang	Gareth C. C.	C		
Chang	Joyce	C		
Chanin	Clifford	C		
Chanis	Jonathan A.	C		
Chao	Elaine L.	C	President	United Way America (wife of Senator Mitch McConnell)
Chao	Victor Tzu-Ping	C		
Chapman	Margaret Holt	C		
Charles	Robert B.	C		
Charpie	Robert A.	C		
Chartener	Robert	C		
Chase	Anthony R.	C		
Chasin	Dana	C	Trustee	Rockefeller Family Fund
Chastelain	John A. D. de	B	Chairman	Independent Int. Comm. On Decommissioning
Chatterjee	Purnendu	C		
Chaudhry	Kiren Aziz	C	Professor	U.C. Berkeley, Political Science
Chaves	Robert J.	C		
Chavez-Thompson	Linda	C	Executive V.P.	AFL-CIO; Sec. (fmr.) Labor Dept.; Newspaper Columnist
Chavira	Ricardo	C	Foreign Edit.	*Dallas Morning News*
Chayes	Abram J.	C	Professor	Howard U., Law School; Adv. Bd. Mbr., Ctr. for Nat. Pol.
Chayes	Antonia Handler	C	Member	Overseas Development Council; Ctr. for Int. Policy
Checki	Terrence J.	C		
Cheever	Daniel Sargent	C	Professor (fmr.)	Boston Univ., Political Science & Int. Relations
Chen	Kimball C.	C	Co-Chairman	Energy Transportation Group, Inc.
Chenault	Kennethy Irving	C	President	American Express Co., Consumer Card & Fin. Svcs.
Cheney	Elizabeth L.	C		
Cheney	Richard (Dick) B.	C,T	Chair., Pres. & CEO	Halliburton Co.;Wyoming, Cong.(fmr.);Dir.,Sec.(fmr.),Def. Dept
Cheney	Stephen A.	C		
Cheremeteff	Kyra	C		

Last Name	First & Mid. Name	Org.	Job Title	Affiliation - Company, Organization
Cherne	Leo	C	Chairman (fmr.)	I.R.C.
Chickering	Allen Lawrence	C	Columnist	San Francisco Chronicle
Chiles	Lawton	T	Governor	Florida
Chino	Yoshitoki	TJ	Vice Chairman	Daiwa Anglo-Japanese Foundation; Advisor, Daiwa Sec. Co.,Ltd.
Choi	Andrey	C		
Chollet	Derek H.	C		
Cholmondeley	Paula H. J.	C	V.P.	Owens Corning
Chorlins	Marjorie	C		
Choucri	Nazli	C		
Chow	Jack C.	C	Int. Coord. & Liason	H. H. S. Dept., Fogerty International Center
Chretien	Jean	BC	Prime Minister	Canada
Chretien	Raymond A.J.	BC	Ambassador	to the US
Christensen	Thomas J.	C		
Christianson	Geryld B.	C	Member	CIA, Ottawa, 1968-'71
Christianson	John F.	C		
Christman	Daniel William	C	Superintendent	West Point
Christman	Walter L.	C		
Christodoulou	Efthymios	BGR	Minister	of Economic Affairs, Greece
Christopher	Warren M.	C,T	Secretary (fmr.)	State Dept.; Chairman, Carnegie Corp of New York
Chubais	Anatoli B.	BRUS	1st V. Prim., Chair. (fmr.)	Russia
Chubb	Hendon	C	CEO	Chubb Insurance Co. of Canada
Churchill	Buntzie Ellis	C	President (fmr.)	World Affairs Council of Philadelphia
Cimbalo	Jeffery L.	C		
Cipolletta	Innocenzo	BI	Director General	Confindustria, Italy
Cirincione	Joseph	C		
Cisler	Walker Lee	B,C	Chf., Pub. Util. (fmr.)	Defense Dept., Supreme Allied Com., Euro. Command
Cisneros	Henry G.	C,T	Secretary (Frm.)	H. U. D. Dept.; Mayor (fmr.), San Antonio; Bd., Ctr./Nat. Pol.
Cisneros	Marc A.	C	Commander (fmr.)	Defense Dept., Fifth U.S. Army
Cittadini	Cesi Il Marchese	BI	President (fmr.)	Association pour l'Etude des Problemes de l'Europe
Claes	Willy	BB	Secretary-General	NATO; Minister of Fgn. Affairs, Belgium
Clapp	Priscilla A.	C	Special Rep.	State Dept., for Food Security
Clarizio	Lynda	C	Partner	Arnold Porter Law Firm, Wash.
Clark	Dick	C	Senator (fmr.)	Iowa; Ambassador-at-Large, US State Dept.
Clark	Howard Longstreth	C	Chairman/CEO (fmr.)	American Express Co.
Clark	J. H. Collum	C		
Clark	Kenneth Bancroft	C	Professor (fmr.)	City College of New York
Clark	Mark E.	C		
Clark	Noreen Morrison	C	Department Chairman	Univ. of Michigan; Director, Aaron Diamond Foundation
Clark	Ralph L.	C	Member	National Science Foundation
Clark	Stephen C.	C		
Clark	Susan Lesley	C		
Clark	Wesley Kanne	C	Comdr.-in-Chief	Defense Dept., Southern Command
Clark	William, Jr.	C		
Clarke	Donald C.	C		
Clarke	J. G.	C	Director	EXXON Corp.
Clarke	Kenneth	BGB	Member	Parliament; Chancellor. (fmr.) of the Exchequer
Clarkson	Lawrence William	C	Corp. Vice President	Boeing Co., Seattle, Planning & Int. Development
Clausen	A. W.	T	Chair. & CEO (fmr.)	BankAmerica Corp.
Clement	Kristin	BN	Deputy Dir. Gen.	Norwegian Confed. Of Business & Industry
Clemons	Steven C.	C	Director	Japan Policy Research Inst.
Clendenin	John L.	C	Director	Coca-Cola Co.
Clercq	Willy, de	TE	Member	Euro. Parliament; Chair., Commission for Fgn. Econ. Rel.
Cleveland	James Harlan	B,C	President (fmr.)	Univ. of Hawaii
Cleveland	Peters Mathews	C		
Clifford	Donald K., Jr.	C	Founder and Pres.	Threshold Management Inc.
Cline	Ray Steiner	C	Chairman	US Global Strategy Council
Cline	William Richard	C	Adv. Bd. Mbr. (fmr.)	Export-Import Bank of US, Wash.
Clinger	William F., Jr.	C	Congressman (fmr.)	Pennsylvania, Chairman, Govt. Reform & Oversight
Clinton	Hillary Rodham	B	Wife	President Clinton
Clinton	William (Bill) J.	B,C,T	President	United States; Governor (fmr.), Arkansas
Cloherty	Patricia M.	C	Pres, & General Ptn.	Patricof Co. (Venture Cap.)
Cloonan	Edward T.	C		
Cloud	Stanley Wills	C	Wash. Contrib. Edit.	Time magazine
Clough	Michael	C	Director	CFR, Domestic Policy & Fgn. Policy
Clurman	Richard Michael	C	Chairman	Columbia Univ., Board of Governors
Coan	Louisa	C		
Cobb	Charles E., Jr.	C	US Ambassador (fmr.)	State Dept., Iceland, Reykjavik
Cobb	Paul Whitlock, Jr.	C		
Cochran	Barbara Cohen	C	Exec. Producer	CBS News
Coffey	C. Shelby, III	C	Editor, Exec. V. Pres.	Los Angeles Times
Coffey	Joseph Irving	C	Professor (fmr.)	Univ. of Pittsburgh
Cohen	Ariel	C		
Cohen	Benjamin Jack	C	Partner	Cahill, Gordon & Reindel, NYC
Cohen	Betsy H.	C		
Cohen	Eliot A.	C	Professor	Johns Hopkins Univ.
Cohen	Herman Jay	C	Assistant Secretary	State Dept., African Affairs
Cohen	Jerome Alan	C	Partner	Paul, Weiss, Riffind, Wharton, & Garrison

Last Name	First & Mid. Name	Org.	Job Title	Affiliation - Company, Organization
Cohen	Joel Ephraim	C	Trustee	Russell Sage Foundation
Cohen	Marshall A.	TC	Counsel	Cassels, Brock & Blackwell, Barristers & Solicitors, Toronto
Cohen	Patricia	C	Political Editor	Rolling Stone Magazine
Cohen	Roberta	C	Guest Scholar	Brookings Inst., Fgn. Pol. Studies
Cohen	Stephen B.	C	Attorney	Georgetown Law Center, Wash.
Cohen	Stephen Frand	C	Commentator	CBS News; Prof., Princeton Univ.
Cohen	Stephen S.	C	Director	Council on Foreign Relations
Cohen	William Sebastian	C,T	Secretary	Defense; Senator (fmr.), Maine, Armed Svcs., Judiciary
Colbert	Evelyn	C	Sr. Res. Analyst	Carnegie Endowment for Int. Peace
Colby	Jonathan E.	C		
Colby	William Egan	C	Director (fmr.)	CIA; Lawyer, Civil. Oper. & Rural Devel. Support, Saigon
Cole	Johnnetta Betsch	C	President	Spelman College; Director, Coca-Cola Co.
Cole	Samual A.	C		
Cole	Thomas Winston Jr.	C		
Coleman	James S.	T	Trustee	Hudson Institute
Coleman	Lewis W.	C		
Coleman	William Thaddeus, Jr.	C,T	Sr. Partner	O'Melveny & Myers; Sec. (fmr.) Transportation
Coles	Isobel	C	Author	"Built-in Impediments"
Coles	James Stacy	C	Pres. (fmr.)	Bowdin College
Collado	Robert E.	T	Chairman (fmr.)	A T & T
Collier	David	C		
Collins	Joseph J.	C	Chairman	Time Warner Cable
Collins	Paula J.	C	Director	Eastman Kodak Co., Trade Relations
Collomb	Bertrand	BF,TE	Chairman & CEO	Lafarge-Coppee, Paris
Colombo	Umberto	TE	Chairman	Foundation LEAD Euirope, Rome
Colonna di Paliano	Don Guido, Prince	BI	Chairmen (fmr.)	La Rinascente
Combs	Richard E., Jr.	C	Director	Newly Independent States Non Proliferation Project
Comstock	Phil	C	Representitive	Int. Guard, Joint Warrighter Ctr.
Conable	Barbara B.	T	Congresswoman	New York; Commissioner, UN Comm. On Global Governance
Condon	Joseph F.	C	Sr. Vice President	Combustion Engineering Int. Sales, Inc.
Cone	Sydney M., III	C	Partner	Cleary, Gottlieb, Steen & Hamilton
Connaughton	James L.	C		
Conners	Leila	C	Founder	TRA Mulitmedia Content Provider
Connolly	Gerald Edward	C	Partner	Quarles & Brady
Connor	John Thomas, Jr.	C	Partner	Sills, Cummis, Radin, Newark
Connor	Joseph E.	C	Partner	Price Waterhouse & Co.
Conroy	Richard	TE	Chairman & CEO	Conroy Diamonds & Gold;Senate Mbr.,Irish Repub.;Ch.,ARCON
Considine	Jill M.	C	President	N.Y. Clearinghouse Assn. (Banking)
Constable	Pamela	C	Staff Writer	*Washington Post*
Conway	Jill Kathryn Ker	C	President (fmr.)	Smith College
Cook	Donald (Don) C.	B,C	Euro. Dip. Cor. (fmr.)	Los Angeles Times
Cook	Frances D.	C	US Ambassador	State Dept., Cameroon, Yaounde
Cook	Gail C. A.	TC	Exec. Vice President	Bennecon Ltd., Toronto
Cook	Gary M.	C	President	Cook Co. (Consulting)
Cook	Gretchen R.	C		
Cook	Howard A.	C	President (fmr.)	Mac Jannet Foundation
Cooke	Goodwin	C	Professor	Syracuse Univ.
Cooke	John F.	C	Board Member	Center for National Policy
Coolidge	Nicholas J.	C		
Coombe	George William, Jr.	C	Exec. Vice Pres. (fmr.)	Bank of America, San Francisco
Coombs	Philip H.	C		
Coon	Jane Abell	C	U.S. Amb. (fmr.)	State Dept., to Bangladesh
Cooney	Joan Ganz	C	Chair., Exec. Comm.	Children's TV Wkshop; Dir., Johnson & Johnson, Xerox
Cooper	Charles A.	C,T	Chairman	C.I.A., Nat. Intelligence Council
Cooper	Chester L.	C	Agent (fmr.)	CIA
Cooper	James H.S.	C	Member	Medical Quality Commission
Cooper	John Milton, Jr.	C,T	Advisory Bd. Member	Center for International Policy
Cooper	Kathleen B.	C		
Cooper	Kerry	C	Member	Stanford A. Winter & Brian L. Weiner Endowment Found.
Cooper	Rebecca J.	C		
Cooper	Richard Newell	B,C,T	Professor	Harvard U.;Dir.,CFR;Und.Sec.(fmr.),St. Dept.,Econ.Afrs.
Cooper	Yvette	TE	Member	British Parliament
Cordesman	Anthony H.	C	Co-Director	Ctr. for Strategic & Int. Studies
Cornelius	Wayne	C	Specialist	Univ. of Cal., Ctr. of U.S.-Mexico Studies
Corrigan	E. Gerald	B,C,T	Partner & Mng. Dir.	Goldman Sachs; Pres. (fmr.), Fed. Res. Bk., NY;Dir.,CFR
Corrigan	Kevin	C	Member	Prodemca, National Council
Cortines	Ramon C,	B	Chancellor	New York City, Board of Education
Corzine	Jon S.	B	Chair. & Sr. Partner (fmr.)	Goldman Sachs & Co.
Costopoulos	Yannis	B		
Cott	Suzanne	C		
Cotta	Alain	TE	Professor	Univ. of Paris, Economics & Management
Cotter	William Reckling	C	President	Colby College
Cotti	Flavio	BCH	Minister	Switzerland, Foreign Affairs
Couloumbis	Theodore A.	BGR	President	Greek Foreign Policy Institute
Courtis	Kenneth	B	1st Vice-President	Deutsche Bank Group
Courtney	William Harrison	C	U.S. Ambassador	State Dept., Kazakhstan
Cousens	Elizabeth M.	C		

Who's Who of the Elite

Last Name	First & Mid. Name	Org.	Job Title	Affiliation - Company, Organization
Coutinho	Vasco Pereira	BF	Chairman	IPC Holding
Covey	James "Jock" P.	C		
Cowal	Sally Grooms	C	US Ambassador	State Dept., Port of Spain, Trinidad & Tobago
Cowan	L. Gray	C	Consultant	Center for Int. Studies, African Studies
Cowen	Jeffery	C		
Cowhey	Peter F.	C	Bureau Chief	State Dept., Int. Bureau Fed. Communications Commission
Cowles	John	T	Trustee/CEO (fmr.)	Cowles Media Company
Cox	Edward F.	C	Member	S.U.N.Y., Planning Committee Steering Committee
Cox	Robert Gene	C	Governor	Oxford Univ., Manchester College
Cradock	Percy	BGB	Ambassador (fmr.)	to China, Great Britain
Crahan	Margaret E.	C	Chairwoman	Hunter College, Env. Justice: Response
Cranborne	Robert M.J.C.	BGB	Leader	Opposition Party, House/Lords
Craner	Lorne W.	C		
Cranston	Alan	T	Senator (fmr.)	California
Cravinho	Joao Cardona G.	BP	Minister	for Infrastructure, Planning & Territorial Admin.
Crawford	John F.	C	Author	"Notes on the Uses of Edgar Poe"
Cressey	Roger W., III	C		
Crichton	Kyle C.	C		
Crile	George, III	C	Editor/Publisher (fmr.)	Medical Tribune; Physician
Crittenden	Ann	C	Reporter (fmr.)	*New York Times*
Crocker	Bathsheba N.	C		
Crocker	Chester Arthur	C	Chairman	US Institute of Peace
Crockett	Andrew	BINT	Gen. Mgr.	Bank for Int. Settlement
Cromwell	Adelaide M.	C	Professor	Boston Univ.
Cronin	Audrey Kurth	C	Professor (fmr.)	Univ. of Virginia, Politics of NATO
Cross	Devon G.	B	Head	Donner Canadian Foundation
Cross	June Victoria	C	Producer	Frontline Station, WGBH-TV
Cross	Sam Y.	C	Manager	Federal Reserve Board, F.O.M.Account
Crowe	William J., Jr.	C,T	US Ambassador	State Dept., U. K.; Chair. (fmr.), Joint Chiefs-of-Staff
Crown	Lester	C		
Cruise	Daniel L.	C		
Crystal	Lester Martin	C	Executive Producer	PBS TV, MacNeil Lehrer News Hour
Cullum	Lee	C	Columnist	Dallas Morning News
Culver	David	TC	Chairman	CAI Capital Corp., Montreal
Culver	John C.	C,T	Senator (fmr.)	Iowa
Cummings	Robert L., Jr.	C	Attorney	Arent, Fox, Kintner, Plotkin & Kahn
Cummiskey	Frank J.	C		IBM
Cumpiano	Flavio	C		
Cuomo	Kerry Kennedy	C	Daughter	of Robert Kennedy, wife of Andrew Cuomo
Cuomo	Mario Matthew	C	Governor (fmr.)	New York
Curran	R. T.	C	President	Foreign Policy Association
Currie	Donald Henry	B	Chairman & CEO	General Instruments Corp., Chicago
Currie	Malcolm Roderick	C	Chairman & CEO	Hughes Aircraft Co., missile systems group
Curtis	Charles B.	C		
Curtis	Gerald L.	C,T	Professor	Columbia Univ., Political Science, East Asian Institute
Cusimano	Maryanne K.	C		
Cutileiro	Jose	BINT	Secretary General	Western European Union
Cutler	Lloyd Norton	C,T	Counsel	to US Pres. Clinton, '94; Adv. Bd. Mbr., Ctr. for Nat. Pol.
Cutler	Walter Leon	C	US Ambassador (fmr.)	State Dept., Tunesia, Saudi Arabia
Cutshaw	Kenneth A.	C		
Cutter	W. Bowman	C	Deputy Assistant	to US President for Economic Policy
Cyr	Arthur	C	Vice President	Council on Foreign Relations, Chicago
Cyr	Raymond	TC	President	Bell Canada Enterprises
Da Silva	Russell J.	C	Partner	Christy & Viener
Daalder	Iao H.	C		
Dahlman	Michael Keith	C		
Dahrendorf	Ralf	BINT	Director (fmr.)	London School of Economic & Political Science
Dale	William Brown	C	Dep. Mng Dir. (fmr.)	International Monitary Fund, Geneva
Dallara	Charles H.	B	Asst. Secretary (fmr.)	State Dept., International Affairs
Dalley	George Albert	C	Partner	Neill, Dalley, Carroll, Nealer & Assev.
Dallin	Alexander	C	Dept. Chairman	Stanford Univ., International Relations
Dalma	Alfons	BA	Editor-in-Chief (fmr.)	ORF, Austrian radio & television
Dalton	Gregory	C		
Dalton	James Edward	C	President	Logicon RDA, Corp.
Dam	Kenneth W.	B,C	Council Member	Brookings Inst.; Deputy Sec. (fmr.), St. Dept.; Dir., CFR
Dam	Marcia W.	C		
Dammerman	Dennis D.	T	V. Chair. & Exec. Officer	General Electric Xompany
Damrosch	Lori Fisler	C		
Danforth	John C	T	Senator	US Senate
Danforth	William Henry	C	President	Washington Univ.; Director, McDonnell Douglas Corp.
Daniel	Ana R.	C		
Daniel	David Ronald	C	Council Member	Brookings Institute; Managing Director, McKinsey & Co.
Danner	Mark	C	Staff Writer	New Yorker magazine
Darman	Richard Gordon	C,T	Director (fmr.)	Office of Management & Budget, Bush Admin.
Dash	Michele Samantha	C		
David	George A.	BGR	Chairman	Hellenic Bottling Company S.A.
David	Jack	C		

Last Name	First & Mid. Name	Org.	Job Title	Affiliation - Company, Organization
David-Weill	Michel	TE	Sr. Partner	Lazard Freres & Co., Paris & New York
Davidson	Daniel I.	C	Attorney	Spiegel McDiarmid, Wash.
Davidson	Ralph Kirby	C	Assoc. Director (fmr.)	Rockefeller Foundation
Davidson	Ralph Parsons	C	Chairman	Time Inc., JFK Center for the Performing Arts
Davignon	Viscounte Etienne	BB,TE	Honorary Chairman	Bilderbergs Soc.Generale de Belgique;V.Ch.(fmr.)Com./Euro.
Davis	Allison S.	C		
Davis	Evan A.	C	Partner	Clearly, Gottlieb, Steen, Hamilton, N.Y..
Davis	Jacquelyn Kay	C	President	National Security Planning Association
Davis	Jerome	C	Division Chief	Transportation Dept., Supply & Space Management
Davis	Kathryn Wasserman	C	President	Shelby Cullom Davis Foundation
Davis	Lynn E.	B,C,T	Under Secretary	State Dept., International Security Affairs
Davis	Maceo N.	C	Chairman & CEO	Int. Resource Exchange Corp.
Davis	Nathaniel	C	Ambassador (fmr.)	Chile
Davis	Shelby Cullom	C	Managing Partner	Cullom Davis & Co.
Davis	Stephen M.	C		
Davis	Vincent	C	Director	Patterson School of Diplomacy & Int. Communications
Davis	Kim Gordon	C		
Davison	Daniel Pomeroy	C	Chairman	Christie, Manson & Woods, Int., Inc. (auctioneers)
Davison	Kristina Perkin	C		
Davison	W. Phillips	C		
Dawisha	Karen Lea	C		
Dawkins	Peter Miller	C	Chairman & CEO	Primerica Financial Services
Dawson	Horace Greeley, Jr.	C	US Ambassador (fmr.)	State Dept., Botswana
Dawson	Marion M.	C	Member-Designate	African Development Foundation
Day	Anthony	C	Sr. Correspondent	Los Angeles Times
Day	Arthur R.	C	US Ambassador (fmr.)	State Dept., to Jaruselem
Days	Drew Saunders, III	C		
De Crane	Alfred C., Jr.	C	Chairman & CEO	Texaco Inc.
de Cuba	Jose	C		
de Janosi	Peter E.	C	Director	IIASA, Luxemburg, Austria
de Menil	George	C	Son	Dominique de Menil, art collector & philanthropist
de Menil	Joy	C		
de Menil	Lois Pattison	C	Author	"Chirac's France in the New Europe"
de Vries	Rimmer	C	Sr. Vice President	Morgan Guaranty Trust Co., NYC
Deagle	Edwin Augustus, Jr.	C	Director	Hughes Aircraft Co., Int. Business Planning
Dean	Jonathan	C	Member (fmr.)	Carnegie Endowment for International Peace
Dean	Robert W.	C	Director	AGC, Membership & Marketing
Deans	Ian	TC	Chairperson	Public Service Staff Relations Board of Canada, Ottawa
Debevoise	Eli Whitney, II	C	Co-Founder	Debevoise, Plimpton, N.Y.
Debs	Barbara Knowles	C	Trustee	Geraldine R. Dodge Foundation
Debs	Richard A.	C	Trustee	Carnegie Endowment; Chairman, Debs, R. A. & Co.
Decherd	Robert W.	T	Chairman	A. H. Belo Corp.
Declercq	Baron Guido	TE	Hon. Chairman	ORDA-B; Hon. Gen. Admin., Catholic Univ., Leuven
Decter	Midge	C	Distinguished Fellow	Institute on Religion & Public Life
Decyk	Roxanne J.	C		
Dedrick	Fred T.	C	Director	Greater Philadephia First Foundation, Econ. Development
Deffenbaugh	Ralston H., Jr.	C	Executive Director	Lutheran Immigration & Refugee Service
Deflassieux	Jean	TE	Chairman	Banque des Eschanges Int.;Hon. Chair.,Credit Lyonnais
Deibel	Terry L.	C	Prof. & Chairman	Defense Dept., National War College, Nat. Security Pol.
del Olmo	Frank	C	Deputy Editor	Los Angeles Times
Del Toro	Carlos	C		
Del Turco	Ottaviano	TE	General Secretary	Italian Socialist Party (PSI), Rome
Delamuraz	Jean-Pascal	B	Vice President	Federal Council; Minister of the Economy
Deleuran	Aage	BDK	Editor-in-Chief	Berlingske Tidende, Denmark
Delorme	Jean-Claude	BC	Chairman	Caisse de depot et placement du Quibec
Deming	Frederick Lewis	B	Director	National City Bancorp
Demirel	Suleyman	BTR	Prime Minister (fmr.)	Turkey
Denham	Robert E.	C		
Denison	Robert J.	C	Vice Chairman	CalArts; Chair. First Security Mgt., N.Y.
Dennis	Bengt	TE	Senior Advisor	Skandinaviska Enskilda Banken, Stockholm
Dennis	Everette Eugene, Jr.	C	Executive Director	Columbia Univ.
Denny	Brewster Castberg	C	Dean (fmr.)	Univ. of Washington, Seattle
Denoon	David Baugh Holden	C	Professor	New York Univ., NYC
Denton	E. Hazel	C	Author	"Srilanka", Harvard Business School
Denton	James S.	C		
DePalma	Samuel	C		
DePoy	Philip E.	C		
Dergham	Raghida	C	President	U.N. Correspondent's Association
Derian	Patricia Murphy	C	Asst. Secretary (fmr.)	State Dept., Human Rights
Derr	Kenneth T.	C		
Derryck	Vivian Lowery	C	President	African-American Institute
Dertouzos	Michael	C		
DeShazer	Mac Arthur	C		
Desmarais	Andre'	TC	Chairman & CEO	Power Corp. of Canada, Montrial
DeSouza	Patrick J.	C	Project Dir.	Nat. Security Council
Destler	I. M.	C	Member(fmr.)	Carnegie Endowment for International Peace
Dethleffsen	Erich	BD	Attendee	Bilderberg Group, 1966

Last Name	First & Mid. Name	Org.	Job Title	Affiliation - Company, Organization
Deutch	John Mark	B,C,T	Director (fmr.)	C.I.A.; Deputy Secretary (Fmr.) Defense Dept., for Acquis.
Deutch	Michael J.	C	Father of	John Deutch, DCI (fmr.)
Deutch	Philip J.	C		
Deutsch	John H.	BC	Professor (fmr.)	Queen's Univ., Canada
DeVecchi	Robert P.	C	President	International Rescue Committee
Devedjian	Patrick	TE	Member	French National Assembly, Paris
Devine	Caroline M.	C		
Devine	M. Colette	C		
Devine	Thomas J.	C		
DeWind	Adrian W.	C	Trustee	Institute for Policy Studies
DeYoung	Karen	C	Member	Washington Post
Di Martino	Rita	C	Director	Fed. Gov. Affairs
Dicke	Gunther F. W.	BD	First VP	Deutsche Bank AG, Organizer '91 BB Conf.
Dickey	Christopher S.	C		
Dicks	Norman D.	C	Congressman	Washington, Appropriations, Select Intelligence/Ranking
Dickson	R. Russell, Jr.	C		
Diebold	John	B,C	President & Chairman	Diebold Group; Chairman, Griffenhagen-Kroeger, Inc.
Diebold	William, Jr.	C		
Diehl	Jackson	C	Asst. Managing Editor	Washington Post
Dieter	Werner H.	BD	Chairman	Mannesmann A.G., Duesseldorf, Germany
Dilenschneider	Robert Louis	C	Principal	Dilenschneider Group, Inc. NYC (public relations)
Dillon	C. Douglas	B,C	Vice Chairman (fmr.)	CFR, '76-'78; Mbr., Brookings Inst.
Dine	Thomas A.	C	Asst. Administrator	St. Dept., A. I. D., Bureau of Euro. & New Ind. States
Dinh	Viet D.	C		
Dinkins	David	C	Mayor (fmr.)	New York
Dion	Stephane	B	Minister	Intergovt. Affairs
DiPaola	Joseph, Jr.	C		
Ditlev-Simonsen	Per	BN	Managing Director	Sverre Ditlev-Simonsen & Co.
Dixon	Carmen R.	C		
Djerejian	Edward Peter	C	US Ambassador (fmr.)	St. Dept., Syria; Asst. Sec. (fmr.),Near E. & S. Asian Afrs.
Dlouhy	Vladimir	TE	Min. of Econ. (fmr.)	Czechoslovakia; Sr. Advisor, ABB
Dobell	Peter C.	TC	Founding Director	Parliament Centre for Fgn. Affairs & Fgn. Trade, Ottawa
Dobriansky	Paula	T	V.P & Wash. Dir.	Council on Foreign Relations
Dobson	Wendy K.	T	Prof. & Director	Ctr. For Int. Business, Toronto Univ.; Deputy (fmr.), G-7
Dodd	Christopher J.	B,C	Senator	Connecticut, Bkg., Hsg. & Urban Afrs., Fgn. Rel., Rules
Dodge	William S.	C	Professor	Hastings of the Law
Doebele	Justin	C	Writer	*Forbes* magazine
Doerge	David J.	C		
Dogramaci	Ihsan	BTR	Professor (fmr.)	Hacettepe Univ., Turkey
Doherty	William C., Jr.	C	Son	Joseph Doherty, formerly with Merrill Lynch
Dohnanyi	Klaus von	BD	Member (fmr.)	Ger. Bundestag; Mayor (fmr.), Freie u. Hansestadt; SPD
Dominguez	Jorge Ignacio	C	Department Chairman	Harvard Univ., Cuban Studies
Donahue	Thomas Reilly	C,T	Sec./Treasurer (fmr.)	AFL-CIO Union; Dir., CFR
Donaldson	Robert Herschel	C	President	Univ. of Tulsa
Donaldson	William Henry	C	Chairman & CEO	New York Stock Exchange; Trustee, Carnegie Endow.
Donilon	Thomas E.	B,C	Chief of Staff (fmr.)	State Dept.; Asst. Sec., for Public Affairs
Donnea	Francois X.	B	Minister (fmr.)	Defense
Donnell	Ellsworth	C		
Donnelly	Harold C.	C		
Donnelly	Sally B.	C	Correspondent	Time magazine, Moscow
Doran	Charles F.	C	Professor	Johns Hopkins Univ., School of Medicine
Dorsen	Norman	C		
Dory	Amanda Jean	C		
Doty	Grant R.	C		
Doty	Paul M., Jr.	C	Director (fmr.)	Harvard Univ., Center for Science
Dougan	Diana, Lady	C	Chairwoman	World Communications Advisory Council
Douglas	Paul W.	C	Chair& CEO (Fnr.)	The Pittston Co.
Douglass	Robert Royal	C	Vice Chairman (fmr.)	Chase Manhattan Bank; Director, Rockefeller Ctr.
Dowling	John N.	C		
Downie	Leonard, Jr.	C	Executive Editor	Washington Post
Doyle	James S.	C	V. P., Exec. Editor	Army Times, The Independent Weekly
Doyle	Michael William	C	Professor	Prinseton Univ.
Draghi	Mario	BI	Director General	Italian Ministry of the Treasury
Draper	William Henry, III	C	CEO	UN Development Programme
Drayton	William, Jr.	C	Mbr. Advisory Coun.	Carnegie Commission for Science Tech. & Government
Drell	Sidney David	C	Executive Director	Stanford Univ., Linear Accelerator Center
Drew	Elizabeth	C	Commentator	NBC, Meet The Press; Columnist; Director (fmr.), CFR
Dreyfuss	Joel	C	Editor-in-Chief	*Our World News*
Drittel	Peter Marc	C		
Dromer	Jean	TE	Chairman	Financiere Agache, Paris
Drouin	Marie-Josee	BC,TC	Executive Dir.	Hudson Inst. of Canada, Montreal
Drucker	Joy E.	C		
Drucker	Richard A.	C		
Druckerman	Pamela	C		
Drumwright	J. R.	C		
Duberstein	Kenneth M.	C	Chief-of-Staff (fmr.)	White House, Reagan Administration
Dubin	Seth H.	C	Partner	Satterle, Stephens, Burke & Burke

Last Name	First & Mid. Name	Org.	Job Title	Affiliation - Company, Organization
Dubow	Arthur Myron	C	President	Fourth Estate, Inc.
DuBrul	Stephen M., Jr.	C	Trustee	Int. House
Ducci	Roberto	BI	Director General (fmr.)	Political Affairs, Minister for Foreign Affairs
Duderstadt	James J.	C	Chairman	National Science Foundation, National Science Board
Due	Johnita P.	C		
Duersten	Althea L.	C		
Duffey	Joseph Daniel	C	Director	Information Agency; President (fmr.), American Univ.
Duffy	Gloria Charmian	C	Dep. Asst. Sec. (fmr.)	Defense Dept., Special Coordinatyor for Threat Reduction
Duffy	James Henry	C	Author	Fiction & Non-fiction books
Dugan	Michael J.	C	Chief-of-Staff (fmr.)	Defense Dept.; Air Force
Dukakis	Michael Stanley	C	Governor (fmr.)	Massachusetts; Candidate for US President (fmr.)
Duke	Angier Biddle	C	US Ambassador (fmr.)	State Dept., El Salvador, Spain, Denmark
Duke	Robin Chandler	C		
Dulany	Peggy	C	Director	Overseas Development Council
Dunbar	Charles F.	C		
Duncan	Charles William, Jr.	C	Director	Coca-Cola Co., Council Member, Brookings Institute
Duncan	John C.	C	Vice President (fmr.)	St. Joe Minerals Corp
Duncan	Richard L.	C	Executive Editor	Time magazine
Dunigan	Andrew	C		
Dunigan	P. Andrew	C		
Dunkel	Arthur	BINT	Director General	GATT (General Agreement on Tariffs & Trade)
Dunkerley	Craig G.	C		
Dunlop	Joan Banks	C	Member	Overseas Development Council
Dunn	Kempton	C	Environ. Analyst	Arthur D. Little (Consultant)
Dunn	Lewis A.	C	Author	"Kuwait, the Outbreak of Hostilities and the Aftermath"
Dunn	Michael M.	C		
Dunston	Stronica	C		
Dupuy	Michel	BC	Asst. Und. sec. (fmr.)	Canada, State Dept.
Dur	Philip A.	C	Rear Admiral	Defense Dept., Navy
Durao Barrosso	Jose Manuel	BP	Minister	Foreign Affairs
Dutton	Frederick G.	C	Special Asst. (fmr.)	White House, to the President
Duval, -Raoul	Michael	C	Limited Partner	Anthem Partners
Dyke	Nancy Bearg	C	Asst. (fmr.)	White House, for Nat. Security Affairs
Dymally	Mervyn Malcolm	C	Congressman (fmr.)	California
Dyson	Esther	C		
Eagleburger	Lawrence S.	C,T	Secretary (fmr.)	State Dept.; Director, Phillips Petroleum
Earle	Ralph, II	C	Deputy Director	Arms Cont. & Disarm. Ag.; Dir.,Lawyers Alliance/World Secur.
Earner	William A.	C		
Easum	Donald B.	C	US Ambassador (fmr.)	State Dept., Nigeria
Eaton	Frederik S.	BC	Chair., Exec. Comm.	Eaton's of Canada
Eberhart	Ralph E.	C	Vice Chief-of-Staff	Defense Dept. HQ U. S. Airforce, Wash.
Eberle	William Denman	C	Chairman	Holders Capital Corp.
Eberstadt	Mary	C	Professor	Hudson Inst.
Eberstadt	Nicholas N.	C		
Ecevit	Bulent	BTR	Member (fmr.)	Turkish Parliament
Echols	Marsha A.	C	Professor	Harvard Univ., Law School
Eckardt	Felix von	BD	Ambassador (fmr.)	United Nations; Mbr. (fmr.) Budnestag; CDU
Eckartsberg, von	K. Gayle	C		
Economy	Elizabeth C.	C		
Ecton	Donna R.	C	President & CEO	Van Houten N. America
Edelman	Albert I.	C		
Edelman	Gerald Maurice	C	Director	Neuroscience Institute
Edelman	Marian Wright	C	President	Children's Defense Fund, Mbr. of Bd., Ctr. for Int. Policy
Edelstein	Julius C. C.	C	Admin. Asst. (fmr.)	to Senator Herbert H. Lehman
Edington	Mark D. W.	T	Author	"Fog of the Familiar Paradigm:On the Dangers/Applied Theory"
Edley	Christopher, Jr.	C	Associate Director	Office of Management & Budget, Economics & Gvt.
Edwards	Claude A.	TC	President	Fed. Superannuates Nat. Assoc.
Edwards	Howard Lee	C	Corp. Secretary	Atlantic Richfield Co.
Edwards	Mickey	C		
Edwards	Robert Hazard	C	President	Bowdoin College
Efros	Laura L.	C		
Eggers	Thomas E.	C	Majority Partner	Computer Sciences Corp.
Ehmke	Horst	TE	Member (fmr.)	German Bundestag, SPD
Ehrlich	Thomas	C	Professor	Indiana Univ. System, Law
Ehrnrooth	Georg	BFIN	President & CEO	Metra Corp., Finland
Eichengreen	Barry	C	Economist	Univ. of Cal., Berkeley
Eilts	Hermann Frederick	C	Department Chairman	Boston Univ.; US Ambassador (fmr.), Saudi Arabia
Einaudi	Luigi R.	C	Sr. Advisor	State Dept., Policy Planning Staff
Einaudi	Mario	C	Professor	Cornell Univ., Center for Int. Studies
Einhorn	Jessica P.	C,T	Managing Director	World Bank, for Finance & Resource Mobilization
Einhorn	Robert J.	C		
Eisendrath	Charles R.	C	Director	Michigan Univ., Journalism Flow. Prog.
Eisner	Michael	C	Chairman	Walt Disney Company
Eizenstat	Stuart E.	C	Under Secretary	St. Dept, Int. Trade; V. Ch., Powell, Goldstein, Frazer & Murphy
Ejiri	Koichiro	TJ	Sr. Bd. Advisor	Mitsui & Co., Ltd.
Ejiri	Takashi	TJ	Attorney	Ashai Law Office
Eldeman	Richard Winston	C		

Last Name	First & Mid. Name	Org.	Job Title	Affiliation - Company, Organization
Eliot	Theodore Lyman, Jr.	B,C	US Hon. Sec. Gen.	Bilderberg Group; US Ambassador (fmr.), Afghanistan
Ellemann-Jensen	Uffe	BDK	Member	Danish Parliament; Minister (fmr.), Foreign Affairs
Ellingwood	Susan K.	C	Asst. Editor	*New Republic*
Elliott	Byron Kauffman	C	Chairman (fmr.)	John Hancock Mutual Insurance Co.
Elliott	Inger McCabe	C		
Elliott	Osborn	C	Professor	Columbia Univ.
Ellis	James Reed	C	Trustee	Henry M. Jackson Foundation
Ellis	Patricia	C	Co-Chairman	Carnegie Endowment, Foreign Policy Group
Ellison	Keith P.	C		
Ellsburg	Daniel	C	Author	The Pentagon Papers
Ellsworth	Paolo	T	Vice Chairman & CEO	General Electric Co., USA
Ellsworth	Robert Fred	C	Chairman	Howmet Corp.; Dep. Secretary, Defense Dept, Ford Admin.
Elson	Edward E.	C		
Ely	John Hart	C	Professor	Stanford Univ., Law School
Ely-Raphel	Nancy Halliday	C	Prin. Dep. Asst. Sec.	State Dept.
Embree	Ainslie Thomas	C	Professor (fmr.)	Duke Univ.
Emerson	Alice Frey	C	Sr. Fellow	Andrew W. Mellon Found.; Dir., Eastman Kodak Co.
Emerson	Steven A.	C	Specialist	Middle East terrorist
Emminger	Otmar	BD	President (fmr.)	Deutsche Bundesbank;Mbr. (fmr.) BIZ, Basel, Switzerland
Emmott	Bill	TE	Editor	"The Economist", London
Enders	Thomas O.	C	Managing Dir.	Salomon Brothers Inc.
Engelen-Kefar	Ursula	BD	Deputy Chair.	Deutscher Gewerkschaftsbund
Engholm	Bjoern	BD	Chairman	Ger. Bundestag; Min. (Fmr.), Trade & Commerce; CDU
English	Robert D.	C		
Enrico	Roger A.	T	Chair. & CEO	PepsiCo, Inc.
Ensor	David B.	C		
Enthoven	Alain C.	C	Professor	Stanfore Univ., Public and Private Management
Entwistle	L. Brooks	C		
Epstein	Barbara	C		
Epstein	Jason	C	V. Pres. & Editor, Dir.	Random House, Inc.
Epstein	Jeffrey E.	T	President	J. Epstein & Co.; Wexner Investment Co.
Epstein	Joshua M.	C	Sr. Fellow	Brookings Inst.
Erb	Guy F.	C		Univ. of Cal., San Diego
Erb	Richard David	C	Deputy Managing Dir.	International Monitary Fund, Washington
Erbsen	Claude Ernest	C	V. Pres. & Director	Associated Press, World Services
Erburu	Robert F.	C,T	Chair. & CEO (fmr.)	Times Mirror Co.;Coun. Mbr., Brookings Inst.;Dir., CFR
Ercel	Gazi	BTR	Governor	Central Bank of Turkey
Ergin	Sedat	B	Bureau Chief	*Hurriyet* , Ankara
Erguder	Ustun	BTR	Rector	Bosporus Univ.
Erkcklentz	Alexander Tonio	C	Partner	Brown Brothers Harriman & Co.
Erkko	Aatos	BFIN,TE	Chairman	Sanoma Corp., Helsinki, Finland
Esperanza	Aguirre y Gil de Biedma	B	President	Spanish Parliament
Espy	Charisse	C		
Espy	Mike	B	Secretary	Agriculture Dept.
Esrey	William T.	T	Chair. & CEO	Sprint Corp.
Estabrook	Robert Harley	C	Publisher (fmr.)	Lakeville Journal, Connecticut
Estrada	Alfredo	C		
Esty	Daniel C.	C	Negotiator	NAFTA
Etxenike	Pedro Miguel	TE	Professor	Basque County U.;(fmr.)Basque Min./Educ.,San Sebastian,Spain
Evans	Carol V.	C		
Evans	Daniel J.	T	Chairman	Daniel J. Evans Assoc.
Evans	Gail H.	C		
Evans	Gordon W.	C	Life Trustee	Int. House
Evans	John C.	C	Advisory Dir.	Morgan Stanley & Co.
Evans	Robert	TE	CEO & Board Member	British Gas Corp., London
Evans	Rowland, Jr.	C	Sy. Col. & C0-Anchor	CNN, Evans & Novak
Evans	Tatjana H.	C		
Ewing	Anthony P.	C		
Ewing	William Hickman, Jr.	C	US Attorney (fmr.)	Justice Dept.
Exter	John	C	Monetary Econ. (fmr.)	Federal Reserve System
Eyton	John Trevor	TC	Member	Canadian Senate; Pres. & CEO, Brascan Ltd., Toronto
Fabian	Larry Louis	C	Sr. V. P. & CEO	CFR; Carnegie Endow., Rockefeller Found.
Fabius	Laurent	BF,TE	Member	Parliament; fmr. Prime Min., fmr. Ch. Parl.
Fairbanks	Charles H., Jr.	C		
Fairbanks	Douglas, Jr.	C	Actor	Hollywood
Fairbanks	Richard Monroe, III	C	Sr. Counsel	Center for Strategic & International Studies
Fairman	David M.	C		
Falco	Mathea	C	Sr. Associate	Carnegie Endowment for International Peace
Falk	Pamela S.	C	Staff Dir.	House of Representatives
Falk	Richard A.	C	Professor	Princeton Univ.
Falkenheim	Ernst G.P.	BD	Attendee	Bilderberg Group, 1966, Wiesbaden, Germany
Falkenrath	Richard A.	C		Harvard Univ.
Fallows	James MacKenzie	C	Editor	U.S. News & Wrld. Retp.; Wash. Edit. (fmr.), Atlantic Mthly.
Fanjul	Oscar	TE	Hon. Chairman	Repsol, Madrid (energy)
Fanning	Katherine Woodruff	C	Adjunct Professor	Boston Univ.
Fanton	Jonathan Foster	C	Trustee	Rockefeller Bro. Fund.; Pres., New School for Social Resch.
Faremo	Grete	TE	Vice President	Storebrand; (fmr.) Norwegian Min. of Devel. Cooperation

Last Name	First & Mid. Name	Org.	Job Title	Affiliation - Company, Organization
Farer	Tom Joel	C	Visiting Professor	Tulane Law School
Farmer	Thomas Laurence	C	Director	Overseas Development Council
Farrington	Thomas A.	C	Chairman	Nat. Ctr. For Afro/American Artists, Boston
Fascell	Dante B.	C	Congressman (fmr.)	Florida
Faure	Edgar	BF	President (fmr.)	French National Assembly
Faure	Lucie, Madam	BF	Author	French
Fawaz	Leila	C	President (fmr.)	Tufts Univ.
Feaver	Peter D.	C	Director	National Security Council, Defense Policy
Feierstein	Mark	C	Policy Advisor	State Dept., O. A. S., to US Representative
Feigenbaum	Evan A.	C		
Feinberg	Richard B.	C		
Feiner	Ava S.	C		
Feinstein	Dianne	B,T	Senator	California; Foreign Operations, Judiciary, Rules & Admin.
Feinstein	Lee Andrew	C		
Feissel	Gustave	C	Resident Rep. (fmr.)	U.N., to Cyprus
Feist	Samuel H.	C		
Feith	Douglas J.	C	Member (fmr.)	White House, Nat. Security Council
Feldman	Mark B.	C	President	International Advisers Inc.
Feldstein	Martin S.	B,C,T	Pres. & CEO	National Bureau of Economic Research; Prof., Harvard U.
Feltman	Jeffrey	C	Author	"Culturism, Autonomy, Women's Rights & Subjugation"
Fenster	Steven R.	C	Limited Ptnr. (fmr.)	Blackstone Group
Feo	Julio	TE	Chairman	Conssultores de Comunicacion y Direccion, Madrid
Ferguson	Charles Henry	C		
Ferguson	Glenn Walker	C	US Ambassador (fmr.)	State Dept., Kenya; President, Radio Free Europe
Ferguson	James L.	C	Chair. & CEO (fmr.)	General Foods Corp.
Ferguson	John Henry	B	Professor (fmr.)	Pennsylvania State Univ.
Ferguson	Ronald E.	C		
Ferguson	William Charles	C	Chairman & CEO	NYNEX Corp.
Ferlic	Suzanne	C		
Fernandez	Jose W.	C		
Ferragamo	Ferruccio	TE	Mng. Director	Salvatore Ferragamo Italia, Florence
Ferrari	Frank E.	C	V.P.	Pro Space Ventures Inc.
Ferraro	Geraldine Anne	C	Congresswoman (fmr.)	New York; US Amb. to the UN Human Rights Comm.
Ferre	Antonio Luis	C	President & Publisher	El Nuevo Dia
Ferre	Maurice A.	C	Advisory Bd. Member	Center for Int. Policy; Advisory Bd., Ctr. for Nat. Policy
Ferrell	Lisa C.	C		
Ferrer	Carlos	TE	Chairman	Ferrer Int. Group; Chair., Int. Vienna Council
Fesharaki	Fereidun	C	Member	East-West Center
Feshbach	Murry	C	Professor	Georgetown Univ.
Fessenden	Hart	C	General Council	Export-Import Bank of US, Wash.
Fetter	Steve	C	Advisory Bd. Member	Center for International Policy
Feyzioglu	Turan	BTR	Dep. Prm. Min. (fmr.)	Turkey
Fields	Bertram M.	C		
Fields	Craig I.	C		
Fierce	Mildred C.	C		
Fife	Eugene V.	C		
Fifield	Russell Hunt	C	Contributer	Wall Street Journal, Asia
Figueras	Ana	C	Asst. Treasurer	Council on Foreign Relations
Finberg	Barbara Denning	C	Exec. Vice President	Carnegie Corp. of New York
Findakly	Hani K.	C		
Finger	Seymour Maxwell	C	Adjunct Professor	City Univ. of New York, NYC
Finkelstein	Lawrence S.	C	Professor	Northern Illinois Univ.
Finlayson	Grant Ellison	C		
Finn	James	C		
Finney	Paul B.	C		
Firestone	Charles M.	C		
Firmage	Edwin B.	C	Professor	Utah Univ., Law
Fischer	David J.	C	President	World Affairs Council
Fischer	Stanley	B,T	1st Dep. Mng. Dir.	IMF
Fisher	Cathleen S.	C	Sr. Associate	Henry L. Stimson Ctr. Wash., (Think Tank)
Fisher	Daniel S.	C		
Fisher	George Myles C.	T	Chairman & CEO	Eastman Kodak Co.
Fisher	Richard B.	T	Chairman	Morgan Stanley Dean Witter
Fisher	Richard W.	C	Member	Heritage Foundation
Fisher	Roger Dummer	C	Trustee	Hudson Inst.; Dir., Harvard Univ., Negotiation Project
Fishlow	Albert	C	Member	CFR, Economic Studies
Fitts	Sarah Watkins	C		
Fitz-Pegado	Lauri J.	C	Asst. Sec.-Designate	Commerce Dept., Foreign Comm. Service
FitzGerald	Frances	C	Member	Overseas Devel. Council; Edit. Bd. Carnegie Endow.
FitzGerald	Garret	BIRL,TE	Prime Minister (fmr.)	Ireland; Member, Irish Dail
Fitzgibbons	Harold E.	C		
Flaherty	Peter	C		
Flanagan	Peter	C		
Flanagan	Stephen J.	C		White House, Nat. Security Council
Flanigan	Peter Magnus	C	Director	Dillon, Read & Co., Inc.
Fleischmann	Alan H.	C		
Fleishman	Rachel	C		

Last Name	First & Mid. Name	Org.	Job Title	Affiliation - Company, Organization
Fletcher	Phillip Douglas	C	President	Con Agra
Flood	A. L.	BC	Chairman	Canadian Imperial Bank of Commerce
Florio	James J.	B	Governor (fmr.)	New Jersey
Flournoy	Michael A.	C	Member	White House, Nat. Security Council
Flournoy	Michael A.	C		
Flynn	George J.	C		
Flynn	Stephen E.	C	Member	US Cost Guard
Foege	William H.	C		
Fogleman	Ronald R.	C	Air Force Chief-of-Staff	Defense Dept., Air Mobility Command
Foley	S. R., Jr.	C		
Foley	Thomas Stephen	B,C,T	Spkr. of House (fmr.)	House of Represenbtatives; Amb. to Japan
Folsom	George A.	C		
Fontaine	Andre	BF	Editor-in-Chief (fmr.)	Le Monde, France
Foote	Edward Thaddeus, II	C	President	Univ. of Miami
Ford	Gerald Rudolph, Jr.	B,C	President (fmr.)	United States
Ford	Henry, II	B	President	Ford Motor Co.
Fore	Henrietta Holsman	B,C	Sr. Associate	CSIS (Ctr. For Strategic & Int. Studies)
Forester	Lynn	B,C	CEO	Netwave Inc. (Communications)
Forman	Shepard	C	Advisory Bd. Member	Center for International Policy
Forrestal	Robert Patrick	C	President	Federal Reserve Syst., Federal Reserve Bank of Atlanta
Forrester	Anne	C		
Forstmann	Theodore J.	C	Founding Ptnr.	Forstmann Little & Company; Dir., Cato Institute
Fort	Randall Martin	C	Deputy Asst. Sec.	State Dept.
Forte	Francesco	BI	Professor (fmr.)	Univ. of Torino
Fortier	L. Yves	TC	Sr. Partner	Ogilvy Renault, Barr. & Solic., Montrial; Can. Amb. (fmr.) UN;
Foster	Brenda Lei	C		
Foulon	Mark	C		
Fowler	Henry Hamill	C	General Partner	Goldman Sachs & Co.; Director, Foreign Policy Assoc.
Fox	Donald Thomas	C	Partner	Fox & Horan, NYC
Fox	Eleanor Mae Cohen	C	Professor	New York Univ., NYC, Law
Fox	Joseph Carter	C	President & CEO	Chesapeake Corp.
Fraga	Arminio	C		
Franck	Thomas Martin	C	Professor	New York Univ., NYC, Law
Francke	Albert, III	C	Partner	Curtis, Mallet-Prevost, Colt & Mosle, NYC
Frank	Andrew D.	C		
Frank	Barney	C	Congressman	Massachusetts, Banking & Finance, Judiciary
Frank	Charles Raphael, Jr.	C	Exec. Vice President	GE Capital Corp.
Frank	Isaiah	C	Professor	John Hopkins Univ.
Frank	Richard A.	C		
Frankel	Andrew V.	C		
Frankel	Francine Ruth	C	Professor	Univ. of Pennsylvania
Frankel	Jeffrey A.	C	Member	White House, Council of Economic Advisors
Frankel	Marvin E.	C	Partner	Kramer, Levin, Naftalis, Nessen, Kamin & Frankel
Franklin	Barbara Hackman	C	Secretary (fmr.)	Commerce Dept.; Director, Dow Chemical Co.
Franklin	George S.	C,T	Director (fmr.)	CFR; (David Rockefeller's roommate at Harvard Univ.)
Franklin	William E.	C		
Fraser	Donald M.	T	Congressman (fmr.)	Minnesotta
Frazer	Jendayi E.	C		
Frederick	Robert R.	C	Chair. & CEO (fmr.)	RCA
Fredericks	J. Wayne	C	Director	Foreign Policy Association
Fredman	Jonathan M.	C		
Freedman	Eugene M.	C		
Freedman	Lawrence	BGB	Head of Department	of War Studies, King's College, U. K.
Freeman	Bennett	C	Deputy Asst. Sec.	State Dept., Public Affairs
Freeman	Charles W., Jr.	B	Asst. Sec. (fmr.)	Defense Dept., for Int. Security
Freeman	Constance J.	C		
Freeman	Harry Louis	C	Secretary (fmr.)	Agriculture; Chair., Worldwatch
Freeman	Orville L.	C	Member	Overseas Devel. Council; Sec. (fmr.), Agriculture
Freeman	Roger C.	C		
Frehner	Walter	BCH	Chairman	Swiss Bank Corp.
Freidheim	Cyrus F., Jr.	C	Vice Chairman	Booz, Allen & Hamilton Inc., NYC
Freidheim	Stephen C.	C		
Frelinghuysen	Peter H. B.	C		
Fremont-Smith	Marion R.	C	Partner	Choate, Hall & Stewart, Boston
Fresco	Paolo	B,T	Chairman	Fiat S.p.A.
Freund	Gerald	C	President	Private Funding Association
Frey	Donald Nelson	C	Director	Clark Equipment Co.
Freytag	Richard A.	C	President & CEO	Citicorp Banking Corp.
Fribourg	Michel	C	Chairman (fmr.)	Continental Grain Co.
Fribourg	Paul	C		
Fried	Edward R.	C	Sr. Fellow	Brookings Institute
Friedberg	Aaron L.	C		Princeton Univ.
Friedman	Bart	C	Sr. Partner	Ciahill, Gordon, & Reindale
Friedman	Benjamin Morton	C	Department Chairman	Harvard Univ., Dept. of Economics
Friedman	David S.	C		
Friedman	Jennifer	C		
Friedman	Jordana D.	C		

Last Name	First & Mid. Name	Org.	Job Title	Affiliation - Company, Organization
Friedman	Stephen James	B,C,T	Sr. Ch. & Ltd. Partner	Goldman Sachs & Co.
Friedman	Thomas L.	B,C,T	Fgn. Affrs. Columnist	New York Times
Friend	Theodore Wood, III	C	President	Eisenhower Exchange Fellowship Inc.
Froman	Michael B. G.	C		
Fromkin	David	C	Professor	Boston Univ., Int. Relations
Fromm	Joseph	C	Asst. Editor (fmr.)	US News & World Report
Fromuth	Peter	C	Special Assistant	State Dept., Mission to the UN
Froot	Kenneth A.	C	Professor	Harvard Univ., Finance
Frost	Ellen Louise	C	Sr. Fellow	Inst. for Int. Econ.; Adv. Bd. Member, Ctr. for Nat. Pol.
Frum	David	B	Polit. Commentator	
Fry	Earl H.	C	Chairman	Brigham Young Univ., Canadian Studies
Frye	Alton	C	Sr. V. P. & Nat. Dir.	Council on Foreign Relations, '94
Frye	William R.	C		
Fuchs	Michael	TE	President	Nat. Federation of German Wholesale & Export Trade
Fudge	Ann M.	C		
Fuerbringer	Otto	C	Professor	Stanford Univ.
Fujii	Hirokai	TJ	President	The Japan Foundation
Fukukawa	Shinji	TJ	Chairman & CEO	Dentsu Inst./Human Stud.;Ex.V.Pres.(fmr.),Kobe Steel Co.
Fukuyama	Francis	C	Sr. Researcher	RAND Corp.
Fuld	Richard S., Jr..	C		
Fuller	Kathryn Scott	C	President & CEO	World Wildlife Fund, Washington
Fuller	William P.	C	President	Asia Foundation
Fullerton	William Bewick	C		
Funabashi	Yoichi	TJ	Columnist	"The Asahi Shimbun"
Fung	Victor K. K.	B,C	Chairman	Hong Kong Trade Development Council.
Furlaud	Richard Mortimer	C	Director	Bristol-Myers Squibb Co.
Futter	Ellen Victoria	C	Chairman	Fed, New York; President, Barnard College, NYC
Gabriel	Charles Alvin	C	Chief-of-Staff (fmr.)	Defense Dept., Air Force
Gaddis	John Lewis	C	Distinguished Prof.	Ohio Univ.
Gadiesh	Orit B.	B,C	Chairman	Bain & Company
Gaer	Felice D.	C	Director	Brown Univ., Advancement of Human Rights
Gaines	James R.	C	Managing Editor	*Time* Magazine
Galbraith	Evan Griffith	C	Int. Dir., Sr. Advisor	Morgan Stanley Group, Inc.
Gallagher	Dennis J.	C	Asst. Legal Adviser	State Dept., Office of Legal Advisor
Gallucci	Robert L.	C	US Amb.-at-Large	State Dept., Political-Military Affairs
Galpin	Timothy J.	C	Principal	Pritchett & Assoc., Dallas
Galvin	John Rogers	B,C	Supr. Ald. Cdr. (fmr.)	Defense Dept., SHAPE, Europe
Galvis	Carlos	C		
Galvis	Sergio J.	C	General Counsel	Council of the Americas; Partner, Sullivan & Cromwell
Gann	Pamela B.	C	Professor	Duke Univ., Law
Gannon	John C.	C		
Ganoe	Charles Stratford	C	Exec. Vice President	FMS Group Inc.
Gantcher	Nathan	C	President & Co-CEO	Oppenheimer
Garber	Larry	C		Michigan Univ.
Garcia-Passalacqua	Juan Manuel	C	Advisory Bd. Member	Center for International Policy
Gard	Robert G., Jr.	C	President	Monterey Inst. of Int. Studies
Gardels	Nathan P.	C	Editor	Global Viewpoint
Gardner	Antony Laurence	C		
Gardner	James Albert	C	President (fmr.)	Lewis & Clark College, Portland
Gardner	Nina Luzzatto	C	Int. Lawyer	
Gardner	Richard Newton	C,T	US Ambassador (fmr.)	State Dept., Spain; Ambassador (fmr.) to Italy
Garel-Jones	Tristan, Lord	TE	Member (fmr.)	British Parl.; Advisor to Union Bank of Switzerland, London
Garment	Leonard	C	White Hse. Council (fmr.)	Nixon Admin.
Garment	Suzanne	C	Resident Scholar	American Enterprise Institute; Author
Garneau	Raymond	TC	Member	Canadian Parliament
Garnett	Sherman	C		
Garrigues Walker	Antonio	TE	Chairman	Garrigues & Anderson, Madrid
Garrison	Mark J.	C	Board Member	Center for Foreign Policy Development, Brown Univ.
Gart	Murray Joseph	C	Counseler (fmr.)	Time Inc.
Garten	Jeffrey E.	C		Yale Univ.; Under Sec. (fmr.) Commerce Dept., Int. Trade
Garthoff	Raymond L.	C	U.S. Amb.	to USIA
Garton Ash	Timothy	BGB	Fellow	St. Antony's College, Oxford
Garwin	Richard Lawrence	C		IBM; Consultant, Los Alamos Scientific Laboratory
Gasteyger	Curt	BCH	Professor (fmr.)	Graduate Institute of International Studies
Gaston	Patricia E.	C		
Gates	Henry Louis, Jr.	C	Professor	Harvard Univ., humanities
Gates	Philomene A.	C	Author	"Suddenly Alone: A Woman's Guide to Womanhood"
Gates	Robert M.	C	Director	National Intelligence Council; Dir., C.I.A. (fmr.)
Gati	Charles	C	Professor	John's Hopkins Univ.
Gati	Toby Trister	C	Asst. Secretary	State Dept., Intelligence & Research Bureau
Gaudiani	Claire Lynn	C	President	Connecticut College
Gause	F. Gregory, III	C	Asst. Professor	Vermont Univ., Political Science
Gay	Catherine	C		
Gayle	Helen D.	C		
Gazzoni Frascara	Giuseppe	TE	Chair. & Mng. Dir.	Gazzoni; Pres., Fed. of Italian Food Ind., Bologna
Gebhard	Paul R.S.	C		
Gedo	Inge	C		

Last Name	First & Mid. Name	Org.	Job Title	Affiliation - Company, Organization
Geertz	Clifford James	C	Professor	Princeton Univ., Institute for Advanced Studies
Geiger	Theodore	C	Chief	Nat. Planning Assoc., Wash., Int. Studies
Geithner	Timothy F.	C		
Gejdenson	Sam	C	Congressman	Connecticut, House Oversight, Int. Relations
Gelb	Amos	C		
Gelb	Bruce S.	C		
Gelb	Leslie Howard	C,T	President	CFR; Columnist, New York Times
Gelb	Richard Lee	C	Pres., Chair. & CEO	Bristol-Myers Squibb Co.
Gell-Mann	Murray	C	Professor	MIT
Genscher	Hans-Dietrich	BD	Foreign Min. (fmr.)	Germany;Mbr.(fmr.)Bundestag;Min.(fmr.)Fgn.Afrs.;FDP
George	John M.	C		
Georges	John A.	T	Chairman & CEO (fmr.)	International Paper Co.
Georgescu	Peter Andrew	C	President	Young & Rubicam, Inc. (advertising agency)
Gephardt	Richard Andrew	C	Congressman	Missouri, Minority Leader
Gerber	Fritz	BCH	Chairman	F. Hoffmann-La Roche AG, Switzerland
Gerber	Louis Emil	C	Sr. Partner	Arter & Hadden, Columbus
Gergen	David R.	B,C,T	Editor-at-Large	US News & World Report; Spec. Asst. to Pres. Clinton
Gergorin	Jean-Louis	BF	Bd. Member	Matra Hachette
Gerhart	Gail M.	C	Author	"Black Power in South Africa"
Germain	Adrienne	C	V.P. & Prog. Dir.	Int. Women's Health Coalition
Gershman	Carl Samuel	C	President	National Endowment for Democracy
Gerson	Allan	C	Attorney	Shapiro & Olander, Baltimore
Gerson	Eliot F.	C		
Gerson	Emelio Gabriel	B	Exec. Vice President	EXXON Corp.; Dir. & Cons., Grace Geothermal Corp.
Gerson	Ralph Joseph	C	Exec. Vice President	Guardian Industries Corp.
Gerstner	Louis V., Jr.	B,C,T	Chairman & CEO	IBM Corp.
Getler	Michael	C	Asst. Managing Editor	Washington Post
Geyelin	Henry R.	C		
Geyelin	Philip L.	C		Washington Post, Newsweek
Geyer	Georgie Anne	C	Syndicated Columnist	Los Angeles Times Syndicate
Geyer	Gerhard	BD	Chairman (fmr.)	ESSO AG, Hamburg; Bd. Mbr. (fmr.) Dresdner Bank AG
Gezgin Eris	Meral	BTR	President	IKV (Econ. Devel. Foundation)
Gfoeller	Joachim, Jr.	C	Principal	Gfoeller Investments, N.Y.
Gfoeller	Michael	C		
Gfoeller	Tatiana C.	C		
Ghiglione	Loren	C		
Giavazzi	Francesco	BI	Professor	Bocconi Univ., Milan, Economics
Gibbons	John Howard	C	Director	Exec. office of the Pres., Office of Sci. & Tech. Policy
Gibbs	Nancy Reid	C		
Gibney	Frank Bray	C	Director	St. Dept., US Commission for Pacific Econ. Cooperation
Gibney	James Suydam	C		
Giersch	Herbert	BD	Director (fmr.)	Institut fuer Weltwirtschaft, Kiel
Giffen	James H.	C	Council Member	Brookings Inst.; Chair. & President, Mercator Corp.
Gigot	Paul A.	B,C	Wash. Columnist	Wall Street Journal
Gil	Andres V.	C		
Gil	Peter P.	C		
Gilbert	Jackson B.	C	2nd Chairman	Espirito Santo Bank of Florida, Miami
Gilbert	Jarobin, Jr.	C	Director	Whitman Corp.
Gilbert	S. Parker	C	Chairman	Morgan Stanley
Gilbert of Dudley	John, Lord	TE	Minister	Def. Procurement;(fmr.)Mbr.,Brit. Parl.;Training/Trans.Min.(fmr
Giles	Frank T. R.	BGB	Deputy Editor (fmr.)	Sunday Times
Gillespie	Michael J.	C	Partner	Debevoise & Plimpton
Gilmore	Kenneth Otto	C	Director	Reader's Digest Assn.
Gilmore	Richard	C	Founder	GIC Group
Gilpatric	Roswell Leavitt	B,C	Counsel	Cravath, Swaine & Moore, N.Y.C.
Gilpin	Robert G., Jr.	C	Professor	Prinseton Univ.
Gingrich	Newton L.	C	Congressman	Georgia; Speaker of the House
Ginn	Sam	C		
Ginsberg	Marc Charles	C		
Ginsburg	David	C	Advisory Bd. Member	Center for International Policy
Ginsburg	Jane C.	C	Professor	Columbia Univ., Law
Ginsburg	Ruth Bader	C	Associate Justice	Supreme Court
Giscard d'Estaing	Valery	BF	President (fmr.)	French Republic, '74-'81; Pres., Euro. Movement Inst.
Glauber	Robert R.	C	Under Secretary	Treasury Dept., Clinton Admin.
Glazer	Nathan	C	Professor	Harvard Univ.
Gleeson	Dermot	BIRL	Attorney General	
Glendon	Mary Ann	C	Professor	Harvard Univ., Law School
Glenn	John H.	T	Senator	Ohio, Armed Svcs., Gvt. Afrs./Ranking, Sel. Intel.
Gleysteen	William H., Jr.	C	Vice President (fmr.)	Council on Foreign Relations; The Japan Society
Globerman	Norma	C		
Gluck	Carol	C		
Glueck	Jeffrey Scott	C		
Glusker	Peter H.	B	Vice President	Prodigy
Godchaux	Frank Area, III	C	Vice President	Colgate-Palmolive Co., NYC
Godiesh	Orbit	B	Chairman	Bain & Company, Inc.
Godsoe	Peter C.	BC,TC	Chairman & CEO	Bank of Nova Scotia
Godwin	I. Lamond	C	Professor	Princton Univ.

Last Name	First & Mid. Name	Org.	Job Title	Affiliation - Company, Organization
Goekjian	Samuel V.	C	Chair. & CEO	Intracon Assoc. (Consultants)
Goheen	Robert Francis	C	Sr. Fellow	Princeton U., Woodrow Wilson Sch.; Amb. (fmr.), India
Goins	Charlynn	C	Member	Int. Planned Parenthood Federation, Pres. Council
Goizueta	Roberto C.	C,T	Chairman & CEO	Coca-Cola; Dir., Eastman Kodak Co., Ford Motor Co.
Gokmen	Oguz	BTR	Head (fmr.)	Minister of Foreign Affairs, Econonics Dept.
Goldberg	Andrew C.	C		
Goldberg	Ronnie Lee	C		
Goldberg	Samuel	C	Director	Foreign Policy Association
Goldberger	Marvin Leonard	C	Professor	Univ. of California, L. A., Physics
Golden	James R.	C	Lt. Col. (fmr.)	US Army
Golden	William Theodore	C	Public Member	Hudson Institute
Goldgeier	James M.	C		State Dept., National Security Council
Goldin	Harrison J.	C	Mayor (fmr.)	New York City
Goldman	Andrew	C	Sr. Policy Analyst	House Republican Research Committee
Goldman	Charles Norton	C	Vice President	ITT Corp., NYC
Goldman	Emily O.	C	Assoc. Professor	Colorado Univ.., Political Science
Goldman	Guido	C	Chairman	First Spring Corp.
Goldman	Marshall I.	C	Assoc. Director	Harvard Univ., Russian Research Ctr.
Goldman	Merle	C	Member	Human Rights Watch
Goldmark	Peter Carl, Jr.	C	President	Rockefeller Foundation
Goldring	Natalie J.	C	Member (fmr.)	Carnegie Endowment for International Peace
Goldschmidt	Neil	C,T	Secretary (fmr.)	Transportation Dept.; Governor (fmr.), Oregon
Goldsmith	Jack Landman, III	C	Chair. & CEO (fmr.)	Federated Department Stores, Inc.
Goldstein	Gordon	C	Author	"Consequences of the Information Revolution"
Goldstein	Jeffrey A.	C	Vice-Chairman	BT Wolfensohn & Co. (Banking)
Golightly	Niel L.	C	Spokesman	Ford Motor Co.
Golob	Paul D.	C		
Gomory	Ralph Edward	C	President	Alfred P. Sloan Foundation
Gompert	David C.	C	V.P. & Dir.	RAND Corp., Defense Research Inst.
Gonensay	Emre	BTR	Minister	Turkish Foreign Affairs
Goodby	James Eugene	C	Dist. Service Prof.	Carnegie Mellon Univ.
Goodman	George Jerome W.	C	Author	(Adam Smith)
Goodman	Herbert Irwin	C	Chairman	Applied Trading Systems, Houston
Goodman	John B.	C	Special Advisor	for Defense, Conversion & Tech.
Goodman	Roy Matz	C	State Senator	New York
Goodman	Sherri Wasserman	C	Deputy Under Sec.	Defense Dept., Environmental Security
Goodpaster	Andrew Jackson	B,C	Cmdr.-in-Chief (fmr.)	Def. Dept.; Superintendent (fmr.), US Military Academy
Goodsell	James Nelson	C	Member	Christian Science Monitor
Goossens	John J.	B	Pres. & CEO	Belgacom
Goossens	John J.	BB	Pres. & CEO	Belgacom
Gordon	Albert Hamilton	C	Chairman	Kidder, Peabody & Co.
Gordon	Duncan L.	BC	Partner	Clarkson, Gordon & Co.
Gordon	John A.	C		
Gordon	Lincoln	B,C	Guest Scholar	Brookings Institute
Gordon	Michael R.	C	Correspondent	New York Times, Pentagon
Gordon	Philip H.	C	Consultant	RAND Corp.
Gorelick	Jamie S.	C		
Gorman	Joseph T.	C,T	Chairman, Pres. & CEO	TRW Inc.; Director, Proctor & Gambel Co.
Gornick	Alan L.	C		
Goss	Porter J.	C		
Gotbaum	Victor	C	Director	CUNY, Ctr. For Social Research
Gotlieb	Allen E.	BC,TC	Chairman	Trilateral Commission, Canada; Ambassador (fmr.) to US
Gottemoeller	Rose E.	C	Director	Nat. Sec. Council, Russian, Ukraine & Eurasian Affairs
Gottfried	Kurt	C	Department Chairman	Cornell Univ.
Gottlieb	Gidon Alain Guy	C	Professor	Univ. of Chicago, Law School
Gottsegen	Peter M.	C		
Goudswaard	Johan M.	BNL	Vice Chairman (fmr.)	Unilever N. V.
Gould	Peter G.	C		
Gourevitch	Peter Alexis	C	Professor	Univ. of California, San Diego
Graff	Henry Franklin	C	Professor (fmr.)	Columbia Univ.
Graff	Robert D.	C		
Graham	Bob	C	Senator	Florida, Intelligence, Vet. Afrs., Fin., Env. & Pub. Wks.
Graham	Carol Lee	C		
Graham	Donald E.	B	Publisher	Washington Post
Graham	Katharine	B,C,T	Chair., Exec. Comm.	Washington Post, Exec. Comm.; Mbr., Brookings Inst.
Graham	Lawrence Otis	C		
Graham	Thomas Wallace	C		
Graham	Thomas Wallace, Jr.	C	General Counsel	US Arms Control & Disarmiment Agency
Graham	William (Bill) C.	TC	Chairman	Canadian H./Commons, Standing Comm. on Fgn. Affairs, Ottowa
Graham	William R., Jr.	C	Science Advisor	to President & Dir. of Office of Sci. & Tech.
Grand	Stephen R.	C		
Grant	James Pineo	C	Director (fmr.)	John Hopkins Univ., International Vol. Services
Grant	Stephen Allen	C	Partner	Sullivan & Cromwell, NYC
Granville	Maurice Fryer	C	Chairman	Texaco Inc.
Gratton	Robert	TC	Chairman & CEO	Power Financial Corp. of Canada, Montrial
Graubard	Stephen Richard	C	Managing Editor	Daedalus
Grave	Frank H. G. de	BNL	Minister	Defense, The Netherlands

Last Name	First & Mid. Name	Org.	Job Title	Affiliation - Company, Organization
Gray	Hanna Holborn	C	President	U. of Chicago;Dir., Atlantic Richfield Co., Concord Coal.
Gray	William H., III	T	Congressman (fmr.)	Louisiana; Pres. & CEO, United Negro College Fund
Grayson	Judy S.	C		
Greathead	R. Scott	C		
Green	Bill	C	Congressman (fmr.)	New York
Green	Carl J.	C	Director	Georgetown Univ., Law Ctr.
Green	Ernest G.	C	Managing Director	Lehman Brothers; Chair., African Development Foundation
Green	Jerrold D.	C	Director	Univ. of Arizona, Ctr. for Mideast Studies
Green	Michael Jonathan	C		
Green	Stephen	TE	Chairman	HSBC Investment Bank, London
Greenberg	Arthur N.	C	Office Director	Veterans Administration, Quality Management
Greenberg	David	C		
Greenberg	Evan G.	C	Dir. & Exec. V.P.	Foreign General Insurance
Greenberg	Karen J.	C	V.P.	OSI, Programs
Greenberg	Maurice R.	B,C,T	Deputy Chair. (fmr.)	Fed, New York; Ch. & CEO, Amer. Int. Gp., Inc.; Dir., CFR
Greenberg	Sanford David	C	Chairman	Realty Capital Inc.
Greene	James C.	C		
Greene	Joseph Nathaniel, Jr.	C	Member	Connecticut College, Ctr. for Int. Studies & Lib. Arts
Greene	Margaret L.	C	Deputy Manager	Fed. Reserve System, Foreign Opperations
Greene	Wade	C		
Greenfield	James L.	C	Mbr. Editorail Bd.	New York Times
Greenfield	Meg	C	Editorial Page Editor	Washington Post
Greenhill	Lord	BGB	Banker (fmr.)	Great Britain
Greenspan	Alan	C,T	Chairman	Fed. Res. Syst.,Bd./Gov.;TC mbr. (fmr.);Dir. (fmr.),CFR
Greenwald	Joseph A.	C	US Ambassador (fmr.)	State Dept., European Communities
Greenway	Hugh Davids Scott	C	Editorial Page Editor	Boston Globe
Greenwood	Ted	C	Program Officer	Alfred P. Sloan Foundation
Gregorian	Vartan	C	President	Brown Univ.
Gregson	Wallace C.	C	Brig. General	Defense Dept., U.S. Marine Corp, Asst. Deputy Chief of Staff
Grenier	Richard	C	Columnsist	*Washington Times*
Griego	Linda	C		
Grieson	Ronald	BGB	Vice Chair. (fmr.)	GEC
Griffin	Anne-Marea	C		
Griffin	Anthony G.S.	BC	Hon. Chair. & Dir.	Guardian Group
Griffith	Alessandra J.	C		
Griffith	William E.	C	Professor	MIT, Political Science
Grilo	Eduardo C. Marcal	BP	Minister	Portugese Education
Grimes	Joseoh A., Jr.	C		
Grimes	Julie M.	C		
Groothaert	Baron Jacques	TE	Honorary Chairman	Generale Bank, Brussels; Ambassador to Belgium
Grose	Peter	C	Research Fellow	Harvard Univ., Ctr. for Scince & Int. Affairs
Gross	Herbert	BD	Attendee	Bilderberg Group, 1955, Garmisch-Partenkirchen, Germany
Gross	Patrick Walter	C	Vice Chairman	American Management Systems, Inc.
Grossman	Gene M.	B	Professor	Princton Univ., Int. Economics
Grove	Brandon H., Jr.	C	US Ambassador (fmr.)	State Dept., Zaire; Dir., Off. of Foreign Scvs. Inst.
Groves	Ray John	C	Chairman & CEO	Ernst & Young, NYC
Grune	George Vincent	C	Chairman & CEO (fmr.)	Reader's Digest Assn.
Grunwald	Henry Anatole	B,C	Editor-in-Chief (fmr.)	Time, Inc.; US Ambassador (fmr.), to Austria
Guedes	Salvador	TE	Bd. Member	Sogrape, Porto, Portugal
Guerra-Mondragon	Gabriel	C	U.S. Ambassador	State Dept., Chile
Guest	Michael E.	C	Foreign Officer	State Dept., to Czech Republic
Guetta	Bernard	BF	Editor-in-Chief	*Le Nouvel Observateur*
Guidi	Marcello	TE	Chairman	ISPI, Milan; Ambassador (fmr.) of Italy
Guindey	Guillaume	BF	President (fmr.)	Compagnie Int. des Wagons-Lits et du Tourisme
Guisinger	Stephen E.	C		
Gullion	Edmund A.	C	Professor	Princton Univ.
Gundlach	Andrew S.	C		
Guptepranay	Haasmimil	C		
Gustafson	Judith	C	Secretary	Council on Foreign Relations
Gustafsson	Stan	BS	Chairman	AB Astra, Sweden
Gutfreund	John H.	C,T	Chair. & CEO (fmr.)	Solomon Bros. Inc.; Council Member, Brookings Inst.
Guth	John H.J.	C		
Guthman	Edwin O.	C	Press Secretary (fmr.)	Justice Dept., to Rob. F. Kennedy
Gutmann	Henning P.	C		
Gutowski	Armin	TE	Director (fmr.)	Hamburger Weltwirtschasftsarchiv (HWWA)
Gwertzman	Bernard M.	C		
Gwin	Catherine B.	C	Member (fmr.)	Carnegie Endowment for International Peace
Gyohten	Toyoo	TJ	President	The Inst. for Int. Monetary Affairs
Gysling	Erich	BCH	Head (fmr.)	Foreign Dept. of
H.R.M.	Sofia	BE	Queen	Spain
Haas	Peter E.	C	Director	Levi Strauss & Co.
Haas	Robert D.	C,T	Chairman & CEO	Levi Strauss & Co.; Council Mbr., Brookings Inst.
Haas	Walter A.	T	Hon. Chairman	Levi Strauss & Co.
Haasen	Uwe	TE	Sup. Adv. Bd. Mbr.	Allianz Versicherung, Munich
Haass	Richard	C,T	Member	Carnegie Endowment for Internsational Peace
Haddad	Yvonne Yazbeck	C	Professor	Georgetown Univ., History
Hadley	Stephen J.	C	Asst. Secretary (fmr.)	White House, for Int. Security Policy

Last Name	First & Mid. Name	Org.	Job Title	Affiliation - Company, Organization
Hafner	Joseph A., Jr.	C	President & CEO	Riviana Foods Inc.
Hagel	Chuck	B	Senator	Nebraska
Hagel	Chuck	C		
Hagen	Katherine A.	C		
Haggard	Stephen	C	Adj. Professor	Univ. of Cal., San Diego, Political Science
Hague	William	BF	Leader	Conservative Party
Hahn	Carl	TE	Supervisory Bd. Mbr.	Volkswagen AG, Wolfsburg
Haig	Alexander Meigs, Jr.	C,T	Secretary (fmr.)	St. Dept.; Chairman & President, Worldwide Assoc., Inc.
Hakim	Peter	C	Member	Inter American Dialogue
Halaby	Najeeb E.	C	Director	CFR, '70-'72; Mbr., Brookings Inst.
Halberstadt	Victor	BNL	Hon. Sec. General	Bilderberg Gp., Europe & Canada; Professor, Leiden Univ.
Hale	David D.	C		
Halefoglu	Vahit	BTR	Minister (fmr.)	Foreign Affairs, Turkey
Haley	John Charles	C	Deputy Chair. (fmr.)	Kissinger & Associates
Hall	Arnold, Sir	BGB	Chair./Mng.Dir.(fmr.)	Hawker Siddeley Group, Ltd.
Hall	C. Barrows	C		
Hall	John P.	C		
Hallerberg	Mark S.	C		
Hallgrimsson	Geir	BICE	Prime Minister (fmr.)	Iceland
Hallingby	Paul, Jr.	C	Sr. Managing Director	Bear Sterns & Co.
Hallstein	Walter	BD	Member (fmr.)	Ger. Bundestag; Pres. (fmr.), European Movement; CDU
Halperin	David R.	C		
Halperin	Morton H.	C	Advisory Bd. Member	Center for International Policy; Dir., ACLU, Wash. office
Halstad	Edward	C		
Halsted	Thomas A.	C	Member (fmr.)	Carnegie Endowment for International Peace
Haltzel	Michael	C	Staff Director	US Inst. Of Peace
Hamalainen	Sirkka	BFIN,TE	Member	Euro. Cent. Bank, Chair., (fmr.) Bank of Finland, Helsinki
Hamburg	David A.	C	President	Carnegie Corp. of NY; Adv. Bd., Ctr. for Nat. Policy
Hamburg	Jill	C		
Hamburg	Margaret Ann	C	Director (fmr.)	White House Press Conf.; New York City Health Commission
Hamilton	Ann O.	C	Director	The World Bank, Population and Humanities
Hamilton	Charles V.	C	Professor	Columbia Univ., Government
Hamilton	Daniel S.	C	Sr. Associate	Carnegie Endowment for International Peace
Hamilton	Doug N.	C		
Hamilton	Edward K.	C	Director	Overseas Devel. Council; Director (fmr.), CFR
Hamilton	Jonathan Carroll	C		
Hamilton	Lee Herbert	B,C,T	Congressman	Indiana, Int. Relations/Ranking, Joint Economic
Hamilton	Michael P.	C	Professor	Adirondack Community College
Hamilton	Ruth Simms	C	Project Director	Michigan State University, African Research Project
Hammonds	D. Holly	C		
Hancock	Ellen M.	C	Sr. V. Pres./Gen. Mgr.	IBM Corp.
Hand	Scott M.	C	President	INCO Limited
Handelman	Stephen	C	Journalist	*Comrade Criminal*
Hannay	David	BGB	Perm. Representative	U.K. Mission to the U.N.
Hanrieder	Wolfram F.	C	Professor (fmr.)	U.C. Santa Barbara, German Foreign Policy
Hanscom	Patricia L.	C	Deputy Director	State Dept., Conventional Arms Control
Hansen	Carol Rae	C	Member	Peace Task Force
Hansen	Keith Eric	C		
Hanson	Robert A.	T	Chairman (fmr.)	Deere & Company
Hanson	Thor	C	Chairman & Director	National Health Council
Hantz	Giselle P.	C		Debevoise & Plimpton
Harari	Maurice	C		
Harding	Harry	C	Dean	George Wash. Univ.; Brookings Inst.; Trustee, Asia Found.
Harding	Sir William	TE	Director	LLoyds Bank, London; British Ambassador (fmr.)
Hardt	John P.	C	Sr. Specialist	Library of Congress, Post-Soviet Economy
Hargrove	John Lawrence	C	Attorney	Amer. Society of Law and Medicine
Harleston	Bernard Warren	C	President	City Univ. of New York, NYC
Harmaia	Jukka	BFIN,TE	President & CEO	Enso-Gutzeit Oy
Harman	Jane L.	C	Congresswoman	California, National Security, Select Intelligence
Harman	Sidney	C	Board Member	Center for National Policy; Sidney Harman Ind.
Harmon	James A.	C		
Harpel	James W.	C	Professor	Harvard Univ., Ctr. for Business and Government
Harper	Conrad Keith	C	Chairman	US Court of Appeals, Admin. & Grievance commission
Harriman	Pamela D. Churchill	C	US Ambassador	St. Dept., France, Hon. Mbr. Exec. Com., Brookings Inst.
Harris	Elisa D.	C	Director	Nat. Sec. Council, Nonproliferation & Export Control
Harris	Fred R.	B	Senator (fmr.)	Oklahoma
Harris	Irving B.	C	Chairman	Pittway Corp., Exec. Committee
Harris	John M.	C		
Harris	Joseph E.	C	Professor	Florida State Univ.
Harris	Martha Caldwell	C	Deputy Asst. Sec.	State Dept., Center for Defense Trade
Harris	Michael	BC	Premier	Ontario
Harrison	Selig Seidenman	C	Sr. Associate	Carnegie Endowment for International Peace
Harrowby	Earl of	TE	Chairman	Private Bank, The, London
Harsch	Joseph C.	B,C	Commentator (fmr.)	NBC, Inc.; Christian Science Monitor
Harshberger	Edward R.	C	Director	Defense Dept., Navy, Acquisition Policy
Hart	Augusta Snow, Jr.	C	Vice Chairman (fmr.)	Quaker Oats Co.
Hart	Bill, Jr.	C		

Last Name	First & Mid. Name	Org.	Job Title	Affiliation - Company, Organization
Hart	Brett J.	C		
Hart	Gary	C	Senator (fmr.)	Colorado; Presidential Candidate
Hart	Parker T.	C		
Hart	Todd C.	C		
Hartman	Arthur A.	B,C	US Ambassador (fmr.)	St. Dept., U.S.S.R.; Bd. Mbr., Center for Fgn. Pol. Devel.
Hartman	J. Lise	C		
Hartwig	Hans	TE	Chairman (fmr.)	Bundesverband des dt. Gross-und Aussenhandels
Haschigian	Ninial	C		
Hasegawa	Norishige	TJ	Counsellor	Sumitomo Chemical Co., Ltd.
Hashida	Taizo	TJ	Counsellor	Fuji Bank, Ltd.
Hashimoto	Toru	TJ	Chairman	Fuji Bank, Ltd.
Haskell	John Henry F., Jr.	C	Managing Director	Dillon, Read & Co., Inc.
Haskins	Caryl Parker	C	Honorary Trustee	Carnegie Corp. of NY; Trustee, Asia Foundation
Hata	Tsutomu	TJ	Prime Minister (fmr.)	Diet, Japanese ; Min. for Fgn. Afrs.; Minister (fmr.), Fin.
Hatfield	Robert Sherman	C	Chairman & CEO	National Executive Services Corp., NYC
Hauge	John R.	C		
Hauser	Rita Eleanore A.	C	Member	Hauser Foundation; Director, CFR
Hauser	William L.	C	Director	CFR
Haussmann	Helmut	BD	Member	German Bundestag, Free Democratic Party
Havel	Theresa Ann	C		
Hawkins	Ashton	C	Exec. V. Pres./Counsel	Metropolitan Museum of Art, Board of Trustees
Hawley	Philip M.	T	Consultant	Broadway Stores, Inc., L. A.
Hayes	Margaret Daly	C		
Hayes	Samuel P.	C	Honorary Director	Foreign Policy Association
Haynes	Fred	C	Division Manager	Commerce Dept., Office of Marketing & Product Mgt.
Haynes	Ulric St. Clair, Jr.	C	Dean	Hofstra Univ., School of Business
Hayward	Thomas B.	C	Admiral (fmr.)	Defense Dept., Chief of Naval Oper.
Hazard	John Newbold	C	Professor (fmr.)	Cambridge Univ.
Healey	Denis	BGB	Chan. to Exchequer	Great Britain
Healy	Harold H., Jr.	C	Partner (fmr.)	Debevoise & Plimton
Healy	Melissa	C	Journalist	*L. A. Times*
Heard	George Alexander	C	Trustee	Ford Foundation; Chancellor (fmr.), Vanderbilt U.
Hearn	Ruby P.	C		
Heath	Edmund	BGB	Prime Minister (fmr.)	Great Britain
Heck	Charles B.	C,T	Director	Trilateral Commission
Hecker	Siegfried S.	C		
Heckmann	Hans	BCH	Vice Chairman	Union Bank of Switzerland
Heckscher	August	C	President (fmr.)	Woodrow Wilson Foundation
Hedelius	Tom C.	BS	Chairman	Svenska Hendelsbanken
Hedstrom	Mitchell Warren	C	Trustee	Ford Foundation; Vice President, Citibank, N. A.
Heep-Richter	Barbara D.	C		
Hegge	Per Egil	B	Editor	*Aftenposten* , Norway
Heginbotham	Stanley J.	C	Member	New York Academy of Sciences
Hehir	J. Bryan	C	Member	Harvard Univ.; Georgetown Univ. TheoligaN
Heiberg	Gerhard	TE	Partner	Norscan Consulting, Oslo; Chair., Aker. Oslo
Heifetz	Elaine F.	C		
Heimann	John Gaines	C	Chairman	Merrill Lynch, Glob.Fin. Inst. Gp.;Mbr. Brookings Inst.
Heimbold	Charles A., Jr.	C		
Heimowitz	James B.	C		
Heineman	Benjamin W., Jr.	C	Sr. Vice President	General Electric Co.; Bd. Member, Ctr. for Nat. Pol.
Heineman	Melvin L.	C		
Heintz	Stephen B.	C		
Heintzen	Harry L.	C		
Heinz	Teresa	C	Chairwoman	Howard Heinz Foundation
Hejlik	Dennis J.	C		
Helander	Robert Charles	C	Mbr. Advisory Bd.	Council of the Amer.; Ptnr., Jones, Day, Reavis & Pogue, NYC
Heldring	Frederick	C	Director	Overseas Development Council
Heller	Richard Martin	C	Managing Partner	Kramer, Levin, Nessen, Mamin & Frankel
Hellman	Frederick Warren	C	Council Member	Brookings Institute; Partner, Matrix Partners
Hellmann	Donald Charles	C	Trustee	American Enterprise Institute
Helm	Robert W.	C		
Helmboldt	Niles E.	C	Member	Overseas Development Council
Helms	Richard McGarrah	C	Director (Fmr.)	CIA; US Ambassador (fmr.), State Dept., Iran
Helprin	Mark	C	Author	"Ellis Island", '81; Bob Dole's speech writer, '96 campaign
Helton	Arthur C.	C		
Henderson	Nicholas	BGB	Ambassador (fmr.)	to Poland, from Great Britain
Hendrickson	David C.	C	Assoc. Professor	Colorado College
Henkin	Alice H.	C	Vice Chairwoman	Human Rights Watch Advisory Commity
Henkin	Louis	C	Professor (fmr.)	Columbia Univ.
Hennessy	John M.	C	President & CEO	First Boston Inc., CS
Hennigar	David J.	TC	Chairman	Crownx Inc., Nova Scotia
Henninger	Daniel Paul	C	Deputy Editor	Wall Street Journal, Editorial Page
Henry	Nancy L.	C		
Hentges	Harriet	C	Exec. Vice President	US Institute of Peace
Herberger	Roy A., Jr.	C	President	The Maricopa Partnership (Finance)
Herbst	Jeffrey	C	Professor	Princeton Univ., Political and Int. Affairs
Herkstroter	Cor A. J.	BNL	Chairman	Royal Dutch Shell, The Neatherlands

Last Name	First & Mid. Name	Org.	Job Title	Affiliation - Company, Organization
Herling	John	C	Edit., Publisher (fmr.)	John Herling's Labor Letter
Hermann	Charles F.	C	Director	Texas A&M Bush School of Government and Public Service
Hernandez	Antonia	C	President	Mexican American Legal Defense & Education Fund
Hernandez-Colon	Rafael	C	Governor	Puerto Rico
Herrero de Minon	Miguel	TE	Lawyer/Int. Consult.	Private; Member (fmr.), Spanish Parliament
Herrhausen	Alfred	BD	President (fmr.)	Deutsche Bank AG, Frankfurt am Main
Herrndorf	Peter A.	BC	Chairman & CEO (fmr.)	TV Ontario; Sr. Visiting Fellow, Toronto Univ.
Herskovits	Jean	C	Professor	State Univ. of New York, African History
Hersman	Rebecca K. C.	C		
Herter	Christian A., Jr.	B,C	Secretary (fmr.)	State Dept.
Herter	Frederic P.	C	President (fmr.)	American Univ.
Hertzberg	Arthur	C	Rabbi (fmr.)	Temple Emanu El
Hertzberg	Hendrik	C	Executive Editor	New Yorker magazine; Speach Writer for Jimmy Carter
Herwarth von Bittenfeld	Hans-Heinrich	BD	Chairman (fmr.)	Deutsche Unilever GmbH; Under Secretary (fmr.)
Herz	Barbara	C	Division Chief	The World Bank, Population and Human Resources
Herzfeld	Charles Maria	C	Fellow (fmr.)	Hudson Institute
Herzog	Maurice	BF	Member (fmr.)	French National Assembly
Herzstein	Jessica	C	Professor	ACOEM Post Graduate Seminars
Herzstein	Robert Erwin	C	Board Member	Coun. of the Amer.; Ptnr. In Chg., Shearman & Sterling, Wash.
Hesburgh	Theodore Martin	B,C,T	President (fmr.)	Univ. of Notre Dame; Director (fmr.), CFR
Heslin	Sheila N.	C		
Hess	John B.	C	Sr. Advisor	Senator Barbara Boxer
Hessler	Curtis Alan	C	Executive	Times Mirror Co.
Hester	James Mcnaughton	C	President	Harry Frank Guggenheim Foundation
Hewitt	William Alexander	B,C,T	Ambassador (fmr.)	Jamaica
Hewlett	Sylvia Ann	C	Director	Nat. Parenting Assoc.
Heyn	Rolf	BD	Attendee	Bilderberg Group, 1955, Garmisch-Partenkirchen, Germany
Heyns	Roger William	C	Board Member	James Irving Foundation
Hiatt	Fred	C		
Hicks	Irvin	C	US Ambassador	State Dept., Republic of Seychelles
Hicks	Irvin, Jr.	C		
Hicks	John F.	C	Asst. Administrator	State Dept., A. I. D., Africa
Hicks	Kathleen H.	C		
Higginbotham	F. Michael	C		
Higgins	Robert F.	C	Assoc. Professor	UCLA, Civil Engineering
Higgins	Tracy Eliane	C		
Highet	Keith	C	Partner	McDermott, Will & Emery
Hight	B. Boyd	C	Partner	O'Melveny & Myers, L. A.
Higuchi	Hirotaro	TJ	Hon. Chairman	Asahi Breweries, Ltd.
Hill	J. French	C	Deputy Asst. Sec.	Treasury Dept., Corp. Finance
Hill	James Tomilson	C	Co-Head	Shearson Lehman Brothers, Investment Banking Div.
Hill	Joseph C.	C		
Hillen	John	C		
Hillenbrand	Martin Joseph	C	Co-Director	Center for East-West Trade Policy
Hillgren	Sonja Dorothy	C	Washington Editor	Farm Journal
Hills	Carla Anderson	C,T	US Trade Rep. (fmr.)	Exec. Off./Bush Admin.; Trustee, Urban Inst.; Dir., CFR
Hills	Laura Hume	C	Sr. Comm. Counsel	Overseas Private Development Corp.
Hilsman	Roger	C	Professor	Columia Univ.
Hilton	Robert Parker, Sr.	C	Vice Director(fmr.)	Defense Dept., Office Joint Chiefs-of-Staff
Himes	James Albert	C	Professor (fmr.)	Univ. of Florida
Hinerfeld	Ruth J.	C	Vice Chairman	UN Association of the US
Hines	Gerald D.	C	Developer	Industrial & Residential. Houston
Hinnekens	Jan	TE	Chairman	Belgian Boerenbond(Farmers Union);Bd.Mbr.,Bank/Belgium
Hinshaw	Randall Weston	C	Professor (fmr.)	John Hopkins Univ., Claremont Graduate School
Hinton	Deane Roesch	C	US Ambassador (fmr.)	State Dept., Kinshasa, Zaire
Hippel, von	Frank N.	C	Professor	Princeton Univ., Public & Int. Affairs
Hirose	Gen	TJ	Honorary Chairman	Nippon Life Insurance, Ltd.
Hirschman	Albert Otto	C	Professor (fmr.)	Harvard Univ.
Ho	Christine M.Y.	C	President	Think Inc. N.Y.
Hoagland	Jimmie Lee	B,C	Associate Editor	Washington Post
Hobbs	Tammany D.	C		
Hoch	Frank W.	C	Limited Partner	Brown Brothers Harriman
Hodgson	James D.	C	Head (fmr.)	O.S.H.A., Nixon Admn.
Hoeber	Amoretta M.	C	President	AMH Consulting
Hoegh	Leif	BN	Owner (fmr.)	Norwegian ships
Hoegh	Westye	BN	Chairman	Leif Hoegh & Co.; Pres., Norwegian Shipowners Assoc.
Hoehn	William Edwin, Jr.	C	Sr. Advisor	to Senator Sam Nunn
Hoenlein	Malcolm, Rabbi	C	Exec. Vice Chairman	Conf. Pres. of Major Jewish Organizations
Hoepli	Nancy L.	C	Editor-in-Chief	Foreign Policy Association
Hoeven	Cess H. van der	BNL	President	Royal Ahold
Hoffenberg	Mark R.	C		
Hoffman	Adonis Edward	C	Sr. Assoc	Carnegie Endowment for Int. Peace
Hoffman	Bruce	C		
Hoffman	Michael L.	C	Bureau Chief	Agriculture Dept., Chemistry Div.
Hoffmann	Dieter H.	TE	Lawyer	Gurland & Lambsdorff;Hd.(fmr.)Unternehmensgruppe Neue He
Hoffmann	Stanley H.	B,C	Director, '83-92	CFR; Editorial Bd., Carnegie Endow.; Harvard Univ.
Hoge	James Fulton, Jr.	B,C,T	Editor	Foreign Affairs magazine, Director (fmr.), CFR

Last Name	First & Mid. Name	Org.	Job Title	Affiliation - Company, Organization
Hoge	Warren M.	C	Asst. Mng. Editor	New York Times Magazine
Hogg	Christopher	BGB	Chairman	Reuters Group plc
Hoguet	George R.	C		Baring Asset Management, Brookline, MA
Hohenberg	John	C	Professor(fmr.)	Columbia Univ.
Hoinkes	Mary Elizabeth	C	General Counsel	Arms Control & Disarmament Agency
Hojdahl	Odd	BN	Vice Chairman (fmr.)	Norwegian Trade Union
Holbrooke	Richard C.	B,C,T	US Ambassador	U.N.Designate;V.Ch.,Credit Suissse First Boston Corp.
Holcomb	M. Staser	C	Exec. Vice President	USAA , San Antonio
Holdren	John P.	C		
Holgate	Laura S. Hayes	C	Co-Author	"Collective Security in a Changing World"
Holl	Jane E.	C	Director	National Security Council, European Affairs
Holland	Mary Sue	C	Division Director	State Dept., Office of Information Security Technology
Hollick	Ann L.	C	Staff Director	State Dept., Economic Policy Staff
Holloway	Dwight F., Jr.	C		
Holm	Niels W.	TE	Chairman	Nat. Inst. of Animal Science & Danish Stds. Assoc.
Holmas	Stephen T.	C		
Holmes	Henry Allen	C	US Amb. at Large	State Dept., Burdensharing
Holmes	Kim R.	C	Vice President & Dir.	Kathran & Shelton Cullom Davis Int. Studies Ctr.
Holst	Johan Jorgen	TE	Minister	Norway, of Defense
Holt	Pat M.	C	Chief of Staff (fmr.)	Senate Foreign Relations Committee
Holtquist	Timothy A.	C		
Holum	John D.	C	Director	US Defense Dept. Arms Control & Disarmament Agency
Home	Lord of the Hirsel	BGB	Chairman (fmr.)	Bilderberg Group
Hood	Robert E.	C		
Hooks	Benjamine Lawson	C	Executive Director	NAACP, NYC
Hoopes	Townsend Walter	C	Vice Chairman	Reseal International Corp., NYC
Hope	Judith Richards	C	Director	IBM; Sr. Ptnr., Paul Hastings, Janofsky & Walker
Hope	Richard O.	C		
Horam	John	BGB	Member (fmr.)	British Parliament
Horelick	Arnold L.	C	V.P. & Dir.	Carnegie Endowment for Int. Peace
Hori	Tetsuya	TJ	President	Long-Term Credit Bank of Japan, Ltd.
Horie	Tetsuya	TJ	Dir. & Sr. Counsellor	The Long-Term Credit Bank of Japan, Ltd.
Horlick	Gary Norman	C	Partner	O'Melveny & Myers, Washington
Hormats	Robert D.	C,T	Vice Chairman	GoldmanSachs;Ast.Sec./St.(fmr.);CarnegieEnd.;Dir.,CFR
Horn	Garfield H.	C	Sr. Counsel	Sullivan & Cromwell, N.Y.
Horn	Karen N.	C	Director	Council on Foreign Relations
Horn	Miriam	C	Sr. Editor	*U.S. News and World Report*
Horn	Sally K.	C	Director	Defense Dept., Threat Reduction Policy
Horner	Matina Souretis	C	President (fmr.)	Radcliffe College
Hornhues	Karl-Heinz	TE	Member	German Bundestag (CDU), Chair. Fgn. Affairs Comm.
Hornik	Richard H.	C		
Horowitz	Irving Louis	C	Professor	Rutgers Univ.
Horta e Costa	Miguel	B	Vice President	Portugal Telecom
Horton	Alan W.	C	Colonel	Defense Dept., US Air Force
Horton	Frank B., III	C	Prin. Deputy	Defense Dept., to Assist. Secretary
Horton	Scott	C	Partner	Patterson, Belknap, Webb & Tyler
Horton	Sharon Freeman	C		
Hosmer	Bradley Clark	C	Superintendent	USAF Academy
Hosomi	Takashi	TJ	Chairman	NLI Resch. Inst.; Ch. (fmr.), Overseas Econ. Coop. Fund
Hoston	Germaine A.	C	Professor	Univ. of Cal. San Diego, Political Science
Hottelet	Richard C.	C	Journalist	CBS News, UPI
Houghton	Amory, Jr. (Amo)	C	Congressman	New York, Int. Relations, Ways & Means
Houghton	James R.	C,T	Chairman & CEO (fmr.)	Corning Inc.
House	Karen Elliott	C	Int. Vice President	Dow Jones & Co.; wife/Peter Kann, Pub., Wall St. Journ.
Houthakker	Hendrik	T	Professor	Harvard Univ., Economics
Houthuys	Jozef	BB	President	C. S. C. Belgique; Vice President, C. M. T.
Hovey	Graham	C	Professor	Univ. of Michigan, Communications Studies
Hovey	Justus Allan, Jr.	C	Staff Member (fmr.)	House of Representatives, Commission of Fgn. Affairs
Howard	John R.	C	Trustee	Louis & Clark College
Howard	Lyndsay	C		
Howard	M. William, Jr.	C		
Howell	Ernest M.	C	Trustee	Asia Foundation; Vice President, Smith Barney
Howell	Peter	C		
Howell of Guildford	David, Lord	TE	Member (fmr.)	British Parliament; Chairman, Foreign Affairs Comm.
Howson	Nicholas C.	C		
Hoyt	Mont Powell	C	Director	Foreign Policy Association
Hrynkow	Sharon Hemond	C		
Huber	Richard Leslie	C	Vice Chairman	Continental Bank Corp./Continental Bank, N.A.
Huber	Robert T.	C		
Huberman	Benjamin	C	Principal	Huberman Consulting Group
Hudson	Manley O., Jr.	C	Partner	Cleary, Gottlieb, Steen & Hamilton
Hudson	Michael Craig	C	Professor	Georgetown Univ.
Huebner	Lee W.	C	President	The American Univ. of Paris
Hufbauer	Gary Clyde	C	Sr. Fellow	Institute for International Economics
Huffington	Roy Michael	C	Founder & CEO (fmr.)	HUFFCO Oil
Hufstedler	Shirley Mount	C	Trustee	Carnegie Endow.; Part., Hufstedler, Kaus & Ettinger
Hughes	Jeffrey L.	C		

Last Name	First & Mid. Name	Org.	Job Title	Affiliation - Company, Organization
Hughes	John	C	Professor	Brigham Young Univ., Journalism
Hughes	Justin	C	Attorney	Manatee, Phelps & Phillips, Santa Monica
Hughes	Thomas Lowe	C,T	President (fmr.)	Carnegie Endowment for Int. Peace, Ch., Mid-Atl. Club
Hughs	Duane L.	C		
Huizenga	John W.	C	Professor (fmr.)	Univ. of Rochester
Hultman	Tamela	C	Exec. Editor	*African News Service*
Hume	Cameron R.	C		
Hume	Ellen	C	Columnist	Wall Street Journal; PBS
Hummel	Arthur W., Jr.	C	U.S. Amb.	USIA
Hundt	Dieter	TE	President	Confederation of German Employers' Assoc. (BDA), Cologne
Hunsberger	Warren S.	C	Chief of Research (fmr.)	State Dept., on Japan and Korea
Hunter	Robert E.	B,C	US Representative	to NATO
Hunter	Shireen T.	C	Sr. Assoc.	Ctr. For European Studies, Brussels
Hunter-Gault	Charlayne	C	Commentator	PBS, McNeil/Lehrer; McNeil Lehrer News
Huntington	Patricia S.	C		
Huntington	Samuel Phillips	C	Trustee	American Enterprise Institute
Huntsman	Jon Meade, Jr.	C	President	Huntsman Chem.; Mbr.(fmr.),St.Dept.,US Pacif.Isl.Jt.Com.Comm.
Hurewitz	Jacob Coleman	C	Consultant	Institute for Foreign Policy Analisis
Hurford	John Boyce	C	Vice Chairman	BEA Associates, NYC
Hurlock	James Bickford	C	Partner	White & Case, NYC
Hurlock	Matthew	C		
Hurst	Robert Jay	C	General Partner	Goldman Sachs & Co.
Hurwitz	Seth L.	C	Counsel (fmr.)	White House, Advisory Committee, Int. Oversight Bd.
Hurwitz	Sol	C	President	Commission for Economic Development, NYC
Hutchings	Robert L.	C		
Hutchins	Glenn H.	C	Member	The Blackstone Group
Hutton	Will	BGB	Editor	*The Observer*
Hutzler	Charles	C	Correspondent	Associated Press-Bejing
Huyck	Philip M.	C	Sr. Advisor	Credit Suisse First Boston Corp
Huyghebaert	'Jan	BB	Chairman	Almanij N.V., Belgium
Hyde	Henry B.	C	Congressman	Illinois, Int. Relations, Chairman, Judiciary,
Hyland	William George	C,T	Distinguished Prof.	Georgetown Univ.; Editor (fmr.), CFR, Foreign Affairs
Ichimura	Shin'ichi	TJ	Director	Int. Centre for the Study of East Asian Devel., Kitakyushu
Igler	Hans	BA	President (fmr.)	Federation of Austrian Industriaslists
Iglesias	Carmen	TE	Member	Royal Spanish Academy of History
Ignatius	David	C	Asst. Mng. Editor	Washington Post
Ihamuotila	Jaako	BFIN	Chairman & CEO	Neste Corp.
Ikenberry	G. John	C	Author	"Salvaging the G-7"
Ikle	Fred Charles	C	Member (fmr.)	Defense Dept., Defense Policy Advisory Commission
Ilchman	Alice Stone	C	Chairman	Rockefeller Foundation; Pres., Sarah Lawrence College
Ilminister, of	Lord Armstrong	TE	Director	R. T. Z. Corp., London
Iloniemi	Jaakko	BFIN	Managing Director	Center for Finnish Business & Policy Studies
Imbert	Claude	BF,TE	Editor-in-Chief	"Le Point", Paris
Immergut	Mel M.	C		
Inan	Kamuran	BTR	Member (fmr.)	Turkish Senate
Inderfurth	Karl F. (Rick)	C	Alt. Representative	State Dept., Special Policy Affairs
Ingersoll	Robert Stephen	C,T	Chairman	Panasonic Foundation
Ink	Dwight A.	C	President (fmr.)	Institute of Public Administration, NYC
Inman	Bobby Ray	C,T	Vice Chairman	CFR; Dir., Xerox Corp.
Inouye	Kaoru	TJ	Honorary Chairman	Dai-Ichi Kangyo Bank, Ltd.
Intriligator	Michael David	C	Professor	MIT
Ireland	Robert Livingston, III	C	General Partner	Brown Brothers Harriman & Co.
Irish	Leon Eugene	C	Partner	Jones, Day, Reavis & Pogue, Wash.
Irvin	Patricia L.	C	Deputy Asst. Sec.	Defense Dept., Humanities & Refugee Affairs
Irwin	John Nichol, II	C	Partner	Patterson, Belknap, Webb & Tyler
Irwin	Steven M.	C		
Isaacs	Maxine	C		
Isaacson	Walter Seff	C	Editor	Time magazine, of New Media
Ischinger	Wolfgang	B	State Secretary	Ministry of Fgn. Affairs, Germany
Iselin	John Jay	C	President	Cooper Union for Advancement of Science & Art
Isenberg	Steven Lawrence	C	Deputy Publisher	Newsday, Inc.
Isham	Christopher	C	Sr. News Producer	ABC, World News Tonight
Ishihara	Hideo	TJ	Chairman	Goldman Sachs (Japan) Ltd.
Ishikawa	Rokuro	TJ	Chairman	Kajima Corp.
Ishikawa	Takeru	TJ	Chairman	Mitsui Marine & Fire Insurance Co., Ltd.
Isik	Hasan F.	BTR	Member (fmr.)	Turkish Parliament
Ispahani	Mahnaz Z.	C	Director	Ford Foundation
Issing	H. C. Otmar	B	Exec. Bd. Member	European Central Bank
Istel	Yves-Andre	C	Vice Chairman	Rothschild, Inc., N.Y.
Ito	Tadashi	TJ	Chairman	Sumitomo Corp.
Itoh	William M.	C		
Ivester	M. Douglas	C		
Izlar	William H., Jr.	C		
Jaans	Pierre	BL	General Manager	Institut Monetaire Luxembourgeois
Jabber	Paul	C	President	Globicaom, Inc.
Jacklin	Nancy P.	C	Partner	Clifford Chance, N.Y.
Jackson	Bruce P.	C	Co-Author	"Space, Power, and Strategy"

Last Name	First & Mid. Name	Org.	Job Title	Affiliation - Company, Organization
Jackson	Eric K.	C	Fellow	Harvard Univ., Social Politics
Jackson	Jesse Louis, Sr.	C	Host	CNN, Both Sides; founder, PUSH; Rainbow Coalition
Jackson	John Howard	C	Professor	Univ. of Michigan
Jackson	Lois M.	C	Member	IBM Corp., Latin America
Jackson	Sarah Jeanette	CC	Sculptor, Graphic Art.	Canada
Jackson	William Eldred	C	Partner	Milbank, Tweed, Hadley & MCCloy
Jacobi	Mary Jo	BGB	Hd./Gp. Pub. Affrs.	HSBC Holdings plc
Jacobs	Eli S.	C	Chairman	Memorex-Telex
Jacobs	John Edward	C	President & CEO	National Urban League, NYC; Director, Coca-Cola Co.
Jacobs	Nehama	C	Director	Wells Fargo Bank
Jacobs	Norman	C	Chairman (fmr.)	Nat. Heritage, Football Licensing Authority
Jacobson	Harold Karan	C	Professor	Univ. of Michigan, Political Science
Jacobson	Jerome	C	Director	Overseas Development Council
Jacoby	Tamar	C	Instructor	New School for Social Research, NYC
Jaffe	Amy Myers	C		
Jaffre	Philippe	BF	Chairman & CEO	Elf Aquitaine
Jagland	Thorbjorn	TE	Member	Norwegian Parliamjent; Chairman, Norwegian Labor Party
Jakobson	Max	BFIN,TE	Ambassador (fmr.)	to US; Consultant & Sr. Columnist, Helsinki
James	Francis J.	C		
Jamieson	John Kenneth	C	Director	Raychem Corp.
Janis	Mark W.	C	Co-Author	"European Rights Law"
Janklow	Morton Lloyd	C	Of Counsel	Janklow, Newborn & Ashley, NYC
Jankowitsch	Peter	B	Minister of State	European Integration & Development Cooperation
Jannott	Horst K.	TE	Chairman	Muenchner Rueckversicherung AG, Munich
Janow	Merit E.	C	Professor	Columbia Univ., Int. Trade
Jansen	Marius B.	C	Professor	Princton Univ., Japanese Studies
Janssen	Baron Daniel E.	BB,TE	Chair., Exec. Comm.	Solvay & Co., Brussels
Janssen	Baron Paul-Emmanuel	TE	Hon. Chairman	Generale de Banque, Brussels
Jaquette	Jane	C	Member	Overseas Development Council
Jarimo-Lehtinen	Marja	BFIN	Organizer	Bilderberg Group, meeting in Helsinki
Jarvis	Nancy A.	C	Chairman (fmr.)	World Affairs Council
Jastrow	Robert	C	Chairman	Mt. Wilson Institute
Jebb	Cindy R.	C		
Jenkins	Sir Michael	BGB,TE	Vice Chairman	Dresdner Kleinwort Benson Group; (fmr.) British Ambassador
Jennings	Peter	B	Anchor & Sr. Editor	ABC News, World News Tonight
Jervis	Robert L.	C	Professor	Columbia Univ.
Jessup	Alpheus W.	C		
Jessup	Philip Caryl, Jr.	C	Secretary-Treasurer	Obor, Inc.
Jeter	Howard F.	B	US Ambassador	State Dept., to Liberia
Job	Peter	BGB	CEO	Reuters Holding PLC
Jochimsen	Reimut	TE	President	Central Bank of Northrhine-Westphalia, Dusselodorf
Joffe	Josef	TE	Foreign Editor	"Sueddeutsche Zeitung", Munich
Joffe	Robert David	C	Member	Brookings Inst.; Partner, Cravath, Swaine & Moore, NYC
Johns	Lionel Skipwth	C	Assoc. Dir.	Office of Science & Technology
Johnson	D. Gail	T		Univ. of Chicago
Johnson	Howard Wesley	C	Chairman	Kenan Systems Corp.; Director, Du Pont Co.
Johnson	James A.	B,T	Chairman & CEO	Fannie Mae
Johnson	Jay L.	C	Chairman	Defense Dept., of Naval Operations
Johnson	Jerome L.	C	V. Chief, Naval Oper.	Defense Dept.
Johnson	L. Oakley	C		
Johnson	Larry D.	C		
Johnson	Lionel Skipwith	C		
Johnson	Nancie S.	C	Vice President	E.I. du Pont de Nemours & Co.
Johnson	Nancy Lee	C	Congresswoman	Connecticut, Ways & Means
Johnson	Robbin S.	C	Corp. V.P.	Cargill Inc., Minn.
Johnson	Robert Henry	C	Member	National Planning Association
Johnson	Samuel Curtis	T	Chairman & CEO	S. C. Johnson & Son, Inc
Johnson	Suzanne Nora	C		
Johnson	Thomas Stephen	C	President (fmr.)	Manufacturers Hanover Corp.
Johnson	Willard Raymond	C	Professor	MIT, political science
Johnson	Willene A.	B	Sr. Officer	New York Fed.
Johnson	Wyatt Thomas, Jr.	C,T	President	CNN
Johnston	J. Bennett	B	Senator (fmr.)	Louisiana, Appropriations, Budget, Energy, Aging
Johnston	Philip	C	President & CEO	C. A. R. E.
Johnstone	Donald J.	B	Sec. General	OECD
Johnstone	V.	B		
Joly	Alain	TE	Chairman & CEO	L'Air Liquide, Paris
Jones	Alan	C		
Jones	Anita K.	C		
Jones	Aubrey	BGB	Chairman (fmr.)	Cornhill Insurance Co., Ltd.
Jones	Benjamin Felt	C		
Jones	David Charles	C	Chairman (fmr.)	Defense Dept., Jt. Chiefs of Staff; Dir., Gen. Electric Co.
Jones	James R.	C,T	US Ambassador	St. Dept., Mexico; Chair./CEO (fmr.), Amer. Stock Exch.
Jones	Kerri-Ann	C		
Jones	Sidney R.	C	Executive Director	Human Rights Watch/Asia
Jones	Thomas V.	C,T	Chairman (fmr.)	Northrop Corp.
Jones	Thomas W.	C		

Last Name	First & Mid. Name	Org.	Job Title	Affiliation - Company, Organization
Jonung	Lars	BS	Professor	Stockholm School of Economics
Joost	Peter Mastrin	C		
Jordan	Amos Azariah, Jr.	C	Vice Chairman	Center for Strategic & International Studies
Jordan	Barbara	T	LBJ Cent. Chr. (fmr.)	Univ. of Texas
Jordan	Eason	C		
Jordan	Vernon Eulion, Jr.	B,C,T	Sr. Partner	Aikin, Gump, Strauss, Hauer & Feld; Dir., RJR Nabisco
Jorden	William John	C	Chairman	US-Panama Consultive Commission
Joseph	Geri Mack	C	US Ambassador (fmr.)	State Dept., Netherlands, The Hague
Joseph	Ira B.	C		
Joseph	James Alfred	C	President	Cummins Foundation
Joseph	Richard A.	C		
Josephson	William Howard	C	Partner	Fried, Frank, Harris, Shriver & Jacobson
Jospin	Lionel	BF	First Secretary	Socialist Party; Minister (fmr.) d'Etat
Joyce	John T.	C	President	Bricklayers & Allied Craft., Int.; V. Chair., Ctr./Nat. Pol.
Julliard	Jacques	TE	Associate Director	Le Nouvel Observateur, Paris
Jumper	John P.	C		
Junz	Helen B.	C	Spec. Trade Repr., Dir.	International Monitary Fund, Geneva
Juster	Kenneth I.	C	Partner	Arnold & Porter
Justman Jacob	Poul Louis	BNL	Chairman (fmr.)	Kon. Ned. Hoogovens & Staalfabrieken N.V.
Kaden	Lewis B.	C	Chairman	Davis, Polk & Wardwell
Kadlec	Robert	C		
Kadono	Kin'ichi	TJ	Senior Advisor	Toshiba Corp.
Kagan	Robert W.	C		
Kahan	Jerome H.	C	Director	Ctr. for Navel Analysis for Regional Issues
Kahin	George McTurnan	C	Honorary Fellow	U. of London, Sch. of Organization and African Studies
Kahler	Miles	C	Professor	Univ. of Cal. San Diego, Int. Relations
Kahn	Harry	C	Founding Sponsor	*The American Prospect*
Kaiser	Karl	BD,TE	Director	Research Inst. of German Society for Fgn. Affairs (DGAP)
Kaiser	Philip Mayer	C	US Ambassador (fmr.)	St. Dept., Hungary; Sr. Cons.,SRI Int.;Adv. Bd.,Nat. Pol.
Kaiser	Robert Greeley	C	News Editor	Washington Post
Kaji	Motoo	TJ	Chairman	The Int. House of Japan
Kakizawa	Koji	TJ	Member	Diet, Japanese ; Parliament V. Minister of Fgn. Affairs
Kalb	Bernard	C	Moderator	CNN, Reliable Sources
Kalb	Marvin	C	Chief Dip. Corr. (fmr.)	CBS, NBC, Moder., Meet the Press; Prof., Harvard U.
Kaletsky	Anatole	BGB	Asst. Editor	*The Times*
Kalicki	Jan H.	C	Sr. Advisor	Center for Foreign Policy Development, Brown Univ.
Kalil	Thomas A.	C	Sr. Director	Nat. Economic Council
Kamarck	Andrew M.	C		Int. Bank for Reconstruction and Development, Wash.
Kaminer	Peter H.	C	Special Master	Supreme Court, State of New York
Kaminsky	Howard	C	President & Publisher	Warner Books, Inc.
Kamiya	Fuji	TJ	Dean	Toyo-Eiwa Women's Univ.; Visiting Professor, Keio U.
Kamiya	Ken'ichi	TJ	Director & Counsellor	Sakura Bank, Ltd.
Kamov	Nikolai	B	Member	Bulgarian Parliament
Kampelman	Max M.	C	Vice Chairman	US Institute of Peace
Kamsky	Virginia Ann	C	Principal	Kamsky Assoc.
Kanak	Donald Perry	C		
Kandell	Jonathan	C	Author	La Capital - The Biography of Mexico City
Kaneko	Hisashi	TJ	President	NEC Corp.
Kanet	Roger Edward	C	Professor	Univ. of Illinois
Kang	C. S. Eliot	C		
Kann	Peter Robert	B,C	Chairman & CEO	Dow Jones & Co.;Pub.,Wall St. Jour.;wife/Karen E. House
Kansteiner	Walter H., III	C		
Kanter	Arnold Lee	C	Sr. Fellow	RAND Corp., Wash.; The Scowcroft Group
Kanter	Rosabeth Moss	C	Professor	Harvard Univ., Business School
Kantor	Mickey	C		
Kaplan	Gilbert E.	C		
Kaplan	Harold J.	C		
Kaplan	Helene L.	C	Board Member	Carnegie Corp. of NY, Mobil Oil Corp.; Dir., CFR
Kaplan	Mark Norman	C	Member of Firm	Skadden, Arps, Slate Meagher & Flom
Kaplan	Stephen S.	C	Member	Brookings Inst.
Kapp	Robert A.	C	President	U.S.-China Business Council
Kapstein	Ethan B.	C	Vice President	CFR, for Studies
Karalekas	Anne	C	Publisher	Washington Post Magazine
Karamanian	Susan L.	C	Vice President	American Society of Int. Law
Karamanlis	Koetas A.	BGB	Leader	Opposition Party
Karatnycky	Adrian	C	President	Freedom House
Karatz	Bruce	C		
Karis	Thomas G.	C	Sr. Resident Fellow	Ralph Bunche Inst.
Karl	Terry Lynn	C	Director	Ctr. for Latin American Studies
Karner	Dietrich	BA	Chair., Mng. Board	Erste Allgemeine-Generali Aktiengesellschaft
Karnow	Stanley	C	Narrator (fmr.)	PBS TV
Karns	Margaret P.	C		Univ. of Dayton
Karras	K.	BGR		
Karsten	C. Frits	BNL	Managing Dir. (fmr.)	AMRO Bk. N.V.; Hon. Treas. (fmr.), Bilderberger Gp.
Kartman	Charles	C	Princ. Dep. Assis. Sec.	State Dept., East Asian and Pacific Affairs
Kasdin	Robert	C		
Kaske	Karlheinz	BD	Chairman (fmr.)	ZVEI - Central Association of Electro-Technical Ind.

Last Name	First & Mid. Name	Org.	Job Title	Affiliation - Company, Organization
Kass	Stephen L.	C	Partner	Carter, Ledyard & Milburn
Kassalow	Jordan S.	C		
Kassof	Allen H.	C		
Kastrup	Dieter	BD	Director	Political Dept., Minister of Foreign Affairs, Germany
Kathwari	M. Farooq	C		
Kato	Koichi	TJ	Member	Diet, Japanese ; Chief Cabinet Secretary (fmr.)
Katz	Abraham	C	Chairman	Council for International Business
Katz	Daniel Roger	C	Co-Author	"Reviving the Rainforest in Southeast Asia"
Katz	Milton	B,C	Advisory Board Mbr.	Univ. of California, Consortium/Competition and Coop.
Katz	Ronald Stanley	C	Partner	Coudert Brothers, San Francisco
Katzenbach	Nicholas deB.	C	Of Council	Riker, Danzig, Scherer, Hyl. & Perr.; Dir. (fmr.), CFR
Katzenstein	Peter J.	C	Staff Member	Smithsonian Inst.
Kaufman	Daniel J.	C		
Kaufman	Henry	C	President	Kaufman & Co.
Kaufman	Robert R.	C		
Kaufmann	William W.	C		
Kawaguchi	Yoriko	TJ	Mng. Director	Suntory Ltd.
Kawakatsu	Kenji	TJ	Chairman	Sanwa Bank, Ltd.
Kaye	Charles R.	C		
Kaye	Dalia Dassa	C		
Kaysen	Carl	B,C	Professor (fmr.)	MIT, Political Economy
Kazemi	Farhad	C	Member (fmr.)	Ford Foundation, Rockefeller Foundation
Kazgan	Gulten (Mrs.)	BTR	Professor (fmr.)	Univ. of Istanbul
Kea	Charlotte G.	C	Spec. Asst. To Asst. Sec.	Commerce Dept., Commercial Services
Kean	Christopher	C		
Kean	Thomas H.	C	President	Drew Univ.; Board Member, Carnegie Corp. of New York
Kearney	Jude	C	Dep. Asst. Secretary	Commerce Dept., Service and Finance
Kearns	David T.	C,T	Dep. Sec. of Educ.	Education Dept.; Chairman (fmr.) XEROX Corp.
Keating	Justin	TE	Minister (fmr.)	Irish Industry & Comm.; Leader (fmr.), Labor Party
Keel	Alton Gold, Jr.	C	US Ambassador (fmr.)	Defense Dept.; N. A. T. O.
Keene	Lonnie S.	C	Sr. Policy Analyst	Exec. Office of the President
Keeny	Spurgeon Milton, Jr.	C	Pres. & Exec. Dir.	Arms Control Association, Wash.
Keersmaeker	Paul de	TE	Chairman	Interbrew, Leuven; (fmr.) Mbr. of thge Belgian Govt.
Keitel	Hans-Peter	BD	Chairman	Hochtief AG
Kelleher	Catherine M.	C	Advisory Bd. Member	Center for International Policy, Center for Nat. Policy
Kellen	Stephen M.	C		
Keller	Edmoud J.	C	Acting Sr. V. Pres.	Council on Foreign Relations
Keller	George M.	T	Chairman (fmr.)	Chevron Corp.
Keller	Kenneth Harrison	C	Sr. V. P.	CFR
Kellerman	Barbara	C		
Kelley	Paul Xavier	C	Commandant (fmr.)	Defense Dept., Marine Corps
Kellner	Peter B.	C		
Kellogg	David	C		
Kelly	Arthur L.	C		
Kelly	James P.	C	Chair & CEO	UPS of America
Kelly	John H.	C	Asst. Secretary	State Dept., Near Eastern & South Asian Affairs
Kelly	John Hubert	C	US Ambassador	State Dept., Finland
Kelman	Herbert C.	C	Fellow	Harvard Univ., Int. Conflict Analysis
Kemble	Eugenia	C	Director	American Fed. of Teachers (Union), Educational Issues
Kemp	Geoffrey	C	Director	Carnegie Endowment, Arms Control Project
Kempe	Frederick Schumann	C	Managing Editor	Wall Street Journal, Europe, Brussels
Kempner	Maximilian Walter	C	Of Counsel	Will & Emery McDermott, NYC
Kendall	Donald M.	C,T	Chairman (fmr.)	PepsiCo Inc.
Kenen	Peter Bain	C	Professor	Princeton Univ., Economics & Finance
Keniston	Kenneth	C	Professor	MIT, Science Technology and Society
Kennan	Christopher J.	C	US Representative	Advisory Council of the Americas
Kennan	Elizabeth Topham	C	President	Mt. Holyoke College; Assoc., Putnam Investments
Kennan	George Frost	C	Professor (fmr.)	Princeton Univ.
Kennedy	Craig	C		
Kennedy	David Michael	B	Professor	Stanford Univ.
Kennedy	Donald	C	Trustee	Carnegie Endowment; President (fmr.), Stanford U.
Kenney	F. Donald	C	Honorary Dir.	Finland Trade
Keohane	Nannerl Overholster	C,T	President	Duke Univ.; Director, IBM Corp.
Keohane	Robert Owen	C	Professor	Harvard Univ., Government
Keough	Donald R.	T	Chairman	Allean & Co., Inc.; President (fmr.), Coca-Cola Co.
Kern	Paul J.	C	Lt. General	Defense Dept., Army Acquisions Corp.
Kerr	Ann	C		
Kerry	John Forbes	C	Senator	Massachusetts, Banking, Commerce, Fgn. Rel., Intell.
Kessler	Denis	TE	Chairman	French Insurance Assoc., (Ffsa), Paris
Kessler	Martha Neff	C	Assit. NIO	CIA, Middle East
Kester	John Gordon	C	Partner	Williams & Connolly, Washington
Keydel	John F.	C		
Kezirian	A. Peter, Jr.	C		
Khalidi	Rashid Islam	C		
Khalilzad	Zalmay	C	Director	RAND Corp., Middle East Studies
Khuri	Nicola Najib	C	Professor	Rockefeller Univ.
Kiep	Walter Leisler	BD,TE	Treasurer	Christian Democratic Party; Member (fmr.), German Parl.

Last Name	First & Mid. Name	Org.	Job Title	Affiliation - Company, Organization
Kiermaier	John	C		
Kiernan	Robert Edward, III	C		
Kiesinger	Kurt-George	BD	Chancellor (fmr.)	Germany; Fed. Chairman (fmr.) CDU Partyt
Kiley	Robert R.	C	President	N.Y.C. Partnership
Kim	Hanya Marie	C		Global Advanced Technology Corp. N.Y.
Kimmitt	Robert Michael	B,C	Managing Director	Lehman Bros.; US Amb. (fmr.), St. Dept., Germany
Kimsey	James V.	C		
Kinde	Lawrence John	C		
King	Charles	C		
King	Henry Lawrence	C	Chair. & Mng. Partner	Davis Polk & Wardwell
King	John A., Jr.	C	Writer	Associated Press
Kintner	William Roscoe	C	Director	US Institute for Peace
Kipper	Judith	C	Director	Overseas Development Council
Kirac	Suna	BTR	Vice Chairman	Koc Holding A.S.
Kiranidiotis	Yannos	BGR	Deputy Minister	for Foreign Affairs, Greece
Kirby	Michael J. L.	TC	Senator	Canadian Senate
Kirk	Grayson Louis	C	Pres. & Trustee (fmr.)	Columbia Univ.; Vice Chairman (fmr.) & Director, CFR
Kirkland	Joseph Lane	C,T	President (fmr.)	AFL-CIO Union ('79-'95); Dir. (fmr.), CFR; TC since '73
Kirkland	Richard I., Jr.	C		
Kirkpatrick	Jeane Duane Jordan	C,T	Sr. Fellow	American Enterprise Inst.; US Ambassador (fmr.), UN
Kissee-Sandoval	Catherine J.	C		
Kissinger	Henry Alfred	B,C,T	Secretary (fmr.)	St. Dept., Nixon, Carter Admin.; Chair., Kissinger Assoc.
Kitamura	Toshi	TJ	Sr. Advisor	Hitachi, Ltd.
Kitchen	Helen	C		
Kitchen	Jeffrey C.	C		
Kittrie	Orde F.	C		
Klasky	Helaine S.	C		
Kleiman	Robert	C		
Klein	David	C	Visiting Professor	Univ. of California, San Diego
Klein	Edward Joel	C	Contributing Editor	Vanity Fair, NYC
Klein	George	C		
Klein	Joe	C	Columnist	Newsweek magazine; Consultant, CBS News
Klein	Ralph P.	BC	Premier	Alberta
Klemperer, von	Alfred H.	C		
Klissas	Nicholas S.	C		
Kloten	Norbert	TE	President (fmr.)	Landeszentralbank, Baden-Wuerttemberg
Klotz	Frank G.	C		
Klurfeld	James Michael	C	Associate Editor	Newsday, Inc.
Knapen	Ben	BNL	Editor-in-Chief (fmr.)	"NRC Handelsblad", The Netherlands
Knight	Andrew	BGB	Editor	"The Economist Newspaper Ltd."; Exec. Chair., News Int., plc
Knight	Edward S.	C	Gen. Counsel	Treasury Dept.
Knight	Jessie J., Jr.	C	Chairman	World Affairs Council, Nom. & Elect. Comm.
Knight	Robert Huntington	C	Director	National Leadership Bank
Knoppers	Antoine T.	B,C	Sr. Vice Pres. (fmr.)	Merck & Co., Inc.
Knowlton	William Allen	C	Representative (fmr.)	Defense Dept., N. A. T. O., US Army
Knowlton	Winthrop	C	Chairman	Knowlton Brother, Inc. (Investing)
Knox	John H.	C		
Kobak	Deborah J.	C		
Kobayashi	Koji	TJ	Chairman (fmr.)	NEC Corp.
Kobayashi	Shoichiro	TJ	Chairman	Kansai Electric Power Co., Ltd.
Kobayashi	Yotaro	TJ	Chairman & CEO	Fuji Xerox Co., Ltd.
Koc	Rahmi M.	BTR	Chairman	Koc Holding, A.S.
Koch	Wendy M.	C		
Kogan	Richard J.	C	President & CEO	Schering-Plough Corp.
Kogg	Christopher	BGB	Chairman	Courtauids plc, U. K.
Kohl	Helmut	BD	Chancellor (fmr.)	Germany; Chairman, CDU Party
Kohler	Horst	TE	President	Deutscher Sparkassen-u. Giroverband, Bonn, Germany
Kohler	Jarl	BFIN	President	Finnish Forest Industries Federation
Kohlhaussen	Martin	TE	Chair., Mng. Bd.	Commerzbank, Frankfurt-am-Main; Pres., Assoc./German Banks
Kohnstamm	Max	BI,TE	President (fmr.)	European Univ.,Florence,fmr.Sec.Gen.,Action/Euro.
Kohut	Andrew	C		Times Mirror Co.
Kojima	Akira	TJ	Director	"The Nikon Keizai Shimbun", and Editorial Page Editor
Kolbe	James T.	C		
Kolodziej	Edward Albert	C	Research Professor	Univ. of Illinois, Political Science
Kolt	George	C	Head	CIA National Intelligence Council, Russia
Koltai	Steven R.	C		
Kondo	Takeshi	TJ	Man. Director	ITOCHU Corp.
Kondracke	Morton	C	Executive Editor	Roll Call
Kono	Shunji	TJ	Chairman	The Tokio Marine and Fire Insurance Co., Ltd.
Kopper	Hilmar	BD	Chairman, Sup. Bd.	Deutsche Bank AG, Frtankfurt am Main
Korb	Lawrence J.	C	Asst. Secretary (fmr.)	State Dept., Bush Admin.; Brookings Inst.
Korbonski	Andrzej	C	Professor	UCLA, Russia and East European Studies
Korn	Jessica	C		
Korry	Edward M.	C	US Ambassador (fmr.)	State Dept., to Ethopia
Korteweg	Pieter	BNL	President & CEO	Robeco Gp., The Netherlands; Hon. Treas., Bilderberger Gp.
Kosai	Yutaka	TJ	Chairman	Japan Center for Economic Research
Kosaka	Kenji	TJ	Member	Japanese House of Representatives

Last Name	First & Mid. Name	Org.	Job Title	Affiliation - Company, Organization
Kosiw	Michael V., Sr.	C		
Kotecha	Mahesh K.	C	Sr. Vice President	Capital Markets Assurance Corp.
Kothbauer	Max	BA	Deputy Chairman	Creditanstalt-Bankverein
Kovanda	Karel	B	Hd. of Mission	Czech Rep. to NATO & WEU
Kraar	Louis	C	Reporter	*Fortune* Magazine
Kraemer	Lillian Elizabeth	C	Partner	Simpson, Thacher & Bartlett, NYC
Kraeutler	Kirk	C		
Kramek	Robert E.	C		
Kramer	David J.	C		
Kramer	Helen M.	C		
Kramer	J. Reed	C	Pre. & Man. Editor	*African News Service*
Kramer	Jane	C	Author	New Yorker magazine
Kramer	Mark Nathan	C	Member	Office of Mgt. & Budget, Coun. on Environ. Quality
Kramer	Michael	C	Chief Polit. Corr.	Time Magazine
Kramer	Steven Philip	C	Professor	Defense Dept., Nat. Defense Univ., Ind. College
Kranenburg	Hendrik J.	C		
Kranwinkle	C. Douglas	C		
Krapf	Franz	BD	Ambassador (fmr.)	Tokyo, Japan
Krasner	Stephen D.	C	Professor	Harvard Univ., Int. Relations
Krasno	Richard M.	C	President & CEO	Inst. of International Education
Krauer	Alex	BCH	Chair. & Mng. Dir.	Ciba-Geigy, Ltd., Switzerland
Krause	Lawrence B.	C	Professor	Univer. Of Cal. San Diego
Krauss	Clifford	C	Writer	*New York Times*
Krauthammer	Charles	C	Syndicated Columnist	Washington Post
Kravis	Henry R.	B,C	Founding Partner	Kohlberg Kravis Roberts; Member, Brookings Institute
Kravis	Marie-Josee	B,T	Sr. Fellow	Hudson Institute
Kreisberg	Paul H.	C	Member (fmr.)	Carnagie Endowment; Director (fmr.), CFR
Krepon	Michael	C	President	Henry L. Stimson Ctr.
Kreps	Juanita M.	C,T	Secretary (fmr.)	Commerce Dept.; Director (fmr.), CFR
Kriegel	J. L.	C		
Krisher	Bernard	C	Editor-at-large	Japan Avenue; Asia Wired
Kristoff	Sandra J.	C	Spec. Asst. to Pres.	National Security Council, Asia-Pacific Economic Affairs
Kristoffersen	Erwin	TE	Head	Int. Abteilung des Deutschen Gewerkschaftsbundes
Kristol	Irving	C	Co-Editor	Public Interest mag.; Dist. Fellow, Amer. Enter. Inst.
Kristol	William (Bill)	B	Editor & Publisher	Weekly Standard mag.; Chair., Project/Republican Future
Krogh	Peter F.	B	Dean	Georgetown Univ., School of Foreign Service
Kross	Walter	C	Commander in Chief	Defense Dept., Transportation Command
Krueger	Anne O.	C	Professor	Stanford Univ.
Krueger	Harvey	C	Director	Bernard Chaus, Inc.
Kruidenier	David	C	Chairman	Cowles Media Co.
Krulak	Charles C.	C	Comandant	Defense Dept., Marine Corps
Kruzel	Joseph J.	C	Deputy Asst. Sec.	Defense Dept., European & N. A. T. O. Policy
Ku	Charlotte	C	Exec. Dir. & Exec. V.P.	American Society of Int. Law
Kubarych	Roger M.	C	Gen. Manager	Henry Kaufman & Co. (Investment)
Kubisch	Jack B.	C		
Kuehlmann-Stumm	Knut Freiherr von	BD	Member (fmr.)	Ger. Bundestag; Vice-Party Whip (fmr.) FDP
Kull	Steven Gordon	C		
Kume	Yutaka	TJ	Chairman	Nissan Motor Co., Ltd.
Kunert	Jiri	T	Chair. & CEO	Zivnostenska Banka, Prague
Kuniholm	Bruce R.	C		
Kuntstadter	Geraldine	C		
Kuntz	Carol R.	C		
Kupchan	Charles A.	C	Member	National Security Council
Kupchan	Clifford A.	C	Member	National Security Council
Kupperman	Robert Harris	C	Sr. Fellow	Los Alamos Laboratory: mbr., Strat. & Int. Studies
Kurth	James R.	C	Professor	Swarthmore Univ.
Kurtzer	Daniel C.	C	Deputy Asst. Sec.	State Dept.
Kusukawa	Toru	TJ	Chairman	Fuji Research Institute Corp.
Kutchins	Alison B.	C		
Kuwata	Yoshio	TJ	Sr. Exec. Mgr.	Hitachi. Ltd.
Kwoh	Stewart	C		
Kyle	Robertr D.	C	Spec. Asst. to Pres.	Office of Policy Development
La Malfa	Giorgio	BI	Professor (fmr.)	Milan State Univ.
Laber	Jeri	C		
Labrecque	Thomas G.	C,T	President & COO	Chase Manhattan Bank; Mbr., Brookings Inst.
Lacharriere	Marc Ladreit, de	BF	Chairman	Fimalac
Ladd	Edward H.	C		
Lader	Philip	C	Administrator	Small Business Administration
Ladner	Joyce A.	C	Vice Chairwoman	Center for National Policy
LaFleur	Vinca S.	C		
Lafontaine	Oskar	BD	Party Leader SPD	Ministry Pres., Saarland; Mbr. German Bundestag
Lahnstein	Manfred	TE	Sup. Board Member	Bertelsmann AG, Gutersloh; Fed. Min. (fmr.), Finance
Laing	Martin, Sir	TE	Chairman	John Laing, London
Laipson	Ellen	C	Member	White House, Nat. Security Council
Laird	Melvin R.	T	Sr. Counsellor	Reader's Digest
Laird	Venessa	C		
Lake	W. Anthony (Tony)	C	Asst. to President	Nat. Security Council; Advisory Bd., Ctr. for Nat. Policy

Last Name	First & Mid. Name	Org.	Job Title	Affiliation - Company, Organization
Lake	William Thomas	C	Financial Consultant	New York City
Lall	Betty Goetz	C	Editor (fmr.)	Bulletin of Atomic Scientists
Lamar	Stephen E.	C		
Lamassoure	Alain	TE	Budget Minister	& Govt. Spokesman, France
Lamb	Denis	C		
Lambert	Baron	BB	Chairman	Compagnie Bruxelles Lambert pour la Fin. et l'Indust.
Lambert	Brett B.	C		
Lambeth	Benjamin S.	C	Specialist	RAND Corp, Russian Military Affairs
Lambsdorff	Count Otto	BD,TE	Partner	Wessing Beerenberg-Gossler
Lamego	Jose	TE	Secretary	State for Fgn. Affairs & Cooperation, Portugal
Lamers	Karl F.	BD	Member	Parliament (Spokesman, Fgn. Affrs. CDU/CSY)
Lamm	Donald Stephen	C	Chairman	W. W. Norton & Co.
Lamont	Lansing	C	Sr. Fellow	Americas Society, Canadian Affairs
Lampley	Virginia A.	C	Spec. Assits.	White House, Nat. Security Affairs
Lampton	David M.	C	President	Nat. Committee on U.S.-China Relations
Lancaster	Carol J.	C	Deputy Administrator	State Dept., Agency for Int. Development
Landau	Christopher	C		
Landau	George Walter	C	President (fmr.)	Coun. of the Amer.;US Amb.(fmr.),St.Dept.,Paraguay,Chile
Landers	James Michael	C	International Editor	Dallas Morning News
Landis-Guzman	Lauren R.	C		
Landy	Joanne	C		Campaign for Peace and Democracy
Lane	Charles M.	C	Sr. Editor	The New Republic
Laney	James Thomas	C	U.S. Ambassador	State Dept., S. Korea; Pres. (fmr.), Emory Univ.
Langdon	George Dorland, Jr.	C	President (fmr.)	American Museum of Natural History, NYC
Langlois	John D.	C		
Lansner	Kermit Irvin	C	Editor, Director	Financial World magazine
LaPalombara	Joseph	C	Professor	Yale Univ., Political Science
Lapham	Lewis Henry	C	Editor	Harper's magazine
Lapidus	Gail W.	C	Sr. Fellow	Stanford Univ., Inst. for Int. Studies
Lardy	Nicholas R.	C		Brookings Institute
Larrabee	F. Stephen	C	Sr. Staff Member	RAND Corp., Int. Policy Dept.
Larre	Rene	BF	Director (fmr.)	Bank of International Settlement
Larson	Charles Robert	C	President	Pioneers Science & Technology History Association
Larsson	Stig	BS	President & Dir. Gen.	Swedish Railways
Lary	Hal B.	C		Univ. of Chicago
Lasser	Lawrence J.	C		
Lateef	Noel V.	C	President & CEO	Foreign Policy Assoc., N.Y.
Lauder	Leonard Alan	C	President & CEO	Estee Lauder, Inc.
Lauder	Ronald S.	C		
Laudicina	Paul A.	C	Vice President	A.T.E. Kearney, Global Business (Consulting)
Lauinger	Philip C., Jr.	C	Principal	Lauinger Publishing Co., Tulso
Lauk	Kurt	BD,TE	Board Member	DaimlerChrysler, Stuttgart
Laurenti	Jeffrey	C		
Laventhol	David Abram	C	Publisher & CEO	Los Angeles Times
Lavin	Franklin L.	C		
Lawlor	Liam	TE	Member	Irish Dail, Dublin
Lawrence	Richard D.	C	Director	Environmental Protection Agency, Eng. Oper. Division
Lawson	Eugene K.	C	1st V. Pres.,V. Chair.	Export-Import Bank
Lay	Kenneth L.	T	Chair. & CEO	Enron Corp.
Layne	Christopher	C	Sr. Fellow	Cato Institute
Lazarus	Steven M.	C	Managing Dir.	Arch Ventures Partner
Leach	James Albert Smith	C,T	Congressman	Iowa, Int. Relations, Chair., Banking & Fin. Services
Leavy	David C.	C		
LeClerc	Paul	C		
Leddy	John M.	C	US Ambassador	USIA
Lede, van	Cees	TE	Chairman & CEO	Akzo Nobel, Arnheim; Pres. (fmr.), Fed./Netherlands Ind.
Lederberg	Joshua	C	V. Chair., Adv. Coun.	Off. of Tech. Assessment; Dir., CFR, '89-
Lederer	Ivo John	C		
Lee	Chong-Moon	C		
Lee	Ernest S.	C		
Lee	Janet	C		
Lee	John J.	C		
Lee	John M.	C		
Lee	William L.	C	Professor	Univ. of Georgia
Lee Williams	Alan	TE	Director	British Atlantic Council; Member (fmr.), Parliament
Lee-Kung	Dinah	C		Oversees Press Club, N.Y.
Leebron	David W.	C		
Leeds	Roger S.	C		
Leet	Mildred Robbins	C		
Lefever	Ernest W.	C	Sr. Fellow	Ethics and Public Policy Center
Leghorn	Richard S.	C		
Legvold	Robert H.	C	Advisory Bd. Member	Center for Int. Policy; Trustee, Carnegie Endowment
Lehman	John F., Jr.	C	Chairman	J. F. Lehman & Co., NYC
Lehman	Orin	C	Advisory Bd. Member	Center for International Policy
Lehman	Ronald F., II	C	Director (fmr.)	Arms Control & Disarmament Agency
Lehr	Deborah H.	C		
Lehrer	Jim Charles	C	Assoc. Ed., Co-Anchor	PBS TV, MacNeil Lehrer News Hour

Who's Who of the Elite

Last Name	First & Mid. Name	Org.	Job Title	Affiliation - Company, Organization
Leich	John Foster	C		
Leigh	Monroe	C	Partner	Steptoe & Johnson, Washington
Leisler-Kiep	Walter	BD, TE	Treasurer	CDU Party; Mbr. (fmr.) German Bundestag
Leister	Klaus-Dieter	TE	Board Member	Westdeutsche Landesbank Girozentrale, Dusseldorf
Leland	Marc Ernest	C	Sr. Advisor	Gordon P. Getty Trust, Washington
Lellouche	Pierre	BF,TE	Member	National Assembly, Paris
Lelyveld	Arthur Joseph	C	Sr. Rabbi (fmr.)	Fairmont Temple, Cleveland
LeMelle	Tilden John	C	Interim President	City Univ. of New York, NYC
LeMelle	Wilbert J.	C	President	Phelps-Stokes Fund; Trustee, Carnagie Endowment
Lempert	Robert J.	C		
Leness	Amanda V.	C		
Lennep	Jonkheer Emile, van	BINT	Sec. General (fmr.)	O. E. C. D.
Lenzen	Louis C.	C	Attorney	Mediation and Arbitration
LeoGrande	William Mark	C	Director	World Policy Journal
Leonard	James F.	C	US Ambassador	State Dept.
Leonard	James G.	C		
Leone	Richard C.	C	President	Twentieth Century Fund
Leonhard	Wolfgang	BD	Professor (fmr.)	Yale Univ., Soviet History
Leprince-Ringuet	Louis	BF	Member (fmr.)	Academie Francaise
Lerner-Lam	Eva	C		
Lescaze	Lee	C	Foreign Editor	Wall Street Journal; Accociate, Foreign Policy Assoc.
Lesch	Ann Mosely	C	Board Member	Human Rights Watch
Leschly	Jan	B	CEO	Smith Kline Beecham p.l.c.
Lesser	Ian O.	C	Researcher	RAND Corp.
Leverkuehn	Paul M. Adolf	BD	Commissioner (fmr.)	German Property, German Embassy, Washington, DC
Levi	Arrigo	BI,TE	Political Columnist	"Corriere dela Sera", Rome
Levin	Gerald	T	Chairman & CEO	Time Warner Inc., NYC
Levin	John A.	C	Principal	John A. Levin and Co., N.Y.
Levin	Michael S.	C	Chairman	e-Steel LLC (USA)
Levin	Neal D.	C		
Levine	Irving Raskin	C	Chief Econ. Cor.(fmr.)	NBC, Wash.; now Dean, Lynn Univ., Sch. of Int. Stud.
Levine	Marne L.	C		
Levine	Mel	C	Congressman (fmr.)	California; Assoc., Builders for Peace
Levine	Susan B.	C	Deputy Asst. Sec.	Treasury Dept., Int. Devel., Dept. of Environmental Pol.
Levinson	Marc	C	Writer	Newsweek Magazine
Levitas	Mitchel Ramsey	C	Sr. Editor	New York Times
Levy	Marion J. Jr.	C	Professor	Princeton Univ., Sociolgy and Int. Affairs
Levy	Maurice	TE	Chairman	Publicis, Paris
Levy	Philip I.	C		
Levy	Reynold	C	Managing Dir.	AT&T, NYC, Int. Pub. Afrs.; Bd. Mbr., Coun. of the Amer.
Levy	Samuel J.	C		
Levy	Walter James	B,C	Oil Consultant	John Hopkins Univ., Sch of Advanced Int. Studies
Levy-Lang	Andre	BF,TE	Chairman	Banque Paribas, Compagnie Financiere de Paribas, Paris
Lewis	Bernard	C	Professor (fmr.)	Princeton Univ.
Lewis	Clifford M.	C		
Lewis	David A.	C		
Lewis	Elise Carlson	C	Asst. Secretary	Council on Foreign Relations
Lewis	Flora	C,T	Sr. Columnist	New York Times, Paris
Lewis	John P.	C	Congressman	Georgia, Ways & Means
Lewis	John Wilson	C	Professor	Cornell Univ., Political Science
Lewis	Loida Nicholas	C	Author/Attorney	"How to Get a Green Card"
Lewis	Samuel Winfield	C	US Ambassador (fmr.)	State Dept., Israel; Dir., St. Dept. pol. plng. staff
Lewis	Stephen Richard, Jr.	C	President	Carleton College; Trustee, Carnegie Endowment
Lewis	W. Walker	B,C	Exec. V. Pres. & Pres.	Avon Products
Leysen	Andre	TE	Chairman & CEO	Gevaert, Antwerp
Li	Lehman	C		
Li	Victor H.	C	Member (fmr.)	Carnegie Endowment for International Peace
Libby	I. Lewis	C		
Lichtblau	John H.	C	Chairman	Petroleum Independent Research Associates, Inc., NYC
Lichtenstein	Cynthia C.	C	Professor	Boston College
Lieber	James Edmund	C		
Lieber	Robert J.	C	Professor	Georgetown Univ.
Lieberman	Henry R.	C		
Lieberman	Jodi B.	C		
Lieberman	Joseph I.	C	Senator	Connecticut, Armed Svcs.,Govt.Afrs.,Envir./ Pub. Wks.
Lieberman	Nancy A.	C		
Lieberthal	Kenneth	C		
Lief	Louis	C	Diplom. Correspond.	US News & World Report
Liesen	Klaus	BD	Chairman	VW AG, Wolfsburg; Chair. (fmr.) Exec. Bd., Ruhrgas AG
Liffers	William Albert	C,T	Vice Chairman	Cyanamid International
Light	Timothy	C	Professor	Michigan Univ.
Lighthizer	Robert E.	C		
Liikanen	Erkki	BINT	Member (fmr.)	European Commission (EC)
Lilienthal	Sally	C	Founder & Pres.	Ploughshares Fund
Lilley	James R.	C	US Ambassador (fmr.)	State Dept., China
Lincoln	Edward J.	C	Sr. Fellow	Brookings Inst.
Lind	Michael E.	C	Sr. Editor	Harper's Magazine, New Republic Magazies

Last Name	First & Mid. Name	Org.	Job Title	Affiliation - Company, Organization
Lindquist	Warren T.	C		
Lindsay	Franklin Anthony	B,C	Mbr. Exec. Committee	National Bureau of Economic Research
Lindsay	George N.	C	Of Counsel	Debevoise & Plimpton, NYC
Lindsay	John Vliet	C	Of Counsel	Mudge, Rose, Guthrie, Alex. & Ferdon; Mayor (fmr.) NYC
Lindsay	Robert V.	C	Honorary Director	Foreign Policy Association
Linen	Jonathan S.	C	Vice Chairman	American Express
Link	Troland S.	C	Board Member	AUC
Linowes	David Francis	C	Professor (fmr.)	Univ. of Illinois
Linowitz	Sol Myron	C,T	Sr. Counsel	Coudert Brothers; Chairman (fmr.), Xerox Int.
Liotard-Vogt	Pierre	BCH	Chairman (fmr.)	Nestle Alimentana S.A.
Lipper	Kenneth	C	Chairman	Lipper Analytical Service; Trustee, Rockefeller Bros. Fund
Lipponen	Paavo	BFIN	Prime Minister	Finland
Lipscomb	Thomas H.	C		Infosafe Systems
Lipset	Seymour Martin	C		George Mason Univ.
Lipsey, von	Rod	C		
Lipsky	John P.	C	Chief Economist	Chase Manhattan Bank
Lipsky	Seth	C	Mem. Ed. Board	*Wall Street Journal*
Lipson	Leon	C	Professor (fmr.)	Yale Univ., Jurisprudence
Liras	G.	BGR		
Lissakers	Karin M.	C	US Executive Director	International Monetary Fund (IMF)
Litan	Robert E.	C		
Litt	David G.	C	US Ambassador	United Arab Emerites
Little	David	C	Sr. Scholor	US Institute for Peace
Litwak	Robert S.	C	Director	Johns Hopkins Univ., Int. Studies
Liu	Maragret	C		
Livanos	G.	BGR		
Livingston	Robert Gerald	C	Advisory Bd. Member	Center for International Policy, Center for Nat. Policy
Llewellyn	J. Bruce	C	Chairman	Coca-Cola Bot. Co., Phil.; Cousin of Colin Powell
Lloniemi	Jaakko	BFIN	Ambassador (fmr.)	to US; Managing Dir., Council of Econ. Organizations
Lockwood	John E.	C		
Lodal	Jan M.	C	Prin. Dep. Under Sec.	Defense Dept., for Policy
Lodge	George Cabot	C	Trustee	Carnagie Endowment; Professor , Harvard Univ.
Loeb	Frances Lehman	C		
Loeb	John Langeloth	C	Vice Chairman	Loeb Partners Corp., NYC
Loeb	Marshall Robert	C	Managing Editor	Time Inc., magazine development
Loewenthal	Richard	BD	Political Scientist	Freie Universitaet Berlin
Logan	Francis Dummer	C	Partner	Milbank, Tweed, Hedley & McCloy
Long	Jeffrey W.	C		
Long	Susan M.	C		
Long	T. Dixon	C		
Long	William J.	C		
Longstreth	Thomas K.	C	Prin. Dep. Asst. Sec.	Defense Dept., Strategy, Requirements & Resources
Loomis	Henry	C	Trustee	Smithsonian Institute
Loranger	Donald E., Jr.	C	Military Fellow (fmr.)	CFR
Lorck	Karl	BN	Managing Dir. (fmr.)	Elkem-Spigerverket
Lord	Bette Bao	C	Chairman	Freedom House; wife of Winston Lord
Lord	Winston	B,C,T	Asst. Secretary (fmr.)	St. Dept., East Asian & Pacific Affairs; Mbr. (fmr.) TC
Lorena	Inmaculada de H.	C		
Lorentzen	Oivind, III	C		
Lougheed	E. Peter	T	Sr. Partner	Bennet Jones Verchere, Barristers & Soilicitors
Louis	William Roger	C	Department Chairman	Univ. of Texas, Austin
Lovdahl	Randall John	C		
Lovejoy	Thomas Eugene	C	Chairman	Manhattan Life Insurance Co., NYC
Lovelace	Jon B., Jr.	C	Chairman	Capital Research & Management Co., L. A.
Low	Stephen	C	President	Association for Diplomatic Studies
Lowenfeld	Andreas Frank	C	Professor	New York Univ., NYC, Law
Lowenkron	Barry F.	C		
Lowenstein	James Gordon	C	US Ambassador (fmr.)	State Dept., Luxemburg; Sr. Consultant, APCO Assoc.
Lowenthal	Abraham Frederic	C	Director, Leader	U. of S. Cal., Int. Studies; Advis. Bd., Ctr. for Nat. Pol.
Lowrey	Dennis Allen	C		
Loy	Frank Ernest	C	President	Ger. Marshall Fund of US;Adv. Bd. Mbr.,Ctr. for Nat. Pol.
Loy	James Milton	C		
Lozano	Ignacio E., Jr.	C	Director	Bank of America
Lozano	Monica C.	C		
Lubbers	Ruud F.M.	BNL	Prime Minister	The Netherlands
Lubin	Nancy	C		
Lubman	Stanley B.	C	Partner	Thelen, Marrin, Johnson & Bridges
Lucas	C. Payne	C	Director	Overseas Devel. Council; Adv. Bd., Ctr. for Nat. Pol.
Luce	Charles Franklin	C	Special Counsel	Metropolitan Life Insurance Co.
Luck	Edward Carmichael	C	President	UN Association of the US
Lucy	William	C	Int. Sec./Treasurer	AFL-CIO, AFSCME
Luers	William Henry	C	Trustee	Rockefeller Bros. Fund; Pres., Metro. Museum of Art, NYC
Luke	John Anderson, Jr.	C	President & CEO	Westvaco Corp., NYC
Lundvall	D. Bjorn H.	BS	President (fmr.)	Telefon AB L.M. Ericsson
Luns	Joseph M.A.H.	BINT	Sec. General (fmr.)	N. A. T. O.
Lustick	Ian S.	C	Professor	Univ. of Pennsylvania, Political Science
Luttwak	Edward Nicolae	C	Chairman in Strategy	Georgetown Univ., Center for Strategic & Int. Studies

Last Name	First & Mid. Name	Org.	Job Title	Affiliation - Company, Organization
Luu	Thien-Ky	C		
Luzon Lopez	Francisco	B	Chairman & CEO	Argentaria
Luzzatto	Ann R.	C		
Lyall	Katherine Culbert	C	President	Univ. of Wisconsin
Lykketoft	Mogens	BDK	Minister	of Finance
Lyman	Princeton Nathan	C	US Ambassador	State Dept., South Africa
Lyman	Richard Wall	C	President (fmr.)	Stanford Univ.; Director, IBM Corp.
Lynch	Edward Stephen	C	Treasurer	ITT Europe, Inc., Brussels
Lynch	Thomas F., III	C		
Lynch	William, Jr.	C	Professor	Brooklyn College
Lynk	Myles V.	T	Attorney	Dewey Ballantine LLP
Lynn	James Thomas	C,T	Sr. Advisor	Lazard Freres & Co.
Lynn	Laurence Edwin, Jr.	C	Director	U. of Chicago, Ctr./Urban Resources & Political Science
Lynn-Jones	Sean M.	C		
Lyons	Gene Martin	C		Harper's Magazine; Prof., Dartmouth College
Lyons	James Edward	C	President	Littlefield Publish., Inc.
Lyons	Richard K.	C	Professor	Univ. of Cal. Berkeley, Business School
Lyons	Richard Kent	C		
Lythcott	George I.	C		Health Dept., N.Y. City
Ma	Christopher Yi-Wen	C		
Maas	Cees	TE	Exec. Bd. Mbr.	Int. Nederlanden Group (insurance), Amsterdam
Mabro	Robert E.	BGB	Director	Oxford Inst. for Energy Studies
Mabus	Raymond Edwin, Jr.	C		
MacArthur	Douglas, II	C		
MacCormick	Charles F.	C		
MacDonald	Gordon James F.	C	Professor	Univ. of California, San Diego
MacDonald	Shawn A.	C		
MacDonald	William A.	BC	Partner	McMillan, Binch
MacDougal	Gary E.	C	Professor	UCLA
MacFarquar	Emily	C	Co-Author	"Non-Govt Org., Early Warning and Preventive Diplomacy"
MacFarquar	Roderick	TE	Member (fmr.)	British Parliament; Professor , Harvard Univ.
MacGillivray	Adrien	C		
MacGregor	Ian K.	C	Chair. & CEO (fmr.)	AMAX, Inc.
Mackay	Leo Sydney, Jr.	C		
MacLaren	Roy	BC,TC	High Commissioner	for Canada in Britain
MacLaury	Bruce King	C,T	President	Brookings Institute
MacMillan	Margaret O.	BC	Editor	International Journal, CIIA
MacMillan	Whitney	T	Chair. & CEO (fmr.)	Cargill, Inc.
Macomber	John D.	C	President & Chairman	Export-Import Bk./US; Prin., JDM Inv. Gp.; Dir., Xerox
Macomber	William B.	C	US Ambassador	State Dept.
Maculan	Alexander R.	BA	Chairman	Maculan Holding AG
Macy	Robert M., Jr.	C		
Madrid	Arturo	C	Professor	Trinity Univ. San Antonio
Maeda	Shonosuke	TJ	President	Toray Industries, Inc.
Magowan	Peter A.	C	Director	Chrysler Corp.
Maguire	John David	C	Chairman	MLK Center for Social Change, Atlanta
Mahoney	Catherine F.	C		
Mahoney	Margaret Ellerbe	C	President	Commonwealth Foundation, NYC
Mahoney	Thomas H., IV	C	Co-Leader	United World Federalist
Mai	Vincent A.	C	President & CEO	AEA Investors Inc.; Bd. Mbr., Carnegie Corp. of NY
Maier	Charles Steven	C	Professor	Harvard Univ.
Majonica	Ernst	BD	Member (fmr.)	Ger. Bundestag CDU; Mbr. (fmr.) European Parliament
Makihara	Minoru	TJ	President	Mitsubishi Corp.
Makins	Christopher J.	C		
Mako	William P.	C		
Malek	Frederic Vincent	C	Chairman	Thayer Capital Partners; Pres. Bush's Campaign Mgr., '92
Malfatti	Franco Maria	BI	Minister (fmr.)	Italian Dept. of Education
Malin	Clement B.	C	V. President	Texaco Inc., Int. Rel.; Bd. Mbr., Council of the Americas
Mallery	Richard K.	C	Exec. Comm. Member	Snell & Wilmer, Phoenix
Malley	Robert	C		
Malmgren	Harold Bernard	C	Managing Director	Malmgren, Golt, Kingston, Ltd., London
Malmgren	Karen Philippa	C		
Malone	Alice Kimball	C		
Mamdani	Mahmoud	C		
Manca	Marie Antoinette	C		
Mandelbaum	Michael E.	C	Fgn. Policy Specialist	Johns Hopkins School of Advanced International Studies
Mandelson	Peter A.	BGB	Member	British Parliament
Manilow	Lewis	C	Chairman	U. S. I. A., Advisory Commission on Public Diplomacy
Mann	Hillary	C		
Mann	Michael D.	C	Director	Security Exchange Commission, Office of Int. Affairs
Mann	Thomas Edward	C	Sr. Fellow	Brookings Institute
Manning	Bayless	C	President (fmr.)	Council on Foreign Relations, '71-77
Manning	Preston	BC	Leader	Reform Party
Manos	Stephanos	TE	Member	Greek Parliament
Mansfield	Edward D.	C	Assoc. Professor	Ohio State Univ., Political Science
Manzi	Jim	C		
Maragall	Pascual	TE	Mayor (fmr.)	Barcelona

Last Name	First & Mid. Name	Org.	Job Title	Affiliation - Company, Organization
Marans	J. Eugene	C	Partner	Cleary, Gottlieb, Steen & Hamilton
Marante	Margarida	BP	Journalist	Television, Portugese
March Delgado	Carlos	TE	Chairman	Banca March, Madrid
Marchick	David	C		
Marcucci	Anna Patricia	C		
Marcum	John Arthur	C	Member	Human Rights Watch
Marder	Murrey	C	Member (fmr.)	Carnegie Endowment for International Peace
Mardin	Serif	BTR	Chairman	American U., Wash. D.C., Dep., Islamic Stud.
Margolis	David Israel	C	Chairman & CEO	Coltec Industries, Inc.
Marinzoli	A. Roger	C		
Mark	David E.	C	US Ambassador (fmr.)	State Dept., to Barundi, Romania
Mark	Gregory A.	C	Secretary (fmr.)	Air Force, Carter Admin.; Chancellor, Univ. of Texas, Austin
Mark	Hans Michael	C	Chancellor	Univ. of Texas, Austin
Mark	Rebecca P.	C	Chair. & CEO	Enron Development Corp.
Markmann	Heinz	TE	Director	Wirtschafts-und Sozialwissenschaftliches Institut (WWI)
Marks	Leonard Harold	C	Chair., Exec. Comm.	Foreign Policy Association
Marks	Paul Alan	C	Professor	Cornell Univ.
Marks	Russell Edward, Jr.	C	Director	Webb, Johnson & Klemmer
Markstaller	Margrit	BCH		
Markusen	Ann R.	C		
Marmor	Theodore R.	C	Professor	Yale Univ., Public Policy & Mgt.
Marr	Phebe A.	C		National Defense Univ.; Mid-East Specialist
Marron	Donald Baird	C	CEO	PaineWebber Inc., NYC
Marshall	Andrew W.	C	Director	Defense Dept., Net Assessment
Marshall	Anthony D.	C	Director	Defense Dept., Net Assessment
Marshall	Charles Burton	C	Consultant	Political Science
Marshall	Dale Rogers	C	President	Weaton College, Mass.
Marshall	Katherine	C		
Marshall	Ray	C	Advisory Bd. Member	Center for International Policy
Marshall	Z. Blake	C		
Martens	Wilfried	BB	Prime Minister	Belgium
Martin	Daniel R.	C	President & CEO	E-Z-EM Inc.
Martin	Edwin McCammon, Jr.	B,C	Member	Overseas Development Council
Martin	Lisa L.	C		
Martin	Lynn	C	Secretary (fmr.)	Labor Dept.
Martin	Malcolm W.	C		
Martin	Paul	BC	Minister	Finance, Canada
Martin	William F.	C	Vice President	Yellow Freight System, Inc.
Martin	William McC., Jr.	C	Council Member	Brookings Institute
Martin-Brown	Joan	C		The World Bank
Martinet	Gilles	TE	Ambassador	France, de; Pres., Assoc. for Euro. Cultural Comm., Paris
Martinez	Armando Bravo	C	Sr. Fellow	World Policy Inst.
Martinez	Leo S., Jr.	C		
Martinez	Vilma Socorro	C	Partner	Munger, Tolles & Olson, L. A.
Martini	Eberhard	TE	Spokesman	Bayerische Hypotheken-und Wechsel Bank, Munich
Martinuzzi	Leo Sergio, Jr.	C	Chairman	Strategic Dimensions, Inc.
Marton	Kati	C	Chairwoman	Committee to Protect Journalists
Marx	Anthony William	C	Professor	Columbia Univ., Political Science
Masera	Rainer S.	B	Dir. General	I.M.I.S. p.A.
Masin	Michael Terry	C	Managing Partner	O'Melveny & Myers, NYC
Mason	Elvis L.	C	Managing Partner	Mason Best Co. (Merchant Banking)
Massey	L. Camille	C		
Massey	Walter E.	C		
Massie	Suzanne	C		
Mastanduno	Michael	C		
Mastanduno	Michael	C		
Mateus	Rui	TE	Chairman	Emaudio International, Lisbon
Mathews	Eugene A.	C		
Mathews	Jessica Tuchman	B,C,T	President	Carnegie End. for Int. Peace
Mathews	Michael S.	C		
Mathews	Sylvia M.	C		
Mathias	Charles McC., Jr.	B,C	Senator (fmr.)	Maryland
Mathis	Brian Pierre	C		J.P. Morgan, N.Y.
Matlock	Jack Foust, Jr.	B,C	US Ambassador (fmr.)	State Dept., U.S.S.R.; Columbia Univ.
Matsui	Robert Takeo	C	Congressman	California, Ways & Means
Matsukata	Naotaka	C		
Matsukawa	Michiya	TJ	Sr. Advisor (fmr.)	Nikko Research Ctr., Ltd.
Matsuoka	Seiji	TJ	Special Advisor	Nippon Credit Bank, Ltd.; Chairman (fmr.)
Matsuoka	Tama	C		
Matteson	William Bleecker	C	Presiding Partner	Debevoise & Plimpton, Paris
Matthews	Eugene A.	C	President	Ashta International (Consulting)
Mattox	Gale A.	C	Staff Member	State Dept., Policy Planning Staff
Mattsson	Bjorn	BFIN	President & CEO	Cultor Ltd.
Matuschka	Count Albrecht	TE	Chairman	Matuschka-Gruppe, Munich
Matuszewski	Daniel C.	C	President	Int. Research and Exchange Board
Maucher	Helmut O.	BCH	Chairman & CEO	Nestle Ltd.
Maude	Francis	TE	Member	British Parliament; Shadow Chancellor of the Exchequer

Last Name	First & Mid. Name	Org.	Job Title	Affiliation - Company, Organization
Maughan	Deryck C.	T	Co-Chair. & Co-CEO	Salomon Smith Barney Inc.
Maull	Hanna W.	TE	Co-Director	German Institut for Foreign Affairs, Bonn
Maxwell	Kenneth	C	Author	
May	Ernest R.	C	Co-Author	"The Kennedy Tapes"
May	Michael M.	C		
Mayer	Gerald M., Jr.	C	Officer	New Hampshire Council on World Affairs
Mayer	Lawrence A.	C	Economist	St. Louis
Mayhew	Alice E.	C		
Maynes	Charles William	B,C	Editor	Foreign Policy magazine; Carnegie Endow./Int. Peace
Maystadt	Philippe	BB	Vice-Prime Minister	Belgium; Minsiter, Finance & Foreign Trade
Mazarr	Michael J.	C	Editor	*Washington Quarterly*
Mazur	Jay	C,T	President	Union of Needletrades, Industrial and Textile Employees
Mc Carter	John W.	C		
Mc Donald	Tom	C		
Mc Keon	Elizabeth	C		
Mc Laughin	Charles J.	C		
Mc Lean	Mora L.	C		
Mc Namara	Thomas E.	C		
McAfee	W. Gage	C		PC Asset Management, Hong Kong
McCain	H. Harrison	T	Chairman	McCain Foods Limited, Toronto
McCain	John	C	Senator	Arizona, Armed Svcs., Commerce, Chair., Science & Tran.
McCall	H. Carl	C	Comptroller	State of New York
McCann	Edward	C	Prin., Invest. Banking	Hamilton & Quist, Inc., NYC
McCartan	Patrick F.	C		
McCarthy	James P.	C	General	Defense Dept., US Air Force
McCarthy	John G.	C	President	American Crop Protection Assoc.
McCarthy	Paul B.	C		
McClary	Topnya D.	C		
McCloy	John J., II	B,C	Commander-in-Chief	Defense Dept., USAF, Headquarters, Euro. Command
McColl	Hugh Leon, Jr.	T	Chair., Pres. & CEO	NationsBank Corp.
McColough	C. Peter	C	Dir. & Treasurer (fmr.)	Council on Foreign Relations; Dir., Xerox Corp.
McCormack	Elizabeth J.	C	Trustee	John D. & Catherine T. MacArthur Foundation
McCormick	David H.	C		
McCouch	Donald G.	C	Sr. Mng. Dir. (fmr.)	Chemical Banking Corp.; Bd. Mbr., Council of the Amer.
McCracken	Paul Winston	B,C,T	Professor (fmr.)	Univ. of Michigan
McCurdy	Dave Keith	C	Congressman (fmr.)	Oklahoma, Arms Services, Science, Space & Tech.
McDermott	James (Jim) A.	C	Congressman	Washington, Ways & Means
McDevitt	Sean Daniel	C		
McDonald	Alonzo Lowry, Jr.	C	Chairman & CEO	Avenir Group, Inc.
McDonough	William J.	B,C	President	Fed, New York
McDougal	Myres S.	C	Professor (fmr.)	Yale Univ. Law School
McDougall	Barbara	BC	Minister	External Affairs
McDougall	Gay J.	C	Member	Int. Human Rights Law Group
McEntee	Joan M.	C	Specialist (fmr.)	Commerce Dept., Military Technology
McFarlane	Jennifer A.	C		
McFarlane	Robert C.	C	Advisor (fmr.)	National Security , Reagan Admin.
McFate	Patricia Ann	C	Program Director	Center for National Security Negotiations
McGhee	George Crews	B,C	Oil Producer	McGhee Production Co.
McGiffert	David Eliot	C	Partner	Covington & Burling, Washington
McGillicuddy	John Francis	C	Chair. & CEO (fmr.)	Chemical Bank Corp., NYC; Dir., Texaco, Inc.
McGinn	Richard A.	B	Chairman & CEO	Lucent Technologies
McGovern	George Stanley	C	Senator (fmr.)	South Dakota; Principal, Mid-East Political Council
McGowan	Alan	C	Director	American Assoc. for the Advancement of Science
McGrath	Eugene R.	C	President & CEO	Consolidated Edison Co., of New York, NYC
McGrath	James A.	TC	Lt. Governor	Newfoundland
McGuire	Raymond J.	C		
McGurn	William	C		
McHale	Thomas R.	C		
McHenry	Donald F.	B,C	US Ambassador (fmr.)	UN; Mbr., Carnegie Endow.; Dir., Coca-Cola Co.
McKenna	Frank	BC	Premier	New Brunswick, Canada
McKeough	W. Darcy	TC	Director	McKeough Sons Co. Ltd., Ontario
McKinney	Robert Moody	C	Chairman	New Mexican, Inc.
McLaughlin	David Thomas	B,C	President & CEO	Aspen Institute
McLean	Sheila Avrin	C	Member	Overseas Development Council
McLin	Jon B.	C		
McManus	Doyle	C		
McManus	Jason Donald	C	Editor-in-Chief	Time Warner Inc., NYC
McNamara	Kathleen R.	C		
McNamara	Robert Strange	B,C,T	President (fmr.)	World Bank; Sec. of Def. (fmr.); Member Brookings Inst.
McNaugher	Thomas L.	C		
McNeill	John Henderson	C	Deputy Gen. Council	Defense Dept.
McNeill	Robert L.	C		
McNerney	Michael J.	C		
McPeak	Merrill Anthony	C	Chief-of-Staff	Defense Dept., Air Force
McPherson	Melville Peter	C	President	Mich. St. Univ.;Grp.Exec.V. P. (fmr.) Bankamerica Corp.
McQuade	Lawrence Carroll	C	Vice Chairman	Prudential Mutual Fund Mgt., NYC
Meacham	Jon	C		

Last Name	First & Mid. Name	Org.	Job Title	Affiliation - Company, Organization
Mead	Dana George	C	Chief Oper. Officer	Tenneco, Inc., Houston
Mead	Walter R.	C		
Meagher	Robert F.	C	Professor	Tufts Univ., Law School
Medina	Kathryn B.	C		
Meers	Sharon I.	C	Co-Author	"Foreign Exchange Regimes"
Mehnert	Klaus	BD	Political Scientist	Editor-In-Chief (fmr.), "Osteuropaq" magazine
Mehren, von	Robert Brandt	C	Partner	Debevoise & Plimpton, NYC
Mehta	Ved Parkash	C	Professor	Vassar College
Meissner	Charles F.	C	Asst. Secretary	Commerce Dept., International Economic Policy
Meissner	Doris M.	C	Commissioner	Justice Dept., Immigration & Naturalization Service
Meister	Edgar	TE	Bd. Member	Deutsche Bandesbank, Frankfort-am-Main
Meister	Irene W.	C	Principal	Irene Meister and Assoc. (Consulting)
Melby	Eric D.K.	C	Sr. Associate	The Forum for Int. Policy
Melkert	Ad P. W.	BNL	Minister	of Social Affairs and Employment
Mello	Judy Hendren	C	President	World Learning
Mello, de	Antonio Vasco	B,TE	Chairman	Sociedad de Reparacao e Montagem de Equip. Ind., Lisbon
Melloan	George R.	C	Writer	Wall Street Journal
Melville	Richard A.	C	Member	MOFTE/CICETE, Bristole, ME
Mendelson	Sarah E.	C		
Mendez	Jose F.	C		
Mendlovitz	Saul H.	C	Professor	Rutgers Univ., Peace & World Studies, Law School
Mendoza	Roberto G.	C		
Menezes Ferreira	Joao de	TE	Director	Euroamer, Lisbon; (fmr.) Mbr. of Portugese Parliament
Menges	Carl B.	C		
Menke	John R.	C		
Menne	Alexander W.	BD	Member (fmr.)	Ger. Bundestag. FDP; Bd. Mbr., Hoechst AG, Frankfurt
Menon	Rajan	C		
Mentzl	Jamie F.	C		
Mentzl	Jamie F.	C		
Merkel	Claire Sechler	C		
Merkel	David A.	C		
Merkel	Hans	BD	Attendee	Bilderberg Mtg., 1967
Merkling	Christian	C	Attorney	Paul Weiss Rifkind Wharton & Garrison
Merlini	Cesare	TE	Chair., Exec. Comm.	Council for the United States and Italy
Meron	Theodor	C	Professor	Oxford Univ., England
Merow	John E.	C	Director	Foreign Policy Association
Merrill	Philip	C	Owner/Pres./Publisher	Washintonian Magazine
Merritt	Jack Neil	C	Director (fmr.)	Defense Dept., Joint Chiefs of Staff
Merszei	Zoltan	C		
Mertes	Alois	BD	Member (fmr.)	Ger. Bundestag; Spokesman (fmr.), Fgn. Afrs., CDU/CSU
Mertus	Julie A.	C		
Mesa-Lago	Carmelo	C	Distinguished Prof.	Univ. of Pittsburgh
Meselson	Matthew Stanley	C	Associate Professor	Harvard Univ., Biology
Messite	Zach	C		
Messner	William Curtis, Jr.	C	Professor	SUNY
Mestrallet	Gerard A.	BF	Chairman & CEO	Suez Lyonnaise des Eaux
Mestres	Ricardo A., Jr.	C		
Metcalf	George R.	C		
Mettler	Ruben F.	C,T	Chairman (fmr.)	TRW, Inc.; Dir., Council on Foreign Relations, '86-'92
Mexia	Antonio	TE	Chairman	Gas de Portugal & Trangas, Lisbon
Meyer	Cord	C	Author	"Facing Reality: From World Federalism to the CIA"
Meyer	Edward Charles	C	Chief-of-Staff (fmr.)	Army, Carter Admin.
Meyer	John Robert	C	Professor	Harvard Univ., Capital Formation & Economic Growth
Meyer	Karl Ernest	C	Editorial Bd. Member	New York Times
Meyer	Michael Ryder	C		
Meyerman	Harold J.	C		
Meyerson	Martin	C	President (fmr.)	Univ. of Pennsylvania
Michelis, De	Gianni	BI	Minister	Foreign Affairs, Italy
Mickelson	Sig	C	Research Fellow	Stanford Univ., Hoover Institute
Mickiewicz	Ellen Propper	C	Subcom. Member	Harvard Univ.
Micklethwait	R. John	BGB	Business Editor	The Economist
Midgley	Elizabeth	C		
Midgley	John J., Jr.	C		
Mihaly	Eugene Bramer	C	Chairman	Mihaly International of Canada, Ltd.
Mikell	Gwendolyn	C	President	Georgetown Univ.
Miles	Edward L.	C	Professor	Univ. of Wash., Seattle
Milestone	Judith B.	C		
Miller	Arjay	T	President (fmr.)	Ford Motor Company
Miller	Charles Daly	C	Chairman & CEO	Avery Dennison Corp.
Miller	Christopher D.	C	Attorney	Martin & Bach, Henderson, KY
Miller	David Charles, Jr.	C	Professor	Computer Science
Miller	Debra L.	C	Director	CSIS, Strengthening of American Communication 1st Report
Miller	Franklin C.	C	Sr. Counselor	Defense Dept., Forces Policy
Miller	Joseph Irwin	C	Chair., Exec. Comm.	Cummins Engine Co., Inc.
Miller	Judith	C	Correspondent	New York Times; Dep. Asst Sec. (fmr.), Def. Dept., Manpower
Miller	Ken	C		
Miller	Linda B.	C	Professor	Wellesley College

Last Name	First & Mid. Name	Org.	Job Title	Affiliation - Company, Organization
Miller	Marcia E.	C	Chairwoman	U.S. Int. Trade Commission
Miller	Matthew L.	C		
Miller	Michelle Beth	C		
Miller	Paul David	C	Inspector General	Federal Labor Relations Authority
Miller	Robert Stevens, Jr.	C	Sr. Partner	James D. Wolfensohn, Inc.
Miller	William Green	C	US Ambassador	State Dept., Ukraine
Millett	Allan R.	C	Professor	Ohio State Univ.
Millington	John A.	C	Vice President	Council on Foreign Relations, Planning & Development
Mills	Bradford	C	Chairman & CEO	Overseas Private Investors, Ltd.
Mills	Karen Gordon	C	Director	N.Y. Univ.
Mills	Susan R.	C	Director	U.N., Dept. of Admin. & Management, Finance Mgmt. Office
Milner	Helen V.	C	Professor	Columbia Univ.
Mims	Valerie A.	C		
Min	Nancy-Ann	C	Associate Director	Office of Management & Budget
Minow	Newton N.	C	Chairman	Carnegie Corp. of New York; Dir., Sara Lee Corp.
Mirsky	Yehudah	C	Spec. Advisor	State Dept., Bureau of Democracy, Human Rights & Labor
Mishkin	Alexander	C		
Mitchell	Arthur M., III	C		
Mitchell	George H., Jr.	C	Attorney-at-Law	O'Connor, Cavanagh, Phoenix
Mitchell	George John	C	Senator (fmr.)	Maine; Majority Leader, Finance, Veterans Affairs
Mitchell	Jacquelyn A.	C	Dean	Buffalo Univ., Graduate School
Mitsotakis	Konstantinos	BGR	Prime Minister	Greece
Mitterbauer	Peter	B,T	President	The Federation of Austrian Industry, Vienna
Mityukov	Ihor	BUKR	Minister	Finance, Ukraine
Miyauchi	Yoshihiko	TJ	Pres. & CEO	ORIX Corp.
Miyazaki	Isamu	TJ	Sr. Advisor	Daiwa Institute of Research, Ltd.
Miyazawa	Kiichi	TJ	Prime Minister (fmr.)	Diet, Japanese, now Member of Diet
Miyoshi	Masaya	TJ	Counsellor	Keidanren
Mize	David M.	C	Brig. General	Defense Dept., Deputy Dir., European Command
Mochizuki	Kiichi	C		Pacific Inst., N.Y.
Moe	Sherwood G.	C		
Moffett	George	C		
Moffett	Julia	C		
Mogi	Yuzaburo	TJ	President & CEO	Kikkoman Corp.
Moisi	Dominique	BF	Deputy Director	IFRI, France
Molano	Walter Thomas	C		
Molinari	Susan K.	C	Congresswoman	New York, Budget, Transportation & Infrastructure
Mommer	Karl	BD	Member (fmr.)	Ger. Bundestag, SPD; Mbr. (fmr.) Council of Europe
Mondale	Walter Fritz	B,C,T	US Ambassador	State Dept., Japan
Monjardino	Carlos A.P.V.	BP	President	Fundacao Oriente, Portugal
Monks	John	BGB	General Secretary	Trades Union Congress (TUC)
Monnier	Claude	BCH	Editor-in-Chief (fmr.)	Journal de Geneve
Monroe	Hunter	C		
Montbrial, de	Thierry	BF,TE	Member	de l'Institut de France
Montgomery	Mark C.	C		
Montgomery	Parker Gilbert	C	Member	Trade Representative, Invironmental Pol. Adv. Comm.
Montgomery	Philip O'Bryan, III	C		
Monti	Mario	BINT,TE	Member	European Commission, Brussels
Moock	Joyce Lewinger	C		
Moody	Jim	C	Congressman (fmr.)	Wisconsin
Moody	William S.	C	Prog. Officer	Rockerfeller Brothers Fund
Moody-Stuart	Mark	TE	Chairman	Shell Transport & Tdg Co.;Gp.Mng.Dir.,Royal Dutch/Shell Gp.
Moore	John J., Jr.	C		
Moore	John M.	C		
Moore	John Norton	C	Chairman (fmr.)	US Inst. for Peace; Adj. Prof., Georgetown Law School
Moore	Jonathan	C	Representative	UN Mission; Sr. Assoc., Carnegie Endow. for Int. Peace
Moore	Paul, Jr.	C	Diocese Bishop	New York
Moose	George E.	C	Alt. Representative	State Dept., African Affairs, UN Security Council
Moose	Richard M.	C	Under Secretary	State Dept., For Management
Mora	Alberto J.	C	Attorney	Holland & Knight, Int. Law
Moragoda	Milinda			Merchantile Merchant Bank
Morali	Veronique	BF	Organizer, '92 Conf.	Bilderberg Group, 1991 Baden-Baden Meeting
Moran	Theodore H.	C	Sr. Advisor	State Dept., Policy Planning Staff
Moratti	Gian Marco	TE	President	Saras-Raffinerie Sade; Chair., Petrolifera Italiana, Rome
Morey	David E.	C	President & CEO	DMG, Inc.
Morgan	Lee L.	T	Chairman (fmr.)	Caterpillar Inc.
Morgan	Thomas E.	C		
Morgenthau	Lucinda L. Franks	C		
Morikawa	Toshio	TJ	President	Sumitomo Bank, Ltd.
Morishita	Yoichi	TJ	President	Matsushita Electric Industrial Co., Ltd.
Morita	Akio	TJ	Chairman	Sony Corp.
Morita	Kazuo	TJ	Vice President	Hitachi, Ltd.
Morley	James William	C	Professor (fmr.)	East Asian Inst., Political Science
Morrell	Gene Paul	C	Vice Chairman	Petro United Terminals, Inc., Houston
Morris	Bailey-Eck	C	Vice President	Brookings Inst., Communications
Morris	Joseph	BC	President (fmr.)	Canadian Labour Congress
Morris	Max K.	C	Chairman	Jacksonville Electric Authority

Last Name	First & Mid. Name	Org.	Job Title	Affiliation - Company. Organization
Morris	Milton D.	C		
Morrisett	Lloyd N.	C	President	Markle Foundation
Morse	Edward L.	C	Publisher	"Petroleum Intelligence Weekly"
Morse	F. Bradford	B,C	Under Secretary	United Nations
Morse	Kenneth Pratt	C	Chairman (fmr.)	Standard Register Co., Dayton
Mosbacher	Robert A.	C	Chairman	Mosbacher Energy Co.; Campaign Mrg., George Bush.'92
Moses	Alfred Henry	C	US Ambassador	St. Dept.,Romania;Ptnr.,Covington & Burling;Pr., Am. Jew. Cong.
Mosettig	Michael David	C	Sr. Producer	PBS TV, MacNeil Lehrer News Hour
Moskow	Kenneth A.	C		
Moskow	Michael H.	C		
Moss	Amber Holmes, Jr.	C	Dean	Univ. of Miami, Graduate School
Moss	David	C		
Moss	Richard H.	C		Battelle Pacific N.W. Nat. Laboratory
Motley	Joel W.	C	Co-Owner	Carmona, Motley & Co.
Motono	Moriyuki	TJ	Advisor to Board	Nomura Securities Co., Ltd.
Mottahedeh	Roy	C	Professor	Harvard Univ., Islamic History
Motulsky	Dan T.	C	Member	CFR, N.Y. Committee
Moyers	Bill D.	B	Executive Director	Public Affairs TV, Inc.; Director (fmr.), CFR
Moynihan	Daniel Patrick	C	Senator	New York, Fin./Ranking, Joint Taxation, Rules & Admin.
Mroz	John Edwin	C	President	Institute for East-West Studies
Mudd	Margaret F.	C		
Mueller	Rudolf	BD	Member	German Bundestag, SPD
Mueller-Armack	Alfred	BD	Economics Scientist	Mbr. (fmr.) "Freiburg Schule";Undersec. (fmr.) Euro. Afrs.
Muenchmeyer	Alwin	TE	President (fmr.)	Deutscher Industrie und Handelstag-"DIHT"
Mujal-Leon	Eusebio M.	C	Chairman	Georgetown Univ., Government Dept.
Mukaibo	Takashi	TJ	Chairman	Japanese Atomic Ind. Forum; Pres. (fmr.), U. of Tokyo
Mulford	David C.	C	Vice Chairman	CS First Boston, Inc.
Mulholland	William D.	B	Trustee	Queen's University
Muller	Charles W.	B	President	Murden & Co.
Muller	Edward R,	C		
Muller	Henry	C	Editorial Director	Time magazine; Board Member, Carnegie Corp. of NY
Muller	Steven	C	President	Johns Hopkins Univ., Fed. Reserve Bank
Mullins	Janet	C		
Mundy	Carl Epting, Jr.	C	Commandant	Defense Dept., Marine Corps
Munger	Edwin Stanton	C	Professor	California Institute of Technology, Political Geography
Munroe	George Barber	C	Chairman & CEO	Phelps Dodge Corp.
Munroe-Blum	Heather	BC	Vice President	Univ. of Toronto, Res. & Int. Rel.
Munthe	Preben	TE	Professor	Univ. of Oslo; Counselor, Norwegian Nobel Institute
Munyan	Winthrop R.	C		New York Times, Dir., Manufacturers Hanover
Murase	Emily Moto	C		
Murase	Jiro	TJ	Managing Partner	Bingham Dana Murase
Muravchik	Joshua	C	Res. Scholar	Georgetown Univ.
Murdock	Deroy	C		
Murdock	Rupert	C	Founder & CEO	News Corp.
Murdy	William F.	C		
Murmann	Klaus	TE	Hon. Chairman	Federation of German Employees Association, (BDA)
Murofushi	Minoru	TJ	President & CEO	ITOCHU Corp.
Murphy	Caryle Marie	C	Fgn. Correspondent	Washington Post, Middle East, Cairo
Murphy	Joseph S.	C	President	City Univ. of New York, Graduate School, NYC
Murphy	Richard W.	C	Sr. Fellow	CFR, Middle East Countries
Murphy	Sean David	C	Staff Assistant	State Dept., Bureau of Political-Military Affairs
Murphy	Thomas S.	C	Chairman & CEO	Cap. Cities ABC Inc.;Dir.,IBM,Johnson & John.,Texaco
Murray	Allen E.	C,T	Chairman, Pres. & CEO	Mobil Corp.
Murray	Douglas P.	C	Member	Overseas Development Council
Murray	Ian P.	C		
Murray	Janice L.	C		
Murray	Leonard, III	C		
Murray	Lori Esposito	C	Asst. Director	Arms Cont. & Disarm. Agency
Murray	Lowell	TC	Minister of State	Senate of Canada
Muse	Martha Twitchell	C	Chairman	Tinker Foundation, NYC; Bd. Mbr., Council of the Amer.
Muskie	Edmund Sixtus	C	Chairman	Ctr. for Nat. Policy; Hon. Director, Foreign Policy Assoc.
Mustard	J. Fraser	BC	President	Canadian Institute for Advanced Research
Myerson	Toby Salter	C	Secretary (fmr.)	Japan Society, Inc., NYC
Myklebust	Egil	BN	CEO	Norsk Hydro
Myrvoll	Ole	BN	Member (fmr.)	Norwegian Parliament
Nabo	Francisco Murteira	BP	President & CEO	Portugal Telecom
Nachmanoff	Arnold	C	Man. Director	Capital Advisors Limited
Nacht	Michael L.	C	Asst. Director	Arms Cont. & Disarm. Agency
Nadiri	M. Ishaq	C	Professor	New York Univ., NYC
Nagai	Yonosuke	TJ	Professor	Aoyama Gakuin Univ.
Nagasue	Eiichi	TJ	Member (fmr.)	Diet, Japanese
Nagl	John A.	C		
Nagorski	Andrew	C	Writer	Newsweek
Nagorski	Zygmunt, Jr.	C		Canadian Diplomatic Corps
Najera	Peter F.	C		
Nakahara	Nobuyuki	TJ	Honorary Chairman	Tonen Corp.
Nakamura	Kaneo	TJ	Counsellor	The Industrial Bank of Japan, Ltd.

Last Name	First & Mid. Name	Org.	Job Title	Affiliation - Company, Organization
Nakamura	Toshio	TJ	Counsellor	The Bank of Tokyo-Mitsubishi, Ltd.
Namkung	K. A.	C		
Narjes	Karl-Heinz	TE	Vice President (fmr.)	Commission of Euro. Union; Mbr. (fmr.) Ger. Bundestag, CDU
Nasher	Raymond D.	C		
Nass	Matthias	BD	Deputy Editor	*Die Zeit*
Nathan	Andrew J.	C		Colombia Univ.
Nathan	James A.	C		
Nathoo	Raffiq A.	C		
Natt	Ted M.	C		
Nau	Henry R.	C	Professor	George Washington Univ., Political Science & Int. Affairs
Navab	Alexander	C		
Naylor	Rosamond Lee	C	Professor	Stanford Univ., Inst. for Int. Studies
Neal	Stephen L.	C	President	Z. Smith Reynolds Foundation
Necci	Antonio Lorenzo	TE	CEO	PS-Ferrovie dello Stato
Negroponte	John Dimitri	C	US Ambassador	State Dept., Philippines
Neier	Aryeh	C	President	Open Society Inst..(by George Soros);Adj.Prof.,N.Y.Univ.,NYC
Neisser	Heinrich	TE	Member	Austrian Parliament; 2nd President, National Assembly
Nelson	Daniel N.	C		
Nelson	Jack	C	Wash. Bureau Chief	L. A. Times; PBS TV, Washington Week in Review
Nelson	Marie E.	C		
Nelson	Mark A.	C		
Nelson	Marlin E.	C	Member	Overseas Development Council
Nenneman	Richard Arthur	C	Editor-in-Chief (fmr.)	Christian Science Monitor
Neuman	Stephanie G.	C	Adj. Professor	Columbia Univ., Int. Affairs
Neumann	Friedrich	TE	Chairman	Arbeitgeberverband Nordrhein-Westfalen
Neustadt	Richard Elliott	C	Professor (fmr.)	Harvard Univ., J. F. K. School of Government
Newberg	Esther R.	C		
Newburg	Andre W. G.	C	General Counsel	Euro. Bank of Reconstruction & Development, London
Newcomb	Nancy	C		
Newell	Barbara Warne	C	Trustee	Carnegie Endowment; Counselor, Florida Dept. of Labor
Newhouse	John	B,C	Dir. of Scholars	Brookings Institute
Newman	Constance Berry	C	Under Secretary	Smithsonian Inst.
Newman	Frank Neil	C		
Newman	Pricilla A.	C		
Newman	Richard T.	C		Lake Forest Capital Management
Newsom	David Dunlop	C	Professor	Georgetown Univ., International Relations
Newton	Quigg	C	President (fmr.)	Colorado Univ.
Ney	Edward N.	C	US Ambassador	State Dept., Canada; Director, Foreign Policy Assoc.
Niarchos	Stavros Spyros	BGR	Head	Niarchos Group; Shipowner
Nicholas	N. J., Jr.	C	Director	Xerox Corp
Nichols	Carole	C		Global Kids, Inc.
Nichols	Nancy Stephenson	C		
Nichols	Rodney W.	C		
Nicholson	Jamie E.	C		
Niehuss	John M.	C	Deputy Asst. Sec.	State Dept., International Monitary Affairs
Niehuss	Rosemary Neaher	C	Director	Foreign Policy Association; member, Kissinger Assoc.
Nielsen	Nancy	C		
Nielsen	Suzanne C.	C		
Nielsen	Waldemar A.	C		
Nierenberg	Claudia	C		NASA, NOAA, Office of Global Programs
Niinisto	Sauli V.	BFIN	Minister	of Finance
Nilsson	A. Kenneth	C		Eureka Group, Inc.
Nimetz	Matthew	C	Partner	Paul, Weiss, Rifkind, Wharton & Garrett
Nishihara	Masashi	TJ	Professor	Nat. Defense Academy, Int. Relations
Nitze	Paul Hilken	B,C	Director (fmr.)	Fgn. Pol. Plng., Truman, Eisenhower & Nixon Admin.
Nitze	William Albert	C	Asst. Administrator	E.P.A.; Pres., Alliance to Save Energy, Wash.
Nix	Crystal	C	Special Assistant	State Dept., Office of Legal Adviser
Nixon	Sir Edwin	TE	Deputy Chairman	National Westminster Bank, London
Nizich	Ivan Astrid	C		
Noam	Eli M.	C		
Noguchi	Teruo	TJ	Chairman & CEO	Koa Oil Co., Ltd.
Noir	Michel	BF	Mayor	Lyon, France; Sec. of State for Foreign Trade (fmr.)
Nolan	Janne E.	C	Sr. Fellow	Brookings Institute
Nolan	Kimberly	C		
Noland	Marcus	C		
Nolte	Richard Henry	C	General Partner	Washburn Island Res. L. P.
Nonacs	Eric S.	C		
Nooter	Robert H.	C	Board Member	Smithsonian Inst.
Norman	William Stanley	C	Exec. Vice President	AMTRAK, Washington
Norquist	Grover Glenn	C		
Norrington	Humphrey	TE	Vice Chairman	Barclays Bank, London
Northrop	Michael F.	C		
Norton	Augustus Richard	C	Professor	Boston Univ.
Norton	Eleanor Holmes	C	Delegate (fmr.)	Dist. of Columbia, Pub. Bldg. & Gnds., Pub. Wks. & Tran.
Nossel	Suzanne F.	C		
Noto	Lucio A.	T	Chair. & CEO	Mobil Corp.
Novak	Michael John	C	Columnist	Forbes magazine; Scholar, American Enterprise Inst.

Last Name	First & Mid. Name	Org.	Job Title	Affiliation - Company, Organization
Novicki	Margaret A.	C		
Nuechterlein	Jeffrey D.	C		
Nugent	Walter Terry King	C	Professor	Univ. of Notre Dame
Nunn	Sam	B	Senator (fmr.)	Georgia, Armed Svcs. Rnkg. Mbr., Gvt. Affrs., Small Bus.
Nye	J. Benjamin H.	B,C,T	Exec. Secretary	Treasury Dept.
Nye	Joseph S., Jr.	B,C,T	Chairman	Nat. Intelligence Council; Dean, Harvard Univ., School of Govt.
Nykopp	Johan	B	fmr. Ambassador	President, Tampella
O'Brien	Dennis J.	C	Professor	Univ. Of Rochester
O'Cleireacain	Carol	C	Member (fmr.)	New York City Office of the Budget; Brookings Inst.
O'Connell	Mary Ellen	C	Professor	Indiana Univ., Int. Law
O'Connor	Sandra Day	C	Associate Justice	Supreme Court
O'Connor	Walter F.	C	Director	Fordham Univ., Taxation and Accounting Program
O'Donnell	Anthony G. S.	BC	Director	of Companies, Canada; Chairman (fmr.), Home Oil Co.
O'Donnell	Kevin	C	Chr. Ex. Com. (fmr.)	SIFCO Industries
O'Flaherty	J. Daniel	C	Member (fmr.)	Carnegie Endowment for International Peace
O'Hare	Joseph Aloysius	C	President	Fordham Univ.
O'Malley	Cormac K. H.	C		
O'Neill	Michael James	C	Vice President (fmr.)	New York Daily News
O'Neill	Paul H.	T	Chairman & CEO	Alcoa
O'Prey	Kevin P.	C		
O'Shaughnessy	Elise	C	Writer	*Vanity Fair*
Oakes	John Bertram	C	Sr. Editor (fmr.)	New York Times
Oakes	John G. H.	C		
Oakley	Robert B.	C	US Ambassador	State Dept., Somalia
Oberdorfer	Don	C	Journalist	Washington Post; Mbr., Johns Hopkins Univ.
Oddsson	David	BICE	Prime Minister	Iceland; Mayor (fmr.), Reykjavik; Chair., Independence Party
Odeen	Philip A.	C	President & CEO	BDM Int.
Odell	John	C	Professor	USC
Odom	William Eldridge	C	Direcctor (fmr.)	National Security Agency (NSA)
Oetker	Rudolf August	BD	Head	Oetker-Gruppe, Bielefeld
Oettinger	Anthony Gervin	C	Member of Faculty	Harvard Univ.
Offergeld	Rainer	BD	Minister (fmr.)	Economic C0-Operation
Offit	Morris Wolf	C	President	Offitbank, NYC; Council Member, Brookings Institute
Ogasawara	Toshiaki	TJ	Publisher-Chairman	"The Japan Times, Ltd."; President, Nifco Inc.
Ogata	Sadako	TJ	High Commissioner	UN High Commission for Refugees
Ogata	Shijuro	TJ	Deputy Gov. (fmr.)	Japan Development Bank
Ogden	Alfred	C	Of Counsel	Reboul, MacMurphy, Hewett, Maynard & Kristoff
Ogden	William S.	C		
Oh	Kongdan	C	Analyst	Korean Policy
Ohga	Norio	TJ	Chair. & CEO	Sony Corp.
Ohnishi	Masafumi	TJ	Chairman	Osaka Gas Co., Ltd.
Okano	Mitsuyoshi	TJ	President	The Suruga Bank, Ltd.
Okawara	Yoshio	TJ	President	Inst. for Int. Pol. Studies; (fmr.) Amb. to the US
Okita	Yoichi	TJ	Professor	Nat. Inst. for Policy Research
Oksenberg	Michael	C,T	Sr. Fellow	Stanford Univ., Asia Pacific Research Ctr.
Okuda	Hiroshi	TJ	President	Toyota Motor Corp.
Okumura	Ariyoshi	TJ	Sr. Advisor	IBJ NW Asset Management Co., Ltd.
Okun	Herbert S.	C	US Ambassador (fmr.)	State Dept., Yugoslavia
Olechowski	Andrzej	B,T	Chairman	Bank Handlowy W Warszawie
Oliva	Lawrence Jay	C	President	New York Univ., NYC
Oliver	April	C	Producer	CNN, Special Assignment
Oliver	Covey T.	C	Professor (fmr.)	Univ. of Pennsylvania, Law School
Olivetti	Roberto	BI	President (fmr.)	Soc. Gen. Semiconduttori S.P.A.
Ollila	Jorma	BFIN	Chairman & CEO	Nokia Corp.
Olmer	Lionel H.	C		
Olmstead	Cecil Jay	C	Member	Steptoe & Johnson, Washington
Olsen	Leif H.	C	President	Leif H. Olso Investments, Inc.
Olson	Ronald L.	C		
Olson	William Clinton	C	Professor (fmr.)	American Univ., Washington
Olvey	Lee D.	C	Vice President	OCLC
Omestad	Thomas E.	C	Associate Editor	Carnegie Endowment, Foreign Policy
Ondaatji	Elizabeth Heneghan	C		
Oort	Conrad J.	BNL	Advisor - Bd. of Mgt.	Algemene Bank Nederland NV
Opel	John R.	C	Director	IBM Corp.
Oppenheimer	Franz Martin	C	Partner	Fort & Schlefer, Washington
Oppenheimer	Michael Frank	C	Exec. Vice President	Futures Group, Inc.
Orban	Viktor	TE	Prime Minister	Hungary
Orlins	Stephen A.	C		
Ornstein	Norman Jay	C	Resident Scholor	American Enterprise Institute, Washington
Orr	Robert C.	C		
Orszag	Peter R.	C		
Osborn	George K., III	C		
Osborne	Richard de J.	C	Treasurer	Council of the Americas
Osisek	Elizabeth M.	C		
Osmer-McQuade	Margaret	C	Vice President (fmr.)	Council on Foreign Relations, Meetings
Osnos	Peter Lionel Winston	C	V. Pres. & Assoc. Pub.	Random House Trade Books
Osnos	Susan Sherer	C		

Last Name	First & Mid. Name	Org.	Job Title	Affiliation - Company, Organization
Osterander	F. Taylor, Jr.	C		
Ostermann	Christian	C		
Ostlund	William Brian	C		
Ostry	Sylvia	BC	Chairman	Univ. of Toronto, Int. Studies
Otero	Joaquin F.	C		
Overholster	Geneva	C		Des Moines Register
Ovitz	Michael S.	C	President	Walt Disney
Owada	Hisashi	TJ	Ambassador (fmr.)	to the U.N.; Vice Minister (fmr.) of Foreign Affairs
Owen	Henry David	C,T	Sr. Advisor	Salomon Bros.; Brookings Inst.; Bd. Mbr., Ctr./Int. Pol.
Owen	Lord	BGB,TE	Chairman	Middlesex Holdings
Owen	Robert B.	B	President	Owen Research Inc.
Owen	Vance	B		
Owens	William Arthur	C	Vice Chairman	Defense Dept., Joint Chiefs of Staff
Oxman	Bernard H.	C		
Oxman	Stephen A.	C	Assistant Secretary	State Dept., European & Canadian Affairs
Oxnan	Robert B.	C		
Oye	Kenneth A.	B	Author	"Cooperation under Anarchy"
Ozceri	Tugay	BTR	Under Secretary	Ministry of Foreign Affairs, Turkey
Packard	David	T	Chairman	Hewlett-Packard Co.
Packard	George Randolph	C	Dean	John Hopkins Univ., Sch of Advanced Int. Studies
Padoa-Schioppa	Tommaso	BI	Exec. Bd. Member	European Central Bank
Page	John M., Jr.	B	Chief Econ.	The World Bank
Paine	George C., II	C	Judge	Justice Dept., Bankruptcy Court, Nashville
Pais	Abraham	C	Professor	Rockefeller Univ.
Pakula	Hannah C.	C		
Palliser	Sir Michael	TE	Vice Chairman	Samuel Montagu & Co.
Palme	S. Olaf	BS	Prime Minister (fmr.)	Sweden
Palmer	Mark	C		
Palmer	Norman Dunbar	C	Member	Orbis, Global Futures Digest, Editorial Board
Palmer	Ronald Dewayne F.	C	US Ambassador (fmr.)	State Dept., Malaysia Kuala Lumpur
Palmieri	Victor Henry	C	CEO	Mutual Life Insurance Co.
Pangalos	Theodoros G.	BGR	Minister	Greece, Foreign Affairs
Panofsky	Wolfgang Kurt H.	C	Director (fmr.)	Stanford Univ., Linear Accellerator
Papademos	Lucas	TE	Governor	Bank of Greece, Athens
Papandreou	George A.	BGR	Alt. Minister	for Foreign Affairs
Paperin	Stuart J.	C		
Papkonstandinov	Michael	BGR	Foreign Minister	Greece
Pardee	Scott E.	C		Yamaichi Int. (America Inc.)
Pardew	James W., Jr.	C		
Parent	Alexander	C		
Park	H. K.	C		
Parker	Barrington D., Jr.	C	Dist. Judge	N.Y.
Parker	Jason H.	C		ACLS
Parker	Jay	C		
Parker	Karen E.	C		
Parker	Maynard Michael	C	Editor	Newsweek magazine
Parkinson	Roger P.	C	Publisher & CEO	*The Globe and Mail*
Parks	Michael Christopher	C		
Parsky	Gerald Lawrence	C,T	Chairman	Aurora Capital Partners, L. A.
Parsons	Richard Dean	C	Chairman & CEO	Dime Savings Bank of N. York, NYC; Pres., Time-Warner
Passer-Muslin	Juliette M.	C		
Passin	Herbert	C	Professor (fmr.)	East Asian Inst., Sociology
Pastor	Ed	C		
Pastor	Robert A.	C		
Patrick	Hugh T.	C	Professor	Columbia Univ., Int. Business
Patricof	Alan J.	C		
Patrikis	Ernest T.	C	Deputy Gen. Counsel	Federal Reserve System, Federal Reserve Bank of NY
Patten	Chris	TE	Governor (fmr.)	Hong Kong; (fmr.) Mbr., British Cabinet
Patterson	Gardner	C	Professor	Princeton Univ., Economics Dept.
Patterson	Hugh B., Jr.	C		
Pattison	James A.	TC	Chair., Pres. & CEO	Jim Pattison Group, Inc., Vancouver
Pauker	Guy J.	C		
Paul	Michael G.	C		
Paul	Ronald Arthur	C	General Counsel	Howmet Corp.
Pavel	Barry	C		
Payne	Donald M.	C	Congressman	New Jersey, Int. Relations, Education & the Workforce
Pearce	William R.	C,T	Vice President	Cargill; Pres. & CEO, I.D.S. Mutual Fund Group
Pearlstine	Norman	C	Editor-in-Chief	Time Warner Inc., NYC; Editor, Time, Inc.
Pearson	John E.	C	Manager	Hoover's Online, Human Resources
Peckham	Gardner G.	C		
Pedersen	Richard Foote	C	Director	California Poly Pomona Univ., International Programs
Pederson	Rena	C	V.P./Editorial Page	Dallas Morning News
Pell	Claiborne	C	Senator (fmr.)	Rhode Island, Foreign Relations, Labor, Rules
Pelletreau	Robert Halsey, Jr.	C	US Ambassador	State Dept., Egypt, Tunisia
Penfield	James K.	C		
Penn	Mark	C	Asian Expert	National Security Council
Penzias	Arno A.	B	V. P. Research	AT&T Bell Labs.

Last Name	First & Mid. Name	Org.	Job Title	Affiliation - Company, Organization
Peratikos	Michael	BGR		
Percy	Charles Harting	C	Chairman & President	Hariri Foundation; Fmr. Senator, Ill.
Perea-Henze	Raul	C		
Pereger	Werner A.	BD	Polit. Correspondent	*Die Zeit*
Peretz	Don	C	Professor	Harvard Univ.
Perez	Antonio F.	C	Professor	Catholic Univ. of America, Law
Perez	David	C		
Perkins	Edward J.	C	Director	State Dept., Personnel; Amb. (fmr.), United Nations
Perkins	George William, II	B	President & Chairman	Financial Marketing System, Inc.
Perkins	James A.	B,C	Member	Overseas Development Council; Dir., CFR
Perkins	Roswell Burchard	C	Partner	Debevoise & Plimpton, NYC
Perle	Richard Norman	C	Resident Fellow	American Enterprise Institute, Public Policy Resolution
Perlman	Janice E.	C	Fdr. & Exec. Dir.	Megacities Project
Perlmutter	Louis	C	Professor	American Univ., Wash.
Permutter	Amos	C		
Perritt	Henry H., Jr.	C		
Perry	Sir Michael	TE	Chairman	Centrica & Dunlop Slazenger Gp.; (fmr.) Ch., Unilever, London
Perry	William J.	B,T	Secretary (fmr.)	Defense Dept.; Prof., Stanford Univ.
Perry	William J.	C		
Peruzzi	Hillary Kircher	C		
Pesmazoglu	John S.	BGR	Dep. Governor (fmr.)	Bank of Greece
Peters	Arthur King	C	President & Owner	A. K. Peters, Co., NYC
Peters	Aulana L.	C	Director	Mobil Oil Corp.; Partner, Gibson, Dunn & Crutcher
Peters	Michael P.	C		
Petersen	Erik R.	C		
Petersen	Holly	C		
Petersen	Howard C.	B,C	Advisor (fmr.)	National Security Council
Petersen	Jan	B	Parliamentary Leader	Censewrvative Party
Peterson	Peter G.	C,T	Chairman	CFR, Blackstone Group; Prin., Concord Coal.
Peterson	Rudolph A.	B,C	Chair., Exec. Comm.	Bankamerica Corp., San Diego
Petree	Richard W.	C	US Ambassador	
Petree	Richard W., Jr.	C		
Petri	Thomas Everet	C	Congressman	Wisconsin, Educ. & Workforce, Transport. & Infrastructure
Petschek	Stephen R.	C		
Pettibone	Peter John	C	Partner	Lord Day & Lord, Barrett Smith, NYC
Petty	John Robert	C	Chairman	Federal National Payables Inc., Washington
Pezullo	Lawrence A.	C	US Special Envoy	State Dept., on Haiti
Pfaltzgraff	Robert Louis, Jr.	C	President	Institute for Foreign Policy Analisis
Pfeiffer	Jane Cahill	C	Chairwoman (fmr.)	NBC, Inc., NYC
Pfeiffer	Ralph A., Jr.	C	Chairman (fmr.)	IBM, World Trade Corp.
Pfeiffer	Steven Bernard	C	Head, Int. Dept.	Fulbright & Jaworski, Washington
Pham	Kien D.	C		Tennaco Inc.
Pharr	Susan J.	C	Member	Harvard Univ.
Phelan	John J., Jr.	C	Chair. & CEO (fmr.)	New York Sock Exchange, NYC
Phelps	Michael E.J.	TC	Chair. & CEO	Westcoast Energy Inc., Vancouver
Philippe	H.R.H. Prince	B	Prince	Belgium
Phillips	Cecil M.	C		
Phillips	Christopher H.	C	US Ambassador	State Dept., Brunei
Phillips	Russell A., Jr.	C	Exec. Vice President	Rockefeller Brothers Foundation
Picker	Harvey	C	Board Member	Academy of Politcal Science
Pickering	Thomas R.	B,C	US Ambassador	St. Dept., Russia, Moscow, '94; Ambassador (fmr.), UN
Piedra	Alberto M., Jr.	C		
Pieezenik	Steve R.	C		
Piel	Gerald	B,C	Chairman (fmr.)	Scientific America, Inc.
Pierce	Lawrence W.	C	Dist. Judge (fmr.)	Southern District of N.Y.
Pierce	Ponchitta A.	C	Director	Foreign Policy Association
Piercy	George T.	C		
Piercy	Jan	C		
Pierer, von	Heinrich	TE	Chair. & CEO	Siemens AG, Munich
Pierre	Andrew J.	C	Sr. Associate	Carnegie Endowment for Int. Peace; Johns Hopkins Univ.
Pierson	Jeffrey D.	C		
Pifer	Alan Jay Parrish	C	Vice President	Carnegie Foundation for Advancement in Teaching
Pigott	Charles M.	C	Director	Boeing Company, Chevron Corp.
Pigott	Maceo Nathaniel	T	Owner	International Resources Exchange Corp.
Pike	John E.	C		
Pillar	Russell I.	C		
Pilling	Donald L.	C	Division Director	Defense Dept., Navy, General Planning
Pilliod	Charles J., Jr.	C	Director	Manufacturers Hanover
Pillsbury	Michael	C		
Pilon	Juliana Geran	C		
Pimenta	Carlos	BP	Member	Eoro. Parliament; fmr. Sec., St.,Environment
Pincus	Lionel Irwin	C	Council Member	Brookings Inst.;Chair./CEO, E.M. Warburg, Pincus & Co.
Pincus	Walter Haskell	C	National Reporter	Washington Post
Pinder	Jeanne	C		
Pinho	Ilidio de	TE	Chairman	Colep, Lisbon
Pinkerton	W. Stewart	C		
Pino	John Anthony	C	CEO	ACT Management

Last Name	First & Mid. Name	Org.	Job Title	Affiliation - Company, Organization
Pinto Balsemao	Francisco	TE	Chairman	SIC; Prime Minister (fmr.), Portugal
Piore	Emanuel Rubin	B	Adjunct Professor	Rockefeller Univ.
Pipes	Daniel	C	Editor	Middle East Quarterly
Pipes	Richard Edgar	C	Professor	Harvard Univ., History
Pirelli	Alberto	BI	Mng. Partner (fmr.)	Pirelli & Co., Milan
Pirelli	Leopoldo	BI	Partner	Pirelli & Co.
Pitts	Joe W., III	C	Professor	Eastern College, St. Davids PA
Pitts	Joseph W., III	C		
Plank	John N.	C		
Platt	Alan A.	C		
Platt	Alexander Hartley	C		
Platt	Nicholas	C	US Ambassador (fmr.)	State Dept., Pakistan
Plattner	Mark F.	C		
Platz	Stephanie S.	C		
Plaut	Peter G.	C		
Plepler	Richard	C		
Plimpton	Calvin Hastings	C	Professor (fmr.)	State Univ. of New York, Downstate Medical Center
Ploetz	Hans-Friedrich, von	BD	State Secretary	Ministry for Fgn. Affairs
Plumeri	Joseph J., II	C		
Pocalyko	Michael N.	C		
Podhoretz	Norman	B,C	Editor-in-Chief	"Commentary"
Pogue	Richard Welch	C	Sr. Partner	Jones, Day, Reavis & Pogue
Pohl	Karl Otto	BD	President	Deutsche Bundesbank
Polanyi	John	BC	Professor	Univ. of Toronto, Canada
Polk	George W.	C		
Polk	William R.	C		
Pollack	Gerald A.	C	Assoc. Director	Commerce Dept., Int. Economics
Pollack	Kenneth M.	C		
Polsby	Neilson Woolf	C	Advisory Bd. Member	Center for International Policy, Center for Nat. Policy
Pompidou	Georges Jean R.	BF	President (fmr.)	French Republic
Pond	Elizabeth	C	Fellow	John D., & Katherine T. Mac Arthur Foundation
Ponneman	Daniel B.	C	Spec. Asst. to Pres.	Nonproliferation & Export Control
Ponto	Juergen	BD	Chairman (fmr.)	Dresdner Bank AG, Frankfurt am Main
Pool	Marquita J.	C		
Popkin	Anne Brandeis	C		
Popoff	Frank P.	C	Chairman & CEO	Dow Chemical Co.
Porrit	Jonathon	BGB	Programme Dir.	Forum for the Future
Porter	John Edward	C	Congressman	Illinois, Appropriations
Portes	Jonathan D.	C		
Portes	Richard D.	C	Sec. General	RES Conference
Porzecanski	Arturo C.	C	Chief Economist	ING-Berings
Porzner	Konrad	TE	Member (fmr.)	German Bundestag; Sec. (fmr.) State, SPD
Posen	Barry R.	C	Professor	MIT, Political Science
Posner	Michael H.	C		Reuters News Service
Posvar	Wesley W.	C	Trustee	Carnegie Endowment; Pres. (fmr.), Univ. of Pittsburgh
Potter	William C.	C	Professor	Monterey Inst. for Int. Studies
Powell	Colin Luther	B,C	Chairman (fmr.)	Defense Dept., Joint Chiefs of Staff
Powell	Jerome H.	C	Assit. Sec. (fmr.)	Treasury Dept., Domestic Finance
Powell	Michael K.	C	Member	Federal Communications Commission
Power	Philip H.	C	Regent	Univ. of Michigan
Powers	Thomas Moore	C	Author & Contr. Edit.	Atlantic mag.
Powers	William Francis, Jr.	C	Exec. Dir. of Research	Ford Motor Co.
Prager	Robert J.	C		
Prasso	Sheri	C		
Precht	Henry	C	Head	State Dept., Iran Desk
Prendergast	Kieran	B	Under Sec. Gen.	for Political Affairs, UN
Press	Frank	C	President	National Academy of Science
Pressler	Larry	C	Senator (fmr.)	S. Dakota, Chair., Commerce; Fgn. Relations, Judiciary
Preston	Lewis Thompson	C	President	Int. Bank of Reconstruction & Devel.; Treas. (fmr.), CFR
Prestowitz	Clyde V.	B	President	Economic Strategy Institute
Prewitt	Kenneth	C	Sr. Vice President	Rockefeller Foundation
Price	Daniel M.	C	Deputy Gen. Counsel	US Trade Representative
Price	Donald K.	B	Professor (fmr.)	Harvard Univ.
Price	Hugh B.	C	Vice President	Rockefeller Foundation; Member, N.Y. Times
Price	John Roy, Jr.	C	Managing Dir. (fmr.)	Chemical Bank Corp., NYC, Govt. & Community Afrs.
Prichard	J. Robert	BC	President	University of Toronto
Prideaux	John Francis, Sir	BGB	Chairman (fmr.)	National Westminster Bank, London
Prieto	Daniel B., III	C		
Profumo	Alessandro	BI	CEO	Credito Italiano
Pruitt	Lisa R.	C		
Pryce	Jeffrey F.	C		
Pryce	William T.	C		
Puchala	Donald J.	C	V.P. of Programs	Univ. of Southern Cal.
Puckett	Allen E.	C		Hughs Aircraft Corp.
Pugh	Richard Crawford	C	Counsel	Cleary, Gottlieb, Steen & Hamilton
Puhringer	Othmar	BA	Chairman	VA-Technologie AG
Pujol	Jordi	BE	President	Generalitat de Catalunya, Spain

Last Name	First & Mid. Name	Org.	Job Title	Affiliation - Company, Organization
Pulling	Thomas L.	C		
Purcell	Susan Kaufman	C	Managing Dir.	Council of the Americas
Pursley	Robert E.	C	Chairman	Logistics Management Inst.
Purves	William	BGB	Gp. Chairman	HSBC Holdings plc
Pury	David, de	BCH	Chairman	de Pury Pictet Turrettini & Co.
Pusey	Nathan Marsh	C		Harvard Univ.
Pustay	John S.	C	Major General	Defense Dept.
Putnam	Robert D.	C,T	Director	Harvard U.; Chairman & CEO (fmr.), Levi Strauss & Co.
Pye	August Kenneth	C	President	Southern Methodist Univ., Dallas
Pye	Lucian Wilmot	C	Professor	MIT, Political Science; Director (fmr.), CFR
Pyle	Cassandra A.	C	Chairwoman	United Nations, Academy for Educ. Devel.
Pyle	Kenneth Birger	C	Professor	Univ. of Washington, Seattle
Quandt	William Bauer	B,C	Sr. Fellow	Brookings Institute; Univ. of Virginia
Quester	George Herman	C	Professor	Univ. of Maryland, Political Science
Quigley	Kevin F. F.	C	Guest Scholar	Georgetown Univ.
Quigley	Leonard Vincent	C	Partner	Paul, Weiss, Rifkind, Wharton & Garrett
Quilter	Peter A.	C		
Quinn	Lochlann	BIRL	Chairman	Allied Irish Bank Gp.
Rabb	Maxwell M.	C	US Ambassador (fmr.)	State Dept., Italy; Chairman, Ecomarine
Rabinowitch	Alexander	C		
Rabinowitch	Victor	C	Sr. Vice President	John D. & Catherine T. MacArthur Foundation
Rademaker	Stephen Geoffrey	C	Repres. Chief Counsel	House of Representatives, Commission of Fgn Afrs.
Radice	Giles H.	BGB	Member	Parliament; Chair., European Movement
Radtke	Robert W.	C		
Radway	Laurence I.	C	Advisory Bd. Member	Center for International Policy, Center for Nat. Policy
Ragone	David Vincent	C	President (fmr.)	Case Western Research Univ., Cleveland
Raimond	Jean-Bernard	BF	Member	French National Assembly; Minister (fmr.), Fgn. Affairs
Raines	Franklin Delano	C,T	Chairman & CEO	Fed. Nat. Mortgage Assoc. (FNMA)
Raisian	John	C	Sr. Fellow	Stanford Univ., Hoover Institute, California
Ralph	Regan Elizabeth	C		
Ralston	Joseph W.	C	Dep. Chief-of-Staff	Defense Dept., Air Force
Ramfors	Bo C.E.	BS	Mng. Dir. & CEO	Skandinaviska Enskilda Banken, Stockholm
Ramirez	Lilia L.	C		
Ramo	Joshua Cooper	C		
Ramo	Simon	C	Consultant	Engineering
Randa	Gerhard	B	Chairman/Mng. Bd.	Bank of Austria
Rangel	Charles B.	C,T	Congressman	New York, Ways & Means/Ranking; Joint Taxation
Ranis	Gustav	C	Professor	Yale Univ., International Economics
Rankin	Clyde E., III	C		
Raphel	Robin L.	C	Asst. Secretary	State Dept., South Asian Affairs
Rappaport	Alan H.	C		
Rashish	Myer	C		
Rasmussen	Nicholas J.	C		
Ratchford	J. Thomas	C	Director	George Mason Univ., Science, Trade & Technology
Rather	Dan	C	Anchor, Mng. Editor	CBS, Evening News
Rathjens	George William	C	Professor	MIT, Dept. of Political Science
Rato Figaredo	Rodrigo de	BE	Parliamentary Leader	Spanish Parliament, Minority Group
Ratti	Giuseppe	TE	Board Member	CoeClerici, Genoa
Rattner	Steve Lawrence	B,C	Head Committee Gp.	Lazard Freres & Co., LLC
Rattray	Gregory J.	C		MIT, PHd. Candidate, Law School
Rauch	Rudolph Stewart, III	C	Managing Editor	Constitution
Raul	Alan Charles	C	Principal	Beverage & Diamond P. C., Washington
Ravenal	Earl Cederic	C	President	Ames Associates, Wash.
Ravenholt	Albert	C	Member	World Affairs Council
Ravitch	Richard	C	Chairman	Aquarius Management Corp.
Ravitch	Samantha F.	C		
Rawl	Lawrence G.	C	Chair. & CEO (fmr.)	EXXON Corp., NYC
Raymond	David Alan	C	President	Ebasco Services Int., NYC
Raymond	Jack	C	President	JR Consulting Servives, Inc.
Raymond	Lee R.	C,T	Chairman & CEO	EXXON Corp.
Reback	Sanford C.	C		
Redman	Charles E.	B	US Ambassador	State Dept., Bonn, Germany, Chief of Mission
Reed	Charles Bass	C	Chancellor	State Univ. System of Florida
Reed	John Shed	B	Chairman & CEO	Santa Fe Southern Pacific Corp.
Reed	Joseph Verner, Jr.	C	Chief of Protocol	State Dept.; Director, Foreign Policy Association
Reese	William S.	C		
Reeves	Jay B. L.	C		
Regan	Edward V.	C	Professor	Bard College, Economic Inst.
Reichart	William M.	C		
Reichert	Douglas D.	C		
Reid	Ogden R.	C	Congressman (fmr.)	(Council of American Ambassadors)
Reid	Whitelaw	C		
Reimer	Dennis J.	C	Chief-of-Staff	Defense Dept., Army
Reinhardt	John Edward	C	Professor (fmr.)	Univ. of Vermont
Reinhart	Carmen M.	C		
Reinharz	Jehuda	C		
Reinke	Fred W.	C		

Last Name	First & Mid. Name	Org.	Job Title	Affiliation - Company, Organization
Reisman	W. Michael	C	Professor	Hebrew Univ., Jurisprudence
Reiss	Mitchell B.	C	Adjunct Professor	Univ. of Washington, Seattle
Reitzle	Wolfgang	BD		BMW AG, Munich
Rell	Eric	BGB	Sr. Advisor	SBC Warburg
Renfrew	Charles B.	C	Director	Chevron; Adv. Bd. Mbr., Ctr./Int. Pol.; Ctr./Nat. Pol.
Renger	Adalbert von	BD	Director	Fed. Industrial Board, Policy Planning
Reppy	Judith V.	C	Professor	Cornell Univ. Peace Studies
Resor	Stanley Rogers	C	Of Counsel (fmr.)	Debevoise & Plimpton, NYC
Reston	James Barrett	B	Co-Chairman	Vineyard Gazette
Revay	Paul	T	Director	Trilateral Commission
Revesz	Richard L.	C	Professor	NYU Law School
Rey	Nicholas A.	C	US Ambassador	State Dept., Poland
Reynolds	A. William	C	Chairman	Fed, Cleveland; Pres. & CEO, GenCorp, Akron
Reynolds	Carolyn A.	C		
Rhinelander	John Bassett	C	Partner	Shaw, Pittman, Potts & Trowbridge
Rhinesmith	Stephen Headley	C	Principal	Rhinesmith & Associates, Inc., NYC
Rhodes	Edward	C	Professor	Univ. of Southern Cal.
Rhodes	Frank Harold Trevor	C	President	Cornell Univ.; Director, General Electric Co.
Rhodes	John Bower, Sr.	C	Of Counsel	Booz, Allen & Hamilton Inc., NYC
Rhodes	Thomas L.	C	Trustee	Heritage Foundation
Rhodes	William Reginald	C	Vice Chairman	Citibank, N.A., NYC
Ribicoff	Abraham A.	C	Senator (fmr.)	Connecticut
Rice	Condoleezza	C	Director	Chevron; Prov.,Stanford U.;Bd. Mbr.,Carnegie Corp.
Rice	Donald Blessing	C,T	President & COO	Teledyne, Inc.; Sec. (fmr.), Defense Dept., Air Force
Rice	Joseph Albert	C	Chair. & CEO (fmr.)	Irving Bank Corp.
Rice	Susan E.	C		
Rice	Susan Elizabeth	C	Director	Nat.Security Council,Global Issues & Multinational Afrs.
Rich	Bryan A.	C		
Rich	John H., Jr.	C		
Rich	Michael David	C	Sr. Vice President	RAND Corp.
Richard	Alain	TE	Minister	Defense, France
Richard	Anne C.	C		State Dept., Research, Plans & Policy
Richards	Paul Granston	C	Professor	Columbia Univ.
Richards	Stephen H.	C		
Richardson	David B.	C		
Richardson	Elliot Lee	C,T	Partner	Milbank, Tweed, Hadley, & McCloy; Dir. (fmr.), CFR
Richardson	Frank H.	C	President & CEO	Shell Oil Co.
Richardson	Gordon	BGB	Governor (fmr.)	Bank of England
Richardson	Henry J., III	C	Member	Overseas Development Council
Richardson	John	C	Chairman (fmr.)	National Endowment for Democracy
Richardson	Richard W.	C		
Richardson	William (Bill) Blaine	B,C	Secretary	Energy Dept.; US Ambassador (fmr.) to the UN
Richardson	William R.	C	Lt. General	Defense Dept., US Army
Richardson	Yolanda C.	C		
Richardson	Yolonda	C	Program Officer	Carnegie Corp. of New York
Richman	Joan F.	C	V. President (fmr.)	CBS News
Richter	Anthony H.	C		
Richter	Anthony H.	C		
Richter	Klaus	TE	Director	Optische Werke G. Rodenstock
Rickard	Stephen A.	C	Dep. Assis. Sec.	State Dept., South Asian Affairs
Ridgway	Rozanne Lejeanne	B,C,T	Co-Chairman	AtlanticCoun.;Amb.(fmr.),Germ.;Dir.,RJR Nab.,Sara Lee
Rieff	David	C		World Policy Institute
Riegle	Donald W.	B	Senator (fmr.)	Michigan, Budget, Finance, Banking, Hsg. & Urban Afrs.
Rielly	John Edward	C,T	Executive Director	CFR, Chicago; Cargagie Endowment
Ries	Hans A.	C		
Riesel	Victor	C	Columnist (fmr.)	*Syndicated Labor*
Riesenhuber	Heinz	TE	Member	German Bundestag; (fmr.) Fed. Min. of Research & Tech., Bonn
Rifkind	Malcolm	BGB	Foreign Secretary	Great Britain
Rifkind	Robert S.	C		
Rindskopf	Elizabeth R.	C	General Counsel	Central Intelligence Agency
Ringel	Johannes	TE	Bd. Member	Westdeutsche Landesbank Girozentrale, Dusseldorf
Ringier	Michael	BCH	Publisher & Chairman	Ringier Inc., Switzerland
Rippon of Hexham	Lord	BGB,TE	Chairman	Unichem & Dun & Bradstreet, London
Ritch	John B., III	C	US Ambassador	Int. Atomic Energy Agency
Rivas-Vasquez	A. Victoria	C		
Rivers	Richard Robinson	C	Advisory Bd. Member	Center for International Policy, Center for Nat. Policy
Rivkin	Donald Herschel	C	Member	Schnader, Harrison, Segal & Lewis
Rivlin	Alice Mitchell	C,T	Vice Chairman	Federal Reserve Board, Federal Reserve System
Rizk	Nayla M.	C	Director	Harvard Business School Assoc. of North Carolina
Rizopoulos	Nicholas X.	C	Vice President	Council on Foreign Relations, Studies
Robb	Charles Spittal	C,T	Senator	Virginia; Armed Services, Foreign Relations, Intelligence
Robbins	Carla Anne	C	Staff Reporter	*Wall Street Journal*
Robert	Joseph E., Jr.	C		
Roberts	Brad	C		
Roberts	Chalmers McGeagh	C	Contrib. Columnist	Washington Post
Roberts	John Joseph	C	Chairman	American International Underwriters Corp.
Roberts	Richard T,	C		

Last Name	First & Mid. Name	Org.	Job Title	Affiliation - Company, Organization
Roberts	Walter Ronald	C	Dip.-in-Residence	George Washington Univ., Washington
Robertson	George	BGB	Secretary	of State for Defence
Robertson	Simon	BGB	Chairman	Kleinwort Benson Group plc
Robins	David	TE	CEO	ING Barings, London
Robinson	Barbara Paul	C		
Robinson	Charles W.	B,C,T	Member	Overseas Development Council, Brookings Institute
Robinson	David Z.	C	Sr. Counselor to Pres.	Carnegie Corp. of New York
Robinson	Davis Rowland	C	Partner	Le Boeuf, Lamb, Leiby & MacRae, Washington
Robinson	Elizabeth L.	C		
Robinson	Eugene Harold	C		
Robinson	James Dixon, III	C	Council Member	Brookings Inst.;Pr., Robinson,J.D.,Inc.; Dir.,Coca-Cola
Robinson	Leonard Harrison, Jr.	C	President	African Devel. Found.; COO, Wash. Strat. Consulting Gp.
Robinson	Marshall Alan	C	Vice President	Daniele Agostino Foundation
Robinson	Pearl T.	C	Member	Tufts Univ.
Robinson	Randall	C	Member	Trans-Africa
Robison	Olin C.	C	Advisory Bd. Member	Center for International Policy, Center for Nat. Policy
Roblin	Duff	TC	Member	Senate of Canada
Rocca	Gianfelice	TE	Chairman	Techint Europe, Milano
Roche	James G.	C	Director (fmr.)	Nat. Ctr. for Volunteer Action
Roche	John P.	C	Professor	Brandeis U, Fletcher Sch./Law & D., Civil & Fgn. Afrs.
Rocke	Mark D.	C		
Rockefeller	David	B,C,T	Ch., Int. Advis. Com.	Chase Manhattan Bank; Hon. Chair., CFR; Chair., TC
Rockefeller	David, Jr.	C	Chairman	Rockefeller Fin. Services, Inc.; Mbr., Brookings Inst.
Rockefeller	John D. (Jay), IV	C,T	Senator	West Virginia, Commerce, Fin., Veterans Affairs/Ranking
Rockefeller	Nicholas	C		Rockvest Int. Development Group
Rockefeller	Rodman C.	C	Board Member	Council on the Americas; Mbr., Pocantico Assoc.
Rockefeller	Sharon Percy	B	President & CEO	WETA-TV and FM radio
Rockwell	Hays H.	C	Bishop	Missouri
Rodgers	William	BGB	Minister (fmr.)	British State, for Defence
Rodman	Peter Warren	C	Sr. Editor	National Review
Rodriguez	Rita Maria	C	Director	Export-Import Bank of US, Wash.
Rodriguez	Vincent Angel	C	Partner	Sullivan & Cromwell, NYC
Rodriguez Inciarte	Matias	BE	Exec. Vice Chairman	BSCH, Spain
Roett	Riordan	C	Director (fmr.)	Chase National Bk., Nat. Rel. of Emerging Markets
Roff	John Hugh, Jr.	C	Chairman	PetroUnited Terminals, Inc., Houston
Rogers	Bernard William	C	Cmdr.-in-Chief (fmr.)	Defense Dept., European Command
Rogers	Edward S.	BC	President & CEO	Rogers Communications, Inc.
Rogers	William D.	C	Editorial Bd. Mbr.	Carnegie Endowment, Foreign Policy magazine
Rogers	William P.	C	Attorney Gen. (fmr.)	Justice Dept., '58-'61; Hon. Dir., Foreign Policy Assoc.
Rognoni	Virginia	BI	Minister	Defense, Italy
Rogovin	Mitchell	C	Partner	Rogovin, Huge & Schiller, Washington
Rohan	Karen	C		
Rohatyn	Felix George	C,T	Senior Partner	Lazard Freres & Co.
Rohlen	Thomas P.	C	Professor	Stanford Univ., School of Humanities
Rojas	Mauricio	B	Assoc. Professor	Lund Univ., Economic History
Rokke	Ervin Jerome	C	President	Defense Dept., National Defense University
Roll of Ipsden	Eric, Lord	BGB,TE	Sr. Advisor	SBC Warburg, London
Roman	Nancy E.	C		
Romano	Sergio	TE	Editorialist	*Corriere della Sera, Milan; Italian Amb. (fmr.), to USSR*
Romberg	Alan D.	C	Member (fmr.)	State Dept.
Romero	Anthony D.	C		
Romero-Barcelo	Carlos Antonio	C	Resident Commission	Puerto Rico; Education & Labor, Natural Resources
Ronchey	Alberto	BI	Dir. & Corresp. (fmr.)	La Stampa, Italy
Rondeau	Ann E.	C		
Roney	John Harvey	C	Partner	O'Melveny & Myers, L. A.
Roosa	Robert V.	B,C	Director	Council on Foreign Relations, '66-'81
Roosa	Ruth AmEnde	C	Author	"Entrepreneurship in Imperial Russia and the Soviet Union"
Roosevelt	Theodore, IV	C	Managing Director	Lehman Brothers, Inc., NYC
Roper	John	TE	Associate Fellow	Royal Institute of Internastional Affairs (RIIA), London
Rosberg	Carl Gustaf	C	Professor (fmr.)	Univ. of California, Berkeley
Rose	Charlie Peete, Jr.	C		
Rose	Daniel	C	Council Member	Brookings Inst.; Dir., Foreign Policy Association
Rose	Elihu	C	Partner	Rose Associates, NYC
Rose	Frederick Phineas	C	Chairman	Rose & Associates (Real Estate Development)
Rose, de	Francois	TE	Ambassador	France, de; Permanent Representative to NATO
Rosecrance	Richard N.	C	Professor	UCLA
Rosen	Arthur H.	C	Chairman	Stanford Univ., Sino-judaic Inst.
Rosen	Daniel H.	C		
Rosen	Jane K.	C		
Rosen	Robert L.	C		
Rosen	Stephen P.	C		
Rosenberg	Ludwig	BD	Trade Union Ldr. (fmr.)	Chairman (fmr.) Deutscher Gewerkschaftsbund (DGB)
Rosenberg	Tina	C		World Policy Institute
Rosenblatt	David S.	C		
Rosenblatt	Peter Ronald	C	Partner	Heller, Rosenblatt & Scheman, Washington
Rosenblum	Mort	C	Spec. Corresp.	*Associated Press*
Rosenfeld	Stephen Samuel	C	Deputy Editor	Washington Post, Editorial Page

Last Name	First & Mid. Name	Org.	Job Title	Affiliation - Company, Organization
Rosenfield	Patricia L.	C	Program Chairman	Carnegie Corp. of New York
Rosengren	Bjorn	B	Minister	Swedish Industry, Employment & Communication
Rosenstock	Robert	C	Chairman	U.N., Int. Law Commission
Rosenthal	A. M.	C	Columnist	New York Times
Rosenthal	Douglas Eurico	C	Partner	Coudert Brothers
Rosenthal	Jack	C	Asst. Managing Editor	New York Times
Rosenthal	Joel H.	C	Author	"Today's Offic Corps, A Repsit. of Vrtu in/Archiac Wld"
Rosenthal	Mitchell	C		
Rosenwald	E. John, Jr.	C		
Rosenzweig	Robert Myron	C	President	Association of American Universities, Washington
Rosin	Axel G.	C		
Roskens	Ronald William	C	President	Action International, Inc., Omaha
Rosovsky	Henry	C,T	Professor	Harvard Univ., Economics
Ross	Anne	C		
Ross	Arthur	C	Director	Foreign Policy Association
Ross	Christopher W.S.	C	US Ambassador	Syrian Arab Republic
Ross	Dennis B.	C	Peace Negotiator	Middle-East Peace Talks, Clinton Admin.
Ross	James D.	C	General	Derfense Dept., US Army
Ross	Robert S.	C		
Ross	Roger	C		
Ross	Thomas Bernard	C	Sr. Vice President	Hill & Knowlton, NYC (P. R. firm)
Rossella	Carlo	BI	Editor	Editrice La Stampa S.P.A.
Rossi	Reino	BFIN	Mng. Director (fmr.)	Finska Socker
Rosso	David J.	C	Attorney	Jones, Day, Reavis & Pogue
Rossotti	Charles Ossola	C	President	American Management Systems, Inc., Arlington
Rostow	Elspeth Davies	C	Vice Chairman	US Inst. for Peace; Prof. (fmr.), Univ. of Texas, Austin
Rostow	Eugene Victor	B,C	Dist. Vis. Resch. Prof.	National Defense Univ.
Rostow	Nicholas	C	Exec. Dir.	Office of Int. Trade and Investment
Rostow	Walt Whitman	C	Professor	Univ. of Texas, Austin, Political Economics
Rotberg	Robert Irvin	C	President	Lafayette College, Pennsylvania
Roth	Katheryn G.	C		
Roth	Stanley Owen	C	Spec. Asst.	Executive Office / Pres., Asian Affairs
Roth	William Matson	C,T	Trustee	Center for Int. Policy; Center for Nat. Policy
Roth	William V., Jr.	C,T	Senator	Delaware, Finance/Chair., Joint Taxation/V. Chair.
Rothkopf	David J.	C	Deputy Under Sec.	Commerce Dept., Int. Trade Policy Development
Rothschild, de	Baron Edmond	BF	Chairman	Banque Rothschild of Paris
Rothschild, de	Baron Guy Edmound	BF	President & Exec. Dir.	Compagnie du Nord, Paris
Rothschild, de	Emma	BGB	Director	Centre, Hist. & Econ.; Fellow, Cambridge U.
Rothschild, de	Evelyn	BGB	Chairman	N.M. Rothschild & Sons
Rottenberg	Linda D.	C		
Route	Ronald A.	C		
Rovine	Arthur William	C	Partner	Baker & McKenzie, NYC
Rowan	Carl. T.	T	President	CTR Productions Inc.
Rowen	Henry Stanislaus	C	President	RAND Corp.; Prof., Stanford Univ., Public Policy
Rowen	Hobart	C	Columnist	Washington Post
Rowny	Edward L.	C	Lt. General	Defense Dept.
Roy	Olivier	BF	Professor	Laboratoire Monde Iranien, CNRS
Rubin	Barnett R.	C	Director	CFR, Ctr. for Preventive Action
Rubin	James P.	C	Communications Dir.	State Dept., Office of the UN Ambassador
Rubin	Nancy H.	C	Hd. Of Deligation	State Dept., U.N. Human Rights Commission
Rubin	Robert E.	B	Secretary (fmr.)	Treasury Dept.; Ch., Thrift Deposit Prot. & Oversight Bd.
Rubin	Seymour Jeffrey	C	Professor (fmr.)	American Univ.
Rubin	Trudy	C	Columnist	Philidelphia Inquirer
Ruckelshaus	Hans	TE	Chairman of Exec. Bd.	Fortis;Ch./Mng. Dir., Amev, Utrecht; Dir. (fmr.), CFR
Ruckelshaus	William D.	C,T	Chairman & CEO	Brwng. Ferris;Adm.(fmr.)EPA;Dep.Gen.(fmr.),Jus. Dpt.
Rudenstine	Neil Leon	C	President	Harvard Univ.
Ruding	H. Onno	TE	Vice Chairman	Citicorp/Citibank, New York; Dutch Minister (fmr.) of Finance
Rudman	Warren Bruce	C	Deputy Chairman	Fed., Boston; Sen. (fmr.), N. H.; Co-Fnd.r, Concord Coal.
Rudolph	Barbara	C	Writer	Time Magazine
Rudolph	Lloyd Irving	C	Professor	Univ. of Chicago, Political Science
Rudolph	Susanne Hoeber	C	Professor	Univ. of Chicago, Political & Social Science
Ruebhausen	Oscar Melick	C	Board Member	Greenwall Foundation
Ruenitz	Robert M.	C		
Ruga	Raimundo L.	C		
Ruge	Friedrich	BD	Vice-Admiral (fmr.)	(fmr.) Heeresgruppe B; (fmr.) Uni-Prof. Tuebingen
Ruggie	John G.	C	Director	Foreign Policy Association
Ruggiero	Pierre	TE	Executive V. Chairman	Fiat, Turin
Ruggiero	Renato	BINT,TE	Dir. General	WTO/OMC,Geneva; Ex.V.P.(fmr.),FIAT S.p.A.,Int.Adv.Bd.
Rugh	William A.	C		
Ruhe	Volker	BD,TE	Minister of Defense	Gernamy; General Sec. (fmr.), Bundestag, CDU
Ruhnau	Heinz	BD	Chairman	Deutsche Lufthansa AG, Koeln
Runge	Carlisle Ford	C	Professor	Stanford Univ., Economics
Rupp	George	C		
Rush	Kenneth	C	US Ambassador (fmr.)	State Dept., France
Rusk	Dean	B,C	Secretary (fmr.)	St. Dept.; Adv. Bd. mbr., Ctr. for Int. Pol. & Nat. Policy
Russell	George F.	T	Chairman & CEO	Frank Russell Company
Russell	Thomas W., Jr.	C	Chair. & CEO (fmr.)	American Brake Shoe Co. (ABEX)

Last Name	First & Mid. Name	Org.	Job Title	Affiliation - Company, Organization
Russin	Elizabeth	C		
Rustow	Dankwart A.	C	Professor	CUNY, Political Science and Sociology
Ruttan	Vernon Wesley	C	Professor	Univ. of Minnesota
Rutzen	Douglas	C	Attorney	Int. Ctr,. For Not-for-Profit Law
Ryan	John Thomas, III	C	Pres., Chair. & CEO	Mine Safety Appliances Co., Pitt.
Ryan	John Thomas, Jr.	C		
Rykens	Paul	BNL	Hon. Treasurer (fmr.)	Bilderberg Group
Saba	Shoichi	TJ	Advisor to the Board	Toshiba Corp. Ltd.
Sabia	Maureen	BC	President & Dir.	Maureen Sabia Int.
Sacks	Paul M.	C	Member	Overseas Devel. Council; Muntinational Strategies, Inc.
Saeki	Kiichi	TJ	Sr. Advisor	Institute for International Policy Studies
Saenz	Thomas A.	C		
Safran	Nadav	C	Professor (fmr.)	Harvard Univ.; author of "The Embattled Ally"
Sagan	Carl Edward	C	Prof., Astronimer	Cornell Univ.
Sagan	Scott D.	C	Assoc. Professor	Stanford Univ., Political Science
Sahlin	Mona	BS	Member	Swedish Parliament
Said	Edward W.	C	Professor	Harvard Univ.
Saito	Yutaka	TJ	Chairman & CEO	Nippon Steel Corp.
Sakoian	Carl	C		
Salacuse	Jeswald William	C	Dean	Tufts Univ.
Salazar	Ana Maria	C		
Salem	George R.	C		
Salgado	Ricardo E. S.	BP	President & CEO	Grupo Espirito Santo
Salk	Jonus Edward	C	Founding Director	Salk Institute of Biological Studies
Salomon	Richard Adley	C	Partner	Mayer, Brown & Platt, Chicago
Salomon	William R.	C	Hon. Chairman	Salomon Brothers Inc.
Samore	Gary	C		
Sampaio	Jorge	BP	President	of Portugal
Sampermans	Francoise	BF	Chairman	Groupe Express
Sample	Steven Browning	C	President	Univ. of Southern California, Los Angeles
Samuels	Barbara C., II	C	Member	Moody's Investors Service, Inc.
Samuels	Michael A.	C	US Amb. (fmr.)	State Dept. to GATT
Samuels	Nathaniel	C	Dep. Under Sec. (fmr.)	State Dept.
Samuels	Richard J.	C	Professor	MIT, Political Science
Samuelson	Paul Anthony	B	Professor	New York Univ., NYC
Sanchez	Miguel A.	C		
Sanchez	Nestor D.	C	Exec. V.P.	George C. Marshall Int. Ctr.
Sanchez	Orlando	C		
Sandberg	Sheryl K.	C		
Sandel	Michael J.	C		
Sander	Alison B.	C		
Sanders	Edward G.	C	Attorney	Sanders, Barnet, Goldman, Simons & Mosk
Sanders	Robin Renee	C		
Sanford	Charles Stedman, Jr.	C	Chairman & CEO	Bankers Trust Co., NYC
Sanford	Terry	C	Senator (fmr.)	North Carolina; Bd. Mbr., World Fed of NC
Santer	Jacques	BL	Prime Minister	Luxemburg
Santo	Espirito	BI	President & CEO	Banco Espirito
Santos	Nicolau	BP	Editor-in-Chief	*Expresso*
Sapiro	Miriam	C	Member	State Dept., Legal Affairs
Saracoglu	Rusdu	BINT	"Mediator"	EU Community
Sarasqueta	Antxon	TE	Exec. President	Muntimedia Capital; Editor, "Echos", Madrid
Sarbanes	Paul S.	C	Senator	Maryland, Banking, Housing/Ranking, Budget, Fgn. Rel.
Sargeant	Stephen T.	C		
Sassen	Saskia	C		Columbia Univ.
Satloff	Robert Barry	C	Member	Wash. Inst. for Near East Affairs
Sato	Kumi	C	President	Cosmo Relations Corp.
Sato	Seizaburo	TJ	Director	Inst. for Int. Policy Studies
Saul	Ralph Southey	C	Chair., Exec. Comm.	Brookings Institute; CIGNA Corp.
Saunders	Harold H.	C	Member	Charles F. Kettering Foundation
Saunders	Paul J.	C		
Saunders	Phillip C.	C		
Sauve	Jeanne (Mrs.)	BC	Minister (fmr.)	Canada, State of Science & Technology
Savage	Frank	C	Chairman	Alliance Capital Management Int.
Savona	Paolo	TE	Minister	Industry ,Italy, of
Sawhill	John Crittenden	C,T	President & CEO	Nature Conservancy; Pres. (fmr.), New York Univ., NYC
Sawoski	Mark	C	Professor	Roger Williams Univ.
Sawyer	John Edward	C	President (fmr.)	Andrew W. Mellon Foundation
Sawyer	L. Diane	C	Co-Anchor	ABC, Prime Time Live
Saylor	Lynne S.	C		
Scalapino	Robert A.	B,C	Director, '82-89	CFR; Adv. Bd. Mbr., Ctr. for Nat. Pol.
Scali	John Alfred	C	Sr. Correspondent	ABC News, Washington
Schacht	Henry Brewer	C,T	Chair. & CEO (fmr.)	Lucent Technologies Inc.; Chair., Carnegie Corp. of NY
Schacht	Serge	TE	Chairman	Compagnie de Distrib. de Mat. Elect.
Schachter	Oscar	C	Professor	Columbia Univ., Law School
Schadlow	Nadia C.	C		
Schaetzel	J. Robert	C,T	Member	Overseas Development Council
Schaffer	Howard B.	C		

Last Name	First & Mid. Name	Org.	Job Title	Affiliation - Company, Organization
Schaffer	Teresita C.	C		
Schaik	Gerard, van	TE	Chairman	Heineken Breweries, Amsterdam
Schake	Kori Naomi	C	Professor	Univ. of Cal. San Diego
Scharping	Rudolf	BD	Minister	Defense, Germany
Schaufele	William E., Jr.	C	US Ambassador	
Schecter	Jerrold	C		
Scheel	Walter	BD	Fed. President (fmr.)	Germany; Chairman (fmr.) Bilderberg Mtg.; FDP
Scheepbouwer	Ad J.	BNL	Chairman & CEO	TNT Post Group
Scheffer	David J.	C	Sr. Advisor & Counsel	State Dept., Office of the Secretary
Scheinman	Lawrence	C	Asst. Director	Arms Cont. & Disarm. Agency
Schell	Orville H., Jr.	C		Author
Schenk	James R.	C		
Schenz	Richard	B	Chairman & CEO	OMV AG. Austria
Scher	Robert M.	C		
Scherpenhuijsen Rom	Willem	TE	Chairman (fmr.)	Internationale Nederlanden Group (insurance), Amsterdam
Schiff	Frank W.	C		
Schifter	Richard	C	Special Asst. to Pres.	National Security Council, Washington
Schiller	Karl	BD	Member (fmr.)	German Bundestag; Prof., Economics; SPD
Schilling	Warner R.	C	Professor	Columbia Univ., Int. Relations
Schlefer	Mark P.	C		
Schlefer	Mark P.	C		
Schleimann	Jorgen	BDK,TE	Sr. Columnist	"Berlingske " Gp./Newspapers, Ch., Euro. Movement, Denmark
Schlesinger	Arthur Meier, Jr.	C	Special Asst. (fmr.)	to US Pres., '61-64; Adv. Bd. Mbr., Ctr. for Nat. Policy
Schlesinger	Jacob M.	C		
Schlesinger	James Rodney	C	Sr. Advisor	Lehman Bros.; Sec. (fmr.), Engy. Dept.;Dir. (fmr.), CIA
Schlosser	Herbert S.	C	President (fmr.)	NBC, Inc.
Schmenann	Anya	C		
Schmertz	Herbert	C	President	Schmertz Co., Inc. (P. R. firm)
Schmertz	Richard	TE	Chairman	Conroy Petroleum; Member/Senate, Irish Republic
Schmidheiny	Stephan E.	BCH	Chairman	ANOVA Holdings Ltd.
Schmidt	Adolph William	B	US Ambassador (fmr.)	State Dept., Canada
Schmidt	Benno Charles, Jr.	C	President & CEO	Edison Project, Knoxville
Schmidt	Helmut	BD,TE	Chancellor (fmr.)	Germany; Co-Editor, "Die Zeit", Hamburg
Schmidt-Chiari	Guido	BI,TE	Chairman	Constantia Gp.; (fmr.) Chair., Creditanstalt Bankverein, Vienna
Schmitz	Ronald	TE	Board Member	Deutsche Bank, Germany
Schmoke	Kurt L.	C,T	Mayor	Baltimore
Schmults	Edward Charles	C	Sr. Vice President	GTE Corp., external relations
Schmults	Otto	TE	Chairman	East-West Trade Commission; Chair. & CEO O. Wolff I.
Schneider	Ernst-Georg	BD	President	Industrie- u. Handelskammer (IHK), Duesseldorf
Schneider	Jan	C	Professor	Medical College of Pennsylvania
Schneider	William	C	Correspondent	CNN; Member, American Enterprise Institute
Schneider-Lenne	Ellen	TE	Board Member	Deutsche Bank, Frankfurt
Schneier	Arthur	C	Rabbi & Hon. Chair.	World Jewish Congress, American Sect.
Schoen	Douglas E.	C		
Schoettle	Enid C. B.	C		National Intelligence Council
Scholten	Rudolf	B	Exec. Bd. Member	Oesterreichische Kontrollbank AG, Austria
Schorr	Daniel Louis	C	Sr. Analyst	National Public Radio, CNN
Schrage	Elliot J.	C		
Schrempp	Jurgen F.	BD	Chair./Bd. of Mgt.	Daimler Chrysler AG
Schreyer	William Allen	C	Chairman	Merrill Lynch & Co.
Schroeder	Christopher M.	C		
Schroeder	Gerhard	BD,TE	Member (fmr.)	German Bundestag; Minister (fmr.) of Defence; CDU
Schroeder	Patricia Scott	C	Congresswoman (fmr.)	Colorado, Armed Svcs., Judic., Post Office & Civ. Svcs.
Schubert	Richard Francis	C	President & CEO	Points of Light Foundation
Schuh	George Edward	C	Dean	Univ. of Minnesota, Humphrey Institute
Schuker	Jill	C	Director	Commerce Dept., Office of Public Affairs
Schulhof	Michael Peter	C	Vice Ch., Pres. & CEO	Sony USA, Inc.
Schultz	William F.	C		
Schumacher	Edward	C		
Schumer	Charles E.	C	Congressman	New York, Banking & Finance, Judiciary
Schurer	Wolfgang	BCH	Chairman	MS Management Service AG
Schuyler	C. V. R.	C		
Schwab	Klaus	BINT	President	World Economic Forum
Schwab	Susan Carol	C	Asst. Secretary (fmr.)	Commerce Dept.
Schwab	William B.	C		
Schwartz	Adam	C		
Schwartz	Eric Paul	C	Director	National Security Council, Global Issues
Schwartz	Ethan	C		
Schwartz	Pedro	TE	Exec. President	Fundesco, Madrid; Prof., Econ., Autonomous Univ. of Madrid
Schwartz	Thomas Alan	C	Assoc. Professor	Vermont Univ.
Schwarz	Benjamin C.	C		
Schwarz	Frederick A. O., Jr.	C	Partner	Cravath, Swaine & Moore, N.Y.C.
Schwarzenberg, of	Prince Karel	TE	Foun. & Dir.	Nadace Bohemiae, Prague; Chancellor (fmr.) to Pres Havel
Schwarzer	William W.	C	US District Judge	California, San Francisco
Schwarzman	Stephen Allen	C	Observer	New York State Finance Control Board
Schwebel	Stephen Myron	C	Judge	International Court of Justice, The Hague
Schweitzer	Louis	TE	Chair. & Mng. Dir.	Regie Renault, Paris

Last Name	First & Mid. Name	Org.	Job Title	Affiliation - Company, Organization
Scidenfaden	Toger	BDK	Editor-in-Chief	"Politiken"
Sciolino	Elaine F.	C	Writer	*New York Times*
Scott	David Wilson	C		
Scott	Hugh	B	Senator (fmr.)	Pennsylvania
Scowcroft	Brent	B,C,T	Asst. to Pres. (fmr.)	National Security Council; Director (fmr.), CFR
Scranton	William W.	C,T	US Ambassador (fmr.)	United Nations, Geneva
Seaborg	Glenn Theadore	C	Department Chairman	Univ. of California, Berkley, Science
Seagrave	Norman P.	C		
Seamans	Robert Channing, Jr.	C	Sr. Lecturer	MIT, Aeronautics & Astronomics
Seaton	James B., III	C		
Segal	Sheldon Jerome	C	Director	Rockefeller Brothers Found., Population Science
Segal	Susan L.	C	Mbr. Advisory Bd.	Council of the Americas; Sr. Mng. Dir., Chemical Bank
Segurado	Jose'	TE	Chairman	Jasinas,Madrid;Hon.Chair.,CEIM;Mbr.(fmr.)Span.Parl.
Seib	Gerald	C	Nat. Policy Corespond.	Wall Street Journal; Accociate, Foreign Policy Assoc.
Seibold	Frederick C., Jr.	C	V.P. & Treas. (fmr.)	Sears World Trade, Wash.
Seidenberg	Ivan	C		
Seidenfaden	Toger	BDK	Editor-in-Chief	Politiken A/S
Seidman	Herta Lande	C	Co-Founder	Tradenet Corp., NYC
Seigenthaler	John L.	C	Admin. Asst. (fmr.)	Justice Dept., to Robert F. Kennedy
Seigle	John William	C	Vice President	Sikorsky Aircraft Div., United Technologies Corp.
Seitz	Frederick	C	President (fmr.)	Rockefeller Univ.
Seitz	Raymond G. H.	T	Vice-Chair.	Lehman Brothers, Europe; Amb. (fmr.) to UK
Sekulow	Eugene A.	C		NYNEX Corp.
Selin	Douglas	C		
Selin	Ivan	C	Chairman	Nuclear Regulatory Commission (NRC)
Semple	Robert B., Jr.	C	Columnist	New York Times
Serfaty	Simon	C	Director	European Studies
Serra	Narcis	BE	Dep. Prime Minister	Spain
Sesno	Frank	C	Anchor	CNN
Sestanovich	Stephen R.	C	US Ambassador	State Dept., at Large
Sewall	John O. B.	C	Maj. General (fmr.)	Defense Dept. Army
Sewall	Sarah	C	Deputy Asst. Sec.	Def. Dept., Peacekeeping & Peace Enforcement Policy
Sewell	John Williamson	C	President	Overseas Development Council
Sexton	William Cottrell	C	Columnist, Edt. (fmr.)	Newsday, Inc.
Shad	John S. R.	B	US Ambassador (fmr.)	State Dept., Netherlands; Director, various companies
Shafer	D. Michael	C	Director	Rutgers Univ., CASE
Shaffer	Gail S.	C	Secretary of State	State of New York
Shailor	Barbara	C		
Shair	Beth L.	C		
Shalala	Donna E.	C,T	Secretary	H. H. S. Dept.; Member (fmr.), TC ; Director, CFR
Shalicashvilli	John M.	C	Chairman	Defense Dept., Joint Chiefs of Staff
Shambaugh	David	C		
Shanker	Albert	T	President	American Federation of Teachers Union
Shapiro	Andrew J.	C		
Shapiro	Eli	C	Chairman (fmr.)	Federal Home Loan Bank, Boston
Shapiro	Harold Tafler	C	President	Princeton Univ.; Director, Dow Chemical Co.
Shapiro	Isaac	C	Partner	Skadden, Arps, Slate Meagher & Flom
Shapiro	Robert B.	B	Chairman & CEO	Monsanto Company
Shaplen	Jason T.	C		
Sharp	Daniel Asher	C	Sr. Int. Advisor	InterMatrix Group
Sharp	Mitchell	TC		Ontario
Shattuck	John	C	Asst. Secretary	State Dept., Democracy, Human Rights & Labor
Shayne	Herbert M.	C		
Sheehan	Kevin P.	C		
Sheeline	Paul Cushing	C	CFO (fmr.)	Intercontinental Hotels Corp.
Sheeline	Umberto	TE	Vice Chairman	Fiat, Turin
Sheffield	James R.	C		
Sheffield	Jill W.	C	Member	Overseas Development Council
Sheinbaum	Stanley K.	C		*New Perspectives Quarterly*
Sheinkman	Jack	B,C	Chairman	Amalgamated Clothing & Textile Workers Union
Sheldon	Eleanor Harriet B.	C	Visiting Professor	Univ. of California, Santa Barbara
Shelley	Sally Swing	C		
Shelp	Ronald Kent	C	President & CEO	NYC Partnership
Shelton	Joanna Reed	C	Prof. Staff Member	US House of Representatives, Ways & Means
Shelton-Colby	Sally A.	C	Member	Georgetown Univ.
Shenk	George H.	C	Partner	Coudert Brothers, San Francisco
Shenk	Maury David	C		
Shepard	Stephen B.	C	Editor-in-Chief	*Business Week*
Shepherd	Mark	T	General Director	Texas Instruments, Inc.
Sherman	Michael	C		
Sherman	Wendy R.	C		
Sherry	George Leon	C	Professor	Occidental College, Diplomacy & World Affairs
Sherwood	Ben	C	News Producer	ABC-TV
Sherwood	Elizabeth D.	C	Deputy Asst. Sec.	Defense Dept., Nuclear Security
Shestack	Jerome Joseph	C	Partner	Wolf, Block, Schorr & Solis-Cohen, Philadelphia
Shevtsova	Lilia	BRUS	Member	Carnegie Moscow Center
Shibusawa	Masahide	TJ	Director	East-West Seminars

Last Name	First & Mid. Name	Org.	Job Title	Affiliation - Company, Organization
Shields	Lisa Katherine	C		
Shiffman	Gary M.	C.		
Shiina	Motoo	TJ	Member	House/Councillors; Japanese Chair., UK-Japan 2000 Gp.
Shiina	Takeo	TJ	Chairman & CEO	IBM Japan, Ltd.
Shimokobe	Atsushi	TJ	Chairman	The Tokio Marine Research Institute
Shiner	Josette	C	Managing Editor	Washington Times
Shinn	James J.	C	Sr. Fellow	CFR
Shiozaki	Yasuhisa	TJ	Member	Japanese House of Councellors
Shipley	Walter Vincent	C,T	Chairman & CEO	Chase; Chr. & CEO (fmr.), Chemical Banking Corp.
Shire	Jacqueline	C		
Shirk	Susan L.	C	Professor	UCLA, San Diego
Shlaes	Amity	C	Editorial Board Mbr.	Wall Street Journal
Shoemaker	Alvin V.	C	Chairman (fmr.)	First Boston Corp.
Shoemaker	Christopher Cole	C		
Shoemaker	Don Cleavenger	C	Columnist	Knight-Ridder Newspapers
Shore	Jennifer	C		
Shore	Peter, Lord	TE	Member	British House of Lords, London
Shorr	David	C		
Showalter	Vinca	C		
Shriver	Donald Woods, Jr.	C	Professor	Christianity Union Theology Seminary, NYC
Shriver	Robert Sargent, Jr.	C	US Ambassador	St. Dept., S.A.L.T.; Adv. Bd., Ctr. for Int. Pol., Nat. Pol.
Shubert	Gustave Harry	C	Sr. Fellow	RAND Corp., Santa Monica
Shulman	Colette	C	Advisor	Ploughshares Fund
Shulman	Marshall D.	B,C	Director	Council on Foreign Relations, '72-'77
Shulman	Stanley S.	C		Stanton Reality Trust
Shultz	George Pratt	C,T	Honorary Fellow	Stanford U., Hoover Inst., Calif.; Sec. (fmr.), State Dept.
Sick	Gary G.	C	Executive Director	Columbia Univ., Gulf/2000 Project; Author
Siegman	Henry	C	Exec. Committee Mbr.	Interreligious Commission on Peace
Sifton	Elizabeth	C	Publisher	Hill & Wang
Sigal	Leon V.	C		
Siglienti	Sergio	TE	Chairman	Banco Commerciale Italiana, Milan
Sigmund	Paul Eugene	C	Professor	Princeton Univ., Politics
Silas	Cecil Jesse	C,T	Chairman & CEO)Fmr.)	Phillips Petroleum Company
Silberman	Laurence Hirsch	C	Judge	Circuit Court of Appeals, Washington
Silk	Leonard Solomon	C	Sr. Fellow	Brookings Institute
Silkenat	James Robert	C	Partner	Winthrop, Stimson, Putnam & Roberts
Silva	Artur Santos	B	President & CEO	BPI Group
Silver	Allison	C		
Silvers	Robert Benjamin	C	Co-Editor	New York Rev. Books
Silvestri	Renato	TE	CEO	Tecnitel, Rome
Silvestri	Stefano	BI	Vice President	Istituto Affari Int.
Silvestri	Umberto	TE	Chairman	STET Int., Netherlands; Chairman (fmr.) Telecom Italia
Simes	Dimitri Konstantin	C	Sr. Assoc. & Director	Carnegie Endow., Study Gp./Russian/Commonw'lth Afrs.
Simmons	Adele Smith	C	President	John D. & Catherine T. MacArthur Foundation
Simmons	P. J.	C		
Simmons	Ruth J.	C		
Simmons	Thomas W.	B	US Ambassador (fmr.)	State Dept., Poland
Simon	David	TE	Chairman	British Petroleum, (BP), London
Simon	Francoise L.	B	Professor	Columbia Univ., Graduate School of Business
Simon	Gunar	BD	Personal Assistant	to Manfred Woerner, Germany
Simon	William E.	C	Secretary (fmr.)	Treasury Dept., Reagan Admin.
Simon of Highbury	David, Lord	TE	Chairman	Brit. Petr., London; Min., (fmr.), Trade & Competitiveness/Euro.
Simonet	Henri	BINT,TE	Member	Belgian Senate
Simons	Julie A.	C		
Simons	Thomas W., Jr.	B	Ambassador	to Poland
Sims	Albert G.	C		
Sims	Robert B.	C	V.P.	*National Geographic Magazine*
Sinclair	Paula J.	C		
Sinding	Steven W.	C	Professor	Prinseton Univ.
Singer	Christine-Eibs	C		Energy House
Siniscalco	Domenico	BI	Professor	Economics; Dir., Fendazione ENI
Sinkin	Richard N.	C		InterAmerican Holding C.
Sisco	Joseph John	C,T	Principal	Sisco Associates, Washington
Sisk	Timothy D.	C	Prog. Officer	U.S. Inst. of Peace
Sito	Jerzy	T	Vice President	Polish PEN Club, Warsa; Amb. (fmr.) to Denmark
Sitrick	James Baker	C	Chair., Exec. Comm.	Coudert Brothers
Skarzynski	Michael P.	C	President	Inferno Network Software
Skidmore	Thomas E.	C	Professor	Brown Univ.
Skinner	Elliott P.	C	Professor	Columbia Univ.
Skinner	Kiron Kanian	C		Hoover Institute
Skolnikoff	Eugene B.	C	Professor	MIT, Political Science
Slade	David R.	C		
Slater	Joseph Elliott	C	Department Chairman	John J. McCloy International Center
Slawson	Paul S.	C	Trustee	Asia Foundation
Sloane	Ann Brownell	C	Private Board Member	Inter-American Foundation
Slocombe	Walker Becker	C	Under Secretary	Defense Dept.; Advisory Board, Center for Nat. Policy
Sloss	Leon	C	Assoc. Councilor	Atlantic Council

Last Name	First & Mid. Name	Org.	Job Title	Affiliation - Company, Organization
Small	Lawrence M.	C	Chief Oper. Officer	Federal National Mortgage Association
Smalley	Patricia Tolles	C	Charter Trustee	Hamilton College
Smart	Stephen Bruce, Jr.	C	Director	Chevron Corp.; Sr. Fellow, World Resources Inst.
Smith	Carleton Sprague	C	President (fmr.)	Music Library Assoc.
Smith	Clint E.	C	Professor	Stanford Univ.
Smith	Clint N.	C		
Smith	David Shiverick	C	US Ambassador (fmr.)	State Dept., Sweden
Smith	DeWitt C., Jr.	C	Major General	Defense Dept.
Smith	Edwin M.	C	Professor	USC, Law School
Smith	Gaddis	C	Professor	Yale Univ., History
Smith	Gare A.	C		
Smith	Gerard C.	T	Amb.-at-Lge., (fmr.)	State Dept.; Chief Negotiator, S. A. L. T.
Smith	Gordon	T	Chairman	Int. Development Research Centre, Canada
Smith	Hedrick Lawrence	C	Commentator	PBS TV, Washington Week in Review
Smith	Jeffrey Hartman	C	Partner	LawFirm
Smith	John	BGB	Member	British Parl., Lab. Party; Shadow Chancellor, Exchequer
Smith	John McCall	C		
Smith	John T., II	C	Bureau Chief	Treasury Dept., Procurement, Tax Sustems Admin.
Smith	Larry K.	C	Counselor	Defense Dept., Office of the Secretary
Smith	Leighton Warren, Jr.	C	Commander in Chief	Defense Dept., Naval Operations
Smith	Malcolm Bernard	C	Chairman	John Simon Guggenheim Memorial Found., Fin. Comm.
Smith	Michael Bryant	C	Professor	Univ. of Connecticut
Smith	Perry M.	C	Brigadear General	Defense Dept.
Smith	Peter	C	Congressman (fmr.)	Vermont
Smith	Peter Bennett	C	Chairman, Credit Com.	Morgan Guaranty Trust Co.; Congr. (fmr.), Vermont
Smith	Peter Hopkinson	C		
Smith	R. Jeffrey	C	Writer	*Washington Post*
Smith	Richard Mills	C	Editor-in-Chief, Pres.	Newsweek magazine
Smith	Stephen Grant	C	Editor	Civilization Magazine
Smith	Theodore M.	C		
Smith	Tony	C		
Smith	Wayne S.	C	Division Director	H. H. S. Dept., Office of Survey & Certification
Smith	William Young	C	President (fmr.)	Defense Dept., Defense Analyses
Smith	Winthrop Hiram, Jr.	C	Exec. V. Pres. & Chair.	Merrill Lynch International
Smythe	Mabel M.	C	Member	Howard Univ., Advisory Commission
Snider	Don M.	C		
Snow	Robert Anthony (Tony)	C	Journalist	Detroit News, USA Today
Snowe	Olympia J.	C	Senator	Maine; Cong. (fmr.), Budget, Armed Svcs., Commerce
Snoy	et d'Oppuers, Baron	BB	Minister (fmr.)	Belgium, Finance
Snyder	Craig	C		
Snyder	David M.	C	Captain	Defense Dept., US Air Force
Snyder	Jack L.	C	Professor	Princton Univ., Int. History
Snyder	Jed C.	C	Team Leader	State Dept., INSS, Middle East & South Asia
Snyder	L. Britt	C		
Snyder	Richard Elliot	C	Chairman & CEO	Paramount Publications, NYC
Snyder	Scott A.	C		
Sobol	Dorothy Meadow	C		Fed. Reserve Bank of NY
Soderberg	Nancy E.	B,C	Deputy Asst. to Pres.	White House, National Security Affairs
Sofaer	Abraham David	C	Legal Advisor	State Dept.; Partner, Hughes, Hubbard & Reed, Wash.
Sohl	Hans-Gunther	BD,TE	Hon. President (fmr.)	Fed. Assoc. of German Ind.; Dir. (fmr.), A.-Thyssen-Huette AG
Sohn	Louis Bruno	C	Dist. Rsch. Prof.	George Washington Univ.
Solana Madarings	Javiar	BINT	Secretary Gen.	N.A.T.O.
Solarz	Stephen Joshua	C	Congressman (fmr.)	New York ; Sr. Counselor, APCO Assoc. Consultants
Solbert	Peter O. A.	C		
Solbes Mira	Pedro	B,T	Member	Spanish Parliament; (fmr.) Min. of Fin. & Agriculture, Madrid
Solomon	Andrew W.	C		
Solomon	Anne G. K.	C	Consultant	N.Y. City
Solomon	Anthony M.	C		Federal Reserve Bank
Solomon	Anthony S.	T	Chairman	Inst. for East-West Security Studies,Econ. Progr., N.Y.
Solomon	Joshua N.	C		
Solomon	Lisa J.	C		
Solomon	Peter J.	C	Founder	Peter J. Solomon Co.
Solomon	Richard Harvey	C	US Ambassador (fmr.)	State Dept., Phillipines
Solomon	Robert	C	Guest Scholar	Brookings Institute
Sommaruga	Cornelio	BCH	President	Int. Committee of the Red Cross
Sommer	Theo	BD,TE	Editor-in-Chief	"Die Zeit", Freie und Hansestadt HamburgGermany
Sonenshine	H. Marshall	C	Partner	Wolfensohn & Co., (Banking)
Sonenshine	Tara	C	Deputy Director	White House, National Security Policy; Newsweek Mag.
Sonne	Christian R.	C		
Sonnenfeldt	Helmut	B,C,T	Guest Scholar	Brookings Inst.; Edit. Bd. Mbr., Carnegie Endow. mag.
Sonnenfeldt	Jean	TE	Director General	French Electric Board, Paris
Sonnenfeldt	Richard Wolfgang	C	Professor	Poly Institute of New York, Brooklyn
Sorensen	Gillian Martin	C	Under Secretary	UN, Special Advisor for Information & Public Policy
Sorensen	Svend O.	BDK	Mng. Director (fmr.)	Den Danske Landmandsbank
Sorensen	Theodore Chaikin	C	Special Counsel (fmr.)	to US Pres.,'61-64; Bd. Mbr.,Ctr. for Int. Pol.;Dir.,CFR
Soros	George	B,C,T	President	Soros Fund Mgt.; Fdr.& Chair., Open Society Institute
Soros	Paul	C	Co-Owner	APEX Silvermines, LTD. Caman Islands

Last Name	First & Mid. Name	Org.	Job Title	Affiliation - Company, Organization
Sousa	Marcelo Robelo de	BP	Leader	PSD Party
Southern	Marcel	TE	Honorary Chairman	French Electric Board, Paris
Southern	Ronald D.	TC	Chair., Pres. & CEO	ATCO Ltd., Calgary; Ch., Canadian Util., Ltd. Edmonton
Southwick	James D.	C		
Sovern	Michael Ira	C	President (fmr.)	Columbia Univ.
Spain	James William	C	US Ambassador	St. Dept., Maldives & Sri Lanka; US Amb. (fmr.), Turkey
Spalter	Jonathan	C	Special Assistant	Defense Dept., Principal Deputy Under Secretary
Spangler	Scott M.	C	Assis. Admin. (fmr.)	USAID
Spar	Debra L.	C		Harvard Univ.
Spector	Leonard S.	C	Sr. Associate	Carnegie Endowment for International Peace
Speedie	David C.	C		
Speidel	Hans	BD	General	Cmdr.-In-Chief (fmr.), NATO land forces, Mid, Europe
Speidel	Kirsten E.	C	Professor	Swarthmore College
Spencer	Edson W.	C,T	Trustee	Carnegie Endowment for International Peace
Spencer	John H.	C	President	Spencer & Spencer, Inc.
Spencer	William Courtney	C	Managing Director	Centre for International Education
Spero	Joan Edelman	C,T	Under Secretary	State Dept., Econ. & Agric. Affairs; Member (fmr.), TC
Speth	James Gustav	C	Und. Sec.-Gen.,Admin.	UN Development Prog.; Bd. Member, Ctr. for Int. Policy
Speyer	Jerry I.	C	Chairman	Columbia Univ., Trustees
Spiegal	John W.	C		
Spielvogel	Carl	C	Director	Asia Society
Spiers	Ronald Ian	C	Under Secretary	State Dept., UN, for Political Affairs
Spindler	J. Andrew	C		
Spiro	Herbert John	C	US Ambassador (fmr.)	State Dept., Cameroon, Equitorial Guinea
Spiro	Peter J.	C	Resident Associate	Carnegie Endowment for International Peace
Spitaels	Guy	BB	Minister	Belgium, of State; Chairman, Socialist Party
Spratt	John McKee, Jr.	C	Congressman	South Carolina, Budget/Ranking, National Security
Springer	Axel Caesar, Sr.	BD	Publisher (fmr.)	Springer-Publishing house; Frei u. Hansestadt Hamburg
Springer	Jenny	C		
Squadron	Howard Maurice	C	Partner	Squadron, Ellenoff, Plesent Sheinfeld & Sork.
Stackpole	D. Andrew	C		
Stacks	John F.	C	Deputy Mng. Editor	Time magazine
Staheli	Donald L.	C	Director	Banker's Trust
Stahl	Lesley R.	B	Correspondent	National Affairs, CBS
Stalson	Helena	C		
Stamas	Stephen	C	Private Invest. Exec.	Windcrest Partners, NYC; Director (fmr.), CFR
Stankard	Francis X.	C		
Stanley	Peter William	C	President	Pomona College, California
Stanley	Timothy Wadsworth	C	President	International Economics Studies Institute
Stanton	Frank	C	Chairman (fmr.)	RAND Corp.
Stanton	R. John, Jr.	C		
Staples	Eugene S.	C		
Starobin	Herman	C	Research Dir. (fmr.)	Int. Ladies Garment Workers Union
Starr	Jeffrey M.	C		
Starr	Stephen Frederick	C,T	Director	Rockefeller Bros. Found.; Adj. Fellow, Hudson Inst.
Stassen	Harold E.	C	Signer	United Nations Charter; Gov. (fmr.), Minnesota
Staunton	Myles	TE	Member	Senate, Irish Republic
Steadman	Richard C.	C		
Stebbins	James H.	C		
Stedman	Louellen	C		
Steeg	Helga	BINT	Executive Director	International Energy Agency
Steel	Ronald	C	Member (fmr.)	Carnegie Endowment for International Peace
Stegemeier	Richard Joseph	C	Chairman & CEO	Unocal Corp.
Steiger	Paul Ernest	C	Managing Editor	Wall Street Journal, NYC
Stein	Elliot, Jr.	C	Man. Director	Commonwealth Capital Partners, L.P.
Stein	Eric	C	Professor (fmr.)	Univ. of Michigan, Law School
Stein	Jonathan B.	C	President	B'nai Israel Usy
Stein	Mark B.	C		
Stein	Paul E.	C	Superintendent	Defense Dept., Air Force Academy
Steinberg	David Joel	C	President	Long Island Univ., Brooklyn
Steinberg	James B.	B,C	Director	State Dept., Policy Planning; Dep., Nat. Security Council
Steinberg	Mark R.	C		
Steinberg	Richard H.	C	Member	Berkeley Roundtable on the Int. Economy
Steinbrener	John D.	C	Advisory Bd. Member	Center for International Policy, Center for Nat. Policy
Steiner	Daniel	C	Lobbyist	to the U.S. Senate
Steiner	Steven E.	C		
Steinfeld	Edward S.	C		
Stempel	John D.	C	Professor	Univ. of Kentucky
Stent	Angela E.	C	Professor	Georgetown Univ., Governmlent
Stepan	Alfred C.	C	Dean (fmr.)	Columbia Univ.
Stephanopolos	George R.	B,C	Senior Advisor (fmr.)	to US President Clinton; Rhodes Scholor
Stern	David Joel	C		
Stern	Ernest	C		J.P. Morgan & Co., Inc.
Stern	Fritz Richard	C,T	Professor	Columbia Univ., History
Stern	H. Peter	C		
Stern	Jeffrey	C		
Stern	Jessica E.	C		

Last Name	First & Mid. Name	Org.	Job Title	Affiliation - Company, Organization
Stern	Paula	C,T	Senior Fellow	Progressive Policy Inst., Pres., The Stern Group
Stern	Todd D.	C		
Sternberger	Dolf	BD	Political Scientist	Prof. (fmr.), Heidelberg; Pres. (fmr.), P.E.N.-Ctr. of Ger.
Sterner	Michael Edmund	C	Managing Director	IRC Group, Inc.
Sternlight	David	C		
Stetson	Anne	C		
Stevens	Charles R.	C		
Stevens	James William	C	Exec. Vice President	Prudential Insurance Co., Newark
Stevens	Norton	C	Private Board Member	Inter-American Foundation
Stevens	Paul Schott	C	Chairman	American Bar Assoc. Standing Committee
Stevenson	Adlaii Ewing, III	B,C	Senator (fmr.)	Illinois
Stevenson	Charles A.	C	Professor	Defense Dept., National War College
Stevenson	H. Dennis	BGB	Chairman	SRU Groupe; Tate Gallery
Stevenson	John Reese		Judge (fmr.)	Permanent Court of Arbitration, The Hague
Stewart	Donald M.	C	President (fmr.)	Spelman College, Director, Ctr. for International Policy
Stewart	Gordon Curran	C	President	Insurance Information Institute, NYC
Stewart	Patricia Carry	C	Vice President	Edna McConnell Clark Foundation, Inc.
Stewart	Ruth Ann	C	Asst. Librarian	Library of Congress, National Programs
Sticht	J. Paul	C	Chair. & CEO (fmr.)	RJR Nabisco, Inc., Winston-Salem
Stid	Daniel D.	C		
Stiehm	Judith Hicks	C	Provost (fmr.)	Florida International Univ., Miami
Stifel	Laurence D.	C		
Stiglitz	Joseph E.	C	Chairman	Council of Economic Advisers
Stiles	Deborah F.	C		
Stiles	Ned B.	C		
Stith-Cabranes	Kate	C	Secretary	Yale Univ., Board of Directors
Stobaugh	Robert Blair	C	Professor	Harvard Univ., Business School
Stockman	David Allen	C,T	General Partner	Blackstone Gp., NYC; Dir. (fmr.), O.M.B.
Stockton	Paul Noble	C		
Stoessinger	John G.	C	Professor	Trinity Univ., Int. Affairs
Stofft	William A.	C	President	Defense Dept., US Army War College
Stoga	Alan	C	Board Member	Council of the Americas; Mng. Dir., Kissinger & Assoc.
Stokes	Bruce	C	Int. Econ. Corr.	National Journal; Fellow, CFR
Stokes	Donald Elkinton	C	Professor	Princeton Univ.
Stokes	Louis	C	Congressman	Ohio, Appropriations
Stoleru	Lionel	BF	Econ. Counsel. (fmr.)	to President of French Republic
Stoltenberg	Gerhard	BD,TE	Member	German Bundestag; Minister (fmr.), Defence; CDU
Stoltenberg	Thorvald	BN,TE	Co-Chairman (UN) (fmr.)	Steering Comm. of the Int. Conf. on former Yugoslavia
Stone	Jeremy Judah	C	President	Federation of American Scientists, Washington
Stone	Michael P. W.	C	Secretary (fmr.)	Defense Dept., Dept. of the Army
Stone	Randall	C		
Stone	Roger D.	C	Campaign Manager	Arlen Spector
Stookey	John Hoyt	C	Chairman & CEO	Quantum Chemical Corp.
Storvik	Kjell	BN	Governor	Bank of Norway
Stratton	Julius Adams	C	President (fmr.)	MIT
Straus	Donald Blun	C	Trustee (fmr.)	Carnegie Endowment for International Peace
Straus	Oscar S., II	C	President	Daniel & Florence Guggenheim Foundation
Straus	R. Peter	C	Chairman	Straus Communications, Inc.
Strauss	Franz-Joseph	BD	Min. President (fmr.)	Free State of Baveria; Fed. Min. (fmr.), Finance; CSU
Strauss	Robert Schwarz	C,T	US Ambassador (fmr.)	St. Dept., Russia; Pt., Akin, Gump, Strauss, Hauer & Feld
Strauss	Simon David	C	Consultant	various industrial firms in US
Strausz-Hupe	Robert	C	US Ambassador (fmr.)	St. Dept., Ceylon, Belgium, Sweden, N. A. T. O., Turkey
Stremlau	John J.	C	Executive Director	Carnegie Corp. of New York
Strmecki	Marin J.	C		
Strock	James Martin	C	Asst. Administrator	E. P. A.; Secretary, St. of California, Environ. Protection
Stromseth	Jane E.	C	Professor	Georgetown Univ., Law
Stromseth	Jane E.	C		
Stroock	Thomas Frank	C	President	Alpha Development Corp.
Stroud	Joe Hinton	C	Sr. Vice President	Detroit Free Press
Strube	Jurgen	BD	CEO	BASF Aktiengesellschaft
Studeman	William Oliver	C	Director (interim)	C.I.A.; Dir. (fmr.), Dept. of Central Intelligence
Styron	Rose	C	Trustee	Nation Institute
Suchocka	Hanna	BPL	Minister	of Justice
Sudarkasa	Michael E. M.	C	Director	Labat-Anderson, Inc., Int. Trade Inv. Promotion Service
Sudarkasa	Niara	C	President	Lincoln Univ., Pennsylvania
Sughrue	Karen M.	C	Vice President	Council on Foreign Relations, Meetings
Suits	Christopher D.	C		
Suleiman	Ezra N.	C	Professor	Princeton Univ.
Sulkin	Seth R.	C		
Sullivan	Barry F.	T	President & CEO	New York City Partnership
Sullivan	Gordon Russell	C	Army Chief of Staff	Defense Dept., US Army
Sullivan	Leon Howard	C	Chairman	Zion Home for Retired
Sullivan	Louis W.	C		
Sullivan	Margaret C.	C	Special Asst. to Sec.	Defense Dept.
Sullivan	Roger Winthrop	C	President (fmr.)	US-China Business Council
Sullivan	William H.	C	Chairman	US-Vietnam Trade Council; Mbr., Dean Whitter
Sulzberger	Cyrus Leo	B	Columnist (fmr.)	New York Times

Last Name	First & Mid. Name	Org.	Job Title	Affiliation - Company, Organization
Summers	Harry G., Jr.	C	Fellow	Defense Dept., Army War College
Summers	Lawrence H.	B,C	Secretary	Treasury Dept.
Sunderland	Jack B.	C	President	America Ind. Oil Co.
Suranyi	Gyorgy	BH	President	National Bank of Hungary
Suslow	Leo A.	C		
Sutherland	Peter D.	BIRL,TE	Chair. & Mng. Dir.	Goldman Sachs Int.,London;Dir.Gen.(fmr.),GATT & WTO
Sutphen	Mona K.	C		
Sutterlin	James S.	C	Professor	Yale Univ.
Sutton	Francis Xavier	C	Consultant	Rockefeller Foundation, USAID, World Bank
Suzuki	Tetsuo	TJ	President	HOYA Corp.
Svanholm	Poul Johan	TE	Chairman	Den Danske Bank; (fmr.) Chair., Carlsberg, Copenhagen
Svedberg	Bjorn	TE,BS	Chairman	Ericsson; (fmr.) Gp. CEO, Skandinaviska Enskilda Banken
Swank	Emory Coblentz	C	US Ambassador (fmr.)	State Dept., Cambodia, '70-73
Swanson	David Heath	C	President & CEO	World Grain Div., Continental Grain Co.
Sweeney	John J.	C	President	AFL-CIO Union
Sweig	Julia E.	C		
Sweitzer	Brandon W.	C		
Swenson	Eric Pierson	C	Sr. Edit./V. Ch. (fmr.)	W. W. Norton & Co.
Swid	Stephen Claar	C	Chairman & CEO	SCS Communications, NYC
Swiers	Peter Bird	C		
Swigert	James W.	C		
Swing	John Temple	C	Exec. V. President	CFR, 1993; President, Fgn. Pol. Assoc.
Szanton	Peter L.	C	President	Saanton & Assoc.
Szporluk	Roman	C	Professor	Harvard Univ., Ukranian History
Tabaksblat	Morris	BNL	Chairman	Unilever N.V.
Taft	Robert	T	Attorner-Partner	Taft, Stettinius & Hollister
Taft	William H., IV	C	US Ambassador (fmr.)	State Dept., N. A. T. O.
Tahir-Kheli	Shirin R.	C		
Taida	Hideya	Tj	Man. Director	Marubeni Corp.
Takagi	Tsuyoshi	TJ	President	ZENSEN (Text.,Gmnt,Chem.,Merch.& Allied Ind.Wkrs.Un.)
Takemi	Keizo	TJ	Member	Japanese House of Councillors
Talbot	Phillips	C	US Ambassador (fmr.)	State Dept., Greece
Talbott	Strobe	C,T	Deputy Secretary	State Dept.; US Ambassador (fmr.), to Russia; Dir., CFR
Taliaferro	Jeffery	C		
Talwar	Puneet	C		
Tamaron	El Marques, de	TE	Director	Instituto de Cuestiones Internacionales y Politica Exterior
Tanaka	Akihiko	TJ	Associate Professor	Univ. of Tokyo, Institute of Oriental Culture
Tanaka	Naoki	TJ	Presodent	The 21st Century Public Policy Institute
Tang	Angelica	C		
Tang	David K. Y.	C	Man. Partner	Preston, Gayes & Ellis; Investment Banker, Hong Kong
Tanham	George Kilpatrick	C	Dep. to V. Pres. (fmr.)	RAND Corp.
Tannenwald	Theodore, Jr.	C	Sr. Judge	US Tax Court
Tanner	Harold	C	President	Tanner & Co., Inc., NYC
Tanter	Raymond	C	Professor	Univ. of Michigan
Tapia	Raul R.	C	Dep. Spec. Asst.	to President Carter
Tapsell	Sir Peter	TE	Member	British Parliament
Tara	Sinan	BTR	Vice President	Enka Construction & Ind. Inc.
Tarnoff	Peter	C,T	Under Secretary	State Dept.; President (fmr.) Council on Fgn. Relations
Tarter	C. Bruce	C		
Tasco	Frank J.	C	Chair. Exec. Comm.	Marsh & McLennan Cos.
Tashkovich	Geligor A.	C		
Tateishi	Nobuo	TJ	Chair. & Rep. Dir.	OMRON Corp
Tatsumi	Sotoo	TJ	President (fmr.)	Sumitomo Bank, Ltd.
Taubman	William Chase	C	Member	Int. Academy Advisory Gp., Russian Fgn. Min. Archives
Tavares	Carlos	TE	Chairman	Banca Nacional Ultramarino, Lisbon
Taylor	Arthur Robert	C,T	President	Muhlenberg College, Allentown, Pennsylvania
Taylor	J. Martin	BGB	CEO (fmr.)	Barclays Bank, London
Taylor	Kathryn Pelgrift	C		
Taylor	William Jesse, Jr.	C	Member	Ctr. for Strat. & Int. Studies; Pres., Taylor Assoc., Inc.
Taylor	Wilson H.	T	Chair., Pres. & CEO	CIGNA Corp.
Taylor	Geoffrey	TE	Chairman	Daiwa European Bank, London
Tedstrom	John E.	C	Investigator	RAND Corp., Russian, Ukranian & Eurasian Affairs
Teece	David John	C	Professor	Univ. of California, Berkeley
Teeter	Robert M.	C		
Teeters	Nancy Hays	C	Director & Trustee	Prudential Mutual Fund Mgt., NYC
Teitelbaum	Michael S.	C	Member (fmr.)	Carnegie Endowment for International Peace
Teles	Jose M. Galvao	BP	Member	Council of State
Telhami	Shibley	C	Assoc. Professor	Cornell Univ., Near Eastern Studies
Tellis	Ashley J.	C		
Teltschik	Horst	BD,TE	Moard Member	BMW AG, Munich; Chancellor-Advicer (fmr.)
Tempelsman	Maurice		Board Member	Center for National Policy
Temple-Raston	Dina Simone	C		
Tenet	George J.	C		(CIA:??)
Tennyson	Leonard B.	C		
Tepper-Marlin	Alice	C	Founder	Council on Economic Priorities
Terkelsen	Terkel M.	BDK	Editor-in-Chief (fmr.)	Berlingske Tidende, Denmark
Terracciano	Anthony Patrick	C	Chair., Pres. & CEO	First Fidelity Bancorp, New Jersey

Who's Who of the Elite

Last Name	First & Mid. Name	Org.	Job Title	Affiliation - Company, Organization
Terry	Sarah M.	C	Assoc. Professor	Tufts Univ.
Teufel	Erwin	BD	Prime Minister	Daden-Wurtemberg
Thatcher	Margaret, Lady	BGB	Prime Minister (fmr.)	Great Britain
Thayer	Artemas Branson	C	Chairman	First Florida Banks Inc., Tampa
Thayer	Lord	TE	Director	RTZ Corp.; Chf. Cabinet Sec. (fmr.) & Prime Minister
Theobald	Thomas Charles	C	Chairman & CEO	Continental Bank Corp., Chicago; Dir., Xerox Corp.
Thery	Jane L. Barber	C		
Thierry	Jacques	TE	Hon. Chairman	Banque Bruxelles Lambert; Ch.,Artois Piedboeuf Interbrew
Thiessen	Marc A.	B,C	Aide	Senate, to Jesse Helms
Thoman	G. Richard	B,C	President & COO	Xerox Corp.
Thomas	Barbara Singer	C	Director	News International, London, Business & Legal Affairs
Thomas	Brooks	C	President	Butterfield House
Thomas	Evan W., III	C	Member	Newsweek Magazine, Author, "The Very Best Men"
Thomas	Franklin Augustine	C	President	Ford Foundation
Thomas	James P.	C		
Thomas	Lee B., Jr.	C	Benifactor of Assoc.	World Resources Inst.
Thomas	Lewis	C	Professor	Cornell Medical School, Medicine
Thomas-Lake	Hillary	C		
Thompson	Gerald F.M.P.	BGB	Chairman (fmr.)	Kleinwort Benson Ltd. (investment bank)
Thompson	James	T		Winston & Strawn
Thompson	Robert L.	C		
Thompson	W. Scott	C	Director	US Inst. for Peace; Mbr. (fmr.), Carnegie Endowment
Thomson	James Alan	C	President & CEO	RAND, Santa Monica
Thomson	James C., Jr.	C		
Thorn	Gaston	TE	Chairman	Bank Int. a'Luxembourg; President (fmr.), EEC
Thornburgh	(Richard L.) Dick	C	Attorney Gen. (fmr.)	Justice Dept.; Under Secretary General (fmr.), UN
Thornell	Richard P.	C	Professor	Harvard Univ., Law School
Thornton	John L.	B	Pres. & co-COO	Goldman Sachs Group, Inc.
Thornton	Thomas P.	C		
Thoron	Louisa	C		
Thorsell	William	BC	Editor	Globe and Mail
Thorup	Cathryn L.	C	Dep. Co-odinator	New Partnership Initiative
Thurman	Maxwell R.	C	Cmdr.-in-Chief (fmr.)	Defense Dept., Southern Command, Panama
Thurow	Lester C.	T	Professor	MIT, Economics, Alfred P. Sloan School of Management
Thygensen	J. V.	BDK	President (fmr.)	Export Credit Council of Denmark
Thygesen	Niels	TE	Professor	Copenhagen Univ., Economics, Enonomic Institute
Tidbury	Antonio	TE	Chairman	S. e Reparacio e Montagem de Eq. Ind.
Tidemand	Otto Grieg	BN,TE	Shipowner	Oslo, Norway; Min. (fmr.) Norwegian Defense & Econ. Afrs.
Tidemann	Heinrich	TE	Chairman	Siemens AG, Munich/Berlin, Munich
Tien	Chang-Lin	C		
Tien	John K., Jr.	C		
Tierney	Paul E., Jr.	C	Chairman	TW Holdings, Inc., S. C.
Tiersky	Ronald	C		
Tigert	Ricki Rhodarmer	C	Chairman	F. D. I. C., Board of Directors
Tiido	Harri	TE	Editor-in-Chief	Radio KUKU Tallinn
Tillinghast	David Rollhaus	C	Partner	Chadbourne & Parke, NYC
Tillman	Seth P.	C		
Timothy-Lankester	Kristen	C		
Timpson	Sarah L.	C	Member	Overseas Development Council
Tindell	Cynthia A.	C		
Tipson	Frederick S.	C		AT&T
Tirana	Amina	C		
Tisch	Laurence Alan	C	Chair., Pres. & CEO	CBS Inc.
Tobias	Randall L.	C	Vice Chairman	AT&T; Dir., Phillips Petroleum Co.
Todaro	Michael P.	C	Author	"Urbanization, Unemployment & Migration In Africa"
Todd	Maurice Linwood	C		
Todman	Terence A.	C	US Ambassador	State Dept., Argentina; Amb. (fmr.), Spain, Denmark
Toepfer	Klaus	BD	Minister	House Building, Ger.; Mbr. (fmr.), Ger. Bundestag; CDU
Toll	Maynard Joy, Jr.	C	Managing Director	First Boston Corp., NYC
Tomabechi	Toshihiro	TJ	Director	Toppan Moore Co., Ltd.; CEO, Tomabechi Consultants
Tomlinson	Alexander Cooper	C	President	Hungarian-American Enterprise Fund, Washington
Ton	Tuong-Vy	C		
Topping	Audrey Ronning	C		
Topping	Seymour	C	President (fmr.)	American Newspaper Editors
Torano	Maria Elena	C		
Tornz	Michael R.	C		
Torres	Art	C	Senator (State)	California
Torres	Esteban Edward	C		
Torricelli	Robert G.	C	Senator	New Jersey; Congressman (fmr.)
Toth	Robert Charles	C	Nat. Security Corresp.	Los Angeles Times
Townley	Preston	C	President & CEO	Conference Board
Townley	Umberto	TE	Mng. Dir. & CEO	STET, Rome (telecommunications)
Townsend	Alair	C	Publisher	*Crain's New York Business*
Toyoda	Eiji	TJ	Honorary Chairman	Toyota Motor Corp.
Toyoda	Tatsuro	TJ	Vice. Chairman	Toyota Motor Corp.
Toyonaga	Keiya	TJ	Vice President	Matsushita Electric Industrial Co., Ltd.
Traa	Maarten, van	TE	Member	Dutch Parliament

Last Name	First & Mid. Name	Org.	Job Title	Affiliation - Company, Organization
Trachtenberg	Stephen Joel	C	President	George Washington Univ.
Train	Harry Depue, II	C	Cmdr.-in-Chief (fmr.)	Def. Dept., Atlantic Flt. & Supreme Allied Commander
Train	John	C	Writer	Wall Street Journal, Worth magazine, Forbes magazine
Train	Russell Errol	C,T	Trustee	Rockefeller Bros. Found.; Chair., World Wildlife Fund, Wash.
Trainor	Bernard Edmund	C	Director	Harvard Univ., National Security Program
Trani	Eugene Paul	C	President	Virginia Commonwealth Univ.
Travis	Martin Bice, Jr.	C	Professor	State Univ. of New York, Stony Brook, Politicl Science
Treat	John Elting	C	Vice Pres. & Partner	Booz, Allen & Hamilton Inc., NYC
Trebat	Thomas J.	C	Man. Director	Citicorp Securities Inc., Emerging Markets Research
Trenin	Dmitri V.	BRUS	Deputy Director	Carnegie Moscow Center
Trenkle	Timothy Paul	C		
Treverton	Gregory F.	C	Director	RAND Corp., Int. Security & Defense Policy Ctr.
Trewhitt	Henry L.	C	Cont. Editor	*Baltimore Sun*
Trezise	Philip Harold	C,T	Sr. Fellow	Brookings Institute
Trice	Robert H., Jr.	C		
Trichet	Jean-Claud	BF	Governor	Banque de France
Trillo Figueroa	Federico	B	VP & Member	Spanish Parliament (Partido Popular)
Trimble	Charles R.	C		
Troeger	Heinrich	BD	Vice President (fmr.)	Dewutsche Bundesbank; Mbr. (fmr.), Bundestag; SPD
Trojan	Vera M.	C		
Tronchetti Provera	Marco	TE	Chair. & CEO	Pirelli, Milan
Trooboff	Peter Dennis	C	Partner	Covington & Burling, Washington
Trotman	Alexander J.	B	Chairman	Ford Motor Company
Trowbridge	Alexander Buel, Jr.	C	Director	NAM, Washington
Trowbridge	Louis V., Jr.	B,T	Chair. & CEO (fmr.)	IBM; Chair. & CEO (fmr.), RJR Nabisco Holding Corp.
Trudeau	Pierre	BC	Prime Minister (fmr.)	Canada
Truitt	Nancy Sherwood	C	Sr. Advisor	The Foundation Ctr.
Truman	Edwin M.	C	Staff Dir., Economist	Federal Reserve System
Tsehai	Elizabeth	C		
Tsipis	Kosta Michael	C	Sr. Research Scientist	MIT
Tsutsumi	Seiji	TJ	Chairman	Saison Corp.
Tu	Lawrence P.	C		
Tucher	H. Anton	C		
Tuck	Edward Hallam	C	Of Counsel	Shearman & Sterling, NYC
Tucker	Katherine K.	C		
Tucker	Nancy Bernkopf	C	Professor	Georgetown Univ., History, Sch. of Fgn. Service
Tucker	Richard F.	C		
Tucker	Robert W.	C	President	INTERED
Tuke	Anthony	BGB	President (fmr.)	Barclays Bank, London
Tuminez	Astrid S.	C		
Tunc	Halil	BTR	Chairman (fmr.)	Federation of Turkish Workers Unions
Tung	Ko-Yung	C,T	Chairman	O'Melveny & Myers, Global Practice Group,
Turck	Nancy B.	C		
Turco	Ottaviano, Del	TE	General Secretary	Italian Socialist Party (PSI), Rome
Turkevich	John	C	Professor	Princeton Univ., Chemistry
Turner	J. Michael	C	Assoc. Professor	Hunter College
Turner	Robert Foster	C	Associate Professor	Univ. of Virginia
Turner	Stansfield	C	Cmdr.-in-Chief (fmr.)	Def. Dept., N. A. T. O., Allied Forces Southern Europe
Turner	William Cochrane	C	Chairman & CEO	Argyle Atlantic Corp., Phoenix
Turner	William I. M., Jr.	TC	Chairman & CEO	EXSULTATE Inc., Montrial
Tuthill	John Wills	B,C	US Ambassador (fmr.)	State Dept., EEC, Brazil
Tyrrell	Robert Emmett, Jr.	C	Editor-in-Chief	American Spectator
Tyson	Laura D'Andrea	B,C,T	Chairwoman (fmr.)	Council of Economic Advisors; Prof., Harvard Univ.
Udgaard	Nils M.	BN	Fgn. Editor	*Aftemposten*
Udovitch	Abraham L.	C	Professor	Princeton Univ., Near Eastern Studies
Uetani	Hisamitsu	TJ	Chairman (fmr.)	Yamaichi Securities Co., Ltd, Tokyo
Uhlig	Mark	C	Writer	*New York Times*
Ullman	Richard Henry	C	Editorial Bd. Mbr.	Carnegie Endow. magazine; Professor, Princeton U.
Ulman	Cornelius M.	C		
Umbricht	Victor H.	BCH	Director (fmr.)	Ciba-Geigy, Ltd., Switzerland
Umemura	Shoji	TJ	Chairman	Nikko Securities Co., Ltd.
Ungar	Sanford J.	C	Member (fmr.)	Carnegie Endowment for International Peace
Ungeheuer	Frederick	C		
Unger	David G.	C		New York Times
Unger	Leonard L.	C	Office Manager	S. E. C., Office of Inspection & Financial Responsibility
Urban	Thomas N.	C	President	Pioneer Hi-Bred Int., Inc.
Urfer	Richard P.	C		
Uri	Pierre	BF	Professor	Paris IX
Urquijo	Jaime Carvajan	B	Chair. & Gen. Mgr.	Iberfomento
Usher	William R.	C	Military Fellow (fmr.)	CFR
Utgoff	Victor A.	C		Institute for Defense Analysis
Utley	Garrick	C	Correspondent	ABC News; Director, CFR
Utton	Albert E.	C	Professor	New Mexico Univ.
Uusmann	Ines J.	B	Minister	Transportation & Communications
Vaarvik	Dagfinn	BN	Editor-in-Chief (fmr.)	Nationen
Vagliano	Alexander Marino	C	Chairman	Michelin Financial Corp.
Vagliano	Sara	C		

Last Name	First & Mid. Name	Org.	Job Title	Affiliation - Company, Organization
Vagts	Detlev Frederick	C	Professor	Harvard Univ., Law
Vaky	Viron Peter	C	Adjunct Professor	George Washington Univ., Dipolmacy
Valdez	Abelardo Lopez	C	Partner	Laxalt, Washington, Perito & Dubuc
Valenta	Jiri	C		
Valenzuela	Artuto A.	C	Deputy Asst. Sec.	State Dept., Mexican Affairs
van Cott	Donna Lee	C	Doctoral Cand.	Georgetown Univ.
van den Haag	Ernest	C	Professor	Fordham Univ., Jurisprudence & Public Policy
van der Vink	Gregory E.	C		Int. Research Inst. for Seismology
van Dusen	Michael H.	C	Min. Chief-of-Staff	House Committee on Int. Relations
van Dyk	(Frederick T.) Ted	C	President	van Dyk, Associates
van Evera	Stephen W.	C	Assoc. Professor	UC Berkeley, Political Science
van Fleet	James Alward	C	Chairman (fmr.)	American-Korean Foundation
van Oranje Nassau	Beatrix Wilhelmina	BNL	Queen	The Netherlands
van Oranje Nassau	Johan Friso Bernhard	BNL	Prince	The Netherlands
Van Ouderan	John	C		
van Vlierden	Constant M.	C	Member	Overseas Development Council
van Voorst	L. Bruce	C	Sr. Correspondent	Time magazine
Vanblen	Tom Clayton	C	Managing Director	Enterprise Consultants, Inc., Washington
Vance	Cyrus Robert	C,T	President Partner	Simpson, Thacher & Barnett; Secretary (fmr.) St. Dept.
Vanden Heuvel	Jon	C		
Vanden Heuvel	Katrina	C	Chairman	UN/USA Board of Governors
Vanden Heuvel	William J.	C	Chairman	U.N. Assoc. of the U.S.A.
Vanderlugt	Robert D.	C		
Vanhala	Matti	BFIN	Chairman	Bank of Finland
Varanini	Jeffery Paul	C		
Varella	Marta B.	C		
Vargas Llosa	Mario	TE	Writer	Member of the Royal Spanish Academy
Vartia	Pentti	BFIN	Mng. Director	Research Inst. Of the Finnish Economy (ETLA)
Vasco de Mello	Antonio	TE	Chairman	Sociedade de Reparacao e Montagem de Equip. Ind., Lisbon
Vasella	Daniel L.	BCH	Chairman & CEO	Novartis AG
Vecchi	Sesto	C		
Vecchio	Mark S.	C		
Vedrine	Hubert	TE	Minister	Foreign Affairs, France
Veiga	Miguel	BP	Lawyer	Portugese
Veil	Simone	TE	Minister (fmr.)	France, de, State for Social, Health & Urban Affairs
Veit	Carol M.	C		
Veit	Lawrence A.	C		
Veliotes	Nicholas Alexander	C	President	Association of American Publishers
Veltroni	Walter (Valter)	BI	Vice Prime Min.	Italy
Venable	Nicole Y.	C		
Veremis	Thomas M.	BGR	Professor	Athens Univ., Political History
Verheugen	Gunter	BD	Secretary General	Social Democratic Party
Verleger	Philip K., Jr.	C		
Vermilye	Peter Hoagland	C	Sr. Advisor	Baring Asset Management
Vernon	Raymond	B,C	Visiting Prof. (fmr.)	World Bank; Professor (fmr.), Harvard Univ.
Verstandig	Toni Grant	C		
Verville	Elizabeth Giavani	C	Deputy Asst. Sec.	State Dept., Bureau of Political-Military Affairs
Verzetnitsch	Fredrich	TE	Member	Austrian Parl. (SPOe); Pres., Austrian Fed. of Trade Unions
Vessey	John W.	C	Chairman (fmr.)	Defense Dept., Joint Chiefs of Staff
Vest	George Southall	C	US Ambassador (fmr.)	State Dept., EEC, Brussels
Victor	Alice	B	Executive Assistant	Rockefeller Fin. Services; Rapporteur, Bilderberger Gp.
Vidal	David J.	C		
Viebranz	Curtis G.	C		
Viederman	Stephen	C		
Viets	Richard Noyes	C		
Vila Marsans	Jose	TE	Chairman	Rhone Poulenc Fibras,Barcelona;Dir.,Banco Central,Madrid
Villalonga	Juan	TE	Chairman	The National Telephone Co. (Telefonica), Madrid
Villar	Arturo	C	Director	Gorbachev State of the World Advisory Board
Villeneuve	Andre-Francois H.	BGB	Exec. Dir.	Reuters Group Holding plc
Vincent	Eric	C		
Vine	Richard D.	C		
Vink	Lodewijk J.R. de	B	President & CEO	Warner-Lambert Company
Viorst	Milton	C	Staff Writer	New Yorker magazine
Virkkunen	Janne	BFIN	Sr. Editor-in-Chief	*Helsingin Sanomat*
Viscusi	Enzo	C	Mbr. Advisory Bd.	Council of the Americas; Rep./ the Amer., ENI Americas
Vitale	Alberto Aldo	C	Chr., Pres. & CEO	Random House, NYC
Vitorino	Antonio	B	Dep. Prime Minister	and Minister of Defence
Vits	Mia de	B	Gen. Secretary	ABVV-FGTB
Vittorelli	Paolo B.	TE	Chairman	Institute Studi Ricerche Defesa, Rome
Voell	Richard Allen	C	President & CEO	Rockefeller Group, NYC (real estate service co.)
Vogel	Ezra F.	B,C	Professor	Harvard Univ.
Vogelgesang	Sandra (Sandy) L.	C	U.S. Ambassador	State Dept., Nepal
Vogelson	Jay M.	C		
Voigt	Karsten D.	TE	Co-ordinator	for German-American Relations, Berlin
Vojta	George J.	C	Vice Chairman	Bankers Trust Co., NYC
Volcker	Paul Adolph	B,C,T	Chairman (fmr.)	Fed.Res.Sys.;Mbr.,Brkgs. Inst.,Dir.,Concord Coal.,CFR
Volgelson	Jay M.	C		

Last Name	First & Mid. Name	Org.	Job Title	Affiliation - Company, Organization
Voljc	Marko	TE	CEO	Nova Ljubljanska Banka, Ljubljana
Volk	Stephen Richard	C	Sr. Partner	Shearman & Sterling, NYC
Voorhoeve	Joris	TE	Member	Dutch Parliament
Voscherau	Henning	BD	Mayor	Hamburg
Votaw	Carmen Delgado	C		Girl Scouts of the USA
Vourloumis	Panagis	TE	Chair.& Man. Dir.	Alpha Finance, Athens
Voutilainen	Pertti	BFIN	President	Merita Bank Ltd.
Vranitzky	Franz	BA	Federal Chancellor (fmr.)	Austria
Vries	Gijs M. de	BINT	Leader	Liberal Group, European Parl.
Vuono	Carl E.	C	General (fmr.)	Defense Dept., US Army
Vuursteen	Karel	BNL,TE	Chairman/Exec Bd.	Heineken N.V., Amsterdam
Waal	Lodewjk J. de	BNL	Chairman	Dutch Confed. of Trade Unions (FNV)
Wachner	Linda Joy	C	Chairwoman & CEO	WARNACO, Inc.
Wacsh	Michael H.	C		
Waddell	Rick	C		
Wadsworth-Darby	Mary	C	Member	Morgan, Stanley & Co., N.Y.
Wahl	Nicholas	C		
Wahlestedt	April	C		
Wakeman	Frederick Evans, Jr.	C	Professor	Univ. of California
Waldegrave	William A.	BGB	Secretary of State	Minister of Agriculture, Fisheries & Food
Waldron	Arthur Nelson	C		
Wales	Jane	C	Associate Director	White House, Interagency Committees
Walinsky	Adam	C	Author	"The Crisis of Public Order"
Walker	Charles E.	C	Chairman	Walker/Free Assoc.
Walker	G. R.	C		
Walker	Jaceques P.	C		
Walker	Jenonne R.	C	Spec. Asst. to Pres.	White House, European Affairs
Walker	John Lockwood	C	Partner	Simpson, Thacher & Bartlett, NYC
Walker	Mary Lynn	C	Partner	Luce, Forward, Hamilton & Scripps, San Diego
Walker	William N.	C	Head	U.N. Observers, Bosnia
Walking	Sarah K.	C		
Wallace	Roger Windham	C		
Wallage	Jacques	BNL	Parliamentary Leader	PvdA (Labor Party)
Wallander	Celeste A.	C		
Wallenberg	Jacob	B	Chairman	Skandinaviska Enskilda Banken
Wallenberg	Marcus, Dr.	B	Chairman	Skanvinavska Enskilda Banken
Wallenberg	Peter	TE	1st Vice Chairman	Skandinaviska Enskilda Banken, Stockholm
Wallerstein	Mitchel B.	C	Deputy Asst. Sec.	Defense Dept., Counterproliferation Policy
Wallich	Christine	C		
Wallison	Peter J.	C	Partner	Gibson, Dunn & Crutcher, Wash.
Walters	Barbara	C	Co-Host	ABC, 20/20
Walton	Anthony J. (Tony)	C	Designer/Illustrator	Theater & Films, Book Illustrator
Walton	Reginald K.	C		
Waltz	Kenneth Neal	C	Professor	Univ. of California, Berkeley, Political Science
Warburg	Sir Siegmund George	BGB	Chairman (fmr.)	S. G. Warburg & Co., Lond.; Ptnr., Kuhn, Loeb & Co.
Ward	Haskell G.	T	President	Ward Associates, Inc.
Ward	Jennifer C.	C		
Ward	John W.	C		
Ward	Katherine T.	C		
Ward	Patrick J.	C		
Ware	Carl	C		
Warner	Edward L., III	C	Asst. Secretary	Defense Dept.
Warner	John William	C		
Warnke	Paul Culliton	C,T	Trustee	Center for Int. Policy; Council Mbr., Brookings Inst.
Warren	Gerald Lee	C	Editor	San Diego Union-Tribune
Warren	J. H.	TC	Prin. Trade Pol. Adv.	Bureau de Quebec, Ontario
Warren	Lewis, Jr.	C		
Warring	Niels	BN	Chairman	Wilhelm Wilhelmsen Limited A/S, Norway
Washburn	Abbott M.	C		
Washburn	John L.	C		
Washio	Etsuya	TJ	President	Japan Trade Union Confederation (RENGO)
Wasserstein	Bruce	C	President	Wasserstein, Perella & Co., NYC; Ch. (fmr.) Maybelline
Watanabe	Fumio	TJ	Counsellor	Tokyo Marine & Fire Insurance Co., Ltd.
Watanabe	Takeshi	TJ	Chairman	Japan Silver Volunteers
Waterbury	John	C	Professor	Prinseton Univ.
Waters	Cherri D.	C	Director	African Development Foundation, Office of Learning
Watson	Alexander Fletcher	C	Asst. Secretary	State Dept., Inter-American Affairs
Watson	Peter S.	C		
Watson	Thomas J., Jr.	C	Chairman	Ctr. for Fgn. Policy Development; US Amb. (fmr.), USSR
Wattenberg	Ben J.	C	Sr. Fellow	American Enterprise Institute; Syndicated Columnist
Watts	Glenn Ellis	C,T	President (fmr.)	Communications Workers of Amererica; Director, CFR
Watts	John H.	C		
Watts	William	C		
Way	Alva O.	C		
Weatherstone	Dennis	C	Chairman & CEO	J. P. Morgan & Co.; Director, General Motors Corp.
Weaver	David R.	C		
Weaver	George L. P.	C		

Last Name	First & Mid. Name	Org.	Job Title	Affiliation - Company, Organization
Webb	Hoyt K.	C		
Webble	Steven	C		
Weber	Doron	C		
Weber	Steven	C		
Weber	Vin	C	Congressman (fmr.)	Minnesota; Empower America mbr.
Webster	William H.	C	Director (fmr.)	CIA, Bush Admin.
Wechmar	Ruediger von	BD	Diplomat	Pres. (fmr.) UN-Generalk Assby.; Mbr., Euro. Parliament
Wechsler	William F.	C		
Wedgwood	Ruth N. Glushien	C		
Weeks	Jennifer R.	C		
Wegener	Henning	BINT	Asst. Sec. General	N. A. T. O., for Political Affairs
Wehrle	Leroy Snyder	C	Chairman	Tie Collar, Ltd.
Weidenbaum	Murray Lew	C	Department Chairman	Washington Univ., Economics
Weigel	George	C	Sr. Fellow	Ethics & Public Policy Ctr.
Weiksner	George B., Jr.	C		
Weil	Frank A.	C	President	Norman Foundation
Weinberg	John Livingston	C	Sr. Chairman	Goldman Sachs & Co.; Director, Du Pont Co.
Weinberg	Serge	TE	Chair. & Dir. Gen.	Pinault-Printemps-Redoute Group, Paris;Ch. (fmr.), Rexel
Weinberg	Steven	C	Professor	Univ. of Texas, Austin
Weinberger	Casper Willard	C,T	Publisher	Forbes magazine; Secretary (fmr.), Defense Dept.;
Weiner	Myron	C	Sr. Staff Member	MIT & Harvard Univ.
Weinert	Richard S.	C		
Weinrod	W. Bruce	C		
Weinstein	Michael M.	C	Editorial Columnist	New York Times
Weintraub	Sidney	C	Professor	Univ. of Texas, Austin
Weisberg	Jacob	C		
Weisman	Steven	C	Editorial Bd. Mem.	*New York Times*
Weiss	Andrew S.	C		
Weiss	Charles, Jr.	C	Professor	Johns Hopkins Univ.
Weiss	Cora	C	Member	Institute for Policy Studies; 30th Anniversary Comm.
Weiss	Edith Brown	C	Vice Chairwoman	Georgetown Univ., Law Ctr.
Weiss	Heinrich	TE	Chairman	SMS Company, Duesseldorf
Weiss	Stanley A.	B	Chairman	Business Executive for National Security, Inc.
Weiss	Thomas G.	C	Professor	Brown Univ.
Weissman	Ivan S.	C		
Weizsaecker	Richard von	BD	Fed. President (fmr.)	Ger.; Mayor (fmr.), Berlin; Mbr. (fmr.), Ger. Bundestag
Welch	Jasper A., Jr.	C		
Welch	John F.	C	Chairman & CEO	General Electric Company; Owner, Kidder-Peabody
Welch	Larry D.	C	Chief-of-Staff (fmr.)	Defense Dept., US Air Force
Weller	Ralph Albert	C	Chairman (fmr.)	Otis Elevator Co.
Wells	Damon, Jr.	C	Owner & CEO	Damon Wells Interests, Houston
Wells	Herman B.	C	Chancellor	Indiana Univ.
Wells	Louis T., Jr.	C	Member	Harvard Univ.
Wells	Samuel F., Jr.	C	Deputy Director	Woodrow Wilson International Center for Scholors
Wells	Walter N.	C		
Wender	Ira Tensard	C	Partner	Patterson, Belknap, Webb & Tyler
Wendt	E. Allan	C	US Ambassador	State Dept., Republic of Slovenia
Wendt	Gerhard M. H.	BFIN	President	Kone Corp.
Wendt	Henry	T	Chairman (fmr.)	SmithKline Beecham
Wertheim	Mitzi Mallina	C	Member	IBM Corp., Federal Sector Div.
Wesbrook	Stephen D.	C		
Weschler	Joanna	C		
Wesley	Edwin Joseph	C	Lawyer	Winthrop Stimson, et al, NYC
Wessel	Michael R.	C	Member	House Democratic Leaders Office
West	J. Robinson	C	Chairman	Gas Ventures Advisers
West	Owen O' Driscoll	C		
West	Togo D.	C	Secretary	Veterans Affairs; Defense Dept., (fmr.) Sec. of the Army
Weston	Burns H.	C	Professor	Iowa Univ., Law
Westrick	Ludger	BD	Fed. Minister (fmr.)	Germany, Special Tasks, CDU; Chief, Bundeskanzleramt
Wexler	Anne	C	Chairman	Wexler, Reynolds, Harrison & Schule, Inc. (P. R. firm)
Wexler	Conrad Moffat	TC	Chairman & CEO	Hollinger Inc., Toronto
Weyerhaeuser	George H.	T	Chairman & CEO	Weyerhaeuser Company
Weymouth	Lally	C	Columnist	*Washington Post*
Whalen	Charles William, Jr.	C	Congressman (fmr.)	Ohio
Whalen	Richard James	C	Chairman	Whalen Co., Inc.
Wharton	Clifton R., Jr.	C,T	Deputy Secr. (fmr.)	State Dept.; Member (fmr.), TC; Director, CFR
Wheat	Francis Millspaugh	C	Vice Chairman	Pomona College, California
Wheeler	John K.	C		
Wheelon	Albert Dewell	C	Visiting Prof. (fmr.)	MIT
Whitaker	C. S.	C	Professor	USC, Los Angeles
Whitaker	Jennifer Seymour	C	Dep.Nat. Director	CFR
Whitaker	Jennifer Seymour	C		
Whitaker	Mark	C	Director	Energy Dept., Defense Nuclear Facility Safety Board
White	John P.	C	Deputy Secretary	Defense Dept.; Chair., Concord Coalition
White	Julia A.	C		
White	P. Maureen	C	US Representative	UNICEF
White	Peter C.	C		

Last Name	First & Mid. Name	Org.	Job Title	Affiliation - Company, Organization
White	Peter G.	BC	Chairman	Unimedia; Head (fmr.), of Prime Minister's office
White	Robert James	C	Columnist	Minneapolis Star Tribune
White	Robert M.	C	Associate Director	Veterans Admin., Compensation & Pension Service
White	Timothy J.	C		
White	Walter H., Jr.	C		Steptoe & Johnson, Wash.
Whitehead	John Cunningham	B,C,T	Chairman	Brookings Institute; Chairman, AEA Investors Inc., NYC
Whitehouse	Charles S.	C	US Ambassador	State Dept.
Whitman	Christine Todd	B,C	Governor	New Jersey
Whitman	Marina v. N.	C,T	Director	Proctor/Gambel;Dist.Vis.Prof.,U./ Mich.;Dir.(fmr.),CFR
Whitney	Craig R.	C	Writer	*New York Times*
Whittemore	Frederick B.	C	Partner	Morgan, Stanley & Co.
Wiarda	Howard J.	C	Author	"Ethnocentricity & Foreign Policy"
Wicker	Thomas Grey	B	Columnist (fmr.)	New York Times
Wickham	John Adams, Jr.	C	Chief-of-Staff (fmr.)	Defense Dept., US Army
Wickman	Krister	BS	Governor (fmr.)	Bank of Sweden
Widmer	Siegmund	BCH	Mayor (fmr.)	Zurich, Member (fmr.), Swedish Parliament
Widner	Jennifer	C	Assoc. Proffessor	Michigan Univ., Political Science
Wieczorek	Norbert	TE	Member	German Bundestag,SPD; Cghair., Comm./ Eoro. Union Affrs.
Wielingen	G. A., van	TC	President & CEO	NuGas Limited, Alberta
Wiener	Carolyn Seely	C	Board Member	Center for National Policy
Wiener	Jonathan Baert	C	Assoc. Professor	Harvard Univ., Risk Analysis
Wiener	Malcolm Hewitt	C	Chairman	Willburn Corp., NYC; Member, Brookings Institute
Wiesel	Torsten Nils	C	President	Rockefeller Univ.
Wieseltier	Leon	C	Literary Editor	New Republic Magazine
Wiesner	Jerome Bert	C	President (fmr.)	MIT
Wijffels	Herman H. F.	BNL	Chairman	Robobank Nederland
Wilbur	Brayton, Jr.	B,C	President	Wilbur-Ellis Co., San Franciscop; Dir., Safeway Stores
Wildavsky	Aaron	C	Professor (fmr.)	UC, Berkelely, Political Science & Public Policy
Wildenthal	Claud Kern	C	President	Southwest Medical School
Wilder	Lawrence Douglas	B	Governor (fmr.)	Virginia
Wilds	Walter W.	C		
Wiley	Richard Arthur	C	Director	Powers & Hall, P.C.
Wiley	W. Bradford	C		
Wilhelm	Harry E.	C		
Wilhelm	Robert E.	C	Sr. Vice Pres. & Dir.	EXXON Corp.;V.,Chair.,Coun. of the Americas; Fgn. Pol. Assoc.
Wilhjelm	Nils	BDK	President	Industrial Mortgage Fund, Denmark; Min. of Ind. (fmr.)
Wilkerson	Thomas L.	C	Maj. General	Defense Dept., Marine Corps Plans
Wilkie	Edith B.	C	Legislative Spec.	CFR
Wilkins	Roger W.	C	Professor	George Mason Univ., History
Wilkinson	Sharon	C	Member	State Dept.
Will	George	T	Panelist	ABC, This Week; Columnist, GFW Inc.
Willey	Fay	C		
Williams	Alan	TE	Member	British Parliament, London
Williams	Avon Nyanza, III	C	Attorney (fmr.)	Nashville, TNN
Williams	Christine	C		
Williams	Earl Carter	C	Director	Wolf Trap Foundation
Williams	Eddie Nathan	C	President	Joint Center for Political & Economic Studies, Wash.
Williams	Harold Marvin	C	President & CEO	J. Paul Getty Trust
Williams	Haydn	C	President (fmr.)	Asia Foundation
Williams	Joseph Hill	C	Chairman & CEO	Williams Companies, Tulsa
Williams	Karen Hastie	T	Partner	Cromwell & Moring, Washington
Williams	Lynn Russell	B	Int. President	United Steel Workers of America
Williams	Maurice Jacoutot	C	Chief US Delegate	State Dept., US-North Vietnam Jt. Econ. Commission
Williams	Melvin F., Jr.	C		
Williams	Paul R.	C		
Williamson	Edwin A.	C		
Williamson	Irving A.	C	Deputy Gen. Counsel	US Trade Representative
Williamson	Richard S.	C		
Williamson	Thomas Samuel, Jr.	C	Solicitor	Labor Dept.; Ptnr., Covington & Burling, Washington
Willrich	Mason	C	CEO (fmr.)	Pacific Gas & Electric, San Francisco
Wilmers	Robert George	C	President & CEO	ENY Savings Bank, NYC
Wilson	Donald Malcolm, III	C	Publisher	Business for Central N.J., Princeton
Wilson	Ernest James, III	C	Director	Overseas Development Council
Wilson	Gretchen	C	Author	"With All Her Might"
Wilson	Heather A.	C		
Wilson	John Donald	C	Sr. Vice Pres. (fmr.)	Chase Manhattan Bank
Wilson	Karen	C		
Wilson	L. R.	BC,TC	Chair., Pres. & CEO	BCE Inc., Montrial
Wilson	Margaret Scarbrough	C		
Wilson	Michael	BC	Minister	of Industry, Science & Technology & Int. Trade, Canada
Wilson	Percy C.	C		
Wilson	Robert N.	T	Vice Chairman	Johnson & Johnson
Wilson	Serena Lynn	C	Member	CFR, Wash. Committee
Wilson	T. A.	T	Chairman (fmr.)	Boeing Company
Wimpfheimer	Jacques D.	C	Member	The Jockey Club of South Africa
Windsor	HRH Prince Philip	BGB	Prince & , Duke of	of England
Winegard	William C.	TC	Chairman	Canadsian House of Commons, Ottawa

Last Name	First & Mid. Name	Org.	Job Title	Affiliation - Company, Organization
Wing	Adrien K.	C	Professor	Iowa Univ., Law
Winokur	Herbert S., Jr.	C	Executive	various companies; NY Historical Society
Winship	Thomas	C	Editor (fmr.)	*Boston Globe*
Winslow	Richard S.	C		
Winston	Michael Russell	C	President	Alfred Harcourt Foundation
Winterer	Philip Steele	C	Partner	Debevoise & Plimpton, NYC
Winters	Francis X.	C	Author	"The Year of the Hare: America in Viet Nam"
Winters	Robert Cushing	T	Chair. & CEO (fmr.)	Prudential Insurance Co. of America
Winthrop	Grant F.	B	Rapporteur	Bilderberg Gp.; Partner, Milbank, Wilson, Winthrop, Inc.
Wirth	David A.	C	Economic Assistant	The World Bank
Wirth	John D.	C	Author	"The CEC"
Wirth	Timothy Endicott	C	Senator (fmr.)	Colorado; State Dept., Under Secretary for Global Affairs
Wischnewski	Hans-Juergen	BD	Member (fmr.)	German Bundestag
Wisner	Frank G., II	B,C	US Ambassador (fmr.)	State Dept., Egypt
Wissmann	Matthias	BD	Fed. Minister	for Transportation
Witkowsky	Anne A.	C	Director	White House, Nat. Security Council
Witunski	Michael	C	Councelor	Atlantic Council Councelor's (Law)
Woerner	Fred F.	C	General	Defense Dept., Southern Command
Woerner	Manfred	BINT	Sec. General	N.A.T.O.
Wofford	Harris Llewellyn	C	Senator (fmr.)	Pennsylvania, Foreign Relations, Labor, Small Business
Wohl	Richard H.	C	Author	"Practice by Foreign Lawyers in Japan"
Wohlforth	William C.	C	Assoc. Editor	*Johns Hopkins Press*
Wohlstetter	Albert J.	B,C	Writer	Wall Street Journal
Wohlstetter	Roberta	C	Author	"Pearl Harbor: Warning and Decision"
Wolf	Charles, Jr.	C	Sr. Fellow	Stanford Univ., Hoover Institute
Wolf	Ira	C		
Wolf	Martin	BGB	Assoc. Editor	The Finantial Times, Economic Commentastor
Wolf	Milton Albert	C	US Ambassador (fmr.)	State Dept., Austria
Wolfensohn	James David	B,C	President	World Bank
Wolff	Alan William	C	Advisory Bd. Member	Center for International Policy
Wolff von Amerongen	Otto	BD,TE	Chairman	East Comm./the German Ind.; Ch. & CEO, Otto Wolff Ind.
Wolfowitz	Paul Dean	B,C,T	Dean	Johns Hopkins Univ., Sch of Advanced Int. Studies
Wolin	Neal Steven	C	Executive Assistant	White House, Office of National Security Affairs
Wolpe	Howard	C	Congressman (fmr.)	Michigan
Wood	Joseph R.	C		
Wood	Suzanne	C		
Woodbridge	David	C	Treasurer	Council on Foreign Relations
Woodcock	Leonard	T	President	United Auto Workers Union
Woods	Ward W., Jr.	C	President & CEO	Bessimer Securities
Wooldridge	Adrian D.	BGB	Fgn. Correspondent	*The Economist*
Woolf	Harry	C	Director	Princeton Univ., Institute for Advanced Studies
Woolsey	R. James	C	Director (fmr.)	C.I.A.; Member, National Security Council
Woolsey	Suzanne H.	C		
Woon	Eden	C	Exec. Director	Washington State China Realtions Council
Worden	Mary Stuart "Minky"	C		
Wormuth	Christine E.	C		
Wray Jr.	Cecil	C	Partner	Debevoise & Plimpton, NYC
Wriggins	W. Howard	C	Professor(fmr.)	Columbia Univ., Int. Politics
Wright	Abi E.	C		
Wright	L. Patrick	C		
Wright	Patrick	BGB	Perm. Under Sec.	of State; Head, Diplomatic Service, U. K.
Wright	Robin	C	Wash. Correspondent	Los Angeles Times
Wright-Carozza	Paolo G.	C		
Wriston	Walter Bigelow	B	Chairman (fmr.)	Citicorp; Director (fmr.), CFR
Wyatt-Walter	Holly	C		
Wyman	Thomas H.	C	Chairman	CBS; Director, General Motors Corp.
Yacoubian	Mona	C		
Yahuda	Michael B.	BGB	Professor	Int. Rel., London School of Economics
Yakushiji	Taizo	TJ	Vice President	Keio Univ.
Yalman	Nur	C	Professor	Harvard Univ., Social Anthropology
Yamamoto	Tadashi	TJ	President	Japan Center for International Exchange
Yamashita	Isamu	TJ	Chairman (fmr.)	Trilateral Commission, Japan
Yanez-Barnuovo	Juan A.	BE	Permanent Rep.	United Nations, from Spain
Yang	James Ting-Yeh	C		
Yang	Linda Tsao	C		
Yang	Phoebe L.	C		
Yankelovich	Daniel	C	Director	Charles F. Kettering Foundation
Yanney	Michael B.	C	Chair & CEO	America First Cos.
Yarmolinsky	Adam	C	Trustee	Center for Int. Policy; Provost, Univ. of Maryland
Yasa	Memduh	BTR	Professor (fmr.)	Univ. of Istanbul
Yasar	Selcuk	BTR	Director (fmr.)	several companies, Izmir
Yashiro	Masamoto	TJ	Exec. V. President	Citicorp/Citibank, NA; Country Corp. Officer
Ybarra	Emelio	TE	Exec. Chairman	Banco Bilbao-Vizcaya, Madrid
Yee	Melinda C.	C		
Yergin	Daniel Howard	C	Research Associate	Harvard Univ.
Yochelson	John N.	C	Member	European Institute, Washington

Last Name	First & Mid. Name	Org.	Job Title	Affiliation - Company, Organization
Yoffie	David B.	C	Professor	Harvard Univ., Business School, Int. Business
Yoneura	Noriyuke	TJ	Man. Director	Fuji Xerox Co. LTD.
Yordan	Jaime E.	C		
Yoshino	Bunroku	TJ	Chairman	Inst. for Int. Economic Studies; Amb. (fmr.) to Germany
Yost	Casimir A.	B,C	Hon. Sec. Gen.	Bilderberg; Dir., Gorbachev State of the World Adv. Bd.
Young	Alison (Alice) I.	C	Division Director	Energy Dept., Planning & Restoration
Young	Andrew	C,T	US Ambassador (fmr.)	United Nations; Congressman (fmr.), Georgia
Young	Edgar B.	C		
Young	Joan P.	C	Administrative Officer	H. U. D. Dept., Office of Ethics
Young	Mervin Crawford	C	Professor	Univ. of Wisconsin
Young	Michael K.	C	Professor	Columbia Univ., Law
Young	Nancy	C	Partner	Richards & O'Neil, NYC
Young	Peter Joel C.	C		
Young	Stephen B.	C	Writer	*Center of the American Experiment*
Youngblood	Kneeland C.	C	Board Memb.	US Enrichment Corp.
Youngman	William Sterling	C	Chairman (fmr.)	American Home Assurance Co.
Yu	Frederick T. C.	C	Professor (fmr.)	Columbia Univ., Int. Journalism
Yu	Peter M.	C		
Yucaoglu	Erkut	BTR	Chairman	Tusiad, Turkey
Yudkin	Richard A.	C		
Yzaguirre	Raul H.	C	President	Nat. Council of La Raza
Zaccaro	Donna A.	C		
Zagoria	Donald S.	C		
Zahn	Joachim	TE	Chairman (fmr.)	Daimler-Benz AG, Sindelfingen/Stuttgart
Zakheim	Dov Solomon	C	CEO	System Planning Corp., Int., Inc.
Zaleski	Michael	C		
Zandano	Gianni	TE	Chairman	Instuto Bancario San Paolo di Torino
Zannoni	Paolo	BI	Sr. Vice President	Defense & Space, Fiat S.P.A., Italy
Zantovsky	Michael	B	Chairman	Comm. On Fgn. Affairs, Defense & Security, Czech Senate
Zarb	Frank Gustave	C	Pres., Chair. & CEO	Smith, Barney, Harris, Upham & Co.; Dir., CFR
Zartman	I. William	C	Professor	Johns Hopkins Univ., Advanced Int. Studies
Zegart	Amy B.	C		
Zeidenstein	George	C	Counsel	Overseas Development Council
Zeikel	Arthur	C		
Zelikow	Philip D.	C	Co-Author	"The Kennedy Tapes"
Zelnick	Carl Robert	C	Pentagon Corresp.	ABC News, Washington
Zemmol	Jonathan I.	C		
Zieba	Father Maciej	TE	Principal	Polish Province of the Dominican Order, Warsaw
Zijlstra	Jelle	BNL	President (fmr.)	The Netherlands Bank
Zilkha	Ezra K.	C	Council Member	Brookings Institute
Zimmerman	Edwin Morton	C	Member	Covington & Burling, Washington
Zimmerman	Peter D.	C	Member	Center for Strategic & Int. Studies
Zimmerman	William	C	Program Director	Center for Political Studies
Zimmermann	Norbert	B	Chairman	Berndorf AG, Austria
Zimmermann	Warren	C	US Ambassador	State Dept., Yugoslavia; Mbr. (fmr.), Carnegie Endow.
Zinberg	Dorothy Shore	C	Sr. Research Assoc.	Harvard Univ., Center for Science & International Affairs
Zinder	Norton Donald	C	Invest. Consultant	Private
Zinni	Anthony Charles	C		
Zinser	Alan	C		
Zipp	Brian R.	C		
Zisk	Kimberly Marten	C		
Zoellick	Robert Bruce	B,C,T	Pres. & CEO	Ctr. For Strategic & Int. Studies
Zogby	James J.	C	President	Arab American Institute
Zolberg	Aristide Rodolphe	C	Professor	New School for Social Research, NYC
Zombanakis	Minos	BGR	Chairman	Group for International Study & Evaluation, Greece
Zonis	Marvin	C	President	Marvin Zonis & Associates
Zorthian	Barry	C	Partner	Alcalde, Rousselot & Fay, Arlington
Zraket	Charles A.	C	Trustee	Hudson Institute; Trustee, MITRE Corp.
Zuckerman	Harriet	C	Sr. Research Scholar	Columbia Univ.
Zuckerman	Mortimer Benjamin	B,C,T	Chr. & Edit.-in-Chief	US News/World Reports, NY Daily News, Atlantic Monthly
Zumwalt	Elmo Russell, Jr.	C	President	Admiral Zumwalt & Consultants, Inc.
Zwan, van der	Arie	TE	Dean	Nijenrode Univ., Breukelen
Zwick	Charles J.	C	Chairman (fmr.)	Southeast Banking Corp.; Trustee, Carnegie Endow.
Zysman	John	C	Professor	US, Berkeley, Political Science

Profile of CFR Membership

Source: 1999 CFR Annual Report
(Below figures as of June 30, 1999)

Location	Number of Members	Percent of Membership
Resident (New York City)	1,167	32
Washington, DC	1,143	32
National (including overseas)	1,295	36
Totals	3,371	100%

Profession	Number of Members	Percent of Membership
Business Executives (Including banking)	928	26
Academic Scholars and Administration	761	21
Nonprofit Institution Scholars and Administration	727	20
U.S. Government Officials	492	14
Journalist, Correspondents, and Communication Executives	366	10
Lawyers	307	8
Other	24	1
Totals	3,605	100%

Council on Foreign Relations
Officers and Directors
in the
Past and Present

CFR Officers

Source: CFR Annual Report, July 1, 1998-June 30, 1999

Office	Last Name	First Name	Years	Office	Last Name	First Name	Years
Chairman	Leffingwell	Russell C	46-53	Vice President	Broda	Frederick C.	96-97
	McCloy	John J.	53-70		Maxwell	Kenneth	96
	Rockefeller	David	70-85		Hufbauer	Gary C.	97-98
	Peterson	Peter G.	85-		Kellogg	David	97-
Vice Chairman	Kirk	Grayson	71-73		Dobriansky	Paul J.	97-
	Vance	Cyrus R.	73-76		Luzzatto	Anne R.	98-
	Dillon	Douglas	76-78		Korb	Lawrence J.	98-
	Wilson	Carroll L.	78-79		Lewis	Elise Carlson	99-
	Vance	Cyrus R.	85-87	Sr. V. President	Frye	Alton	93-
	Christopher	Warren	87-91		Keller	Kenneth H.	93-
	Brown	Harold	91-92		Fabian	Larry L.	94-95
	Inman	Bobby Ray	92-93		Peters	Michael P.	95-
	Kirkpatrick	Jeane D. Jordan	93-94	Secretary	Gay	Edwin F.	21-33
	Greenberg	Maurice R.	94-		Dulles	Allen W.	33-44
President	Davis	John W.	21-33		Altschul	Frank	44-72
	Wickersham	George W.	33-36		Swing	John Temple	72-87
	Davis	Norman H.	36-44		Gustafson	Judith	87-
	Leffingwell	Russell C.	44-46	Treasurer	Gay	Edwin F.	21-33
	Dulles	Allen W.	46-50		Shepardson	Whitney H.	33-42
	Wriston	Henry M.	51-64		Hunter	Clarence E.	42-51
	Kirk	Grayson	64-71		Josephs	Devereux C.	51-52
	Manning	Bayless	71-77		Bell	Elliott V..	52-64
	Lord	Winston	77-85		Hauge	Gabriel	64-81
	Swing	John Temple	85-86		Peterson	Peter G.	81-85
	Tarnoff	Peter	86-93		McColough	C. Peter	85-87
	Frye	Alton	93		Preston	Lewis T.	87-88
	Gelb	Leslie H.	93-		Burke	James E.	88-89
Hon. President	Root	Elihu	31-37		Woodbridge	David	89-94
Exec. V. Pres.	Swing	John Temple	86-93		Murray	Janice L.	94-
Vice President	Cravath	Paul D.	21-33	Exec. Director	Armstrong	Hamilton Fish	22-28
	Davis	Norman H.	33-36		Davis	Malcolm W.	25-27
	Gay	Edwin F.	33-40		Mallory	Walter H.	27-59
	Polk	Frank L.	40-43		Franklin	George S.	53-71
	Leffingwell	Russell C.	43-44	Dir. of Studies	Bidwell	Percy W.	37-53
	Dulles	Allen W.	44-46		Mosely	Philip E.	55-63
	Bowman	Isaiah	45-49		Ullman	Richard H.	73-76
	Wriston	Henry M.	50-51		Lowenthal	Abraham F.	76-77
	Rockefeller	David	50-70		Campbell	John C.	77-78
	Altschul	Frank	51-71		Kreisberg	Paul H.	81-87
	Josephs	Devereux C.	51-52		Gleysteen	William H., Jr.	87-89
	MacEachron	David W.	72-74		Rizopoulos	Nicholas X.	89-94
	Swing	John Temple	72-86		Keller	Kenneth H.	94-
	Frye	Alton	87-93		Kapstein	Ethan B.	95-96
	Greysteen	William H., Jr.	87-89		Maxwell	Kenneth	96
	Millington	John A.	87-		Hufbauer	Gary C.	97-98
	Osmer-McQuade	Margaret	87-93		Korb	Lawrence J.	98-
	Rizopoulos	Nicholas X.	89-94	Editor of	Coolidge	Archibald Cary	22-28
	Sughrue	Karen M.	93-98	Foreign Affairs	Armstrong	Hamilton Fish	28-72
	Lowenthal	Abrahyam F.	95-		Bundy	William P.	72-84
	Murry	Janice L.	95-		Hyland	William G.	84-92
	Vidal	David J.	95-97		Hoge	James F., Jr.	92-
	Kapstein	Ethan B.	95-96				

CFR Directors

Source: CFR Annual Report, July 1, 1998-June 30, 1999

Last Name	First Name	Years	Last Name	First Name	Years
Allaire	Paul A.	93-	Erburu	Robert F.	87-
Allen	Robert E.	93-96	Feldstein	Martin S.	98-
Allison	Graham T., Jr.	79-88	Finletter	Thomas K.	44-67
Altschul	Frank	34-72	Finley	John H.	21-29
Anderson	Robert O.	74-80	Foley	Thomas S.	88-94
Arledge	Roone	98-	Foster	William C.	59-72
Armstrong	Hamilton Fish	28-72	Franklin	George S.	72-83
Aspin	Les	95	Fraser	Leon	36-45
Baeza	Mario L.	95-	Frye	Alton	93
Bell	Elliott V.	53-66	Gay	Edwin F.	21-45
Blumenthal	W. Michael 72-7	79-84	Gelb	Leslie H.	93-
Bowman	Isaiah	21-50	Gelb	Richard L.	79-88
Brown	Harold	83-92	Gerstner, Jr.	Louis V.	95-
Bryson	John E.	92-	Geyelin	Philip L.	77-87
Bundy	William P.	64-74	Gray	Hanna Holborn	95-98
Burden	William A. M.	45-74	Greenberg	Maurice R.	92-
Burke	James E.	87-95	Greenspan	Alan	82-88
Bush	George H. W.	77-79	Halaby	Najeeb E.	70-72
Bzezinski	Zbigniew	72-77	Hamilton	Edward K.	74-83
Cheney	Richard B. 87-89	93-95	Harriman	W. Averell	50-55
Christopher	Warren	82-91	Harrison	W. Averell	50-55
Clendenin	John L.	89-94	Haskins	Caryl P.	61-75
Cohen	William S.	89-	Hauge	Gabriel	64-81
Coolidge	Archibald Cary	21-28	Hauser	Rita E.	93-97
Cooper	Richard N.	93-94	Hesburgh	Theodore M.	76-85
Corrigan	E. Gerald	93-95	Hills	Carla A.	94-
Cravath	Paul D.	21-40	Hoffmann	Stanley	83-92
Crowe	William J., Jr.	90-93	Hoge	James F., Jr.	80-84
Cullum	Lee	96-	Holbrooke	Richard C.	91-93, 96-
Cutler	Lloyd N.	77-79	Horn	Karen N.	92-95
Dam	Kenneth W.	92-	Hormats	Robert D.	91-
Davis	John W.	21-55	Houghton	James R.	92-96
Davis	Norman H.	21-44	House	Karen Elliott	87-
Dean	Arthur H.	55-72	Houston	David F.	21-27
Deutch	John	99-	Howland	Charles P.	29-31
Dillon	Douglas	65-78	Hunter	Clarence E.	42-53
Dodds	Harold W.	35-43	Hunter-Gault	Charlayne	92-98
Donahue	Thomas R.	90-	Inman	Bobby Ray	85-93
Donovan	Hedley	69-79	Jessup	Philip C.	34-42
Douglas	Lewis W.	40-64	Johnson	Joseph E.	50-74
Drew	Elizabeth	72-77	Josephs	Devereux C.	51-58
Duggan	Stephen P.	21-50	Kahn	Otto H.	21-34
Dulaney	Peggy	95-	Kaplan	Helene L.	94-96
Dulles	Allen W.	27-69	Katzenbach	Nicholas deB.	75-86
Einhorn	Jessica P.	95-	Kirk	Grayson	50-73

Last Name	First Name	Years	Last Name	First Name	Years

CFR Directors

Source: CFR Annual Report, July 1, 1998-June 30, 1999

Last Name	First Name	Years	Last Name	First Name	Years
Kirkland	Lane	76-86	Scowcroft	Brent	83-89
Kirkpatrick	Jeane D. Jordan	85-94	Shalala	Donna E.	92-93
Kissinger	Henry A.	77-81	Shepardson	Whitney H.	21-66
Kreps	Juanita M.	83-89	Shephard	William R.	21-27
Labouisse	Henry R.	65-74	Shulman	Marshall D.	72-77
Lederberg	Joshua	89-	Shultz	George P.	80-82
Leffingwell	Russell C.	27-60	Sorensen	Theodore C.	93-
Lippmann	Walter	32-37	Soros	George	95-
Lord	Winston	77-85	Spofford	Charles M.	55-72
Lord	Bette Bao	98-	Stamas	Stephen	77-89
Mai	Vincent A.	'97-	Stevenson	Adlai E.	58-62
Mallory	Walter H.	45-68	Talbott	Strobe	88-93
Manning	Bayless	71-77	Tarnoff	Peter	86-93
Mathias	Charles McC., Jr	86-92	Taylor	Myron C.	43-59
'May	George O.	27-53	Tyson	Laura DD'Andrea	'97-
McCloy	John J.	53-72	Utley	Garrick	93-
McCulough	C. Peter	78-87	Vance	Cyrus R. 69-76	81-76
McDonough	William J.	95-	Volcker	Paul A. 75-70 ?	88-
McHenry	Donald F.	84-93	Wallace	Martha Redfield	72-82
McPherson	Harry C., Jr.	74-77	Warburg	Paul M.	21-32
Mettler	Ruben F.	86-92	Warner	Edward	40-49
Mitchell	George J.	95-	Warnke	Paul C.	72-77
Mitchell	Wesley C.	27-34	Watts	Glenn E.	87-90
Moskow	Michael H.	98-	Wharton	Clifton R., Jr.	83-92
Moyers	Bill	67-74	Whitman	Marina v.N.	77-87
Neal	Alfred C.	67-76	Wickersham	George M.	21-36
Perkins	James A.	63-79	Williams	John H.	37-64
Peterson	Peter G. 73-83	84-	Williams	Franklin Hill	75-83
Polk	Frank L.	21-43	Wilson	Carroll L.	64-79
Preston	Lewis T.	81-88	Woolley	Clarence M.	32-35
Pye	Lucian W.	66-82	Wriston	Henry M.	43-67
Reed	Philip D.	45-69	Wriston	Walter B.	81-87
Reed	John S.	89-92	Young	Owen D.	27-40
Richardson	Elliott L.	74-75	Zarb	Frank G.	94-96
Riefler	Winfield W.	45-50	Zoellick	Robert B.	94-
Rivlin	Alice M.	89-92			
Robinon	James D., III	88-91			
Rockefeller	David	49-85			
Rogers	William D.	80-90			
Roosa	Robert V.	66-81			
Ruckleshaus	William D.	79-83			
Rudman	Warren B.	'97-			
Savage	Frank	95-			
Sawyer	Dioane	98-99			
Scalapino	Robert A.	82-89			

Dual & Triple Membership
in these
Elite Organizations

Dual & Triple Membership in Elite Organizations

Last Names	First Names	Org.	Day Job	Affiliation - Agency, Company, Country
Abshire	David M.	C,T	President	Ctr. for Strat. & Int. Stud.; Amb. (Fmr.), N. Atlan. Coun.
Ackermann	Josef	B,T	Board Mbr.	Deutsche Bank, Frankfurt-am-Main
Agnelli	Umberto	BI,TE	V. Chair. & Mng. Dir.	IFI; Chairman, IFIL, Turin
Ahlstrom	Krister Harry	BFIN,TE	Chairman	Ahlstrom Group, Helsinki
Albert	Michel	B,T	Member	l'Inst.de France;Mbr.,Coun./Mon.Pol.,Banque de France
Allen	Robert E.	C,T	Director	Pepsico, Inc.; Dir., CFR
Anderson	John Bayard	C,T	Congressman (Fmr.)	Illinois; '80 candidate for President
Anderson	Robert Orville	B,C	Chairman (Fmr.)	Atlantic Richfield Co. (ARCO)
Araskog	Rand Vincent	C,T	Chair., Pres. & CEO	ITT Corp.
Argyros	Sterios	BGR,TE	Member	European Parliament
Armacost	Michael Hayden	C,T	President	Brookings Inst.; Mbr.,Asia Found.; Amb. (fmr.), Japan
Armstrong	Anne Legendre	C,T	Chairman	Ctr. for Strat. & Int. Stud.; US Amb. (Fmr.), U. K.
Babbitt	Bruce Edward	C,T	Secretary	Interior Dept.
Ball	George Wildman	B,C	Sr. Mng. Director	Lehman Brothers; fmr. Undersec., State
Bell	David Elliott	B,C	Exec. Vice President	Ford Foundation
Bennet	Douglas Joseph, Jr.	B,C	Assistant Secretary	State Dept., International Organization Affairs
Benson	Lucy Peters Wilson	C,T	President	Benson & Associates, Amherst & Washington
Berger	Samuel R. (Sandy)	B,C	Asst. to President	National Security Affairs
Bernabe'	Franco	BI,TE	CEO	Telecom Italia, Rome
Biedenkopf	Kurt	BD,TE	Ministry President	Free State/Saxony; Mbr. Comm. on Global Governance
Bildt	Carl	BE,TE	Prime Minister (fmr.)	Sweden; Mbr., Swedish Parl.; Chair, Moderate Party
Birrenbach	Kurt	BD,TE	Chairman (fmr.)	August-Thyssen-Huette AG; Mbr. (fmr.) CDC, EP
Bjerregaard	Ritt	BDK,TE	Member	Euro. Commission;Mbr., Parl., Danmark ; Chr., SDP Gp.
Black	Conrad M.	BC,TC	Chairman & CEO	Hollinger Inc., Toronto
Blackwill	Robert D.	B,C	Member (Fmr.)	Nat. Sec. Council; Lecturer, JFK School, Harvard Univ.
Blumenthal	Werner Michael	C,T	Limited Partner	Lazard Freres & Co.; Director (Fmr.), CFR
Borges	Antonio	BP,TE	Dean	INSEAD
Bosworth	Stephen W.	C,T	US Ambassador	S. Korea
Bowie	Robert R.	B,C	Member	Overseas Development Council
Boyd	Charles Graham	B,C	Dep.Cmd./Chief(fmr.)	Defense Dept., US European Command
Bradley	Tom	C,T	Mayor (fmr.)	Los Angeles
Bradley	William (Bill) L.	B,C	Senator (fmr.)	New Jersey; Fin., Energy & Nat. Res.; Rhodes Scholar
Brady	Nicholas Frederick	B,C	Secretary (Fmr.)	Treasury Dept.; Director, NCR Corp.
Brimmer	Andrew F.	C,T	Director	Du Pont (E. I, Du Pont De Nemours & Co.)
Brock	William E., III	C,T	Chairman	Blackstone Gp., NYC; Sec. (Fmr.), Labor Dept., '85-'87
Brown	Harold	C,T	Secretary (fmr.)	Def. Dept.; Councelor, Ctr. for Strategic & Int. Stud.
Brundtland	Arne Olav	BN,TE	Sr. Research Fellow	Norwegian Institute of International Affairs, Oslo
Bryan	John H.	B,T	Chairman & CEO	Sara Lee Corp.
Buckley	William Frank, Jr.	B,C	Editor-at-Large	National Review; PBS-Firing Line
Bundy	McGeorge	B,C	Chairman	Carnegie Univ., Com. for Reducing Nuclear Danger
Burke	James E.	C,T	Director	IBM Corp.; Director, CFR
Bush	George Herbert W.	C,T	President (Fmr.)	United States; Director (Fmr.), CIA, CFR
Cabot	Louis Wellington	B,C	Chairman (Fmr.)	Brookings Institute; Chairman (Fmr.), Cabot Corp.
Caldwell	Philip	C,T	Sr. Managing Director	Lehman Brothers, Inc.; Director, Digital Equip. Corp.
Calkins	Hugh	C,T	President & Director	Initiatives in Urban Education
Camps	Miriam	B,C	Vice President (Fmr.)	State Dept., Planning Council
Carlucci	Frank C., III	C,T	Adjunct Fellow	Hudson Inst.;Sec.(Fmr.), Def. Dept.; V. Ch., Carlyle Gp.
Carter	Jimmy	C,T	President (Fmr.)	United States; Member, CFR
Carvajal Urquijo	Jaime	BE,TE	Chairman	Iberfomento; Chairman, Ford, Espana
Chace	James	B,C		World Policy Journal
Chafee	John Hubbard	C,T	Senator	Rhode Island, Finance, Intelligence, Small Business
Cheney	Richard (Dick) B.	C,T	Chair., Pres. & CEO	Halliburton;Wyoming, Cong.(fmr.);Sec.(fmr.),Def.Dept.
Christopher	Warren M.	C,T	Secretary (fmr.)	State Dept.; Chairman, Carnegie Corp of New York
Cisler	Walker Lee	B,C	Chief, Pub. Util.(Fmr.)	Defense Dept., Supreme Allied Com., Euro. Command
Cisneros	Henry G.	C,T	Secretary	H.U.D. Dept.;Mayor (Fmr.), San Antonio
Cleveland	James Harlan	B,C	President (Fmr.)	Univ. of Hawaii
Cohen	William Sebastian	C,T	Secretary	Defense; Senator (fmr.), Maine, Armed Svcs., Judiciary
Coleman	William Thaddeus, Jr.	C,T	Sr. Partner	O'Melveny & Myers; Sec. (fmr.) Transportation
Collomb	Bertrand	BF,TE	Chairman & CEO	Lafarge-Coppee, Paris
Cook	Donald (Don) C.	B,C	Euro. Dip. Cor. (fmr.)	Los Angeles Times
Cooper	Charles A.	C,T	Chairman	C.I.A., Nat. Intelligence Council
Cooper	John Milton, Jr.	C,T	Advisory Bd. Member	Center for International Policy
Crowe	William J., Jr.	C,T	US Ambassador	State Dept., U. K.; Chair. (fmr.), Joint Chiefs-of-Staff
Culver	John C.	C,T	Senator (fmr.)	Iowa
Curtis	Gerald L.	C,T	Professor	Columbia Univ., Political Science, East Asian Institute
Cutler	Lloyd Norton	C,T	Counsel	US Pres. Clinton, '94; Adv. Bd. Mbr., Ctr. for Nat. Pol.
Dam	Kenneth W.	B,C	Council Member	Brookings Inst.; Dep. Sec. (Fmr.), St. Dept.; Dir., CFR
Darman	Richard Gordon	C,T	Director (Fmr.)	Office of Management & Budget,Bush Admin.
Davignon	Viscounte Etienne	BB,TE	Honorary Chairman	Bilderbergs; Soc. Gen. de Belgique;V.Ch.(fmr.) Euro.
Diebold	John	B,C	President & Chairman	Diebold Group; Chairman, Griffenhagen-Kroeger, Inc.
Dillon	C. Douglas	B,C	Vice Chairman (Fmr.)	CFR, '76-'78; Mbr., Brookings Inst.
Dodd	Christopher J.	B,C	Senator	Connecticut, Bkg., Hsg. & Urban Afrs., Fgn. Rel., Rules
Donahue	Thomas Reilly	C,T	Sec./Treasurer (fmr.)	AFL-CIO Union; Dir., CFR
Donilon	Thomas E.	B,C	Chief of Staff (fmr.)	State Dept.; Asst. Sec., for Public Affairs
Drouin	Marie-Josee	BC,TC	Executive Director	Hudson Institute of Canada, Montreal

Last Names	First Names	Org.	Day Job	Affiliation - Agency, Company, Country
Eagleburger	Lawrence S.	C,T	Secretary (Fmr.)	State Dept.; Director, Phillips Petroleum
Einhorn	Jessica P.	C,T	Managing Director	World Bank, for Finance & Resource Mobilization
Eliot	Theodore Lyman, Jr.	B,C	US Hon. Sec. Gen.	Bilderberg Group; US Ambassador (Fmr.), Afghanistan
Erburu	Robert F.	C,T	Chair. & CEO (fmr.)	Times Mirror;Coun. Mbr., Brookings Inst.;Dir., CFR
Erkko	Aatos	BFIN,TE	Chairman	Sanoma Corp., Helsinki, Finland
Fabius	Laurent	BF,TE	Member	Parliament; fmr. Prime Min., fmr. Ch. Parl.
Feinstein	Dianne	B,T	Senator	California; Fgn. Oper., Judiciary, Rules & Admin.
Fischer	Stanley	B,T	1st Dep. Mng. Dir.	IMF
FitzGerald	Garret	BIRL,TE	Prime Minister (Fmr.)	Ireland; Member, Irish Dail
Ford	Gerald Rudolph, Jr.	B,C	President (fmr.)	United States
Fore	Henrietta Holsman	B,C	Sr. Associate	CSIS (Ctr. For Strategic & Int. Studies)
Forester	Lynn	B,C	CEO	Netwave Inc. (Communications)
Franklin	George S.	C,T	Director (fmr.)	CFR; (David Rockefeller's roommate at Harvard Univ.)
Fresco	Paolo	B,T	Chairman	Fiat S.p.A.
Fung	Victor K. K.	B,C	Chairman	Hong Kong Trade Development Council.
Gadiesh	Orit B.	B,C	Chairman	Bain & Company
Galvin	John Rogers	B,C	Supr. Ald. Cdr. (fmr.)	Defense Dept., SHAPE, Europe
Gardner	Richard Newton	C,T	US Ambassador (fmr.)	State Dept., Spain; Ambassador (fmr.) to Italy
Gelb	Leslie Howard	C,T	President	CFR; Columnist, New York Times
Gigot	Paul A.	B,C	Wash. Columnist	Wall Street Journal
Gilpatric	Roswell Leavitt	B,C	Counsel	Cravath, Swaine & Moore, N.Y.C.
Godsoe	Peter C.	BC,TC	Chairman & CEO	Bank of Nova Scotia
Goizueta	Roberto C.	C,T	Chairman & CEO	Coca-Cola; Dir., Eastman Kodak Co., Ford Motor Co.
Goldschmidt	Neil	C,T	Secretary (fmr.)	Transportation Dept.; Governor (fmr.), Oregon
Goodpaster	Andrew Jackson	B,C	Cmdr.-in-Chief (fmr.)	Def. Dept.; Superintendent (fmr.), US Military Academy
Gordon	Lincoln	B,C	Guest Scholar	Brookings Institute
Gorman	Joseph T.	C,T	Chairman & CEO	TRW Inc.; Director, Proctor & Gambel Co.
Gordon	Lincoln	B,C	Guest Scholar	Brookings Institute
Gorman	Joseph T.	C,T	Chair., Pres. & CEO	TRW Inc.; Director, Proctor & Gambel Co.
Gotlieb	Allen E.	BC,TC	Chairman	Trilateral Commission, Canada; Ambassador(fmr.)to US
Greenspan	Alan	C,T	Chairman	Fed.Res.Syst.,Bd./Gov.;TC mbr.(Fmr.);Dir.(Fmr.),CFR
Grunwald	Henry Anatole	B,C	Editor-in-Chief (fmr.)	Time, Inc.; US Ambassador (fmr.), to Austria
Gutfreund	John H.	C,T	Chair. & CEO (fmr.)	Solomon Bros. Inc.; Council Member, Brookings Inst.
Haas	Robert D.	C,T	Chairman & CEO	Levi Strauss & Co.; Council Mbr., Brookings Inst.
Haass	Richard	C,T	Member	Carnegie Endowment for Internsational Peace
Haig	Alexander Meigs, Jr.	C,T	Secretary (fmr.)	St. Dept.; Chairman & Pres., Worldwide Assoc., Inc.
Harmaia	Jukka	BFIN,TE	President & CEO	Enso-Gutzeit Oy
Hamalainen	Sirkka	BFIN,TE	Member	Euro. Cent. Bank, Chair., (fmr.) Bk./Finland, Helsinki
Harsch	Joseph C.	B,C	Commentator (fmr.)	NBC, Inc.; Christian Science Monitor
Hartman	Arthur A.	B,C	US Ambassador (fmr.)	St. Dept., U.S.S.R.;Bd.Mbr.,Center/Fgn. Pol. Devel.
Heck	Charles B.	C,T	Director	Trilateral Commission
Herter	Christian A., Jr.	B,C	Secretary (fmr.)	State Dept.
Hesburgh	Theodore Martin	B,C	President (Fmr.)	Univ. of Notre Dame; Director (Fmr.), CFR
Hewitt	William Alexander	B,C	Ambassador (Fmr.)	Jamaica
Hills	Carla Anderson	C,T	US Trade Rep. (fmr.)	Exec. Off./Bush Admin.; Trustee, Urban Inst.; Dir., CFR
Hoagland	Jimmie Lee	B,C	Associate Editor	Washington Post
Hoffmann	Stanley H.	B,C	Director, '83-92	CFR; Editorial Bd., Carnagie Endow.
Hormats	Robert D.	C,T	Vice Chairman	Goldman Sachs; Ast. Sec./St. (fmr.); Carnegie End.
Houghton	James R.	C,T	Chairman & CEO (fmr.)	Corning Inc.
Hughes	Thomas Lowe	C,T	President (fmr.)	Carnegie Endowment for Int. Peace, Ch., Mid-Atl. Club
Hunter	Robert E.	B,C	US Representative	to NATO
Hyland	William George	C,T	Distinguished Prof.	Georgetown Univ.; Editor (Fmr.), CFR, Foreign Affairs
Imbert	Claude	BF,TE	Editor-in-Chief	"Le Point", Paris
Ingersoll	Robert Stephen	C,T	Chairman	Panasonic Foundation
Inman	Bobby Ray	C,T	Vice Chairman	CFR; Dir., Xerox Corp.
Jakobson	Max	BFIN,TE	Ambassador (Fmr.)	to US; Consultant
Janssen	Baron Daniel E.	BB,TE	Chair., Exec. Comm.	Solvay & Co., Brussels
Jenkins	Sir Michael	BGB,TE	Vice Chairman	Dresdner Kleinwort Benson Group; (fmr.) British Amb.
Johnson	James A.	B,T	Chairman & CEO	Fannie Mae
Johnson	Wyatt Thomas, Jr.	C,T	President	CNN
Jones	James R.	C,T	US Ambassador	St. Dept., Mexico; Ch./CEO (fmr.), Amer. Stock Exch.
Jones	Thomas V.	C,T	Chairman (Fmr.)	Northrop Corp.
Kaiser	Karl	BD,TE	Director	Research Inst. of German Society for Foreign Affairs
Kann	Peter Robert	B,C	Chairman & CEO	Dow Jones & Co.;Pub.,Wall St. Jour.;wife/Karen House
Katz	Milton	B,C	Advisory Board Mbr.	Univ. of Cal., Consortium/Competition and Coop.
Kaysen	Carl	B,C	Professor (Fmr.)	MIT, Political Economy
Keohane	Nannerl Overholser	C,T	President	Duke Univ.; Director, IBM Corp.
Kearns	David T.	C,T	Dep. Sec. of Educ.	Education Dept.
Kendall	Donald M.	C,T	Chairman (Fmr.)	PepsiCo Inc.
Keohane	Nannerl Overholser	C,T	President	Duke Univ.; Director, IBM Corp.
Kiep	Walter Leisler	BD,TE	Treasurer	Christian Dem. Party; Member (Fmr.), German Parl.
Kimmitt	Robert Michael	B,C	Managing Director	Lehman Bros.; US Amb. (Fmr.), St. Dept., Germany
Kirkland	Joseph Lane	C,T	President (fmr.)	AFL-CIO Union ('79-'95);Dir. (fmr.), CFR; TC since '73
Kirkpatrick	Jeane Duane Jordan	C,T	Sr. Fellow	American Enterprise Inst.; US Ambassador (Fmr.), UN
Knoppers	Antoine T.	B,C	Sr. Vice Pres. (Fmr.)	Merck & Co., Inc.
Kohnstamm	Max	BI,TE	President (Fmr.)	European Univ. Institute, Florence
Kravis	Henry R.	B,C	Founding Partner	Kohlberg Kravis Roberts; Member, Brookings Institute

Last Names	First Names	Org.	Day Job	Affiliation - Agency, Company, Country
Kravis	Marie-Josee	B,T	Sr. Fellow	Hudson Institute
Kreps	Juanita M.	C,T	Secretary (Fmr.)	Commerce Dept.; Director (Fmr.), CFR
Labrecque	Thomas G.	C,T	President & COO	Chase Manhattan Bank; Mbr., Brookings Inst.
Lambsdorff	Count Otto	BD,TE	Partner	Wessing Beerenberg-Gossler
Lauk	Kurt	BD,TE	Board Member	DaimlerChrysler, Stuttgart
Leach	James Albert Smith	C,T	Congressman	Iowa, Int. Relations, Chair., Banking & Fin. Services
Leisler-Kiep	Walter	BD, TE	Treasurer	CDU Party; Mbr. (fmr.) German Bundestag
Lellouche	Pierre	BF,TE	Member	National Assembly, Paris
Levi	Arrigo	BI,TE	Political Columnist	"Corriere dela Sera", Rome
Levy	Walter James	B,C	Oil Consultant	John Hopkins Univ., Sch of Advanced Int. Studies
Levy-Lang	Andre	BF,TE	Chairman	Banque Paribas, Compagnie Financiere de Paribas, Paris
Lewis	Flora	C,T	Sr. Columnist	New York Times, Paris
Lewis	W. Walker	B,C	Exec. V. Pres. & Pres.	Avon Products
Liffers	William Albert	C,T	Vice Chairman	Cyanamid International
Lindsay	Franklin Anthony	B,C	Mbr. Exec. Committee	National Bureau of Economic Research
Linowitz	Sol Myron	C,T	Sr. Counsel	Coudert Brothers; Chairman (Fmr.), Xerox Int.
Lynn	James Thomas	C,T	Sr. Advisor	Lazard Freres & Co.
MacLaren	Roy	BC,TC	High Commissioner	for Canada in Britain
MacLaury	Bruce King	C,T	President	Brookings Institute
Martin	Edwin McCammon,Jr.	B,C	Member	Overseas Development Council
Mathias	Charles McC., Jr.	B,C	Senator (fmr.)	Maryland
Matlock	Jack Foust, Jr.	B,C	US Ambassador (fmr.)	State Dept., U.S.S.R.; Columbia Univ.
Maynes	Charles William	B,C	Editor	Foreign Policy magazine, Carnagie Endowment
Mazur	Jay	C,T	President	Union of Needletrades, Industrial and Textile Employees
McCloy	John J., II	B,C	Commander-in-Chief	Defense Dept., USAF, Headquarters, Euro. Command
McCracken	Paul Winston	B,C	Professor (Fmr.)	Univ. of Michigan
McDonough	William J.	B,C	President	Fed, New York
McGhee	George Crews	B,C	Oil Producer	McGhee Production Co.
McHenry	Donald F.	B,C	US Ambassador (fmr.)	UN; Mbr., Carnegie Endow.; Dir., Coca-Cola Co.
McLaughlin	David Thomas	B,C	President & CEO	Aspen Institute, Aspen, Colorado
Mello, de	Antonio Vasco	B,TE	Chairman	Sociedad de Reparacao e Montagem de Equip.Ind.,Lisbon
Mettler	Ruben F.	C,T	Chairman (Fmr.)	TRW, Inc.; Dir., Council on Foreign Relations, '86-'92
Mitterbauer	Peter	B,T	President	The Federation of Austrian Industry, Vienna
Montbrial, de	Thierry	BF,TE	Member	de l'Institut de France
Monti	Mario	BINT,TE	Member	European Commission, Brussels
Morse	F. Bradford	B,C	Under Secretary	United Nations
Murray	Allen E.	C,T	Chair., Pres. & CEO	Mobil Corp.
Newhouse	John	B,C	Dir. of Scholars	Brookings Institute
Nitze	Paul Hilken	B,C	Director (fmr.)	Fgn. Pol. Plng., Truman, Eisenhower & Nixon Admin.
Oksenberg	Michael	C,T	Sr. Fellow	Stanford Univ., Asia Pacific Research Ctr.
Olechowski	Andrzej	B,T	Chairman	Bank Handlowy W Warszawie
Owen	Henry David	C,T	Sr. Advisor	Salomon Bros.;Brookings Inst.; Bd. Mbr., Ctr./Int. Pol.
Owen	Lord	BGB,TE	Chairman	Middlesex Holdings
Parsky	Gerald Lawrence	C,T	Chairman	Aurora Capital Partners, L. A.
Pearce	William R.	C,T	Vice President	Cargill; Pres. & CEO, I.D.S. Mutual Fund Group
Perkins	James A.	B,C	Member	Overseas Development Council; Dir., CFR
Perry	William J.	B,T	Secretary (fmr.)	Defense Dept.; Prof., Stanford Univ.
Petersen	Howard C.	B,C	Advisor (Fmr.)	National Security Council
Peterson	Peter G.	C,T	Chairman	CFR, Blackstone Group; Prin., Concord Coal.
Peterson	Rudolph A.	B,C	Chair., Exec. Comm.	Bankamerica Corp., San Diego
Pickering	Thomas R.	B,C	US Ambassador	St. Dept., Russia, Moscow,'94; Ambassador (fmr.), UN
Piel	Gerald	B,C	Chairman (fmr.)	Scientific America, Inc.
Podhoretz	Norman	B,C	Editor-in-Chief	"Commentary "
Powell	Colin Luther	B,C	Chairman (fmr.)	Defense Dept., Joint Chiefs of Staff
Putnam	Robert D.	C,T	Director	Harvard U.; Chairman & CEO (fmr.), Levi Strauss & Co.
Quandt	William Bauer	B,C	Sr. Fellow	Brookings Institute
Raines	Franklin Delano	C,T	Chairman & CEO	Fed. Nat. Mortgage Assoc. (FNMA)
Rangel	Charles B.	C,T	Congressman	New York, Ways & Means/Ranking; Joint Taxation
Rattner	Steve Lawrence	B,C	Head Committee Gp.	Lazard Freres & Co., LLC
Raymond	Lee R.	C,T	Chairman & CEO	EXXON Corp.
Rice	Donald Blessing	C,T	President & COO	Teledyne, Inc.; Sec. (fmr.), Defense Dept., Air Force
Richardson	Elliot Lee	C,T	Partner	Milbank, Tweed, Hadley, & McCloy; Dir. (Fmr.), CFR
Richardson	William (Bill) Blaine	B,C	Secretary	Energy Dept.; US Ambassador (fmr.) to the UN
Rielly	John Edward	C,T	Executive Director	CFR, Chicago; Cargaige Endowment
Rippon of Hexham	Lord	BGB,TE	Chairman	Unichem & Dun & Bradstreet, London
Rivlin	Alice Mitchell	C,T	Vice Chairman	Rederal Reserve Board, Federal Reserve System
Robb	Charles Spittal	C,T	Senator	Virginia; Armed Services, Fgn. Rel., Intelligence
Rockefeller	John D. (Jay), IV	C,T	Senator	W. Virginia, Commerce, Fin., Veterans Affairs/Ranking
Rohatyn	Felix George	C,T	Senior Partner	Lazard Freres & Co.
Roll of Ipsden	Eric, Lord	BGB,TE	Sr. Advisor	SBC Warburg, London
Roosa	Robert V.	B,C	Director	Council on Foreign Relations, '66-'81
Rosovsky	Henry	C,T	Professor	Harvard Univ.
Rostow	Eugene Victor	B,C	Dist. Visit. Rsch. Prof.	National Defense Univ.
Roth	William Matson	C,T	Trustee	Center for Int. Policy; Center for Nat. Policy
Roth	William V., Jr.	C,T	Senator	Delaware, Banking, Finance, Housing & Urban Affairs
Ruckelshaus	William D.	C,T	Chairman & CEO	Brwng. Ferris;Adm.(fmr.)EPA;Dep.Gen.(fmr.),Jus. Dpt.
Ruggiero	Renato	BINT,TE	Dir. General	WTO/OMC; Ex.V.P.(fmr.),FIAT S.p.A., Int. Adv. Bd.

Last Names	First Names	Org.	Day Job	Affiliation - Agency, Company, Country
Ruhe	Volker	BD,TE	Minister of Defense	Gernamy; General Sec. (fmr.), Bundestag, CDU
Rusk	Dean	B,C	Secretary (fmr.)	St. Dept.; Adv. Bd. mbr., Ctr. for Int. Pol. Policy
Sawhill	John Crittenden	C,T	President & CEO	Nature Conservancy; Pres. (fmr.), New York Univ., NYC
Scalapino	Robert A.	B,C	Director, '82-89	CFR; Adv. Bd. Mbr., Ctr. for Nat. Pol.
Schacht	Henry Brewer	C,T	Chair. & CEO (fmr.)	Lucent Technologies; Chair., Carnegie Corp. of NY
Schaetzel	J. Robert	C,T	Member	Overseas Development Council
Schleimann	Jorgen	BDK,TE	Sr. Columnist	"Berlingske " Group of Newspapers, Ch., Euro. Mvmt.
Schmidt	Helmut	BD,TE	Chancellor (fmr.)	Germany; Co-Editor, "Die Zeit", Hamburg
Schmidt-Chiari	Guido	BI,TE	Chairman	Constantia Gp.; (fmr.) Ch., Creditanstalt Bankverein
Schmoke	Kurt L.	C,T	Mayor	Baltimore
Schroeder	Gerhard	BD,TE	Member (fmr.)	German Bundestag; Minister (fmr.) of Defence; CDU
Scranton	William W.	C,T	US Ambassador (fmr.)	United Nations, Geneva
Shalala	Donna E.	C,T	Secretary	H. H. S. Dept.; Member (fmr.), TC ; Director, CFR
Sheinkman	Jack	B,C	Chairman	Amalgamated Clothing & Textile Workers Union
Shipley	Walter Vincent	C,T	Chairman & CEO	Chase; Chr. & CEO (fmr.), Chemical Banking Corp.
Shulman	Marshall D.	B,C	Director	Council on Foreign Relations, '72-'77
Shultz	George Pratt	C,T	Honorary Fellow	Hoover Inst., Stanford U., Calif.; Sec. (Fmr.), St. Dept.
Silas	Cecil Jesse	C,T	Chair. & CEO)Fmr.)	Phillips Petroleum Company
Simonet	Henri	BINT,TE	Member	Belgian Senate
Sisco	Joseph John	C,T	Principal	Sisco Associates, Washington
Soderberg	Nancy E.	B,C	Deputy Asst. to Pres.	White House, National Security Affairs
Sohl	Hans-Gunther	BD,TE	Hon. President (fmr.)	Fed. Assoc./German Ind.;Dir.(fmr.), A.-Thyssen-Huette
Solbes Mira	Pedro	B,T	Member	Spanish Parl.; (fmr.) Min. of Fin. & Agriculture, Madrid
Sommer	Theo	BD,TE	Editor-in-Chief	"Die Zeit", Freie und Hansestadt HamburgGermany
Sonnenfeldt	Helmut	B,C	Guest Scholar	Brookings Inst.; Edit. Bd. Mbr., Carnagie Endow. mag.
Spencer	Edson W.	C,T	Trustee	Carnegie Endowment for International Peace
Spero	Joan Edelman	C,T	Under Secretary	State Dept., Econ. & Agric. Affairs; Member (Fmr.), TC
Starr	Stephen Frederick	C,T	Director	Rockefeller Bros. Found.; Adj. Fellow, Hudson Inst.
Steinberg	James B.	B,C	Director	State Dept., Policy Plannintg
Stephanopolos	George R.	B,C	Senior Advisor (fmr.)	to US President Clinton; Rhodes Scholor
Stern	Fritz Richard	C,T	Professor	Columbia Univ., History
Stern	Paula	C,T	Senior Fellow	Progressive Policy Inst., Pres., The Stern Group
Stevenson	Adlaii Ewing, III	B,C	Senator (Fmr.)	Illinois
Stockman	David Allen	C,T	General Partner	Blackstone Gp., NYC; Dir. (Fmr.), Of. of Mgt. & Budget
Stoltenberg	Gerhard	BD,TE	Member	German Bundestag; Minister (fmr.), Defence; CDU
Stoltenberg	Thorvald	BN,TE	Co-Chairman (UN)	Steering Comm. of the Int. Conf. on former Yugoslavia
Strauss	Robert Schwarz	C,T	US Ambassador (fmr.)	St. Dept., Russia;Pt., Akin, Gump Strauss,Hauer & Feld
Summers	Lawrence H.	B,C	Secretary	Treasury Dept.
Sutherland	Peter D.	BIRL,TE	Chair. & Mng. Dir.	Goldman Sachs, London;Dir.Gen.(fmr.),GATT & WTO
Svedberg	Bjorn	TE,BS	Chairman	Ericsson; (fmr.) Gp. CEO, Skandinaviska Enskilda Bank
Talbott	Strobe	C,T	Deputy Secretary	State Dept.; US Ambassador (fmr.), to Russia; Dir., CFR
Tarnoff	Peter	C,T	Under Secretary	State Dept.; President (fmr.) Council on Fgn. Relations
Taylor	Arthur Robert	C,T	President	Muhlenberg College, Allentown, Pennsylvania
Teltschik	Horst	BD,TE	Moard Member	BMW AG, Munich; Chancellor-Adviced (fmr.)
Thiessen	Marc A.	B,C	Aide	Senate, to Jesse Helms
Thoman	G. Richard	B,C	President & COO	Xerox Corp.
Tidemand	Otto Grieg	BN,TE	Shipowner	Oslo, Norway
Train	Russell Errol	C,T	Trustee	Rockefeller Br. Fnd.; Ch., World Wildlife Fund, Wash.
Trezise	Philip Harold	C,T	Sr. Fellow	Brookings Institute
Trowbridge	Louis V., Jr.	B,T	Chair. & CEO (Fmr.)	IBM; Chair. & CEO (Fmr.), RJR Nabisco Holding Corp.
Tung	Ko-Yung	C,T	Chairman	O'Melveny & Myers, Global Practice Group,
Tuthill	John Wills	B,C	US Ambassador (fmr.)	State Dept., EEC, Brazil
Vance	Cyrus Robert	C,T	President Partner	Simpson, Thacher & Barnett; Secretary (fmr.) St. Dept.
Vernon	Raymond	B,C	Visiting Prof. (Fmr.)	World Bank; Professor (Fmr.), Harvard Univ.
Vogel	Ezra F.	B,C	Professor	Harvard Univ.
Vuursteen	Karel	BNL,TE	Chairman/Exec. Bd.	Heineken N.V., Amsterdam
Warnke	Paul Culliton	C,T	Trustee	Center for Int. Policy; Council Mbr., Brookings Inst.
Watts	Glenn Ellis	C,T	President (fmr.)	Communications Workers of Amererica, Director, CFR
Weinberger	Casper Willard	C,T	Publisher	Forbes magazine; Secretary (Fmr.), Defense Dept.;
Wharton	Clifton R., Jr.	C,T	Deputy Secr. (fmr.)	State Dept.; Member (fmr.), TC; Director, CFR
Whitman	Christine Todd	B,C	Governor	New Jersey
Whitman	Marina v. N.	C,T	Director	Proctor/Gmbl.;Dist.Vis.Prof.,U./ Mich.;Dir.(fmr.),CFR
Wilbur	Brayton, Jr.	B,C	President	Wilbur-Ellis Co., San Franciscop; Dir., Safeway Stores
Wilson	L. R.	BC,TC	Chair., Pres. & CEO	BCE Inc., Montrial
Wisner	Frank G., II	B,C	US Ambassador (fmr.)	State Dept., Egypt
Wohlstetter	Albert J.	B,C	Writer	Wall Street Journal
Wolff von Amerongen	Otto	BD,TE	Chairman	E. Comm./the German Ind.; Ch. & CEO, Otto Wolff Ind.
Wolfensohn	James David	B,C	President	World Bank
Yost	Casimir A.	B,C	Hon. Sec. Gen.	Bilderberg; Dir., Gorbachev State of the World Adv. Bd.
Young	Andrew	C,T	US Ambassador (fmr.)	United Nations; Congressman (fmr.), Georgia
Zuckerman	Mortimer Benjamin	B,C	Chair. & Ed.-in-Chief	US News/World Reports,NY Daily News,Atlantic Monthly

Last Names	First Names	Org.	Day Job	Affiliation - Agency, Company, Country
Allaire	Paul Arthur	B,C,T	Ch.,CEO/Ch.,Ex.Com.	Xerox Corp.; Dir., Sara Lee Corp.; Dir., CFR
Allison	Graham Tillety, Jr.	B,C,T	Advisory Bd. Member	Center for National Policy; Director (Fmr.), CFR
Andreas	Dwayne Orville	B,C,T	Chairman & CEO	Archer Daniels Midland Co
Bartley	Robert Leroy	B,C,T	Editor	Wall Street Journal
Bergsten	C. Fred	B,C,T	Sr. Fellow	Brookings Institution
Bowie	Robert R.	B,C,T	Member	Overseas Development Council
Brademas	John	B,C,T	Congressman (fmr.)	New York; Dir., Texaco Inc.; Pres. (fmr.), NYU.
Brzezinski	Zbigniew	B,C,T	Counselor	Johns Hop.,Ctr./Strat. & Int. Stud.; Nat. Sec. Advis. (fmr.)
Chafee	John Hubbard	B,C,T	Senator	Rhode Island, Environ. & P.W./Chair., Fin., Sel. Intellig.
Clinton	William (Bill) J.	B,C,T	President	United States; Governor (Fmr.), Arkansas
Cooper	Richard Newell	B,C,T	Professor	Harvard U.; Dir.,CFR; Und. Sec. (Fmr.),St. Dept.,Econ. Afrs.
Corrigan	E. Gerald	B,C,T	Partner & Mng. Dir.	Goldman Sachs; Pres. (fmr.), Fed. Res. Bk., NY;Dir.,CFR
Davis	Lynn E.	B,C,T	Under Secretary	State Dept., International Security Affairs
Deutch	John Mark	B,C,T	Director (fmr.)	C.I.A.; Deputy Secretary (Fmr.) Defense Dept., for Acquis.
Feldstein	Martin S.	B,C,T	Pres. & CEO	National Bureau of Economic Research; Prof., Harvard U.
Friedman	Stephen James	B,C,T	Sr. Partner & Co-Ch.	Goldman Sachs & Co.
Friedman	Thomas L.	B,C,T	Columnist	New York Times
Foley	Thomas Stephen	B,C,T	Spkr. of House (fmr.)	House of Represenbtatives; Amb. to Japan
Friedman	Stephen James	B,C,T	Sr. Ch. & Ltd. Partner	Goldman Sachs & Co.
Friedman	Thomas L.	B,C,T	Fgn. Affrs. Columnist	New York Times
Gergen	David R.	B,C,T	Editor-at-Large	US News & World Report; Spec. Asst. to Pres. Clinton
Gerstner	Louis V., Jr.	B,C,T	Chairman & CEO	IBM Corp.
Graham	Katharine	B,C,T	Chair., Exec. Comm.	Washington Post, Exec. Comm.; Mbr., Brookings Inst.
Greenberg	Maurice R.	B,C,T	Deputy Chair. (fmr.)	Fed, New York; Ch. & CEO, Amer. Int. Gp., Inc.; Dir., CFR
Hamilton	Lee Herbert	B,C,T	Congressman	Indiana, Int. Relations/Ranking, Joint Economic
Hesburgh	Theodore Martin	B,C,T	President (fmr.)	Univ. of Notre Dame; Director (fmr.), CFR
Hewitt	William Alexander	B,C,T	Ambassador (fmr.)	Jamaica
Hoge	James Fulton, Jr.	B,C,T	Editor	Foreign Affairs magazine, Director (fmr.), CFR
Holbrooke	Richard C.	B,C,T	US Ambassador	U.N. Designate;V.Chair.,Credit Suissse First Boston Corp.
Jordan	Vernon Eulion, Jr.	B,C,T	Sr. Partner	Aikin, Gump, Strauss, Hauer & Feld; Dir., RJR Nabisco
Kissinger	Henry Alfred	B,C,T	Secretary (fmr.)	St. Dept., Nixon, Carter Admin.; Chair., Kissinger Assoc.
Lord	Winston	B,C,T	Asst. Secretary (fmr.)	St. Dept., East Asian & Pacific Affairs; Mbr. (fmr.) TC
Mathews	Jessica Tuchman	B,C,T	President	Carnagie End. for Int. Peace
McCracken	Paul Winston	B,C,T	Professor (fmr.)	Univ. of Michigan
McNamara	Robert Strange	B,C,T	President (Fmr.)	World Bank; Sec. of Def. (Fmr.); Member Brookings Inst.
Mondale	Walter Fritz	B,C,T	US Ambassador	State Dept., Japan
Nye	J. Benjamin H.	B,C,T	Exec. Secretary	Treasury Dept.
Nye	Joseph S., Jr.	B,C,T	Chairman	Nat. Intel. Council; Dean, Harvard Univ., School of Govt.
Ridgway	Rozanne Lejeanne	B,C,T	Co-Chairman	AtlanticCoun.;Amb.(fmr.),Germ.;Dir.,RJR Nab.,Sara Lee
Robinson	Charles W.	B,C,T	Member	Overseas Development Council, Brookings Institute
Rockefeller	David	B,C,T	Ch., Int. Advis. Com.	Chase Manhattan Bank; Hon. Chair., CFR; Chair., TC
Scowcroft	Brent	B,C,T	Asst. to Pres. (fmr.)	National Security Council; Director (fmr.), CFR
Sonnenfeldt	Helmut	B,C,T	Guest Scholar	Brookings Inst.; Edit. Bd. Mbr., Carnegie Endow. mag.
Soros	George	B,C,T	President	Soros Fund Mgt.; Fdr.& Chair., Open Society Institute
Tyson	Laura D'Andrea	B,C,T	Chairwoman (fmr.)	Council of Economic Advisors; Prof., Harvard Univ.
Volcker	Paul Adolph	B,C,T	Chairman (fmr.)	Fed.Res.Sys.;Mbr.,Brkgs. Inst.,Dir.,Concord Coal.,CFR
Whitehead	John Cunningham	B,C,T	Chairman	Brookings Institute; Chairman, AEA Investors Inc., NYC
Wolfowitz	Paul Dean	B,C,T	Dean	Johns Hopkins Univ., Sch of Advanced Int. Studies
Zoellick	Robert Bruce	B,C,T	Pres. & CEO	Ctr. For Strategic & Int. Studies
Zuckerman	Mortimer Benjamin	B,C,T	Chr. & Edit.-in-Chief	US News/World Reports,NY Daily News,Atlantic Monthly

Members and Attendees of the
Bilderberg Conferences
in the
Past and Present

Bilderberg Officers and Committee Members

Source: "THE SPOTLIGHT" Reprint, Sept. 1991, On The Bilderbergers, Irresponsible Power, and the 1975, 1991 through 1999 issues of "THE SPOTLIGHT", published by

Liberty Lobby, Inc., 300 Independence Ave, SE, Wash., DC 20003 + very special efforts by Klaus Kopf

Years of Attendance Documented

Last Name	1st & Middle Names	Country of Job	Office, Post or Affiliation	54	55	56	57	58	59	60	62	63	64	66	67	68	71	74	75	91	93	94	95	96	97	98	99
Armgard	HRH Prince Bernhard	Neatherlands	Chairman (Fmr.)	x	x	x	x	x	x	x	x	x	x	x	x	x	x	x	x			x	x	x	x	x	x
Carrington	Lord Peter	U.K.	Chairman																			x	x	x	x	x	x
Davignon	Viconte Etienne	Belgium	Honorary Chairman								x							x				x	x	x	x	x	x
Coleman	John S.	U.S.	Chairman (Fmr.)		x	x																					
Roll of Ipaden	Sir Eric	U.K.	Chairman (Fmr.)															x	x			x	x	x	x	x	x
Zeeland	Viscounte Paul, van	Belgium	Vice President	x	x	x	x	x																			
Retinger	Dr. Joseph Hieronim	Poland	Honorary Secretary General for Europe	x	x	x	x	x	x																		
Beugel	Ernst H., van der	Netherlands	Honorary Secretary General for Europe											x	x	x	x	x	x			x	x	x	x	x	x
Halberstadt	Victor	Netherlands	Honorary Sec. Gen. for Europe & Canada																			x	x	x	x	x	x
Lamping	Arnold T.	Netherlands	Deputy Secretary General for Europe	x	x																						
Johnson	Joseph E.	U.S.	Honorary Secretary General for U.S.							x	x	x	x	x	x	x	x										
Eliot	Theodore L., Jr.	U.S.	Honorary Secretary General for U.S.														x										
Yost	Casimir A.	U.S.	Honorary Secretary General for U.S.																			x	x	x	x	x	x
Rykens	Paul	Netherlands	Honorary Treasurer								x	x															
Meynen	Johannes	Netherlands	Honorary Treasurer										x	x	x	x											
Karsten	Christian F.	Netherlands	Honorary Treasurer												x	x		x	x								
Oort	Conrad J.	Netherlands	Honorary Treasurer														x			x							
Heinz	Henry John, II	U.S.	Advisory Committee Member	x	x	x	x	x	x	x	x	x	x	x	x	x											
Mueller	Dr. Rudolph	Germany	Advisory Committee Member	x	x	x	x	x	x	x	x	x	x	x													
Nebolsine	George	Italy	Advisory Committee Member	x	x	x	x	x	x	x	x	x															
Quaroni	Pietro	Italy	Advisory Committee Member					x	x	x	x		x														
Rijkens	Paul	Netherlands	Advisory Committee Member	x	x	x	x	x	x	x	x																
Dean	Arthur Hudson	U.S.	Co-Chair, Steering Committee	x	x	x	x	x	x	x	x	x	x	x	x	x	x	x	x								
Heinz	Henry John, II	U.S.	Co-Chair, Steering Committee	x	x	x	x	x	x	x	x	x	x	x	x	x	x	x	x								
Rusk	Dean	U.S.	Co-Chair, Steering Committee			x	x	x	x	x	x	x	x	x	x	x											
Smith	Gen. Walter Bedell	U.S.	Co-Chair, Steering Committee (CIA Director, f			x	x																				
Agnelli	Giovanni	Italy	Steering Committee Member					x	x	x	x	x	x	x	x	x	x	x	x	x	x	x	x	x	x	x	x
Airey	Sir Terence	U.K.	Steering Committee Member	x	x																						
Amerongen	Otto Wolff, von	Germany	Steering Committee Member							x	x	x	x	x	x	x	x	x	x	x	x	x	x	x	x	x	x
Arliotis	Charles C.	Greece	Steering Committee Member												x	x											
Ball	George W.	U.S.	Steering Committee Member	x	x		x	x	x	x	x	x	x	x	x	x	x	x	x								
Baumgartner	Wilfred S.	France	Steering Committee Member				x	x	x	x	x	x	x	x													
Bennett	Sir Frederic	U.K.	Steering Committee Member						x	x	x	x	x	x	x	x	x	x	x		x						
Birgi	Muharrem Nuri	Turkey	Steering Committee Member				x	x	x	x	x	x	x	x	x	x											
Boveri	Walter E.	Switzerland	Steering Committee Member						x	x	x	x	x	x	x	x	x										
Cavendish-Bentnick	Victor	U.K.	Steering Committee Member	x	x	x	x																				
Christiansen	Hakon	Denmark	Steering Committee Member			x	x	x	x	x	x	x	x	x	x	x	x	x									
Collado	Emelio Gabriel	U.S.	Steering Committee Member							x	x	x	x	x	x	x	x										
Cowles	Gardner	U.S.	Steering Committee Member				x	x	x	x	x	x	x	x	x		x										
Duncan	James S.	Canada	Steering Committee Member						x	x	x	x	x														
Erler	Fritz	Germany	Steering Committee Member					x	x	x	x	x	x														
Fanfani	M. Amintore	Italy	Steering Committee Member											x	x												
Ferguson	John Henry	U.S.	Steering Committee Member	x	x	x	x	x																			
Hauge	Gabriel	U.S.	Steering Committee Member										x	x	x	x	x	x									
Hauge	Jens Christian	Norway	Steering Committee Member												x	x											
Hoegh	Leif	Norway	Steering Committee Member	x	x											x		x									
Jackson	Charles D.	U.S.	Steering Committee Member	x	x	x	x	x	x	x	x	x	x														
Kleffens	Eelco N., van	E.C.S.C.	Steering Committee Member	x	x				x	x	x	x	x														
Maudling	Reginald	U.K.	Steering Committee Member							x	x	x	x	x													
Mueller	Dr. Rudolf	Germany	Steering Committee Member	x	x	x	x	x	x	x	x	x	x	x													

179

Who's Who of the Elite

Last Name	1st & Middle Names	Country of Job	Office, Post or Affiliation	54	55	56	57	58	59	60	62	63	64	66	67	68	71	74	75	91	93	94	95	96	97	98	99
Murphy	Robert Daniel	U.S.	Steering Committee Member	x	x	x	x	x	x	x	x	x	x	x	x	x											
Nebolsine	George	U.S.	Steering Committee Member	x	x	x	x	x	x	x	x	x	x	x	x												
Quaroni	Pietro	Italy	Steering Committee Member	x	x	x	x	x	x	x	x	x	x	x													
Rockefeller	David	U.S.	Steering Committee Member	x	x	x	x	x	x	x	x	x	x	x	x	x	x	x	x	x	x	x	x	x	x	x	x
Rykens	Paul	Netherlands	Steering Committee Member	x	x	x	x	x	x	x	x	x	x														
Sarmento Rodrigues	Manuel M.	Portugal	Steering Committee Member	x	x	x	x	x	x	x	x	x	x														
Schmid	Professor Carlo	Germany	Steering Committee Member				x	x	x	x	x	x	x														
Snoy et d'Oppuers	Baron	Belgium	Steering Committee Member			x	x	x	x	x	x	x	x	x	x	x	x	x	x								
Stone	Shepard	U.S.	Steering Committee Member							x	x	x	x	x	x	x		x	x								
Taverne	Dick	U.K.	Steering Committee Member										x	x	x	x		x	x								
Terkelsen	Terkel M.	Denmark	Steering Committee Member	x	x	x	x	x	x	x	x	x	x	x	x	x		x									
Valletta	Vittorio	Italy	Steering Committee Member	x	x	x	x	x	x	x	x	x	x														
Wallenberg	Marcus	Sweden	Steering Committee Member				x	x	x	x	x	x	x	x	x	x							x	x			
Zellerback	James David	U.S.	Steering Committee Member	x	x		x	x	x	x	x	x	x	x	x												

Last Name	1st & Middle Names	Country of Job	Office, Post or Affiliation	54	55	56	57	58	59	60	62	63	64	66	67	68	71	74	75	91	93	94	95	96	97	98	99
Australia																											
Officer	Sir Keith					x																					
Austria																											
Androsch	Hannes	Minister	Finance															x									
Czernetz	Karl								x	x		x														
Dalma	Alfos	Editor-in-Chief	ORF. Austrian Radio & TV															x	x	x							
Igler	Hans	President	Confederation of Austrian Industrialist																		x						
Jankowitsch	Peter	Minister of State	European Integration & Dev. Cooper.										x								x						
Karner	Dietrich	Chairman of Mng. Bd.	Erste Allgemeine-Gen. Aktiengesellschaf																			x	x	x	x	x	
Kothbauer	Max	Deputy Chairman	Creditanstalt-Bankverein																					x	x		
Lendavi	Paul															x										
Maculan	Alexander R.	Chairman	Maculan Holding AG																				x		x		
Mitterbauer	Peter	Chairman	Miba AG																								x
Molden	Dr. Fritz P.	Chief Editor	"Die Presse"			x			x		x			x													
Portish	Hugo																								x		
Puhringer	Othmar	Chairman	VA-Technologie AG																						x	x	
Randa	Gerhard	Chairman & CEO	Bank of Austria AG																		x					x	
Schenz	Richard	Chairman & CEO	OMV AG																							x	
Schmidt-Chiari	Guido	Chairman of Mng. Bd.	Creditanstalt Bankverein									x															
Scholten	Rudolf	Member Bd. Of Exec. Dir.																									
Thurn	Max Graf										x			x												
Vranitzky	Franz	Federal Chancellor (fmr:	Oesterreichische Kontrollbank															x	x				x	x	x	x	x
Withalm	Hermann														x											
Zimmer-Lehmann	Georg													x												
Zimmermann	Norbert	Chairman	Berndorf AG																	x			x	x	x	x	x
Belgium																											
Ansiaux	Hubert									x	x			x	x												
Bauwens	Mascell															x											
Becu	Omer L.	President	Int. Confed. of Free Trade Unions	x	x			x					x														
Boel	Baron Renne									x																	
Bonvoisin	Baron Pierre	President	Banque de la Soc. Gen. de Belgique	x	x			x		x	x		x			x											
Cadieux	Jean-Louis	Deputy Director Gen.	Foreign Affairs, E.E.C.						x	x	x		x							x							
Camu	Louis	Chairman	Banque de Bruxelles					x	x	x	x		x														
Claes	Willy	Minister	Foreign Affairs					x			x											x	x				
Cool	Pierre-August								x		x															
Davignon	Viconte Etienne	Executive Chairman	Societe Generale de Belgique											x				x		x		x	x	x	x	x	x
De La Vallee Poussin	Etienne	Senator			x	x		x																			
Dehousse	Fernand	Senator	Ch. European Comm./Saar Referendum		x			x						x						x					x		
Donnea	Francois X.	Minister (fmr.)	Defense															x									
Drapier	Jean	Lawyer			x	x		x		x	x		x														
Fayat	Henri	Minister						x		x	x		x														
Goossens	John J.	Pres. & CEO	Belgacom																					x			
Guillaume	Baron Jules					x		x		x																	

Last Name	1st & Middle Names	Country of Job	Office, Post or Affiliation	54	55	56	57	58	59	60	62	63	64	66	67	68	71	74	75	91	93	94	95	96	97	98	99
Houthuys	Jozef	President	C.S.P. Belgique; VP C.M.T.																						x		
Huyghebaert	Jan	Chairman	Almanj-Krediet-bank Group																			x		x	x	x	x
Janssen	Daniel E.	Dir., Dep. Gen Mgr.	U.C.B., S.A.																				x		x	x	
Kerchove d'Ousselghem	Nicholas W., de	Assistant	"Ecole des Sciences politiques et sociales																								
Lambert	Baron Leon	Chairman	Comp. Bruxelles Lamberet p. la Fin. et l'l					x											x								
Larock	Victor	Member	Parliament; fmr. Min., Foreign Affairs						x						x												
Lefevre	Theo																										
Martens	Wilfried	Prime Minister																									
Maystadt	Philippe	Vice Prime Minister	Minister of Finance & Fgn. Trade																	x							
Motz	Roger	Senator	Fmr. Chair., Liberal Party; fmr. Min.																					x			
Philippe	H.R.H.	Prince																						x			
Ryckmans	Pierre				x																					
Segers	Paul W.	Minister	Transport						x		x																
Simonet	Henri	Vice President	Comm. of the European Communities										x		x												
Snoy et d'Oppuers	Baron	Managing Director	"Comp. d'Outremer pour l'Ind. et la Fin."				x	x	x	x	x	x	x			x		x	x								
Solvay	Jacques																	x	x								
Spaak	Paul Henri																										
Spitaels	Guy	Chairman	Socialist Pt'y., Minister of State									x															
Vallee Poussin, de la	Etienne									x			x							x							
Vits	Mia de	Gen. Secretary	ABVV-FGTB				x	x			x			x													
Willems	Jean		"Fondation Universitaire"				x	x	x	x	x	x	x														
Zeeland	Viscoute Paul, van	Member	Parl., Fmr. Prime Min.; V. P., BB Conf.				x	x	x	x	x	x	x														
Bulgaria																											
Kamov	Nikolai	Member	Parliament																						x		
Canada																											
Aird	John B.	Sr. Partner	Aird, Zimmerman & Berlis															x									
Allard	J. V.																										
Amiel	Barbara	Columnist	Maclean's weekly newsmagazine																				x				
Axworthy	Lloyd	Minister	for Foreign Affairs												x												
Bassett	Isabel	Parl. Asst.	to Min. of Finance, Gvt./Ontario																			x					
Bassett	John W. H.								x																		
Beaton	Leonard										x	x	x			x											
Belanger	Michael															x	x									
Black	Conrad M.	Chairman	Telegraph Group Limited								x	x	x									x	x	x	x	x	x
Bruce	Fraser W.	President	Northern Aluminium Ltd.						x	x			x														
Cadieux	Marcell												x														
Chastelain	John A.D. de	Chairman	Ind. Int. Com. on Decommissioning																						x		
Chevier	Lionel	Member	Parliament; fmr. Min. of Transport					x																			
Chretien	Jean	Prime Minister	Canada																					x		x	
Chretien	Raymond A.J.	Ambassador	to the US																						x		
Coldwell	M. J.																										
Courtis	Kenneth	1st Vice-President	Deutsche Bank Group																			x		x			
Cross	Devon G.	Head	Donner Canadian Foundation																		x					x	
Davidson	Ian D.											x															
Delorme	Jean-Claude	Chairman	Caisse de depot et plqacement du Quibec																x								

Who's Who of the Elite

182

Last Name	1st & Middle Names	Country of Job	Office, Post or Affiliation	54	55	56	57	58	59	60	62	63	64	66	67	68	71	74	75	91	93	94	95	96	97	98	99
Deutsch	John H.	Professor	Queens Univ., Economics											x						x							
Dion	Stephane	Minister	Intergovt. Affairs																							x	
Dodge	William									x																	
Drouin	Marie-Josee	Executive Director	Hudson Institute of Canada											x				x	x								
Duncan	James S.	Chairman	Hydro-electric Power Commission, Ontar								x	x	x	x													
Dunton	A. Davidson													x													
Dupuy	Michael	Asst. Undersecretary	State, External Affairs					x	x	x	x			x													
Dupuy	Peirre	Ambassador	to France		x																						
Eaton	Frederik S.	Chair., Exec. Comm.	Eatons of Canada											x											x		
Eayrs	James												x														
Faribault	Marcel													x													
Fleming	Donald M.	Minister	Finance					x					x	x									x				
Flood	A. L.	Chairman	Canadian Imperial Bk. of Commerce							x				x									x				
Foulks	Charles																								x		
Frum	David	Polit. Commentator										x		x													
Gibson	J. Douglas																										
Godsoe	Peter C.	Chairman & CEO	Bank of Nova Scotia										x								x						
Gordon	Duncan L.	Partner	Clarkson Gordon & Co.					x	x	x				x				x									
Gordon	Walter L.	Mgt. Consultant						x	x	x	x	x	x	x													
Gotlieb	Allan E.	frm. Ambassador	to United States								x	x	x	x	x	x	x					x	x				
Griffin	Anthony G. S.	Chairman	Home Oil Compant Ltd.								x	x	x		x	x	x						x				
Harris	Mishael	Premier	Ontario																								
Heeney	Arnold D.P.	fmr. Ambassador	to US; Ch. Int. Jt. Comm., Water Resour				x				x	x	x		x												
Herrndorf	Peter A.	Chair. & CEO (fmr.)	TV Ontario												x							x				x	
Holmes	John W.										x					x											
Klein	Ralph P.	Premier	Alberta												x							x					
Lambert	Allen T.																										
Lamontagne	Maurice	President	Queen's Privy Council for Canada										x		x												
Leger	Jules																										
Lesage	Jean																										
MacDonald	William A.	Partner	McMillan, Binch															x			x						
MacLaren	Roy	High Commissioner	for Canada in Britain																			x		x		x	
MacMillan	Margaret O.	Editor	International Journal, CIIA																						x	x	
Manning	Preston	Leader	Reform Party																								
Marchand	Jean																										
Martin	Paul	Minister	Finance				x				x	x	x		x							x					
McDougall	Barbara	Minister	External Affairs																		x						
McKenna	Frank	Premier	New Brunswick																		x	x					
McKinnon	Neil													x													
McLean	William F.														x		x										
Michener	Roland																										
Molson	Hartland de M.																	x								
Morris	Joseph	President	Canadian Labour Congress																								
Munroe-Blum	Heather	Vice President	Univ. of Toronto, Res. & Int. Rel.																						x		
Mustard	J. Fraser	President	Canadian Institute for Advanced Research																			x					
Ostry	Sylvia	Chairman	Univ. of Toronto, Ctr. for Int. Studies													x								x			
Parizeau	Jacques																										

Who's Who of the Elite

Last Name	1st & Middle Names	Country of Job	Office, Post or Affiliation	54	55	56	57	58	59	60	62	63	64	66	67	68	71	74	75	91	93	94	95	96	97	98	99
Pearson	Lester B.	Prime Minister									x		x		x	x											
Polanyi	John	Professor	Univ. of Toronto, chemistry															x									
Prichard	J. Robert	President	University of Toronto																				x				
Rasminsky	Louis																									
Ritchie	Ronald S.																									
Robertson	Norman A.	High Commissioner	London	x								x		x		x											
Rogers	Edward S.	President & CEO	Rogers Communications Inc.																					x			
Ronning	Chester A.			x									x		x												
Ryan	Claude																									
Sabia	Maureen	President & Dir.	Maureen Sabia Int.												x										x		
Sauve	Mrs. Jeanne	Minister of State	Science & Technology										x				x										
Sauve	Maurice																										
Stanfield	Robert L.																										
Stone	Thomas	Ambassador	To The Netherlands	x			x							x													
Thornbrough	Albert A.																										
Thorsell	William	Editor	"The Globe & Mail"																			x					
White	Peter G.	Chairman	Unimedia, fmr. Head of Prime Min.'s Offic																			x	x				
Wilgress	L. Dana			x					x	x	x	x															
Wilson	L. R.	Chair, Pres. & CEO	BCE Inc.						x	x	x		x														
Wilson	Michaiel	Minister	Industry, Science & Tech. & Int. Trade																		x						
Winters	Robert H.	Industrialist							x	x	x		x				x										
Czech Republic																											
Kovanda	Karel	Hd. of Mission	Czech Rep. to NATO & WEU																							x	
Zantovsky	Michael	Chairman	Czech Senate, Comm. On Fgn. Affairs, Defense & Security																								x
Denmark																											
Andersen	Bodil Nyboe	Governor	Central Bank of Denmark				x		x																		
Andersen	K. B. M.P.	fmr. Minister	Foreign Affairs														x										
Axel	H.R.H.	Prince				x			x																		
Bjerregaard	Ritt	Commissioner	European Communities																			x					
Christiansen	Hakon	Managing Director	East-Asiatic Company Ltd.			x			x	x																	
Deleuran	Aage	Editoe-in-Chief	"Berlingske Tidende"				x		x	x																	
Djerregaard	Ritt	Member	Parliament, Labor Party; Ch., Labour Gp.									x															
Ellemann-Jensen	Uffe	Chairman	Liberal Party; Mbr., Parliament										x					x									
Haekkerup	Per	Minister	Foreign Affairs									x	x		x	x											
Knudtzon	Harold	General Manager	"Den Danske Landmandas Bank"	x	x																						
Kraft	Ole Bjorn	Member	Parliament, Fmr. Foreign Minister	x	x	x	x		x	x	x	x	x														
Krag	Jens Otto	Minister	Foreign Trade, Foreign Afdfairs	x	x	x	x		x	x	x	x	x							x							
Kristensen	Thorkil	Member	Parliament, Fmr. Min. of Finance			x	x		x	x	x																
Lykketoft	Mogens	Minister	of Finance																								x
Matthiasen	Neils																										
Neilsen	Einar	Deputy Chairman	Danish Trade Unions					x																			
Norgaard	Ivar												x														
Schleiman	Jorgen	Commentator	Foreign Relations, Danish Radio												x												
Seidenfaden	Toger	Editor-in-Chief	Politiken A/S																						x	x	x
Sorensen	Svend O.	Managing Director	Den Danske Landemandsvank														x							x	x	x	x

Last Name	1st & Middle Names	Country of Job	Office, Post or Affiliation	54	55	56	57	58	59	60	62	63	64	66	67	68	71	74	75	91	93	94	95	96	97	98	99
Terkelsen	Terkel M.	Editor-in-Chief	"Derlingske Tidende"	x	x	x	x											x	x								
Thygesen	J. V.	President	Export Credit Council																x								
Wilhielm	Nils	President	Ind. Mortgage Fund; fmr. Min. of Industry										x														
Finland																											
Ahlstrom	Krister	President & CEO	Ahlstrom Group																			x					
Aho	Esko	Prime Minister	Republic of Finland																			x					
Ahtisaari	Martti	President	Republic of Finland																			x	x	x	x		
Ehrnrooth	Georg	President & CEO	Metra Corp.																		x						
Erkko	Aatos	Publisher	"Helsingin Sanomat"															x									
Hamalainen	Sirkka	Chairman	Bank of Finland																			x					
Harmaia	Jukka	President & CEO	Enso-Gutzeit Oy																				x				
Ihamuotila	Jaako	Chairman & CEO	Neste Corp.																			x	x	x	x		
Iloniemi	Jaakko	Managing Editor	"Centre/Finnish Bus. & Policy Stud."																x					x	x		
Jakobson	Max	Gen. Manager	Council of Economic Organizations																			x					
Jarimo-Lehtinen	Mirja	Organizer	1994 BB Conference																			x					
Kohler	Jarl	President	Finnish Forest Industries Federation																			x					
Lipponen	Paavo	Prime Minister	Finland																				x				
Mattsson	Bjorn	President & CEO	Cultor Ltd.																						x		
Niinisto	Sauli V.	Minister	of Finance																								
Nykopp	Johan	fmr. Ambassador	President, Tampella										x	x	x									x	x	x	
Ollila	Jorma	Chairman & CEO	Nokia Corp.												x									x	x	x	
Rossi	Reino	Managing Director	Finska Socker														x										
Tuomioja	Sakari S.	Chairman	Bank of Finland					x		x																	
Vanhala	Matti	Chairman	Bank of Finland							x												x					
Virkkunen	Janne	Sr. Editor-in-Chief	Helsingin Sanomat																						x		
Vartia	Pentti	Mng. Director	Research Inst. Of the Finnish Economy (ETLA)								x														x		
Voutilainen	Pertti	President	Merita Bank Ltd.																			x					
Wendt	Gerhard M. H.	President	Kone Corp.																		x						
France																											
Aaron	Raymond	Professor	Sorbonne, Political Writer						x	x					x												
Alphand	Herve	fmr. Secretary Gen.	Foreign Office						x	x								x									
Andre	Robert	President	Syndicat du Petrole			x	x																				
Attali	Jacques	Professor	Ecole Polytechnique, Economics																	x							
Baumel	Jacques	Senator, Sec. Gen.	"Union pour la Nouvelle Republique"						x	x				x	x	x											
Baumgartner	Wilfred S.	Governor	Banque de France; fmr. Min., Finance			x	x	x	x	x		x	x	x	x	x											
Beaumont	Guerin, de	Member	Parliament			x	x					x															
Bebear	Claud	Chairman & CEO	AXA Group																				x				
Boucher	Eric Le	Chief Editor	International, Le Monde																								x
Bourbon Busset	Comte, de	President							x	x				x	x												
Brutelle	Georges								x	x				x	x												
Casanova	Jean C.													x													
Catroux	Diomede	Vice President	European Centre for Int. Trade				x											x									
Cavasse	Felicia	Organizer	1992 Bilderbern Conference																		x						
Chalandon	Albin	Fmr. Minister	Member, Parliament													x		x									
Clement-Cuzin	Rene	Chairman	Assoc. Metroploe-Cutremere; fmr. Min.	x									x														

Last Name	1st & Middle Names	Country of Job	Office, Post or Affiliation	54	55	56	57	58	59	60	62	63	64	66	67	68	71	74	75	91	93	94	95	96	97	98	99
Collom	Bretrand	Chairman & CEO	Lafarge Coppee																						x	x	x
Commin	Pierre								x																	
Coutinho	Vasco Pereira	Chairman	IPC Holding				x																			x	
Croisillier	Francois																								x		
Defferre	Gaston	Mayor	Marseille; Deputy Nat Assemble								x	x	x														
Dreyfus	Pierre										x																
Duchet	Roger	Member	Parliament	x	x				x	x	x	x															
Duhaml	Jacques														x											
'Estaing	Valery Gisard, de	President (fmr.)																									
Fabius	Laurent	Member	Parliament; fmr. Prime Min., fmr. Ch Pa												x							x					
Faure	Edgar	President	National Assembly												x		x					x					
Faure	Madame Lucie	Member	Parliament, fmr. Minister					x									x										
Faure	Maurice	Member	Parliament						x	x	x	x	x	x			x										
Fontaine	Andre	Editor-in-Chief	"Le Monde"														x										
Fouchier	Jacques, de																									
Gallois	Pierre M.	General (Retired)	Industrialist, Specialist in Nuclear Proble					x							x												
Garde	Jean, Da La						x							x												
Georges-Picot	Jacques																									
Gergorin	Jean-Louis	Bd Member	Matra Hachette								x													x	x		
Guetta	Bernard	Editor-in-Chief	Le Nouvel Observateur																						x		
Guichard	Baron Olivier																									
Guindey	Guillaume	President	Comp. Int. des Wagons-Lits et du Tour.								x	x		x			x										
Hague	William	Leader	Conservative Party								x																
Hartung	Henri														x	x										
Herzog	Maurice	fmr. Secretary	State; Mayor, Chamonix											x			x										
Huvelin	Paul																									
Imbert	Claude	Chief Editor	"Le Point"																	x		x					
Jaffre	Philippe	Chairman & CEO	Elf Aquitaine																		x	x					
Jongh	E. L. Tanugi, de											x														
Jospin	Lionel	1st Secretary	Socialist Party, Fmr. Minister d'Etat																				x				
La Malene	Christian, de	Member	Parliament, Mbr. European Parliament																x								
Lacharriere	Marc Ladreit, de	Chairman	Fimalac																	x							
Lagarde	Comte Jean Vyau, de	Ambassade	to Mexico									x															
Lecanuet	Jean								x																	
Lellouche	Pierre	Fgn. Affrs. Spokesman	Rassemblement pour la Republique																					x			
Leprince-Ringuet	Louis	President	Org. Francise du Mouvement Europeen						x		x						x										
Letourneau	Jean																									
Levy-Lang	Andre	Chair., Bd. of Mgt.	Banque Paribas; Ch., Comp. Fin. de Parit								x									x				x			
Lipkowski	Jean, de	Member	Parliament, Mbr. European Parliament									x											x	x			
Marjolin	Andre								x		x	x	x													
Marjolin	Robert E.			x					x																	
Massigli	Rene	Sec. General (fmr.)	O.E.E.C								x	x															
Maurois	Andre								x		x	x	x													
Mendes-France	Pierre										x				x											
Mestrallet	Gerard	Chair./Exec. Bd. & CEO	Suez Lyonnaise des Eaux																							x	
Moisi	Dominique	Deputy Dir.	IFRI																							x	
Mollet	Guy	Secretary General	Socialist Party, Deputy Prime Min.	x	x																					x	x

Last Name	1st & Middle Names	Country of Job	Office, Post or Affiliation	54	55	56	57	58	59	60	62	63	64	66	67	68	71	74	75	91	93	94	95	96	97	98	99
Monnet	Jean	President	Action Comm., United States of Europe						x																		
Montbrial	Thierry, de	Director	French Inst. of Int. Rel.; Prof., Ecole Po															x	x				x	x	x	x	
Morali	Veronique	Organizer	1992 BB Conference																x								
Morisot	Georges	President	La Libre Entreprise				x		x	x																	
Noir	Michael	Mayor	Lyon; fmr. Secretary of State, Fgn. Trade															x		x							
Pattrat	Antoine	Cief de Cabinet	Foreign Ministry	x							x	x															
Piette	Jaques	Economist, Member	Parliament	x					x	x	x	x	x														
Pinay	Antoine	Minister	Finance, Fmr. Prime Minister	x	x	x			x	x	x	x	x	x	x												
Pleven	Rene													x	x												
Pompidou	Georges	Banker																									
Raimond	Jean-Bernard	Member	Parliament; fmr. Minister of Fgn. Affairs																		x						
Rothschild	Baron Edmond de	Banker														x	x	x									
Roux	Ambroise	Banker																						x			
Roy	Olivier	Professor	Laboratoire Monde Iranien, CNRS											x													
Rueff	Jacques	Chairman	Groupe Express						x	x	x	x	x														
Sampermans	Francoise	Chairman																					x				
Segard	Jacques																		x								
Stoleru	Lionel	Economic Counselor	Presidency of the Republic			x																					
Teitgen	Pierre-Henri	Vice President	Council of Ministers						x	x					x								x				
Trichet	Jean-Claud	Governor	Banque de France																							x	
Tron	Ludovic	Professor																									
Uri	Pierre E.	Professor	Paris IX, Mbr, French Econ. & Soc. Cou						x		x	x		x		x		x									
Villiers	Georges	President	"La Federation"																								
Voisin	Andre			x					x		x	x															
Yrissou	Henri	Chairman								x																	
Germany.																											
Abs	Herman J.	Chairman (fmr.)	Deutsche Bank AG, Frankfurt am Main				x	x	x	x	x	x	x	x	x	x	x	x	x	x	x	x	x	x	x	x	x
Amerongen	Otto Wolf, von	Chairman & CEO (fmr.)	East Committee of the German Industry		x	x	x	x	x	x	x	x	x	x	x	x	x	x	x	x	x	x	x	x	x	x	x
Bahr	Egon Karlheinz	Director	IFS Hamburg; Fed. Min./special tasks; SF													x						x					
Barzel	Rainer	Member (fmr.)	Bundestag; fmr. Pres., Bundestag; CDC m															x									
Becker	Kurt	Editor (fmr.)	"Koelner Stadt-Anzeiger", Koeln																	x							
Beitz	Berthold	Chairman (fmr.)	Friedrich Krupp GmbH, Essen				x	x	x	x	x	x	x	x	x	x											
Berg	Fritz	President (fmr.)	Federation of German Industry (BDI)	x	x	x	x	x	x	x	x	x	x	x	x	x											
Bertram	Christoph	Dipl. Correspondent	"Die Zeit", Hamburg; Pr. Min. (fmr.)																x								
Birrenbach	Kurt	Chairman (fmr.)	August-Thyssen-Huette AG; fmr. mbr CDl			x	x	x	x	x	x	x	x	x	x	x	x	x	x								
Blessing	Karl	President (fmr.)	Deutsche Bundesbank				x		x																		
Boden	Hans C.	President (fmr.)	Allgemeine; Int. Trade Chamber			x	x	x	x	x								x									
Brandt	Willy	Chancellor (fmr.)	FRG; fdr. Comm. on Global Governance,							x												x					
Brauer	Max	Mayor (fmr.)	Freie u. Hansestadt Hamb.;mbr.Bundesta	x	x																						
Brautigam	Hans-Otto	Minister	of Justice, Brandenburg																								
Breuel	Birgit	Member of Board	Treuhandanstalt																	x					x	x	
Burda	Hubert	Chairman	Burda Media																					x		x	
Cartellier	Ulrich	Board Member	Deutsche Bank, A.G.																		x						
Dahrendorf	Ralf	Director (fmr.)	London School of Economics														x	x									
Dehousse	Fernand	Chairman	Consultativ Assy. of Europe												x												
Deist	Heinrich									x																	

Who's Who of the Elite

Last Name	1st & Middle Names	Country of Job	Office, Post or Affiliation	54	55	56	57	58	59	60	62	63	64	66	67	68	71	74	75	91	93	94	95	96	97	98	99
Dethleffsen	Erich	Editor, General, Ret.	"Wirtschaftstolitische Gesellschaft"											x													
Dicke	Gunther F. W.	First VP	Deutsche Bank AG, Organizer '91 BB Cor																x								
Dieter	Werner H.	Chairman	Mannesmann AG														x										
Dohnanyi	Klaus, von	Mayor (fmr.)	Freie u. Hansestadt Hamb.;fmr.mbr.Bunde															x									
Drexelius	DR. W.	Senatssyndicus (fmr.)	Freie u. Hansestadt Hamb.; att. Mayor Bra					x																			
Eckdardt	Felix, von	Ambassador (fmr.)	UN, NYC;fmr. mbr. Bundestag,CDU										x	x													
Emminger	Otmar	President (fmr.)	Deutsche Bundesbank; fmr mbr. BIZ											x													
Engelen-Kefar	Ursula	Deputy Chair.	Deutscher Gewerkschaftsbund																		x						
Engholm	Bjorn	Prime Minister	Schleswig-Holstein; Chairman, SPD												x												
Erhard	Ludwig	Minister	Economic Affairs, mbr., Bundestag; CDU	x			x	x		x	x		x	x													
Erler	Fritz	Vice President	Bundestag, Parl. Socialist Party				x	x	x	x	x																
Falkenheim	Ernst G. P.	Attendee	Bilderbergs, Wiesbaden meeting				x	x			x	x	x														
Focke	E. G.	Attendee	Bilderbergs, Marienlyst, Denmark meetin				x	x	x	x	x	x	x														
Geyer	Gerhard P. Th.	Chairman (fmr.)	ESSO, Hamb.;fmr Bd.Mbr.,Dresdner Bank	x				x	x		x		x	x													
Giersch	Herbert	Director	Inst. fur Weltwirtschaft an der Universitat															x									
Gross	Dr. Herbert	Journalist/Economist	'55 BB mtg., Garmisch-Partenkirchen	x			x	x		x	x																
Halberstadt	Victor	Professor	Leiden Univ., Public Economics																			x	x	x			
Hallstein	Dr. Walther	Secretary of State	Chair., Executive Commission, EEC	x			x	x	x	x	x		x														
Haussmann	Helmut	Member	Parliament (Free Democratic Party)											x													
Herwarth von Bittenfeld	Hans-Heinrich	Chairman (fmr.)	Deutsche Unilever GmbH' fmr. Undersec.	x			x	x	x	x	x	x															
Heyn	Rolf																					x	x				
Ischinger	Wolfgang	State Secretary	Ministry of Fgn. Affairs																							x	x
Issing	H. C. Otmar	Bd. Member	European Central Bank																						x	x	
Jaeger	Richard	Vice President	Bundestag				x	x																			
Kaiser	Karl	Director	German Inst. for Fgn. Affairs														x										
Kastrup	Dieter	Director	Political Dept., Minister of Foreign Affai	x																							
Keitel	Hans-Peter	Chairman	Hochtief AG																			x					
Kiep	Walther Leisler	Treasurer	CDU; fmr. mbr. Bundestag														x	x									
Kiesinger	Kurt-George	Chairman	Bundestag, Fgn. Policy Comm.	x			x	x	x	x	x		x	x													
Kohl	Helmut	Chancellor	FRG; Chairman, CDU Party																x								
Kopper	Hilmar	Chairman, Sup. Bd.	Deutsche Bank AG, Frtankfurt am Main																			x	x	x			
Krapf	Hans	Chief	Political Div., Min. of Fgn. Affairs									x	x	x													
Krapf	Franz	Ambassador (fmr.)	to Tokyo, Japan																								
Kuhlmann-Stumm	Knut Freiherr von	Member (fmr.)	Bundestag; fmr. Vice-Party Whip, FDP												x												
Lamers	Karl F.	Member	Parliament (Spokesman, Fgn. Affrs. CDU																			x					
Lauk	Kurt	Mng. Vice Chairman	AUDI AG, Ingolstadt																x								
Leverkuehn	Paul M. Adolf	Member	Parl.; Property Comm., Ger. Emb., NYC	x	x				x																		
Lowenthal	Richard	Political Scientist	Freie Universitaet Berlin																								
Majonica	Ernst	Member (fmr.)	Bundestag, CDU; fmr. mbr., Eoro. Parl.						x	x		x	x														
Mehnert	Klaus	Edit.-in-Chief (fmr.)	"Osteuropa" magazine						x												x						
Menne	Dr. W. Alexander	Member (fmr.)	Bundestag; Pres, Assoc./German Chem.	x					x	x			x	x													
Merkel	Hans	Attendee	'67 BB mtg, Cambridge, England						x			x	x														
Mommer	Karl														x											
Mueller	Dr. Rudolf	Lawyer	Chair., Wirtschaftspolitische Gesellscha	x	x	x	x	x	x																		
Mueller-Armack	Alfred	Member (fmr.)	Freiburger Schule:fmr.Undrsec.,Euro. Afr						x	x									x								
Nass	Matthias	Deputy Editor	Die Zeit																							x	x
Pereger	Werner A.	Polit. Correspondent	Die Zeit																								x

188

Last Name	1st & Middle Names	Country of Job	Office, Post or Affiliation	54	55	56	57	58	59	60	62	63	64	66	67	68	71	74	75	91	93	94	95	96	97	98	99
Ploetz	Hans-Friedrich, von	State Secretary	Ministry for Fgn. Affairs																							x	
Pohl	Karl Otto	President	Deutsche Bundesbank																	x							
Ponto	Jurgen	Chairman	Dresdner Bank A.G.															x									
Ritterbach	Manfred E.		IWUG-Institute, Duesseldorf																								
Rosenberg	Ludwig	Chief of Dept.	Fgn.Afrs.; fmr.Ch.,Deutsche Gewerkschaf	x					x	x																	
Ruge	Friedrich	Vice-Admiral (fmr.)	fmr. Herresgruppe B;fmr.Univ.Prof.,Turt							x											x						
Ruhe	Volker	Minister of Defense	FRG; mbr., Bundestag; CDU																			x					
Ruhnau	Heinz	Chairman	Deutsche Lufthansa Ag																		x						
Scharping	Rudolf	Minister	Defense																								x
Scheel	Walter	Fed. President	FRG; fmr. mbe. & Chair., Bundestag; FDf													x											
Schiller	Karl	Member (fmr.)	Bundestag; Prof., Economics; SPD									x		x													
Schmid	Professor Carlo	Vice President	Bundestag, Prof., Univ. of Frankfurt								x	x	x	x													
Schmidt	Helmut	Chancellor (fmr.)	FRG; Co-Editor, "Die Zeit", Hamburg														x										
Schmidt	Carlo	Member (fmr.)	Bundestag; SPD	x	x			x	x	x	x	x															
Schneider	Ernst-Georg	President (fmr.)	Chamber of Commerce, Dusseldorf	x	x																						
Schrempp	Jurgen F.	Chair./Bd. of Mgt.	Daimler-Chrysler AG																			x	x	x	x	x	
Schroeder	Gerhard	Member (fmr.)	Bundestag															x									
Senger und Ettrelin	Frido, von																										
Sohl	Dr. Hans-Gunther	Managing Director	Ausust Thyssen Hutte	x					x	x																	
Sommer	Theo	Editor-in-Chief	"Die Zeit"															x	x								
Speidel	Hans	Cmdr.-in-Chief (fmr.)	NATO land forces, Middle Europe												x												
Springer	Sr. Axel Caesar	Publisher	Springer-Publishing house, Hamburg				x																				
Sternberger	Prof. Dr. Dolf	Editor	"Die Gegenwart"													x											
Stoltenberg	Gerhard	Member	Bundestag; fmr. Minister of Defense; CDl						x	x																	
Strauss	Franz-Joseph	Min. President (fmr.)	Free St/Baveria; fmr.Fed.Min/Fin.;CSU								x	x									x						
Strube	Jurgen	CEO	BASF Aktiengesellschaft																		x						
Teufel	Erwin	Prime Minister	Daden-Wurtemberg								x	x											x				
Troeger	Heinrich	Vice President (fmr.)	Deutsche Bundesbank; fmr. mbr., Bundes	x							x	x															
Verheugen	Gunter	Secretary General	Social Democratic Party																x								
Voscherau	Henning	Mayor	Hamburg																				x				
Westrick	Ludger	Fed., Minister (fmr.)	Spec. Tasks; CDU; Chf., Bundeskanzlerat											x	x		x										
Wischnewski	Hans-Jurgen	Member (fmr.)	Bundestag																							x	
Wissmann	Matthias	Fed. Minister	for Transportation																								
Greece																											
Argyros	Sterios	Governor	National Mortgage Bank of Greece																		x						
Arliotis	Charles C.	Minister	of Defense											x	x												
Arsenis	Gerasimos	Minister																				x					
Athanassiades	Bodossaki	Industrialist						x	x	x																
Carras	Costa	Director	various companies																	x		x	x	x	x		
Chrristodoulou	Efthymios	Minister	Economic Affairs																		x						
Costopoulos	Yannis	Minister																								x	
Couloumbis	Theodore A.	President	Greek Foreign Policy Institute																				x				
David	George A.	Chairman	Hellenic Bottling Company S.A.																x								
Kanellopoulos	Penayotis	Member	Parliament																		x						
Karras	K.			x	x																					x	x
Kiranidiotis	Yannos	Deputy Minister	for Foreign Affairs																							x	x

Last Name	1st & Middle Names	Country of Job	Office, Post or Affiliation	54	55	56	57	58	59	60	62	63	64	66	67	68	71	74	75	91	93	94	95	96	97	98	99
Livanos	G.																										
Liras	G.																				x						
Mitsotakis	Konstantinos	Prime Minister	Greece																	x							
Niarchos	Stavros S.																				x						
Pangalos	Theodoros G.	Minister	for Foreign Affairs																				x				
Papandreou	George A.	Alt. Minister	for Foreign Affairs																				x	x			
Papkonstandinov	Michael	Foreign Minister	Greece																			x					
Peratikos	Michael																					x					
Pesmazoglou	John S.	Deputy Gov. (fmr.)	Bank of Greece												x					x							
Pipinelis	Panayotis N.	Foreign Min. (fmr.)	Fmr. Ambassador to USSR					x	x	x	x	x			x												
Stratos	Christofore												x													
Veremis	Thomas M.	President	Eliamep; Prof., Polit. Hist., Athens Univ.																	x						x	x
Zombanakis	Minos	Chairman	Group for Int. Study & Evaluatipon																x			x					
Hungary																											
Suryanyi	Gyorgy	President	National Bank of Hungary																			x					
Iceland																											
Benediktsson	Bjarni											x	x														
Bjarnason	Bjorn	Member	Parliament, Ind. Pty.; Min. Culture & Edi												x									x			
Hallgrimsson	Geir	Prime Min. (fmr.)													x	x		x									
Oddsson	David	Prime Minister																					x			x	x
Schmidheiny	Stephan E.	Chairman	ANOVA Holdings Ltd.																					x		x	
Thoroddsen	Gunnar													x													
Ireland																											
Bruton	John	Leader	of Fine Gael.																				x	x			
Fitzgerald	Garret	Minister	Foreign Affairs															x									
Gleeson	Dermot	Attorney General																				x					
Quinn	Lochlann	Chairman	Allied Irish Bank Gp.																					x			
Sutherland	Peter D.	Chair. & Mng. Dir.	Goldman Sachs Int.; Ch., Brit. Petroleum																	x	x	x	x	x	x	x	x
Italy																											
Agnelli	Giovanni	Hon. Chairman	FIAT S.p.A.					x	x	x	x	x	x				x			x	x	x	x	x	x		
Agnelli	Umberto	Chairman	IFIL						x	x										x	x						
Ambrosetti	Alfredo	Chairman	Ambrosetti Group.																			x					
Anzilotti	Enrico	Governor (fmr.)	Somaliland									x		x													
Bassetti	Piero							x	x	x																	
Bernabe	Franco	Mng. Dir. & CEO	Telecom Italia																				x	x			
Bettiza	Enzo	Journalist	"Corriere della Sera"														x					x					
Cafiero	Raffaele	Senator					x	x																			
Cantoni	Giampiero	Chairman	Banca Nationale del Lavoro						x	x																	
Carli	Dr. Guido	Governor	Bank of Italy.					x	x	x	x							x									
Cavalchini	Luigi G.	Perm. Representative	European Union																				x				
Cefis	Eugenio																x									
Cerretelli	Adriana	Correspondent	"Il Sole/24 Ore."								x	x															x
Chiusano	Vittorino																										

Last Name	1st & Middle Names	Country of Job	Office, Post or Affiliation	54	55	56	57	58	59	60	62	63	64	66	67	68	71	74	75	91	93	94	95	96	97	98	99
Cipolletta	Innocenzo	Director General	Canfindustria																					x			
Cittadini Cesi	Il Marchese	President	Assoc. por l'Etude des Prob. de l'Europe																								x
Colonna di Paliano	Prince Guido	Chairman	La Rinascente														x										
Draghi	Mario	Director General	Ministry of the Treasury																			x	x				
Ducci	Roberto	Director General	Political Affairs															x	x								
Fanfani	M. Amintore	Prime Minister (fmr.)	Sec. Gen., Christian Democrat Party						x	x					x												
Ferrari Aggradi	Mario	Prime Minister (fmr.)												x													
Forte	Francesco	Professor	Univ. of Torino, Finance																x								
Fresco	Paolo	Chairman	Fiat S.p.A																								x
Gasperi	Alcide, de	Fmr. Prime Minister		x																							
Giavazzi	Francesco	Professor	Bocconi Univ., Milan, Economics								x																
Giordani	F.	President	Nat Nucleur Research Committee											x													
La Malfa	Giorgio	Professor	Milan State Univ., Economics								x	x															
La Malfa	Ugo	Member	Parliament						x																		
La Pira	Giorgio.	Mayor	Florence		x																						
Masera	Rainer S.	Dir. General	I.M.I.S. p.A.																	x							
Micheli	Alighiero, De	Minister	Foreign Affairs								x																
Michelis	Gianni, De	Editor-in-Chief	"La Stampa"															x	x	x							
Levi	Arrigo	Editor-in-Chief	"La Stampa"									x	x														
Lolli	Ettore	Dep. Gen. Manager	"Banca Nacionale del Lavore"									x	x	x													
Longo	Imbriani						x	x		x	x	x	x														
Malagodi	Giovanni F.	Member	Parliament, Sec. Gen. Liberal Party				x	x		x	x	x	x	x													
Malfatti	Franco Maria	Minister	Education, Undersec., Ind. & Commerce										x	x				x									
Messeri	Girolamo											x	x	x													
Monti	Mario	Commissioner	European Commission (EC)																	x	x	x		x			
Olivetti	Roberto	Board Member	European Central Bank													x											
Padoa-Schioppa	Tommaso	Board Member	European Central Bank																		x	x					
Pastore	Giullion	Managing Director	Italconsulte							x	x	x	x	x	x	x											
PecEi	Aurelio	Managing Director	Italconsulte				x	x		x	x	x	x	x	x	x											
Pedini	Mario													x													
Petrilli	Giuseppe.								x		x	x	x	x	x	x											
Piovene	Guido	Writer																									
Pirelli	Alberto	Minister	of State				x	x	x	x	x	x	x	x	x												
Pirelli	Leopoldo	Minister	of State								x	x	x	x	x	x		x									
Profumo	Alessandro	CEO	Credito Italiano																						x		
Quaroni	Pietro	Ambassador (fmr.)	Germany, France, USSR				x	x	x	x	x	x	x	x													
Rognoni	Virginia	Minister	Defence																	x							
Ronchey	Alberto	Director (fmr.)	"La Stampa"													x											
Rossella	Carlo	Editor	Editrice La Stampa S.P.A.																					x			
Rossi	Paolo	Member	Parliament								x		x	x													
Ruggiero	Renato	Exec. Vice Chairman	FIAT S.p.A., Int. Adv. Bd.; fmr. Min., Tra																			x	x	x			
Rumor	Mariano													x													
Saraceno	Pasquale	Professor	Economics						x	x	x	x	x														
Scaglia	Giovanni Battista	Member	Parliament; V. Chair., Chriatian Dem. Pt				x	x	x	x	x	x	x														
Scarpa	Gino				x								x														
Silvestri	Stefano	Vice President	Istituto Affari Int.																						x		
Siniscalco	Domenico	Professor	Economics; Dir., Fendazione ENI																								x

Who's Who of the Elite

191

Last Name	1st & Middle Names	Country of Job	Office, Post or Affiliation	54	55	56	57	58	59	60	62	63	64	66	67	68	71	74	75	91	93	94	95	96	97	98	99
Spinelli	Altiero																										
Stille	Ugo	Editor	"L'Unità"													x											
Valletta	Vittorio	President	FIAT S.p.A.	x	x										x												
Veltroni	Valter	Editor	"L'Unità"																					x			
Vittorelli	Paolo	Senator											x	x													
Zannoni	Paolo	Sr. Vice President	Defence & Space, FIAT S.p.A.										x	x		x		x									
Luxembourg																											
Jaans	Pierre	General Manager	Institut Monetaire Luxembourgeois																x		x							
Santer	Jacques	Prime Minister																				x						
Netherlands																											
Armgard	H.R.H. Beatrix	Queen																									
Armgard	H.R.H. Bernhard	Prince	Chairman Bilderberg Conferences	x	x	x	x	x	x	x	x	x	x	x	x	x	x	x	x	x	x	x	x	x	x	x	x
Armgard	H.R.H. Claus	Prince													x	x											
Aukes	Albert G.	Economist							x																			
Banck	Maja	Executive Secretary	Bilderberg meetings																		x	x					
Bergh	Maarten A. van den	Gp. Mng. Dir.	Royal Dutch/Shell																			x					
Beugel	Ernst H. van der	Vice President	Royal Dutch Airlines,fmr.Min./State.Fgr						x			x	x						x		x	x					
Beyen	Johan Willem										x	x	x													
Biesheuvel	Barend W.																									
Blaisse	Pieter A.	Member	Parliament				x	x							x												
Bolkestein	Fritz	Parliamentary Leader	VVD (Liberal Party)															x					x				
Boon	Hendrik N.	Ambassador	to Venezuela						x		x																
Brinkhorst	Laurens-Jan	Minister of State	Foreign Affairs															x									
Dankert	Piet																									
Goudswaard	Johan M.	Vice Chair. of Board	Unilever N.V.	x																	x						
Grave	Frank H. G. de	Minister	Defense														x										
Halberstadt	Victor	Professor	Leiden Univ., Public Economics					x													x	x	x				
Herkstroter	Cor A. J.	Chairman	Royal Dutch Shell															x				x	x				
Hirschfeld	H. M.	Economic Advisor	Government	x					x		x	x															
Hoeven	Cess H van der	President	Royal Ahold																		x						
Justman Jacob	Poul Louis	Chairman	Kon. Ned. Hoogov. & Staalfabr. N.V.					x	x	x							x										
Kapteyn	P. J.		Amsterdam					x														x					
Karsten	Christian F.	Honorary Treasurer	Bilderberg Conferences	x					x			x										x					
Kloffens	E.N., van	Chairman (fmr.)	U.N. Assembly, Minister of State												x		x	x									
Knapen	Ben	Editor-inChief	"N.R.C. Mandelsblad"																	x							
Koningsberger	Victor J.	Professor	State Univ. of Utrecht						x			x															
Korteweg	Pieter	President & CEO	Robeco Group													x						x					
Koster	Herman J., de	President	Federation of Netherlands Industries										x	x							x	x		x			
Kraam Houckgeest	Andreas E., van											x		x												
Kuin	Pieter														x											
Kymmell	Jaap																									
Lamping	Arnold T.	Dep. Sec. General	for Europe						x		x	x	x	x	x							x					
Loudon	Jonkeer Jon H.														x											
Lubbers	Ruud F. M.	Prime Minister															x	x		x	x						
Luns	Joseph M. A. H.	Minister	Foreign Affairs	x	x												x	x		x	x						

Last Name	1st & Middle Names	Country of Job	Office, Post or Affiliation	54	55	56	57	58	59	60	62	63	64	66	67	68	71	74	75	91	93	94	95	96	97	98	99
Mathon	Theodore E.E.H.	Minister	of Social Affairs and Employment																							x	
Melkert	Ad P. W.	Minister	A.K.U.																					x		
Meynen	Johannes	Managing Director																								
Oldenbroeck	J. H.	Secretary	Int. Confed. of Free Trade Unions		x		x	x		x	x		x		x	x											
Oort	Conrad J.	Advisor - Bd. of Mgt.	Algemene Bank Nederland NV															x									
Oosterhuis	H.	Member	Parliament, Pres., Neth. Trade Unions	x	x		x		x	x	x	x	x														
Ooyevaar	J. J.					x			x																		
Otten	Pieter F. S.	Chairman	Phillips Gloeilampenfabrieken			x	x		x	x	x																
Rijkens	Paul	Chairman	Unilever, N.V.	x		x	x		x	x	x		x														
Roijen, van	Jan H.						x		x	x																	
Roy	Bertia le												x														
Royen	J. Herman, van																										
Rykens	Paul	Chairman	Midec S.A., fmr Chair., Unilever N.V.	x					x	x	x		x	x													
Samkaalden	Ivo																										
Sandberg	Herman W.														x											x
Scheepbouwer	Ad J.	Chairman & CEO	TNT Post Group	x					x		x		x														
Steenberghe	Maximilien P. L.	Minister (fmr.)	Economic Affairs, Dir. of Companies	x					x		x			x													
Tabaksblat	Morris	Chairman	Unilever N.V.																				x				
Tinbergen	Jan																										
Udink	Verend J.														x											
Vermeer	Evert A.							x	x	x	x															
Verrijn Stuart	G. M.								x	x	x			x												
Vlekke	B. H. M.	Secretary General	of the Netherlands Society of Int. Affairs	x				x	x	x				x													
Vries	Egbert, de	Professor	Instiotute of Social Studies					x	x				x	x													
Vuursteen	Karel	Chairman	Heineken N.V.																			x	x				
Waal	Lodewijk	J. de	Trade Unions (FNV)																		x		x				
Wallage	Jacques	Parliamentary Leader	PvdA (Labor Party)																			x					
Walsem	Graff, van	Bd. Member	Philips Industries Eindhoven				x		x	x			x														
Waslem	H. F. , van																									x	
Wijffels	Herman H. F.	Chairman	Robobank Nederland																							x	
Zijlstra	Jelle	President	Netherlands Bank; Ch., Bk. /Int. Settlem.						x	x	x			x													
New Zealand																											
Webb	Sir T. Clifton																										
Norway																											
Brundtland	Arne Olav	Sr. Research Fellow	Norwegian Institute of Int. Affairs																	x							
Clement	Kristin	Dep. Dir. Gen.	Confed. Of Business & Ind.																		x						
Ditlev-Simonsen	Per	Managing Director	Sverre Ditlev-Simonsen & Co.																								
Engen	Hans K.				x				x	x	x															
Hauge	Jens Christian	Minister	of Justice		x				x	x	x		x		x	x											
Hegge	Per Egil	Editor	Aftenposten				x											x									
Hoegh	Leif	Chairman	Norwegian American Line	x					x	x	x		x	x	x			x									
Hoegh	Westye	Chairman	Leif Hoegh & Co. A.S.A.															x	x			x	x	x	x		
Hojdahl	Odd	Vice Chairman	Norwegian Trade Union									x															
Jahn	Gunnar	Fmr. Governor	Bank of Norway					x							x												
Lange	Halbard	Minister	Foreign Affairs			x			x					x	x												

Last Name	1st & Middle Names	Country of Job	Office, Post or Affiliation	54	55	56	57	58	59	60	62	63	64	66	67	68	71	74	75	91	93	94	95	96	97	98	99
Lindebraekkee	Sjur D.J.	President	Bergens Privatbank		x	x	x							x													
Lorck	Karl	Managing Director	Elkem-Spigerverket														x										
Melander	Johan A.													x	x											
Moe	Finn	Member	Parliament, Vice Pres. Council of Europe	x	x				x	x				x	x												
Munthe	Preben												x													
Myklebust	Egil	CEO	Norsk Hydro																							x	
Myrvoll	Olle	Member	Parliament													x											
Petersen	Jan	Parliamentary Leader	Censerwative Party																					x			
Skaug	Arne																									
Stoltenberg	Thorvald	Co-Chairman	Int.Conf./Fmr. Yugoslavia;fmr.Min.Fgn.											x								x	x				
Storvik	Kjell	Governor	Bank of Norway																			x	x				
Tidemand	Otto Grieg	Ship Owner																									x
Udgaard	Nils M.	Fgn. Editor	*Aftemposten*										x	x	x	x											x
Vaarvik	Dagfinn	Editor-in-Chief	"Nationen"; Chairman, Centr. Party												x			x									
Warring	Niels																x									
Willoch	Kaare I.	Chairman	Wilh. Wilhelmsen Ltd. A/S							x				x													
Pakistan																											
Chaudhri	Sir Zafrulla Kahn	Judge	Perminent Court of Int. Justice	x																							
Zafrulla Kaahn	Sir Muhammad			x					x					x												
Poland																											
Olechowski	Andrzej	Chairman	Central Europe Trust, Poland																	x	x	x	x	x	x	x	x
Retinger	Dr. Joseph Hieronim	Hon. Secretary Gen.	for Europe, BB Group	x	x	x	x	x	x	x																	
Suchocka	Hanna	Minister	of Justice																							x	
Portugal																											
Amaral	Joaquim Freitas do Ama	Member	Portugese Parliament																								
Balsemao	Franciusco Pinto	Prime Min. (fmr.)																		x	x	x	x	x	x	x	x
Borges	Antonio	Dean	INSEAD																				x				
Carrilho	Maria	Professor	Sociology																			x					
Cravinho	Joao Cardona G.	Minister	Infrastructure, Planning & Territorial Admin.																			x					
Durao Barrosso	Jose Manuel	Minister	Foreign Affairs																		x						
Espirito Santo Silva	Manuel R.															x										
Grilo	Eduardo C. Marcal	Minister	Education												x												
Horta e Costa	Miguel	Vice President	Portugal Telecom																								x
Marante	Margarida	Journalist	TV																						x		
Mathias	Marcello J. N. D.																		x							
Mello	Vasco de	Vice. Chair & CEO	Grupo Jose de Mello										x														
Monjardino	Carlos A. P. V.	President	Fundacao Oriente																							x	
Nabo	Francisco Murteira	President & CEO	Portugal Telecom																				x				
Nogueira	Alberto F.																									x
Pimenta	Carlos	Member	Eoro. Parliament; fmr. Sec. St.,Environt																		x						
Salgado	Ricardo E. S.	President & CEO	Grupo Espirito																				x		x		
Sampaio	Jorge	President	Portugal																					x			
Santos	Nicolau	Editor-in-Chief	Expresso																								x
Sarmento Rodrigues	Manuel M.	Commodore, Ret.	fmr. Min. of Overseas Territories					x	x	x																	

Last Name	1st & Middle Names	Country of Job	Office, Post or Affiliation	54	55	56	57	58	59	60	62	63	64	66	67	68	71	74	75	91	93	94	95	96	97	98	99
Silva	Artur Santos	President & CEO	BPI Group																								x
Sousa	Marcelo Robelo de	Leader	PSD Party																							x	
Teles	Jose M. Galvao	Member	Council of State																						x		
Ulrich	Ruy Ennes			x																							
Veiga	Miguel	Lawyer																				x					
Vitorino	Antonio	Dep. Prime Minister	and Minister of Defence																					x			
Russia																											
Chubais	Anatoli B.	1st V Prim., Chair. (fmr.)																							x	
Shevtsova	Lilia	Member	Carnegie Moscow Center																								x
Trenin	Dmitri	Deputy Director	Carnegie Moscow Center																								x
Spain																											
Aguirre y Gil de Biedma	Esperanza	President	Spanish Senate																								x
Almunia Amann	Joaquin	Sec. General	Socialist Party																								x
Borban	H.R.M. Sofia	Queen	of Spain								x	x										x	x				
Carvajal Urquijo	Jaime	Chairman	Dresdner Kleinwort Benson S.A.																					x			
Esperanza	Aguirre y Gil de Biedma	President																				x					
Luzon Lopez	Francisco	Chairman & CEO	Argentaria									x										x					
Pujol	Jordi	Parliamentary Leader	of Minority Group (Partido Popular)									x										x	x	x			
Rato Figaredo	Roderigo de	Exec. Vice Chairman	Banco de Santander													x											
Rodriguez Inciarte	Matias	Dep. Prime Minister																					x	x			
Serra	Narcis	Member	Spanish Parliament, Socialist Party																			x	x				
Solbes Mira	Pedro	VP & Member	Parliament (Partido Popular)																				x				
Trillo Figueroa	Federico	Chair. & Gen. Mgr.	Iberfomento																	x			x				
Urquijo	Jaime Carvajan	Perm. Representative	to United Nations																				x				
Yanez-Barnuovo	Juan A.																						x				
Sweden																											
Aman	Walter	Secretary General	Central Org. of Salaried Employees																								x
Asland	Anders	Sr. Associate	Carnegie Endow. for Int. Peace					x						x													
Aspling	Sven		Investo AB																		x	x	x	x	x		
Barnevik	Percy	Chairman	Investo AB											x							x		x	x	x		
Bergstrom	Hans	Political Editor	"Dagens Nyheter"																			x	x				
Bildt	Carl	Prime Minister (fmr.)	Sweden				x	x	x												x	x	x	x	x		
Boheman	Erik	Ambassador (fmr.)	to U.K.				x	x	x																		
Dahlman	Sven												x													
Erlander	Tage F.						x	x	x					x												
Geijer	Arne	Chairman	AB Astra								x																
Gustafsson	Stan	Chairman	AB Astra																	x							
Heckscher	Gunnar													x												
Hedelius	Tom C.	Chairman	Svenska Handelsbanken																							x	
Holmberg	Yngve														x											
Iveroth	Axel											x		x												
Jacobsson	Per									x																
Jonung	Lars	Professor	Stockholm School of Economics, Econo...																	x							
Kling	Herman											x		x												

Last Name	1st & Middle Names	Country of Job	Office, Post or Affiliation	54	55	56	57	58	59	60	62	63	64	66	67	68	71	74	75	91	93	94	95	96	97	98	99
Lange	Gunnar	President & Dir. Gen.	Swedish Railways												x												
Larsson	Stig	President	Telefon AB L. M. Ericsson																			x					
Lundvall	D. Bjorn H.															x			x								
Ohlin	Bertil	Prime Minister		x										x		x											
Palme	S. Olof J.													x					x								
Ramfors	Bo C. E.	Mng. Dir. & Gp. CEO	Skandinaviska Enskilda Banken															x									
Rojas	Mauricio	Assoc. Prof.	Lund Univ., Econ. History																						x	x	
Rosengren	Bjorn	Minister	Industry, Employ. & Comm.																								x
Sahlin	Mona	Minister	Parliament																					x			
Sandler	Rickard	Member																					x				
Svedberg	Bjorn	President & CEO	Skandinaviska Enskilda Banken	x				x	x																		
Tingsten	Herbert L. G.	Chief Editor	"Dagens Nyheter"					x	x			x												x			
Uusmann	Ines J.	Minister	Transportation & Communications									x	x									x					
Waldenstrom	Martin	Industrialist								x																	
Wallenberg	Jacob	Chairman	Skandinaviska Enskilda Banken	x				x	x	x	x	x	x	x	x	x	x										
Wallenberg	Marcus, Dr.	Chairman	Skanvinavska Enskilda Banken	x				x	x	x	x	x	x	x	x	x	x	x	x				x	x			
Wickman	Krister	Goverenor	Bank of Sweden; Fmr. Min. Fgn. Affairs													x	x										

Switzerland

Last Name	1st & Middle Names	Country of Job	Office, Post or Affiliation	54	55	56	57	58	59	60	62	63	64	66	67	68	71	74	75	91	93	94	95	96	97	98	99
Ackermann	Josef	President, Exec. Bd.	Chedit Suisse																			x					
Boveri	Walter E.	Chairman	Brown, Boveri & Co.					x	x	x		x	x	x	x												
Broggini	Gerardo							x	x					x	x												
Burckhardt	Carl J.																										
Butler	Hugo	Editor-in-Chief	Neue Zurcher Zeitung						x	x												x					
Cotti	Flavio	Minister	Foreign Affairs																					x	x	x	
Delamuraz	Jean-Pascal	Vice President	Federal Council; Minister of the Economy																		x	x		x	x		
Frehner	Walter	Chairman	Swiss Bank Corp.																			x					
Gasteyger	Curt	Professor	Graduate Inst. of Int. Studies														x										
Gerber	Fritz	Chairman	F. Hoffmann-La Roche AG															x				x					
Gysling	Erich	Head	Fgn. Dept. of "Weltwoche"														x										
Heckmann	Hans	Vice Chairman	Union Bank of Switzerland															x									
Jolles	Paul											x															
Krauer	Alex	Chairman & Mng. Dir.	Ciba-Geigy Ltd											x								x					
Liotard-Vogt	Pierre	Chairman	Nestle Alimentana S.A.												x				x			x					
Markstaller	Margrit														x												
Maucher	Helmut O.	Chairman & CEO	Nestle Ltd						x	x											x						
Monnier	Claude	Editor-in-Chief	"Journal de Geneve"					x	x	x												x					
Petitpierre	Max	Chairman	de Pury Pictet Turrettini & Co.																								
Pury	David, de	Chairman										x										x					
Reinhardt	Eberhard	Publisher & CEO	Ringier Inc.								x											x	x	x	x	x	x
Ringier	Michael	Director	European Cultural Center, Author																								
Rougemont	Denis, de													x	x							x					
Schaffner	Hans	Chairman	ANOVA Holdings Ltd.				x	x																			
Schmidheiny	Stephan	Chairman	MS Management Service AG																		x	x					
Schurer	Wolfgang														x	x						x	x					
Schwarz	Urs	President	Int. Committee of the Red Cross																								x
Sommaruga	Cornelio																						x			

Last Name	1st & Middle Names	Country of Job	Office, Post or Affiliation	54	55	56	57	58	59	60	62	63	64	66	67	68	71	74	75	91	93	94	95	96	97	98	99
Umbricht	Victor H.	Head (fmr.)	Swiss Treasury; President, CIVA-Geigy L															x								x	x
Vasella	Daniel L.	CEO	Novartis AG																							x	
Widmer	Siegmund	Mayor	Zurich; Mbr. Fed. Parliament																x								
Wilhelm	Arthur										x																
Turkey																										
Akbil	Semih	Head	Info. Dept., Ministry of Fgn. Affairs																								
Alp	Ali Hikmet	Ambassador	Perminent Representative to the C.S.C.E																			x					
Alpkartal	Nureddin F.	Member	Parliament						x	x				x													
Ariburun	Tekin	Commander-in-Chief	Turkish Air Force						x	x	x													x			
Bayar	Ugur	Chairman	Privatazation Admin.																								
Belge	Burnham	Member	Parliament						x				x														
Beyazit	Selahaltin	Director	various companies						x			x	x	x	x					x	x	x	x	x			
Bilgin	Dinc	Chairman	Sabah A.S.																				x				
Birgi	Muharrem Nuri	Ambassador (fmr.)	to N.A.T.O., U.K.				x	x	x	x		x	x	x	x			x	x								
Boyazit	Selattin	Director	Compa				x																				
Boyner	Cem	Chairman	New Democracy Movement																	x							
Caglayangil	Ihsan S.	Minister	Foreign Affairs																x								
Cem	Ismail	Minister	for Foreign Affairs								x													x			
Cetin	Hikmet	Deputy Prime Minister	fmr. Minister for Foreign Affairs																								
Demirel	Suleyman	Prime Minister											x									x					
Diker	Vecdi	Chairman	Turkish Fed. Road Transport						x					x													
Dogramaci	Ihsan	Professor	Hacettepe Univ., Medacine, Rector																x								
Ecevit	Bulent	Member	Parl., Ldr./Rep. People's Pty., fmr. Pr. M									x		x					x								
Eczacibasi	Nejat F.											x				x											
Ercel	Gazi	Governor	Central Bank of Turkey																					x	x		
Ergin	Sedat	Bureau Chief	*Hurriyet* , Ankara																						x		
Erguder	Ustun	Rector	Bosporus Univ.																	x							
Esenbel	Melih	Dep. Prime Minister								x	x		x							x							
Feyzioglu	Turan	Dep. Prime Minister	Leader of Repub. Trust Pty., Fmr. Prof., L											x				x									
Gezgin Ens	Meral	President	IKV (Econ. Devel. Foundation)																			x					
Gidel	Nail																										
Gokmen	Oguz	Head	Econ. Dept., Ministry Affairs							x								x									
Gonensay	Emre	Minister	Foreign Affairs																					x			
Halefoglu	Vahit	Minister (fmr.)	Foreign Affairs							x										x							
Inan	Kamuran	Member	Senate, Chair., Fgn. Rel. Committee													x											
Isik	Hasan F.	Member	Parliament, fmr. Min. of Fgn. Affairs							x									x								
Kazgan	Gulten (Mrs.)	Professor	Univ. of Istambul, Faculty of Economics							x																	
Kirac	Suna	Vice Chairman	Koc Holding A.S.																			x					
Koc	Rahmi M.	Chairman	Koc Holding A.S.										x	x											x	x	
Mardin	Serif	Chairman	American U., Wash. D.C., Dep., Islamic S																				x				
Menderes	Adman	Prime Minister							x	x																	
Ozceri	Tugay	Undersecretary	Ministry of Foreign Affairs							x	x									x							
Sarper	Selim								x	x														x			
Tara	Sinan	Vice President	Enka Construction & Ind. Inc.																				x				
Tokay	Selahattin	General	Chief of Operations, Gen. Staff						x	x			x					x									
Tokus	Ahmet												x														

Last Name	1st & Middle Names	Country of Job	Office, Post or Affiliation	54	55	56	57	58	59	60	62	63	64	66	67	68	71	74	75	91	93	94	95	96	97	98	99
Tunc	Halil	Chairman	Fed., Turkish Workers Unions, Mbr., Sen																								
Turkmen	Liter																										x
Yasa	Memduh	Professor	Univ. of Istambul, Faculty of Economics															x									
Yasar	Selcuk	Director of companies	Izmir																x								x
Yucaoglu	Erkut	Chairman	Tusiad																								
Zorlu	F. R.	Minister	Foreign Affairs				x	x	x																		
Ukraine																											
Mityukov	Ihor	Minister	Finance																								x
United Kingdom																											
Edingurgh	H.R.H. Philip	Prince &, Duke of	of England										x														
Airey	Sir Terence	Member	Steering Committee Member, Bilderbergs	x	x					x	x	x	x	x													
Assheton	Rt. Hon. Ralph	Member	Parltiament	x						x	x	x	x														
Astor	the Hon. F. David L.	Editor	"The Observer"			x	x	x		x	x	x	x														
Barbour	Walworth							x	x	x																	
Barran	David H.											x		x												
Becu	Omer								x	x																	
Beddington-Behrens	Sir Edward	Chairman	European Movement						x	x	x	x															
Bennett	Sir Frederic	Member	Parliament, Steering Committee Member					x	x	x	x	x	x	x	x	x	x	x									
Bevan	Aneurin						x	x																			
Blair	Tony	Prime Min.	England		x																x						
Boothby	Sir Robert	Member	Parliamewnt	x	x					x	x	x	x	x													
Bridgeman	Sir Maurice R.										x	x	x		x											
Brown	George A.	Member	Parliament, Fmr. Minister				x					x		x													
Brown	Gordon	Member	Parliament, Labour Party												x						x						
Browne	E. John P.	Group CEO	British Petroleum Co., plc																			x	x				
Buchan	the Rt. Hon. Alaster	Director	Institute for Startegic Studies										x	x													
Buchanan	Robin W.T.	Sr. Partner	Bain & Company Inc. UK																			x	x				
Buzzard	Sir Anthony	Director	Vickers Armstrongs Ltd.	x				x		x																	
Callaghan	James	Chairman (fmr.)	Christies, Fmr. Sec. Gen., N.A.T.O.						x	x	x	x															
Carrington	Lord Peter	Chairman	Christie's Int. plc; fmr. Sec. Gen., N.A.T.																	x	x	x	x	x	x		
Clarke	Kenneth	Member of Parl.	Chancel. (fmr.) of the Exchequer																x		x	x					
Cavendish-Bentnick	Victor	Ambassador (fmr.)	to Poland, Argentina, BB Strg. Comm. M				x		x	x	x	x	x	x													
Chambers	Sir Paul											x														
Clitheroe	the Lord							x																		
Cochrane	Sir Ralph	Air Chief Marshall	Industrialist			x		x		x																	
Cohen	the Honorable						x	x	x	x	x	x	x													
Cooke	B. D.									x																
Cradock	Percy	Ambassador (fmr.)	to China; fmr. Fgn. Pol. Adv. to Prime M																			x					
Cranborne	Robert M.J.C.	Leader	Opposition Party, House/Lords																					x			
Crowther	Sir Geoffery	Chief Editor	"Economist"				x			x	x	x	x	x													
Darvall	Frank O.							x																		
Davies	Rt. Hon. Clement	Member	Parliament	x					x	x	x	x															
Delmer	D. Sefton								x	x																
Dundee	Lord	Minister										x															
Elliot	Sir William	Minister	State, for Foreign Affairs	x					x	x		x	x														

Last Name	1st & Middle Names	Country of Job	Office, Post or Affiliation	54	55	56	57	58	59	60	62	63	64	66	67	68	71	74	75	91	93	94	95	96	97	98	99
Epsom	the Lord Geddis of	Member	Parliament																								
Foster	Sir John G.	Member			x	x																					
Franks	Rt. Hon. Sir Oliver	Chairman	Lloyd's Bank		x	x												x									
Freedman	Lawrence	Head of Dept.	Kings College, War Studies																		x						
Gaitskell	the Rt. Hon. Hugh T.N.	Chancellor (fmr.)	Exchequer; Leader of Parl. Labour Party				x	x																			
Garton Ash	Timothy	Fellow	St. Antony's College, Oxford																					x			
Geddes	C.J.	Chairman	T.U.C. 1954-'55		x																						
Geddes	Reay												x														
Giles	Frank T.R.	Deputy Editor	"Sunday Times"														x										
Gladwyn	the Lord											x	x														
Glendevon	the Lord											x	x														
Gordon Walker	Patrick	Member	Parl., Fmr. Sec. St./Commonwealth Rela					x																			
Greenhill	the Lord	Perm. Sec. (fmr.)	Fgn. & Commonwealth Office														x										
Grieson	Ronald	Vice Chair. (fmr.)	GEC																								x
Grimond	Joseph	Leader	Parliamentary Liberal Party				x	x	x	x																	
Gubbins	Sir Colin McVean	Major General Ret.	Form. charge of SOE.		x	x	x	x	x	x																	
Hall	Sir Arnold													x												
Hall Patch	Sir Edmund														x											
Hampden	the Viscount																									
Hannay	David	Perm. Representative	U.K. Mission to the U.N.																	x							
Harlech	the Lord													x												
Harsch	Joseph C.																									
Healey	Denis W.	Chancellor	of the Exchequer, Steering Committee M	x	x	x	x	x	x	x	x	x	x	x	x	x											
Heath	Edward R. G.										x	x	x	x	x											
Henderson	Nicholas	Ambassador (fmr.)	to Poland, France, US							x	x		x						x								
Hogg	Christopher	Chairman	Reuters Group plc																			x					
Hogg	Quintin															x										
Hope	Lord John	Secretary of State	Foreign Affairs	x						x	x																
Horam	John	Member	Parliament, Economic Consultant															x									
Hutton	Will	Editor	The Observer																					x			
Hyde	H. Montgomery																									
Ismay	Gen. R.H., Lord	Secretary General	N.A.T.O.	x	x					x	x		x														
Jacobi	Mary Jo	Hd./Gp. Pub. Affrs.	HSBC Holdings plc															x									
Jay	Rt. Hon. Douglas P. T.	Member	Parliament, Finan. Sec. to Treasury	x			x	x		x	x		x														
Jellicoe	the Earl	First Lord	Admiralty				x	x		x	x		x	x													
Jenkins	Michael	Vice Chairman	Dresdner Kleinwort Benson				x	x		x	x		x											x			
Job	Peter	CEO	Reuters Holdin plc															x						x			
Jones	Aubry	Chairman	Cornhill Insurance Co.										x														
Kaletsky	Anatole	Asst. Editor	The Times																							x	
Karamanlis	Koetas A.	Leader	Opposition Party																						x	x	
Kesarton	Sir Frank																									
Keswick	John			x			x	x		x	x		x														
Kilmuir	the Earl of	Lord Chancellor		x			x	x		x	x																
Kipping	Sir Norman	Director General	Fed. of British Industries	x			x	x		x	x		x														
Kleffens	Eelco N., van	Minister	of State, Fmr. Fgn. Minister	x			x	x		x	x		x														
Kleinwort	Cyril																										
Knight	Andrew	Executive Chairman	News International plc																	x			x			x	x

Last Name	1st & Middle Names	Country of Job	Office, Post or Affiliation	54	55	56	57	58	59	60	62	63	64	66	67	68	71	74	75	91	93	94	95	96	97	98	99
Knollys	the Viscount	Chairman	Vickers, Ltd.																						x		
Knollys	the Viscount																									
Kogg	Christopher	Chairman	CourtauidaS plc															x									
Mabro	Robert E.	Director	Oxford Inst. for Energy Studies																					x			
Mandelson	Peter	Member	Parliament																							x	
Maudling	Rt. Hon. Reginald	Member	Parl.; Min., Supply; Steering Comm. Mb								x	x	x														
Micklethwait	R. John	Business Editor	The Economist																					x	x	x	
Monks	John	General Secretary	Trade Union Congress (TUC)																				x	x			
Montgomery Hyde	H.	Member	Parliament	x																							
Montgomery of Alamein Viscount		Field Marshall					x																				
Mountbatten of Burma	the Earl												x	x												
O'Neill	Sir Con																									
Oppenheim	Sir Duncan					x										x										
Ormsby-Gore	Sir David	Minister of State	for Fgn. Affairs, Mbr. of Parliament								x	x	x		x												
Owen	David	Lord	for Fgn. Affairs, Mbr. of Parliament																		x						
Pilkington	Sir Harry	President	Fed. of British Ind.; Dir., Bk. of England	x	x			x		x	x		x														
Plowden	the Lord							x			x		x			x											
Pomian	John								x																		
Porrit	Jonathan	Programme Dir.	Forum for the Future																						x		
Powel	J. Enoch														x	x										
Purves	William	Gp. Chairman	HSBC Holdings plc																x								
Radice	Giles H.	Member	Parliament; Chair., European Movement																		x						
Rell	Eric	Sr. Advisor	SBC Warburg																	x							
Richardson	Gordon	Governor	Bank of England										x				x										
Rifkind	Malcolm	Foreign Secretary																					x				
Rippon	Geoffrey	Member	Parliament														x										
Robens	Alfred	Member	Parliament; fmr min, Labor & Nat. Svce						x	x	x																
Roberts	Sir Alfred	Chairman	Int. Committee of the T.U.C.					x	x	x	x																
Robertson	George	Secretary	of State for Defence																								
Robertson	Simon	Chairman	Kleinwort Benson Group plc																			x	x				
Rodgers	William	Minister of State	for Defence														x										
Roll of Ipaden	Sir Eric	Sr. Advisor	SBC Warburg Dillon Read										x				x	x	x				x		x	x	
Rothschild	Emma	Director	Centre, Hist. & Econ.; Fellow, Cambridge																			x					
Rothschild	Evelyn de	Chairman	N.M. Rothschild & Sons										x		x												
Shawcross	Lord																									
Shonfield	Andrew A.													x												
Slessor	Sir John	Marshall	Royal Air Force	x																							
Smith	A. H.	Chairman	United Africa Company						x	x	x	x	x														
Smith	John	Member	Parl., Labor Pty.; Shadow Chanc., Excheq						x	x	x								x								
Steel	Sir J. Lincoln S.					x		x	x	x	x															
Stevenson	John M.	Chairman	SRU Groupe; Tate Gallery																			x					
Stewart	H. Dennis	Member	Parliament								x	x															
Taverne	Michael	Member	BB Steering Committee								x	x															
Taylor	Dick	CEO (fmr.)	Barclays Bank plc								x																
Tennant	J. Martin																			x	x	x	x	x	x	x	x
Thatcher	Peter F. D.	Member	Parliament, Leader of the Opposition														x										x

Last Name	1st & Middle Names	Country of Job	Office, Post or Affiliation	54	55	56	57	58	59	60	62	63	64	66	67	68	71	74	75	91	93	94	95	96	97	98	99
Thompson	Gerald F. M. P.	Chairman	Kleinwort Benson Ltd.															x									
Tiarks	Henry F.							x	x	x	x			x											x	
Turner	Sir Mark																								x	
Villeneuve	Andre-Francois H.	Exec. Dir.	Reuters Group Holding plc																								x
Waldegrave	William A.	Secretary of State	Minister of Agriculture, Fisheries & Food									x		x									x				
Warburg	Sir Sigmund													x												
Wheeler	Sir Charles													x	x											
Williamson	the Lord Thomas	General Secretary	Nat. Union of Gen. & Munic. Workers	x	x									x													
Wilson	Harold											x		x												
Woldeingham	the Lord Robens of					x					x			x												
Wolf	Martin	Assoc. Editor	"The Financial Times"																						x		
Woodhause	Christopher M.											x														
Woodhouse	the Hon. Montague													x												
Wooldridge	Adrian D.	Fgn. Correspondent	The Economist																							x	x
Wren	Walter T.						x							x												
Wright	Patrick	Perm. Undersecretary	of State & Head of Diplomatic Service																	x							
Yahuda	Michael B.	Professor	Int. Rel., London School of Economics											x									x				
Younger	Kenneth										x			x												
United States																											
Acheson	Dean Gooderham	Secretary (fmr.)	State Dept.	x	x			x	x	x	x		x	x													
Achilles	Theodore C.							x		x	x			x												
Allaire	Paul Arthur	Chairman	Xerox Corp.																	x	x	x	x	x	x	x	
Allison	Graham Tillett, Jr.	Member	Defense Dept. Policy Bd.														x										
Anderson	Robert Orville	Chairman & CEO	Atlantic Richfield Co.												x												
Andreas	Dwayne O.	Chairman	Archer-Daniel-Midland Co., Inc.										x								x		x				
Armacost	Michael H	President	Brookings Institute																			x					
Ball	George Wildman	Sr. Mng. Director	Lehman Brothers; fmr. Undersec., State	x	x			x	x	x	x			x													
Barbour	Walworth	Ambassador (fmr.)	Israel					x		x	x																
Bartley	Robert Leroy	Editor	Wall Street Journal												x							x					
Bayh	Evan	Senator, D.	Indiana,																						x		
Beebe	Frederick Sessions	Chairman (fmr.)	Washington Post											x													
Bell	David E.	Administrator (fmr.)	U.S. A.I.D.										x														
Bell	Elliott Vance	Editor (fmr.)	Business Week					x		x	x			x													
Bennet	Douglas J.	Asst. Secretary	State Dept., for Int. Org.																			x					
Bennett	Jack F.	Director & Sr. V.P.	EXXON Corp.															x									
Bentsen	Lloyd M.	Secretary (fmr.)	Treasury Dept.																				x	x			
Berger	Samuel R.	Asst. to President	for National Security																				x			x	
Bergsten	C. Fred	Sr. Fellow	Brookings Institution																		x			x			
Bingham	George Barry	Chairman (fmr.)	Int. Press Institute	x	x			x		x				x													
Bernstein	Richard	Book Critic	New York Times																						x		
Black	Eugene R.	Pres. & Chair. (fmr.)	Int. Bank of Reconstruction & Devel.			x		x		x	x			x													
Blackwell	Robert D.																				x						
Blum	Robert			x				x	x	x																	
Bolling	Richard										x																
Boskin	Michael Jay	Chairman (fmr.)	President's Council of Econ. Advisors																	x							
Bowie	Robert Richardson	Director (fmr.)	Harvard Univ., Ctr. for Int. Affairs		x				x		x		x	x													

Last Name	1st & Middle Names	Country of Job	Office, Post or Affiliation	54	55	56	57	58	59	60	62	63	64	66	67	68	71	74	75	91	93	94	95	96	97	98	99
Boyd	Charles G.	Exec. Director	Nat. Security Study Group																							x	x
Brademas	John	President (fmr.)	NYU																								
Brady	Nicholas Frederick	Secretary (fmr.)	Treasury Dept.																x								
Brandt	Karl	Member (fmr.)	Pres.'s Council of Econ. Affairs						x				x														
Brewster	Kingman, Jr.	President (fmr.)	Yale Univ.										x														
Brooke	Edward, Senator	Senator (fmr.)	Massachusetts													x											
Brown	Irving			x																							
Bruce	David K. E.	Ambassador (fmr.)	Germany; United Kingdom						x				x														
Bryan	John H	Chairman & CEO	Sara Lee Corp.																			x	x	x			
Brzezinski	Zbigniew	Counselor	Ctr. for Strategic & Int. Studies														x	x									
Buckley	William F., Jr.	Editor-at-Large	"National Review"														x	x					x				
Bundy	McGeorge	President (fmr.)	Ford Found.;fmr.Spec.Asst./Pres./Nat.Se				x		x		x	x	x														
Burgess	W. Randolph	Chief of US Mission	N.A.T.O. & European Regional Org.				x		x		x	x															
Burt	Richard R.	U.S. Ambassador	Germany																								
Cabot	Louis Wellington	Chairman (fmr.)	Brookings Instit.; fmr. President, Cabot											x	x												
Camps	Miriam	Sr. Research Fellow	Council on Foreign Relations															x									
Case	Clifford Philip	Senator (fmr.)	New Jersey				x		x		x	x	x														
Chace	James	Managing Editor	CFR, "Foreign Affairs"													x											
Chafee	John Hubbard	Senator	Rhode Island, Environ. & P.W./Chair., F																	x							
Cisler	Walter Lee	Chairman & CEO	Detroit Edison				x		x		x	x	x														
Cleveland	Harlan	Ambassador (fmr.)	NATO									x	x	x	x												
Cleveland	Harold Van B.											x	x	x	x												
Clinton	Hillory Rodom	Wife	President Clinton																					x			
Clinton	William Jefferson	President	United States															x									
Cole	David Lee															x											
Coleman	John S.			x	x																						
Collado	Emelio Gabriel	Executive V.P.	Exxon Corp.						x		x	x	x	x	x	x	x	x									
Cook	Donald C.	Dipl. Corresp. (fmr.)	Los Angeles Times																			x					
Cooper	Richard Newell	Professor	Harvard Univ., Yale Univ.														x	x									
Copeland	Lammot du Pont	President (fmr.)	E. I. du Pont de Nemours & Co.										x														
Cordier	Andrew Wellington	Dean (fmr.)	Columbia Univ., Graduate School																								
Corrigan	E. Gerald	Chair., Int. Advisors	Goldman Sachs; Pres. (fmr.), Fed. Res. B																		x						
Cortines	Ramon C.	Chancellor	NYC Board of Education																			x					
Corzine	Jon S.	Chair. & Sr. Partner (fm	Goldman Saches & Co.													x								x			
Cowles	Gardner	Editor-in-Chief	Cowles Communications	x	x																			x			
Dallara	Charles H.	Asst. Secretary (fmr.)	State Dept., International Affairs							x														x			
Dam	Kenneth W.	Professor	Univ. of Chicago Law School															x	x				x				
Davis	Lynn E.	Undersecretary	State Dept., Arms Control																			x	x				
Day	Robert A., Jr.	Chairman	Trust Cpmpany of the West																								
Dean	Arthur Hudson	Ambassador (fmr.)	UN Conf. on the Law of the Seas						x		x	x	x	x	x	x	x										
Deming	Frederick Lewis	Director	National City Bancorp																			x					
Deutch	John Mark	Director (fmr.)	Central Intelligence Agency												x									x			
Dewey	Thomas Edmund	Governor (fmr.)	New York State							x					x										x		
Diebold	John	President, Chairman	Diebold Group (Consultant)												x												
Dillon	C. Douglas	Chairman (fmr.)	Rockefeller Foundation																								
Dodd	Christopher J.	Senator, D.	Connecticut																							x	
Dodge	Joseph M.	Chairman	Detroit Bank	x					x		x	x															

Last Name	1st & Middle Names	Country of Job	Office, Post or Affiliation	54	55	56	57	58	59	60	62	63	64	66	67	68	71	74	75	91	93	94	95	96	97	98	99
Donilon	Thomas E.	Chief of Staff (fmr.)	State Dept.: Asst. Sec., for Public Affairs																						x		x
Donovan	Hedley Williams	Editor-in-Chief	Fortune magazine																								
Dulles	Allen W.	Director	Central Intelligence Agency (CIA)						x					x													
Eliot	Theodore Lyman, Jr.	Trustee	Asia Foundation																	x							
Espy	Mike	Secretary	Agriculture Dept.																			x					
Evans	Daniel J.	Senator	Washington																								
Feinstein	Diane	Senator	California																		x						
Feldstein	Martin S.	Pres. & CEO	Nat Bureau of Economic Research																					x	x		x
Ferguson	John Henry	Deputy Dir. (fmr.)	State Dept., Policy Planning Staff	x	x	x																					
Finletter	Thomas Knight	U.S. Perm. Rep.	NATO						x	x	x																
Finley	Murray H.	President	Amalg. Cloth. & Text. Wkrs. Union																								
Flanders	Ralph E.	Senator (fmr.)	Vermont	x						x	x																
Florio	James J.	Governor (fmr.)	New Jersey																				x				
Foley	Thomas S.	Spkr. of House (fmr.)	House of Representatives										x														
Ford	Gerald R.	President (fmr.)	United States															x									
Ford	Henry, II	Chairman (fmr.)	Ford Motor Company												x												
Forester	Lynn	Pres. & CEO	FirstMark Holdings, Inc.																							x	
Foster	William Chapman	President & Chairman	United Nuclear Corp.									x	x														
Frankel	Max											x															
Frazer	Donald	Senator	Minnesota														x										
Freeman	Charles W., Jr.	Asst. Secretary (fmr.)	Defense Dept., Int. Security												x									x			
Frelinghuysen	Peter H. B.	Senator	New Jersey, fmr. Congressman													x											
Friedman	Stephen James	Sr. Ch. & Ltd. Partner	Goldman Sachs & Co.						x																		
Friedman	Thomas L.	Fgn. Affrs. Columnist	New York Times																				x				
Fulbright	James William	Senator	Arkansas						x	x	x	x	x	x													
Gadiesh	Orit	Chairman	Bain & Company																			x					
Gallagher	Cornelius E.	Congressman										x															
Galvin	John Rogers	Supr. Ald. Cdr. (fmr.)	Defense Dept., SHAPE, Europe												x					x							
Garner	Robert L.			x																							
Gergen	David R.	Editor-at-Large	US News & World Report; Spec. Asst. to						x													x					
Gerstner	Louis V., Jr.	Chairman & CEO	IBM Corp.																		x	x					
Gigot	Paul	Wash. Columnist	The Wall Street Journal																				x				
Gilpatric	Roswell Leavitt	Counsel	Chavath, Swaine & Moore						x	x	x	x	x														
Godiesh	Orbit	Chairman	Bain & Company, Inc.																			x					
Golden	Clinton S.	Trade Unionist		x																							
Goodpaster	Andrew Jackson	Comd.-in-Chief (fmr.)	Def. Dept., Supr. Alld. Comnd., Europe												x	x		x									
Gordon	Lincoln	Guest Scholar	Brookings Inst.				x		x	x	x	x	x														
Gossett	William T.	Chairman										x															
Graham	Donald E.	Publisher	Washington Post																					x			
Graham	Katharine	Chairman	Washington Post					x												x	x	x					
Gray	Gordon	Secretary (fmr.)	Defense Dept.	x																							
Greenberg	Maurice R.	Deputy Chair. (fmr.)	Fed, New York; Ch. & CEO, Amer. Int. G																	x							
Grossman	Marc	Asst. Secretary	State Department																						x		
Gruenther	Alfred M.	General (fmr.)	Supreme Allied Commander - Europe	x					x	x	x	x	x														
Grunwald	Henry A.	Managing Editor	"Time Magazine"															x									
Hafstad	Lawrence R.																										
Hagel	Chuck	Senator, R.	Nebraska																								x

Last Name	1st & Middle Names	Country of Job	Office, Post or Affiliation	54	55	56	57	58	59	60	62	63	64	66	67	68	71	74	75	91	93	94	95	96	97	98	99
Hamilton	Lee H.	Congressman	Indiana																								
Harris	Fred R.	Senator (fmr.)	Oklahoma																						x		
Harsch	Joseph Close	Wash. Correspondent	NBC				x							x													
Hartman	Arthur A.	Ambassador (fmr.)	former Soviet Union														x	x									
Hauge	Gabriel	Chairman	Mfg. Hanover Trust Co.											x				x									
Hays	Brooks	Congressman (fmr.)	Arkansas	x	x	x	x	x	x	x	x																
Heilperin	Michael A.	Professor	Inst. of Int. Studies, Geneva	x	x	x	x	x	x		x																
Heinz	Henry John, II	Chairman (fmr.)	H. J Heinz Co.; Us Rep., E.C.E.						x	x	x	x		x	x	x	x	x									
Herter	Christian Archibald	Secretary (fmr.)	State Dept.					x	x	x	x	x															
Herter	Christian A.	Undersecretary	State Dept.				x																				
Hesburg	Theodore M., Rev.	President (fmr.)	Holy Cross Univ.														x	x									
Hewitt	William A.	Chairman (fmr.)	Deere & Co.								x	x	x	x													
Hickenlooper	Bourke Blakemore	Senator (fmr.)	Iowa								x	x															
Hoagland	Jim	Assoc. Editor	*Washington Post*																						x	x	
Hochschild	Harold K.	Chairman	American Metal Co.								x	x	x														
Hoffman	Paul Gray	US Ambassador (fmr.)	United Nations	x	x			x	x	x	x																
Hoffman	Stanley			x				x	x						x												
Hoge	James F., Jr.	Editor	*Foreign Affairs* (CFR)																						x		
Holbrooke	Richard C.	Asst. Secretary	St Dept., European & Canadian Afrs.																			x	x	x	x	x	x
Holifield	Chet	Congressman											x	x		x											
Horelick	Arnold L.	Director	RAND/UCLA Ctr./Stdy./USSR Behav.																								
Hormats	Robert D.	Director	Goldman Sachs Int												x					x							
Horning	Donald Frederick	Director (fmr.)	President's Office of Science & Tech.										x														
Huber	Robert W.	Sr. Vice President	IBM														x	x									
Humelsine	Carlisle										x																
Hunter	Robert E.	US Representative	to NATO																		x						
Irwin	Donald J.															x											
Jackson	Charles D.	Vice President	Time Inc.	x	x		x	x	x	x	x																
Jackson	Henry M.	Senator (fmr.)	Washington state					x	x	x	x		x	x		x											
Jackson	William H.										x	x	x			x	x	x									
Javits	Jacob K.	Senator (fmr.)	New York	x	x							x	x														
Jay	Nelson Dean	Banker	J. P. Morgan & Co. Inc.					x	x	x	x	x	x														
Jennings	Peter	Anchor & Sr. Editor	ABC News, World News Tonight																			x					
Johnson	James A.	Chairman & CEO	Fannie Mae																					x			
Johnson	Joseph E.	Secretary (fmr.)	State Dept.	x	x		x	x	x	x	x	x	x	x	x	x	x										
Johnston	J. Bennett	Senator	Louisiana, Democrat																x								
Jordan	Vernon Eulion, Jr.	Partner, Sr.	Akin, Gump, Strauss, Hauer & Feld																	x	x		x	x	x	x	x
Kann	Peter Robert	Chair. & CEO	Dow Jones & Co., Pub., Wall St. Journ.																				x				
Katz	Milton	Professor	Suffolk Univ. Law School																								
Kaysen	Carl	Professor	MIT												x												
Kearns	David T.	Chairman	Xerox Corp.																								
Keenan	George F.	Ambassador (fmr.)	to U.S.S.R., 1952	x	x				x		x		x														
Keener	Jefferson Ward	Pres. & CEO (fmr.)	B. F. Goodrich Co.												x												
Kennedy	David Michael	Professor	Stanford Univ.	x				x							x	x											
Kennedy	David M.																										
Kimmitt	Robert Michael	Managing Dir.	Lehman Broithers Inc.																			x					

Last Name	1st & Middle Names	Country of Job	Office, Post or Affiliation	54	55	56	57	58	59	60	62	63	64	66	67	68	71	74	75	91	93	94	95	96	97	98	99
Kissinger	Henry A.	Secretary (fmr.)	State Dept.				x										x			x	x	x	x	x	x	x	x
Knoppers	Antonie T.														x										x	x	x
Kraft	Joseph														x										x	x	x
Kravis	Henry R.	Founding Partner	Kohlberg Kravis Roberts & Co.																				x	x		x	x
Kravis	Marie-Josee	Sr. Fellow	Hudson Institute																				x	x		x	x
Kristol	William (Bill)	Editor & Publisher	Weekly Standard magazine																			x					
Krogh	Peter F.	Dean	Georgetown U., Sch. of Fgn. Service																		x						
Leschly	Jan	CEO	SmithKline Beecham																						x	x	x
Levy	Walter James	Economic Consultant	Private																								
Lewis	William Walker	Exec. V. Pres. & Pres.	Avon Products																						x		
Lieftinck	Pieter	President	IMF-IBRD						x	x		x	x	x													
Lindsay	Franklin Anthony	President	Itek; Mbr, Smithsonian Inst, Adv. Coun									x	x	x	x			x									
Litchfield	Lawrence, Jr.	Chairman (fmr.)	ALCOA							x		x	x	x													
Littlejohn	Edward			x																				x			
Lord	Winston	Asst. Secretary	State Dept.												x			x									
Maillard	William S.																										
Martin	Edwin McCammon, Jr.	Partner, Sr.	Hale & Dorr, Wash.				x		x	x		x	x	x													
Mason	Edward S.			x			x		x	x	x																
Mathews	Jessica Tuchman	President	Carnegie End. for Int. Peace															x	x	x							
Mathias	Charles McCurdy, Jr.	Senator (fmr.)	Maryland												x	x	x	x	x								
Matlock	Jack Foust, Jr.	Fellow, Sr. Research	Columbia Univ.													x								x			
Maynes	Charles William	Editor	Foreign Policy																			x					
McCloy	John J.	Chairman (fmr.)	Chase Manh. Bk.,Fmr. Hi. Com., Germ.				x		x	x	x		x	x		x											
McConald	David J.									x	x		x	x													
McCormack	James									x																	
McCracken	Paul Winston	Professor	Univ. of Michigan												x			x	x								
McDonald	David J.																										
McDonough	William J.	President	Fed. Res. Bank of New York																					x		x	
McGee	Gale W.	Senator (fmr.)	Wyoming													x			x								
McGhee	George Crews	Owner	McGhee Production Co. (oil); fmr. Amb.	x			x		x	x		x		x		x											
McGill	Ralph E.	Chairman & CEO	Lucent Technologies																								
McGinn	Richard A.	Chairman & CEO	Lucent Technologies																						x		
McHenry	Donald F.	Research Professor	Georgetown Univ., Dipl. & Int. Afrs.																			x					
McLaughlin	David Thomas	President & CEO	Aspin Institute																		x						
McNamara	Robert Strange	President (fmr.)	World Bank													x			x								
McNaughton	John T.																										
Mitchell	James P.	Secretary (fmr.)	Labor				x								x												
Mondale	Walter Fritz	Ambassador	Japan															x									
Monroney	A. S. Mike	Senator	Oklahoma						x	x	x	x	x	x	x												
Morse	F. Bradford																										
Mosely	Philip E.	Professor	Columbia Univ., Russian Inst.	x			x		x	x	x	x	x	x	x	x											
Moyers	Bill D.	Executive Editor	Publiv Affairs TV, Inc.												x	x											
Muller	Charles W.	President	Murden & Co.														x			x		x					
Murphy	Robert Daniel	Chairman (fmr.)	Corning Glass Int.	x			x		x	x	x	x	x	x													
Nash	Frank C.																										
Neal	Alfred C.	President	Committee for Economic Development							x	x	x	x	x	x	x											
Nebolsine	George	Lawyer	Consultant, Dept. of State	x	x	x	x	x	x	x	x	x	x	x	x	x											

Last Name	1st & Middle Names	Country of Job	Office, Post or Affiliation	99	98	97	96	95	94	93	91	75	74	71	68	67	66	64	63	62	60	59	58	57	56	55	54
Newhouse	John																										
Nitze	Paul Henry	Secretary (fmr.)	Navy			x													x	x	x	x	x	x	x	x	x
Norstad	Lauris	General (fmr.)	Supreme Allied Commander - Europe				x	x								x	x				x	x	x	x			
Nunn	Sam	Senator	Georgia				x	x																			
Nye	Joseph S., Jr.	Chairman	National Intelligence Council						x																		
Paepcke	Walter P.																				x	x					
Page	John M., Jr.	Chief Econ.	The World Bank			x																					
Parker	Cola G.	Industrialist	Mbr., Commission/Fgn. Econ. Policy																	x	x	x	x			x	x
Patterson	Morehead																			x	x	x					
Payne	Frederick B.																							x			
Penzias	Arno A.	V. P. Research	AT&T Bell Labs.					x																			
Perkins	George William, II	Pres. & Chair.	Financial Marketing System, Inc.																	x							
Perkins	James Alfred	Chairman (fmr.)	Cornell Aero. Labs.													x	x	x	x								x
Perry	William J.	Secretary (fmr.)	Defense Dept.				x																				
Peterson	Howard C.	President (fmr.)	Fidelity-Philadelphia Trust																			x					
Peterson	Rudolph A.	Director	Bank America Natl. Trust & Savings															x	x								
Pfaltzgraff	Robert L., Jr.	President	Inst. for Fgn. Pol. Analysis											x													
Pickering	Thomas R.	US Ambassador	St. Dept., Russia, Moscow, '94, Ambassad						x																		
Piel	Gerald	Chairman (fmr.)	Scientific America, Inc.													x	x										
Piore	Emanuel Rubin	Adjunct Professor	Rockefeller Univ.													x	x										
Podhoretz	Norman	Editor	"Commentary"				x																				
Porkins	George H.	Perm. Representative	North Atlantic Council																							x	
Powell	Colin L.	Chairman (fmr.)	Joint Chiefs of Staff			x																					
Price	Don K.	Professor (fmr.)	Harvard Univ.																					x			
Pritchard	Joel McFee	Member	Congress									x	x														
Quandt	William Bauer	Sr. Fellow	Brookings Inst.							x																	
Rabi	Isidor Isaac	Chairman (fmr.)	Association of Universities										x	x													
Rattner	Steven	Deputy Executive	Lazard Freres & Co., LLC							x																	
Reed	John Shedd	Chairman & CEO	Santa Fe Southern Pacific Corp.							x																	
Reinhardt	G. Frederick	Counsellor	State Dept.; fmr. Ambassador														x										
Reston	James Barrett	Co-Chairman	Vineyard Gazette											x													
Reuss	Henry																										
Reuther	Walter Philip	Vice President (fmr.)	AFL-CIO Union															x	x								
Richardson	Bill	Secretary	Energy Dept.			x																					
Ridgway	Rozanne Lejeanne	Co-Chairwoman	Atlantic Council of the US							x	x																
Riegle	Donald W.	Senator	Michigan										x														
Rhodes	William R.	Vice Chairman	Citibank, N.A.		x																						
Roberts	Henry Lithgow														x												
Robinson	Charles W.	Undersecretary	State Dept., Economic Affairs									x	x														
Rockefeller	David	Chairman	Chase Man. Bk., Rockefeller Gp., Inc.	x	x	x	x	x	x	x	x	x	x	x	x	x	x	x	x	x	x	x	x	x	x	x	x
Rockefeller	Nelson Aldrich	President (fmr.)	Rockefeller Brothers Foundation			x																					
Rockefeller	Sharon Percy	President & CEO	WETA-TV and FM radio				x																				
Roosa	Robert V.	Vice President (fmr.)	Fed. Res. Bk./NY, Pt, Brown Bros. Harri										x					x	x	x	x	x	x				
Ross	Michael				x	x																					
Rostow	Eugene Victor	Dist. Vis. Rsch. Prof.	National Defense Univ.																			x	x				
Prendergast	Kieran	Under Sec. Gen.	for Political Affairs, UN		x																						
Prestowitz	Clyde V.	President	Economic Strategy Institute		x																						

Last Name	1st & Middle Names	Country of Job	Office, Post or Affiliation	54	55	56	57	58	59	60	62	63	64	66	67	68	71	74	75	91	93	94	95	96	97	98	99
Rumsfeld	Donald Henry	Chairman & CEO	General Instruments Corp., Chicago															x	x								
Rusk	Dean	Professor	U. of Georgia; Sec. (Fmr.), St. Dept.		x	x			x	x	x		x			x											
Ryan	John T.															x											
Samuelson	Paul Anthony	Professor	NYU																								
Scalapino	Robert A.	Research Professor	Univ. of Calif.										x								x						
Schmidt	Adolph William	Ambassador (fmr.)	Canada								x		x														
Schnitzler	William F.	Sec.-Treasurer (fmr.)	AFL-CIO Union		x						x		x														
Scott	Hugh	Senator (fmr.)	Pennsylvania																								
Scowcroft	Brent	Asst. to (fmr.)	President of US																			x					
Shad	John S. R.	Ambassador (fmr.)	Neatherlands																	x							
Shapiro	Robert B.	Chairman & CEO	Monsanto Company																								x
Sheinkman	Jack	Chairman	Amal.Cloth.& Text.Wkrs.Un.,AFL-CIO																			x	x	x			
Shulman	Marshall D.	Professor	Harvard Univ., Int. Politics									x	x														
Simons	Thomas W., Jr.	Ambassador	to Poland																		x						
Smith	Howard Page	Admiral (fmr.)	Supr. Allied Commandewr - Atlantic			x	x																				
Smith	Walter Bedell	General	Director (fmr.), C.I.A.			x	x																				
Soderberg	Nancy E.	Dep. Asst. to Pres.	White House, Nat. Sec. Afrs.																				x				
Sonnenfeldt	Helmut	Counselor (fmr.)	State Dept.														x										
Soros	George	President	Soros Fund Management																				x	x			
Spang	Joseph P., Jr.	Chairman (fmr.)	Gillette Co.	x	x	x																					
Sparkman	John	Senator	Alabama		x																						
Spofford	Charles M.	Chairman	North Atlantic Council Deputies		x	x			x	x	x	x	x														
Stahl	Lesley R.	Correspondent	National Affairs, CBS																						x		
Steinberg	James B.	Director	State Dept, for policy planning												x				x								
Stephanopoulos	George	Senior Advisor	to President Clinton																				x	x			
Stevenson	Adlai Ewing, III	Senator	Illinois							x	x				x	x											
Stone	Shepard	President	Int. Assoc./Cult. Freedom; Dir., Ford Found.						x	x	x	x	x	x	x	x	x	x	x								
Stone	Thomas A.									x																	
Sulzberger	Arthur Hays	Chairman (fmr.)	Chattanooga Publishing Co.				x		x	x	x																
Sulzberger	Cyrus Leo	Columnist (fmr.)	NY Times					x	x	x	x					x	x										
Summers	Lawrence H.	Dep. Secretary	Int. Affrs., Treasury Dept.																						x		
Thoman	G. Richard	President & CEO	Xerox Corp.										x												x	x	
Thornton	John L.	President & co-COO	Goldman Sachs Group, Inc.																							x	
Trotman	Alexander J.	Chairman	Ford Motor Company																					x			
Trudeau	Pierre	Prime Minister (fmr.)	Canada													x	x										
Tuthill	John Wills	Director	Georgetown Univ.												x	x											
Tyson	Laura d'Andrea	Dean	Haad School of Business, Berkeley																								x
Vernon	Raymond	Professor (fmr.)	Harvard Univ.										x		x												
Victor	Alice	Executive Assistant	Rockefeller Financial Services, Inc.																	x			x				
Vink	Lodewijk J.R. de	President & CEO	Warner-Lambert Company																						x		
Vogel	Ezra F.	Professor	Social Sci., Harvard Univ.																			x					
Vogt	John W., Lt. Gen.	Director (fmr.)	US Joint Chiefs of Staff												x	x											
Volcker	Paul Adolph	Chairman	BT Wolfensohn																			x					
Vorys	John M.	Congressman				x	x																				
Weinberg	Sidney					x	x																				
Weiss	Stanley A.	Chairman	Business Exec. for Nat. Security, Inc.																	x		x	x			x	x
Whitehead	John Cunningham	Judge	Nebraska State District, Columbus			x														x		x				x	x

Who's Who of the Elite

Last Name	1st & Middle Names	Country of Job	Office, Post or Affiliation	54	55	56	57	58	59	60	62	63	64	66	67	68	71	74	75	91	93	94	95	96	97	98	99
Whitman	Christine Todd	Governor	New Jersey																							x	
Wicker	Thomas Grey	Columnist (fmr.)	NY Times				x									x											
Wilbur	Brayton, Jr.	President	Wilbur-Ellis Co: Dir., Safeway Stores																		x						
Wilcox	Francis O.																										
Wilde	Frazar B.	Chairman (fmr.)	Connecticut Gen. Life Insurance Co.	x			x		x	x																	
Wilder	Lawrence Douglas	Governor (fmr.)	Virginia						x	x			x														
Wiley	Alexander	Senator					x		x	x																	
Williams	Lynn Russell	International President	Unit. Steelwkrs/America (union)																	x							
Winthrop	Grant F.	Partner	Mlbank, Winthrop & Co.																		x	x					
Wisner	Frank G.	Undersecretary	Defense Dept., for policy																		x						
Wohlstetter	Albert																									
Wolfensohn	James David	President	The World Bank										x											x	x	x	x
Wolfowitz	Paul Dean	Dean	John Hopkins Univ., Sch./Adv. Stud.																					x	x	x	
Wriston	Walter Bigelow	Chairman (fmr.)	Citicorp																				x	x	x	x	x
Yost	Casimir A.	Hon. Sec. Gen.	for U.S. at Bilderbach Conferences																				x	x	x	x	x
Zellerbach	James David	President	Crown Zellerbach	x	x																						
Zoellick	Robert Bruce	Exec. VP/Gen. Cnsl.	Fannie Mae, Wash.																		x						
Zuckerman	Mortimer B.	Editor	US News & World Report																								
International																												
Beer	Henrik	Secretary General	League of Red Cross Societies								x	x															
Bokros	Lojos	Sr. Advisor	The World Bank																						x		
Bonino	Emma	Member	European Parliament																						x		
Booth	Alan R.		World Council of Churches											x													
Bottelier	Pieter P.	Chief of Mission	World Bank, Resident Mission, China																				x				
Brittan	Leon	Vice President	European Commission																					x			
Brock	Hans, van den	Commissioner	European Communities																			x					
Brosio	Manlio		N.A.T.O.											x	x												
Crockett	Andrew	Gen. Mgr.	Bank for Int. Settlement																				x				
Cutileiro	Jose	Secretary General	Western European Union																					x			
Dunkel	Arthur	Director General	GATT															x									
Dunlap	Clarence R.		S.H.A.P.E.						x		x																
Fischer	Stanley	1st Dep. Managing Dir.	IMF																					x	x		
Johnstone	Donald J.	Sec. General	OECD																					x			
Kohnstamm	Max	President	Euro. U.,Florence,fmr.Sec.Gen.,Action/E									x	x				x	x		x	x	x	x				
Larre	Rene	Director	Bank for International Sattlements															x									
Lemnitzer	Gen. Lyman L.	Chairman	Monetary Comm.,E.E.C.;Sec.Gen.,O.E.C								x																
Lennep	Jonkheer Emille, van		IMF-IBRD									x					x	x									
Lieftnick	Pieter	Director										x															
Liikanen	Erkki	Member	European Commission (EC)																							x	
Mansholt	Sicco L.	Vice President	E.E.C.												x												
Puget	Andre		S.H.A.P.E.						x		x		x														
Rey	Jean		E.E.C.						x		x		x														
Santo	Espirito	President & CEO	Banco Espirito										x														
Saracoglu	Rusdu	"Mediator"	EU Community																	x							
Schuyler	C. V. R.		S.H.A.P.E.				x		x		x																
Schwab	Klaus	President	World Economic Forum (Italy)																			x				x	x

Last Name	1st & Middle Names	Country of Job	Office, Post or Affiliation	54	55	56	57	58	59	60	62	63	64	66	67	68	71	74	75	91	93	94	95	96	97	98	99
Schweitzer	Pierre-Paul	Managing Director	IMF										x	x													
Solana Madarings	Javiar	Secretary Gen.	N.A.T.O.																							x	
Southard Jr.	Frank A., Jr.		IMF								x			x													
Steeg	Helga	Executive Director	International Energy Agency																	x							
Stikker	Dirk U.	Secretary General	N.A.T.O.								x		x	x													
Thurston	Raymond		N.A.T.O.										x	x													
Visser 't Hooft	Willem A.		World Council of Churches													x											
Vries	Gijs M. de	Leader	Liberal Group, European Parl.																					x	x		
Wegener	Henning	Asst. Secretary Gen.	NATO, Political Affairs																	x							
Woods	George D.		IBRD											x													
Woerner	Manfred	Secretary General	N.A.T.O.																	x	x						
Wyndham White	Eric	Executive Secretary	G.A.T.T.										x	x													

Unidentified at publication date

Braathen	Erik																			x							
Brady	Connor																			x							
Braitwaite	Rodric																			x							
Brederode	Santos Nuno																			x							
Brinkman	L. C.																			x							
Cebrian	Juan Luis																			x							
Johnstone	V.																			x							
Mozer	Alfred E.												x													
Owen	Vance																			x							
Saint-Mluex	A.								x																	

Bilderberg Conferences

Dates, Places of Meetings, and Agendas

Source: Copy of an official Bilderberg document acquired by Klaus Kopf, RIE's German Distributor.

May 29-31, 1954 - Bilderberg Hotel, Oosterbeek, The Netherlands
Subjects;
A. The attitude towards communism and the Soviet Union
B. The attitude toward dependent areas and people overseas
C. The attitude toward economic policies and problems
D. The attitude toward European integration and the European Defense Community

March 18-20, 1955 - Barbizon, France
Subjects:
A. Survey of Western European-USA relations since the first Bilderberg Conference
B. Communist infiltration in various Western countries
C. The uncommitted people:
  • Political and ideological aspects
  • Economic aspects

September 23-25, 1955 - Garmisch-Partenkirchen, Germany
Subjects:
A. Review of events since the Barbizon Conference
B. Article 2 of the North Atlantic Treaty Organization
C. The political and strategic aspects of atomic energy
D. The reunification of Germany
E. European unity
F. The industrial aspects of atomic energy
G. Economic problems:
  • East-West trade
  • The political aspects of convertibility
  • Expansion of international trade

May 11-13, 1956 - Fredenborg, Denmark
Subjects:
A. Review of development since the last Conference
B. The causes of the growth of anti-Western bloc, in particular in the United Nations
C. The role played by anti-colonialism in relations between Asians and the West
D. A common approach by the Western world towards China and the emergent nations of South and East Asia
E. The communist campaign for political subversion or control of the newly emancipated countries of Asia
F. How the West can best meet Asian requirements in the technical and economic fields

February 15-17, 1957 - Rockefeller owned hotel, St. Simons Island, Georgia, USA
Subjects:
A. Review of events since the fourth Bilderberg meeting in May, 1956
B. Nationalism and neutralism as disruptive factors inside Western Alliances
C. The Middle East
D. The European policy of the Alliance, with special reference to the problems of Eastern Europe, German reunification and military strategy

October 4-6, 1957 - Fiuggi, Italy
Subjects:
A. Survey of developments since the last Conference
B. Modern weapons and disarmament in relations to Western security
C. Are existing political and economic mechanisms within the Western community adequate?

September 13-15, 1958 - Palace Hotel, Buxon, England

Subjects:

A. Survey of events since the last Conference

B. The future of NATO defense

C. Western economic cooperation

D. The Western approach to Soviet Russia and communism

September 18-20, 1959 - Yesilkoy, Turkey

Subjects:

A. Review of developments since the last Conference

B. Unity and division in Western policy

May 28-29, 1960 - Burgenstock, Switzerland

Subjects:

A. State of the world situation after the failure of the Summit Conference

B. New political and economic developments in the Western world

April 21-23, 1961 - Castin, Canada

Subjects:

A. What initiatives are required to bring about a new sense of leadership and direction within the Western community?

B. The implications for Western unity of changes in the relative economic strength of the United States and Western Europe

May 18-20, 1962 - Saltsjobaden, Sweden

Subjects:

A. The political implications for the Atlantic community of its members' policies in the United States

B. Implications for the Atlantic community of prospective developments

May 29-31, 1963 - Cannes, France

Subjects:

A. The balance of power in the light of recent international development

B. Trade relations between the USA and Europe in the light of the negotiations for Britain's entry into the Common Market

C. Trade relations between the Western world and the developing countries

March 20-22, 1964 - Rockefeller owned hotel, Williamsburg, Virginia, USA

Subjects:

The consequences for the Atlantic Alliance of:

A. Apparent changes in the communist world
  • Soviet internal development
  • The Communist Bloc

B. Possible changes in the attitude of the USSR to the West

C. Recent developments within the Western world:
  • Political
  • Military
  • Economic

April 2-4, 1965 - Villa D'Este, Lake Como, Italy

Subjects:

A. Monetary cooperation in the Western world

B. The state of the Atlantic Alliance

March 25-27, 1966 - Wiesbaden, Germany

Subjects:

A. Should NATO be reorganized, and if so how?

B. The future of world economic relations especially between industrial and developing countries

March 31-April 2, 1967 - Cambridge, England
Subjects:
A. • Do the basic concepts of Atlantic cooperation remain valid for the evolving world situation?
   • If not, what concepts could take their place?
B. The technological gap between America and Europe with special reference to American involvement in Europe

April 26-28, 1968 - Mont Tremblant, Canada
Subjects:
A. The relations between the West and the Communist countries
B. Internationalization of business

May 9-11, 1969 - Marienlyst, Denmark
Subjects:
A. Elements of instability in Western society
B. Conflicting attitudes within the Western world towards relations with the USSR and the other Communist states of Eastern Europe in the light of recent events

April 17-19, 1970 - Bad Ragaz, Switzerland
Subjects:
A. Future function of the university in our society
B. Priority in foreign policy

April 23-25, 1971 - Woodstock Inn (owned by Rockefellers), Woodstock, Vermont, USA
Subjects:
A. The contribution of business in dealing with current problems of social instability
B. The possibility of a change of the American role in the world and its consequences

April 21-23, 1972 - Knokke, Belgium
Subject:
The state of the Western community in the light of changing relationships among the non-communist industrialized countries and the impact of changing power relationships in the Far East on Western security

May 11-13, 1973 - Saltsjobaden, Sweden
Subjects:
A. The possibilities of the development of a European energy policy and the consequences of European-North American relations
B. Conflicting expectations concerning the European Security Conference

April 19-21, 1974 - Hotel Mont d'Arbois (owned by Baron Edmond de Rothschild), Megeve, France
Subject:
Prospects for the Atlantic world

April 25-27, 1975 - Golden Dolphin Hotel, Cesme, Turkey
Subjects:
A. Inflation: its economic, social and political implications
B. Recent international political developments:
   • The present status and prospects to resolve the Arab-Israeli conflict and the effect on relations among NATO members
   • Other recent developments affecting the relations among NATO countries

April 22-24, 1977 - Torquay, England
Subjects:

North American and Western European attitudes towards:

A. The future of the mixed economies in the Western democracies
B. The Third World's demand for restructuring the world order and the political implications of these attitudes

April 21-23, 1978 - Princeton, New Jersey, USA
Subjects:

A. Western defense with its political implications
B. The changing structure of production and trade: consequences for the Western industrialized countries

April 27-29, 1979 - Baden Austria
Subjects:

A. The present international monetary situation and its consequences for World cooperation
B. The implications of instability in the Middle East and Africa for the Western World
C. Other current issues bearing on European-American relations

April 18-20, 1980 - Aachen, Germany
Subject:

America and Europe: Past, Present, and Future

A. New threats and old Allies: prospects for the security of Europe and America
B. The Americans and the Alliance in 1980
C. Economic relations between North America and Europe
D. Energy policy, monetary policy, foreign trade and payments relations between Europe and the United States of America
E. Europe and the United States - yesterday and tomorrow

May 14-17, 1981 - Burgenstock, Switzerland
Subject:

Challenges of the 1980's

A. What should Western policy be toward the Soviet Union in the 1980s?
B. Obstacles to effective cooperation of Western policies
C. How can the Western economies put their house in order?

May 14-16, 1982 - Sandefjord, Norway
Subjects:

A. Divergent policies and attitudes in the North Atlantic Community
B. What can arms control achieve?
C. Middle East: Issues at stake
D. Economic issues: dogmas and realities
E. Current events:
   • The Falkland Islands crisis
   • East-West relations: Poland, trade and finance

May 13-15, 1983 - Montebello, Canada
Subjects:

A. East-West relations: constraints, detente or confrontation
B. Issues in medium-term prospects for growth in the world economy:
   • Protectionism and employment
   • Risks in banking and finance
C. Current events: U.S. foreign policy in the Middle East and Central America

May 11-13, 1984 - Saltsjobaden, Sweden
Subjects:
A. Western power and the Middle East: a case study in Atlantic relationships
B. The state of arms control negotiations
C. Future employment trends in the industrialized democracies
D. Current events: continental drift: economic and political
E. The Soviet Union, the West and the Third World; a case study: Central America

May 10-12, 1985 - Rockefeller owned hotel, Rye Brook, New York, USA
Subjects:
A. Divergent social and economic trends in the Atlantic World
B. How should the West deal with the Soviet Bloc?
C. S.D.I.
D. How should the West deal with developing countries?
E. Current events: the current status of the budget in Congress and the European perspective on that situation
F. Operating the Alliance

April 25-27, 1986 - Gleneagles, Scotland
Subjects:
A. The Soviet Union under Gorbachev: foreign policy implications
B. The Western global response to the Soviet changes
C. The fragmentation of the world economy: debt, currency disorder, protectionism, and uneven growth
D. Current events: terrorism
E. South Africa

April 24-26, 1987 - Villa D'Este, Italy
Subjects:
A. Strategy toward the USSR
B. Policy toward trade and protectionism
C. The public sector and economic growth
D. Current events: China
E. The arms control debate

June 3-5, 1988 - Telfs-Buchen, Austria
Subjects:
A. What can be done with the world economy: alternative scenarios
B. How to handle a world awash with public and private debt?
C. The German question revisited
D. The new information era
E. Briefing on the Moscow summit
F. The impact of glasnost
G. Future strategy of the Alliance
H. The Gulf and Afghanistan

May 12-14, 1989 - La Toja, Spain
Subjects:
A. Domestic developments in Eastern Europe: policy implications for the West
B. Can the Alliance be sustained by military and arms control issues alone?
C. The long-term economic design of the E.C.: European sovereignty?
D. Current events: U.S.-Soviet relations
E. Greater political and monetary union of Europe: European sovereignty?
F. Global relationships: surpluses, deficits and protectionism
G. Environmental constraints

May 11-13, 1990 - Rockefeller owned hotel, Glen Cove, New York, USA
Subjects:
A. The new Soviet (Dis) Union
B. Strategy issues
C. Economic relations with Eastern Europe
D. Can Western values be applied universally?
E. Germany
F. The future of NATO and the European Community
G. Japan: political changes

June 6-9, 1991 - Baden-Baden, Germany
Subjects:
A. Eastern Europe: economic prospects
B. Developments in the Soviet Union: political and economic impacts on the Alliance
C. The Middle East: political fallout and future prospects
D. Economic and financial threats to the Alliance
E. The practical agenda for the Alliance
F. Do we have the institutions to deal with the agenda?
G. Recent developments in Yugoslavia
H. The situation in South-Africa
I. The Treuhand experience

May 21-24, 1992 - Evian-Les-Bains, France
Subjects:
A. Prospects for the former Soviet Republics
B. What should be done for Eastern Europe?
C. Whither the United States?
D. The World economy
E. Whither Europe?
F. Soviet Union: the view from Moscow
G. The migration issue
H. The evolving west/west relationship

April 22-25, 1993 - Vouliagmeni, Greece
Subjects:
A. What kind of Europe will the U.S. have to deal with?
B. Current events: Former Yugoslavia
C. Restoring confidence in leadership and institutions
D. Prospects for Global Trade
E. U.S. domestic policy concerns
F. The outlook for Japan's economy
G. Cost of indifference toward the former Soviet Union
H. Current events: Italy
I. Foreign policy concerns of the Clinton Administration
J. Crisis management

June 2-5, 1994 - Helsinki, Finland
Subjects:
A. Redefinition of the Atlantic relationship in a time of change
B. The changing face and perspective of America
C. Europe - Cohesion or Confusion
D. Economic instability ahead
E. Jobs, where are they and how will the West create them
F. The political changes of Islamic Fundamentalism
G. Russia - How will its internal evolution affect its external behavior
H. GATT: Risk ahead
I. The issue of non-proliferation: North Korea
J. China - The consequences of convulsion or stability

June 8-11, 1995 - Grand, Park & Palace hotels, Burgenstock, Switzerland

Subjects:

A. What is NATO supposed to do?
B. Is there work for all?
C. Atomization of society: Impact on political behavior of new technology
D. Looking (Back) at Washington
E. Current events: Turkey and the Atlantic Alliance
F. Is there still a North Atlantic Community?
G. Should the European Union integrate further, and why?
H. Our agendas for WTO and World Bank
I. Current events: Former Yugoslavia
J. Peacekeeping in an UNstable World
K. Lessons of the New Currency Crises
L. Practical steps toward better Global Governance and Rules

May 30 - June 2, 1996 - Canadian Imperial Bank of Commerce Leadership Center, King City, Ontario, Canada

A. Status Report on the Alliance
B. Former Yugoslavia
C. Russia: Political Forces and Economic Prospects
D. Europe: the Politics of EU Enlargement
E. Has Europe's Economy Run Out of Steam?
F. Will the Enlarged Union Survive EMU's Success or Failure?
G. The US Agenda
H. The Israeli Election
I. How and How Much can the Western World Grow Economically?
J. WTO and the World Bank: Briefing
K. Where is China Going?

June 12-15, 1997 - Renaissance Pine Island Resort, Lake (Sidney) Lanier Island, about 57 miles NE of Atlanta, Georgia, USA

Subjects:

A. Racial Harmony
B. World Without Borders
C. Most Favored Nation (MFN) for China
D. European Union
E. American Union

May 14-18, 1998 - Turnberry, Scotland (Turnberry Hotel, 55 miles from Glasgow)

Subjects:

A. The Atlantic Relationship in a time of change
B. NATO
C. Asian Crisis
D. European Monetary Union
E. Growing Military Disparity
F. Japan
G. Multilateral Organizations
H. Europe´s Social Model
I. EU/ US Market Place

June 3-6, 1999 - Caesar Park Penha Longa, Sintra, Portugal (40 miles N. W. of Lisbon)
Subjects:
A. Atlantic Relationship in a Time of Change
B. NATO
C. Genetics
D. Emerging Markets
E. The New Economy
F. European Politics
G. US Politics
H. International Financial Architecture
J. Russia

June 1-4, 2000 - Hotel Chateau du Lac at Genval, 9 miles south of the Brussels, Belgium airport.
Subjects:
    A. US Elections
    B. Globalization
    C. New Economy
    D. The Balkans
    E. EU Enlargement
    F. The European Far Right

May 24-28, 2001 – Quality Hotel, Stenungsbaden, Sweden, 30 KM North of Gothenburg.
Subjects:
    A. Defense
    B. China/Japan
    C. Russia
    D. Europe
    E. Productivity
    F. Agriculture
    G. Middle-East
    H. Globalization

May 30 – June 2, 2002 – Westfields Marriott Hotel, Chantilly, Virginia, Near the Dulles International Airport
Subjects:
    A. Terrorism
    B. Trade
    C. Post Crisis Reconstruction
    D. Middle East
    E. Civil Liberties
    F. US Foreign Policy
    G. Extreme Right
    H. World Economy
    I. Corporate Governance

Summary of the Elite

Summary of the Distribution of the Elite in the United States		
Name of Agency or Department	Present Members In Office	Former (but recent) Past Members
Universities	479	71
News Media	313	36
Think Tanks	312	37
Industry	177	40
Law Firms	160	3
Investment Organizations	148	10
Miscellaneous	120	8
State Department	118	84
Foundations	103	7
Executive Office of the President	74	31
Defense Department	67	66
Commercial Banks	64	15
Consultants	61	1
Federal & International Banking	33	14
House of Representatives	32	25
Other Government Agencies	30	2
Senate	24	27
United Nations	20	27
Charities, Race & Religion	13	4
Other Federal Courts	12	2
Commerce Department	10	7
State Governments	10	5
Treasury Department	9	19
Unions	9	6
Central Intelligence Agency	7	16
Public Relations & Advertising	5	- -
City Governments	5	4
Supreme Court	4	2
Health & Human Services Department	3	4
Energy Department	3	2
Agriculture Department	2	1
Justice Department	1	9
Housing & Urban Development Department	1	3
Transportation Department	1	2
Labor Department	1	1
Interior Department	1	- -
Education Department	1	- -
F.B.I.	0	2
Sub-Totals	2433	591
United States Grand Total	3024	- -

Name of Agency or Department	Present Members In Office	Former (but recent) Past Members
Think Tanks		
Overseas Development Council	36	- -
CFR Officers & Directors	34	11
Carnegie Foundations	33	15
Brookings Institute	32	1
Center for International Policy	25	- -
Foreign Policy Association	15	- -
RAND Corporation	15	2
Council of the Americas	12	1
Hudson Institute	8	1
Center for National Policy	7	- -
American Enterprise Institute	7	- -
US Institute for Peace	7	1
Human Rights Wastch	6	- -
Center for Foreign Policy	4	- -
Institute for Policy Studies	3	- -
Bilderberg Group	3	- -
Asia Society	2	1
World Affairs Council	2	1
Others	<u>61</u>	<u>3</u>
Sub Totals	312	37
Universities		
Harvard University	50	6
Columbia University	33	10
Universities of California	29	4
Princeton University	28	2
Stanford University	24	2
Georgetown University	20	- -
Mass. Institute of Technology	16	5
Yale University	9	2
Cornell University	9	- -
Univ. of S. Cal.	8	- -
Johns Hopkins University	7	3
University of Michigan	7	2
New York University	7	- -
University of Chicago	7	- -
George Washington University	7	- -
University of Texas	6	1
City University of New York	6	- -
Brown Univ.	6	- -
Boston University	5	1
Rockefeller University	5	1
Tufts Univ.	5	1
Others	<u>190</u>	<u>32</u>
Sub Totals	479	71

Name of Agency or Department	Present Members In Office	Former (but recent) Past Members
Industry		
Petroleum Refining	31	8
Telecommunications	14	1
Food	12	5
Chemicals	12	1
Computers & Office Equipment	10	3
Aerospace	9	3
Electronic & Electrical Equipment	9	1
Motor Vehicles & Parts	8	3
Beverages	7	2
Metals	7	--
Pharmaceuticals	6	3
Scientific, Photographic & Control Equipment	6	--
Industrial & Farm Equipment	5	4
Apparel	5	--
Forest & Paper Products	4	1
Soap & Cosmetics	4	--
Pipelines	3	1
Trains & Trucking	3	--
Electrical & Gas Utilities	2	1
Internet	2	--
General Merchandisers	1	1
Building Materials	1	--
Healthcare	1	--
Truck Leasing	1	--
Waste Management	1	--
Construction	1	--
Hotels & Motels	0	1
Other	12	--
Sub Totals	177	40
Law Firms		
Debevoise & Plimpton	10	2
O'Melveny & Myers	6	--
Cleary, Gottlieb, Steen & Hamilton	5	--
Coudert Brothers	5	--
Cravath, Swainew & Moore	4	--
Paul, Weis, Rifkind, Wharton & Garrett	4	--
Steptoe & Johnson	4	--
Sullivan & Cormwell, NYC	4	--
Covington & Burlington	3	--
Gibson, Dunn & Crutcher	3	--
Jones, Day, Reavis & Pogue	3	--
Patterson, Belknap, Webb & Tyler	3	--
Skadden, Arps, Slate, Meagher & Flom	3	--
Sheraman & Sterling, NYC	3	--
Winthrop, Stimson, Putnam & Roberts	3	--
Others	97	1
Sub Totals	160	3

Who's Who of the Elite

Name of Agency or Department	Present Members In Office	Former (but recent) Past Members
Investment Organizations		
Goldman Sachs & Co.	7	1
Lehman Brothers, Inc., NYC	6	1
Lazard Freres & Co.	4	- -
ITT Corp.	4	- -
Dillon, Read & Co., Inc.	3	- -
Merrill Lynch & Co.	3	- -
Salomon Brothers	3	2
Prudential	3	1
Others	<u>115</u>	<u>5</u>
Sub Totals	**148**	**10**
Foundations		
Rockefeller Foundations	16	1
Carnegie Corp. of New York	14	- -
John P. & Catherine T. MacAuthur Foundation	6	- -
Ford Foundation	6	1
Andrew W. Mellon Foundation	3	1
Others	<u>74</u>	<u>5</u>
Sub Totals	**103**	**7**
Commercial Banks		
Chase (Chase Manhattan + Chemical)	5	7
Citibank, NYC	3	1
J. P. Morgan	4	- -
Credit Suisse First Boston	3	1
Bankamerica Corp.	2	1
Other	<u>47</u>	<u>5</u>
Sub Totals	**64**	**15**

Who's Who of the Elite

Name of Agency or Department	Present Members In Office	Former (but recent) Past Members
Mainstream News Media		
Book Publishing		
Various Authors	51	- -
Random House, Inc.	3	- -
W.W. Norton & Company	1	1
Others	10	2
Sub Totals	65	3
Newspaper Publishing		
New York Times	22	4
Washington Post	21	- -
Wall Street Journal	16	- -
Los Angeles Times	10	1
Associated Press	4	- -
Dallas Morning News	4	1
Times Mirror Company	2	- -
Others	68	14
Sub Totals	125	16
Magazine Publishing		
Time Warner, Inc.	15	3
Newsweek magazine	6	- -
New Yorker magazine	5	- -
US News & World Report	6	1
New Republic magazine	3	- -
Harpers	3	- -
Reader's Digest Association	2	1
Newsday, Inc.	2	1
National Review	2	- -
Others	51	6
Sub Totals	95	12
Television Broadcasting Networks		
ABC	13	- -
CBS	8	2
CNN	7	- -
PBS	6	1
NBC	3	5
Others	8	- -
Sub Totals	45	9
Motion Pictures	2	1
Radio Broadcasting	1	- -
Mainstream News Media Sub Totals	313	36

Name of Agency or Department	Present Members	Former (but recent)
Federal Government	In Office	Past Members
State Department	118	84
Executive Office of the President	74	31
Defense Department	67	66
Treasury Department	9	19
Commerce Department	10	7
Agriculture Department	2	1
Health & Human Services Department (HHS)	3	4
Central Intelligence Agency (CIA)	7	16
Energy Department	3	2
Housing & Urban Development Department (HUD)	1	3
Justice Department	1	9
Transportation Department	1	2
Labor Department	1	1
Interior Department	1	- -
Education Department	1	- -
Federal Bureau of Investigation (FBI)	0	2
Other Government Agencies	30	2
Sub Totals	329	249
Congress		
House of Representatives	32	25
Senate	24	27
Sub Totals	56	52
United Nations	20	27
Federal Courts		
Supreme Court	4	2
Other Federal Courts	12	2
Sub Totals	16	4
Consultants		
Booz, Allen & Hamilton Inc., NYC	3	- -
Kissinger & Assoc.	1	1
Others	57	- -
Sub Totals	61	1
Federal & International Banking		
Federal Reserve System	14	10
Export-Import Bank of US	5	1
World Bank	8	2
International Monetary Fund	2	1
Others	4	- -
Sub Totals	33	14

Who's Who of the Elite

Name of Agency or Department	Present Members In Office	Former (but recent) Past Members
Miscellaneous	120	8
State Governments	10	5
Charities, Race & Religion	13	4
Unions	9	6
Public Relations & Advertising	5	- -
City Governments	5	4
Sub Totals	162	27
United States Total	2498	596
Name of Country		
United States	2498	596
Japan	104	7
Germany	90	55
Great Britain	70	18
Canada	70	9
Italy	56	11
France	51	17
International	37	4
Spain	33	1
Portugal	30	1
The Netherlands	27	9
Greece	22	1
Finland	21	3
Sweden	21	3
Belgium	20	3
Turkey	18	15
Switzerland	17	6
Norway	17	5
Austria	16	2
Ireland	9	2
Denmark	8	4
Poland	6	- -
Czech Republic	4	1
Luxembourg	3	- -
Iceland	3	1
Russia	2	1
Hungary	2	0
Bulgaria	1	- -
China	1	- -
Ukraine	1	- -
	3258	775

Council on Foreign Relations
Committees

The CFR started out as a New York organization. It later expanded to include Washington, DC as part of the "Council". Then it added Committees in most of the larger cities across the nation. The *1992 Council on Foreign Relations Annual Report* states, on Pages 122-126:

"*Created in 1938, the Committees of Foreign Relations are membership organizations affiliated with the Council. The Committees, which serve as the Council's main form of outreach, are located in 37 cities nationwide; their members are selectively chosen from among leading figures in their communities, representing a cross section of the professions, government, academia, and the media* (emphasis added). *Committee members meet regularly to discuss foreign policy issues of current salience with officials and experts in the field of international affairs. Like the Council, the Committees encourage candid disclosure by holding their meetings on a not-for-attribution* (emphasis added) *basis.*

... Furthermore, 19 meetings addressed the 'New World Order'- an area not covered in past seasons - and new international institutions.

... In October, a small delegation of Committees representatives attended a series of briefings at the NATO and European Community headquarters in Brussels. Organized by NATO for the Committees, the program focused on the implications of the Alliance's evolving military structures for the United States and for the global security system (emphasis added).*"*

The CFR Committees are located in the following cities:

Albuquerque	Honolulu	Providence
Billings	Houston	Rochester
Birmingham	Indianapolis	St. Louis
Boise	Little Rock	St. Paul/Minneapolis
Boston	Los Angeles	Salt Lake City
Casper	Louisville	San Francisco
Charlottesville	Miami	Santa Barbara
Cleveland	Nashville	Tampa Bay Area
Dallas	Omaha	Tucson
Denver	Philadelphia	Tulsa
Des Moines	Phoenix	Wichita
Detroit	Portland, Maine	Worcester
	Portland, Oregon	

Many of the CFR members, who's affiliation has not been determined at this printing, are most likely associated with the above Committees.

Council on Foreign Relations
Corporate Member Roster

<u>Corporate Program</u> - *The Council on Foreign Relations, 1995 Annual Report, page 65, states:*

The Corporate Program provides programs of special interest to U.S. and foreign corporations, financial institutions, law firms, and other organizations involved in international business. The Program gives executives the opportunity to exchange views with their peers from other parts of the business world and from the public and private sectors, and to reflect on a wide variety of international issues. Corporate members are urged to designate executives who are the most concerned with the subject under discussion to be their representatives at given events, as well as to extend invitations to other executives to broaden their involvement in the Program.

Among the benefits of corporate membership are:
• Access to top political and economic leaders, from the United States and abroad
• Participation in intimate, <u>off-the-record</u> (emphasis added) discussions with experts in all areas of international affairs
• Interaction with other executives, Council members, and Senior Fellows in the most comprehensive program of foreign policy analysis and discussion available
• Dinners organized exclusively for chairs and presidents, and for their spouses
• Timely discussions of breaking issues
• Subscription to "Foreign Affairs"

Council on Foreign Relations - Corporate Member Roster

Source: Page 140, Council on Foreign Relations 1995 Annual Report

Company Name	Company Name
AGIP Petroleum Company	The Chatterjee Group
AGIP USA, Inc.	Chemical Banking Corporation
Alliance Capital Management	Chevron
Amerada Hess Corporation	China Times Express
American Airlines	CIBC Wood Gundy
American Council on Germany	Citibank/Citicorp
American Express Company	Clayton Dubilier & Rice
American International Group	Cleary, Gottlieb, Steen & Hamilton
American Standard Companies, Inc.	The Coca-Cola Company
Amoco Corporation	Community Energy Alternatives
Archer Daniels Midland Company	The Consulate General of Japan
Arnhold and S. Bleichroeder, Inc.	Corning Incorporated
Arthur Anderson & Co., SC	Coudert Brothers
ASARCO Incorporated	Cowen & Company
AT&T International	CPC International
Atlantic Richfield Company	CS First Boston
Avon Products, Inc.	Davis Polk & Wardwell
Baker & McKenzie	Debevoise & Plimpton
Banco Santander	Deere & Company
Bank Audi (USA)	Deloitte & Touche
Bank Julius Baer	Deutsche Bank AG
Bank of Montrial	Dillon, Read & Co., Inc.
The Bank of New York	Directorship
The Bank of Tokyo	Donaldson, Lufkin & Jenrette
Bankers Trust Company	The Dow Chemical Company
Banque Indosuez	Dow Jones & Company, Inc.
Banque Paribasa Corporation	Eli Lilly & Co.
Bates Worldwide	Ernst & Young
BDO Seidman	Estee Lauder Companies
BEA Associates	The Export-Import Bank of Japan
Bear, Sterns & Co.	EXXON Corporation
Sanford C. Bernstein & Co.	First Chicago Corporation
Bertelsmann Corporation	Fischer Francis Trees & Watts
The Blackstone Group	Ford Motor Company
Bloomberg Financial Markets	French-American Chamber of Commerce
BMW (US) Holding Corp.	Gavin Anderson & Company
The Boeing Company	General Electric Company
Booz, Allen & Hamilton	Goldman, Sachs & Co.
Bristol-Myers Squibb Company	Guardmark
British Airways	H.J. Heinz Company
British-American Chamber of Commerce	Hypo-Bank AG
Brown Brothers Harriman & Co.	IBJ Schroeder Bank and Trust Company
Cahill Gordon & Reindel	IBM
Caltex Petroleum Corporation	Institute of International Bankers
Capital Cities/ABC	ITT Corporation
Cargill, Inc.	JETRO New York
Caxton Corporation	John A. Levin & Co., Inc.
CDC North America	Johnson & Johnson
Champion International Corporation	Jones, Day, Reavis & Pogue
Chancellor Capitol Management, Inc.	J.P. Morgan & Co., Inc.
The Chase Manhattan Bank	Kohlberg Kravis Roberts & Co.

Company Name	Company Name
KPMG Peat Marwick L.L.P.	Reuters America
Kroll Associates	The Rockefeller Group
Lagardere/Matra Hachette	Royal Bank of Canada
Lazard Freres & Co. LLC	RWS Energy Services
Lehman Brothers	Salomon Brothers Inc.
Lockheed Martin	Scarbroughs
Loral Corporation	Schlumberger Limited
MacAndrews & Forbes Holding, Inc.	Scudder, Stevens & Clark, Inc.
Mark Partners	Joseph E. Seagrams & Sons
Marks & Murase	Shearman & Sterling
Marsh & McLennan Companies	Shell Oil Company
Marubeni America Corporation	Siemens Corporation
Marvin & Palmer Associates	Sierra Capital Management
McKensey & Company, Inc.	Simpson, Thacher & Barnett
Mercedes-Benz of North America	Smith Barney Inc.
Merrill Lynch International	Sony Corporation of America
MetLife International	Soros Fund Management
Mine Safety Appliances Company	Southern California Edison Company
Mitsui & Co. (U.S.A.), Incv.	Standard & Poor's Rating Group
Mobil Corporation	Sullivan & Cromwell
Moody's Investors Service, Inc.	Summit International Associates
Morgan Stanley & Company, Inc.	Techint, Inc.
Morningside/Springfield Group	Texaco, Inc.
Mutual Life Insurance Company of New York	TIAA-CREF
Newsweek	Time Warner
Nippon Steerl U.S.A., Inc.	Times Mirror
Nomura Research Institute America	Titan Industrial Corporation
NYNEX Corporation	Towers Perrin
Occidental Petroleum	Toyota Motor Corp. Services of N. America, Inc.
Oil Capital Ltd., Inc.	TRW
Omega Advisors, Inc.	Union Camp Corporation
Oxford Analytica	United States Trust Company of New York
Paul Ray Berndtson	United Technologies
PepsiCo	Viatel Inc.
Pfizer	E.M. Warburg, Pincus & Co.
Pioneer Hi-Bred International	Weil, Gotshal & Manges
Poten & Partners	White & Case
Price Waterhouse & Co.	World Gold Council
The Proctor & Gamble Company	Wyoming Investment Corporation
The Prudential Insurance Company of America	Xerox Corporation
The Putnam Companies	Young & Rubicam
Reliance Group Holdings, Inc.	

Trilateral Commission
Executive Committee
Source: TC Web Site for 1999 - http://www.trilateral.org/

Last Name	First & Mid. Name	Job Title	Affiliation - Company, Country, Org.
Albert	Michel	Member	Council for Monetary Policy of the Banque de France
Argyros	Stelios	Member	European Parliament
Bergsten	C. Fred	Director	Institute for International Economics, US
Berthoin	Georges	Int. Hon. Chair.	European Movement
Braga de Macedo	Jorge	Professor	of Economics, Nova University at Lisbon
Brzezinski	Zbigniew	Advisor (fmr.)	to President for National Security
Carmoy, de	Hervé	Chairman	Banque Industrielle et Mobilière Privée, Paris
Colombo	Umberto	Chairman	Fond. LEAD (Leadership for Env. and Devel.), Rome
Einhorn	Jessica P.	Managing Director	for Finance and Resource Mobilization, World Bank
Ejiri	Koichiro	Senior Advisor	to the Board, Mitsui & Co., Ltd.
Fanjul	Oscar	Honorary Chairman	Repsol, Madrid
Fortier	L. Yves	Senior Partner	Ogilvy Renault, Barristers & Solicitors, Montreal
Fresco	Paolo	Vice Chairman	The General Electric Company; Executive Officer
Gyohten	Toyoo	President	The Institute for International Monetary Affairs, Japan
Haas	Robert D.	Chairman and CEO	Levi Strauss & Co.
Herrero de Miñon	Miguel	Member (fmr.)	of Spanish Parliament
Jakobson	Max	Ambassador (fmr.)	Finnish, United Nations
Janssen	Baron Daniel	Chairman	of the Executive Committee, Solvay, Brussels
Jenkins	Sir Michael	Vice Chairman	Kleinwort Benson Group, London; fmr. British Amb.
Kissinger	Henry	Chairman	Kissinger & Assoc.; Secretary (fmr), State Dept.
Maas	Cees	Mbr. Exec. Bd.& CF O	the ING Group, Amsterdam;
Makihara	Minoru	President	Mitsubishi Corporation
Miyazawa	Kiichi	Member	House of Representatives, Japan
Monti	Mario	Member	the European Commission, Brussels
Murofushi	Minoru	Pres. & CE O	ITOCHU Corporation, Japan
Nye	Joseph S., Jr.	Dean	Kennedy School of Government, Harvard University
Okawara	Yoshio	Executive Advisor	Keidanren (Japan Federation of Econ. Organizations)
Saeki	Kiichi	Senior Advisor	Institute for International Policy Studies, Japan
Schmidt-Chiari	Guido	Chairman	Constantia Gp.; fmr. Ch., Creditanstalt Bankverein
Shore	Peter	Member	of the House of Lords, London
Staunton	Myles	Member	of Senate, Irish Republic
Stoltenberg	Thorvald	Fgn. Min. (fmr,)	of Norway
Svedberg	Björn	Chairman	Ericsson, Stockholm
Thygesen	Niels	Professor	Univ. of Copenhagen, Economics, Economics Institute
Wieczorek	Norbert	Member	of the German Bundestag
Wolff von Amerongen	Otto	Chairman	East Committee of the German Industry

Organization Charts
of the

Elite

Graphic representation of the makeup of the *Elite* can easily illustrate the interrelationships of these people, and their secret organizations. The following tables and charts are intended to serve this purpose. To find the details regarding these interrelationships, the reader should refer to my companion book, *They Don't Dare Let Us Tell The People*.

While the previous tables contain facts furnished by the CFR, and TC from their own documents; their "day jobs", and affiliations found in information furnished by the TC, plus researched from *Who's Who in America '94-'98*, by Marquis; and the BB information found in *THE SPOTLIGHT,* by Liberty Lobby; the following organizations charts are my conclusions, and predictions, or my best informed opinions based on the preceding facts, represented in graphic form.

There is no absolute proof, nor will there be any proof that they are trying to dominate the entire world, until their goals are accomplished. I sincerely hope that I am mistaken as to their intent. It is up to you to carefully absorb the preceding facts, and arrive at your own conclusions. However, do not expect to have your conclusions confirmed by the *Elite's* mass media, because they are a part of this cabal, and have other agendas.

Level of Involvement by Elite Members

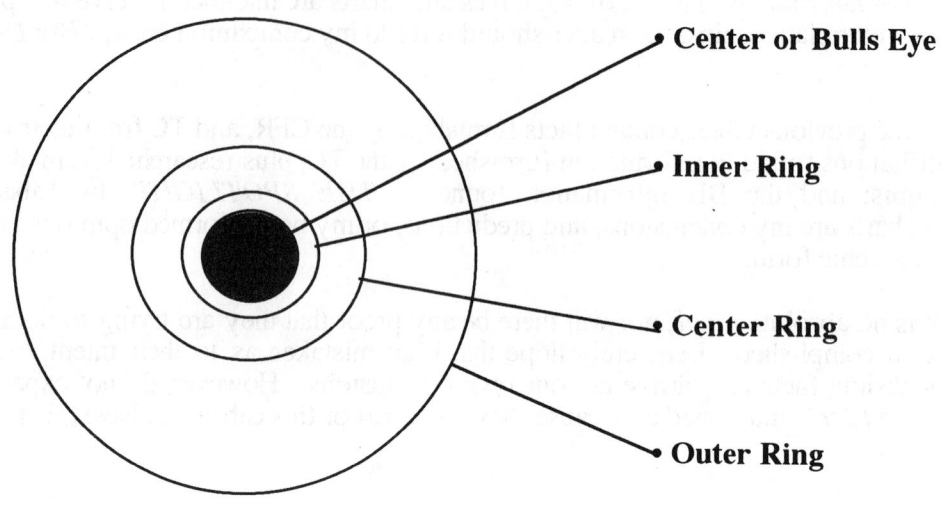

Center or Bulls Eye

Inner Ring

Center Ring

Outer Ring

- **Center or Bulls Eye** - Is made up of the Czar, and the members of the Inner Circle. They are the decision-makers, and are therefore 100% informed, and involved in the Global Union movement. The Rothschilds and David Rockefeller are the only "obvious" member of this group. We can speculate about the members of the Inner Circle, but we will probably never have these speculations confirmed.
- **Inner Ring** - This group is made up of the Officers & Directors, and triple members of all three *Elite* groups. They are probably 90% informed by the Czar, and the members of the Inner Circle, and are heavily involved in the Global Union movement. (see the preceding listing, and following charts for these members)
- **Center Ring** - This group is made up of the leaders, implementers, and double members of the three *Elite* Groups, and who are probably 80% informed by the Czar, and the members of the Inner Circle, and are moderately involved in the Global Union movement.
- **Outer Ring** - These members are included for camouflage purposes only, and are made up of many of those who belong to only the CFR. These members are aware of only about 50%, or less of the goals, and objectives of the Global Union movement. A large number of these people are members for ego, and social reasons only, and would very likely resign immediately, when they find out what the Global Union is "really" up to. An example is Douglas Fairbanks, Jr., the Hollywood actor, who probably falls completely off the above target. He would be classified as true camouflage. Another example of another possible member of the Outer Ring is Ben J. Wattenberg. He would be in the Outer Ring if he told the absolute truth on C-SPAN, with Bryan Lamb, on August 29, 1995, when he stated "I plead guilty to being a member of the CFR, and I only pay my dues, but never, or rarely attends their meetings". If he were truthful, I would place him in the Outer Ring. On the other hand, the CFR's bylaws absolutely prohibit their members from discussing this *Elite* organization. For this reason, he could have just been complying with their bylaws, and in all reality, he may be a very active member, and really belongs in one of the inner rings.

Inner Circle

Finding irrefutable proof of the makeup of the members of the "inner circle" is now, and will forever be, very difficult, and improbable. These people are the super-rich, and/or super-powerful, they are above, and beyond the laws of the world, and they shun public exposure. They do not want the world to be aware of their immense wealth for fear of exposure to notoriety, and/or physical harm. <u>Most</u> of them will never appear on the various lists of the world's richest people, such as the annual lists of the richest individuals, and families that appear in *Forbes* magazine. Those listed on the following Inner Circle chart are purely speculation on my part, but logic plays a major role in their selection. There are some that I have listed that may not belong to these secret groups. On the other hand, there are very likely some that belong to the inner circle, and I have not included them, because they remain so deeply in the shadows.

Czar

All of the proceeding information leads me to believe that David Rockefeller is <u>clearly</u> the Czar of the Global Union. He was first included as a member of the Council on Foreign Relations in the December, 1942 issue of their annual report. He was a Director from 1949-'85; Vice President from 1950-'70; Chairman from 1970-'85; and Honorary Chairman since 1985. He helped create the Bilderbergs in 1954, has been a member of the BB Steering Committee since its founding; is the only member that has attended every one of its meetings since its inception, and presented a paper at the first meeting titled *Economic Problems*. He personally created the Trilateral Commission in 1973; was Chairman for a number of years; and is currently the Honorary Chairman of the TC. He founded, and is Honorary Chairman of the Council of the Americas. Among other things, he is currently Chairman of the International Advisory Committee for Chase Manhattan Bank, N.A. In this position he personally directs the activities, and the vast wealth of the combined Chase Manhattan, and Chemical banks. It is my sincere belief that <u>nothing of significance</u> happens within these secret *Elite* organizations that he does not directly or indirectly control. During the Cold War, there was, and probably still is, a special scrambled, and cleared telephone line between the US President, and the Soviet leader in Moscow. It is highly unlikely that this speculation will be confirmed, but I would hypothesize that this phone is a two-line phone, with the other line going directly to David Rockefeller's office, and home. Perhaps the proof is in the Senate Banking Committee hearings, headed by Alfonse M. D'Amato, on December 13, 1995, investigating the Whitewater scandal, discussed the conversations between Hillary Clinton, and several members of the White House staff over a special phone line that was not routed through the White House switchboard.

Members of the Inner Circle

Members of the Inner Circle

Japanese Elite

Yoshiaki Tsutsumi interests
Minoru Mori interests
Akira Mori interests
Yasuo Takei interests
Kinoshita interests
Masatoshi Ito interests
Iwasaki interests
Busujima interests
Otsuka interests
Eitaro Itoyama interests
Hisakichi Yamaguchi interests
Junichi Murata interests
Ryoichi Jinnai interests
Rinji Shino interests
Ohga interests
Toyoda interests
Yoshimoto interests
Otani interests
Kenkichi Nakajima interests
Kazuo Matsuda interests
Uehara interests
Mitsui interests
Mitsubishi interests
Sumitomo interests
Itochu interests
Marubeni interests
Nissho Iwai interests
Toyota interests
Hitachi interests
Tomen interests
Tsai interests

N. American Elite

George F. Baker interests
James Stillman interests
Rockefeller interests
Schiff interests
Lehman Bros. interests
Kuhn, Loeb US interests
J. P. Morgan interests
Ryan interests
Warburg US interests
Cox interests
Payne interests
Sterling interests
Peabody interests
Brown Brothers interests
Rothschild US interests
Harriman interests
Goldman, Sachs interests
Warren Edward Buffett
Cargill interests
du Pont interests
John Werner Kluge
Mellon interests
Kenneth R. Thomson
Irving interests
Edgar M. Bronfman
Carlos Slim Helu interests
Emilio Azcarraga Milmo
Richard M. DeVos
Jay Van Andel
Jeronimo Arango
Rupert K. Murdoch
Herst interests
Donald E. Newhouse
Samuel I. Newhouse
Zambrano interests
Ronald O. Perelman
Fisher interests
Sumner M. Redstone
Mickey Arison
McCaw interests
Phipps interests
Walter Haefner interests
Hans Rausing interests
Rafik Hariri interests
Koc interests
Bill Gates

European Elite

House of Rothschild interests
Bank of England Governors
Brown, Shipley interests
Morgan, Grenfell interests
Lazard Brothers interests
J. Henry Schroder interests
Warburg interests
Queen Beatrix of Netherlands
Queen Elizabeth of England
Queen Sofia of Spain
Israel Moses Self interests
Kuhn, Loeb German interests
Wallenberg interests
Albrecht interests
Quandt interests
Henkel interests
Haniel interests
Erivan Haub interests
Otto interests
Schickedanz interest
Friedrich Kasrl Flick, Jr.
von Finck interests
Boehringer interests
von Siemens interests
Otto Beisheim interests
Schmidt-Ruthenbeck interests
Herz interests
Rolf Gerling interests
Adolph Merckle interests
Leo Kirch interests
Oetker interests
Sacher/Hoffmann interests
Agnelli interests
David Sainsbury interests
Stavros Niarcos interests
Garry Weston interests
Costas Lemos interests
Liliane Bettencourt interests
Seydoux/Schlumberger interests
Mulliez interests
Brenninkmeyer interests

House of Rockefeller — House of Rothschild

Czar, Global Union

David Rockefeller

Evolution of the Global Union

The Elite have attempted to unite the world under one controlling governing body for thousands of years. The efforts date back to pre-Christ, but were more apparent during the Genghis Khan era in 1220 BC; followed by the Roman Empire around 753 BC; and on and on; the League of Nations and such conquerors as Joseph Stalin, and Adolf Hitler made their attempts.

The Global union has been evolving for hundreds of years, but the present format started in the early 20th century. Formal meetings on the structure and objectives were held in the very first 1954 Bilderberg Conference, and the plan is on schedule for completion around the period 2010 – 2015. This evolution is depicted in the following charts.

European Evolution

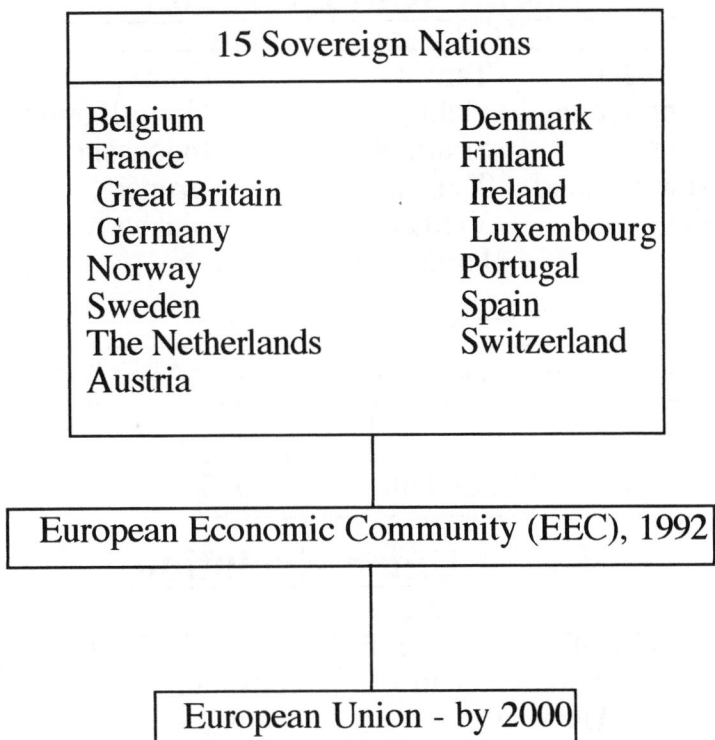

15 Sovereign Nations

Belgium	Denmark
France	Finland
Great Britain	Ireland
Germany	Luxembourg
Norway	Portugal
Sweden	Spain
The Netherlands	Switzerland
Austria	

European Economic Community (EEC), 1992

European Union - by 2000

American Evolution

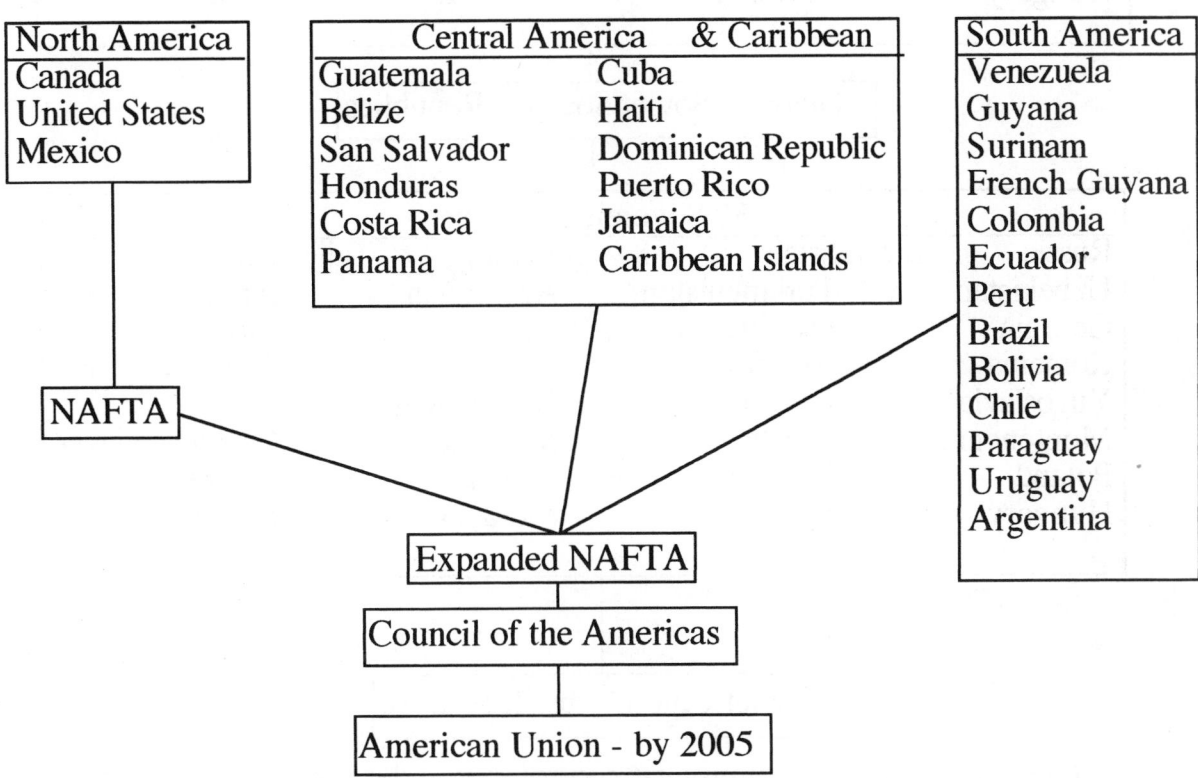

North America
Canada
United States
Mexico

Central America   & Caribbean

Guatemala	Cuba
Belize	Haiti
San Salvador	Dominican Republic
Honduras	Puerto Rico
Costa Rica	Jamaica
Panama	Caribbean Islands

South America
Venezuela
Guyana
Surinam
French Guyana
Colombia
Ecuador
Peru
Brazil
Bolivia
Chile
Paraguay
Uruguay
Argentina

NAFTA

Expanded NAFTA

Council of the Americas

American Union - by 2005

Pacific Rim Evolution

16 Sovereign Nations		
Australia	Taiwan	China
Hong Kong	Philippines	Hong Kong
Japan	South Korea	Indonesia
New Zealand	Thailand	Brunei
Singapore	Vietnam	Malaysia
	Papua New Guinea	

Asian Pacific Economic Cooperation (APEC), 1994

Asian Union - by 2010

Soviet Union Evolution

32 Sovereign Nations			
Russia	Kazakhstan	Kyrgyzstan	Tajikistan
Uzbekistan	Turkmenistan	Azerbaijan	Armeni
Georgia	Ukraine	Belarus	Mollova
Romania	Bulgaria	Mace	Albania
Yugoslavia	Bosnia	Herzegovina Serbia	
Montenegro	Croatia	Macedonia	Czechoslovakia
Poland	Lithuania	Lastvia	Estonia
Hungary	Slovenia	Moravia	Bohemia

Union of Soviet Socialist Republics

32 Sovereign Nations			
Russia	Kazakhstan	Kyrgyzstan	Tajikistan
Uzbekistan	Turkmenistan	Azerbaijan	Armeni
Georgia	Ukraine	Belarus	Mollova
Romania	Bulgaria	Mace	Albania
Yugoslavia	Bosnia	Herzegovina	Serbia
Montenegro	Croatia	Macedonia	Czechoslovakia
Poland	Lithuania	Latvia	Estonia
Hungary	Slovenia	Moravia	Bohemia

Soviet Union* - by 2010-2015

* This time not under Communist control, but under direct *Elite* control.

New Global Union

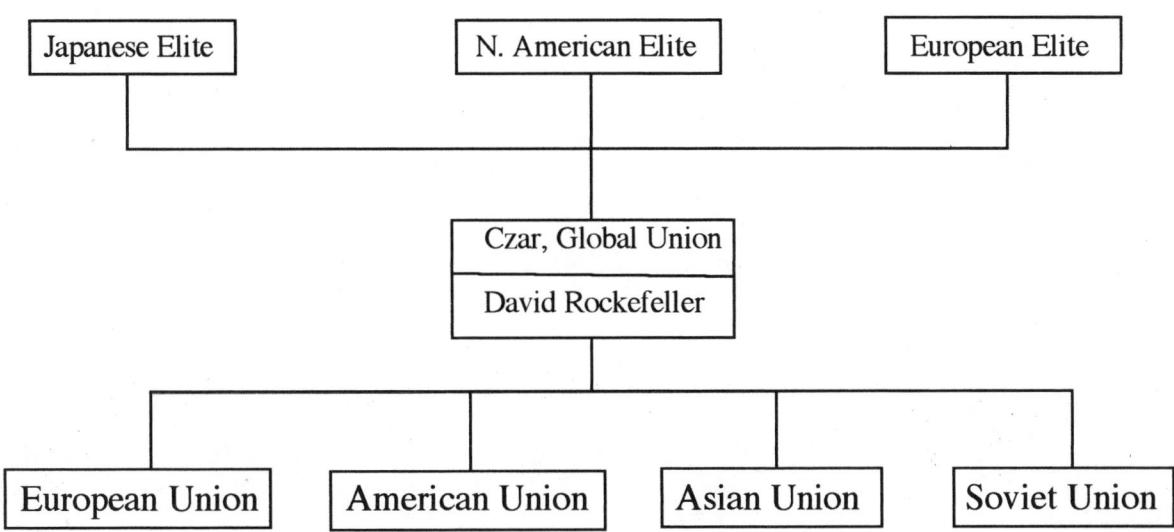

Note: The nations that are now located between Russia and Western Europe may be included it either the European Union or the next Soviet Union. The name of the next Soviet Union may be changed to another term to avoid the stain of the atrocities committed by the former Soviet Union leaders.

The Three Major Secret Organizations

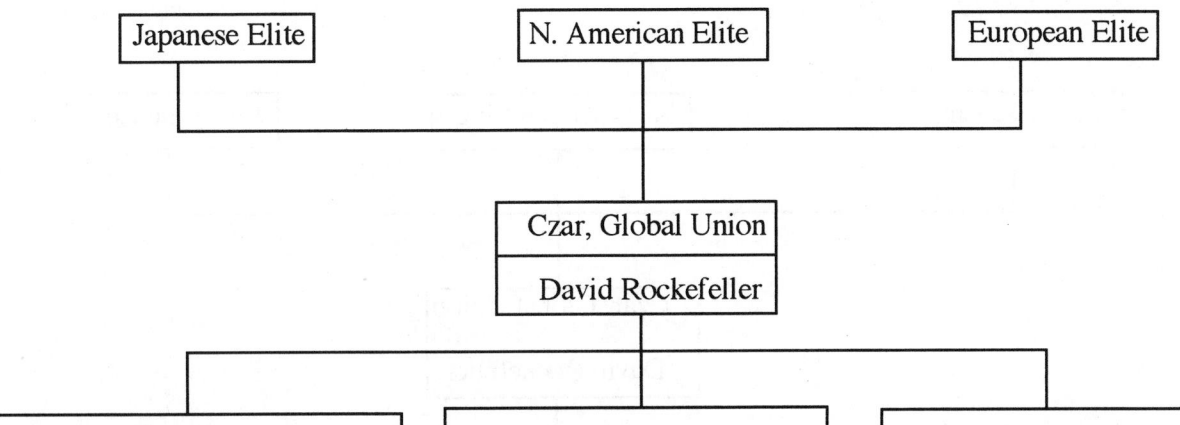

| Japanese Elite | N. American Elite | European Elite |

Czar, Global Union

David Rockefeller

Council on Foreign Relations

Honorary Chairman
David Rockefeller

Chairman
Peter G. Peterson

Vice Chairman
Maurice R. Greenberg

President
Leslie H. Gelb

Sr. V.P. C.O.O.
Michael P. Peters

Vice President, Wash. Program
Paula J. Dobrinsky

V. P. Corp. Affairs & Publisher
David Kellogg

V. P., Studies
Lawrence J. Korb

V.P., Membership & Fellowship
Elise Carlson Lewis

Vice President
Abraham F. Lowenthal

V.P. Meetings
Anne R. Luzzatto

Vice President & Treasurer
Janice L. Murray

Secretary
Judith Gustafson

Bilderberg Group

Chairman
Peter Carrington

Honorary Secretary General
Europe & Canada
Victor Halberstadt

Honorary Secretary General
United States
Casper A. Yost

Honorary Treasurer
Conrad J. Oort

Trilateral Commission

Founder & Hon. Chairman
David Rockefeller

Japanese Chairman
Yotaro Kobayashi

Japanese Deputy Chairman
Shijuro Ogata

Japanese Director
Tadashi Yamamoto

N. American Chairman
Paul A. Volcker

N. Amer. Deputy Chairman
Allen E. Gotlieb

N. Amer. Director
Charles B. Heck

European Chairman
Otto Graf Lambsdorff

European Deputy Chairman
Antonio Garrigues Walker

European Director
Paul Revay

Specific Areas Under Direct Control of the Elite

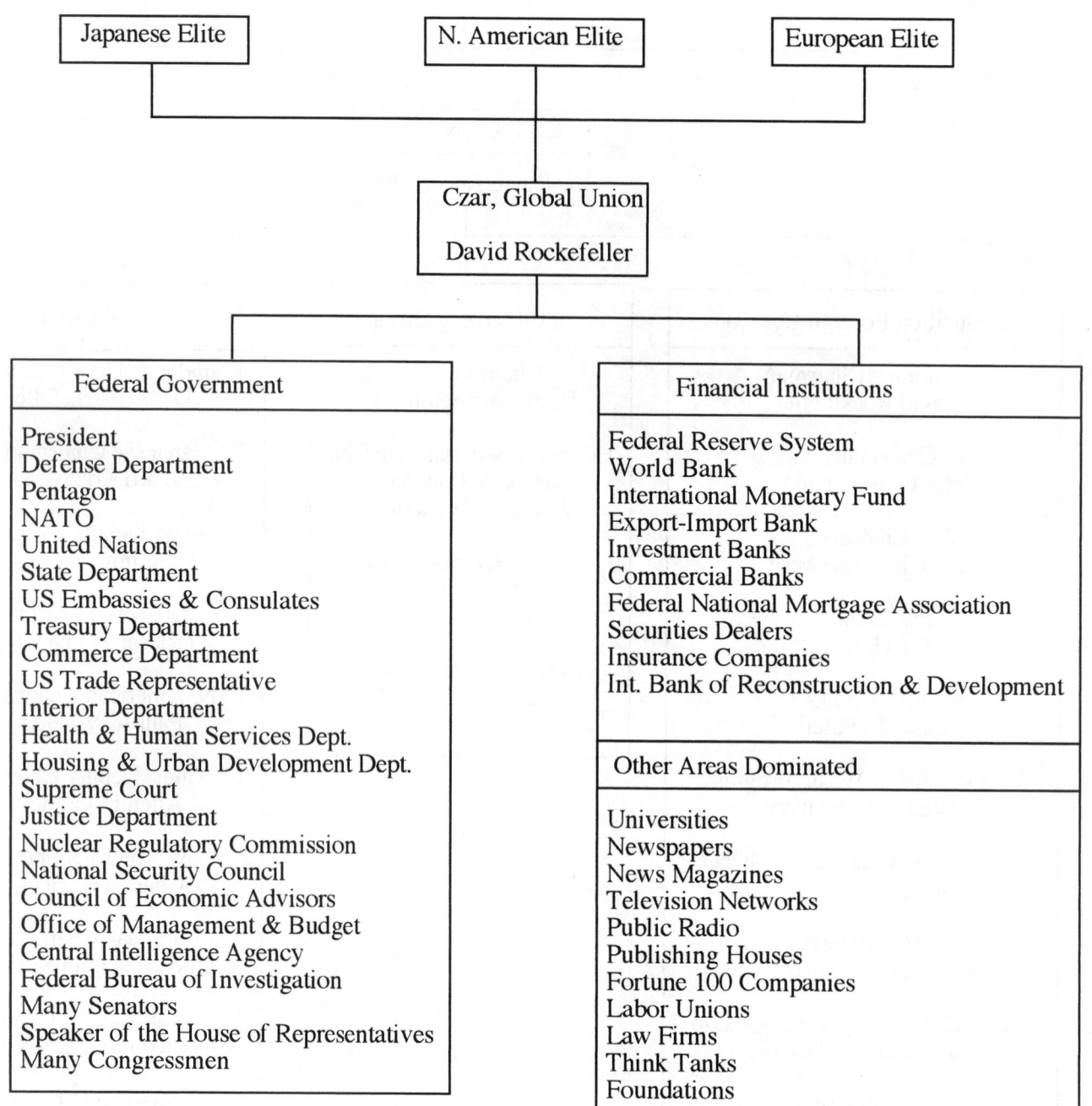

| Japanese Elite | N. American Elite | European Elite |

Czar, Global Union

David Rockefeller

Federal Government

President
Defense Department
Pentagon
NATO
United Nations
State Department
US Embassies & Consulates
Treasury Department
Commerce Department
US Trade Representative
Interior Department
Health & Human Services Dept.
Housing & Urban Development Dept.
Supreme Court
Justice Department
Nuclear Regulatory Commission
National Security Council
Council of Economic Advisors
Office of Management & Budget
Central Intelligence Agency
Federal Bureau of Investigation
Many Senators
Speaker of the House of Representatives
Many Congressmen

Financial Institutions

Federal Reserve System
World Bank
International Monetary Fund
Export-Import Bank
Investment Banks
Commercial Banks
Federal National Mortgage Association
Securities Dealers
Insurance Companies
Int. Bank of Reconstruction & Development

Other Areas Dominated

Universities
Newspapers
News Magazines
Television Networks
Public Radio
Publishing Houses
Fortune 100 Companies
Labor Unions
Law Firms
Think Tanks
Foundations

What Our Founding Fathers Said About
The Money Merchants

"I see in the near future a crisis approaching that unnerves me, and causes me to tremble for the safety of our country. Corporations have been enthroned, an era of corruption will follow, and the money power of the country will endeavor to prolong its reign by working upon the prejudices of the people, until the wealth is aggregated in a few hands, and the republic is destroyed. The Government should create, issue, and circulate all the currency, and credits needed to satisfy the spending power of the Government, and the buying power of consumers. By the adoption of these principals, the taxpayers will be saving immense sums of interest. Money will cease to be master, and become the servant of humanity." - ABRAHAM LINCOLN

"The modern theory of the perpetuation of debt has drenched the earth with blood, and crushes its inhabitants under burdens ever accumulating. If the American people ever allow private banks to control the issue of their currency, first by inflation, then by deflation, the banks...will deprive the people of all property until their children wake-up homeless on the continent their fathers conquered...the issuing power should be taken from the banks, and restored to the people, to whom it properly belongs." - THOMAS JEFFERSON

"History records that the money changers have used every form of abuse, intrigue, deceit, and violent plans possible to maintain their control over governments by controlling money, and its issuance." - JAMES MADISON

"If Congress has the right under the Constitution to issue paper money, it was given them to use themselves, not to be delegated to individuals or corporations." - ANDREW JACKSON

"If ye love wealth greater than liberty, the tranquillity of servitude greater than the animating contest for freedom, go home from us in peace. We seek not your counsel, nor your arms. Crouch down, and lick the hand that feeds you. May your chains set lightly upon you; and may posterity forget that ye were our countrymen." - SAMUEL ADAMS

Note: The above quotations were supplied by Still Productions, P.O. Box K, River & Wesson St., White Springs, FL 32096.

Federal Reserve System

Probably 90% of the US citizens think that the Federal Reserve System is one of the branches of the federal government (most think that it is part of the Treasury Department), because of the term "Federal" in its name. This is no accident. It is a psychological ploy to con the Americans into accepting their deception. It is not "Federal", and there is no "Reserve". The following tables, and organization charts are provided to clear up this myth. For a detailed discussion of the Fed, please refer to *They Don't Dare Let US Tell the People*.

Federal Reserve System

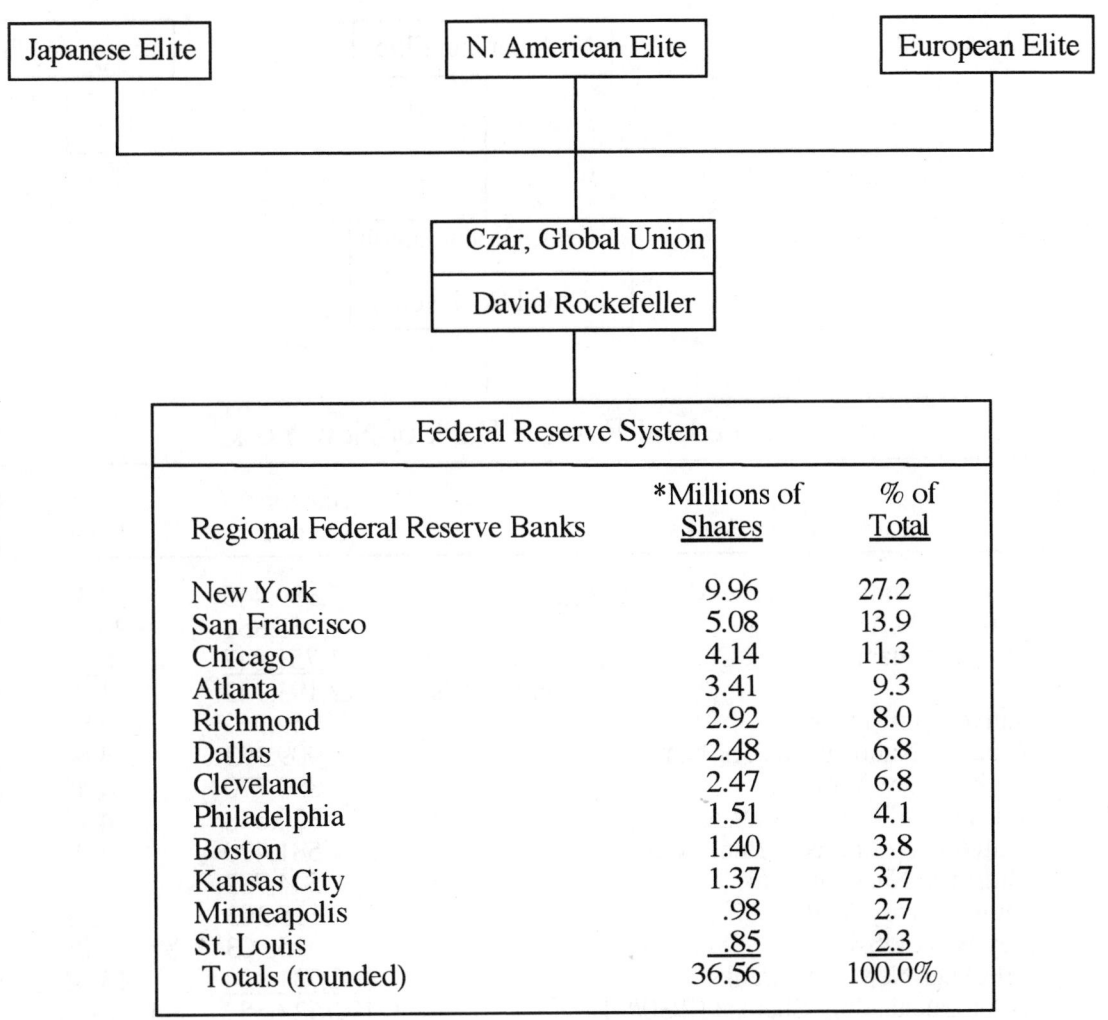

| Japanese Elite | N. American Elite | European Elite |

Czar, Global Union

David Rockefeller

Federal Reserve System

Regional Federal Reserve Banks	*Millions of Shares	% of Total
New York	9.96	27.2
San Francisco	5.08	13.9
Chicago	4.14	11.3
Atlanta	3.41	9.3
Richmond	2.92	8.0
Dallas	2.48	6.8
Cleveland	2.47	6.8
Philadelphia	1.51	4.1
Boston	1.40	3.8
Kansas City	1.37	3.7
Minneapolis	.98	2.7
St. Louis	.85	2.3
Totals (rounded)	36.56	100.0%

* Courtesy of the Board of Governors of the Federal Reserve System (as of 12/30/94)

Federal Reserve Bank of New York

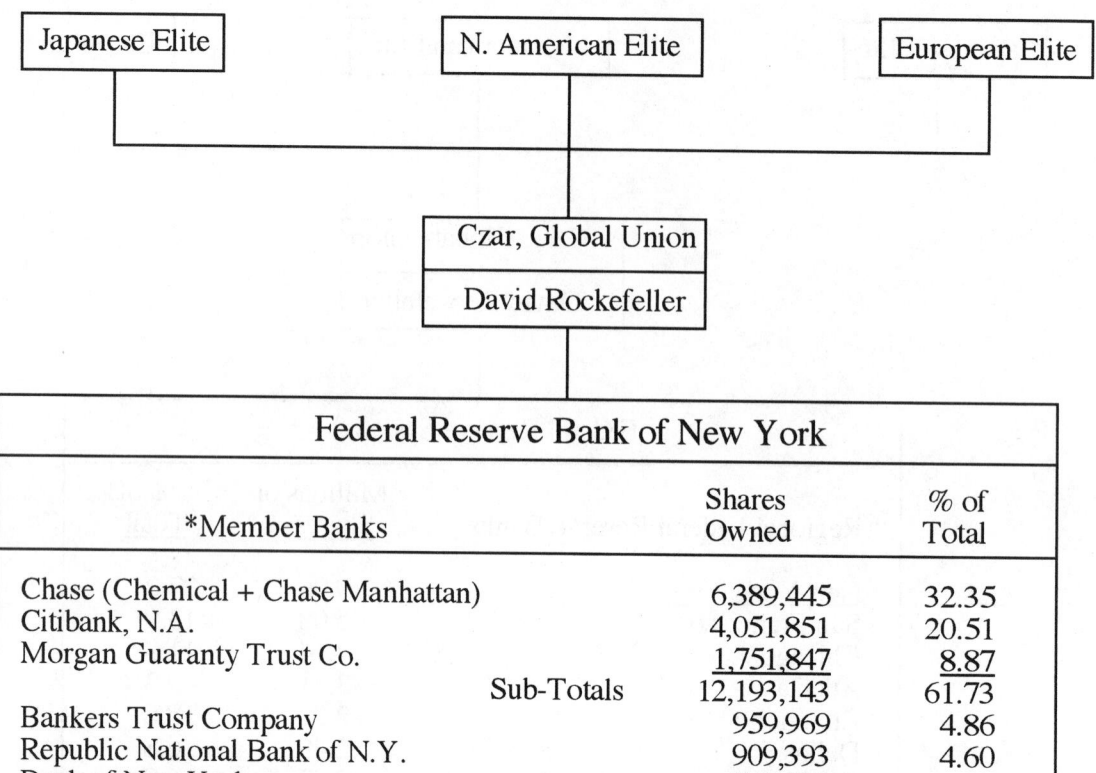

Japanese Elite	N. American Elite	European Elite

Czar, Global Union

David Rockefeller

Federal Reserve Bank of New York		
*Member Banks	Shares Owned	% of Total
Chase (Chemical + Chase Manhattan)	6,389,445	32.35
Citibank, N.A.	4,051,851	20.51
Morgan Guaranty Trust Co.	<u>1,751,847</u>	<u>8.87</u>
Sub-Totals	12,193,143	61.73
Bankers Trust Company	959,969	4.86
Republic National Bank of N.Y.	909,393	4.60
Bank of New York	880,770	4.46
Marine Midland Bank, N.A.	820,648	4.15
National Westminster Bank, USA	581,420	2.94
Midlantic National Bank	544,782	2.76
United Jersey Bank	115,303	.58
Key Bank USA, N.A.	15,903	.08
All Other New York Banks	<u>2,731,324</u>	<u>13.83</u>
Total Outstanding Shares (12/30/94)	19,752,655	100.00%

* Courtesy of the Board of Governors of the Federal Reserve System (as of 12/30/94)

Chase

(Chase Manhattan Bank)

Years	Chairmen	*Elite* Member
'34-'53	Winthrop W. Aldrich	CFR
'53-'60	John J. McCloy	BB,CFR
'61-'69	George Champion	CFR
'69-'81	David Rockefeller	BB,CFR,TC
'81-'90	Willard C. Butcher	CFR
'90-'95	Thomas G. Labrecque	CFR,TC

(Chemical Bank)

Years	Chairmen	*Elite* Member
-'47	Frank K. Houston	CFR
'47-'54	N. Baxter Jackson	No
'54-'65	Harold H. Helm	No
'65-'73	William S. Renchard	CFR
'74-'83	Donald C. Platten	CFR
'84-'95	Walter V. Shipley	CFR

Citibank

Years	Chairmen	*Elite* Member
'09-'18	James Stillman*	No
'18-'19	James A. Stillman*	No
'21-'29	Eric P. Swenson	CFR
'29-'33	Charles E. Mitchell	CFR
'33-'40	James H. Perkins	CFR
'40-'48	Gordon S. Rentschler	CFR
'48-'52	William Gage Brady, Jr.	CFR
'52-'59	Howard C. Sheperd	CFR
'59-'67	James Stillman Rockefeller	CFR
'67-'70	George S. Moore	CFR
'70-'84	Walter B. Wreston	CFR
'84-	John S. Reed	CFR

Morgan Guaranty Trust Co.

Years	Chairmen	*Elite* Member
-'43	J.P. (Jack) Morgan, Jr.	No
'43-'48	Thomas Lamont	CFR
'48-'50	Russell C. Leffingwell	CFR
'50-'55	George Whitney	No
'55-'65	Henry C. Alexander	CFR
'65-'67	Thomas S. Gates	CFR
'69-'71	John M. Meyer, Jr.	CFR
'72-'76	Ellmore C. Patterson	CFR
'79-'80	Walter H. Page	CFR
'81-'90	Lewis T. Preston	CFR
'91-	Dennis Weatherstone	CFR

New York Federal Reserve Bank

Dates	Chairman	*Elite* Member
'14 - '28	Benjamin Strong, Jr.*	No
'28 - '40	George L. Harrison	CFR
'41 - '56	Allan Sproul	CFR
'56 - '75	Alfred Hayes	CFR
'75 - '80	Paul A. Volcker	CFR
'80 -'984	Anthony M. Solomon	CFR
'84 - '93	E. Gerald Corrigan	CFR
'93 -	William J. McDonough	CFR

*The CFR did not exist prior to 1921

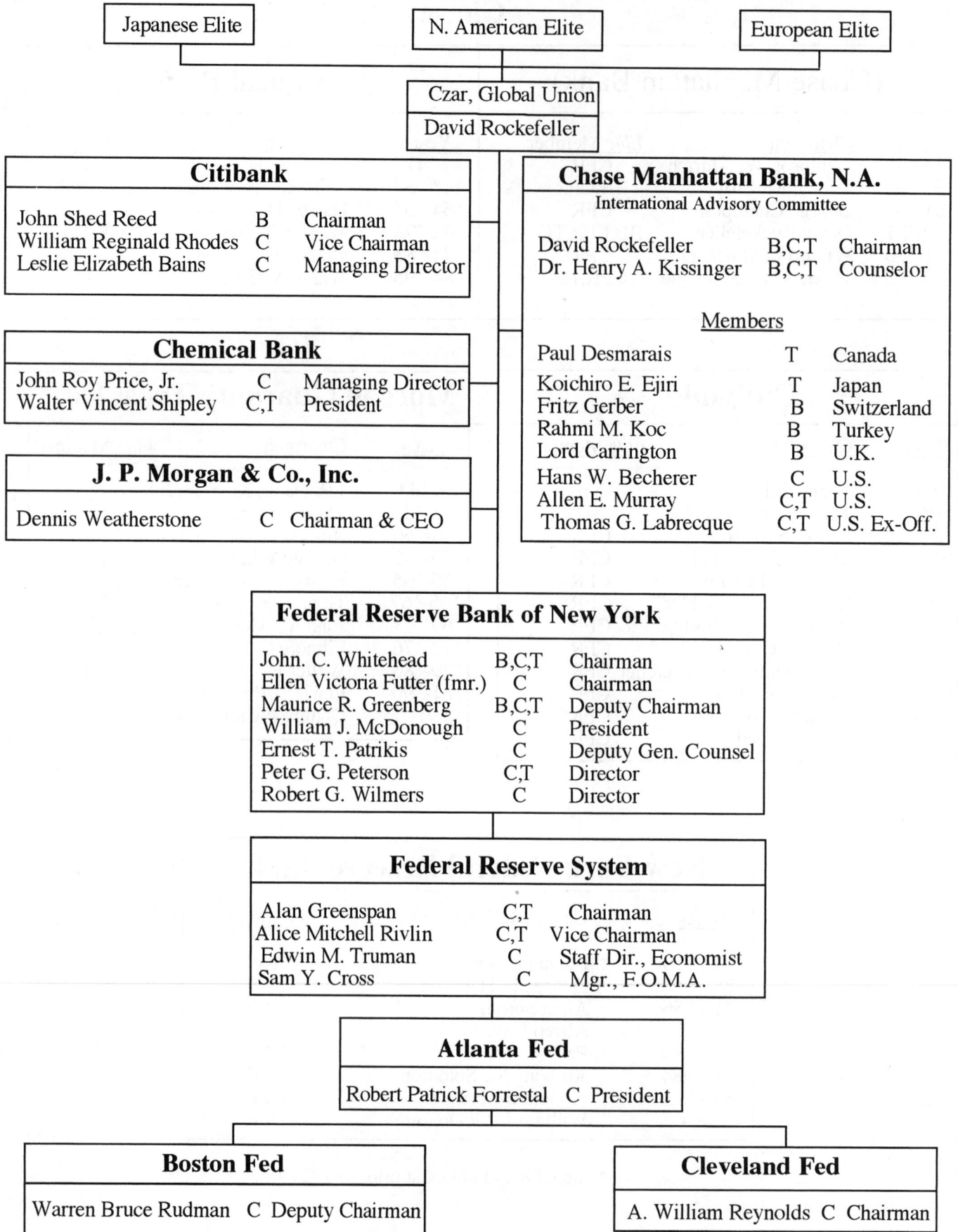

Elite Members of the Federal Reserve

| Japanese Elite | N. American Elite | European Elite |

Czar, Global Union
David Rockefeller

Citibank

John Shed Reed	B	Chairman
William Reginald Rhodes	C	Vice Chairman
Leslie Elizabeth Bains	C	Managing Director

Chemical Bank

| John Roy Price, Jr. | C | Managing Director |
| Walter Vincent Shipley | C,T | President |

J. P. Morgan & Co., Inc.

| Dennis Weatherstone | C | Chairman & CEO |

Chase Manhattan Bank, N.A.
International Advisory Committee

| David Rockefeller | B,C,T | Chairman |
| Dr. Henry A. Kissinger | B,C,T | Counselor |

Members

Paul Desmarais	T	Canada
Koichiro E. Ejiri	T	Japan
Fritz Gerber	B	Switzerland
Rahmi M. Koc	B	Turkey
Lord Carrington	B	U.K.
Hans W. Becherer	C	U.S.
Allen E. Murray	C,T	U.S.
Thomas G. Labrecque	C,T	U.S. Ex-Off.

Federal Reserve Bank of New York

John. C. Whitehead	B,C,T	Chairman
Ellen Victoria Futter (fmr.)	C	Chairman
Maurice R. Greenberg	B,C,T	Deputy Chairman
William J. McDonough	C	President
Ernest T. Patrikis	C	Deputy Gen. Counsel
Peter G. Peterson	C,T	Director
Robert G. Wilmers	C	Director

Federal Reserve System

Alan Greenspan	C,T	Chairman
Alice Mitchell Rivlin	C,T	Vice Chairman
Edwin M. Truman	C	Staff Dir., Economist
Sam Y. Cross	C	Mgr., F.O.M.A.

Atlanta Fed

| Robert Patrick Forrestal | C | President |

Boston Fed

| Warren Bruce Rudman | C | Deputy Chairman |

Cleveland Fed

| A. William Reynolds | C | Chairman |

"The modern banking system manufactures money out of nothing. The process is perhaps the most astonishing piece of slight of hand ever invented. Banking was conceived in iniquity, and born in sin. Bankers own the earth. Take it away from them, but leave them the power to create money, and with the flick of a pen, they will create enough money to buy it back again. Take this great power away from them, and all great fortunes like mine will disappear. And, they ought to disappear, for then this would be a better and happier world to live in. But if you want to continue to be the slaves of the bankers, and pay the cost of your own slavery, then let bankers continue to create money, and control credit." - Sir John Stamp (former governor of the Bank of England)

"Whoever controls the volume of money in our country is absolute master of all industry, and commerce... and when you realize that the entire system is very easily controlled, one way or another, by a few powerful men at the top, you will not have to be told how periods of inflation, and depression originate."
- President James Garfield a couple of weeks before he was assassinated on July 2, 1881.

"We the people, are the rightful masters of both the Congress, and the Courts. Not to overthrow the Constitution, but to overthrow the men who have perverted it." - Abraham Lincoln

THINK ABOUT IT

How Can We Eliminate the Massive Federal Debt?

Our national debt is now well above five trillion dollars (if they counted every debt obligation, and accounted for them in the same manner as they require the public to account for them, the <u>REAL</u> Fed debt is $39 TRILLION). Did you ever wonder who we owe all of this money to? Will it ever be possible or even practical, to pay it off? Who benefits when the debt continues to increase?

None of our government leaders seem to be very concerned about such a huge debt. Why?

How much interest is due? Who collects the interest? Who stands to benefit if the national debt is never paid off? Could it be those public-spirited people who collect their share of the interest?

Where is all the gold that used to be stored in the vaults at Fort Knox?

There are people who know the answers to the above questions. Our government propaganda mills call such people "conspiracy nuts", or "hate groups". Have you bothered to check out what the conspiracy nuts are trying to tell you? <u>Do you care?</u>

If it can be shown that any person, or any group of people, is using an especially advantageous position of power to gain an excessive financial profit from the U.S. government, then it may be possible to declare such excessive profit as a motive for insurrection against the government of the United States.

Section 4 of Amendment 14 of the U.S. Constitution states that ". . . *neither the United States nor any State shall assume or pay any debt or obligation incurred in aid of insurrection or rebellion against the United States, . . . but all such debts, obligations, and claims shall be held illegal, and void*".

At the present time, there are apparently many people who are using their advantageous positions to get their hands on 'government' money, including the owners of the Federal Reserve banking system. It is now evident that the owners of the Federal Reserve Banks are making an excessive profit from interest on the national debt-the greater the debt, the more the interest, the greater the profits to the bank owners.

In other words, it may be possible (if any lawyers are willing to try) to prove that the national debt is an illegal debt, and that the owners of the Federal Reserve Banks are guilty of insurrection, or rebellion against the United States.

Think about it, make copies, and pass this on to your friends. Do not depend on the news media to inform you. - Cecil Jack Ross

Why Should We Care?

Even though these Elite organizations go to a lot of effort, and expense to remain secret, the word seems to get out anyway. There have been dozens of very good books written since the beginning of this century on this subject, but they remain rather obscure, because the Elite conspire to suppress them.

The BB's are the most secretive of the three. When the BB's meet, they clear out all people in the buildings where they are to meet, they completely de-bug all the rooms, bring in their own cooks, waiters, housekeepers, heavily armed security guards, etc., and they do not allow outsiders anywhere near the meeting place just before, during, and immediately after they meet. These very powerful people do not meet to discuss the latest recipe for blueberry pancakes, or the melting rate of snow at the South Pole. When they meet, they more than likely discuss, and decide:

<u>Wars</u> - They decide when wars should start, how long they should last, when they should end, who will, and will not participate, the changes in boundaries of countries resulting from the outcome of these wars, who will lend the money to support the war efforts, and who will lend the money to rebuild the countries after they have been destroyed by war.

<u>Money</u> - They own the central banks, such as the Federal Reserve System in the US, and similar organizations in all major countries throughout the world, and therefore are in a position to determine discount rates, prime rates, money supply levels, the prices of gold, and other precious metals, and very tightly control who, and/or what countries should receive loans (guaranteed by the taxpayers of the respective countries).

<u>Governments</u> - They decide who will be allowed to run for the offices of President, Prime Minister, Chancellor, Governor General, or other names applied to the leaders of all major countries around the world.

<u>Stocks, Bonds, & Commodities</u> - Since the Elite own the major banks, and the Central banks, they know exactly what interest rates, and money supply levels will be, so it is very likely that they regularly run these exchanges up, and down to their financial gain.

<u>News and other information</u> - They directly or indirectly own all the major news media, and can therefore tell the public exactly what they want them to hear, and deny the public the information they do not want them to see, hear, or read.

<u>Wages and salaries</u> - They directly or indirectly own all the major banks, businesses, industries, and the like, and therefore can suppress wages and salaries by either shipping the production jobs to the cheapest labor rates around the world, by importing the technical specialists from the cheapest countries around the world, and by employing mostly temporary, and/or part time workers in their home countries. The labor unions do not resist such efforts, because the labor leaders are members of the *Elite* as well.

I don't know about you, but these above activities seriously concern me, because my children, and grandchildren will suffer many times greater than we do today under the control of these EVIL MONSTERS (I have tried to find worse terms for them, but this is the best that I can think of to describe them.). My ancestors finally decided to leave Ireland for the New World in 1772 because of economic suppression. The absentee landlords and money merchants had raised the rents on the tenant farmers of Ireland three times in just one year, and the farmers could no longer afford to ply their trade. These brave people risked their lives in this new undeveloped land rather than continue to be persecuted by the *Elite* of that period. The writers of our Constitution took great care in drafting this fine document so as to protect us from *Elite* domination. This secret cabal is again conquering us in ever-increasing ways, and I, for one, have had enough. The best way to stop this oligarchy's efforts is "SUNSHINE". *Who's Who of the Elite* is my spotlight on this conspiracy.

Can they be stopped?

Yes, they can be stopped. But only if everyone works very hard at the solutions, for nothing happens on its own, and apathy is NOT the answer.

However, violent efforts are inappropriate because: (1) it is wrong to break our laws; (2) many innocent people will be killed or wounded, and their property destroyed; (3) The Elite control our courts, the Pentagon, the U.N., NATO, N.S.A., C.I.A., F.B.I., B.A.T.F., our Senate and House of Representatives, and directly or indirectly control all local law enforcement agencies.

All efforts to stop the Elite must be legal, such as:

1. Everyone must go to the poles in each election, and vote for their independent party candidates of choice. Once the independents have gained control of our state and federal governments, perhaps that is the time to eliminate the party system completely, and have very candidate for public office run on their own efforts and merits, with financing only from individuals who have resided for at least 5 years in the district or area that they propose to represent. Violation of the new campaign financing proposal should be a felony with stiff monetary fines, and jail time for the convicted offenders. All elections must be reduced to two months for the primary, and one month for the general elections, and all voting must be on a Saturday and Sunday. All votes should be on paper ballots counted by precinct Citizens Oversight Committees. The last place on each list of candidates on the ballots must be "NONE OF THE ABOVE", and if this is selected by a majority of the voters, a new slate of candidates must be submitted for vote, until one candidate receives 50% + one vote of all the votes cast. Then the Electoral College must be eliminated entirely with the President and Vice President elected by popular vote only. All this should be accomplished by a Constitutional Amendment approved by both houses of Congress, and approved by 38 states. Constitutional Amendments should not be done by a Constitutional Convention, because the Elite would take charge, and our Constitution would be eliminated, or changed so drastically that it would be unrecognizable.

2. Every state that does not already have the privilege should have the citizens circulate petitions demanding Initiative, Referendum and Recall privileges.

3. We must also demand Initiative, Referendum and Recall at the federal level as well.

4. After the citizens have Initiative, Referendum and Recall privileges, and the independent people have control again, then the first thing that should be done is to pass state, and federal laws prohibiting anyone from being appointed, elected or otherwise employed in any public office or position that has been a member of any secret organization for the previous five years, including the Klu Klux Klan, Black Panthers, Islamic Jihad, Red Brigade, Bilderbergs, Bohemian Club, Council on Foreign Relations, and/or Trilateral Commission. These laws should exclude the typical "grandfather" clauses, so that once these laws are passed, anyone who meets this definition must resign immediately. If anyone wanted to belong to these groups, and hold public office, then these organizations must change their rules so that every meeting, including board of director's meetings, must be opened up to attendance by the public, and the press, with two weeks advance notice published in the local press stating the date, time, and place of all meetings, along with the agendas of all meetings.

5. The Federal Reserve Act must be repealed, and the exclusive right to create money and credit must be restored to the US Treasury Department, as stipulated in the US Constitution.

6. The present practice of "fractional reserve" banking requiring only 10% reserves for banks must, within one year, be raised to 100% reserves. Without this change, banks would continue to have the ability to create money and credit, which should be exclusively reserved for the Treasury Department.

7. The US national debt should be completely eliminated by a one-time exchange of non-interest bearing Treasury Notes for all of the outstanding interest bearing Treasury Bonds.

8. The Treasury Department should be designated as the sole lender to states, counties, and municipalities for capital projects that are now financed by municipal bonds, and the like; the rate charged for these loans should be fixed by law at 3%; Congress should be allowed to change this interest rate if 80% of those "eligible" to vote on the change vote in the affirmative; and any changes to this rate must only be in effect for 365 days, when it would automatically revert to 3% again.

9. The Treasury Department should offer loans to banks at the fixed rate of 3% on the condition that they must not add more than 5% of true annual interest to the loans to any borrower of these funds. Violation of this requirement must be a felony with stiff monetary fines and jail time penalties for violating this provision, with the fines and jail time being given to the chief executive officer of the erring bank.

10. Inflation should not be controlled by varying interest   rates, but by varying the supply of money and credit.

11. The Internal Revenue Act should be revoked because it is severely regressive, is extremely complicated, and 100% of the money collected by the IRS is now deposited into the Federal Reserve System under provisions of the Internal Revenue Act, and these taxes are never seen by the Treasury Department. All money used by the federal government is borrowed from holders of Treasury bonds at interest from the Federal Reserve System, mutual funds, etc.

12. Every law passed by Congress must first pass the test of the Constitution. If the proposed bill is not specifically allowed by the Constitution, it becomes null, and void. Every bill submitted for approval by both houses of Congress must be single-issue bills, and must not contain any amendments that are not clearly and specifically related to the proposed bill. All bills proposed that require increases or decreases in taxes or other revenue streams must be approved by at least 80% of all those eligible to vote on the bill in both houses of Congress.

This is just a start on needed changes, but if enacted, we will again have government by, and for the people.

"For we wrestle not against flesh and blood, but against principalities, against powers, against the   rulers of the darkness of this world, against spiritual wickedness in high places."–Ephesians (6: 12)
"Expose the works of darkness." - Ephesians (5:11)

"No man is good enough to govern another man without that other's consent." - Abraham Lincoln in a 1854 letter to Congress. Further in this letter he reminded them that:

"These United States of America can never be destroyed   from forces outside its borders. If America falls, it will fall from within. Brought down by apathy. When good people do nothing, Anarchy reigns."

"Still, if you will not fight for the right when you can easily win without bloodshed, if you will not fight when your victory will be sure, and not so costly, you may come to the moment when you will have to fight with all the odds are against you, and only a precarious chance for survival. There may be a worse case. You may have to fight when there is no chance of victory, because it is better to perish than to live as slaves." *Churchill*

"We the people are the rightful masters of Congress and the courts, not to overthrow the Constitution, but to overthrow men who pervert the Constitution." - Abraham Lincoln

The aim of socialism is not only to abolish the present division of mankind into small states, and all national isolation, not only to bring the nations closer to each other, but also to merge them. The merging of states is inevitable." - Lenin in his *Imperialism and the Right to Self-determination*

"The coming of a world state is longed for by all the worst, and most distorted elements. This state, based on the principles of absolute equity of men, and a community of possessions, would banish all natural loyalties. In it no acknowledgment would be made of the authority of a father over his children, or of God over human society."
- Pope Benedict XV, July 25, 1920

In 1836, President Andrew Jackson forced the closing of the Second Bank of the U.S. by revoking its Charter. He is said to have been met by the Moneychangers who approached him in the drawing room of the White House, whereupon Jackson said:

"Gentlemen, I have had men watching you for a long time, and I am convinced that you have used the funds of the bank to speculate in the breadstuffs of the country. When you won, you divided the profits amongst you, and when you lost, you charged it to the bank. You tell me that if I take the deposits from the bank, and annul its charter, I shall ruin ten thousand families. That may be true, gentlemen, but that is your sin! Should I let you go on, you will ruin fifty thousand families, and that would be my sin! You are a den of vipers, and thieves. I have determined to rout you out, and by the Eternal God, I will rout you out!"

The few who can understand the system **(the international banking system)** *will be so interested in its profits, or so dependent on its favors, that there will be no opposition from that class, while on the other hand, the great body of the people are mentally incapable of comprehending the tremendous advantage that derives from the system, will bear its burdens without complaint, and perhaps without even suspecting that the system is inimical to their interest.*
- Rothschild Brothers of London

". . . the powers of financial capitalism had another far-reaching aim, nothing less than to create a world system of financial control in private hands able to dominate the political system in each country and the economy of the world as a whole". - *Tragedy and Hope*, by Carroll Quigley, page 324

"The case for government by the Elite is irrefutable ... government by the people is possible, but highly improbable." - J. William Fulbright, former Chairman of the Senate Foreign Relations Committee, at a 1963 symposium.

THE GHOST FROM VALLEY FORGE
(Author unknown)

I had a dream the other night I didn't understand,
A figure walking through the mist, with flintlock in his hand.
His clothes were torn, and dirty, as he stood there by my bed,
He took off his three-cornered hat, and speaking low he said:

We fought a revolution to secure our liberty,
We wrote the Constitution, as a shield from tyranny.
For future generations, this legacy we gave,
In this, the land of the free, and home of the brave.

The freedom we secured for you, we hoped you'd always keep,
But tyrants labored endlessly while your parents were asleep.
Your freedom gone-your courage lost-you're no more than a slave,
In this, the land of the free, and the home of the brave.

You buy permits to travel, and permits to own a gun,
Permits to start a business, or to build a place for one.
On land that you believe you own, you pay a yearly rent,
Although you have no voice in choosing how the money's spent.

Your children must attend a school that doesn't educate,
Your moral values can't be taught, according to the state.
You read about the current "news" in a very biased press,
You pay a tax you do not owe, to please the IRS.

Your money is no longer made of silver or of gold,
You trade your wealth for paper, so life can be controlled.
You pay for crimes that make our Nation turn from God to shame,
You've taken Satin's number, as you've traded in your name.

You've given government control to those who do you harm,
So they can padlock churches, and steal the family farm.
And keep our country deep in debt, put men of God in jail,
Harass your fellow countryman while corrupted courts prevail.

Your public servants don't uphold the solemn oath they're sworn,
Your daughters visit doctors so children won't be born.
Your leaders ship artillery, and guns to foreign shores,
And send your sons to slaughter, fighting other people's wars.

Can you regain your Freedom for which we fought, and died?
Or don't you have the courage, or the faith to stand with pride?
Are there no more values for which you'll fight to save?
Or do you wish your children live in fear, and be a slave?

Sons of the Republic, arise, and take a stand!
Defend the Constitution, the Supreme Law of the Land!
Preserve our Republic, and each God-given right!
And pray to God to keep the torch of freedom burning bright!

As I awoke he vanished, in the mist from whence he came,
His words were true, we are not free, and we have ourselves to blame.
For even now as tyrants trample each God-given right,
We only watch, and tremble--too afraid to stand, and fight.
If he stood by your bedside in a dream while you're asleep,
And wonder what remains of your right he fought to keep.
What would be your answer if he called out from the grave?
Is this still the land of the free, and home of the brave?

Beating a Rigged Game

By Nikki Case

It's an open secret: Apparently, someone is doing more than just corner the market; they're trying to corner the world. Call them globalist, global capitalists, CFR, Bilderbergers, the Insiders, the Establishment, the Knights, the Illuminatti ^ they're all the same greedy bloodsuckers and they're all members of the same clubs. I call them elitists; a more exact name would be to call them what they are - the latest super bug: Millennium Parasites. They strive to enslave and feed on the world.

They disguise themselves as friends of 'big business' or free enterprise. This is a lie. They loathe free enterprise and have all but destroyed it by cornering every market, swallowing every competitor and monopolizing all possible economies. It's all about 'the money, honey,' and they want it all. Other disguises include posing as actors, statesmen, diplomats, and politicians. It's still about money, translated 'power.'

Satisfaction will elude these parasites, no matter the billions they amass, as long as there are free men with the potential to earn even a fraction of what these elitists spend on one Lear jet ride. Commoners are a threat. Threats must be neutralized. Threats demand control. Control can be accomplished easily: It calls for a rigged game.

Rigged games have been around forever. In a game of Hearts, it's as simple as eliminating a certain suite of cards; there are also loaded dice; formulas for chess and other gimmicks. The parasites use these principles and similar gimmicks to achieve their 'global neighborhood' agenda, alias global control alias-totalitarian world government, the 'New World Order, or Global Union.'

They've attacked and all but eliminated morality, religion, any kind of free press, and robbed those protesting of hope. Why? Morality breeds discipline, responsibility, and order, thus freedom and independence. As for religion: Hope can't be allowed, or any kind of faith ^ these might inspire a fight ... a victory even. Better rig the game.

How?

The ultimate parasitic weapon has been television, newspapers, and magazines. Employing formulas of indoctrination through the now monopolized media, messages were sent: 'Everyone does it.' 'All kids have sex.' 'Religion is extreme.' 'Conservatives are extreme.' 'Commitment is bad ^ it's literally extreme.' 'Morality is relative.' 'Lies about sex are okay.' 'Parents are oppressors - disobey.' 'The government will do it all for you, if you're willing to sacrifice a large portion of your income, never smoke, wear a seatbelt, and use politically correct language.' 'Universal harmony can only be obtained through the sacrifice of sovereign nations, and the gobbling of their culture, religion, and individual rights.' 'Be nationality-less, culture-less, faceless 'Stepford' children ^ it's for the children.' 'Live for the moment, because AIDS only happens if you don't use a condom and abortion is available on demand ^ even if you're six months along.' 'Cheat, after all, this is the age of 'no fault' divorce.' 'Give your child a latch-key.' 'Guns kill all by themselves ^ never mind defending yourself or checking crime ^ ban them.' 'Don't nurture your child ^ use day care! You need a BMW!" 'Materialism is everything. The government will fix anything else ^ with your money.'

Originally, most thinking people objected to these formulaic messages acted out and sold via sitcoms, soap operas, drama series, and sensationalized movies. Thinking viewers objected to the violence, the lack of values, and the 'sleeping around,' done even by young teens.

Sadly most of the protestors shut up, suffered, and then accepted the messages when the media refused to acknowledge the people's protests, flooding protestors with 'New World Order' messages instead. Here the people failed. They allowed indoctrination in their living rooms and in their children's ears.

After all, who could give up TV? Magazines? The 'in' newspapers? And wasn't it probably true ^ most kids 'did it' at thirteen? Lawyers twisted the law to win cases, whether right or wrong? Powerful men 'slept around'? Women did too? Doctors were no exception? Immorality was normal, especially under certain circumstances? Heck, nobody's to blame, and blaming is extreme, right? It's out to be an 'extremist' and so many things are extreme, yeah?

Distractions, like 'sleight of the hand' in magic and poker, are another part of the game. Give the people 'Monica,' Kosovo, emphasize 'violence' and 'school shootings' rather than the documented fact that 'an armed society is a civil society' and people won't notice when you sell the country's security to Communists. They won't notice when you legislate 'thought control' in the name of 'hate crimes' (after all, it sounds good, doesn't it?). They won't notice that the Constitutional proviso for 'search and seizure' is a protection no longer available via another great sounding program: 'The War on Drugs.' Oh yes, and this war is being waged on citizens, *property owners, and teenagers ˆ not on Cuban importers, the KLA (known heroin dealers), or Chinese importers. Oh no, it's the hard working people you have to watch out for ˆ those yuppies and property owners, they're the ones with 'freedoms' that must be curtailed. Right?*

Well, the elitists own the media, so the dice were loaded long ago. Most of the stations and all but a few of the newspapers have been sending these messages for decades. Communications has been compromised, and the Internet, once taxed by the UN via Gore and subsequently regulated (perhaps through Art Bell and his new lawsuit) will be swallowed as well. Small ISP's will go out of business, and elitist owned conglomerates will emerge: Ted Turner will surely grab enough of the pie to turn the Net into another mindless, spin machine for the zombified as soon as possible.

Planned Parenthood talks to the teens almost as often as schoolteachers do, and the banks have already started practicing the 'know your customer' agenda, though Congress shot it down. Let's face it, the millions of us still awake realize we're fighting a rigged game. So many are crying, "Is there any way to win?" You betcha.

We Know Who They Are

That's right, we know who's in bed with who and which companies are owned by these parasites. Do you have the guts to boycott these people and their companies, turn off their owned and sponsored programs? I do.

I'll never turn on CNN again, even if they're the only ones airing the first landing on Mars. Barnes and Noble won't get my business. I'll order from Amazon instead. And what about Microsoft? Gates just accepted his first Bilderberg meeting invitation. Hmmm ... seems he sold out, after all. No more Windows or mediocre software for me ˆ Linux will do just fine. The head of ATT will be there too. Life-Line will get my long distance business. Yes, there seem to be so many of them ... all rolling in cash and lusting for even more exaggerated power. Still, I refuse to continue paying for my own enslavement. How about you? Read on.

They're Outnumbered

Another 'oh yes.' It's two or three hundred parasites versus millions of people demanding their continued freedom. Each of us can make a difference. Tell ten of your friends, relatives, and co-workers who these people are and what they're striving for: Cornering the Globe the way Rockefeller cornered the oil business decades ago.

Do this every week. If even one in ten sees the light, that's another freedom lover willing to say, 'NO.' 'No' to globalized slavery; 'No' to monopolized trade; 'No' to NAFTA; 'No' to GATT; 'No' to 'thought crimes,' 'Internet Licenses,' 'sixty percent tax brackets,' and 'NO' to the 'overturning of the Constitution,' the 'dividing of Canada,' 'the dissolving of any kind of freedom under a sovereign government.' It's one more person who'll say 'No' to the monopolized financing of inflation driven slavery and the abolishment of the 'small but local banks and independent lenders' courtesy of the 'World Bank.' Another who'll say 'NO' to 'secular humanism' as the 'one world' or 'global neighborhood' religion. Another who'll work to beat a rigged game.

This one person will tell others, and the numbers will grow. Let us unite and spread the word. Exposure to sunlight kills all parasites ˆ expose those who would feed off our labors to secure their comfort - and that of their heirs - and I promise you, they'll retreat.

Make sure you hit them in the pocketbook too. Don't add one more nickel to the parasite 'Bondage Campaign' coffers. There are millions of us! Let's deny power to a handful of them! Write the government letters; write letters to the editor of your local and national newspapers; call talk radio and scream until you're heard. These people own traceable monopolies: Complain to your government until they're investigated and penalized. Complain until they're taxed the way you are. Refuse to buy their products and services. Turn off your TV. Write them and their sponsors and tell them you've done so. Spread the word. It's your freedom they're after. Don't help them by staying silent for fear of ridicule. Above all, don't finance your own slavery. Boycott and expose: Call them on their loaded dice. Win when they forfeit.

There is a cure for parasites. Expose them, starve them out, and drive them from your environment. Let them know the 'jig' is up. Stop playing a rigged game. This is the way to win. You couldn't start too soon. Withdrawal and recovery may be a little painful, but the healthy effort ˆ with time and commitment - will secure freedom for you, your children, and their children.

Close

As stated in the Preface, and repeated here, it is extremely important that the reader understand that this book is absolutely <u>not</u> intended to incite violent actions by anyone.

Wanton attacks on innocent people, violent revolution or armed insurrection is <u>not</u> the answer. The bombing of the federal building in Oklahoma City is heinous, and absolutely unforgivable. This was the act of a very troubled, deranged, evil, and isolated small group of radical extremist, violent criminals.

A violent effort to rid the US, and the world of the control of the *Elite* is a mistake for at least the following reasons:

1. It is wrong. It is wrong to violate our laws, and to endanger innocent people by violent acts.

2. It is illogical. It is impossible for <u>any</u> armed group to defeat the military capabilities of the *Elite*. They <u>own</u> the US military, NATO, the Secret Service, the CIA, the Supreme Court, and many of the lower courts. They control either directly or indirectly, most of the state, county, and local law enforcement agencies. To ignore this fact is pure lunacy. Those who blew up the federal building in Oklahoma City clearly fit this lunacy description.

Nevertheless, the heinous act in Oklahoma City should not deter us from using every moral, ethical, political, and legal process at our disposal to stop the *Elite* takeover of the US, and the rest of the world.

For some recommended answers of how to stop the *Elite*, I suggest reading my companion book; *They Don't Dare Let Us Tell the People*.

"THERE COMES A TIME WHEN SILENCE IS BETRAYAL ..."
- Martin Luther King, Jr.

Sunshine will cure many ills. My job is to shine this high intensity spotlight on the *Elite*. It is now your obligation to pass this knowledge on to anyone who will listen, for we cannot count on the mainstream media, for they are part of the problem. If you encounter someone who just won't listen, or who just wants to argue, don't waste your time, just walk away, because there are millions of uninformed citizens who are eager to learn the TRUTH. Thanks for your interest, your confidence, and your help. - Robert Gaylon Ross, Sr.

Other Recommended Reading

America's Rise to World Power: 1898-1954 (1955), by Foster Rhea
    Dulles, Harper & Rowe, 49 E 33rd St., New York, NT 10016
America's Secret Establishment, by Antony C. Sutton
    RIE, 24505 Old Ferry Road, Spicewood, TX 78669
Annual Reports of the Council on Foreign Relations, by the CFR
    58 E. 68th St., New York, NY 10021
Battling Wall Street, The Kennedy Presidency (1994), by Donald Gibson
    Sheridan Square Press, 145 West 4th Street, New York, NY 10012
Best Enemy Money Can Buy (1986), by Antony C. Sutton
    RIE, 24505 Old Ferry Road, Spicewood, TX 78669
Blindside (1995), by Eamonn Fingleton
    Houghton Mifflin Company, 215 Park Ave. S., New York, NY 10003
Call to Serve, by James "Bo" Gritz
    Lazarus Publishing Company, Box 472 HCR-31, Sandy Valley, NV 89019
Circle of Intrigue, by Texe Marrs
    Living Truth Publishers, 1708 Patterson Road, Austin, Texas 78733
Conspirators' Hierarchy: The Story of the Committee Of 300, by Dr. John Coleman
    America West Publishers, P.O. Box 3300, Bozeman, MT 59772
Defrauding of America, by Rodney Stitch
    RIE, 24505 Old Ferry Road, Spicewood, TX 78669
Descent into Slavery, by Des Griffin
    Emissary Publications, 9205 SE Clackamas Rd., Clackamas, OR 97015
Dope, Inc. (1986), by Editors of Executive Intelligence Review
    New Benjamin House, Box 20551, New York, NY 10023
Emerging Viruses (1996), by Leonard G. Horowitz, D.M.D, M.A., M.P.H.
    Tetrahedron, Inc., 20, Drumlin Road, Rockport, MA 01966
Establishment's Man (1992), by James Drummey
    Western Islands, Box 8040, Appleton, WI 54913
Gestapo Chief (1995), by Gregory Douglas
    R. James Bender Publishing, P.O. Box 23456, San Jose, CA 95153
How to Read the Federalist (1961), by Holmes Alexander
    Western Islands, Box 8040, Appleton, WI 54913
Federal Reserve Monster (1922), by Sam Clark & Wallace Campbell
    Emmisary Publications, P.O. Box 642, S. Pasadena, CA 91030
Imperial Brain Trust, by Laurence H. Shoup and William Minter
    Monthly Review Press, New York, NY
Land Use: Washington Grabs for Control (1975), by Gary Allen
    Western Islands, Box 8040, Appleton, WI 54913
Media Bypass magazine by Tree-Top Communications, Inc.
    P.O. Box 5326, Evansville, IN 47716
Men of Wealth, by John T. Flynn
    Simon and Schuster, New York, NY
My Memories of Eighty Years, by Chauncey M. Depew
    Charles Scribner's Sons, New York, NY
None Dare Call It Conspiracy, by Gary Allen
    Concord Press, P.O. Box 2686, Seal Beach, CA 90720
None Dare Call It Treason 25 Years Later, by John A. Stormer
    Liberty Bell Press, P.O. Box 32, Florissant, MO 63032
Our Global Neighborhood, The Report of the Commission on Global Governance
    by The United Nations, Published by Oxford University Press, Inc., New York
Project L.U.C.I.D., by Texe Marrs
    Living Truth Publishers, 1708 Patterson Rd., Austin, TX 78733
Save Your Job, Save Our Country, by Ross Perot with Pat Choate
    Hyperion, 114 Fifth Ave., New York, NY 10011

Secrets of the Federal Reserve, by Eustace Mullins
    Bankers Research Institute, P.O. Box 1105, Staunton, VA 24401

Secular Humanism, (1979), by Homer Duncan
    Missionary Crusader, 4606 Ave. H, Lubbock, TX 79404

Shall It Be Again, by John Kenneth Turner
    B. W. Huebsch, Inc., New York, NY

Square Peg for a Round Hole (1993), by Officer J. W. Hughes
    P.O. Box 27801, Concord, CA 94527

Stealing of America, (1983), by John W. Whitehead
    Crossway Books, Westchester IL, 60153

Soviet Impact on the Western World, (1947), by Edward Hallett Carr
    McMillan & Company, London, England

Ten Myths about Paper Money, (1983), by Congressman Ron Paul
    Foundation for Rational Economics & Education
    P.O. Box 1776, Lake Jackson, TX 77566

Texas In The Morning (1997), by Madeleine Duncan Brown
    RIE, 24505 Old Ferry Road, Spicewood, TX 78669

The Big Foundations (1972), by Waldemar A. Nielsen
    Columbia University Press, New York, NY

The Chairman, by Kai Bird
    Simon & Schuster, Rockefeller Ctr., 1230 Ave. of the Americas, NY, NY 10020

The Coming Conflict with China (1997), by Richard Bernstein and Ross H. Munro
    Alfred A. Knopf, New York

The Communist Manifesto (1974), by Karl Marx
    American Opinion, P.O. Box 8040, Appleton, WI 54913

The Creature from Jekyll Island (1994), by G. Edward Griffin
    American Opinion Publishing, Inc., P.O. Box 8040, Appleton, WWI 54913-8040

The Empire of the City, by E. C. Knuth
    Emissary Publications, P.O. Box 642, S. Pasadena, CA 91080

The Essence of Security (1968), by Robert S. McNamara
    Harper & Rowe, 49 E 33rd St., New York, NT 10016

The Fearful Master: A second look at the United Nations (1964), by G. Edward Griffin
    Western Islands, Box 8040, Appleton, WI 54913

The Federal Reserve Conspiracy (1995), by Antony C. Sutton
    RIE, 24505 Old Ferry Road, Spicewood, TX 78669

The Fourth Reich: Toward an American Police State (1993), by Don McAlvany
    Southwest Radio Church, Box 1144, Oklahoma Coty, OK 73101

The Franklin Cover-Up (1996), by John DeCamp
    RIE, 24505 Old Ferry Road, Spicewood, TX 78669

The Hitler Book (1984), by Elga Zepp Larouche
    New Benjamin House, Box 20551, New York, NY 10023

The Insiders, by John F. McManus
    The John Birch Society, P.O. Box 8040, Appleton, WI 54913

The Mystery of the Carefully Crafted Hoax, forward by Ted Gunderson
    Nebraska Leadership Conference, Box 30165, Lincoln, NE 68503

The Naked Communist, by W. Cleon Skousen
    The Ensign Publishing Co., P.O. Box 2316, Salt Lake City, UT

The New World Order, by Pat Robertson
    Word Publishing, Park West II, Suite 650, 1501 LBJ Freeway, Dallas, TX 75234

The Ruling Class, Inside the Imperial Congress, by Eric Felten
    The Heritage Foundation, 214 Massachusetts Ave. NE, Wash., DC 20002

The Secret Societies, by Charles William Heckethorn
    University Books, New Hyde Park, New York

The Seicus Circle (1977), by Claire Chambers
    Western Islands, Box 8040, Appleton, WI 54913

The Shadow of Power, by James Perloff
    Western Islands, P.O. Box 8040, Appleton, WI 54913

The Spotlight, by The Liberty Lobby
   300 Independence Ave. SE, Washington, DC 20003
The Struggle for World Power: Revolution & Counter-Revolution (1971),
      by George Knupffer
   The Plain Speaking Publishing Co., 43 Bath Rd., London, England W4 1LJ
The Trap (1994), by Sir James Goldsmith
   Carroll & Graf Publishers, 260 5th Ave., New York, NY 10001
They Don't Dare Let Us Tell the People, by Robert Gaylon Ross, Sr.
   RIE, 24505 Old Ferry Road, Spicewood, TX 78669
Trance Formation of America, by Kathy O'Brien and Mark Phillips
   RIE, 24505 Old Ferry Road, Spicewood, TX 78669
Tragedy and Hope, by Dr. Carroll Quigley
   The Macmillan Company, New York, NY
Trilaterism 1980, by Holly Sklar
   South End Press, 116 St. Botolph St, Boston, MA 02115
Valley of Decision (1988), by Sterling Lacy
   Dayspring Publications, Box 7677, Texarkana, TX 75505
Why A Bankrupt America, by Devvy Kidd
   Project Liberty, P.O. Box 741075, Arvada, CO 80006-9075
What Happened to the American Dream (1993), by Larry Burkett
   Moody Press, c/o MLM, Chicago, IL 60610
With No Apologies, by Senator Barry M. Goldwater
   William Morrow & Company, 1350 Ave. of the Americas, NY, NY 10019

Order form for Books, Audio & Video Tapes for Sale by RIE
Prices for **one** item in U.S. $, including shipping & handling, (including sales tax for Texas only)

Books	Texas	Other States	Canada	Mexico	Western Europe	Pacific Rim	Amount
America's Secret Establishment	$26.20	$24.95	$27.95	$27.95	$29.95	$29.95	_____
America's Secret Establishment (hard cov.)	$31.51	$29.95	$32.95	$32.95	$34.95	$34.95	_____
Best Enemy Money Can Buy	$20.94	$20.00	$23.00	$23.00	$25.00	$25.00	_____
CIA & MKULTRA Mind Control	$31.56	$30.00	$33.00	$33.00	$35.00	$35.00	_____
CIA & Human Biological Testing	$31.56	$30.00	$33.00	$33.00	$35.00	$35.00	_____
Elite Serial Killers	$42.13	$39.95	$42.95	$42.95	$44.95	$44.95	_____
Elite Serial Killers (signed copy)	$47.13	$44.95	$47.95	$47.95	$49.95	$49.95	_____
End of the United States of America	$11.50	$10.50	$11.50	$11.50	$13.50	$13.50	_____
Federal Reserve Conspiracy	$20.94	$20.00	$23.00	$23.00	$25.00	$25.00	_____
Friends of the Ezekiens (science fiction)	$10.00	$ 9.00	$11.00	$11.00	$14.00	$14.00	_____
International Jew (4-volume Set)	$49.50	$48.00	$51.00	$51.00	$55.00	$55.00	_____
Protocols of the Learned Elders of Zion	$18.50	$17.00	$20.00	$20.00	$25.00	$25.00	_____
Texas in the Morning	$36.82	$34.95	$37.95	$37.95	$39.95	$39.95	_____
Texas in the Morning (signed copy)	$41.82	$39.95	$42.95	$42.95	$44.95	$44.95	_____
Trilaterals Over America	$20.94	$20.00	$23.00	$23.00	$25.00	$25.00	_____
Who's Who of the Elite, 2000 Edition	$36.82	$34.95	$37.95	$37.95	$39.95	$39.95	_____
Who's Who of the Elite, 2000 (signed)	$41.82	$39.95	$42.95	$42.95	$44.95	$44.95	_____
Who's Who of the Elite, 1995 Edition	$20.94	$20.00	$23.00	$23.00	$25.00	$25.00	_____
Who's Who of the Elite, 1995 (Signed)	$25.95	$25.00	$28.00	$28.00	$30.00	$30.00	_____
VHS Video Tapes							
Clint Murchison Meeting (2 Hr.)	$26.20	$24.95	$27.95	$27.95	$29.95	$29.95	_____
American Union by 2005-06 (1.5 Hrs.)	$26.20	$24.95	$27.95	$27.95	$29.95	$29.95	_____
Audio Tapes							
Texas in the Morning	$10.75	$10.00	$16.00	$16.00	$19.95	$19.95	_____

Normal shipping is by USPS.
(UPS cannot deliver to a P. O. Box))   Add for UPS delivery in the U.S. $3.00

Shipping deductions for multiple items: 2 items -$3, 3 items -$7, 4 items -$10, 5 items -$15   - _____

Total $ _____

Due to the slowdown in U.S. mail service, we suggest that you pay an extra $3.00 per book for UPS delivery.

Visa/Master Card No.: _____   Expires: _____

Name: _____   Phone: _____

Address: _____

City: _____ State/Country: _____ Zip Code: _____

Mail a copy of this completed form including a personal check, bank draft, or money order payable to **RIE** to:

RIE
5404 Reimers Road
Spicewood, TX 78669
Order the above items with VISA/MasterCard by calling our toll-free number in the U.S. and Canada:
Toll Free 800-410-5571, or in the Austin, Texas area 512-264-1901
Please keep the toll-free number open for sales. For non-sales related questions, call 512-264-1901.
Check our web site at: **www.4rie.com**

Registration Form

This is <u>not</u> an order form, but is simply a means provided to give the reader an opportunity to be notified when additional **RIE** books will be made available for purchase. We have several books under development at this time, and we will notify you when they are ready to be distributed. Our mailing list is confidential, and will not be shared with, or sold to anyone. You can copy this form, or simply provide the same information on a postcard, or in a letter.

(Please Print)

First Name: _____ Middle Initial: _____ Last Name: _____

Postal Box: _____ Street: _____ Apt No.: _____

City: _____ State: _____ Postal Zip Code: _____-_____

<u>Mail this form to</u>:
RIE,
5404 Reimers Road,
Spicewood, TX 78669

<u>Thanks for registering with RIE.</u>